POLITICAL MOBILIZATION

*A Sociological Analysis of
Methods and Concepts*

SOCIETY TODAY AND TOMORROW

General Editor: A. H. Halsey
*Fellow of Nuffield College and Head of the Department
of Social and Administrative Studies, Oxford*

∗

THE SECONDARY MODERN SCHOOL
by William Taylor *Principal Lecturer in Education, Bede College,
Durham*

THE CUTTESLOWE WALLS: A Study in Social Class
by Peter Collison *Department of Social and Administrative
Studies, Oxford*

CRIME AND THE SOCIAL STRUCTURE
by John Barron Mays *Eleanor Rathbone Professor of Social
Science, University of Liverpool*

SOCIETY IN THE MIND: Elements of Social Eidos
by Charles Madge *Professor of Sociology, University of Birmingham*

THE FAWLEY PRODUCTIVITY AGREEMENTS
by Allan Flanders *Senior Lecturer in Industrial Relations, University of Oxford*

CONSTITUENCY POLITICS: A Study of Newcastle-under-Lyme
by Frank Bealey, J. Blondel, W. P. McCann

MODERN BRITISH POLITICS: A Study of Parties and Pressure
Groups
by Samuel H. Beer *Professor of Politics, Harvard University*

PROFESSIONAL EMPLOYEES: A Study of Scientists and Engineers
by Kenneth Prandy

Political Mobilization
A SOCIOLOGICAL ANALYSIS OF
METHODS AND CONCEPTS

J. P. NETTL

FABER AND FABER LTD
24 Russell Square
London

First published in mcmlxvii
by Faber and Faber Limited
24 Russell Square London W.C.1
Printed in Great Britain by
Western Printing Services Limited Bristol

© *J. P. Nettl* 1967

Contents

CONTENTS

Acknowledgements

One of the best ways of recognizing that a routine activity is becoming professionalized is the fact that its trivial courtesies turn into ritual symbols. Acknowledgements in the social sciences are a good example. Distinguished names are invoked as having advised or commented – or merely given their general blessing; they are then promptly absolved from any responsibility and dismissed. I have adopted a different method. Since the compressed yet wide-ranging nature of this essay cannot permit full expiation of my total intellectual debt, I shall first thank those who have helped by giving *inter vivos*, by talking, criticizing and in some cases just *being*. Then I shall list the main works that have provided guide and anchor in the formulation of ideas about the subject matter of this book. Finally there are some references to my own work, many of which relate to attempts to deal in greater detail with some of the problems encountered while writing this book.

Outstanding among those who have contributed personally is Roland Robertson, whose critical devotion to Parsonian social theory convinced me, after grave initial doubts some years ago, of its enormous heuristic potential. His dogged refusal to be browbeaten in argument has saved me from many errors and misinterpretations. It is no exaggeration to say that without him this book could not have been written, and therefore no pronouncement by me can absolve him from a stake in it. I also asked Eric Hobsbawm to use his wide historical knowledge, compounded by an intellectual suspicion of modern sociological theory, to pronounce upon the validity of the basic argument and some of the historical generalizations; the fact that this little boat survived both sociological Scylla and historical Charybdis deserves the traditional sailors' paean of thanksgiving.

Next in order of indebtedness comes Philip Williams. He too was asked to assess the legitimacy of the argument as a whole *in spite of* its (to him) repellent sociological appearance and anti-liberal bias. He also

11

ACKNOWLEDGEMENTS

gave me a lot of useful criticism on matters of fact. Moshe Tczudnowski of the Hebrew University of Jerusalem made some useful comments, both critical and approving, of the analysis. Finally Richard Rose took time off from a British General Election (*horribile dictu!*) to purge the manuscript of many linguistic and conceptual spasms. In the course of his editing he held a looking-glass up to the very soul of this book, and thus brought about a much more fundamental last-minute revision than I had intended – an essential revision, as I now realize.

Bits and pieces of this analysis have been presented at various seminars in my own and other universities; some of the discussions have proved helpful in sharpening my ideas. If I now close my acknowledgements by saying that what follows is, like the pavement artist's, 'all my own work', this is not intended to absolve the aforementioned from being accessories before the fact, but merely represents the frustrations of an English academic working without benefit of institutional or financial assistance in fields in which his American colleagues are generously assisted with finance, research help and above all the chance to have stimulating people to talk with. It is in the context of informal or semi-formal interaction within universities that British academic life is at its most parochial – except on matters appertaining to the educational process in general, and to one's own university in particular.

The frequent manifestations of formal structure-functionalism are rooted, as they must be, in the large and somewhat diffuse body of Talcott Parsons' writings scattered through thirty years. The works most relevant here are:

The Structure of Social Action, 1937
Essays in Sociological Theory, 1947
The Social System, 1952
Towards a General Theory of Action, 1951 (with Edward Shils, eds.)
Working Papers in the Theory of Action, 1953 (with Robert Bales and Edward Shils, eds.)
Family Socialization and Interaction Process, 1955 (with Robert Bales and others)
Economy and Society, 1956 (with Neil J. Smelser)
Structure and Process in Modern Societies, 1960
'Pattern Variables Revisited', *American Sociological Review*, XXV, 1960
Theories of Society, 1961 (with Edward Shils and others)

12

ACKNOWLEDGEMENTS

'The Point of View of the Author', in Max Black (ed.), *The Social Theories of Talcott Parsons*, 1961
Social Structure and Personality, 1964
'On the Concept of Influence', *Public Opinion Quarterly*, XXVII, 1963
'On the Concept of Political Power', *Proceedings of the American Philosophical Society*, CVII, 1963
'Voting and the Equilibrium of the American Political System', in E. Burdick and A. J. Brodbeck (eds.), *American Voting Behaviour*, 1959

My acceptance of Parsons' method, concepts and theories is by no means uncritical; but most of his basic vision of what society is about happens also to be mine. Whenever I have amended his concepts and analysis for my own purposes, reference is made to that effect. The odd thing is that for me at least Parsons' own work has been most illuminating, and has provided the greatest stimulus, precisely at the periphery of his discussion where logic and the relation to the empirical begin to break down.

Implicit in my intellectual and methodological debt to Talcott Parsons is a parallel debt to Neil Smelser, who has most usefully and rigorously applied Parsons' ideas and methods to particular social processes and situations. The main works are:

Social Change in the Industrial Revolution, 1959 *Theory of Collective Behaviour*, 1962

I have also been greatly influenced in my whole conceptual approach and focus of interest by the work of Karl W. Deutsch. Particular reference should be made to his writing on nationalism and the communication processes involved:

Nationalism and Social Communication, 1953
'Social Mobilization and Political Development', *American Political Science Review*, LV, 1961

In addition *The Nerves of Government*, 1963, has provided my basic entry point into the whole notion of cybernetic models and of the importance of information flow in political science.

The monumental contribution of Stein Rokkan, both to the analysis of grassroots political structure and behaviour for comparative purposes, as well as the formulation of cross-national hypotheses for comparing politics at almost every level of abstraction, has influenced my own approach enormously. Rokkan's research is part of

13

ACKNOWLEDGEMENTS

the basic architecture of this book. His work is scattered widely in journals and books, and cannot be summarized here; frequent detailed reference to it will be found in the text.

Mention must also be made at this stage of a somewhat more critical absorption of much of the writing on the concept of system in political science, particularly the work of two political scientists, Easton and Almond. The main references are:

David Easton, *The Political System: An Enquiry into the State of Political Science*, 1953
    'An Approach to the Analysis of Political Systems', *World Politics*, IX, 1957
    A Framework for Political Analysis, 1965
    A Systems Analysis of Political Life, 1965
Gabriel A. Almond, 'Comparative Political Systems', *Journal of Politics*, XVIII (1956)
    The Politics of the Developing Areas, 1960, Introduction
    The Civil Culture, 1963 (with Sidney Verba)
    'Political Systems and Political Change', *American Behavioral Scientist*, VI, 1963
    'A Developmental Approach to Political Systems', *World Politics*, XVII, 1965
Gabriel A. Almond and G. Bingham Powell, *Comparative Politics: A Developmental Approach*, 1966

A more diffuse debt to a whole number of American political scientists and sociologists, particularly Harold Lasswell, Robert Dahl and Seymour Lipset, must also be acknowledged here.

In this general section I should also state clearly that I have adopted the basic approach to the sociology of knowledge which is spelt out in the work of Karl Mannheim, particularly in *Ideology and Utopia*, 1936.

In the field of political theory, I must acknowledge above all the very considerable influence of Sheldon S. Wolin, *Politics and Vision, Continuity and Innovation in Western Political Thought*, 1960, even though it focuses a different conceptual apparatus upon the same basic preoccupations as this essay.

Carl J. Friedrich, *Man and His Government*, 1963, must be taken into account in any work connected with problems of human governance simply because, as Deutsch has said, 'there is nothing like it'. The same applies to the historical discussion of sociological thought by Raymond Aron, *Main Currents in Sociological Thought*, 1966.

14

ACKNOWLEDGEMENTS

The pioneering work of Erving Goffman in analysing the structure of apparently random face-to-face contact, and in helping to crystallize roles in the plethora of situations in which individuals find themselves, has made a great and pervasive impact on my *manner* of thinking. I have particularly found *The Presentation of Self in Everyday Life* very fruitful in discussing some of the implications of political behaviour and roles in hitherto uncharted situations. The whole conception of a dramaturgical analogy for politics arises largely from this source of inspiration.

Two writers have held me captive; one is Amitai Etzioni with his original analysis of the sociological problems of compliance in organizations: *The Comparative Analysis of Complex Organizations*, 1961. The other is Ralf Dahrendorf, *Class and Class Conflict in Industrial Society*, 1959; *Gesellschaft und Freiheit*, 1961; *Gesellschaft und Demokratie in Deutschland*, 1965. Dahrendorf has an intuitive sense for social structure and analytical order, for the way societies are 'built', and what in them matters more and what less. Both he and Etzioni are examples of that rare phenomenon: social analysts who automatically and naturally think sociologically, and therefore light up almost every subject they write about with original insights. My own debt to both ranges through all their writing on social change and, in Etzioni's case, all the way to the field of international relations, especially his *The Hard Way to Peace*, New York, 1962, 'The Epigenesis of Political Communities at the International Level', *American Journal of Sociology*, LXVIII (1963), and *Political Unification: A Comparative Study of Leaders and Forces*, New York, 1965.

At a somewhat more specific level of influence stands the work of a number of social scientists who have highlighted different aspects of politics or society. The work of Harry Eckstein on pressure groups, and on theoretical problems connected with them, has been authoritative (*Pressure Group Politics*, 1960, and various articles). His other, more adventurous work on a societal scale has proved stimulating, even though I do not always go all the way with method or conclusions (*A Theory of Stable Democracy*, 1961; *Internal War*, 1964).

Similarly, mention must be made of the work of Edward Shils, particularly his analysis of elite and intellectual roles and attitudes in developing countries. A good deal of Shils' work is scattered in the form of articles in a very wide variety of journals, but the most important references are:

ACKNOWLEDGEMENTS

'The Intellectuals and the Powers: Some Perspectives for Comparative Analysis', *Comparative Studies in Society and History*, I (1958).

'Political Development in the New States', *Comparative Studies in Society and History*, II (1960).

The Intellectual Between Tradition and Modernity, The Hague, 1961.

Political Development in the New States, The Hague, 1962.

The most recent statement by Shils of his approach to the study of developing countries is 'Opposition in the New States of Asia and Africa,' *Government and Opposition*, I, 2 (January 1966).

Anyone interested in the general problem of political modernization or development must inevitably owe a substantial debt to David Apter, initially for his two important area studies on Ghana and Uganda, then for his gradual approach towards a theory of modernization originally laid out piecemeal in various articles but finally put together between hard covers in *The Politics of Modernization*, 1965.

Less elegant but in many ways more congenial for its substantive content (because much better capable of appreciating the subjective value problems of developing societies, and therefore approachng more closely the three-step prismatic form of analysis used here) is the outstanding work of S. N. Eisenstadt. His work is relevant to the whole sociological problem of development, but especially to that of bureaucracy. With regard to the latter I have found especially helpful and illuminating Crozier's analysis of problems contingent in bureaucratic phenomena in developed societies, as distinct from those writers more fully committed to Weberian rationality:

Michel Crozier, *The Bureaucratic Phenomenon*, 1964.

'De l'étude des relations humaines à l'étude des relations de pouvoir', *Sociologie du Travail*, I, 1961.

Perhaps this is a good lead-in for acknowledging debts to two other writers, debts which extend far beyond their immediate contribution to the study of bureaucracy; Herbert Simon's work on the action and process aspect of individuals in bureaucracies, *Administrative Behaviour*, 1945, and, with James March, *Organizations*, 1958. Complementary to this is the discriminating and elegant adaptation of various outside models for solving sociological problems in *Models of Man: Social and Rational*, 1957.

A further number of more scattered debts needs brief acknowledgement. Eric Hobsbawm's *Labouring Men*, 1964, a collection of essays, sets out, among other things, to make 'sense' of events and

ACKNOWLEDGEMENTS

actions which sociologists have been only too happy to consign to the general dustbin of *anomie*–a fact which led me to reconsider many existing aspects of so-called rational and irrational behaviour. W. J. M. Mackenzie enters the present essay specifically with only one very minor work–'The Export of Electoral Systems', *Political Studies*, V, 1957. The seemingly casual presentation of his argument nonetheless represents one of the earliest critiques of the patronizing manner in which the relationship between developed and developing societies was commonly discussed, and his approach foreshadowed many of the conceptual changes of the next decade. His mild suggestion that there was no good *a priori* reason why developed countries should always be the norm and developing countries the deviants set me off on a very basic train of thought.

Finally room must be made for two acknowledgements of a rather diffuse kind. Ernest Gellner's *Words and Things*, 1959, and more particularly *Thought and Change*, 1964, require mention. The author is, I think, covering very much the same ground and with the same object in view. I read the latter book only after my own approach had been more or less committed in some detail; our ideas complement each other substantially in that we seem to arrive at similar conclusions, though the style of discourse, the coverage of empirical material and the methods used are very different. In a sense the same thing is true of the–for me–outstanding work of Samuel Huntington. Again the methodological commitment is very different from my own, but the socio-political *Weltanschauung* appears similar. Among the many researchers and students into problems of modernization in America I find the closest echo to basic problems in Huntington's work. In particular these ideas come out of two long articles: 'Political Development and Political Decay', *World Politics*, XVII, 3 (April 1965), pp. 386–430; 'Political Modernization; America vs. Europe', *World Politics*, XVIII, 3 (April 1966), pp. 378–414; and the part on the United States in the outstanding comparative analysis *Political Power: USA/USSR* (with Z. Brzezinski), 1964.

In addition to those singled out here a host of other writers are cited; some favourably, some critically. Detailed reference to these has been made where necessary. The present bibliographical note is really intended to serve as a manifest acknowledgement for basic ideas and orientations borrowed directly or at one remove.

In the course of writing this book a host of detailed problems presented themselves, often unexpectedly, and eventually imposed

ACKNOWLEDGEMENTS

an absolute need for further investigation and clarification which could not always be filled within the framework of the present book. Some of the results were published separately–planets revolving round this central essay, as it were. Since frequent reference to them has been made in the text, they are best listed here.

i. The problem of selecting a satisfactory concept of system from among the available offerings (which turned out to be much less alike in their implications than I had realized) led to 'The Concept of System in Political Science', *Political Studies*, XIV, 3 (October 1966).

ii. The attainment of national independence as a unique phenomenon in time but general in its contemporary application to the process of social and political change in the Third World gave rise to 'The Inheritance Situation' (cf. also the definition of inheritance below, p. 35).

This analysis took as its starting point some ideas which had arisen from previous work on Social Democracy in the Marxist context and published under the title: 'The German Social Democratic Party as a Political Model, 1890–1914', *Past and Present*, No. 30, April 1965.

iii. The problem of temporal change in the emphasis of different social subsystems or functions (as defined by Parsons) led to an attempt to evolve a phase-model of social functions, more particularly to suggest a shift from the dominant emphasis on economics towards an increasingly political reference in the developing world today. The implications were examined in an article with Roland Robertson, 'Industrialization, Development or Modernization?', *British Journal of Sociology*, XVII, 3 (September 1966).

iv. This in turn gave rise to a more detailed assault on the problem of whether an international social (as opposed merely to a political or conflict) system exists within the context of which modernization and development might more fruitfully be discussed on a comparative basis. The result was 'Modernization and International Systems'.

A much expanded version of 'Industrialization, Development or Modernization', together with 'The Inheritance Situation' and 'Modernization and International Systems', constitute parts one, two and three respectively of a book of essays written jointly by Nettl and Robertson under the title *The International Context of Modernization*, due for publication under the same imprint later in 1967.

Introduction

PURPOSE AND METHOD

This book aims to persuade. Its primary purpose is to find means of understanding the present state of political societies in the world. 'A sociologist contributes most when he reports what he observes in such a fashion that his account rings true to insiders, but also in such a fashion that they themselves would not have written it.'[1] In order to do this within manageable and readable proportions, I have concentrated on one particularly political process which is not only central to all political activity, but makes political change comprehensible as something other than a series of set pieces or tableaux.[2] For this one needs to focus on process–a process which operates universally in all societies at any time. I hope that the choice of political mobilization as the central process in question will not only concentrate attention on a particularly crucial aspect of social life, but also provide a key to the comparative study of societies which others may find useful for empirical studies in the future.

The great advantage of selecting political mobilization is that it does justice to the need to treat developed and developing countries as *sui generis* in so far as their priorities and socio-economic requirements are concerned. This is an essential condition in the selection of any comparative process for study. The approach adopted here tries to show the particular values and goals to which social structures are related in different societies, and to discuss the instrumental utility of these structures in relation to such values and goals. The terms 'developed' and 'developing' are relative enough to be adopted as initial categories representing two different types of society. There is

---

[1] Barney G. Glaser and Anselm L. Strauss, *Awareness of Dying*, London, 1966, Introduction.
[2] H. Bergson, 'Die Wahrnehmung der Veränderung', in *Denken und Schöpferisches Werden*, Meisenheim, 1948, p. 165.

no attempt to impose on developing countries a value system extra-polated from our own developed world, and I have tried to the best of my ability to avoid any normative judgements based on the achievement criteria of our own value systems–perhaps even to the extent of appearing to make the developing world the norm, and the Western world the deviant. And why not? This approach, then, makes it possible to seek out and compare both political structures and political processes common to developed and developing societies, without becoming entangled in the equally important but different problem of their respective value systems.

As between the observer and the observed there are, in my analysis, two steps rather than one: the observer is not only required (1) to judge structures and processes directly, but also (2) to judge or view them through the eyes of the participants (as expressed by their cultural system and their goal and value orientations). Only then can comparisons be made. These comparisons are accordingly derived from incidental similarities of structure and process, from which in turn common values and goals may or may not be deduced. This is exactly the opposite process from postulating common goals, and then testing their more or less efficient attainment from structural and process phenomena. The essential difference is that comparison does not in the least depend on common values or goals. Having agreed that situations in which societies find themselves may be defined very differently between one society and another, we can better study political mobilization as a continuing process and compare its manner, the means used to achieve it, its scale and intensity and its level of impact. However, considerable and continual stress has then to be laid on the multiple relationship between the observer, the participant and the process observed. This necessitates frequent discussion of the implications of the various forms of 'objective' analysis currently used by social scientists; I firmly believe that these are not only the reflection of, but in turn also help to create, the process they are seeking to analyse. Such a binary form of discussion admittedly makes for complexity, but does, I think, represent a distinct departure from the usual approach which divides fairly sharply into either the extrapolation of people's ideas on the one hand (political theory or philosophy; discussion of culture and values), or into the allegedly neutral study of structures, roles and actions on the other (empirical sociology and sociological theory). The continual dialogue adopted here is sometimes awkward but may perhaps prove rewarding.

INTRODUCTION

The attempt to run such a binary analysis has led to the extensive use of footnotes for the purpose of discussing at some length the relevant contribution of social scientists to any empirical or analytical problem. Though some of this discussion inevitably boils up into the text from time to time, I have tried where possible to keep the empirical discussion above the line and the methodological discussion below it. Those who want to ignore the latter should skip the footnotes.

It will also be obvious that no attempt has been made to do comprehensive justice to the vast literature which exists in all the various areas which the present argument at one time or another invades. No one will have much difficulty in discovering omissions. This applies particularly to evidence of historical events. The brief excursions into history are essentially summaries; to illustrate them from the works of other writers would require a very extended discussion. I hold strongly to the view that the impressive infrastructure of footnotes, common in much American sociological analysis, is no doubt in part a concession to the pressures of respectability in the industry of academic production, but is also the consequence of a growing service industry–the writing of 'special' history pre-digested for sociologists, a sort of academic baby-food. As evidence this does not add as much to the discussion as is often believed.[1] What it does do however is to make clearer the relationship between ideological bias and the argument or material in question. Consequently it has seemed preferable to grasp the bull by the horns and use the work of other social scientists, not only for its substantive contribution but also as evidence of certain trends of thought.

I am very conscious that in choosing process as the main focus I have chosen the most difficult aspect of social and political analysis. We are structure-bound all the way–from the empirical material with which social scientists work, right down to the constraints of the language we use. In spite of all the difficulties involved, I am committed to the view that social and political analysis must increasingly move from structure to process–from a static to a dynamic vision–if we are to make any progress (the impasse in which the study of class in Britain has landed itself through structure-bound constraints of method is one good example of this situation; it has taken a historian to point this out).[2] On the other hand the so-called

[1] This problem presented itself demandingly to me in the course of writing a lengthy piece of history recently: *Rosa Luxemburg*, London, 1966.

[2] E. P. Thompson, *The Making of the English Working Classes*, London 1964.

21

INTRODUCTION

behaviourists have not so far helped much either. They too adopt the foreshortened focus of objective analysis, and tend to concentrate on the manageably parochial–the summated or grossed-up individual (not to mention the vulgar British variant of Butler and others who deal only in the trivia of elections). There are accordingly some real situational difficulties to be pleaded as an excuse for inelegance of method and partly also of style; for a tendency to leap about from problem to problem instead of following the desired unilinear method instilled in us by philosophical argument.

Language presents a special difficulty. First style. There are three choices with this sort of book. To write only in good (or at least accepted) English means reducing the level of analysis to the lowest common factor of universal but not very illuminating concepts. The universality anyhow soon turns out to be bogus, since it assumes that what we mean by, say, justice or democracy or police or even lunch will necessarily mean the same thing to everyone else. As against this, to write pure sociologese means imposing incessantly a highest uncommon multiple even where it is not strictly necessary. Any attempt to do justice simultaneously to the material and to the non-technical reader in turn means a mixed bag and does away with any unity of style. But for present purposes the last option seems the least evil, and has accordingly been adopted; where the problem is one of cross-societal comparison of structure or process, jargon is used; where the issue is one of explanation or illustration, the discussion reverts to English. Only the finished product can justify the method; English (as opposed to American) reviewers are welcome to lament the outrage to linguistic purity of which, in the social sciences, they have appointed themselves the special guardians.

A second problem is that of simultaneity. Language establishes an unconscious chronological hierarchy; you can only say one thing at one time–elegantly. In social science the problem often is one of relating any statement to a number of statements that have gone before, a process of accretion that requires many things to be held

---

Cf. W. G. Runciman, *Relative Deprivation and Social Justice*, London 1966; Ralf Dahrendorf has recently pointed up the vital difference between class or elite as *abstract* concept or *real* social factor. Both exist–the difference between them is a central variable in the analysis of society, in his case Germany. See *Gesellschaft und Demokratie in Deutschland*, Munich 1965, pp. 258 ff, 293–307, for the concepts of 'abstract' and 'established' elites. Those familiar with his previous work, especially *Class and Class Conflict in Industrial Society*, will note the extent to which this latest book represents a departure from his previous conceptual position on class and elite.

constant and relevant like numbers read into a computer. The only way I have been able to cope with this is by the use of constant, possibly tedious reminders; it may be that, by putting myself forward as a standard for how much reminding is needed, I have either over-taxed or underrated the memory capacity of the reader.

Closely related to the problem of language is that of objectivity—that ugly wart which no amount of professional *maquillage* will disguise. Although the present analysis uses a method and a form of discourse for which many users, with much self-satisfaction, claim objectivity and neutrality, the questions I shall be discussing are far too contentious for me to get away with a scientific (or scientistic) claim to be wearing the Emperor's clothes of invisibility. In any case a frank admission of wishing to persuade settles nothing; it merely avoids one dilemma and promptly poses another. The attempt to be objective and the belief that the attempt succeeds have turned into a sort of self-sustaining merry-go-round: the use of certain 'neutral' concepts is supposed to facilitate objective analysis and in turn 'proves' the objectivity of the analysis in question. There is therefore a strong case to be made for avoiding such concepts altogether. This however leads directly into an equally frustrating blind alley. It is an occupational disease of British academics writing about society to convince themselves that by writing 'good' English and using simple, everyday words, the complexities of society can be adjusted to the procrustean demands of that mythical beast, the intelligent general reader. Accordingly a good deal of British sociology today is deter-minedly parochial, if not downright trivial. Our nose is grimly kept a bare inch above the squiggly furrow of facts. Alternatively the apparatus of a liberal education is brought to bear on the complexities of German-American sociology and hunts them mercilessly with the cry of ugliness and mystification. But it is a victory of style over understanding—a pyrrhic victory. For more than fifty years British social analysis has neither defined nor solved any problems on a societal scale and has contributed nothing to the development of sociological theory. All that has been achieved is to keep the language sacred and mystical—at the expense of gross over-simplification of the social problems involved.[1]

We are witnessing a transatlantic duel. The only way in which I

---

[1] It is perhaps relevant that the definition of ideology provided by the Oxford English Dictionary combines emphasis on 'visionary speculation' with 'the manner of thinking characteristic of a class or individual, and the ideas at the basis of some economic or political theory'.

have been able to deal with this very real divergence is not to make a choice but to do the splits. Social analysis on the American scale and of the American complexity demands a special language. For one thing, there are enough scholars in the field to form at least a partial linguistic consensus; this focuses arguments and disagreements on matters of substance. Secondly, much of the discussion deals with unfamiliar things like systems which need a whole new structure of terms and concepts. Thirdly, sociology is rapidly becoming international; the language of the discipline unites where the language of nations divides. Insofar as I have discussed the conclusions of many American sociologists (and expressed any disagreement over substance) I have done so in their own terms and not by an elegantly arrogant attack on their language. At the same time I have adopted a polemical posture over matters which belong to the field of ideology—a field for which polemics are still eminently suitable. The result may therefore be that I shall please neither American sociologists nor British critics. Nonetheless, the task of examining critically not only substantive problems but also the way they have been tackled imposes a requirement to deal simultaneously in both modes of discourse.

In one sense therefore this book is a selfconscious attempt at synthesis, bringing together the different approaches to the study of problems of political change on the two sides of the Atlantic. I have found this attempt at synthesis helpful in reaching an understanding of, and explaining, social change in any one society, and in comparing changes across national boundaries. The problem of developing countries is, by almost unanimous agreement, the most important one facing us today—and 'us' means both the academic social scientists and the participant member of society in whatever position of influence and power he may find himself.

Changes in developing countries, or in the Third World, take place with bewildering speed and frequency; between completion of this manuscript and its eventual perusal by the reader a number of regimes cited and discussed will have disappeared or greatly changed. This is evidence of the epiphenomenal nature of their political institutions, a factor which is repeatedly stressed in this analysis. Provided base and superstructure are firmly distinguished, provided also that the stressful and changing nature of developing societies is borne in mind, this occasional 'out-of-dateness' of specific reference does not matter much. I now have only one sense of regretful omission—the perhaps excessive reliance on the Soviet model at the expense of the

INTRODUCTION

Chinese in discussing intensive, ideologically articulate mobilization based on a dominant party. Since I am here primarily concerned with the view of the Soviet experience taken by developing countries rather than with analysis of that experience itself, this appeared legitimate–the more so as the Chinese model provided less of an *industrialization* model than the Soviet Union, and was much less well known or accessible. Nonetheless the almost exclusive emphasis on Soviet experience to 'fill' this important model with empirical examples fails to do justice to the important Chinese variants, especially since the Chinese challenge to Soviet exclusiveness and supremacy in the diffusion of the Communist model is currently stronger than ever. All this was less apparent when the book was being written. It may well be that if, as I suspect, industrializing perspectives come to play a less prominent role in development problems, and national integration as well as mass mobilization become ends as well as merely means, the Chinese model may become increasingly relevant as against that of the Soviet Union. This may be closely linked to the outcome of the Sino-Soviet dispute in its structural form. It is therefore necessary to repair this omission at least in part by a brief and cautionary reference at this point.

The practical purposes of the present essay, then, are:

1. to find variables and concepts for the study of comparative political process that are both simple and yet have considerable organizing power. These variables and concepts move on three different dimensions: culture, function and process. The book is accordingly arranged under three basic headings. A summary of the variables put forward here for the analysis of political change is sketched out in the first part of the conclusions.

2. to bring developed and developing societies into one coherent discourse and to find a means of differentiating between them that is not culture bound.

3. to examine critically the ideological implications of much contemporary social analysis and to attempt to isolate the ideological components of my own analysis as much as possible.

4. to suggest a model for the empirical study of these problems in the future.

5. to discuss the process of political mobilization in some detail as a central component of the political process and to use it as a means of analysing the problem of political and social change. The approach is not intended to be historical, though reference has frequently to be made to historical periods and events.

INTRODUCTION

DEFINITION OF CORE CONCEPTS

A. *Culture*

There are two basic alternatives.

One is overarching and covers social processes and structures in their historical and intellectual setting. This on the whole is the way anthropologists use the concept of culture. The other, which has been adopted here, is more limited. It treats culture as an abstraction from interactive social processes and discusses it separately from them. Parsons first used the concept in this manner: the cultural system was defined as the highest level in the systems hierarchy cultural system-social system-personality system-biological system. Recently Parsons has inclined more towards the broader, more inclusive definition of culture; by referring to the socio-cultural system he has tended to treat it once more as analytically inseparable from interactive processes.

In the present discussion culture has been kept as 'separate' as possible without straining at reality. But instead of an abstract system on a vertical scale of hierarchies, it has been treated as a catchment area for interactive processes, capable of conceptual autonomy for purposes of analysis. Thus political culture, with which we are here particularly concerned, becomes the culture surrounding political interaction, as evidenced by the political system (for this see below, p. 27f.). Though not wholly defining the processes and structures of interaction, it provides the setting for their style, tone and colouring. The colour dimension is a useful analogy; culture transforms black-and-white shapes of a comparable kind into an individually coloured social context.

An analytical distinction has further to be drawn between the overall social culture, which is the total cultural surround or catchment area for the sum of interactions of a whole society, and the political (or religious, economic, legal or what have you) culture which colours a limited functional sector of activities (or subsystem) within society as a whole.

The best operational definition for present purposes is a partial synthesis of two different versions of the concept. On the one hand 'culture consists of patterns, *explicit and implicit, of and for behaviour acquired and transmitted by symbols*, constituting the distinctive achievement of human groups, including their embodiment in artifacts; the essential core of culture consists of traditional (i.e. historically derived and selected) ideas and especially their attached values;

culture systems may, *on the one hand be considered as products of action, on the other as conditioning elements of further action*.[1]

This definition emphasizes the feedback quality of culture; shaping or colouring action and in turn being reinforced by action. But it established no priority between these interdependent categories which, at least analytically, require separating and arranging in some order of priority. Accordingly culture for present purposes is better defined as relating primarily to the conditioning element of action. The product of action, in combination with cultural influence, will be termed ideology and discussed under that concept. We have thus an initial predisposition to the notion of orientations as governing action, which belong to culture; the reflection of action on culture and on the form of further action, which tend to constitute more particular and unique phenomena in each individual society or part of that society, belong more properly to the area of ideology. This distinction is important because it covers in part the involvement of social scientists with the material they analyse. Thus the latter is an ideological problem, while the abstract view of orientations, analytically separated from action, forms the area of cultural investigation.

The other, more precise definition of culture, with which the earlier and wider definition can be constrained, and which also carries the desired emphasis on orientation, is provided by Almond and Verba in the form of a 'psychological orientation towards social objects'. These authors view culture as relating and linking the micro and macro aspects of social process and emphasize its causative function as a conditioning element of action rather than as its product.[2]

B. *System*

(i) In *one* sense system is the bounded area of a total society as a concrete entity. This makes it a concrete supra-system.[3] Insofar as

[1] A. L. Kroeber and Clyde Kluckhohn, *Culture: A Critical Review of Concepts and Definitions*, Papers of the Peabody Museum of American Archaeology and Ethnology XLVII (1952), p. 181 (my italics). Cf. Kroeber, *The Nature of Culture*, Chicago 1952. For the dependence of sociology upon the concept of culture, see Pitirim A. Sorokin, *Society, Culture and Personality: Their Structure and Dynamics*, New York 1947.

[2] Gabriel A. Almond and Sidney Verba, *The Civic Culture*, Princeton 1962, pp. 14, 32–35, 73–75. See also the more system-integrated analysis in Gabriel A. Almond and G. Bingham Powell, *Comparative Politics: A Developmental Approach*, Boston 1966, Sections 2 and 3.

[3] The definition of supra-system, and the classification of systems into concrete, abstract and conceptual, may be found in the authoritative analysis of James G. Miller, 'Living Systems: Basic Concepts', *Behavioral Science*, X, 3,

Parsons deals with the empirical analysis of actual societies, divided into abstract functional subsystems, this seems to be the sense in which he too uses the concept of system (though it could well be argued that he intends the concept of system to be abstract throughout). However, the equilibrium postulate for systems implicit in the Parsonian concept has not been adopted here – mainly because it has little relevance to the present analysis.

(ii) I have also adopted the outline of functional subsystems, and Parsons' basic classification of functions served by these subsystems. These are: Goal attainment function–political subsystem, adaptive function–economic subsystem, integrative function–subsystem of normative control (the structures and collectivities through which people are integrated within society through the diffusion of social norms), pattern maintaining and conflict management function–latency subsystem (primary groupings, families, etc., the locus of culture production in the system). The notions of boundary and systemic interrelationships have also been adopted. In this context the concept of system is here used in its *second*, abstract sense.

There is however one important distinction between the terminology used to describe subsystem here, and that used by Parsons and those who have applied Parsonian method to the analysis of particular societies. The term subsystem is used *only* in an abstract sense; where a concrete group or collection of structures is to be designated, a different term is employed in each case. Thus the notion of political subsystem is an abstraction, while the polity is a more selfconsciously concrete entity.[1] The reference to abstract subsystem should therefore not be confused with reference to structural entities like polity, economy, etc. These are arrangements of structures and processes in the conventional manner used by participants; political in this context is what everybody in society accepts as being related to the polity, while economic refers to processes generally accepted as relating to the economy. The structure of the present analysis accordingly moves simultaneously at two levels; an empirical level of polity and economy, and an analytical level of political subsystem and economic subsystem. The concrete analyses of input and output provided by

(July 1965), pp. 193–237, especially pp. 200–9, 218. This is based on Miller's forthcoming book, *Living Systems*, the most comprehensive analysis of comparative systems to date.

[1] Parsons uses subsystem in both concrete and abstract form; polity and political subsystem are interchangeable. Cf. William C. Mitchell, *The American Polity: A Social and Cultural Interpretation*, New York/London 1962, which is an attempt to analyse the United States in fairly rigorously Parsonian terms.

Easton, Almond and others apply (insofar as their model is relevant here) to the concrete polity, or the political institutions, not to the political system as here defined. The latter is essentially a grouping of abstract interrelationships: actions, roles and structures viewed by the observer as serving the societal function of goal attainment. The attribution of actions, roles and structures by the observer to the political system has been separated from their attribution to the polity by participants. Accordingly the concept of system has been used as a sensitizing or scanning concept to 'collect' actions, roles and structures for simultaneous reference at any one time. The concrete existence of process and structures is not changed, but their analytical relationship to each other may be. This will be very clear if it is emphasized that the political system (or, more correctly, sub-system) is to be defined as that 'area' of society serving the function of goal attainment broadly as defined by Parsons.

On the other hand politics or the political will be defined as empirically related to central government (see immediately below). This is not a contradiction but a differentiated definition to correspond to two different levels of analysis. It does however imply different allocations to the sphere of what is political at these different levels.[1]

C. *Politics*

There are two current uses of the word politics which differ considerably, more in their implications than in their superficial characteristics. Both have much to recommend them. With the convergence of modern political science and sociological theory, the once extreme claims by political theorists for autonomy, supremacy and especially universality of their subject have been somewhat moderated, so that politics is now often defined (1) merely as the area of formal government in its widest sense, including all processes directly and indirectly associated with it;[2] (2) in an alternative interpretation, used by some political scientists and many sociologists, as focusing on certain roles and processes which exist in any situation, collectively or structure –

[1] A fuller explanation of the alternatives among concepts of system presently available, and of the criteria that have led me to adopt this one, are set out in Nettl, 'The Concept of System in Political Science', op. cit.

[2] The old sense of all-inclusive politics is in turn a corruption of an even older meaning of the word. It clearly originates from Aristotle's *politeia*, the sort of constitution in which every citizen had a share, but in the Middle Ages was adapted to distinguish government involving and deriving from the people (*dominium politicum*) from government vested in the King (*dominium regale*). In this context the word political carries a prescriptive and preferential designation.

irrespective of whether these latter are concerned with government or not. The referent for this second definition is the notion of power. To this extent the potential or actual use of power implies the presence of the 'political' in many subsystems of society–economic, religious, etc. Not that there is any agreement about the meaning of power; this 'dispersed' definition of politics has merely diffused the reference from one subsystem throughout all of society.

The first, governmental definition of politics has in the main been adopted here. This is largely for reasons of analytical convenience and in order to confine the discussion to manageable size and proportion. As already mentioned, the functional attribution of politics in a society is in terms of societal goal attainment. In almost all empirical situations this means mainly (though not exclusively) the institutional structure of government. Similarly the reference of political orientation is to the government and its activities, an orientation to be at length discussed later in the context of political culture, mobilization and participation. Accordingly the word politics is mainly used to describe the complex of institutional structures and processes relevant to central government (with the necessary connotation of territorial discontinuity). At times necessity dictates that it be used (with a specific note to that effect) more in the sociologist's sense of relevance to matters of power and authority in any social structure including, but not confined to, central government. As a rule politics is to social action as political culture is to social culture– a distinct sector or differentiated subsystem within a larger whole.

There is at present little agreement on the precise definition of the status of politics. The process of sociological 'shrinking' of the primary and all-embracing nature of politics, which began with Marx and Max Weber, has continued–in spite of occasional efforts at re-expansion–right up to its crystallization as just one of four equal social subsystems by Parsons. For many writers the political system still retains some considerable primacy in society.[1] The most

[1] Cf. the development of the concept of the political system by Easton and Almond. A similar assumption of primacy is present in the work of Robert A. Dahl, e.g. 'The Concept of Power', *Behavioral Science*, II, 3 (July 1957), pp. 201–15; *Who Governs?*, New Haven 1961; *The Analysis of Politics*, New York 1963. See also Harold D. Lasswell and Abraham Kaplan, *Power and Society*, New Haven 1950. For a specific resuscitation of the maximal claim for politics see Herbert J. Spiro, 'Comparative Politics: A Comprehensive Approach', *American Political Science Review*, LVI, 3 (September 1962), pp. 577–95; also Spiro, *Government by Constitution: The Political Systems of Democracy*, New York 1959. This is quite apart from political theorists like Friedrich, who make the claim much more overtly and specifically.

usual locus of relevance is still the state, or 'what is general to a society . . . the inclusiveness of political society contrasted with the parochialisms of family, class, local community and sect' (Wolin). The most usual medium is power, in the last resort defined as 'legitimate, heavy sanctions' or 'physical force' (Weber), or more recently, in an economic analogy, as 'cash' contrasted with a nexus of prestige or influence in the form of 'credit' (Deutsch).[1]

The tendency to think in terms of a political *system* (insofar as this is not merely a fashionable term) has thus brought about a partial redefinition of scope and means, but the status of political *functions* would still seem to require some corresponding redefinition. There are writers, particularly Parsons, for whom the notion of an *a priori* primacy for the political does not arise, and whose definition of politics is largely functional, in the sense of goal attainment. The notion of primacy becomes a dependent variable according to the situation. Parsons has ordered these situations in a general phase-model, according to which a certain primacy is assigned to different subsystem and functions at different periods. This analysis is accepted here, with some amendments; it will be argued that according to such a phase-model the goal attainment function and the political system are relatively salient in developing countries at this moment — in fact this constitutes an important part of the definition of contemporary development.[2]

In so far as concrete locations are concerned, then, I have used central government as referent. At a higher level of abstraction a functional notion of politics as goal attainment has been adopted, with its implications of a political subsystem. The level of analysis is indicated where the discussion of politics makes this necessary. Insofar as politics relates to government, we are dealing with the polity. Insofar as it relates to societal goal attainment we are dealing with the political system. I have tried to avoid the use of the term power as much as possible, preferring an affectionate bow in the direction of Deutsch's cash and analogy.

[1] Deutsch's analogy (*The Nerves of Government*, pp. 120 ff.) is likely to find increasing acceptance among political scientists and political sociologists, especially since he has nudged Parsons in this direction — though Parsons has expressly departed from the handsome simplicities of the Deutsch analogy for something more complex and symbolic; see Talcott Parsons, 'On the Concept of Political Power', *Proceedings of the American Philosophical Society*, CVII, 1963, pp. 232–62.

[2] This is argued at some length in 'Industrialization, Development or Modernization', op. cit.

INTRODUCTION

It should finally be noted that politics, in addition to being a series of social actions in a system, is also an academic discipline–while sociology is *only* such a discipline. Hence politician, or political activist, is a distinct role, while being a member of a society (the social equivalent) is not. This point has considerable implications with regard to the two respective forms of analysis, which will be elaborated as they arise in due course.

D. *Mobilization*

This is the central concept of the essay. The following definitional limitations should be clearly noted.

(i) Mobilization is taken to mean a process which is induced, not a mere state or level which can be worked out either from 'hard' objective indices, or simply abstracted from subjective notions like participation, levels of cognition, etc. These latter are treated as second-order consequences here. Ideally the most fruitful way of measuring relative states of mobilization through time, or between different societies, would be by use of reference group theory within an action framework. Though I have not attempted to develop such an apparatus in detail here, the whole concept of mobilization is related in its comparative or measurable aspects to the notion of substantial changes in defining new referents for different sections of the population, as well as to the success of an elite in forcing acceptance of its new reference groups, both normative and comparative.

(ii) Mobilization is also analysed as a function in terms of the social system. In this context it will be discussed in its manifest and latent forms, and an attempt will be made to fit the function of political mobilization into the broader political function of goal attainment.

(iii) My use of the concept of mobilization is neutral with regard to *purpose*. No attempt is made to classify different experiences of mobilization at different times in accordance with any latent or declared purpose. As will already be clear from the functional definition given just above, the concern here is more with the instrumental process in relation to the existential goals and values than with any overall assessment of the normative or ethical purposes of mobilization.

(iv) In concentrating on process it is necessary to define precisely what is involved. Mobilization is essentially (1) attitudinal–a commitment to action, and (2) a means of translating this commitment

32

into action or observed behaviour. This is a composite process involving several stages:

(*a*) the existence of values and goals requiring mobilization.

(*b*) action on the part of leaders, elites or institutions seeking to mobilize individuals and groups.

(*c*) the institutional and collective means of achieving this mobilization.

(*d*) the symbols and references by which values, goals and norms are communicated to, and understood as well as internalized by, the individuals involved in mobilization.

(*e*) the process by which mobilization takes place in terms of individual interaction, the creation and change of collectivities and structures, the crystallization of roles, the effect on subsystems and their boundaries.

(*f*) estimates of the numbers of people (or proportion of a population) mobilized and the degree of such mobilization for different sectors or strata of the population.

E. *Development*

Though not enamoured of a term with such evolutionary under-tones, I have used it for lack of anything better to convey the basic dichotomy which differentiates more and less developed countries. The concept usually carries strong economic connotations of growth, some of which will be spelt out and criticized in detail later. Insofar as development is more specifically attached to socio-political as-pects, it tends to be strongly synonymous with the concept of socio-political *change*. Development is used here in a temporally restricted sense; the complex of aspirations and actions attached to the concept by participants in the contemporary world. There is a large element of self-definition involved; countries are called de-veloping or developed not because of some 'objective' scale of indices of achievement, but mainly because they see themselves respectively as developed or developing. This type of approach presents difficulties where the analysis is in any way concerned with scaling; in the present context this is not the case, and the concepts 'developed' and 'developing' merely provide a crude initial entry into the substantive analysis itself.

Accordingly I do not subscribe to the notion that a particular type of development or developmental process is especially appropriate to generating social change. Such is the implication of contingency attached to the theory of structural differentiation (cf. especially

Eisenstadt who has elaborated and made operational the concepts of political and social development as special processes). Rather the words developed and developing are used as an initial means of differentiating particular societies in accordance with their own view of themselves (ideology) and their commitment to economic development (value system). The notion of developed and developing societies thus implies a commitment to a tentative system of international stratification, left here rather gross and unrefined.[1] It should perhaps be stated that to qualify for the description of a developing society, evidence of the commitment to developmental perspectives on the part of an entire society is not required; the articulation of development goals by an effective ruling elite or legitimate institutionalized leadership is sufficient for present purposes.

Particular mention must also be made of the use of the words predeveloped or 'traditional' in discussing certain societies. The concept of traditional is mainly used as an abstraction to characterize a state of affairs or society prior to the articulation of developmental goals. As such it refers also to particular components of social structure or action in order to distinguish these analytically from developmental or 'modern' components. Insofar as reference is made to traditional societies these are societies who do not appear to have reached the stage either of objective economic development or of any subjective desire to participate in the processes associated with it. Cases where the objective economic criteria negate development but the relevant commitment and symbols exist are impossible to allocate to any of our three categories; they have to be treated on their merits and often assigned somewhat arbitrarily. Selfconscious adhesion to existing international strata provides some evidence of self-definition and is a good guide to assignment. Thus Ethiopia has little objective economic or social development but acts internationally with the developing Third World; the Argentine has many of the indices of being developed but also acts internationally as a developing country. Both are accordingly included in this category.[2]

Such a definition should not, of course, be taken to imply that countries which are here called developed and have been included in this general category are no longer preoccupied with growth – or in-

[1] This is developed at some length in 'Modernization and the International System', op. cit.

[2] A good discussion of this problem of classification with reference to South America is K. H. Silvert, 'The Politics of Economic Change', Paper presented to a Conference on Latin America at the Royal Institute of International Affairs, London, February 1965.

deed that there is such an 'end' as complete and final 'development'.[1] All that is implied is a judgement on the relevance of development as variously understood and practised, in the value systems and in the consequent adaptation of structure and process. Many of the problems associated with development, particularly the central one of mobilization, continue to have relevance to societies that are modern or developed by any definition.

The concept of modernization or modernity is frequently associated with that of development, either being sometimes viewed as instrumental to the attainment of the other. Modernization is highly relativistic: a compound self-definition in terms of goals which are a constantly moving target. Like the Marxist word progressive, modern is self-defining as well as summating. Its occasional use here is mainly as a blanket term signifying the self-applied characterization of a high level of development, particularly as distinguished from those societies seeking to emulate it or those 'traditional' ones which have not yet begun to try.

For present purposes, then, development and modernization are entry concepts rather than substantive working ones. As the present analysis proceeds, they will be seen to become increasingly redundant and are replaced by a more detailed classification based on the core concept of mobilization. This is not to suggest that concepts like development or modernization are useless. Being strongly relativistic, they have a place in any *international*—as opposed to the present *cross-national*—analysis. In *The International Context of Modernization* a sustained attempt has been made to define and make operative both these concepts in their appropriate international context; to that extent it is intended to be complementary to the present volume.

F. *Inheritance*

Inheritance is intended to convey a special socio-political situation as defined by the participants. It serves primarily as a lead into the particular situational pattern from which many of the developmental values, structures and processes arise, and which largely sets the manner of their evolution. As such it has cultural connotations; the inheritance situation acts as a common socialization process into the international system for ex-colonies and by derivation for many developing countries. The concept of inheritance is based on the

[1] Such ideological preoccupations cluster round both the extremes of social-economic analysis; Marx and the Communists with their 'final' Communist society, Rostow with his 'last-stage' societies of mass consumption.

assumption of a multi-faceted but dominant reference group relationship between ex-colonies and imperialist countries, real or postulated, arising from an analogy with the legal inheritance of a benefit.

More specifically inheritance refers to the orientation and actions of an elite expecting and preparing to take over from its predecessors. The most common and 'purest' type of inheritance is the attainment of independence by colonies, but social revolution and even substantial reform often carry inheritance aspects in their situation. The concept of inheritance and its application to developing countries will be elaborated repeatedly in the text below.[1]

G. *Political Philosophy and Political Theory*

These terms are used more or less interchangeably to describe the thinking on an abstract level about the government of man and the nature of the state from Plato and Aristotle onwards.[2] As such the intention is to contrast it with sociology and sociological theory. Readers may feel that the distinction has been drawn much too sharply, particularly where modern political theory or modern theories of politics are concerned, let alone political science.[3] The latter seems to me to be an attempt precisely to bridge this chasm. But I have found the distinction heuristically useful, in that there appears to be a real division between the two types of thought and one which is based on a fundamental difference about assumptions. Political theory or philosophy is concerned with problems of legiti-

[1] The concept itself, and its application to empirical situations, have considerable relevance to the present discussion; detailed reference should be made to 'Inheritance', op. cit.

[2] This identification of political theory with political philosophy is usual, though attempts have been made to distinguish between them. Most recently see Eric Weil, 'Philosophie politique, théorie politique', *Revue française de science politique*, IX (1961), pp. 267–94. Theory is there treated as relativistic, prescriptive and practical (Sartre is cited), while philosophy is a more basic discussion, an analysis of and choice between theories on fundamental, unchanging grounds. Personally I doubt whether the difference matters, and I am sure it does not matter here.

[3] The status of political science as a science, and as distinct from political theory or philosophy, is in itself a somewhat agonizing problem of definition and self-appraisal which need not be gone into here. Reference may be made to Carl J. Friedrich, 'Political Philosophy and the Science of Politics', in R. Young (ed.), *Approaches to the Study of Politics*, Evanston, Illinois, 1958, pp. 172–89; 'Philosophy and the Social Sciences', in H. Feigl and M. Brodbeck (eds.), *Readings in the Philosophy of Science*, Minneapolis 1953, section VII. For present purposes modern political science can be taken as having the same orientations and aims as sociological theory, except where specifically distinguished in the text.

macy of rule and justification of acts, and attempts to formulate universal principles by which the action and motivations of individuals can be judged, while sociology is not and does not.[1]

A further point of division between the two is concerned with method. Political theory is committed to tackling normative problems and the distillations of normative criteria while sociology focuses on these mainly in order to remove them from its substantive argument. In political theory 'ought' problems are therefore to the fore; something is reasonable (in the sense of 'it follows that . . .') and/or desirable ('to be preferred . . .'). Sociology on the other hand puts forward proposals and hypotheses about relationships, which, under the weight of empirical evidence, will, it is hoped, eventually stand as theories or even laws. If sociology is not yet at this stage, it is because we do not yet have fully adequate theories and means of testing them, rather than because sociologists accept that the material does not lend itself to the formulation of such laws.

Political theory or philosophy on the one hand, and sociology and sociological theory on the other, in some sense occupy antipodean positions and fill complementary areas of enquiry. Yet at times they confront each other antagonistically. Believing as I do that this contrast between two modes of thought has contributed to certain major difficulties in the analysis of society today, I have illustrated sections of the argument in this essay with examples of their varying contributions.

[1] A representative (of American scholars) discussion of the differences between them is R. Bendix and S. M. Lipset, 'Political Sociology: An Essay and Bibliography', *Current Sociology*, VI (1957), p. 87. Political science is described as investigating the effect of the state on society, while political sociology concerns itself with the effect of society on the state. The difference is thus reduced to direction of influence between two agreed phenomena. A recent discussion, which differentiates between them carefully and in detail, is W. G. Runciman, *Social Science and Political Theory*, Cambridge 1963. Though I think Runciman oversimplifies by attacking the alleged incompatibilities between them as merely the marginalia of disciplinary intolerance and exaggeration, his attempt to show their interdependence and harmony does incidentally provide an illuminating analysis of their respective content and concerns.

Part I
Culture

CHAPTER ONE
Centre and Periphery in Society and Social Science

The notion of society as an entity – at least as a unit of analysis – is a common starting point in many branches of social science. Yet the fact is that few modes of analysis can do justice to the concept of society – even the concept of social system presents many difficulties. As a rule this discrepancy between the unitary implications of the concept and its lack of empirical application is ascribed to the nature of societies themselves – the existential material to which analysis relates. If society is not a meaningful concept it is because there may not be any obvious societies. (Not to mention the even sadder fact that too many social scientists, especially in Britain, simply evade the problem by refusing to rise above the safe but parochial level of 'indisputable' collectivities like parties, churches, trade unions or families.)

Let us for a moment make the opposite assumption – that societies exist in a meaningful way, and that the difficulties are due to the fact that the tools of social science cannot readily be co-ordinated to do justice simultaneously (1) to the sophisticated demands of different academic disciplines, and (2) to the integrated functional reciprocity of a society. The implications of this postulate are that it may be the methodological, intellectual and above all structural separation of social science that prevents justice being done to the study of whole societies. The model of structural differentiation as evidence of social modernization posits the controlling unity of a universalist orientation; in the case of the social sciences we may have structural differentiation without any universals.[1] The reason could be precisely this: social science is not a society and therefore has no universals of its own, yet on the other hand it transports its lack of universals into the subject matter with which it deals. Two qualifications underline the

---

[1] Cf. below, pp. 330 ff.

likelihood of this explanation. First, historically, the increase of specialization and proliferation of methodological preoccupations coincides with a shrinking of the horizon of relevance; we have moved from the universal arena of the theologian via the political theorists' area of state or nation to the individual of the psychologist and behaviourist. As against this, the professionalization of sociology in America has provided a counter movement; the new professional universals seem to coincide with a resuscitation of societal (as opposed to social) perspectives.

If this connection between the social sciences and received views of society is valid, then a more detailed examination of social science problems in this regard may help to explain some of the difficulties of analysis on a societal scale. This applies particularly to the problem of culture. It has already been defined earlier as an activating concept, which colours structure and process and assigns a common dimension to them.[1] Now we suggest that culture may also provide a very specific link for the social sciences, heuristically necessary to enable a connection to be re-established between disciplines which have become over-separate and autonomous for various reasons. In this context culture thus becomes a variable which serves to link disciplines instead of a boundary to separate them.

Following on this discussion it will then be suggested that the idea of culture as a link between disciplines can also usefully be applied to social subsystems. Analytically culture thus has a twofold function: to activate and colour social subsystems by providing a conceptual measure for their orientational content, and also to act as a connecting link between different subsystems, so that boundary exchanges between subsystems pass through two respective frontier areas or subcultures.

Every social science has its catchwords. These are deliberately vague conditioning concepts that follow at the end of a string of precise argument. At first sight, it is alleged, they help to embed the argument in reality. Take a mathematical model of economic devel-

---

[1] See for instance Gabriel A. Almond and S. Verba, *The Civic Culture*, Princeton 1963. The need for such research, though without any specific conceptualization under the term 'culture', is spelt out in considerable detail by Stein Rokkan, 'The Comparative Study of Political Participation: Notes Toward a Perspective on Current Research', in Austin Ranney (ed.), *Essays on the Behavioral Study of Politics*, Urbana, Illinois, 1962, pp. 47–90, especially pp. 55–66.

opment. To make such a model, there must be a great many assumptions and abstractions. These make it neat but 'unreal', of little empirical relevance. At the end some tentative general remarks will therefore often be made, to relate the argument to existential reality. In our example, the author will usually say that the application of his model depends, of course, on the political climate, the sort of government in power, the ability to raise the required taxation, etc., etc. These, he will emphasize, are not his (an economist's) problem. 'Theories about motivations and attitudes, and about the rational or irrational behaviour of different sectors of society ... are of little economic interest or urgency. The economist can easily name the social requirements for economic development; but he expects the sociologist to indicate how to surmount the social and institutional obstacles to growth and how to foresee the social consequences of given measures ...'[1] If the economist does attempt to come to grips with them, he will be berated for an excursion into foreign territory for which he is not qualified.

But the notion that any area of scientific enquiry is encased in a surrounding twilight of 'reality' is a scientistic inversion of the real priorities; it is the surround which is real, and the central area of analysis which is artificial. In any case the apologia for incompetence refers, not so much to diffuse 'reality' as to other areas of enquiry which may be equally scientific, but are of a different discipline and method to the one central for our postulated social scientist. 'Reality' is thus an egocentric definition of disciplinary autonomy. In fact the frontier of relevance is not defined by the line at which abstraction ends and reality begins (however much it may often seem like this), but by the limitations of methodological means at hand, and ignorance of more suitable alternatives. Such limitations are partly genuine, partly imposed by the academic convention of self-disciplined specialization; the risks of poaching are great. Our economist may know much more about politics or sociology than he lets on, but prefers to keep his apologia very general for fear of poaching in a 'foreign' jurisdiction.

Yet there is at the same time nothing haphazard or accidental about these catchwords. In the social sciences they play a necessary role. Indeed, the field they cover is a geographically inevitable suburb on the outskirts of the discipline itself, whose existence actually makes the scientific development of the discipline possible; without

[1] Victor L. Urquidi, *The Challenge of Development in Latin America*, New York 1964, p. 77.

them, the necessary definitional precision of science could not be attained. I shall call this field a catchment area.[1]

There are two interesting aspects to these catchment areas. First they–and only they–make possible any analogy between the social and the physical sciences; without them, there would be no such thing as social *science*. Specifically, catchment areas make exactitude possible in inexact (i.e. non-repetitive) circumstances, by facilitating the removal of non-comparable variables in a theoretical (universally valid) system, *and then permitting them to be reintroduced at the end in the form of extraneous qualifications*. Secondly, the cultivation efforts in catchment areas are not a methodological commitment; like judges' *obiter dicta*, they cannot be quoted or held against the theory to which they relate nor against its author. Magically, they condition the theory but cannot invalidate it.[2]

The main catchment area of modern politics is political culture. This is a new concept, both in its analytical and operational distinc-

[1] Perceptive readers may have noticed that twice in this paragraph the word 'field' has been used. This legal-agricultural word–with its connotation of obvious discontinuities, of womb-like infertility (until fertilized by research), of specialized cash crops–is good linguistic evidence of the compartmentalization of academic effort. In this metaphor disciplines, with their notion of joint or shared endeavour and interactive learning, really become specialized co-operative or collective farms (with multi-product farms corresponding to universities). Catchment areas here correspond to marginal land (marginal in the sense of being capable of profitable utilization in different ways). As will be seen if the metaphor is retained in the mind throughout perusal of the following pages, this catchment land can be used in various ways; cultivated to produce what the main farm area produces, cultivated to produce what other neighbouring farms produced, or left fallow. This corresponds to the subsequently developed notions of autonomy, colonization and simple though eventually retrograde isolation.

[2] For a recent formulation of a theory of interdisciplinary differentiation in the social sciences see Max Gluckman (ed.), *Closed Systems and Open Minds: The Limits of Naïvety in Social Anthropology*, Edinburgh 1964. This book is concerned with the same problems as the present chapter though it solves them in a different way–by postulating valid areas of autonomy for each discipline, and then classifying permissible and impermissible excursions across frontiers. Demarcating autonomous areas is called circumscription. Summarizing and simplifying the conclusions put forward by work in neighbouring disciplines (with the necessary assumption of internalizing them) is called compression. These activities are permitted under certain, fairly rigorous conditions which are outlined in the lengthy conclusion–by Gluckman and Devons– on the empirical work contained in the volume. In short, naïve trespasses into neighbouring disciplines by the use of compression are permitted only in fields which are considered to be genuinely peripheral, i.e. of secondary importance. This thesis necessarily involves a definition of what is central and peripheral to each discipline and therefore depends on the functional accuracy of such definitions. There is also difficulty with the wider implications of this method. It assumes a world of disciplines divided into autonomous entities, each one

tiveness and in respect of the focus of empirical research in it. Yet the relevant area of concern is of course much older, going back to Bagehot, de Tocqueville and a whole generation of work on 'national character' as well as to Weber's analysis of the connection between achievement and socio-religious culture.[1] Particularly the development of comparative politics has made the need for identifying the catchment area all the more urgent, a catchment area moreover in which all the inconvenient peculiarities of each political society, which cannot be 'compared' and thus hold up the creation of concepts of general, or at least cross-national validity, may be trapped and carted away. Thus we may compare the executives, legislatures, political parties and interest groups of Britain, France, Germany and Russia, and ascribe the incomparable to political culture. We may–if we are conscientious–analyse it a bit; often with a dose of overselective and schematic history. Initially, the concept of political culture thus seems to offer a simple way out of a genuine difficulty. Like all simple escapes from real intellectual difficulties, the manner in which this catchment area (and indeed all catchment areas) can be made operational can easily become stereotyped. Thus imports from catchment areas are liable, methodologically and substantively, to be secondary derivations or abstractions rather than primary findings. Yet we cannot do without imports, since the social sciences are inevitably interdependent; for *some* purposes at least society must be perceived as a complex but single system. There is a permanent dilemma: increasingly autonomous development in each of the social sciences which separates it from the others, and simultaneously a growing need to relate these sciences to each other– hence the increasing specialization of research in the catchment areas. At a certain stage a catchment area becomes so specialized as to justify its elevation into a new, separate discipline (social anthropology between anthropology and sociology, or social psychology between psychology and sociology). This in turn creates new catchment areas. I shall call the opening up or development of catchment areas colonization.

How to escape from this dilemma? There seem to be two main

---

relevant to a particular aspect or sector of social enquiry–the constraining tyranny of the 'field' once more. Translated into social terms this is precisely equivalent to the assumption that subsystems of society are autonomous and at all times equally salient; the concept of society thus becomes a mere abstraction.

[1] Some of the major works on Germany, Britain, the Soviet Union and the United States are cited in *The Civic Culture*, note 9, pp. 13–14.

possibilities, intellectual collaboration and dialectic substitution. The first is an attempt at a methodological and personal get-together, which defines the problem in terms of a lack of communication facilities. 'Let's have a conference with the economists (sociologists, philosophers, etc.). Let's read and internalize each other's pace-making texts.' Most important, 'let's encourage research (and the institutionalized expression of it through special academic posts) in the frontier areas, the problem areas that divide and at the same time hold the social sciences together'.[1] This, it is hoped, will eliminate catchment areas. The assumption is that catchment areas are an unscientific and temporary nuisance, due to a failure to communicate.

This method (to continue our analogy) might be called the customs union. Imports are now 'free', and efforts are made to use them to the best advantage in the home industry. To use the techniques of functional anthropology on complex industrial societies, for instance, is now fashionable. Of course it also makes intellectual sense. Much really illuminating research in the social sciences—and, for all I know, in the physical sciences as well—breaks up the bricks and mortar of the familiar into 'neutral' raw material before it can create new shapes and forms; information theory is a very good example. For our purposes the interesting thing is that such a breakthrough often occurs first on the disciplinary frontiers, in the catchment areas. Conscious of this valuable potential, each discipline now tries to occupy the catchment areas for itself on the grounds that it is exclusively the concern of the central subject. Instead of assigning political culture—the catchment area of political studies—to history and psychology, political scientists increasingly occupy it as a fertile area which can fructify their researches in the acknowledged central areas of political studies. So our methodological get-together has not really produced a customs union or free trade at all; having discovered the historians' and psychologists' tools for colonizing political culture we adopt the tools—but reserve the right of exploitation to ourselves. The catchment area still exists, 'owned' perhaps by us but exploited with borrowed tools.[2]

[1] Cf. E. H. Carr '. . . the more sociological history becomes, and the more historical sociology becomes, the better for both. *Let the frontier between them be kept wide open for two-way traffic.*' (*What is History?*, 1962, p. 84; my italics.) For a more pessimistic view, which confines the historical relevance of certain sociological techniques to 'subordinate social systems [only] such as industry, the family, or the organization of science', see Jean Floud, *History and Theory*, IV, 2, (1965), p. 275.

[2] This provides the exact 'academic' illustration of Parsons' theory of structural differentiation mentioned earlier. See particularly Parsons and

But science is not static. Borrowed techniques do not remain in the catchment areas. Functional anthropology for instance has permeated all political and social studies (except in Britain). Some disciplines seem to colonize their neighbours, while others whose methodology may perhaps be weak or out of date tend easily to absorb 'foreign' development. This in itself would make a fascinating comparative study. Politics seems at present to be a fat colonial prize, and has recently been heavily penetrated by sociology. (Whether the study of politics really has, or ever has had, any particular methodology of its own is very much open to question.)

Unlike bits of land, however, ownership and control of catchment areas are not exclusive. In the social sciences these can be simultaneously occupied and exploited by two or several disciplines. Thus social psychology is at one and the same time the frontier area for studies of individuals in their collective orientation, and the frontier area for sociology in its study of collectivities as affected by individual psychology. Nor is there any *a priori* reason why such overlapping should produce either collaboration or differentiation; the same catchment area may sometimes be shared or disputed. In many cases there may not even be awareness that there is a common catchment area. 'In 1955 the author chanced upon an education journal devoted to reviewing research studies on the diffusion of new educational ideas. This was the first convergence between two research traditions, education and rural sociology, that had both been investigating the spread of new ideas for over 17 years!'[1]

This has obvious relevance to society as well. Problems are often unjustifiably viewed as amenable exclusively to one type of remedy, or *either* to one remedy *or* another, but not amenable to both and only to both. It has taken a long time to accept the interrelation of politics with economics–and the understanding is not by any means complete. A different example is the difficulty of institutionalizing the co-operation between the social services, like mental and physical health, and the law; between education and socialization, etc. It becomes clear yet again to what extent problems of social integration on one hand, and intellectual or academic integration on the other are closely related.

Smelser, *Economy and Society*, 1956; and Parsons, Bales and others, *Family, Socialization and Interaction Process*, 1955; also Neil J. Smelser, 'Toward a Theory of Modernization' in Amitai and Eva Etzioni (eds.), *Social Change*, New York 1964.

[1] Everett M. Rogers, *Diffusion of Innovations*, New York 1962, p. 21. Cf. also the specific instances given on pp. 22 ff.

Nor does the interaction of academic disciplines relate only to the catchment areas, and thus remain a boundary problem. This brings up the other, substitution, method of dealing with the problem of catchment areas, to meet the neighbouring discipline head on and absorb it into the discipline itself. This is difficult–if it were easy, the 'import' would not have been confined to a catchment area in the first place. There is more to this than a mere extension of normal inter-disciplinary accommodation. The borrowed techniques do not occupy the catchment areas direct from abroad. Instead they get there via the home discipline, 'internalized' by that discipline and its practitioners for the purpose of conquest. In analysing political culture, we do not invite sociologists or psychologists in (if they are in already we try to drive them out)–we *become* sociologists and psychologists. To this extent the main discipline is affected by the import even *before* the catchment area is colonized with new techniques. Instead of this:

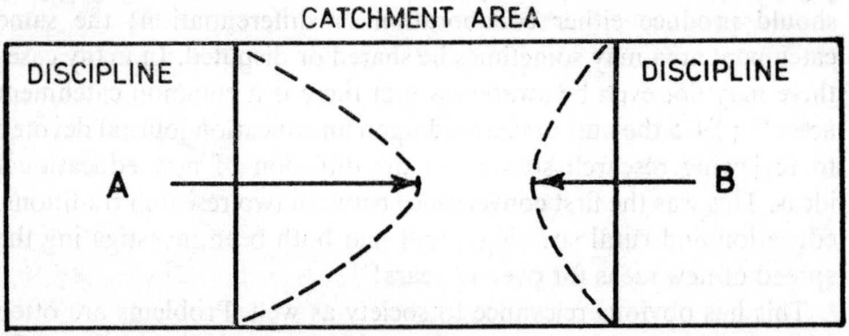

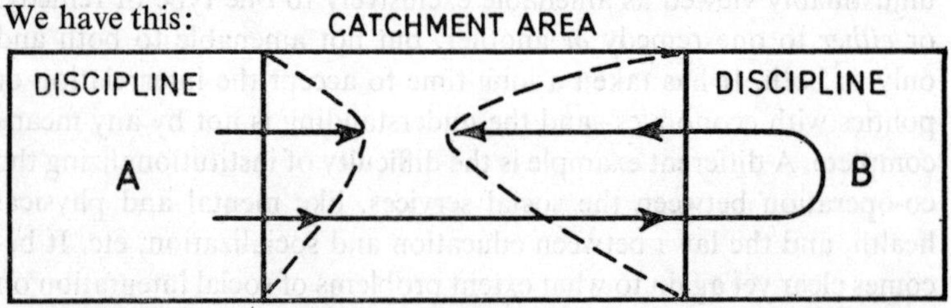

Diagram 1

This might be described as the dialectic (instead of the evolutionary) concept of creativity–the notion that juxtaposition or enforced interaction of the unfamiliar, the incongruent, the apparently irrelevant even, often produce a new and valuable synthesis. Koestler makes just this claim in his analysis of artistic creation; and it has been summed up neatly by an elegant philosopher as 'converting paradoxes into platitudes and vice versa'.[1] At first sight this notion of drastic or vital confrontation seems to negate the relevance of the concept of catchment areas by making them redundant. But it may in fact enhance its importance. For the confrontation between disciplines is never stark but more or less conditioned. While the awareness of paradox between disciplines and of its creative possibilities may come with brutal suddenness, its subsequent use (certainly the explanation of any synthesis) is gently and relativistically cushioned. For instance we know enough about metaphor to realize how constrained is the dramatic illumination of the unexpected or unfamiliar, and how much social time its permeation and acceptance take. In this context therefore catchment areas act as a means of acclimatizing and domesticating the foreign. Such quarantine is *psychologically* necessary for the users. Once more this problem is as much social as academic; new techniques are usually diffused most rapidly by being made to appear as logical extensions of the familiar.[2]

One particular catchment area may illustrate this argument–one that is of central relevance to the present essay. Theories of economic development all trail socio-political catchment areas behind them. The very success of the development panacea has made 'the development plan' into a magic formula–with the result that economists who normally extrapolate from, or analyse the consequences of, a technology rooted in the postulate of rational behaviour now find their tools and concepts employed to further the ends of a modern version of tribal magic. Either they have had to increase their catchment areas furiously to keep up, or relegate much so-called development planning in practice to a limbo that has nothing to do with economics at all.[3] Any such inversion of the normal size ratio between substantive discipline and catchment area or fringe is both uncomfortable and unprofessional (it is at this point that the need for philosophical enquiry into the basic assumptions of disciplines

[1] Arthur Koestler, *The Act of Creation*, London 1964; Isaiah Berlin, 'Does Political Theory still Exist?', in P. Laslett and W. G. Runciman *Philosophy, Politics and Society*, Second Series, Oxford 1962, p. 1.

[2] Everett M. Rogers, *Diffusion of Innovations*, op. cit. Cf. M. Landau 'On the Use of Metaphor in Political Analysis', *Social Research*, XXVIII (1961), pp. 331–53; James F. Davidson, 'Political Science and Political Fiction', *Am. Pol. Sc. Rev.*, LV, 4 (December 1961), pp. 851–60.

[3] Cf. Andrew M. Watson and Joel B. Dirlam, 'The Impact of Underdevelopment on Economic Planning', *Quarterly Journal of Economics*, LXXIX, 2, May 1965; also Albert Breton, 'The Economics of Nationalism', *Journal of Political Economy*, LXXII (1964), pp. 376–86.

becomes urgent).[1] Accordingly the catchment area of development economics (the social and political setting for economic planning) has recently been rigorously colonized by socio-political development studies. It is perfectly possible in theory to accept the political *rationality*–and the political *purpose*–behind a lot of economic planning and development in emerging countries and project some sort of an economic growth model from them, even though it may look very odd and out of balance. It is equally possible (and has been done) to carry out the exercise the other way round and deduce a *political* model from existing growth patterns that happen not to make any *economic* sense (and therefore cannot be used as an economic model).[2] In each case a towering catchment area has been internalized and broken up into manageable shape with borrowed techniques.

The problem is old though it has not always been squarely faced in modern politics or sociology. Making as it does large claims for the area it covers, sociology particularly is sensitive to the constant need to import and export techniques, to synthesize paradoxes or contrasts for heuristic purposes, and to pay special attention to its catchment areas.[3] It may well be this crucial sensitivity, which arises both from the complexity of the subject studied as well as the saliency of its frontier areas as a discipline, that makes it (wrongly) prone to the attacks of methodological scoffers. By denying the existence of sociology, they may in fact be denying the existence of society.[4]

The same colonization has now been attempted in the catchment area of politics–political culture. The techniques are those of sociology and psychology; political theory as such has no tools for the job. Political culture can, according to these attempts, now be grouped into kinds (e.g. unitary and divisive); more important still, it can be divided into patterns and variables by which cultures can then be graded on a scale.[5] From being a general catchment concept, political

[1] Cf. Joseph Cropsey, 'On the Relation of Political Science and Economics', *Am. Pol. Sc. Rev.*, LIV 1 (March 1960), pp. 3–14.

[2] Nettl and Robertson, 'Industrialization, Development or Modernization?', op. cit.

[3] Cf. the discussion by Talcott Parsons, 'Some Problems Confronting Sociology as a Profession', *American Sociological Review*, XXIV (1959), pp. 547–59.

[4] See recently W. G. Runciman, 'Sociologese', *Encounter*, XXV, 6 (December 1965), pp. 45–47. Some of these problems were raised by Georg Simmel, *Grundfragen der Soziologie*, Leipzig 1917.

[5] Cf. G. A. Almond and Sidney Verba, *The Civic Culture*, op. cit.

culture is thus on the way to becoming one of the major avenues by which politics and especially comparative politics may be approached. Substantively there is increasing evidence of emphasis on culture, though the specific conceptualization is still new and relatively rare, and hence used with much caution.[1]

But there still remains the level-of-analysis problem. It is no accident that political analysis can more easily accommodate culture and relate it to process when dealing with an empirical study of one or a few countries. It is far more difficult to incorporate the concept of culture into any balanced theory or theoretical construct of cross-national political or social life. One such overall attempt is that of Talcott Parsons. As already pointed out in the introductory definition of the concept of culture, he assigns a whole 'system' of culture to the top of his hierarchy of human systems. In addition he assigns the function of culture production in the social system to the latency subsystem, thus giving it some primacy (the intake boundary of the L subsystem is partially blocked off, suggesting more output than input for the subsystem). There is a whole range of problems connected with Parsons' analysis and representation of culture, but it does represent an attempt to incorporate the problem into consistent systems analysis. This is very important. The present analysis puts forward an alternative method by which culture can be related to

[1] Though not specifically political, the culture retrieval operations of the 1937 Yale Cross-Cultural Survey have pride of place; see George P. Thurdock, 'The Cross-Cultural Survey', *American Sociological Review*, V (1940), pp. 361–70; *An Outline of World Cultures*, third edition, New Haven 1963; F. W. Moore (ed.), *Readings in Cross-Cultural Methodology*, New Haven 1961 (Human Relations Area Files). The pioneering studies in politics are probably Harold D. Lasswell, Nathan Leites, *et al.*, *Language of Politics*, New York 1949; Lasswell, Daniel Lerner and I. de Sola Pool, *The Comparative Study of Symbols*, Stanford 1952. The specific emphasis on political culture *eo ipso* began cautiously with Almond who, in *Politics of Developing Areas*, 1960, still uses culture mainly by postulate, as a residual category. For Almond and Verba, *Civic Culture*, 1963, it becomes the central reference, though the authors exercise restraint in the claims they make for its explanatory power. But cf. Seymour Martin Lipset, *The First New Nation*; Lucian W. Pye, *Politics, Personality and Nationbuilding*; *Burma's Search for Identity*; L. Binder, *Iran: Political Development in a Changing Society*, and other recent area studies for increasing operational emphasis on the specific concept of culture. See also Lucian W. Pye and Sidney Verba, *Political Culture and Political Development*, Princeton 1965, a series of brief area studies. Herbert J. Spiro, 'Comparative Politics: A Comprehensive Approach', *Am. Pol. Sc. Rev.*, LVI, 3, (September 1962), pp. 577–95, emphasizes style rather than culture as one of the central variables, but substantively his analysis assigns absolute priority to culture as directly governing the political process. Carl J. Friedrich and Karl W. Deutsch announce a specifically political systems application of the Human Relations Area Files material in progress.

process, both at the empirical level and at the abstract level of systems. For catchment areas are essentially an analytical concept, and can be used both for system and subsystem analysis as well as providing a means of coming to grips with empirical problems. Hence the attempt here to relate the problems of analysis to the 'reflected' (and 'reflecting') problems of society.[1]

If political culture can be analytically incorporated into the conceptual framework of both systems analysis and comparative politics, it will help to enrich all other concepts and condition their use. The relationship between legislatures and executives, or the pattern and scope of interest groups, will make much more sense if illuminated by the particular colour of a recognizable *type* of political culture. If the German state need no longer be explained by a politicized or popularized continuum of Hegelian Reason, but can be identified *inter alia* as the product of what Almond and Verba call a largely parochial-detached subject culture, or as a bureaucratic collectivity of authoritarian personalities;[2] if ministerial instability in Italy is related to a civic culture of cynical or 'alienated' non-participation— then clearly the *area* of researchable politics (as a system of related variables) has been increased. Whether or not we like the particular method in question, or agree with its results, we cannot afford to ignore this colonization of a catchment area.

But it must be absolutely clear that in operational (rather than conceptual) terms political culture is not a substantive discovery—let alone solution—of a 'new' cluster of problems. Political culture is not a thing, or a fact, or even a sector of hitherto undiscovered relevance. It is merely a rearrangement (possibly improvement?) of the intellectual order of things, a new structural relationship between disciplines in academic 'society' and in social systems. It resembles the effect on certain social structures of any social change. By capturing, holding and rapidly colonizing the catchment area of political culture *with the tools of sociology* (conceptual as well as operational—sample surveys, intense participant observation, latent structure analysis), politics or political science is defending itself against the sociological offensive; it is keeping sociology as a discipline out of its concerns. It is somewhat like the barbarian settlement policy of the later Roman and Chinese empire, like the incorporation of more developed subject

---

[1] For a more extended discussion of Parsons on culture and a confrontation of the two alternative approaches, see the longer version of this chapter published in *American Behavioral Scientist*, IX, 10 (June 1966), pp. 39–46.

[2] T. W. Adorno and others, *The Authoritarian Personality*, New York 1950.

nations by the Ottomans.[1] Thus the real function of catchment areas is to combine the two methods mentioned earlier of breaking down the autonomy and isolation of disciplines as well as systems and sectors: on one hand a concession to bellicose neighbours which simultaneously provides a valid defence, on the other a creation of spectrally or culturally mixed combinations which provide areas of communication between one discipline and another. The more specialized a discipline has become, the greater the need for catchment areas around it; the more thorough the specialization achieved by its neighbours, the greater the need for self-defence by old, diffuse, 'imperialist' disciplines like politics. The reason why the catchment concept of political culture has been put forward in this essay is therefore twofold. It is a useful concept within which to analyse certain types of facts about social systems (mostly not new)–a concept moreover, as we hope to show, that is capable of comparative categorization. Secondly its use may help to revive political analysis in particular from its present integrative sterility and explain its over-adaptive deference *vis-à-vis* sociology and other disciplines (or, alternatively, Marxism).

Before we examine the particular colonization involved in political culture, let us ask once again (and more empirically) to what extent colonization of catchment areas is really progress of self-deception. The fact that catchment areas are an important rearrangement of existing conceptions and not a discovery of new ground (let alone an invention) has already been emphasized. There is also the fact that particular forms of analysis may become fashionable, and translate any

---

[1] One classic example of precisely such a process of defence-by-adoption in the 'war' between politics and sociology is Gabriel A. Almond, 'Political Systems and Political Change', *American Behavioral Scientist*, VI, 10 (June 1963), pp. 3–10; and 'A Developmental Approach to Political Systems', *World Politics*, XVII, 2 (January 1965), pp. 183–214. Here the process can be studied in an ongoing form through the work of one political scientist. For one thing, Almond's notion of politics suddenly (1963) demonstrates an unexpected general systems approach but one that actually particularizes the concept of system in the direction of the concept of sovereignty evolved in classical political theory (cf. also 'The Concept of System', op. cit., p. 320). Secondly he incorporates into politics some anthropological-sociological system functions (three) and system survival capabilities (four in 1963, five in 1965), all bearing a superficial resemblance to those of Parsons. Finally Almond adopts fully sociological perspectives by expressly equating dysfunctional inputs (destructive of equilibrium) with the locus of social change or development. This point is developed from simple malfunctioning (1960) via situational compression of adjustments in capability systems (1963) to a final definition of dysfunction as intra- or inter-system inputs making for change. Truly any peripheral [political] barbarian too can now shout *civis sociologicus sum*–if he wants!

excessive emphasis resulting from academic fashionableness into a corresponding emphasis on the particular aspect of society with which they happen to be concerned. Thus the new concept of political culture may be promoted to explain far too much–partly because jaded academic palates are as much tickled by the new and recent as anybody else's, partly because catchment areas have a (logical) habit of being wider in scope than any individual piece of heartland research, and thus give a greater return in terms of apparent relevance. Political culture provides the context for the analysis of groups, institutions, processes, individuals. But this is not the same as creating a collectivity for analytical purposes. Any analytical move towards bigger units or blocks must, one would suppose, be a genuine synthesis of comparable agglomerations of things, not just the inflation of catchment areas as contexts. If, say, legislatures, executives, judiciaries, bureaucracies and informal agencies can be meaningfully synthesized into 'government'–not just a collective word, but a *collectivity* capable of meaningful comparison with other such collectivities–then comparative politics at once becomes more scientific. The use of a catchment area as a new collectivity, merely because neighbouring techniques have been used for colonization and are therefore more fashionable than the discipline's own particular techniques, is intellectually a pyrrhic victory. To accept as axiomatic that the fashionable import must be more relevant is an admission of defeat. It *may* be justified, but *need* not be. The elevation of a former catchment area into a new, central and superior conceptual collectivity does not automatically justify the all-round acceptance of new techniques–unless the discipline was already so feeble as to let its own central preoccupations become another discipline's catchment area. This would for instance be the case if sociology–its particular kind of imagination and its evolving techniques–were really able to explain political processes, institutions and events better than the means adopted by political scientists over the years–or if philosophy proved to be no more than the mere superstructure of economic relations after all.

One good way of testing the justification of incorporating newly colonized catchment areas is to find out to what extent the colonization is really tautological. It is perhaps a sad commentary on modern specialization that we often use the techniques of one discipline to demonstrate something that we already knew with the (perhaps drab) tools of another. Or we simply prove the obvious–like the fact that those who frequently visit public libraries take out more books than those who visit rarely (a well-publicized example of recent research).[1] This illustration has been chosen deliberately for it is *both* an example of obviousness and low-grade relevance–so what if there is little correlation between visiting and using–and yet at the same time *could* throw an interesting light on the public library as a social centre for the otherwise deprived; what is irrelevant and obvious in one context may illuminate something important in another. This problem is at the very core of all sociological reference, and consti-tutes an important part of what makes the sociological imagination different from any other. In the case of Almond and Verba's *Civic Culture*, the questionnaire about German attitudes to government illustrates little more–though in different *words* and with a different and more formal *technique*–than what most historians already know. (The authors will reply 'guessed' instead of 'knew'.) To that extent any acclaim for the *Civic Culture* questionnaire is a denigration of history. The same thing applies to the 'proof' of the participant attitude prevailing in Britain and the United States (De Tocqueville!). This warning does not of course invalidate the colonization of catch-ment areas, it merely puts it into the right perspective.

Ultimately the problem is one of balance and interrelationships. The colonization of the catchment area of political culture at the empirical level provides a better understanding of particular societies. At the theoretical and comparative level it can provide a better understanding of the context within which systems operate, and in what way components are related. Here we must distinguish between improvement and precision of knowledge that we already have and mere relabelling, also between the reallocation of priorities as to what is more or less relevant or important and the addition of genuinely new variables for the analysis of society–the creation of *tools*. So far we have discussed culture as a concept; how it fits into academic social science and how it might be fitted into the study and understanding of society. Now we must see whether the concept lends itself (1) to any form of quantitative measure, or (2) to any useful means of qualitative classification, and (3) whether any such classi-fications are merely descriptive or can be used to explain process in the social system.

[1] Hans L. Zetterburg, *Social Theory and Social Practice*, New York 1962.

CHAPTER TWO
Political Culture-Level

SUMMARY

A discussion of political culture in the framework of any systems analysis must do justice both to the problem of measuring quantity, and also attempt to find a means of comparing quality. Though in many senses quality is the first-order problem, convenience dictates a discussion of quantity first. An attempt will be made to find concepts for the criteria of measurement; in what way can culture be defined for purposes of quantitative measurement? The criterion chosen is, simply stated, knowledge and evaluation of problems of government, with particular reference to the orientation towards institutionalized authority. Some examples will be given of the types of problems involved. Next, and closely connected with this, is the relationship between political culture and the notion of participation. Almond and Verba in the *Civic Culture* have relied mainly on participation as a means of classifying political cultures; a brief critique of this approach is undertaken. At the same time the problem of ideology and consciousness in the context of political culture must be raised here. Next it will be necessary to search for indices in order to measure varying levels of culture and some possible alternatives are examined. An important distinction between 'hard' indices of acculturation, and 'soft' indices related to orientations is emphasized. Finally, the notion of a continuum of levels of political culture is broken down into five different thresholds, according to which individual societies, and sectors of society, can be classified and compared.

Without a discussion of quality there cannot really be any discussion of quantity or extent of culture, otherwise we do not really know what we are measuring.[1] However, there are good reasons for beginning here with a discussion of quantity. For one thing, a dis-

[1] See e.g. Colin Cherry, *On Human Communications*, New York 1957, pp. 256–73. Cf. Deutsch, *Nerves of Government*, pp. 87–88.

cussion of quantity introduces at an early stage a crucial problem in any discussion of politics; namely the declining levels of culture as we move from centre to periphery in the social system. By dealing with this problem first, it is easier at a later stage to identify the location of issues and actions in accordance with the declining level of culture as we move out from centre to periphery, and to view them as more or less salient in accordance with their distance from the centre, as expressed in terms of culture levels.[1]

Secondly, the language of politics is more conducive to qualification than to quantification. Thus, by taking quantification first, some initial familiarity can be obtained with the particular approach to be used in the present analysis.[2] But for this purpose it will be necessary to define at least the approximate nature of what is being quantified; a more refined analysis of content being reserved for the later discussion of quality.

A political culture may be said to exist when political authority, and the processes relating to that authority, are effectively internalized by members of the society. Political authority in this context may be defined as the institutionalization of societal goal attainment. For the observer, therefore, culture consists of a pattern or patterns of knowledge, evaluations and communications relating to political authority.

As one is never sure in cases of definition whether conceptual definition is better served by example or by explanation (or explanation immediately followed by its own example, in a neat parade of pairs like candidates for Noah's Ark) it might be useful to spell out more fully the meaning of the core concepts of authority, goal attainment, function and political system, in terms of the orientation of those whose level of culture we may wish to measure. The more differentiated the political sub-system in relation to other sub-systems and of society as a whole, the greater the specific crystallization of political culture (in terms of the previous discussion, the greater the catchment area of politics). If we take culture, in accordance with Parsons' definition, as a total system analytically separated from the social system, we would have to discuss the level of political culture not only as a separate, specifically political, phenomenon, but also consider

---

[1] This incorporation of distance in terms of saliency as a cultural problem is one more valuable contribution of the model put forward by Herbert J. Spiro, 'Comparative Politics: A Comprehensive Approach', op. cit.

[2] Some interesting aspects of the problem of language in the context of quantification and qualification are raised in G. Scott Williamson and Innes H. Pearce, *Science, Synthesis and Sanity*, London 1965.

it as part of an undifferentiated cultural system generally. By using the notion of catchment areas, however, we are able to treat political culture as a specific phenomenon from the start, and consider an undifferentiated culture, which is unable to incorporate any specific notions of political authority, as a form of low acculturation and consequently as evidence of a low level of political culture.

Also, by taking political authority as the main referent, we avoid a host of difficult problems which either broaden the concept of political culture excessively, or define it in a culture-bound or prescriptive sense. Thus problems of sanctions–which also exist outside politics; of legitimacy–which is not always accorded by members of a society; and of the allocation of values, on which there may also not be universal agreement, are all avoided in this definition. The problem of positive versus negative evaluation of authority, of allegiance or disaffection, is left open; both evaluations would represent a certain level of political culture indifferently as between a pattern of positive or negative attitudes. Also it is most emphatically *not* suggested that acculturation as described here implies any strengthening of central values; this is a much more positive factor of normative integration which may be part of acculturation, but is not essential to it.[1]

A further component of measuring political culture in this context is provided by the emphasis on communication. Knowledge and evaluation, the main criteria of culture level, are meaningless except in the context of communication structures. While we do not necessarily have to study these structures in order to make judgements about the level of political culture, these can serve as useful means of discovering orientations resulting from knowledge and evaluation, and therefore provide some indices as to culture levels. Culture is altogether the most difficult aspect of politics to measure, and consequently it is desirable to maintain as many options as possible in reserve to enable us to make useful judgements about culture levels.

Now some examples. The referent of political authority and its institutionalization will most usually be the State and its government. But there are, of course, political cultures which focus almost exclusively around political parties, like the Chinese Communists in Yunan after the Long March, and the German SPD in its 'isolated' period before the First World War. The relative weight given to party

---

[1] Such an identification is however attempted by Edward Shils, 'Centre and Periphery', *The Logic of Personal Knowledge: Essays Presented to Michael Polanyi on his Seventieth Birthday*, London 1961, pp. 117–30.

and state in many countries where dissident, tightly organized and self-sufficient parties exist, varies from situation to situation; where stable denial of legitimacy to a state exists, and is instead accorded to a party, we clearly already have quite a high level of political culture. This was the situation in Germany under the Weimar Republic both as regards Communists and National Socialists, also in France during the long history of the disaffection of the Right under the Third Republic. Even a revolutionary insurgent is therefore part of the political culture of a society–however much he may dissociate himself from the polity or the society as such. The main criterion for deciding whether the incorporation of institutionalized authority within such parties or movements belongs to a political culture or not depends largely on the framework within which particular situations arise. Thus it is conceivable for a religious movement like the Moslem Brotherhood to articulate a particular orientation towards leadership which denies the basis of political legitimacy of the secular state and yet still be part of a political culture. Where on the contrary such movements take place in total disregard of the state, neither specifically in favour nor opposed to it, we would speak of a low level of political culture and treat the orientation towards a religious leader as not providing evidence of a political culture. This is the case with Millenarian leaders in Latin America and in Polynesian Cargo cults. Nearer home we have this sort of problem in assessing the cultural aspects of involvement as regards member of sects like the Salvation Army in its militant phase towards the end of the nineteenth century.

The boundary of political culture is thus not to be measured in terms of commitment as such, but implies a judgement on the form and nature of such commitment. A Vietnamese or Laotian peasant who is blackmailed or otherwise forced into support of the Viet Cong or Pathet Lao respectively may be committed as a result of personal force, but he is not necessarily acculturated–though he may become acculturated in time and may evaluate his situation politically rather than personally in accordance with higher levels of knowledge. Similarly insurgent Radfan tribesmen on the Yemen-Aden border may or may not be acculturated in their dissidence, depending on whether their response is the automatic loyalty given to fellow members of a tribe or a more or less evaluated protest against the British or the South Arabian Federation. Similar problems arise with many other dissident movements in developing countries, like the Karens in Burma and the Nagas in India. Even though we may be in no position to answer such questions accurately, it is nonetheless important to recognize where the conceptual boundary of political culture falls. This is particularly the case when assessing the evidence of mobilization through political parties in developing countries. There is far too much emphasis on the instrumentality of such parties at the centre of the political system, and not nearly enough on the effect of such parties on the level of political culture at the periphery. We do not usually have the evidence to distinguish, say in a case like that of the Convention Peoples' Party in Ghana under the Nkrumah regime, between the personal element of force and the political-cultural element of involvement at the grassroots level of mobilization. Indeed the two aspects are, or become, interrelated. In any case it will be argued later that the function of these parties ought to be viewed, at least in part, as connected with the diffusion of political culture. As recent research has shown, similar functions of culture production and diffusion were in the past performed by political parties at the periphery in what are today developed countries with high all-round levels of political culture.[1]

The present definition of political culture in no way calls for any particular view about the nature of political authority and its institutionalization. In this sense the definition of political culture is broad, since it leaves open the problem of what and whose political authority is in question. Moreover, there is no need to view the internalization of political authority as referring to any constant form or locus of authority. These may well change, particularly in a revolutionary situation, where allegiance and legitimacy are transferred from one, possibly central, structure to other, possibly local, regional, tribal, religious, or ethnic institutions, and back again. The distinction is important, for while allegiance and evaluation may shift, slowly or rapidly, the *level* of acculturation is not reversible—except conceivably over a long period of time. Indeed, this fact actually helps to explain the tendency, at a certain level of acculturation, for rapid shifts of allegiance to take place. At such levels evaluative attention becomes closely focused on problems of legitimacy attribution; the increasing awareness and evaluation of government naturally tend to produce a

[1] See for instance S. Rokkan and H. Valen, 'The Mobilization of the Periphery', in S. Rokkan (ed.), *Approaches to the Study of Political Participation*, Bergen 1962, pp. 111–59. Some English evidence on similar lines is provided by N. Gash, *Politics in the Age of Peel*, London 1953; H. J. Hanham, *Elections and Electoral Management: Politics in the Time of Disraeli and Gladstone*, London 1959; J. Cornford, 'The Transformation of Conservatism in the Late Nineteenth Century', *Victorian Studies*, VII (1963), pp. 35–66. Similar work exists for the United States, France, Germany and Finland.

predisposition to be more critical. As Deutsch has said, in this sense 'nations all over the world are becoming increasingly hard to govern'.[1] Of course a rising level of political culture does not in itself imply either more criticism or greater difficulty for government, but it suggests at least a possibility that governmental competence and levels of political culture do not necessarily move in step; while we are accustomed in the West to the idea that the former usually precedes the latter, there is no good reason why the reverse situation should not hold in many developing countries. The argument of this essay will put forward the notion that this imbalance between the level of political culture in different sectors of a society, and the corresponding accommodation of government to such levels, is one of the main features of politics in many developing countries.

We can in fact go rather farther than this. The product of research, both of vulgar psephology and more sophisticated behavioural analysis, constantly reminds us of the sizeable pockets of lack of knowledge, of contradiction between evaluation and action, of indifference in the [presumably] high levels of culture in developed societies.

How are we to match this up with the far greater knowledge, more 'rational' alignment of action with evaluation, and interest or involvement in formal politics, in countries like Italy or Greece – not to speak of the obviously participant activities of rioters or demonstrators and counter-demonstrators in developing societies like India, Ghana or Nigeria? Much of the difference arises from the quality of political culture, particularly with regard to the saliency and range of the political subsystem in society, which we shall examine in the next chapter. But there is also a problem of culture levels. Indifference may be evidence of latent allegiance and satisfaction, but lack of knowledge and low information constraint is likely to fall conceptually across both quality and level problems of culture (a more specific discussion of the functional aspects of the results of behavioural analyses of voters and voting is undertaken below, note to Ch. V, pp. 148–61). This is where the catchment area concept is useful; we may find a differentially much higher level of political culture in many of today's developing societies both as compared to other catchment areas or aspects of culture, like economics and integration, and – what is more significant – compared to political culture in many developed societies, where the level of political culture is lower than that of other subsystem or sector cultures.

[1] Karl W. Deutsch, 'The Future of World Politics', *Political Quarterly* XXVII, January/March 1966, pp. 20–22.

This initial discussion of the parameters of political culture should conclude with an attempt to differentiate the notion of culture from that of ideology. This is relevant both to a discussion of the level or quantity of culture, as well as to the problem of quality raised in the next chapter. It is a very important distinction. The elaborate and sophisticated attempt to investigate the whole area of political culture by Almond and Verba is more concerned with quality than quantity, though the authors are conscious that the one cannot be discussed without the other. In taking parochial, subject and participant as main culture variables, they fuse the two aspects of quantity and quality to a large extent; the shift from parochial to a subject culture in any one society is notionally a rise in level as well as quality, while the shift from a subject to a participant orientation is probably more of a qualitative one. This appears to cause confusion. As already suggested, there may be rapid shifts in transfer of allegiance, and substitution of one legitimate authority for another, in periods of great social change. These are better viewed in the context of participation and allegiance than in terms of culture levels (or even culture quality); such problems are in large measure ideological rather than cultural.[1]

[1] This distinction is based on an acceptance of the definition of ideology as being especially a reflection of both culture *and* the processual and object phenomena of socio-political life, in accordance with the approach put forward by Mannheim, *Ideology and Utopia*, op. cit. Accordingly the over-comprehensive definition of culture put forward by Kroeber and Kluckhohn (above, pp. 26–7) is now broken down into the cultural component–the conditioning element of action–and the ideological component–the product of action and objects.

This convenient distinction should not however obscure the very close connection between culture and ideology. It is perhaps significant that the proximity of these concepts, and their empirical interaction in society, have eluded most social scientists; culture is what everyone has, ideology however is usually the lamentable prerogative of the other fellow. One of the few who are highly conscious of the connection is the social anthropologist Clifford Geertz. See his introduction and contribution 'The Integrative Revolution', in Geertz (ed.), *Old Societies and New States*, New York 1963, pp. 105–57; *Peddlers and Princes*, Chicago 1963; 'Ideology as a Cultural System', in David E. Apter (ed.), *Ideology and Discontent*, New York 1964, pp. 47–76. There is also some discussion of this interrelationship in Edward A. Tiryakian (ed.), *Sociological Theory, Values, and Sociocultural Change*, Glencoe 1963. Reference may also be made to a very recent debate, of which an attempt to define the *meaning* of ideology forms part: Joseph LaPalombara, 'Decline of Ideology: A Dissent and an Interpretation', *Am. Pol. Sc. Rev.*, LX, 1 (March 1966), pp. 5–16; Seymour Martin Lipset, 'Some Further Comments on "The End of Ideology"', ibid., pp. 17–18. However, our present definition of ideology, and the interpretation of Mannheim, differ substantially from that of LaPalombara and his reading of what Mannheim really meant.

Thus a shift from a parochial culture to one that can handle cognition and evaluation of the centre can be, but need not be, an index of an increase in the level of culture. It could hardly be claimed that the move towards European unification in the last decade represents a higher level of political culture in Europe; there is also no *a priori* reason why the creation of central government in a relatively arbitrary area like Nigeria should by itself provide evidence of higher cultural levels. These are empirical questions that cannot be decided by conceptualizing growth in the form of a shift from smaller to larger units. Where such a shift involves a more specific differentiation of political authority, and produces more specific cognitions and evaluations, a heightening of the level of political culture may justifiably be claimed as having taken place. This however is quite a different problem to any transfer of allegiance.

By removing the whole problem of how political authority is evaluated from the discussion of culture level, the need to judge the element of distortion in evaluation falls away. Here once more we part company from the implications of the *Civic Culture*, where in the last resort the judgement on political cultures is based on some notion of alignment between orientations and realities. Indeed, the orientations *become* realities; as the examples of individual respondents show, a preponderance of alienated *respondents* provides evidence of an *alienated political culture*. This is then graded in accordance with some notional scale of what culture should be–in the case of Almond and Verba, instrumental for the maintenance of stable democracy. Participation on the other hand is viewed as beneficial, and is defined as a more realistic view of the possibilities of exercising one's individual competence. This view of rationality, as an alignment between a disposition to participate and evidence of actual participation, fails to accommodate the intervention of symbols and the whole problem of ideological distortion.[1] For purposes of assessing the level of culture, it makes little difference whether the evaluation of authority and its institutionalization is based on myth or 'reality'. Thus societies with a high level of culture may ascribe mythical functions to structures, processes and even people, regard secondary roles or functions as primary, and ascribe mere ritual significance or no significance at all to vital loci of power. The level of British political culture is not reduced by exposing as myth or ideology the widespread belief that parliament is the fount of sovereignty, or that elections are

[1] Cf. the critical discussion of *Civic Culture* by Rokkan in *Am. Pol. Sc. Rev.*, LVII, 3 (1964), pp. 676–9.

effective means of exercising popular control of parliament. Similarly, the fact that the widely held belief that American elections settle allocation of power, make decisions between policies and authoritatively gratify interests, is partly an ideological distortion or a myth does not invalidate the claim for American political culture to be at a relatively high level.[1] The important contribution to culture production in developing countries of constant flourishes of crude symbols like imperialism cannot be over-emphasized.[2] Political culture in the Soviet Union may be said to have been raised substantially by the symbolic projection of Trotsky as the arch-villain. It may well be that this need to emphasize the absence of any necessarily rational component in political culture as such is heightened by the implicit connotations of evolutionary self-improvement and progress contained in the word 'culture', and that those who use it cannot easily escape this constraint. Hence the need to emphasize the other, biological, sense of the word—a nourishment bed for cell growth.

What specific indices are useful in isolating different levels of political culture? Deutsch has put forward a set of such indices by which measures of culture level might be obtained. Instead of the concept of culture, he uses social mobilization—mobilization being viewed as a state of conscious as well as unconscious commitment by the mobilized rather than a deliberate process of induction as we have defined it here. For present purposes, however, we may take his analysis as applying to culture. Deutsch makes no attempt to differentiate specifically between political and other elements of culture, though it is perfectly feasible to divide his indices into more or less political components. The indices in question range widely over economic criteria like income, consumption *per capita*, GNP *per capita*; political indices like participation in elections, educational indices like literacy rates, reading newspapers, exposure to modern technology, use of communication equipment like letters and telephones, etc.[3]

However, these indices are not easily used in an analysis that attempts to separate culture analytically from process, since they give no direct indication as to orientations. An investigation of any particular society in accordance with Deutsch's criteria will lead initially

---

[1] Murray Edelman, *The Symbolic Uses of Politics*, Urbana, Illinois, 1964.
[2] This is discussed in detail in Nettl, 'Inheritance', op. cit.
[3] See Karl W. Deutsch, 'Social Mobilization and Political Development', *American Political Science Review*, LV, 3 (September 1961), pp. 493–514.

to disjunctions, not unlike those produced by analyses of class; but disjunctions that are indifferent between orientation and action. Consequently it is suggested that while this approach may be very useful in providing a focus of interest for research into cultural levels, it does not itself provide direct evidence of such levels. This can only be obtained by interpreting the data specifically in terms of orientations–in the case of political culture in terms of the internalization of authority. Deutsch's indices of mobilization would have to be rewritten in terms of internalization and evaluation. A signpost for studying such problems is provided by Almond and Verba with their assessment of orientations from survey techniques. Consequently a possible research method in this direction would be some compromise between Deutsch's indices and the Almond and Verba method of evaluating them.[1]

More precisely, reference group theory suggests a possible manner of dealing with the problem. By reformulating indices of mobilization in comparative reference group terms, and establishing adequate reference groups as a result of sampling techniques, it would be possible to classify respondents in accordance with their use of such reference groups in viewing both the political process as a whole and themselves within it. This method emphasizes Deutsch's principle of 'neutral' involvement rather than that of participation–an essential distinction. Yet at the same time the investigation of orientations must be related particularly to the catchment area of political culture. Accordingly an objective approach might be provided which also avoids treating individuals merely as discrete units to be grouped into locational clusters according to scales of exposure to, or possession of, 'things'.

The work of Stein Rokkan is very significant in combining a rigorous methodological use of hard data and an ability to interpret it conceptually in accordance with great historical understanding. Though again there is no specific attempt to isolate culture analytically, the combination of historical knowledge and hard data makes possible a clear understanding of process in its cultural setting.[2]

[1] A tentative suggestion of some such method is put forward by James Coleman in *The Politics of the Developing Areas*, op. cit. pp. 532–3.

[2] The main references are: S. Rokkan (ed.), *Approaches to the Study of Political Participation*, Bergen (Norway) 1962, also his contributions in Otto Stammer (ed.), *Politische Forschung*, Cologne 1960; a general discussion of research and conceptual strategies in 'The Comparative Study of Political Participation: Notes Toward a Perspective on Current Research', in Austin Ranney (ed.), *Essays on the Behavioral Study of Politics*, Urbana 1962, pp. 47–90, especially 55–66; 'Comparative Cross-National Research', in Richard L.

POLITICAL CULTURE-LEVEL

There is after all no point in necessarily investigating culture as such alone; the purpose of analytical separation is only to furnish a better understanding of the discussion of processes.

On to this combination of historical information, crystallization of reference groups and investigation of orientations towards them, there may then be superimposed evidence of communication channels in each society. This might best be done in terms of feedback; different levels of culture could be distinguished in accordance with the feedback obtained from the political process in general, the institutions of political authority in particular, and from the extent of their absorption into the orientations of individuals and groups in society. A variety of models of such feedback processes exist, all emphasizing the nature, sophistication and extent of communication channels, as well as the possible blockages that might arise.[1]

With these definitions of indices and criteria of culture, and the various means of formulating concepts of culture level, we can now suggest some thresholds to mark off different levels of culture. These thresholds are intended to represent analytical categories to facilitate the ordering and conceptualization of what is essentially a continual process. We would not like to suggest that these categories should become reified so as to transpose what mathematicians call the analysis of continuity into the analysis of discreteness. The problem is very similar to–indeed a function of–that important area known as centre-periphery relation. As Lerner has recently suggested, this continuous process of interaction also can best be stated in terms of steps.[2]

Merritt and S. Rokkan, *Comparing Nations*, New Haven 1966, pp. 3–36. See also his contribution in E. Allardt and Y. Littunan (eds.), *Cleavages, Ideologies and Party Systems: Contributions to Comparative Political Sociology*, Helsinki 1964; and in the forthcoming volumes Robert A. Dahl (ed.), *Political Opposition in Western Democracies*, New Haven 1965; J. LaPalombara and Myron Weiner (eds.), *Political Parties and Political Development*, Princeton 1966; and the forthcoming S. M. Lipset and S. Rokkan (eds.), *Party Systems and Voter Alignments*, due 1967.

[1] For these see *inter alia* Deutsch, *Nerves of Government*, op. cit. Easton, *A Systems Analysis of Political Life*, op. cit., as well as some of the more directly cybernetic approaches to social communication.

[2] See particularly Daniel Lerner, 'Some Comments on Center-Periphery Relations' in Richard L. Merritt and Stein Rokkan (eds.), *Comparing Nations*, New Haven 1966, pp. 259–65, and also *passim*. Lerner categorizes the growth of centre-periphery relations, which is in many senses analogous to, and a part of, culture diffusion in terms of disinterest, difference promotion, and dissidence reduction. The first two categories of disinterest and difference promotion are closely related to categories 1 and 2 in our analysis below, and dissidence reduction has also partial bearing on our categories 3 and 4. In the case of these latter categories, elements of cultural competition between centre and peri-

The steps we propose are as follows:

1. Starting from a notional level of total ignorance, the first such threshold would be a situation in which an awareness of institutionalized political authority exists. This involves some contact, whether in terms of interaction or mere hearsay, with the reference group of the polity and its institutional structure–primarily government. In such a situation the flow of communication would be outward from the institutional structure of the polity only; there would be little or no feedback. Such situations appear to exist at the periphery of many societies, particularly in those cases where a new and central authority has recently been established, and is beginning to supplant the exclusive orientation of peripheral members towards a totally undifferentiated tribal or communal system. This is the classic stage of 'opening up' areas hitherto hardly affected by activities of government, such as the recent efforts of the Brazilian government to 'incorporate' the interior province of Amazonas.

2. The second threshold would be the emergence of some form of role relationship, in which there begins to exist an awareness of authority functions and corresponding roles. Some internalization of the existence of government is coupled with a crude initial evaluation of certain roles and functions. The outward flow of communication from the centre will have increased; there may be some very weak initial response in terms of feedback, but not necessarily. This threshold is reached when the initial tasks and possible primary functions of government make themselves felt, when government appears in the form of conqueror, tax collector or policeman, and feedback may appear in terms of resentment or rebellion. This happens when attempts to incorporate peripheral areas of a country are made, and corresponds to the state of affairs at the periphery of many developing countries today. Historically we would find evidence of it in the territorial expansion of the Russian and American state and society in the nineteenth century, and in some of the British, French and Dutch imperialist ventures.

3. The next step is the emergence of a notion of system–some form of inter-relatedness between various authority functions and a simultaneous view of institutionalized authority in general, in terms of a variety of functions and roles. This stage corresponds to substantial internalization and the beginning of mature evaluation. Outward

---

phery appear, though our emphasis on the internalization of institutionalized authority as the main component of political culture undermines the competitive potential except in certain special cases.

communication is once again increased and is matched by some feedback in terms of demands, supports and/or denials of support for government. At this threshold the indices of acculturation put forward by Deutsch all register fairly high levels; we move from internalization increasingly to the assessment of evaluation as criteria of culture level. Such is the situation which applies to the middle sectors in many developing countries, and represents the periphery in developed countries with a relatively high level of political culture.[1]

4. The final threshold is where evaluation matches the level of internalization, so that there is little disparity between cognition as such and meaningful evaluation of some sort. The process of government, in terms of action, role and function, is evaluated by people in terms of their own situation and response. We have, therefore, a strong notion of involvement. Communication flows steadily (though not necessarily with great accuracy) in both directions; this feedback is matched by adjusted output on the part of government. In this situation we can speak of an advanced level of political acculturation, and find examples of it in some of the middle sectors of developed countries, as well as in the tight cluster of those immediately involved as participants or competitors at the centre of politics in developing countries—the elite.

Clearly these thresholds are only meaningful in terms of comparisons—either between different sectors of one society, or between similar sectors in different societies. Notional levels of acculturation could then be plotted against proportions of population. A comparison between a 'typical' developed and a 'typical' developing country is depicted in diagram 2. The vertical axis expresses the four thresholds of acculturation, the horizontal axis the population from 0 (none) to 100 (all). Curve A thus represents the levels of acculturation for different sectors of the population in a developed society, while curve B represents the society in an early stage of development with a narrow political culture. The thickened part of the line notionally represents the respective middle sectors in a developed and developing society.

It might be useful to compare this depiction of potentially empirical situations to that of three ideal-typical societies—or rather the cultural abstraction that could be deduced from these ideal-typical cases. In diagram 2, curve X, a horizontal line, represents perfect democracy

---

[1] The notion of such middle levels and their crucial role has been analysed by Deutsch, *Nationalism and Social Communication*, Cambridge (Mass.), 1963, particularly pp. 97–126.

of the Rousseau or anarchist variety, in which equal acculturation is postulated for all members. Curve Y, on the contrary, represents the rigidly stratified society of a Platonist kind, in which the divisions of society are based on functional differentiation arising from *a priori* talents, knowledge and capacity for evaluation. Finally Z, an amendment of Y, represents the Marxist depiction of late capitalist society,

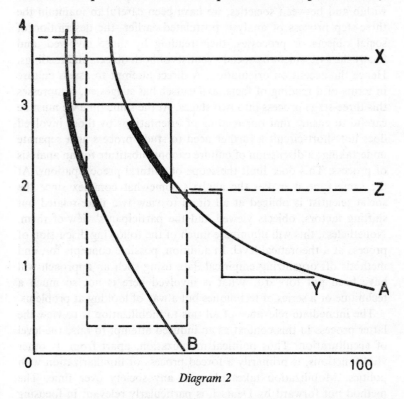

Diagram 2

in which a small revolutionary elite is in sole possession of fully internalized and evaluated perception of political authority. There is a medium-sized group of uncomprehending capitalists and satraps who are unable to evaluate the logic of history. Finally there is a larger section of class-conscious proletarians, whose knowledge and evaluation are greater than that of the 'dying' capitalist class. It will be noted that both in curve Y (the Platonist model) and curve Z (the Marxist model) the notional division of society into classes suggests that such stratification produces sharp disjunctions in levels of acculturation between different classes. Naturally the implications of this cannot be accepted; the boundaries between classes are not marked as clearly as this, and we have already noted that levels of acculturation are generally to be viewed as irreversible except over very long periods of time.

In setting out possible approaches to the study of political culture, and formulating thresholds which enable comparisons to be made within and between societies, we have been careful to maintain the three-step process of analysis postulated earlier–the description of social objects or processes, their reading by those involved, and finally the assessment by social scientists of both objects and readings. Hence the accent on orientation. A direct attempt to assess culture in terms of a reading of facts, as Deutsch has suggested, compresses this three-stage process into two stages. At the same time we must be careful to ensure that our reading of orientations by those involved does not short-circuit a further need to study process as a separate undertaking; a discussion of culture cannot substitute for an analysis of process. This does limit the scope of cultural preoccupations. At the same time it makes the analysis somewhat complex since the social scientist is obliged at all times to view two inter-related but shifting factors, objects viewed and the participants' view of them. Nonetheless, this will illuminate much of the following discussion of process at a theoretical level. In addition, possible concepts for, and methods of, organizing empirical data using such an approach will have been put forward. What is involved here is not so much a technique or a series of techniques but a way of looking at problems.

The immediate relevance of all this to mobilization is to view the latter process in this context as an induced attempt to raise the level of acculturation. Thus political mobilization, apart from its other vital functions, is primarily a forced process of familiarization with politics. Mobilization takes place in any society over time. The method put forward by Deutsch is particularly relevant in focusing attention on aspects of social communication in those societies where institutional authority is not preoccupied with problems of mobilization, and where consequently the observer's awareness of this process may be lost. In countries where mobilization is deliberate, where we have a commitment to compression of time and social distance, where one of the main functions of politics is the rapid involvement of peripheral members of society, it is easier to view mobilization as a deliberate process and to regard it as in large part aimed at culture formation. In discussing mobilization in its various aspects the primacy of this function should be borne in mind. Institutionalized authority in developing countries may be said to make the deliberate escalation of society up the stepladder of acculturation one of its main tasks. It is therefore not likely to be able to borrow successfully from political models in which the perceived process of political acculturation hardly exists any longer, or only in an attenuated form, and where the notion of such acculturation and the possibilities of its growth have been discovered by political scientists almost behind the backs of political leaders.

CHAPTER THREE

The Quality of Political Culture:
a Pattern Variable

SUMMARY

In this chapter an attempt will be made to analyse political culture in terms of a pattern variable. First we must be clear about the relative status of the political subsystem within society as a whole, and to recognize that this is not constant but shifting–both through time and as between different societies. This problem can be treated as part of a phase model affecting all four subsystems. For present purposes the discussion is confined to the relationship between the political subsystem and its supra-system–society. Two variables are adumbrated–the density or saliency of the subsystem (a purely analytical concept), and its range (the coefficient of political system and polity). The culture connotations of these concepts are discussed.

Next the central culture pattern variable elitist-constitutional is introduced. This 'grosses up' the two variables of density and range. In addition it subsumes a fundamental orientation towards politics–the disposition to emphasize manifest or latent structures, to assign value and primacy to institutions or to elites. Examples of such different cultures are discussed. Since elites are a crucial component of the variable, some attempt is made to arrive at a clear and concise definition of the concept. Concepts closely related to elite are then discussed: class, nation, ideology. The relevance of the two patterns to political mobilization is examined. In an appendix at the end of the chapter a random example is appended of how the suggested pattern variable might be superimposed on a particular piece of empirical research.

Perception of a differentiated political system plays an important part in any rise of the level of political culture, just as structural differentiation is a crucial feature of development itself. We by-passed this factor in the last chapter, merely pointing up the important analytical distinction between the ideological problem of shifting allegiances from parochial to central orientations on the one hand, and the genuine cultural factor of internalizing as well as evaluating differentiated political authority. These are different dimensions. The shift from parochial to 'national' preoccupations, which Parsons has more than adequately covered with his particularism-universalism pattern variable, *may* be evidence of growing acculturation, but may equally be the product of shifting allegiance or changing ideologies. To define this as modernity is one possible view of what constitutes that elusive and inconstant nymph. Each situation must be examined on its merits. But we are still left with the much less prescriptive factor of differentiation. This constitutes an important component of the present attempt to present culture in terms of a pattern variable, according to which individual political cultures can be identified and classified.

By considering political processes and structures as a functional subsystem of society, we can first of all assign to it a notion of *space* in the social system. This will vary in range, both between societies and at different periods in any one society. Thus a shift in goals may draw into the process of goal attainment a whole range of structures previously outside it. If economic welfare and redistribution, coupled with a strong priority for growth in industrial production, become a central social goal, we find the political system incorporating economic structures which previously might not have been considered within the purview of social goal attainment. This is one way of regarding the shift towards the welfare state in Western Europe over the last fifty years, a view that arises from a system approach to society. Similarly the divorce of religion from politics since the Middle Ages suggests a contraction of goal attainment functions away from the organizations and processes of religion. The Soviet Union for a long period demanded the subordination of families and other primary groupings to the broad social goals postulated by the political elite, the Communist Party. Once again we had here the extension of the range of the political subsystem at the expense of the latency subsystem. Clearly the notion of social space, filled by different subsystems at different times and in different societies, suggests a fruitful approach to problems of comparison. In analytical terms, the concept of system space represents the coefficient of what the social scientist evaluates as properly belonging to the subsystem in question, and the structures and processes allocated by the 'real'

THE QUALITY OF POLITICAL CULTURE:

society to the polity, the economy, etc. in accordance with the habitual perception of the participants.

Secondly the political subsystem can be considered according to the dimension of *weight* relative to other subsystems. Such weight would be expressed in terms of saliency. Different emphasis will be given at different times to political, economic or integrative problems, implying a shift not so much in orientation but of priorities within given orientations. This sort of change can take place only on the upper rungs of cultural levels; it implies a sophisticated matching of evaluation with cognition, and will affect feedback and consequent adjustment to a considerable extent. Above all it implies evaluation of some considerable differentiation of subsystems—irrespective of whether it is matched by 'genuine' structural differentiation as viewed by the observing social scientist. Accordingly we find widespread adjustment to changes in saliency in developed societies; in developing countries such changes are likely to be confined to elite participants. There is plenty of empirical evidence for both types of situation. We have the much discussed phenomenon of depoliticization in America, Sweden and elsewhere.[1] This would seem to suggest not so much any physical decline of politics, but a 'lightening' of the political subsystem in society, possibly coupled with an extension of its range; the goals of society shift to economic areas and problems but are pursued with less intensity. More dramatically we have the 'depoliticization' of Guizot in 1840–8 with the famous slogan 'enrichissez vous', which covers Adenauer's Germany after 1948 just as accurately (and whose breakdown under Erhard in 1966 signified a 'repoliticization'). The saliency of the political system can also increase sharply, an orientation summed up by Nkrumah's

[1] Ulf Himmelstrand 'A Theoretical and Empirical Approach to Depoliticization and Political Involvement', *Acta Sociologica*, VI (1962), especially pp. 91–95, and literature cited there, especially the work of Herbert Tingsten. Cf. also the cross-national analysis of S. M. Lipset and J. Linz, *The Social Bases of Political Diversity*, Stanford 1956, chapter VII; Lipset, 'The Changing Class Structure and Contemporary European Politics', *Daedalus*, XCIII, 1 (1964), pp. 271–303; R. A. Dahl (ed.), *The Opposition in Western Democracies*, New Haven 1965; R. Bendix (ed.), *Nation-Building and Citizenship*, New York 1964. The major philosophical statements of this trend as a universal phenomenon associated with modernity in general, and economic prosperity in particular, are in Raymond Aron, *The Opium of the Intellectuals*, New York 1962; Talcott Parsons, 'An Approach to the Sociology of Knowledge', *Transactions of the Fourth World Congress of Sociology*, Milan 1959, pp. 25–49; Edward Shils, 'The End of Ideology?', *Encounter*, V (November 1955), pp. 52–58; S. M. Lipset, *Political Man*, op. cit., pp. 403–17; Daniel Bell, *The End of Ideology*, Glencoe (Illinois) 1960, pp. 369–75, and *passim*.

exhortation: 'Seek ye first the Kingdom of Politics', which applies to many developing countries. Accordingly the empirical findings of those who proclaim the end of ideology–which can only be ignored at considerable peril–ought to be understood in the context of a differential emphasis of different subsystems through time rather than in terms of a measurable decline of a quantitative factor called 'ideology'.[1]

With these three initial criteria–evaluated subsystem differentiation, range and saliency of the political subsystem–an attempt can now be made to evolve a pattern variable of a specifically cultural kind, one that will be positively useful in making comparisons of different cultures. This rescues culture from being the residually unique, *ad hoc* component of most comparative socio-political analysis. The pattern variable is specifically one relating to *political* culture; it may be useful for the analysis of other aspects of culture but no attempt will be made to apply it beyond the catchment area of politics. The notion of such a variable, and its particular differential focus, has been adapted from Parsons' well-known pattern variable diffuseness-specificity. However, as will be seen, the pattern variable here operates on at least two non-parallel dimensions, as befits a cultural context, while Parsons' use is unidimensional. *It is suggested, then, that there are two basic patterns of political culture, constitutional and elitist, and that all existing political cultures can be located somewhere along an axis between the ideal-typical extremes.*[2]

[1] See most recently S. M. Lipset, 'Some Further Comments on "The End of Ideology"', *Am. Pol. Sc. Rev.*, LX, 1 (March 1966), pp. 17–18.

[2] A very rough sketch or glimpse of an approach based on some of the ideas and distinctions that are elaborated in what follows may be found in Parsons' review of Lipset, *Political Man: The Social Bases of Politics*, New York 1960, and Kornhauser, *The Politics of Mass Society*, London 1960, under the title of 'Social Structure and Political Orientation', *World Politics*, XIII, 1 (October 1960), pp. 112–29, especially pp. 127 ff. Cf. also Samuel P. Huntington, 'Political Modernization; America Vs. Europe', *World Politics*, XVIII, 3 (April 1966), pp. 378–414, for a partially similar characterization of politics.
Previous attempts to classify culture according to stated variables for comparative purposes are rare. Usually they begin with rather gross and elusive prescriptions like modern or traditional; cf. Richard Rose, 'England: A Traditionally Modern Political Culture', in Pye and Verba, *Political Culture and Political Development*, pp. 83–129. (I suspect that what is meant in this case is a culture that has always–i.e. traditionally–been regarded as modern!) A more formal attempt is David E. Apter, 'The Role of Traditionalism in the Political Modernization of Ghana and Uganda', *World Politics*, XIII, 1 (October 1960), pp. 45–68. This produces the socio-political culture categories of consummatory (Ashanti) and instrumental (Buganda). Though there is some correlation between these categories and those put forward here some difficulties arise with Apter's classification. The main one is that it confuses the social

THE QUALITY OF POLITICAL CULTURE:

1. *System Differentiation and System Autonomy*

The first dimension is concerned with the autonomy of the political subsystem and its culture surround. This is not the same as its differentiation, but may arise out of it; differentiation is a precondition for autonomy. Thus an autonomous political subsystem is one that provides for specific authority relations and processes of authority-legitimation which differ from those in other subsystems. An undifferentiated social system will fuse authority structures just as it will not have distinct politics, economics, etc. But even within a differentiated system we may find the same intersystem authority structures and institutions; the differentiation is now exclusively one of *roles*. Thus the upper ranks of the Soviet Communist Party or the Communist Party of China furnish authoritative leadership in the polity, the economy, the cultural subsystem, the army, etc.[1] Similarly in Britain we tend to speak of a homogeneous elite providing leadership in the political and almost every other field; the real attack on the amateur establishment was initially not based so much on the fact that it is recruited from a limited body of men but because of the lax disregard for the need even to accept any measure of role differentiation in accordance with the perceived requirements of leadership

---

impact of processes with a definite cultural orientation; the Ashanti would accordingly play everything hot (value orientedly), the Buganda cool (interest specifically). And in the last resort this classification merely resolves once more into traditionalistic and modernizing dispositions.

[1] Whether or not these upper ranks correspond to an elite in any meaningful sense of the word will emerge more clearly after we have examined the definition of elite for present purposes more closely below, pp. 91–6. It is worth pointing out that there has been little doubt among both Communist and Western analysts of the homogeneity of the top Soviet leadership; in the case of Soviet analysis this is based on common ideological commitment and schooling, in the case of Western analysts on the more classic socio-cultural plus authority criteria. It is only in the context of the recent search for evidence for theories of convergence between highly industrial nations, sparked off by American social scientists, that a view of the Soviet Union as ruled by differentiated and varied elites has crept in. See for instance Robert C. Angell and J. David Singer, 'Social Values and Foreign Polity Attitudes of Soviet and American Elites', *Journal of Conflict Resolution*, VII (December 1964), pp. 329–391, and Sidney I. Ploss, *Soviet Politics Since the Fall of Khrushchev*, Foreign Policy Research Institute, Philadelphia 1965 (cyclostyled), for extreme views. Cf. also V. V. Aspaturian in Roy C. Macridis and Robert E. Ward, *Modern Political Systems: Europe*, Englewood Cliffs 1963. All these studies tend, however, to take the notion of differentiated and competing elites as a starting point rather than as something to be demonstrated in a context of group differentiation and group action. Thus Angell and Singer take their six Soviet elites as military, scientific, cultural, labour, government and economic, though the disjunctions between these are never spelt out and in the Soviet case look highly dubious.

in different sectors or subsystems.[1] On the other hand there are many societies where authority structures and institutions are specific to the polity, where the political subsystem is, in the present context, relatively autonomous. In addition to any functional and structural specificity of the subsystem, authority within it is recruited and institutionalized in a specific manner relating to the subsystem. In such societies we would find both a specific political elite and/or specific political institutions of a highly differentiated kind. The reasons for focusing on authority criteria are twofold:

(a) because this relates the problem specifically to culture in accordance with the definition of political culture given earlier, and distinguishes it from process or structure; (b) because it focuses on autonomy rather than mere differentiation. The latter may be a question of roles, the former encompasses recruitment and institutionalization in addition to role definition.

It is important to recognize the boundaries of what is implied here. The emphasis on autonomy or lack of it only acquires heuristic value when we start making comparisons. Thus authority in any political subsystem is only more or less autonomous by comparison with other subsystems in the same society, or other political subsystems in other societies. Moreover the concept of autonomy tells us nothing about either saliency or range of the political subsystem. Thus in situations where authority in subsystems is relatively autonomous we still do not necessarily know anything about the relative status and power of political subsystem elites and institutions in relation to those of other subsystems; do the politicians dominate, or the businessmen; what happens when important business corporations or trade unions are in conflict with government? Similarly, where little autonomy appears to exist it is still not immediately possible to generalize about the recruitment of overarching (across subsystems) elites; are they initially recruited through the political subsystem, as in the Soviet Union, or are they merely of diffuse social status, conceivably recruited in the

[1] This emerges clearly from the contribution of Thomas Balogh in Hugh Thomas (ed.), *The Establishment*, London 1959, and Anthony Sampson, *The Anatomy of Britain*, London 1962. Cf. Sampson second thoughts in *The Anatomy of Britain Today*, London 1965. Many other works make the same point with regard to different sectors of society; J. P. Nettl, 'Consensus or Elite Domination: The Case of Business', *Political Studies*. Specific analyses of the British elite in politics are W. L. Guttsmann, *The British Political Elite*, London 1963; R. T. McKenzie, *British Political Parties*, second edition, London 1963; T. Lupton and C. Shirley Wilson, 'The Social Background and Connections of Top Decision-Makers', *The Manchester School*, XXVII, 1 (January 1959), pp. 30–31.

latency subsystem as in Britain? Though vital, these are essentially empirical questions; leaving them open does not invalidate the notion of focusing on subsystem autonomy as a main component of a cultural pattern variable.

2. *Institutionalization of Authority*

Autonomy is only one dimension. To it must be added the additional important dimension of relative institutionalization of authority within the subsystem. Considered also as a variable this to some extent helps to organize the problem of autonomy, as well as adding an additional component to it. The addition is concerned with enquiring to what extent and in what way autonomously generated authority in the political subsystem finds specific institutional expression. This is especially crucial for the political subsystem; politics, by virtue of its goal attainment function, is especially concerned with authority problems.[1] We may find that an assessment of subsystem autonomy and of specific institutionalization of subsystem authority gives conflicting answers in empirical cases. In contemporary Western Germany we have an increasingly autonomous political subsystem recruiting distinct political elites; but compared to, say, France this is not matched by any correspondingly high level of autonomous institutionalization.[2] Similarly a systems analysis of Britain and the Soviet Union indicates diffuseness rather than autonomy of the political subsystem; there is little specifically political authority but rather a pyramidal social structure embracing society as a whole. To use Lenski's terminology, status crystallization across subsystems is high.[3] Yet there are substantial differences between Britain and the

---

[1] There is general agreement over this special relationship, even between those who follow a functional approach to society and generally forbear to assign *a priori* primacy to any one function, and those who view politics simultaneously as the primary social activity (concerned with the authoritative allocation of values, etc.), and the queen of the social sciences. Though Friedrich inclines to the latter view, his discussion of the relationship between politics and authority problems is comprehensive and valuable (*Man and His Government*).

[2] This emerges from the illuminating discussion of just this problem by Ralf Dahrendorf, *Gesellschaft und Demokratie in Deutschland*, Munich 1965, pp. 245–326, especially pp. 293 ff.

[3] See Gerhard E. Lenski, 'Status Crystallization: A Non-Vertical Dimension of Social Status, *American Sociological Review*, XIX (1954), pp. 405–13; 'Social Participation and Status Crystallization', ibid., XXI (1956), pp. 458–64. The notion of crystallization has been developed for a more directly political context in the form of membership crystallization across subsystems; differentiated subsystems lead to lower membership crystallization, undifferentiated

USSR when we come to add the problem of institutionalization of authority within subsystems. The British polity has evolved very precise and durable institutions which are held in reverence, and only through control of these does the pyramidal or diffuse elite exercise authority within the political subsystem. (It will be noticed that we speak deliberately of a distinct polity with durable institutions, and a diffuse and relatively unautonomous political system in one and the same society; this contrast between concrete polity and abstract political subsystem is an important aspect of a certain type of society.) The Soviet polity on the contrary is as diffuse as the political system. Political institutionalization of authority is far less than in Britain; institutions of a specific political kind are less durable and inspire little or no reverence–in short, institutionalization of political authority is as limited as the autonomy of the subsystem, and polity and political system are congruent in their measure of diffuseness. Thus Britain and the Soviet Union are similarly placed on the dimension of subsystem autonomy, but differ considerably on the dimension of institutionalization of authority in the subsystem.

The way the latter dimension organizes the former is with regard to the relative weight or saliency of the political subsystem. Take the two sets of societies already used as an example. In the Soviet Union the pyramidal, diffuse elite is recruited politically but is institutionalized in the Communist Party which overlays and compresses authority positions in all subsystems. In Britain the almost equally pyramidal, diffuse elite is not specifically recruited in politics but across various functional subsystems, yet it is institutionalized in authority structures which are distinctly autonomous in different subsystems. Though these two situations show considerable empirical differences, we might say that from a cultural-orientational point of view the result is similar; lack of subsystem autonomy and lack of autonomous institutionalized authority in the subsystem–even though the British case emphasizes formal polity structure and the Soviet case does not. In the British case we have an effective downgrading of the saliency of the political subsystem even though the institutions of the polity are stable and revered–they are, as it were, left high and dry. In the Soviet Union we have a highly salient political subsystem in which the subsystem institutions are of little consequence; the overarching Communist Party, though emerging and recruited from

---

subsystems to higher crystallization. For this see contributions of Allardt and Himmelstrand in S. Rokkan (ed.), *Approaches to the Study of Political Participation*, Bergen 1962, pp. 67–110.

the political subsystem, dominates all subsystem institutions every-where. The effective cultural orientation in both cases is much the same: a predisposition towards an elitist orientation with regard to priorities in evaluating authority. It is specifically a cultural phen-omenon because it connects the individual to the whole (combining micro- and macro-politics) and because it is concerned with the predispositions to action and the evaluation of action.

In the case of Germany and France (both countries with a tradi-tion of a strong and autonomous state) we have less clearly established patterns. Germany represents a conflictual situation between autonomous institutions and elites, between subsystem autonomy and diffuseness. Even in the National Socialist period the political elite never obtained the same measure of domination across sub-systems as the CPSU in the Soviet Union; nonetheless this was the most markedly elitist reversion from the Weimar attempt to create intersystem autonomy and differentiated institutionalization of authority. Since 1945 there have been crosspatterns; an attempt to reach more formal means of institutionalizing of authority, coupled with some increase in political subsystem autonomy (though this has not gone as far is often asserted).[1] Hence Dahrendorf's 'half-way house' depiction of empty boxes; institutions occupied by differen-tially recruited elites who are yet unable to provide *either* homogeneous *or* competitive authority. In France and Italy by contrast we have a longstanding tradition of strong subsystem autonomy, and specifi-cally institutionalized leadership–at least in the political subsystem. Status crystallization across elites is low; these are the societies of socially unacceptable political leaders.[2] Yet the absence of any homo-genous elite across subsystems, the reasons for which are deeply em-bedded in the history of the two societies, is not matched by any very profound reverence for, or durability of, political institutions. The maintenance of differentiated and highly autonomous elites in the last resort takes precedence over any emphasis on their institutionalization. In a sense the Fifth Republic has attempted to alter this order of prior-

[1] The cautionary view in this regard is suggested by Lewis J. Edinger, 'Post Totalitarian Leadership: Elites in the German Federal Republic', *Am. Pol. Sc. Rev.*, LIV, 1 (March 1964), pp. 58–82. See recently W. Zapf, *Wandlungen der deutschen Elite*, Munich 1965, for more detailed empirical evidence. The problem of homogeneous versus differentiated elites is discussed on lines very similar to the present on pp. 196 ff.

[2] There is no need to turn to the analyses of historians or political scientists for illustrations; the classic French comedy of the nineteenth and early twentieth century makes the point emphatically. See particularly de Caillavet, de Flers and Arène's classic but still frequently performed comedy *Le roi s'amuse*, 1908.

ities indirectly, by reducing the *saliency* of the political subsystem while maintaining its traditional *autonomy*; this has meant encouraging the competitive potential of non-political elites, from the economy and the state bureaucracy. Whether this will also alter the longstanding cultural orientation towards institutions remains to be seen; it is too early to say whether the saliency of specific subsystem institutions will be matched by a greater reverence for them and thus a tendency for greater durability. Accordingly we place France somewhat farther away from an elitist orientation than Germany.

Finally we come to the type of society whose political culture stands at the opposite end of the continuum from that which we have described as elitist. The United States has a strongly differentiated political subsystem, an autonomously recruited and specific authority structure within it, and above all one that is based on formal institutions. These are stable objects of reverence and utility. But the important distinction between the United States and, say, France is not so much in the capacity for survival of specific institutions (a weak indicator in a purely cultural sense) but in the vital role which the institutions play in the formation and crystallization of elites. Both societies have relatively autonomous subsystems and highly autonomous political elites, but in France they control the institutions which are fashioned and refashioned in their required image, while in the United States the political elite or elites become such by virtue of their connection with formal political institutions, whether at city, state or federal level.[1] Thus elections are significant in recruiting and promoting political leadership, but much less significant in effecting the distinct and different elites in other subsystems. This type of society and the pattern of political culture to which it relates might be called constitutional, in the sense that the word sensitizes the significance and saliency of political institutions, and the relationship and interaction between them,[2]

[1] This point is implied in the title, and made explicit in the contents, of the article by Andrew Hacker, 'The Elected and the Anointed: Two American Elites', *Am. Pol. Sc. Rev.*, LV, 3 (September 1961), pp. 539–49.

[2] The use of the word constitutional in this context may appear unusual. The reasons for giving it a cultural connotation, and applying it in contrast to a disposition to elitist behaviour, will become clearer as it is used to discuss different empirical situations and societies. There is in fact no general agreement over the correct or conventional use of the word constitution or constitutional; the notion is open for use in a new way. The difficulties arise partly from the long period of Anglo-Saxon hegemony in constitutional tradition and from the consequent peculiar English imprint on the notion of constitutionalism. This is perhaps particularly significant in view of the fact that British political culture has here been classified as elitist rather than constitutional.

This preliminary discussion leaves us with some indication of the nature of the two cultural patterns, elitist and constitutional. They are not simple dichotomies of an either/or kind, as indeed no cultural phenomena can be. Nor on the other hand are they analytical polarities like universalism–particularism or specificity–diffuseness; this would be impermissible reductionism. Rather the patterns put forward here are multi-variable patterns in which subsystem autonomy or diffuseness, autonomy or diffuseness of authority structures, institutional or elite primacy within the subsystem, all play a part. They are essentially explanatory tools rather than explanations or organizations of facts; hence the heuristic rather than axiomatic manner of setting out their meaning and implications. A possible diagrammatic depiction of the proposed pattern variable would look like this:

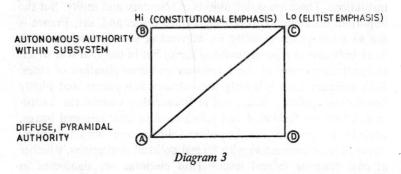

Diagram 3

Societies located in area ABC have a constitutional culture, those in CDA an elitist one. Points B and D represent ideal typical cultures of the constitutional and elitist variety respectively. It should be noted that the AB axis subsumes the problem of subsystem autonomy (this is not an exclusively cultural criterion, covering as it does in large part the social scientists' evaluation rather than that of participants; we shall revert to the problem again in the context of socio-political congruence in chapter VI).

Before investigating the application of this pattern variable on a

For a recent discussion of different usages see Giovanni Sartori, 'Constitutionalism: A Preliminary Discussion', *Am. Pol. Sc. Rev.*, LVI, 4 (December 1962), pp. 853–64; also the debate between Morris-Jones, ibid., LIX, 2 (June 1965), pp. 439–40, and Sartori pp. 441–4. Sartori in a private communication suggests that his discussion, though it challenges the purely English version, gives no comfort to the present use of the term constitutional, but it nonetheless suggests that something more fundamental than a mere dispute over the definition of the term constitutional is at issue.

wider range of specific societies, a more detailed and rigorous definition may now be attempted. Even so the definitions that follow are
still to a large extent preliminary; the potential value of the pattern
can be better assessed after relationship and interaction with other
variables used in the present analysis have been established and tested.
The definitions will take the two patterns in the inverse order to the
one in which they were introduced. The reason is that this enables us
to move from the notion of the relatively autonomous political subsystem outwards towards more diffuse subsystems, which means
making the rest of society increasingly relevant to politics.

The Constitutional Political Culture

Primarily this type of political culture cognizes and evaluates
politics as a distinct process strongly differentiated from all others;
authority similarly is differentiated as between political and other
forms – say economic or religious. Political roles will be clearly crystallized, and we shall find that they relate to, and are connected with
certain specific institutions, collectivities and even individuals. There
will be a wide consensus of political role expectations, suggesting a
distinct *classe politique*. There will be good boundary maintenance
by the political subsystem – of which the autonomous state is perhaps
the most common concrete expression. The notion also involves a
cultural propensity to be able to live with dissonance of information;
the recognition of differentiated and relatively autonomous subsystems, of a distinct polity separate from questions of family or from
economic problems, raises the threshold of tolerance for dissonant
information emanating from sectors that are evaluated as different.
Possibly in addition such dissonance may tend to be resolved by
questioning the source of information rather than its content; the
status of authority would thus be questioned before the autonomy of
the subsystem. Indeed, particular occupants of authority institutions
within the subsystem would tend to be judged by the evaluation of
their messages.[1]

On the other dimension a constitutional political culture emphasizes the institutional structure. Authority is perceived as vested in
manifestly political institutions. Politics is viewed in terms of the
relationship between institutions, and in turn between institutions
and individuals or groups. This process of interrelation between

[1] The problem of consonance and dissonance, and ways of resolving the
latter, are summarized in Robert Lane and David Sears, *Public Opinion*,
Englewood Cliffs, New Jersey, 1964, pp. 47–56.

individuals and institutions will be as clearly defined and openly symbolized as possible. Definition, systematization and open symbolization of these relationships is a major preoccupation of such cultures. The constitutional pattern of political culture articulates the fundamental alternative of take it or leave it at a relatively early stage of any political conflict; accept the definitions of the situation or reject them. 'Holity' with regard to the system–all or nothing–is a probable and consequential tendency, with corresponding political brittleness; major changes are relatively infrequent but substantial.[1] Leadership is essentially institutional; based on manifest structures and institutions. Brokerage–the neutralization or compromise of leadership–is confined to persons who act between institutions. Elites are thus essentially institutional; they are formed in the political subsystem by virtue of their clustering around formal institutions like the legislature and institutionalized collectivities like parties, and depend for their survival on these institutions. We might call them politically institutionalized elites.

In practice this pattern of culture includes some apparently strange bedfellows. In a country like France, the identification of elites with manifest political institutions appears high, and conversely the rejection of one coincides with the rejection of the other. Thus both in approval and rejection, the identification of individuals and elites with institutions is considerable. (A good way of judging this is to examine the status and role of the ex-occupant of office in different societies in relation to the status and role which he had during his previous occupancy.) Manifest *alteration* of the constitution is preferred to its latent *adaptation*. Where the level of political culture is high and reaches a sophisticated level of cognition about relationships, as in France, the rate of institutional change will be relatively lower than in a country like Brazil, where the political culture level is much lower and more narrowly confined to the centre. There political

---

[1] This suggests a partial orientation towards a consummatory rather than instrumental attitude. For a presentation of these patterns as cultural variables see David E. Apter, 'The Role of Traditionalism in the Political Modernization of Ghana and Uganda', *World Politics*, XIII, 1, (October 1960), pp. 45–68; also more generally Apter, *The Politics of Modernization*, Chicago 1965. Though the handling of the discussion there leaves some doubt as to the precise area to which these summary concepts apply–they are social scientists' judgements on process rather than on participants' evaluations– these patterns need not be confined to analysing developing societies but have relevance to developed ones, including Apter's own. Cf. also the discussion and diagrammatic presentation of Spiro, 'Comparative Politics', op. cit., and his *Government by Constitution*, op. cit.

relationships are seen as simple by the large majority of those who are only marginally involved. Hence political change is frequent, consummatory challenges take place much more often in the political subsystem (though these are not on any account to be confused with social revolution. We are talking here about politics. The *social* structure may be much more stable and unchanging). Changes in the constitution are thus more frequent than a change of elites–compared, say, to France, where both tend to change simultaneously, and even more compared to the United States, where institutions long outlive elites. Political roles are very narrowly defined and highly professionalized (there is high consensus of expectations). The focus of power is patent. There are few *éminences grises* in Latin America for long; they either become *éminences claires* or cease to be eminences altogether. (The rise of Rojas Pinilla in Colombia and of Peron in the Argentine illustrates this process very clearly.)

Among developed countries nearly all major West European societies, as well as the United States and Canada, tend to have more or less constitutional political cultures. In all these cases, the institutions of the state have played a major role in the crystallization of politics, and–efficient or inefficient–they have altered at various times mainly in the direction of greater conformity with perceived reality of current functional requirements. The political or legal constitution itself has become a major ideological reference point, to be supported or attacked. An academic by-product of this orientation is that the development of the social sciences has emanated, though often painfully, from the faculties of Law–except perhaps the 'refugee' science of modern sociology in America; law and [ex] lawyers have been central in the growth of the academic social sciences, and have not, as in England, remained immured in a self-sufficient academic cul-de-sac or acted, as in the Soviet Union, merely as the relevant technical handmaiden to socio-political instrumentality.[1]

A very important feature of certain constitutional cultures–almost a specific sub-category of such cultures–is the constitutional conflict model. Here the institutional arrangements are so patterned as to provide for built-in conflict, as a means of (*a*) focusing on the constitution as the most important political referent; and (*b*) of using

---

[1] An incidental criterion of difference between constitutional and elitist political cultures is the social *function* of law. The Parsonian identification of the legal systems with the integrative function seems to approximate much more closely to elitist societies, whereas in constitutionalist societies the legal 'system' seems to be shared between the integrative and goal attainment function– and nowhere more so than in the United States!

THE QUALITY OF POLITICAL CULTURE:

built-in and manageable institutional conflict as a means of preventing or resolving possible social conflicts. This is noticeably the case in the United States. What, in legal parlance, began as the most elaborate institutionalization of the *division* of powers is in sociological terms really a structured *conflict* of institutions sanctified by the constitution, if not one of its most hallowed features. Sociologically speaking the famous doctrine of the separation of powers means little. The concept only takes on empirical meaning in terms of a manifest conflict between institutions – and more meaning still if this institutional conflict is considered in the context of its *latent* function of preventing or overcoming class conflict or any conflict arising out of social stratification (partly by diverting *attention*, partly by diverting *energy*). In the eighteenth century, when the doctrine of separation of powers was at its height, such a manifest conflict function was but dimly understood, while the latent substitution function was not understood at all.

Once again the methodology and preoccupations of social science can in this case be seen to reflect as well as influence the empirical situation with which they are concerned – though allegedly as a neutral observer. It is thus hardly an accident that American stratification theory has developed and heavily leant towards horizontal or functional theories of differentiation, which in its present context may justifiably be viewed as the sociological equivalent of a doctrine of separation of [institutional] powers, in which conflict is seen both as competitively beneficial and entirely containable.[1] On the other hand

---

[1] See particularly Kingsley Davis and Wilbert E. Moore, 'Some Principles of Stratification', *American Sociological Review*, X (1945), pp. 242–9; Bernard Barber, *Social Stratification*, New York 1957. Parsons himself, though he has refined these theories somewhat, has also adopted a horizontal theory of differentiation for his subsystem model. Based as it is mainly on roles, however, the boundaries of summated strata are very hard to define, and we are finally left with kinship relationships as a means of disjunction. For this elaboration, see particularly Talcott Parsons, 'An Analytical Approach to the Theory of Social Stratification' (1940); 'A Revised Analytical Approach to the Theory of Social Stratification, (1953), both in *Essays in Sociological Theory*, (Revised Edition), Glencoe, Illinois 1954. Similar problems arise with regard to the study of the sociology of education. Obviously formal education plays a vital role in socialization and class formation. A very suggestive contribution to the characterization of elitist societies is offered by Ralph H. Turner,' Modes of Social Ascent Through Education; Sponsored and Contest Mobility', reprinted in A. H. Halsey, Jean Floud and C. A. Anderson (eds.), *Education, Economy and Society*, New York 1961. See also in general Edward Shils, *The Torment of Secrecy*, Glencoe 1956. It must be understood that these classifications of educational systems lead to an elitist-egalitarian dichotomy, and cannot therefore be more than tangentially relevant to the more specifically political variable elitist-constitutional with which we are here concerned.

sociologists working in, and on, societies with a more elitist orientation, like Britain or the Soviet Union, rely on vertical theories of
differentiation. They also place much greater emphasis on class as a
heuristic tool (the problem of class as an existential phenomenon
will be raised later) than their colleagues living in, and concerned
with, constitutional cultures.

The Elitist Political Culture

We have already stressed one feature of this type of political culture, the relative lack of autonomy of authority within the subsystem,
both as regards recruitment of elites and the area of elite status. A
very important additional aspect of elitist political cultures is the
relationship between elites and institutions. In an elitist political
culture institutions tend to be symbolic, acting merely as fronts for
relationships that cannot be formally expressed. 'One of the problems we are confronted with is that through the very great efforts of a
relatively small body of people . . . it has been possible to make the
organization as a whole and its central machinery do almost anything. It has achieved quite remarkable successes but I think it has
done it in spite of the [institutional organization] rather than because
of it.'[1] This relative downgrading of institutional autonomy and
saliency suggests two possible variants in what might be called
the relevance of institutions to socio-political processes, both of which
characterize elitist cultures. One variant is the situation which has
recently been most aptly described as institutional Darwinism; a
death and renewal rate of institutions which obviously assigns them
mere epiphenomenal significance only.[2] We find this phrase also
present in the Soviet Union, though decreasingly, and in most
peoples' democracies–with the significant exception of China, which
will be discussed later. The second variant might be described as
institutional symbolism, a situation in which institutions remain
apparently unchanging through long periods of time, but their original significance and saliency are 'hollowed out' so that there is a
discrepancy between their apparent 'status' and their real significance.

[1] This extremely apt characterization of the institution-elite relationship in
typically elitist societies is not in fact a sociologist's analysis of Britain, but
Lord Franks' attempt to sum up the relationship between the elite and the
formal structure in the government of the University of Oxford. See *Report of
Commission of Enquiry*, Vol. I, Oxford 1966.
[2] This phrase or concept comes from David Schoenbaum, 'Class and Status
in the Third Reich', Unpublished Oxford Doctoral Thesis 1964–a highly
perceptive analysis of 'elitist' Nazi Germany.

This represents the position in a country like Great Britain. Both variants, however, differ from constitutional political cultures where the main focus of process and action is located in institutions which accordingly represent 'reality' or saliency in the political subsystem. We have already joined both Britain and the Soviet Union together in the elitist culture category in terms of subsystem differentiation and institutionalization of authority; the present emphasis on the status of institutions *per se* confirms this initial category assignment.

Further definition suggests that elitist political cultures will emphasize consensus and its corollary, obscurity, as against definition and proclamation. Political relationships will be viewed as informal and indistinct. Differentiation tends to be confined to the relatively 'low' hierarchical level of roles rather than collectivities. In extreme cases even political roles fail to crystallize clearly and differentiatedly; role consensus is low because roles are not seen to be sharply defined.[1] A well-articulated consensus usually exists to maintain the *status quo* or at least to adapt institutions gradually to new functions and roles. Such adaptations or minor changes are frequent, but substitution of people is divorced from changes in–and even more from changes of–the polity; there is substitution of people within elites *instead of* changes of elites. Political leadership is vested in elites, which implies a strong element of ascription. Brokerage, where it exists, is now carried out by institutions–the 'neutral' institution so beloved of those who equate pluralism with sophistication. The tendency would be for the evaluation of political information to be made consonant more quickly, *usually* by an opinion change and occasionally by a reassessment of information sources. Messages are more apt to be judged in accordance with the perceived status and authority of the source than in constitutional cultures. In elitist political cultures the political subsystem will often embrace a wider range of institutions and a greater complex of roles than in the more constitutional cultures. As will be argued later in some detail, rapid and large-scale social change often coincides with the emergence of a definitely elitist orientation which will, at any rate temporarily, also enhance the saliency of the political system. But no stable correlation of the saliency aspect with elitist cultures can be established. Finally

[1] One of the best ways of analysing the strength or weakness of role consensus and the crystallization of specific roles is the manner of recruitment to the 'profession' to which the role relates. In elitist societies there is an unwillingness to use neutral, market tests of job selection or job seeking, the criteria are diffuse and often unknown, expressive rather than instrumental (e.g. the Administrative Class of the British Civil Service).

an elitist culture will produce less subsystem autonomy and poor boundary maintenance, especially at the higher or elite levels of the authority structure.

As noted, the elitist type includes Britain and the Soviet Union – indeed most Communist countries with perhaps the interesting exception of China – still a much more constitution- (or institution-) oriented culture than any other Communist society. This culture variable in fact cuts across the usual democratic-Communist dichotomy. Elitist types of culture also include many developing countries, most notably Ghana under Nkrumah and Algeria under Ben Bella, though in many developing countries there is insufficient structural differentiation of the political subsystem to enable us to speak of any specifically political culture at all. As both political institutions and political elite-roles are new phenomena, no really stable patterns of political culture can have emerged. Indeed the concept of elite is more of a sociological convenience than a social fact in many development situations. In most developing countries moreover the attempt to formalize political relations is too recent to have become divorced from personal dependence on an individual ruler. If the present ruling elite or charismatic leader changes, to what extent will the institutional structure change too (Algeria since Ben Bella's overthrow; Ghana since Nkrumah's)? This is still one of the big underlying questions in India – otherwise apparently a moderately stable constitutional culture.

Then there are countries like Greece where an apparently constitutional type of political orientation is confronted by the culture surrounds of neighbouring systems with a very different and strongly elitist orientation. This situation is quite common in centralized, ethnically united countries where political development and technology at the centre have far outrun social change at the periphery and in the middle sectors (Argentine, Middle East, Greece and Turkey). Political parties in this situation have the patina of modern structure and mobilization, but are in fact mostly personal *coteries* except at election times – a typical stage in the development of para-participation in democracies. As long as one elite controls the formal constitutional structure an unusual degree of stability results; however, when competing elites representing various social sectors and even ideologies struggle for constitutional power the political subsystem becomes very unstable (e.g. Syria, Iraq; the recent confrontation in Greece between Papandreou's Centre Union and the old sociopolitical elite suggests that this phenomenon may still be recurring there). In yet other countries, internal political conflicts, instead of being *for* control of institutions by elites, are based on different institutions or even hierarchies within the subsystem, each 'representing' different elites. The polity output of the executive may not suit the army; the polity input through the legislature may not suit the executive of the regions, and so on. This was the situation in post-Peron Argentina and in Brazil under Goulart, and also represents to some extent the picture in Turkey during the last years of Menderes. In all these cases, an emerging, specifically political culture is in conflict with the older, more widespread culture of other subsystems, the social culture; this increases the freedom of unstructured action on the part of elites clustering round particular institutions and based on particular hierarchies. In many developing countries it is thus very difficult to speak of any distinct type of established political culture or any subsystem autonomy; instead of interacting, subsystems and their cultural catchment areas in effect cut across and conflict with each other, often with rapid changes in respective saliency and range.

As soon as the problem becomes one of comparing developing with developed societies, the difference in the levels of political culture of various sectors of the population takes primacy over any attempt to compare the patterns of quality; the latter are initially less likely to emerge with sufficient clarity to make comparison worth while. When one or several interest groups in developing countries in effect embrace the entire acculturated urban population they are not merely interest groups within a polity–they *become* the acculturated polity. For instance, until recently we were able to excise almost all Bolivia's Indians–50 per cent of the population–from any study of Bolivian politics for most purposes, except perhaps those working in the tin mines and in La Paz. Similarly, it may be argued that in Syria for the last decade the political system effectively consists of the army and its supporters; all political conflicts have primarily been fought out *within* the armed forces, each one of whose factions has its clients in society at large. As against this, in countries where the level of political culture towards the periphery has risen above the minimal thresholds, the *quality* of involvement still varies greatly between elites and the crucial middle sector of society; that is why the problem of culture level gives way increasingly to problems of quality patterns as societies develop.

The present analysis obviously begs the problem of pluralistic versus monolithic societies in cultural terms; the whole prescriptive business of so-called democratic progress. Pluralism based on structural differentiation is one of several possible responses to socioeconomic development, and is thus a concept concerned with process rather than one concerned with culture–let alone a judgement on better or worse types of culture. As will be argued later, it is not to be identified as the prime index of development, or even an implicit component of it. Instead we shall offer the possible variant of compressed differentiation for certain modernizing and modern societies. This concept suggests an attempt to *counteract* differentiation at the top authority levels, to combine some role differentiation with diffuse elitist supervision and control of society by de-emphasizing subsystem autonomy at the levels of collectivities and norms.[1] The variant has considerable mobilizational relevance, as will be shown in chapter 8; in the present context it may be viewed in the context of an elitist form of culture production through undifferentiated mobilization. At this stage, in order further to clarify the pattern variable itself, and in particular to set it in the context of subsystem differentiation and of pluralism with its ideological overtones, it is probably desirable to relate the present discussion to the concepts of elites, class, nation and ideology.

1. *Elites*

One of the things we share with Marxism (or better, which Marxism shares with the capitalist ideology it analyses) is the tendency for prime referents to drift from specificity to diffuseness in the course of much use. Let a word be contentious (academically or politically) and be bandied around in the course of combat, and it will soon lose its precise meaning. The more it hurts, the less it means. Words cease to define or explain, but merely substitute for definition and explanation. Thus elites. Elites rule; those who rule are an elite. The circulation of elites is now old hat for social change. This etiolation of meaning has the additional advantage that it smooths the way for pluralism (either no mention of elites at all or their proliferation all over society like spring flowers after a hard winter, until the ideal society becomes simply a complicated and self-balancing elitemolecule–a model that reached its apotheosis in the extreme version of group theory).[2]

[1] See also Nettl and Robertson, 'Industrialization, Development or Modernization?', *British Journal of Sociology*, op. cit., pp. 282–3 and 'Modernization and International Systems'.

[2] The proponents of group theory (Bentley, Truman, etc.) are in a sense really the philosophic heirs of nineteenth-century individualism and market

The concept of elite has to fulfil two conditions in the present context.

1. It implies *some* evidence of social cohesion among the designated members of an elite. This may be very specific, in the form of an elite group (leadership of a political party, officers from a specific army or even regiment, etc.). It may also be rather more loose, with evidence of common life chances established by, say, education or religion but without any indices of group behaviour other than in connection with authority functions. This latter reservation is important. Common or shared authority functions, within as well as across subsystems do usually produce evidence of group behaviour; what is here demanded of the concept of elite is evidence of cohesion *prior* to the attainment of authority positions. This condition accordingly relates to elite *formation*.[1]

2. The other condition concerns actual or potential access to positions of authority. Condition 1 suggests that those who rule are not necessarily an elite, but condition 2 postulates that those without access to authority either within or across subsystems should not be described as an elite either. (The alternative between authority within and across subsystems accommodates *inter alia* conflict systems in which elites struggle for control of a subsystem and eventually for a whole society.) This condition is more orthodox, and follows most of the

---

economics, which Wolin has so well described as propagating 'a society without a community' (*Politics and Vision*, op. cit. p. 351). They simply substitute groups for the rationally self-seeking individual whose efforts benefit society—which in turn is defined as merely a summation of individuals. Elites in groups correspond to the self-seeking individual's head, the members of the group are made up of his limbs and tools—or working capital. A somewhat analogous idea seems in the process of resuscitation under the guise of general systems theory. Cf. Nettl, '*Systems*', op. cit., p. 323. The problem of distinguishing conceptually and empirically between individual behaviour and group behaviour is very important in this connection. Methodological strategies in this connection are offered in Paul F. Lazarsfeld and Morris Rosenberg (eds.), *The Language of Social Research*, Glencoe 1955, Section IV; Hanan C. Selvin and W. O. Hagstrom, 'The Empirical Classification of Formal Groups', *American Sociological Review*, XXVIII (1963), pp. 399–411.

[1] See Harold D. Lasswell and Morton A. Kaplan, *Power and Society: A Framework for Political Inquiry*, New Haven 1950; S. F. Nadel, 'The Concept of Social Elites', *International Social Science Bulletin*, VIII, 3 (1956), pp. 413–424. More empirically Robert E. Lane, *Political Life: How People Get Involved in Politics*, Glencoe 1959; Lasswell and Daniel Lerner (eds.), *World Revolutionary Elites: Studies in Coercive Ideological Movements*, Cambridge (Mass.) 1965. A brief account of the relevant concepts and definitions is T. B. Bottomore, *Elites and Society*, London 1964, pp. 1–41. A useful bibliography of recent research on elite formation, using quantitative data, is given in Merritt and Rokkan, *Comparing Nations*, op. cit., pp. 567–8.

classic definitions from Pareto to Aron and Bottomore.[1] It relates to elite *circulation*.

All this has special relevance for the political subsystem where elite formation is a prime function–at least a manifest one.[2] We are here especially interested in the relationship between elites and institutions in a cultural context. In an elitist political culture elites are formed extra-institutionally, their authority is structured by creating or capturing institutions. Leadership will be primarily by elites, but finds expression through institutions. In constitutional cultures by contrast institutions are themselves concerned with elite formation (Lasswell's precept is thus a special case). Elites crystallize by institutional association, and leadership will primarily be institutional.[3] In

[1] See particularly Raymond Aron, 'Social Structure and the Ruling Class', *British Journal of Sociology*, I, 1 (1950), pp. 1–16 and I, 2 (1950), pp. 126–43; 'Classe Sociale, classe politique, classe dirigeante', *European Journal of Sociology*, I, 2 (1960), pp. 260–81; Bottomore, *Elites and Society*, pp. 42–62, 105–21. Cf. also Harold D. Lasswell, Daniel Lerner and C. Easton Rothwell, *The Comparative Study of Elites*, Stanford 1952. It is to be noted that Lasswell's specific definition of what constitutes an elite in this context–'the holders of high positions in a given society' (*Comparative Study*, p. 6)–is much looser than the one used here.

[2] Though we need not go as far as Lasswell in suggesting that elite formation is the exclusive function of politics (*Power and Society*).

[3] Hence the difficulty of attempting an elitist interpretation of a constitutional culture like the United States. C. Wright Mills, *The Power Elite*, New York 1959, attempts to create cross-subsystem elites by postulate, but instead of an elite we are only left with a number of individuals with considerable authority and authority roles, and with evidence of interaction. That, rather than error, explains why the Mills analysis of the United States has had relatively little response there, and why it has been so fiercely attacked. See particularly Robert A. Dahl, *A Preface to Democratic Theory*, Chicago 1956, 'A Critique of the Ruling Elite Model', *Am. Pol. Sc. Rev.*, LII, 2 (June 1958), pp. 463–9, 'The Concept of Power', *Behavioral Science*, II, 3 (July 1957), pp. 201–15; *Who Governs?*, New Haven 1961; Nelson W. Polsby, *Community Power and Political Theory*, New Haven 1963; Andrew Hacker, 'The Elected and the Anointed', op. cit. A recent summary of the debate is by Geraint Parry, 'Elites and Polyarchies', Political Studies Conference, London, March 1966, cyclostyled, who points up the relevance of alternative societal models as the real factor in this debate.

The present formulation of a cultural variable along elitist/constitutional lines cuts across the whole debate about the validity of a polyarchic or elitist model. The proponents of both types have increasingly tended to postulate universal validity for their model; accordingly the problem has shifted from the applicability of these models to their universal validity as theoretical constructs. A continental political scientist has already attacked this claim for universalization several years ago on grounds of logic and proof (Giovanni Sartori, *Democratic Theory*, Detroit 1962, p. 114). We have here gone one step farther by using the debate as a means of differentiating two different types of society– which in a sense (though unintentionally) may act as a compromise between the incompatible claims of the two schools. Probably the extension of findings in terms of priorities elites precede institutions in elitist cultures, while institutions precede elites in constitutional ones.[1]

Not that elites and institutions are in any way alternative or incompatible. Even in wholly constitutional societies elites exist, but they may not have such important political functions except by virtue of the institutions with which they are associated. It is, for instance, not good enough to shrug off post-war India simply as ruled either by an elite or by institutions and individuals, according to academic discipline or orientation. Within the polity India is institutionally led; its traditional elites are essentially apolitical and are in the process of partial, often painful and reluctant, politicization (non-competitive caste adapting and changing into competitive caste associations). Even more absurd, because cruder in method and intent, is the analysis of *cuartelazos* or governmental coups in many South American republics simply in terms of circulating elites (one interesting view holds that South American government is essentially a business run for the benefit of a few cartellized hierarchies, and governmental overthrow by the military merely a brutal displacement of the board by a self-interested shareholders committee).[2] There are and probably always will be elites in different subsystems. In so far as they fill political institutions, act through them, and depend on them to 'lead' politically, they are secondary in the present context. In so far as they provide extra–(or contra)–institutional leadership and authority in politics, they are of primary relevance here.[3]

---

particular empirical cases to universal validity is a good example of social science ideology at its most virulently unobjective.

[1] This ranking of priorities is to be sharply distinguished from the pattern variable which is occasionally put forward as a means of accommodating elitism comparatively–that of elitist-egalitarian (cf. Lipset, *Political Man; The First New Nation*). This is more of an ideological than a cultural phenomenon, and in any case implies the somewhat unsociological notion that some societies can dispense with elites altogether.

[2] See Merle Kling, 'Towards a Theory of Power and Political Instability in Latin America', *Western Political Quarterly*, IX (1956), pp. 21–35. Though this author may not like or accept my *Executive Suite* analogy of his hypothesis, I shall use and elaborate his idea again later, below, pp. 361–4. See also K. H. Silvert, 'The Politics of Economic Change', op. cit., pp. 13 ff.

[3] The most specific discussion of elites in developing countries is Edward Shils, *Political Development in the New States*, The Hague 1962. But however important as a 'horizontal' concept, the word elite is never analysed functionally, or vertically. For Shils, elites are simply the newcomers; they are elites in so far as they influence or control power.

Various authors have of course tackled the problem empirically in country studies. Good treatment of elites in particular settings is contained in David E. Apter, *Ghana in Transition*, New York 1963; L. Binder, *Iran: Political Development in a Changing Society*, Berkeley and Los Angeles 1962. Lucian W. Pye,

For present purposes an elite is half-way between a social stratum, whose membership is based on common location on scales of indices which may or may not be collectively perceived by those concerned, and a collectivity whose cohesion is based on a common structure and process of action, or a common function. Possibly the best definition is one where the two elements coincide not derivatively (common location due to membership of a collectivity or vice versa), but separately. It is also clear that education is one of the major indices involved. A comparative analysis of elites might therefore begin with the question of common emergence of social identity; at what age, or in what age group, do people see themselves and are they seen by others to belong to a distinct status group or category?[1] In elitist cultures, for instance, this will be relatively early and strongly connected with education, family background, etc. In constitutional cultures such crystallization or elite formation will take place rather later, and the determinants will show greater variation from one subsystem to another, with education tending to provide indices of professionalization as a means to status crystallization.[2] In a sense both the precise differentiation of elite indices, and the complex

---

Politics, Personality and Nation Building: Burma's Search for Identity, New Haven and London 1962. More general comparative treatment is to be found in D. Lerner, *The Passing of Traditional Society*, New York 1958; Rupert Emerson, *From Empire to Nation: The Rise to Self-Assertion of Asian and African Peoples*, New York 1962. S. N. Eisenstadt has treated this problem systematically and comparatively in his writing.

Shils is also responsible for the inflation of the concept 'intellectual' into something hovering between a modernizing elite and a ruling class (see 'Political Developments in the New States', *Comparative Studies in Society and History*, II (1960), pp. 275 ff.: 'The Intellectuals and the Powers: Some perspectives for Comparative Analysis', *Comparative Studies . . .* I (1958); 'Intellectuals, Public Opinion and Economic Development,' *World Politics* X (1958), pp. 232–55; and most emphatically *The Intellectual Between Tradition and Modernity*, The Hague 1961). He has been followed by other American writers on new states, e.g. J. H. Kautsky in Kautsky (ed.), *Political Change in Underdeveloped Countries*. Even American domestic history is now being reinterpreted as a form of 'intellectual' revolution – quite feasibly when there is such a flexible definition of the word intellectual to hand; cf. Lipset, *The First New Nation*, chapter II. Curiously enough, this trend towards diffuse terminology follows current Soviet writing on the exactly equivalent concept of intelligentsia. See T. P. Thornton (ed.), *The Third World in Soviet Perspective*, Princeton 1964, pp. 24–26. For an attempt to break down the broad concept of intellectual into sociologically usable, measurable and above all comparable categories of occupation, see Theodor Geiger, *Aufgaben und Stellung der Intelligenz in der Gesellschaft*, Stuttgart 1949, pp. 1–24, 81–101.

[1] See for instance S. N. Eisenstadt, *From Generation to Generation*, Glencoe 1956.
[2] Some very suggestive methodological criteria for measuring elite differentiation are put forward by W. Zapf, *Wandlungen der deutschen Elite*, op. cit.

differential relationship between institutions and elites, are themselves evidences of a developed society (and not merely of developed socio-logical concepts and notions); historical analyses of elites are usually much more directly related to a history of institutions.[1]

Reference has already been made to the way in which the elitist model of societies has been used by political scientists to postulate a certain type of universal development in modern society. According to this theory, societies either tend to be simply elite-governed, with the majority of citizens apathetic (thus negating the empirical validity of classical democratic theory), or to consist of differential elites competing in the form of polyarchies, making possible greater levels of participation by citizens–though not necessarily in the context of voting (thus supporting the validity of democratic theory). The present analysis has cut across these two conflicting views of society, and has rather presented their implications in terms of models for two different alternative types of developed societies. But in present-ing these two alternative models, we are stating certain propositions regarding the nature of elites without thereby entering into the debate about participation–an entirely different problem. Recent analysis recognizes this fact; by postulating a notion of consensus among elites which are socially differentiated is it, perfectly possible to have a society like the United States which does consist of differentiated, conflicting elites and yet shows considerable evidence of political apathy. Even with the existence of differentiated elites, therefore, democratic theory is in danger. From our point of view, however, the

---

[1] Reference in this connection may be made to two recent cases of historical research connected with elites. Lawrence Stone, *The Crisis of the Aristocracy 1558–1641*, Oxford 1965, offers a very wide-ranging and perceptive study of the decline of the peerage, contrasted with the rise of the gentry in this period. We have thus an example of elite circulation. The point of departure is the institu-tional locus of the two elites; the House of Lords and the Court in the case of the peerage, the House of Commons in the case of the gentry. However, the crystallization of the elite concept is not based on any narrow institutional focus, but emerges from economic, social, educational and other indices. We are dealing here with two 'genuine' elites in the modern sense.

By contrast Keith Hopkins, 'Elite Mobility in the Roman Empire', *Past and Present*, No. 32 (December 1965), pp. 12–26, is not able to offer such a clear view of elites. This is not due to any inadequacy of research, but rather to the difficulties inherent in the subject. 'There is little quantitative evidence of social mobility in Rome ... Rome had an estate system of stratification with legal distinctions between strata. In accordance with this, Romans expected a high degree of status congruence' (p. 26). This suggests that we are dealing more with relative status and power of *a priori* strata than with any elite formation across or within broader disjunctions of stratification. Accordingly the issue here is more one of mobility between predetermined classes.

validity or otherwise of democratic theory is quite irrelevant; indeed
it is felt that its intrusion into empirical analysis is more likely to lead
to confusion than to clarification of problems.[1]

2. *Class*

It would seem that emphasis on class differentiation, and the use of
class conflict as a factor (or *the* factor) in social change, does not
greatly affect the analysis of political culture patterns. It represents an
alternative rather than a complementary scheme of social analysis,
but one which creates considerable difficulties of definition and
which has strong ideological overtones.[2] The notion of class domination, whether accepted as a heuristic or a dialectical tool or not at all,
does not prevent the division of cultures into constitutional or elitist
types. Communist political cultures also divide conceptually into
these two alternatives; the Soviet Union where the elite has broadened
over the last four decades, but which still has a distinctly elitist
political culture, as against China which is much more constitution-
oriented. Class configurations do not in fact alter the nature of the
problems posed and discussed here; indeed the whole point is to
discuss politics in terms of its own autonomous variables which do
not substitute for others (economic, social) but at the same time
relate to and interact with them.[3] The variables of politics, to be
useful, must apply to all types of polities and their so-called opposites

[1] This confusion emerges clearly from the debate between Walker and Dahl
in *Am. Pol. Sc. Rev.*, LX, 2 (June 1966), pp. 285–305. Dahl defends his critique
of the ruling elite model against Walker, who in fact has never attacked it; by
postulating consensus, however, Walker suggests that from the point of view of
participation, the result of Dahl's polyarchic model comes to much the same
result as Mills's ruling elite model. As far as democratic theory is concerned
both prove to be elitist rather than egalitarian or participant models.

[2] Most writers on the influence of class on political problems generally, and
political culture problems in particular, admit the diffuseness of the concept on
the one hand, and the great variations in the assessment of class as a social
factor – depending on the location of the respondent – on the other. For Britain,
see F. M. Martin, 'Social Status and Electoral Choice in Two Constituencies',
British Journal of Sociology, III, 3 (1952); Elizabeth Bott, *Family and Social
Network*, London 1957; in general Richard Rose, 'England: A Traditionally
Modern Political Culture', in Pye and Verba, *Political Culture and Political
Development*, op. cit., pp. 106 ff.; Rose, *Politics in England*, Boston 1964, pp.
16 ff. and references there. A cross-cultural, theoretical analysis of this problem,
mainly in a political context, is Stanislaw Ossowski, *Class Structure in the
Social Consciousness*, London 1963. These difficulties continue in spite of the
attempt of Ralf Dahrendorf to rescue the concept of class from its ideological
implications and the apparently irreconcileable problems of finding a generally
acceptable definition, and to put it to use as a heuristic tool (*Class and Class
Conflict in Industrial Society*).

[3] An interesting example of the irrelevance of class as a tool in studying

–capitalist/socialist, developed/primitive, 'authoritarian'/'democratic'. To make any sense, politics and the political system may not be summoned into analytical existence only at a certain level of social or economic (or even religious) development. Politics is always 'there'; it is subsystem, functional and structural differentiation that ease the task of identifying it as a distinct process. Consequently any definition of class will do for present purposes except one; the 'simple' authority definition of class offered by Dahrendorf.[1] For such a notion of class simply subsumes that of elite. (But class *is* a symbolic mobilizing referent and will be discussed as such later.)

3. *Nation*

The concept of nation is a far more useful one with regard to problems of political culture production and patterns of quality. There is for one thing no conceptual overlap between nation and elite, as there is between elite and class. In addition the relevance of nation to culture production is strongly centred on the political subsystem, while that of class is far less obvious. The concept of nation in fact plays a whole series of different roles in politics, some of which we shall have to discuss further (i.e. as a factor in political mobilization). For the moment it will only be discussed in the context of subsystem autonomy, as a means of identifying our patterns of elitist or constitutional cultures. What is at issue here is the *emphasis* of nationalism; this changes as between the one type of culture and the other. In constitutional cultures the notions of foreign or domestic spheres, and of foreign or domestic *politics* within the subsystem, are relatively distinct. This is shown by the structural and personal differentiation between them, by the separation of decision-making loci, and finally by the phenomenological selection of criteria for decisions between one sphere and the other. De Gaulle personifies this distinction very clearly; so do the varying but often contradictory

mobilization in developing countries is the analysis of the 'classlessness' of Brazilian peasant unrest in North East Brazil in Benno Galjart, 'Class and "Following" in Rural Brazil', *America Latina*, VII (1964), pp. 2–24. Cf. the discussion of Peasant Leagues by Anthony Leeds, 'Brazil and the Myth of Francisco Julião' in Joseph Maier and R. W. Weatherhead (eds.), *Politics of Change in Latin America*, New York 1964.

[1] *Class and Class Conflict*, op. cit.; *Gesellschaft und Freiheit*, Munich 1961, especially ch. 9, pp. 197–236. An interesting recent application of this approach is in Richard N. Adams, 'Dual Sectors and Power in Latin American Social Structure', Conference Paper, London RIIA, February 1965. But however convincing, this profile of Latin American society is no more than a model of horizontal social stratification, with the state partly as umpire, partly as a self-interested third party to the [social] action.

intra- and extra-mural attitudes to communism in developing countries like Egypt. The notion that these spheres, and the corresponding collectivities and roles, are and must be distinct and somehow different in kind has a long tradition reflected in political institutions, in political thought and in politics as an academic discipline (though in the latter sphere there is now some deliberate dedifferentiation in methodological specialization and orientational commitment as between domestic and international studies).

In many elitist cultures this differentiation is also symbolically maintained, but here loses much of its structural validity. The latent instrumentality of external relations for the internal goal attainment and integration subsystems is much more common in elitist cultures. Conceptually it brings together (for our purposes of analysis) the crude mobilization of anti-imperialism in Ghana and anti-Zionism in Egypt with (say) the independent deterrent or the strong Pound Sterling in Britain, and the neutrality of Sweden or Switzerland. In the latter two countries the establishment of such a wide consensus over foreign policy seems functionally related to the claim of pluralism and free competition in domestic affairs. Thus the vital factor in maintaining viable domestic pluralism within a single national framework may be the establishment of a working consensus over foreign policy, which is then imported and 'used' in the domestic field – often as the main component of the domestic consensus. In Sweden and Switzerland the 'success' and stability of the polity are held to be functionally related to a particular kind of foreign policy; in Britain and America the consensus is greater on foreign than on domestic policy, and its domestic application is peculiarly the reflection (often refracted and distorted) of an identity of views over foreign policy. For instance the strong Pound Sterling, essentially a commitment with domestic implications and upheld by domestic policies, is presented as a foreign policy necessity, if not commitment.[1] Similarly

[1] Some incidental and tentative suggestions about the need for foreign policy 'tools' in tuning and operating the domestic consensus in Britain are made in Peter Nettl and David Shapiro, 'Appearance or Realities – A British Approach', *Journal of Common Market Studies*, II, 1 (1963), 24–36. Though there the implication was not specifically drawn it is now suggested that foreign policy in Britain is one of the major sources of strength for the extra-institutional elite. One of the difficulties in analysing this whole problem is precisely the fact that the process of importing foreign policy issues into the domestic sphere is not an institutional one – foreign and domestic policy *institutions* are still remarkably well separated – but is performed by elitist 'smuggling' on the quiet. Thus for instance we find the atomic deterrent figuring as an internal 'prestige' issue at several elections, while at other times it has been a more 'usual' matter of defence.

American interwar attitudes to international treaties and conventions were often in part a rationalization of deliberate policies of domestic inaction–as well as being the product of more obvious isolationism. America has become less and less of an elitist and more of a constitutional society in the last twenty years–though it has always been relatively strongly constitution-oriented. The frequent denunciations of a conspiracy to import greater domestic centralization under the guise of foreign policy imperatives, which motivated the support for the Bricker amendment, have had little echo as a clear and present danger. Yet such denunciations are based on an acute sense of history (even de Tocqueville predicted the centralizing effects of foreign policy on the United States). Such importation, far from being of historical interest only, still persists. The only difference is that now an international system more conscious of, and susceptible to, planning in all its forms has been used to commit America informally to a more active form of planning at home–above all to create an atmosphere more favourable to it.[1] This in spite of the fact that foreign aid appropriations continue to be rigidly limited to an annual basis, and a great amount of symbolic uncertainty always attaches to the final passage through the legislature and to the amount that is finally voted.

The concept of nation obviously has an important place among the referents of political culture–generally far greater than class. We shall see this as an open, deliberate, almost self-conscious factor when we look at developing countries; the foregoing brief discussion of the more latent, diffuse, tangential reference to nation in developed societies will merely serve to show that such reference is at a fairly constant level in both developed and developing societies, even though the symbols may change.

4. *Ideology*

We have defined this as the reflection of process and structure in the consciousness of those involved–the *product* of action. Other definitions exist, but there is no point in justifying our choice since a lengthy discussion would lead far away into the realms of the sociology of knowledge.[2] Ideology is much more easily recognized (by

[1] This is argued by Andrew Shonfield, *Modern Capitalism: The Changing Balance of Public and Private Power*, London 1965, pp. 72–73.

[2] A recent review of the literature and definitions appertaining to this concept is in Joseph J. Spengler, 'Theory, Ideology, Non-Economic Values, and Politico-Economic Development', in Ralph Braibanti and J. J. Spengler (eds.), *Tradition, Values and Socio-Economic Development*, Durham (North Carolina)

an outside observer) in constitutional cultures as a commitment for or against; the classical mode of analysis of political theory or philosophy relates men to institutions, and/or restructures the latter to accord with some ideal scheme. The reason for this apparent manifestness of ideology in constitutional societies is almost certainly connected with the state; total, consummatory or anti-system opposition finds expression in opposition to a state much more easily than in a diffuse rejection of 'society'. The fact that revolutionary Marxism found its concrete expression in autocratic societies by overthrowing a strongly articulated state rather than (as Marx seemed to suggest) in strongly stratified societies through the destruction of a ruling class is perhaps a much more significant irony than the more usual one which points up Marxist revolutionary success in backward, largely agrarian societies. The 'decline of ideology' is thus a more easily recognisable phenomenon, without necessarily being greater, in societies where the state plays an important role. In such societies the state as such has simply become less *contentious*, and ideological questions have increasingly been transferred to types of leadership and representation within the state. In this respect the recent tendency in constitutional or state-oriented societies has been to approximate more closely to the pattern of ideology formation and assertion in elitist societies – latent, diffuse and harder to articulate (therefore harder to analyse) precisely. Above all ideology has become increasingly conservative: to maintain the state or system, and to act within it.[1]

Hence it seems more fruitful to speak of changes in the nature of ideology instead of any overall decline. Our present definition of ideology suggests that attempts to measure it quantitatively for comparative purposes are not useful, and that the suggestion of over-all decline has little meaning. The issue is a change in form, content

---

1961, pp. 3–56. See also the discussion in Joseph LaPalombara, 'Decline of Ideology: A Dissent and an Interpretation', *Am. Pol. Sc. Rev.*, LX, 1 (March 1966), pp. 5–16.

[1] It is probably no accident that sociologists, who view the political sub-system primarily in terms of party-politics arising out of social strata and elites, are more disposed to regard conflict reduction as a decline of ideology, while those who start from the existence of a state, and its acceptance or rejection, tend to view conflict reduction in terms of integration. For a good example of the latter see recently Michelle Perrot and Annie Kriegel, *Le socialisme français et le pouvoir*, Paris 1966, especially pp. 151–217. This quite fundamental difference in approach is compounded by the difficulties presented by the concept of ideology, first as between Marx's class definition and the subsequent, historical incidence of anti-state revolutions, secondly in the considerable differences over the meaning and scope of ideology. For this see once more the recent debate between LaPalombara and Lipset in *Am.Pol.Sc.Rev.*, LX, 1, op. cit.

and symbols–not in quantity. First there is the difference between manifest and latent ideology (differences in form); secondly the tendency in elitist cultures–especially in pluralistic elitist cultures–for ideology to emphasize what is and therefore claim to be free from utopian or prescriptive content, in fact not be an ideology at all (difference in kind); thirdly, elitist ideology comes from apparently 'spontaneous' sources like a cave echo, from practicals–often bureaucrats–and not from intellectuals (difference in location). A conservative ideology, in the guise of no ideology at all, will find its reflection in a value system that is oriented towards the maintenance of certain fundamental institutions as the most important social task or purpose (democracy, the American-British or whatever way of life, the Empire, private enterprise, neutrality, etc.). Such a conservative value system may elude those observers who expect to see values concretely asserted, preferably as a departure from 'what is', but they are just as real, and just as much values for all that. Thus the competitive polity, as first put forward by Schumpeter, may be seen to be as firmly rooted in ideology as the market economy; inherently there is no reason why 'pluralism' may not have as much ideological content as monolithic conformity or 'autocracy'.[1] Similarly the taxonomy of social usefulness or instrumentality in accordance with scientific or technological capability is ideologically based on a view of fitness to contribute to society which is first cousin to the accordance of authoritative legitimacy to 'qualified' or achieving elites.[2]

Note to Chapter III
Constitutional/Elitist Political Culture as a Tool for Empirical Analysis

It may finally be useful to test the pattern variable randomly on a recent piece of research not specifically concerned with theoretical

---

[1] Josef Schumpeter, *Capitalism, Socialism and Democracy*, New York 1950.
[2] For this see e.g. David Apter, 'Ideology and Discontent', ibid., pp. 30–39. Cf. the social scientists' professional variant of this notion–the plea that even a universal acceptance of general systems method would not really put systems analysts into an unassailable position of instrumental indispensability in society –for science, too, is a system requiring systems analysis! Kenneth E. Boulding, 'Political Implications of General Systems Research', *General Systems*, VI (1961), pp. 6–7. A theoretical attack on this position and its ideology, argued from the basis of an ethical theory of democratic participation, is by G. Duncan and Steven Lukes, 'The New Democracy', *Political Studies*, XI, 2 (June 1963), pp. 156–77; for an American statement see Lane Davis, 'The Cost of Realism: Contemporary Restatements of Democracy', *Western Political Quarterly*, XVII (1964), pp. 37–46; Christian Bay, 'Politics and Pseudopolitics', *Am. Pol. Sc. Rev.*, LIX, 1 (1965), pp. 39–51, op. cit. Cf. also the implications of this ideology on election studies, below, pp. 148–61.

analysis, or for that matter towards the analysis of political culture. This will help to put the suggested method in more workaday clothes than any general remarks about different societies.

In the course of an article reviewing this research the question of allocating its conclusions to one of a number of theoretical models of the polity (not of system range) was posed. Various models were tested against the hard findings of the research and found wanting. The reviewing author sought, and attempted to provide, a better model. This is an attempt to steal the clothes both of researcher and reviewer.[1]

Specifically Lowi criticizes both behaviourist group theory and conventional (Wright Mills') elite theory. He culls examples from the book to show that, within the context of the 'unique' problem studied by the authors, neither the assumptions of group theory nor of elite theory apply sufficiently often to provide a valid framework for analysis of modern American politics.

Lowi proposes an alternative classification of socio-political action in accordance with three 'arenas': distributive, regulatory and re-distributive. To each one of these arenas he assigns certain types of unit reference, certain relations between units, different power structures, stabilities and foci of interest which he calls primary decision loci. This is an interesting classification of areas of political action, each giving rise to distinctive features.[2]

[1] Theodor J. Lowi, 'American Business, Public Policy, Case Studies and Political Theory', *World Politics*, XVI (July 1964), pp. 677–715; reviewing Raymond A. Bauer, Ithiel de Sola Pool and Lewis A. Dexter, *American Business and Public Policy: The Politics of Foreign Trade*, New York 1963. Readers of this note are referred to the article and the book for the full setting of the present comments.

[2] Compare this with the recent preoccupation with system capability theory—a specifically 'political' application of the ideas most recently put forward by Parsons in *Structure and Process in Modern Societies* (1960). See for instance Francis X. Sutton, 'Social Theory and Comparative Politics' in H. Eckstein and David E. Apter (eds). *Comparative Politics*, pp. 67–81, David Apter, ibid., pp. 82–94, G. A. Almond, e.g. in 'A Developmental Approach to Political Systems', *World Politics*, XVII, 2 (January 1965), pp. 183–214. Almond has five *categories* of capability—instead of Lowi's three *arenas*: extractive, regulative, distributive, symbolic, responsive. In some ways these categories are rather odd. How can one isolate extraction from allocation—unless of course extractive capability simply means taxation plus seizure plus military recruitment? Symbolic capability is variously defined as 'means of communication with other systems' and 'affirmations of values, displays of political symbols, statements of policies and intents'—hardly the same thing. Distribution seems to be concerned with values—an old Almond idiosyncrasy which raises far more problems than it solves (originally based on a definition by David Easton, *The Political System*, New York 1953, but since relegated by him).

The authors of the book find what is essentially a conflict between group self-interest and prevailing ideologies. Assertions of sectional interests do not depend on exclusive membership of groups; rather such sectional interests seem enhanced where overlapping of group membership exists. Also ideology (in this case a prevailing view either common to the various different group members, or common to the 'targets' within government on which articulated interests focus their impact) often appears to prevail against the articulation of conflicting interests. The issue in question was tariff policy. A clear feeling emerges from the book, and is emphasized by the reviewer, that institutions can and do resist the influence of group pressures through an assertion of the ideology of the 'public interest'. Both book and review are American and the 'public interest' is of course nowhere equated specifically with ideology; the infusion of ideology into the argument is mine.

This situation is especially comprehensible if we recognize the United States to be a constitutional society as defined above. Opinion clusters develop in all institutions; though Congress exists as a means of articulating these interests, it also leads an autonomous life of its own as an institution. The assertion of the public interest by institutions, and the crystallization of elites who are legitimately able to make these assertions by exercising authority through the institutional structure, become analytically comprehensible as part of a pattern. Lowi himself tends once more to use elites in the tautological sense— applying to anyone who has authority for whatever reason. This is particularly noticeable in his classification of action arenas which suggests different types of elites in the three different arenas. Particularly in the case of the redistributive arena he speaks of 'conflictual elites–elite and counter elite' which in fact is nothing else but an unnecessary introduction of the word elite into the confrontation between different views and interests.

If we apply this method of analysis to Britain for a moment, we would find the result somewhat different. The division of political activity into these three arenas would be much less marked. The institutional assertion of the public interest as a separate ideology is fused more closely with the expression of legitimacy for any particular form of public policy expressed at a recent election. In so far as there is such institutional assertion it is more likely to be routinized,

---

However this may be, it is important to notice the common assumption of system in all these models. The differences between them ultimately hinge on different definitions of what constitutes a system.

emanating from elite collectivities like the civil service as much as from the institutions of 'democratic politics' like government, cabinet, parliament. In short the formal institutions are much more neutral.[1]

This may at first sight seem more like a concession to group theory, but this is not the case. Rather we have a vitiation of conflict due to an elite-dominated consensus. One of the features of constitutional societies is precisely that the arena of politics can be sliced up meaningfully into arenas with different configurations and that the institutional structure of government seems to allow, and indeed encourage, conflict between such sectors. In elitist societies this division is much less clear and a configuration of Lowi's type would not make much analytical sense in Britain, or say, the Soviet Union.[2] This would

[1] In this context it is legitimate to pose the question whether the dearth of studies in Britain of the *American Business and Public Policy* type is due only to lack of money (it 'reads' expensive), or whether the implications of an elitist culture mean that such studies, their framework and even their methodology, cannot 'solve' problems in that sort of society, since the necessary premises do not exist to the same extent. British research on business policy completely skirts the question of impact on government. Either it is concerned with commercial or organizational policy (treating firms or industries as autonomous entities), or, in so far as government enters into it, such research regards the latter's influence on business as the only flow worth studying. Since the crude left-wing assertions of backstairs manipulation of government policy by the armaments industry some thirty years ago, detailed studies of pressure groups have been significantly confined to professional associations like the British Medical Association. In this respect British tradition has been well upheld by (ironically) S. E. Finer who concludes *Anonymous Empire*, London 1958, a classificatory study of all forms of pressure groups including business, with a plea for more light on such dangerous goings-on. A. M. Potter, an American, takes his survey of British pressure groups (*Organized Groups in British National Politics*, London 1961) much more casually, as does Beer (*Modern British Politics*, London 1965).

[2] It may not be too fanciful to suggest that the structure-boundedness of traditional political analysis is a concession to a (wrongly) perceived world of constitutional societies. Sociological analyses of politics, based on notions of stratification, are much more recent; only since their appearance have structural concepts been transferred from political to social institutions. Broadly speaking, we are offered these two methods as alternative ways of studying given societies, and currently stratification analysis is held to be subsuming the use of the more obvious institution-based analysis, such as the work of Sir Ivor Jennings, etc. The tendency is away from a view of a constitutional world. By transferring the notion of constitutionalism to a cultural context, and classifying political cultures primarily into constitution or elitist oriented, an attempt is made not so much to compromise between conflicting views and forms of analysis, but to do justice to an existential reality which incorporates both forms. This sort of swing in methodological and analytical fashion among academics in the social sciences very often does not really pose the apparent surface alternative of either/or, but unjustifiably makes into an alternative what is essentially a genuine dichotomy.

105

indicate that, whatever the other attractions or repulsions of the elitist-constitutional variable, it has at least considerable organizing power and relevance to many different empirical situations.[1]

[1] There is [almost] a choice–if one is prepared to scan one's material methodologically as well as substantively–between tightly defined concepts of limited application, and vaguer concepts of greater organizing power. With subjects of a wholly societal range, the latter seem *prima facie* preferable. The number of axiomatic or tight concepts and variables required to do justice to so wide-ranging a subject as culture–assuming that it were possible to classify, explain and justify them all–would certainly exceed the attention span of any reader other than one who merely gorged on references. A good recent discussion of these problems with regard to the social sciences is in Karl W. Deutsch, 'On Theories, Taxonomies and Models as Communication Codes for Organizing Information', *Behavioral Science*, XI, 1 (January 1966), pp. 1–17. A measurement scale correlating organizing power and variables necessary for maximal application, based on this research, is suggested in Karl Deutsch, J. David Singer and Keith Smith, 'The Organizing Efficiency of Theories: The N/V Ratio as a Crude Rank Order Measure', *American Behavioral Scientist*, IX, 2 (October 1965), pp. 30–33. This is precisely the sort of test to which the pattern variable put forward here might well be submitted in competitition with other alternatives.

CHAPTER FOUR

Political Acculturation and Political Mobilization: Problems of Scale and Quality

SUMMARY

Mobilization is introduced as the main focus of our enquiry in this chapter. First some preliminary indications of its importance are given. Reference is made to the significance of the fact that the concept of mobilization has tended to disappear–at any rate that it is absent–from much modern political and sociological analysis. Though claiming to be functional in greater or lesser degree, much of this analysis tends to define system and function in such a way as (1) to substitute input and output analysis *instead of* mobilization; (2) to use the apparatus of structure-functionalism, with its value-norm-collectivity-role hierarchy and its focus on structural differentiation, as a depiction of a defensive social mechanism against 'outside' mobilization. It is suggested that this form of analysis treats mobilization as an outside and 'hostile' onslaught on the social system, and neglects the intrinsic social function of mobilization altogether–an ideological problem once again. This distortion has particularly important consequences in the correlation and analysis of developing and developed societies. A brief attempt is made to demonstrate how the concepts and hierarchies of structure-functionalism can be used just as successfully in terms of intrinsic or internally induced mobilization, especially by using the elitist-constitutional variable of political culture discussed in the last chapter. Finally some general relationships between scale and form of mobilization, and the patterns of culture, is projected.

It seems hard to conceive of any attempt to study political parties comparatively without assigning a central place to mobilization. Yet with very few exceptions this is the present state of the discipline.

POLITICAL ACCULTURATION

It is worth noting briefly where contemporary political science and sociology stand, in order to highlight why they have relatively little to offer for the analysis of developing countries.[1] For there mobilization is clearly perceived as crucial–by the participants

[1] Thus comparative analysis of political parties has not really risen above the threshold of classification or taxonomy to the next one of explanation. Since political analysis took note of the specific phenomenon of political parties, we have moved from Michels' and Ostrogorski's analysis of structure and integrative function to the methodologically more sophisticated comparative taxonomies of Duverger, *Political Parties*, and Sigmund Neumann, 'Toward a Comparative Study of Political Parties', in Neumann (ed.), *Modern Political Parties*, Chicago 1956. The latter analysis does partly approach the legitimacy-interest differentiation laid out later in the present essay. Some functional perspectives also can be briefly glimpsed in some of the critiques of Duverger; see Colin Leys, 'Models, Theories and the Theory of Political Parties', in Harry Eckstein and David E. Apter, *Comparative Politics*, New York 1963, pp. 305–15. For a critical overview of the state of the discipline at the height of the classification stage see Frederick C. Engelmann, 'A Critique of Recent Writings on Political Parties', *The Journal of Politics*, XIX (1959), pp. 423–40. A significant departure from the general preoccupation with classification is the work of Stein Rokkan himself and that done under his direction. See *Party Systems and Voter Alignments*, Glencoe 1966; 'Electoral Mobilization, Party Competition and National Integration', in Joseph LaPalombara and Myron Weiner (eds.), *Political Parties and Political Development*, Princeton 1966, and other contributions in this volume. See also various Norwegian studies, especially H. Valen and K. Katz, *Political Parties in Norway*, Oslo 1964 and also a few studies of Israel in this connection: B. Akzin, 'The Role of Parties in Israeli Democracy', *Journal of Politics*, XVII (1955), pp. 507–45; Amitai Etzioni, 'Kulturkampf ou coalition: Le cas d'Israel', *Revue française de science politique*, II (1958), pp. 311–35; Lester G. Seligman, *Leadership in a New Nation*, New York 1964, Chapter V. These studies all assign a central and integrated function to political mobilization. For a discussion of parties in a wider political context, which deliberately (and successfully) attempts to bridge the autonomous structural and system approaches and incorporates behavioural variables as well, see Avery Leiserson, *Parties and Politics: An Institutional and Behavioral Approach*, New York 1958. Much of the pioneering work in relating structural and behavioural problems of political parties to each other and to the wider social context is based on American parties. See the overview in Clinton Rossiter, *Parties and Politics in America*, Ithaca (N.Y.) 1960; in greater detail David B. Truman, *The Congressional Party*, Englewood Cliffs 1959, and, most recently and comprehensively, Samuel J. Eldersveld, *Political Parties: A Behavioral Analysis*, Chicago 1964. Eldersveld's book is particularly important in that it attempts an up-to-date definition and conceptualization of parties, taking into account the many functions and variables which have to be accommodated. For this, and the suggested concept of stratarchy, see *Political Parties*, Chapter I and pp. 115 ff. An attempt, perhaps the most successful to date, to elaborate a systematic theory of parties and party systems, using both behavioural and sociological or structural variables, is the work of Giovanni Sartori, *Partiti e sistemi di partito*, Florence 1965; *The Theory of Parties Revisited*, forthcoming. For further discussion of the difficulty of applying research on parties in developed countries to those in developing countries, see below, chapters VII and XI.

as much as the observer. The reason may be that both Western participants and Western observers (in the sense of the developed West) tend to think of politics as something that people do (actions)– rather than as something that is done to or happens to them (effects). We try to find out what happens in terms of what people set out to do, what they actually achieve and how they achieve it. We look at political parties in terms of their aims, composition and structure. When we come to include the notion of a system in the analysis we tend to look at the end product delivered to (or at) 'government' in terms of demands and supports; the greater the impact at that narrow end, the more we are interested. We assume political parties to have a functional (or dysfunctional) relationship with existing government. Indeed ideologically it often seems difficult, even from the way the architecture of analysis is laid out, to comprehend a political party other than as a channel in the political input process. Even the language we normally use is a conceptual trap; politics is a sphere of activity and a politician a practitioner, while no agreed term for the study of the subject has yet emerged (political science, theory or just political studies).[1]

Some modern political analysis based on systems has established what is in fact an ideological order of priorities. It is perhaps significant that this applies especially to Easton and Almond, both of whom tend to treat the political system as to some extent a unique system, and have not attempted to integrate their analysis of the political system into the framework of a social system as a whole.[2] By concentrating on an input-output notion of system, a priority for assessing effectiveness is established which focuses on the structure as more or less effective in processing input into output, and which tends to identify stability of structure with perceived effectiveness, and therefore legitimacy. Instead of viewing inputs and outputs as boundary exchanges between systems, an odd locational contradiction arises by which individuals or groups are viewed as part of a system for some purposes (e.g. gatekeeping), but as unattached or loose, part of *no* system, for others. This is both an ideological and a methodological confusion; ideological because of the emphasis on

[1] The precisely opposite constraint of language and concepts in sociology and economics has already been pointed out (Ch. I); there it is the participant who suffers from terminological diffuseness rather than the student. Moreover, there is an agreed *object* of study (society, economy); the word polity is still a relatively academic term, even though *politeia* in fact existed long before the precise differentiation of a society or an economy.

[2] This is elaborated in Nettl, 'Systems', op. cit. especially pp. 315 ff, 327 ff.

stability, methodological because it confounds the concrete level of polity and the abstract level of system.

This 'narrow' type of functionalism is thus not so much a general theory of politics but a conceptualization of a special case. The limiting factors are

(1) the applicability of the model only to highly developed countries,

(2) the applicability, imposed by structural emphasis on stability, to evolutionary rather than revolutionary societies,

(3) the emphasis on input and output which implies a pluralistic democracy of a special kind – one in which there is no tradition of any autonomous, selfconscious state, where the notion of 'neutral' institutions making up the structure of the political subsystem substitutes for the notion of a very un-neutral or *engagé* state.

In terms of development perspectives such an analysis postulates a model of perfection to which developing societies approximate to a greater or lesser extent; development becomes a stage in a predetermined process. There are thus implicit prescriptive elements in the analysis, as well as explicit ones.[1] Since the present essay will attempt to argue that today's developing countries are themselves a unique model, and that comparison between developed and developing societies may throw as much light on the problems of the former as on any shortcomings of the latter, the type of input-output functionalism mentioned here cannot be of very much help. 'In the process of offering to developing countries some indication of our "electoral" experiences we will perhaps learn as much about our own political practice as about that of others.'[2]

If we forget about the conceptualization and location of inputs for the moment and stick to mobilization as the most relevant political function for present purposes, the problem of pre-ordained grading largely disappears. Even if one did insist on using it, the marking should if anything be in inverse order. For a manipulated mobiliza-

[1] Cf. Almond in *World Politics*, XVII, 2 (January 1965), 198: 'Empirical studies of the performance of political systems, of the *what* of politics (in addition to the *who* and *how*) should enable us to grapple operationally with what we mean when we speak of good and evil, just and unjust, political systems'. Cf. also Almond and Powell, *Comparative Politics*, op. cit., Introduction.

[2] W. J. M. Mackenzie, 'The Export of Electoral Systems', *Political Studies*, V (1957), p. 254. Cf. also the arguments of Ernest Gellner (*Thought and Change*, London 1964, pp. 143 ff.) against Michael Oakeshott's contention in *Rationalism in Politics and Other Essays*, London 1962, pp. 330 ff. that studying developing countries as a means to understand developed ones is useless.

tion–based on earthly not heavenly symbols, achievements and not ascriptions–which encompasses its purpose quickly and relatively honestly in the pioneering circumstances of, say, Ghana, Egypt or Tanzania, is perhaps to be graded higher than a mobilization decked out with the myth and symbols of participation, like a British or Swedish general election. The point that will be argued at some length in the next two chapters is that both are essentially products as well as means of mobilization as much as institutionalized occasions for making rational choices. At some stage of historical development, every society undergoes one or several processes of mobilization; when such mobilization is political, it creates or develops the growth and strength of the polity, and may well extend the range as well as increasing the saliency of the political system. It is also the major accelerating factor in both the extent and level of political acculturation. Mobilization is therefore one of the most important functions for the achievement of which so many sophisticated Western and Soviet political techniques have been imported into developing countries. Yet the significant feature of Western ideology is the outraged denial that mobilization is in fact the most important, the central, function of many political collectivities, i.e. parties, interest groups, etc.

This becomes clear if we take a closer look at the implications of some of the sociological theories directed specifically at problems of socio-political mobilization as a process. It is, as we have seen, an axiom by now–and a perfectly acceptable one–that development in general and industrialization in particular involve some increasing differentiation of structures and roles. Amorphous, diffuse, multipurpose structures and roles give way to more clearly articulated, single-purpose, specific ones. The analogy, expressly or implicitly, comes from economics; it is essentially the application to social activity of the empirically valid observation that a technologically modern economic system requires ever increasing specialization–the division of labour so important for Adam Smith as well as Emile Durkheim. Yet in its social transplantation this economic concept creates several difficulties: (1) the concept of differentiation is based on the assumption of a general diffusion of development or modernity; that differentiation across system boundaries will make the affected areas or structures of both systems equally 'modern'. This assumption of system complementarity contained in the common assertion that routinized application of modern economic production techniques necessarily corresponds to a notional equivalent level of learning and personality adaptation by the practitioners is not always borne out by the evidence.[1] (2) The notion of differentiation is anchored in abstractions (roles, structure, groups), rather than in people. The same people and institutions play different roles consecutively (promotion, demotion, acting ranks). They play temporary roles (civil servants in administrative tribunals, rotating chairmen of university departments). (3) Functional differentiation may often be more a matter of role emphasis rather than genuine role differentiation (Parliament as legislature and simultaneously as a forum for redress of grievances, the American President as commander in chief, Kosygin as Chairman of the Council of Ministers of the USSR and a senior member of the Party Praesidium). (4) The perception of specificity and differentiation is sometimes more ideological than real. The increasing limitation of choices in elections—and the multiplication of elections themselves—can simplify the electoral process into something like ringing the change up on a till. The polity, to function properly, might appear to call for such mechanistic efficiency (a by-product of a political 'market' ideology); all the elements of a ritualized and mobilization which continue to affect the participants through time as well as making them *perform* for one specific electoral occasion are pushed out of sight. The notion of orderly, efficient elections is very much an ideological prop of 'democratic', pluralistic societies, and so this aspect is emphasized in considerable excess of its 'real' exclusivity or even saliency. (There even exists an economic theory of democracy which purports to show—not without reason and evidence—that, given a low level of knowledge, the acceptance of considerable over-simplification of choice by political parties is in fact 'cheaper' than any attempt to reach higher levels of cognition which would enable a more sophisticated evaluation of choices to be made—but also result in a demand for multiple choices in the first place).[2] Most of the sociological findings about what elections do to people have not yet penetrated the tauter traditional concerns of

[1] For a particularly striking example concerning Central American Indians in factories, see M. Nash, *Machine Age Maya: The Industrialization of A Guatamalan Community*, New York 1948. The 'lazy' concepts of industrialization and modernization thus need breaking up into subsystem areas. This intersystem approach also provides a challenge to the status of Deutsch's indices of social learning through economic contact (above, p. 64).

[2] Anthony Downs, *An Economic Theory of Democracy*, New York 1957. A detailed empirical application of this theory as applied to American elections is in A. Campbell, *et al.*, *The American Voter*, New York 1960. But although Downs' material points to a potential and quantifiable cost of acquiring knowledge, his reference to its application is in terms of [lack of] influence by peripheral participants in the political system—the foregoing of opportunity costs.

many political scientists – except at moments of crisis or disillusion – they as a rule still postulate the purpose of elections as given and merely measure their efficiency and their relevance in this context. Thus the sackcloth-and-ashes period of sterling crisis following the British general election of October 1964 produced the following autocritique from one of our leading academic students of politics . . . 'looking back on these two major exercises in democratic politics [elections in Britain and the United States] it is comparatively easy, I think, to see why our respective forms of competitive party politics have been so widely rejected by the new nations . . . [44 per cent of the electorate electing a government] is an anomaly . . . which we have learnt to live with [*sic*] but which seems both preposterous and unworkable in many of the newer countries . . . there are many other features of our election which must seem anomalous and unattractive . . .'[1] But 'in rejecting . . . the curious Westminster model . . . too many of the newer countries have assumed that some form of one-party dictatorship is the only possible alternative.' Candidates for ideas are still advised to look West – only now (as a last resort) it is to Switzerland.

(5) Finally, and in some ways most important in the present context, is the manner in which the concept of structural differentiation has been handled in relation to mobilization. This has been almost entirely *defensive*. Differentiation is thus frequently emphasized when sociologists are talking about strain and social actions to adjust to strain – either offensively (Smelser's notion of collective behaviour) or defensively (social control). Collective behaviour in fact implies an *antithesis* to institutional action; it is by definition un- (and therefore anti-) institutional.[2] The notion of the dynamic of social strain or conflict is central to much modern sociology, and explains the whole problem of escalation (or, as sociologists sometimes call it, value-addition). As the intensity and scope of social action need to increase in order to be effective, so the various differentiated structures, functions and beliefs are drawn into an increasingly generalized conflict – either by aggregation or by shortcircuiting (or better, compression).[3] Compression in terms of mobilization or collective behaviour initially commits more resources and not less. But it may

[1] Robert McKenzie, 'Perils of the Party Game', *Observer*, 6th December 1964.
[2] Neil J. Smelser, *Theory of Collective Behaviour*, op. cit. The social control aspect of differentiation is analysed in Smelser's earlier work, *Social Change in the Industrial Revolution*, op. cit.
[3] This concept of shortcircuiting or compression, which we have already put forward as an important variant to differentiation with regard to social change,

also involve an efficiency factor in so far as it allocates resources in accordance with requirements through rapid restructuring of action components, like a general who makes his heavily supported breakthrough on a narrow front. In developing countries such 'fronts' are often socially narrow and symbols tend to be largely value oriented.

Differentiation is accordingly not only a more efficient means of channelling upwards a growing complex of demands and downwards of decisions, but also a social mechanism making for stability. It is defensive, like the honeycomb of self-sealing compartments in a ship's hull, which confines the incoming rush of water (*inward* social action) to a number of spaces which are sealed off and 'sacrificed', but preserve the rest of the ship. The point of Smelser's value-oriented movements is that they are total, and aggregate or *compress* action through *all* compartments, and therefore the entire social vessel. It will readily be obvious that if this is so, then the idea of increasing pluralistic participation – which in the most common usage is merely the active political principle of increasing differentiation – also becomes in part an ideological device to scatter and confine any desire or effort for radical social action. This is one way in which 'modern' society can be viewed. The differentiation of political functions, the increasing alienation of one function from another (used deliberately in the Marxist sense of a process of discrete *meaningfulness* leading to collective *meaninglessness*), and finally the prescriptive grading of one function against another – these are bastions of stability, of resistance to social change. Hence the paradox that organized, structured movements in most industrial societies tend to be maximally norm-oriented, while value-oriented movements are loosely structured, relatively unorganized – and, as a rule, ineffective. To be effective, in turn, they must take on hyperorganizational perspectives, like Communist and Fascist *Gefolgschaft* parties. The easier and more common option is individual or group withdrawal.[1] It is therefore not surprising to find contemporary political discourse (in Oakeshott's sense) either boring and muted, or holisti-

---

corresponds closely to Deutsch's concept of strategic simplification in communication: substituting for 'gross operations with major physical resources ... much simpler operations by means of symbols' (*Nerves of Government*, p. 252; adapting an idea of Toynbee's).

[1] One version of the general effect of withdrawal on elites, and their response, is Harold D. Lasswell, 'Political Constitution and Character', *Psychoanalysis and Psychoanalytical Review*, XLVI (1959), pp. 3–18; 'The Garrison-state Hypothesis Today', in S. P. Huntington (ed.), *Changing Patterns of Military Politics*, Glencoe 1962. In general see Lasswell, *Psychopathology and Politics*

cally antipathetic. Those who upgrade the importance of limited, differentiated conflict in politics as meriting the full political energies and commitment of participants are considered cranks.[1] Perhaps this is why we look to mechanical, politically extraneous 'objective' factors like industrialization, development and demography to *do* as well as to *justify* the work of large-scale social change for us. Clearly Marxism is only one of several philosophies which co-ordinates social action to 'outside' preconditions. We shall have occasion to return to the problem of democratic determinism again later.

There are only three processes of systematic long-term social mobilization *en masse*; military, religious and political. Since all three fulfil broadly similar functions in creating community, they have much in common. For one thing, they all relate people tightly together in a distinct and often novel form, by evolving particular structures and by giving people common goals and reference groups. In doing so, mobilization processes either substitute new priorities for previous ones, or creates conscious priorities on a general scale for the first time, where none existed previously.[2]

Now, how does political mobilization differ from other forms of mobilization and from the notion of social mobilization generally? One possibility is to analyse the problem in terms of subsystems;

(1930) reprinted in *The Political Writings of Harold D. Lasswell*, Glencoe 1951. Some brief remarks with particular relevance to the situation of the intellectual in this context may be found in Nettl, 'Rosa Luxemburg Today', *New Society*, 184, 7 April 1966, pp. 11–13.

[1] Like Bernard Crick, *In Defence of Politics*, London 1962. The point about Crick is that he is not interested in justifying or praising *any* value system (I doubt whether he accepts Smelser's 'scale'). For him, politics has nothing to do–or should have nothing to do–with values, but only with norms. Groups and their conflicts are the best means of achieving that sort of politics. But whether this upgrading of norm-oriented conflict *removes* or merely *ignores* values is another question. Is this not just a sophisticated (or idiosyncratic) way of asserting a consensus ideology of 'what is'? *The Reform of Parliament*, London 1964–the strengthening of the institution *par excellence* of norm-oriented conflict–thus follows *In Defence of Politics* as logically as night follows day!

[2] An outstanding theoretical analysis of West European party cleavages and their historical basis, using an adapted Parsonian system for locating conflicts comparatively according to two sets of variables, is to be found in the two Rokkan chapters already mentioned, S. M. Lipset and Stein Rokkan, 'Cleavage Structures, Party Systems and Voter Alignments: An Introduction', draft chapter (November 1965) for *Party Systems and Voter Alignments*, op. cit. and Rokkan, 'Electoral Mobilization, Party Competition and National Integration', in Joseph LaPalombara and Myron Weiner (eds), *Political Parties and Political Development*, op. cit.

politics is one, normative integration, economic activity and kinship relations are others. We can measure their interaction in terms of changing range and density; thus we may often find one system predominant at any one time (dominant religion during the reformation, kingship in 'primitive' societies, economics in communist societies)–the phase model. The relevance of this method has already been discussed in the course of the analysis of political culture in the preceding chapter. A second possibility is to introduce politics at an upper stage of the progression of value-addition in forms of collective behaviour. Thus panics, crazes, hostile outbursts are not basically political, though they may take political forms and have political consequences. But norm and value-oriented movements have largely political reference, though they do not necessarily exhaust themselves exclusively in political action – at that level they become part of society's goal-attainment function. The moment we are dealing with norms and beyond, we are also dealing with the norm or decision-making machinery and are therefore in politics. A third version– which is really a logical extension of the latter alternative–is simply to define the political context narrowly or broadly (change of policy, change of policy-making personnel or structure, change of the value components of the structure) and to take that part of *any* given social action, or of *any* social situation for that matter, which we think is rightly Caesar's and leave the rest to God or the sociologist (economist, psychologist, theologian). This really implies a completely different definition of politics–in terms of authority roles or actions concerned with the exercise of power. Such a definition approximates most closely to the Lasswell/Kaplan and Dahl definition of politics and the Dahrendorf model of society (cf. above, pp. 30, 98). The political process now becomes a component of social action all the way through the hierarchy from values down to individual roles. In one sense it is probably the most satisfactory method, since it avoids arbitrary and brittle classifications of process and action. However, it suffers from the grave disadvantage (for present purposes) that it makes the political component of action or situations almost impossible to isolate. Comparison becomes very difficult–and comparison in terms of change is the main purpose of this essay.

The second of the three methods of analysing political mobilization in accordance with the scale and level of its societal impact is most easily related to the previous discussion of constitutional or elitist political cultures. In a strongly constitutional polity, norm-oriented attack on, as well as defence of, the existing rules of the game will quickly reach the limits of the normatively possible; if it carries sufficient impetus escalation to value-orientation will be manifest and dramatic. This is because constitutional societies tend to incorporate their formal structures into their prescriptive ideology, and into the general definition of their given situation. Malfunctioning is therefore rapidly and closely identified with institutions; any part is held to be functionally dependent on the whole (and is defended in these terms) and both antipathetic political action as well as sympathetic assertion escalate easily to value-orientation.[1] We see this clearly in countries like France, Germany and Italy, in 'new' democracies like Turkey and Nigeria–the choices available to Federal President and Prime Minister following the partially boycotted elections in Nigeria in December 1964 are a good illustration of the ideological alternative. We see it again in the debates in the United States over the status and functions of the Supreme Court–an institution whose actions appear remarkably prone to be viewed in value-oriented terms. In Apter's definition, all these are consummatory cultures as far as the dimension of their major political institutions is concerned.[2]

In elitist societies, by contrast, conflict over norms encompasses a much larger but more self-contained area. Escalation is more difficult, because the institutional structure of the polity is porous, flexible and in the last resort expendable. (Was it the realization that contemporary political radicalism merely tilted at windmills, deliberately exposed in the form of targets, that first caused Karl Marx to look to a class reality behind structural fictions?) We have this situation primarily in Britain and the Soviet Union, to a lesser extent in post-war Germany and Japan; among the newer countries in Pakistan and Indonesia. On the institutional dimension these are thus relatively instrumental political cultures. Perhaps it should be emphasized that the issue here is the social possibility for antipathetic normative movements to escalate into value-oriented ones, not the functional instrumentality or structural conduciveness for mobilization offered by emerging elitist or constitutional polities, which will be discussed later.

[1] This identification of the 'health' of institutions with the 'health' of the whole, of structure with system, explains the *definition* of system given by political theorists working in a constitution-oriented cultural environment. See for instance Carl J. Friedrich, *Man and His Government*, op. cit. p. 25; cf. the slightly more relaxed formulation in 'Political Pathology', *Political Quarterly*, XXXVII, 1 (1966), p. 71.

[2] See David E. Apter, 'The Role of Traditionalism in the Political Modernization of Ghana and Uganda', op. cit. Cf. above, p. 84, note 1.

Of course there are difficult, apparently composite cases like India, Switzerland and Sweden. In India we simply do not yet know what kind of cultural orientation will prevail in the polity. Is the structure independent of, or indifferent to, those presently managing it? Is Congress a stable political party, or an insufficiently differentiated womb for the Indian political universe? Can antipathetic political mobilization be contained in a struggle for norms, however acute (which might include the transformation of the political and institutional structure), or will it escalate to engulf the very existence of the Indian Union? A substantial amount of evidence regarding norm-oriented mobilization and counter-mobilization in India has accumulated as a result of the issue of linguistic states. Between the period of the division of Bombay State into two new linguistic states in 1956, and the similar division of the Punjab (PEPSU) in 1966, there has been regular and highly organized rioting of the traditional collective behaviour type. At times this has escaped the control of the authorities, who on the whole have maintained that each new linguistic state must be the last. Some food rioting has exhibited the same symptoms. Yet these severe challenges have so far been contained at a norm-oriented level, often even at a collectivity level; partly by concessions, partly by the ready collapse or deflation of the movements after a short while. The gloomier predictions for India have not yet come to pass–though the resistance and authority of Mrs. Gandhi's government seemed severely shaken by the end of 1966.[1]

With Sweden and Switzerland the difficulty is analytical rather than phenomenological. Yet the dividing line between the two patterns of constitutional and elitist culture analytically falls right here, precisely because these two countries are in many ways 'neighbours'. Some consideration of the difference between them may well illuminate the patterns themselves. Switzerland would accordingly be classed as a constitutional culture and Sweden as an elitist one. But both societies would be located near the centre of the dividing line in diagram 3 on p. 82. In Switzerland the political system is narrow in range but salient. The political framework, the constitution, is a strong cultural referent. Elites are largely the product of institutions. Above all, a great deal of the political value system is effectively built into the constitution. Unlike Sweden, the whole Swiss concept of neutrality is constitutional and highly value-orientated, not 'political' and normative. By the same token Sweden seems to qualify for elitist

[1] For such a gloomy view of India see Selig H. Harrison, *India: The Most Dangerous Decades*, Princeton 1960.

status. The political system is more wide ranging and less salient, extending well beyond the structures of the formal polity. Elites are extra-institutional, though there is rather more interelite competition and subsystem differentiation than, say, in England, and much more social mobility. The concept of an elitist culture (or an elitist society) is of course neutral as to size or composition of elites.

Finally it would be useful to consider the nature of mobilization in the context of the four basic components of the social hierarchy— roles, collectivities, norms, values. To some extent this is a simple progression, as we have seen. Mobilizing people makes them either into a mob (if non-institutional but based on some general belief) or a collectivity by coercion (if institutional but not based on a general belief; press-gangs, enforced savings, etc.). Mobilizing people plus norms equals the minimum of *political* action. Mobilizing people plus values might be called a revolution or, if institutionally induced, a mobilized nation-at-arms. But in real life things are not often as simple as this. No doubt social or political action increases in scope and intensity as issues move from the lowest level of roles to antipathy or support for norms or even values. But the effect we have already described as compression or shortcircuiting prevents these components from being simple alternatives or even additives. The mobilization of collectivities (or conversely their identification as social and political obstacles to mobilization) need not end with escalation to the next highest category on our scale: norm-oriented action. In elitist societies antipathy to individuals is often a sign and means of escalation from normative preoccupations to value-oriented ones: individuals may become the symbol of norm-oriented change ('Neville Chamberlain must go' in 1940 approaches this level). We shall find customs of colleagueal solidarity and of ritual colleagueal sacrifice in which men are first over-identified with institutions and then just as excessively de-identified. We shall also find important differences in the significance of political abandonment and personal disgrace (compare Eden in 1938 and 1956; Selwyn Lloyd in 1962 with Hore-Belisha in 1939 or with Profumo in 1963). Still more striking examples can be culled from the history of the Soviet Union. In elitist political cultures institutions and men clearly stand in a flexible, changing and often confused relationship.

In the other case of constitutional cultures leadership is from the start much more closely identified with structured collectivities and norms. Political character assassination of individuals is more difficult in constitutional than in elitist cultures (as in the US or

France, for instance). However useful to a charismatic leader the build-up of a personal image may be, he will, in a constitutional culture, sooner or later attempt to institutionalize his leadership and make it independent of his own particular person or achievement— where the equivalent leader of elitist societies is more likely to try to legitimize it by permanent political mobilization in terms of a personality cult. (Compare Kemal Ataturk with Lenin, Ayub Khan with Nkrumah, Nasser with Ben Bella; in the latter case we have an interesting constitutional reaction to such excessive charismatic mobilization in Boumedienne's army coup of 1965.) Thus in constitutional societies individual leaders play first a steadily increasing and then a steadily declining role in the escalation of social action. The maximum point of personality role in leadership is reached at the level of norm-orientation, where a strongly articulated role consensus ties people to norms and institutions in a formal and often quite rigid manner. We need only consider the role of different American presidents, the two presidents of the Weimar Republic, and the post-war prime ministers of Turkey to see how institutions and personality not only affect each other, but *have* to affect each other. When it comes to the still higher stakes of value-oriented action people decline into hostages (Tsar Nicholas II and family), representatives (the haphazard, ethnic group-by-group and firm-by-firm expropriation of foreigners in Egypt between 1953 and 1963), and finally role-playing symbols (Chief Awolowo or Pétain first in office and later on trial).

In short, the concept of differentiation presents considerable difficulties for any analysis of mobilization except in a purely defensive context. Since we must accommodate an offensive, intrinsic or internally induced form of mobilization as well—especially if we are to do justice to developing countries—the concept of differentiation, like that of input, will have to be treated as something of a special case, and make room for dedifferentiation or compression in certain cases and for certain societies. The culture pattern variable we have evolved helps in pointing up certain relationships between differentiation and mobilization in different societies. The correlation between differentiation and mobilization helps in turn to classify certain marginal societies, like Switzerland and Sweden.

Part II
FUNCTION

CHAPTER FIVE

The Function of Political Mobilization

SUMMARY

Having considered political culture and its relationship to political mobilization, we now investigate the function of mobilization in the political system. First the experience of the developed West is briefly examined; political–as opposed to religious or military–mobilization is the collective and structured expression of commitment and support within society. Such expression may take the form of political parties or quasi-parties–interest groups, movements, etc., anything that has a well-articulated structure (quasi-*groups* are thus by definition excluded from the present context). Moreover such parties arose and developed around cleavages–at least initially. Later the cleavages generally became mediated by issues, while the parties became self-sustaining collectivities activated by, or creating, issues, generally in connection with elections.

In terms of function, this historical development is set against a dichotomous pattern of an interest-articulating function and an authority-legitimating function. These are viewed as the two essential functions of modern political mobilization *as a process*. The historical change from cleavage to issue as institutionalized through mass elections corresponds in many societies to a dedifferentiation or confusion of the two functions; often they can no longer be separated either structurally or processually. Only the flourish of symbols is able to maintain an ideological view of elections as instrumental to the fulfilment of these functions. The special relevance of elections, and of research based on electoral preoccupations, is examined further in a note at the end of the chapter.

This confusion is discussed in terms of the political ideas of the present time and the last two hundred years. Where such dedifferentiation has taken place, it is regarded as the consequence of a superimposition of the authority-legitimating function on structured collectivities originally serving mainly an interest-articulating function. As a result of this superimposition, parties have become greatly transformed in structure.

A classification of Western societies is put forward, based on the differentiation or confusion of the two functions. A number of specific polities are examined in accordance with this pattern; it is argued that where historical cleavages have been maintained–and not transposed into 'mere' electoral issues–the two functions also tend to remain differentiated, or rather the polity is more conducive to efforts to maintain or resolve such differentiation. Finally the process of cleavage mobilization based on interests is contrasted with issue-specific mobilization for the legitimation of authority. Once again the question of relevance of the Western model for developing countries is raised and the model found wanting.

What is the function of political mobilization in society? Since there has been much discussion about the ideological demobilization of modern society on the one hand, coupled on the other with the notion of *growing* mobilization suggested by a cultural analysis, the problem must first be treated historically. Everyone appears to agree that there have been changes in mobilization; it is over the direction of the change that no agreement exists.

When we speak of function in this context we have to broaden this concept somewhat. Mobilization is not a structure in the strict, possibly in any, sense; the assignment of a systemic function according to structure-functionalism has little meaning. Indeed it could well be viewed as a dysfunction in a strictly systemic context; some writers of considerable sophistication certainly suggest such an interpretation, for instance Huntington, who argues that mobilization and political institutionalization of process are, or may be, dichotomous.[1] It is therefore proposed to adopt a somewhat wider definition of the concept in this case which includes notions of meaning and direction and which is based on process and action. The discussion itself will make clear just what is intended.[2]

[1] Samuel P. Huntington, 'Political Development and Political Decay', *World Politics*, XVII, 3 (April 1965), pp. 386–430.
[2] A full statement of this larger 'meaning' of function, supplementary to the narrower concept of structure-functionalism, is contained in a recent book by Alain Touraine, *Sociologie de l'Action*, Paris 1966. Touraine seeks to investigate the 'orientation' of processes of action–in terms of 'creation, innovation, attribution of meaning . . . the *raison d'être* of social movements'.

THE FUNCTION OF POLITICAL MOBILIZATION

Political mobilization is a form of social mobilization which corresponds to a particular era and certain special needs. In a sense it is historically the last and latest of the forms of mobilization, following religious and military mobilization as potential alternatives or complementarities. This aspect of substitution and complementarity is important, for although the propensity of a society to become mobilized may vary over time, the form such mobilization will take is perhaps governed by more general factors which are not entirely within the control of each society but correspond to some form of international culture. The historical decline of religious mobilization is too well known to need elaboration. As for military mobilization, though its extent or inclusive range has increased continually through time (in strangely close proportion to the extension of the franchise!), its saliency or primacy has not, except temporarily at moments of national crisis or war. In Europe and America the emphasis has been on the aspect of a soldier's growing 'civility' and professionalization, at least since the First World War. In other countries the civilian and military functions have become partially fused, so that army service fulfils essential socialization and value-orientation functions, as in Switzerland, Israel, Brazil and now increasingly in Arab countries.[1] Part of the 'missing' component of political mobilization is thus supplied by remnants of military mobilization serving political functions. At the same time many countries which continue to rely on techniques of military mobilization today do so in highly political, value-orientated terms which go well beyond the 'defence of the fatherland' (China, Indonesia, Viet Cong, the French in Algeria, the FLN etc.). Thus emerging countries tend often to fuse military and political mobilization.[2]

Political and religious mobilization are essentially cleavage mobilizations; as religious cleavages declined in the West after the seventeenth century the corresponding form of mobilization also either declined or became transposed into a political version. Political collectivities increasingly incorporated the expression of religious cleavage. In fact the attenuated religious cleavage between Protestants and Catholics provides one of the three major bases of political cleavage in many countries of the West, which we shall look at in

[1] For the 'nation-in-arms' concept, see David S. Rapoport, 'A Comparative Theory of Military and Political Types', in S. P. Huntington (ed.), *Changing Patterns of Military Politics*, op. cit., pp. 77–96.

[2] For a discussion and reference to the literature of structure congruence between military and political mobilization see S. P. Huntington, 'Political Development and Political Decay', op. cit.

more detail later. Military mobilization is on a somewhat different dimension, since it does not itself provide a basis for cleavage – except perhaps during the period of the private, almost self-sufficient mercenary army in Europe from the sixteenth to the eighteenth century. It is normally to be viewed as an instrument of mobilization based in the last two hundred years on the 'ready-made' international cleavage created by national states. In this sense military mobilization is therefore a cross-cutting cleavage to that created by politics; indeed it has often served in the West as a temporary means of overcoming domestic political cleavage in times of crisis or war, and is much more specifically viewed as such by many developing countries, as already suggested. In such cases, however, it is conceptually more fruitful to consider it as the variant of political mobilization which we shall call national or constitutional mobilization when discussing it as a process in greater detail. Once more this is a concession to the uniqueness of developing countries today; what has to be considered as a relatively differentiated form of mobilization in the West, with its special processes and symbols, is fused or dedifferentiated in many developing countries.

Political mobilization, then, is to be considered as differential commitment and support for collectivities based on cleavages. Such cleavages obviously vary widely from society to society, and through time. In England the cleavages of political mobilization date back to the seventeenth century, and the mobilization connected with them took their reference in the last resort from the Puritan revolution and the revolution of 1688. Moreover the existence of an elected House of Commons, and the process of election to it, provided an initial if mainly symbolic form of mobilization in the eighteenth century; personal interest thinly disguised as a political issue within a narrow electorate, as Namier has shown us. Compared to the rest of Europe, the English case is a peculiar one, in that first of all the different areas of cleavage have never been very clear cut, secondly the structure of the collectivities has tended to dictate the cleavages instead of the more common or probable inverse relationship, and finally because new cleavages like those arising from industrialization have again been aligned with, and superimposed upon, older cleavages. The elitist political culture, moreover, has ensured that this superimposition of cleavages, instead of summating conflict, has in fact helped to reduce it. Contrary to the expectation of many Conservatives in the 1820's and 1830's, therefore, the extension of the suffrage did not polarize society. The elite-controlled apparatus of mass parties was created about half-way during the process of extending the suffrage, between 1860 and 1890, and succeeded in imposing the old competitive group pattern of politics on to the newly created mass parties.[1] The basic cleavages of modern European politics existed, but in attenuated form subsumed by the structure of the political system and the symbols of the collectivities.

In the rest of Western Europe the cleavages are a much more dominant feature in the structure of political systems. Instead of being the product of an existing political subsystem within a society, as in England, they in fact helped to create and shape the political subsystem; society itself is in part the product of institutionalized conflict based on such cleavages. These latter have traditionally governed in large part the shape, size, number and structure of political collectivities. It is this reverse order of priorities and causality in European political systems, in confrontation with England and to a large extent the United States, which explains the structural politicization of European collectivities based on such cleavages: the fact that the spectrum of conflict tends to be represented by political parties more or less based, historically at least, on one of the major cleavages. This formal structure of conflict delayed the emergence of groups which, though interest-specific in their orientations, nonetheless avoided the formal political process institutionalized around the competitive electoral system–the plethora of interest and pressure groups as we know them today. In England and America, on the other hand, the cleavages are more directly the product of the political systems' structure; the historic social cleavages of society failed, therefore, to find full or adequate expression in the form of parties and tended accordingly to become partly institutionalized in the form of groups which did not compete electorally. Hence it is not surprising that interest in the analysis of groups–as opposed to parties–should originate in the United States, move from there to England, and only recently engage the attention of social scientists in Europe.

What are these cleavages? They can be organized under five main headings, each corresponding to a major conflict in Europe at a distinct epoch. Each has left a social cleavage of some kind, on to which the next major conflict has then superimposed a new cleavage,

[1] See the recent study of the Liberal party in the relevant years; John Vincent, *The Formation of the Liberal Party, 1857–1868*, London 1966. For the Conservatives see J. Cornford, 'The Transformation of Conservatism in the late nineteenth century', *Victorian Studies*, VII (1963), pp. 35–66.

so that the political systems of Europe are in effect an accretion of different conflicts, expressed in terms of cleavage collectivities which are structured partly in accordance with each separate cleavage and partly represent a fusion or summation of conflicts.[1]

1. *The Reformation Cleavage.* This is essentially a religious conflict which has become transposed into a political cleavage in more recent times. (Holland, Germany, Switzerland.)

2. *The French Revolution Cleavage.* This is a more diffuse but wider ranging cleavage, finding political expression in terms of church vs. state, conservative vs. rationalist, private vs. public priorities. This cleavage is most strongly marked in countries with a strong state tradition.

3. *The Industrialization Cleavage.* This too is a widely extended cleavage, institutionalized as a line-up of employers vs. workers, free vs. planned enterprise, earned vs. redistributed value, etc. It is almost universally reflected in European and American politics, either in relatively distinct structural form or 'mixed' with other cleavage structures.

4. *The Urban-Rural Cleavage.* Antedates the industrialization cleavage but cross-cuts with it in many countries, and largely dominated the latter in pre-war Eastern Europe and Austria.

5. *The Centre-Periphery Cleavage.* Now only an echo of its former importance (though possibly resuscitated in part through recent 'Celtic fringe' Liberalism in England); once important in countries like Norway and Spain, especially where superimposed on a linguistic cleavage. The growth of universalist perspectives in a national-social framework has to some extent submerged the saliency of such historical cleavages in each society. There is a strong element of latency about their status today; they are as it were the first-line reserve of mobilization when issues arise which relate to the cleavages in question, and to which those mobilized are consequently sensitive in a particular degree. Accordingly, where there is a tendency to a greater or lesser extent for political parties to become activated by particular issues, we may justifiably consider such parties as relating cleavages to issues, and issues to cleavages, in the political system. Parties thus fulfil the function of bridging or connecting the self-consciously ideological aspect of cleavage with the more objectively

[1] This summary of cleavages follows the discussion in Rokkan and Lipset, 'Cleavage Structures . . .' op. cit. For an attempt to discuss the summation or fusion in terms of respective saliency of each of these cleavages in different countries, see particularly pp. 53–62 of draft introduction.

instrumental aspect of resolving issues. As such, parties are structurally mixed: they can in practice never be wholly ideological since
this would destroy almost all relevant mobilizing potential, nor can
they be wholly issue-specific as this would be structurally impossible
in a political system within a developed, relatively universalistic
society. Hence even emphatically ideological parties such as communists adopt issue-specific attitudes (and often cause themselves
much agony and internal dissent in doing so), while complete issue-
specificity has remained the utopian *reductio ad absurdum* of the
otherwise very perceptive pioneering analysis of Moisei Ostrogorski.[1]
What enshrines this middle position, and prevents the *logically*
perfectly possible adoption of an extreme ideological or issue-specific
attitude on the part of political parties, is the dependence of the latter
on an electoral process which, in spite of apparently wide variation
between different countries, in fact heavily constrains the structure
and orientation of political collectivities. Groups which are not
affected by electoral participation, like attitude or interest groups,
civil or military bureaucracies or, say, professions, are immediately
able to act much more ideologically or issue-specifically and still
survive—such as the John Birchers in America at one extreme and the
Anti-Vivisection League in Britain at the other.

All this may perhaps seem somewhat obvious were it not for the
fact that modern social science has tended to substitute quite a
different polarity. Instead of a pattern of ideology→*issue* specificity
as evidence of historical change in politics (usually labelled modernity), the pattern that is put forward is one of ideology→*interest*
specificity, sometimes referred to as consummatory→instrumental.
The major difficulty with the latter polarity is that it poses a false
alternative. Far from being different in kind, the pursuit of interest
may well be ideological, while the pursuit of ideology or consumma-
tion may well be viewed not only as *an* interest but as *the* interest. In
pursuing once again the goal of equating a decline in the intensity of
commitments to cleavage, and the consequent encapsulation of particular cleavages within a prior first-order commitment to society or
nation, with an overall reduction of ideological issues, social scientists insist on redefining interest not as perceived by participants
but as something perceived only by themselves. The pursuit of

[1] For a critical analysis of this prediction for the future of Anglo-American
political parties, see S. M. Lipset's introduction (in draft) to a recent edition of
Ostrogorski's *Democracy and the Organization of Political Parties*, New York
1964, first published in France in 1903.

ideological perspectives thus tends to become a residual attribution of orientation or action which the observing social scientist is unable to accommodate in accordance with any rational perception of the actors' possible interest. In other words such an attribution implies either irrationality in terms of ascribed interests, or dysfunction in terms of system, or both.[1] It will be obvious that, short of perspectives which view developing countries as infants compared to the developed adult world, there is no way in which such a polarity of ideology vs. interest-specificity can do much to explain developing countries.[2]

The reason for the common crystallization of this, essentially misleading, polarity has perhaps been first the wish to relate the decline of cleavage mobilization to some polar pattern of behaviour in functional terms, and secondly to accommodate the notion of differentiation in this context. Thus diffuse, consummatory mobilization has been joined up with specific, cross-pressured interest mobilization

---

[1] The working definition of rationality in this context is taken from Robert A. Dahl and Charles E. Lindblom, *Politics, Economics and Welfare*, New York 1953, p. 38: 'Action designed to maximize goal achievement given the goal in question and the real world as it exists'. This contains difficulties; hence the notion of rationality is here used mainly as a notional absolute to be measured against empirical reality, rather than as a description of certain acts but not of others, according to some criteria of achievement. For this we shall use instrumental. We shall use rational accordingly more in terms of a judgement on consistency in the perceived acts of others, or between premise and acts, than as a judgement on the perceived acts in terms of an assessment of their probable goals. Rationality here has nothing to do with function, instrumentality has.

[2] At this point the present analysis appears to part company at least with the terminology of Rokkan, 'Cleavage Structures' who uses the ideology-interest specific variable not so much to *explain* actions (as do many others of lesser sophistication) as to *locate* cleavages or conflicts comparatively. Though naturally any analysis based on issue resolution alone leaves out the entire vital cleavage dimension, and therefore all historical explanation, such an analysis does at least remove the danger of this dangerously constraining notion of opposing ideology and interest specificity, and focuses on issue instead. For such an analysis see H. Spiro, 'Comparative Politics', op. cit. Though not necessarily comparative, systematic studies of issue resolution have a respectable tradition by now. In political science, see for instance R. M. Thrall, C. H. Coombs and R. L. Davis (eds), *Decision Processes*, New York 1954; D. Braybrooke and C. E. Lindblom, *A Strategy of Decision: Policy Evaluation as a Social Process*, New York 1963. Problems of issue resolution also enter strongly into the preoccupation of R. A. Dahl and many others who study power in communities. Finally such problems are at the root of the attempts to apply economic theory to politics, especially the work of Downs; 'An Economic Theory of Political Action in a Democracy', *Journal of Political Economy*, LXV (April 1957), pp. 135–50; *An Economic Theory of Democracy*, New York 1957.

in one continuum relating to evolution or change towards modernity. This joining up appears to have the additional advantage that it corresponds to the notion of an increasingly differentiated political subsystem, to which we have already subscribed here. But in fact this wish is a bad stepfather to the thought; ideology and interest-specificity are different dimensions, and cannot therefore be connected in this way.[1] To accommodate interest-specificity in any comparative or pattern-variable analysis of political collectivities we need an additional variable to be added to that of cleavage–issue-specificity. That variable consists of interest orientations on the part of political parties as one component, and is contrasted to authority-legitimation on the other. The historical development of cleavage structures towards partial accommodation of issue-specific orientations on one dimension is thus set against the functional dichotomy interest articulation-authority legitimation on the other. The cleavage-issue dimension is concerned with scale of conflict and source of commitment, the interest-authority dimension with the functional focus of actions, processes and structures without any connotation of intensity. The two dimensions are thus properly complementary.

Interest articulation refers to the function of articulating the specific interests of members or mobilized supporters as perceived by them; no *a priori* competition for power or the capture of institutionalized positions of authority in the polity is implied. Authority legitimation refers to the function of allocating legitimacy to one group, or several competing groups, of leaders within the context of a political system. Theoretically both functions can be served by any conceivable process, violent or non-violent, elective or non-elective, manifest or latent. In practice we may, in our discussion of the developed West, confine ourselves almost invariably to the electoral process, in the context of which these functions are normally exercised. This fact constrains the collective-structural expression of the functions in European political systems as firmly as it governs the superimposition of issues on to originally ideological cleavage structures.

[1] One way round this problem is to adopt the Parsonian concept of hierarchical *level*, and thus to speak of conflict as tending to 'reduce' [in level] from values to norms, as already discussed in ch. 4. But this is not directly a polar variable, but a conceptual and analytical location of level in accordance with the observer's attribution; it cannot tell us much about the specific function of any political structure or action (alternatively, it begs the question of functional relevance by a self-defining attribution of function to either a higher or a lower social level; an action simply becomes functional as value oriented or norm oriented).

THE FUNCTION OF POLITICAL MOBILIZATION

A good way to tackle the role of political mobilization with regard to these two functions is again through a brief historical review, but this time one in which we are concerned not only with what happened but also with how political thinkers have evaluated trends and events; we are dealing here with abstract *functions* rather than with real, even if conceptually foreshortened, facts like cleavages. One of the crucial differences, perhaps *the* crucial difference, between the two dimensions in question is that on the cleavage-issue dimension the problem of authority in the political system is a secondary, derived one. Mobilization is initially neither concerned with supporting or opposing authority nor with according or denying legitimacy; this depends on the institutional orientation in each case and is constant neither in the direction of mobilization for or against the established leadership in the subsystem, nor in intensity or level of mobilized commitment as we have outlined these in ch. 4. On the other dimension of interest articulation-authority legitimation the problem of authority is crucial and orders the empirical location of any particular society in the dichotomous pattern. For the authority legitimation function is concerned primarily with according legitimacy to elites, leaders or institutions, either by choosing from among alternatives, or by confirming or denying legitimacy to established authority in one of its several institutionalized forms. The interest articulation function, on the other hand, is initially indifferent to the 'who' of authority, and seeks mainly to guide it in the required direction of 'what'. As we shall see, this analytically quite basic distinction cannot necessarily be maintained or reflected in terms of distinct processes and structures; for instance frustrated interest articulation may become strongly concerned with the allocation and denial of legitimacy, while the decision between competing candidates for authoritative legitimacy may be strongly coloured by group or individual interest. One of the ways of comparing political sub-systems will indeed prove to be not only the relative emphasis on one or other function in empirical cases of political mobilization, but the extent to which the two functions are structurally and processually differentiated. As with the cleavage-issue dimension, extreme positions are logically unlikely; here also we must take a mixed or prismatic view.[1]

Political theory, like politics itself, has always been much con-

---

[1] This very useful conceptual analogy of a prism in which two dichotomous patterns of behaviour, in this case traditional and modern, are mixed and

cerned with the question of sovereign authority–its justification, its extent (or better, quantity measured in terms of power) and, since Bentham, with the values according to which it should function and select its criteria of effectiveness. But, though the slant of the enquiry changed, its focus and object did not: the extent and form, and of course justification, of the impact of sovereign authority on individuals. Even Rousseau for all his innate sociological perspective did not consider the effects of natural interaction arising out of the structural problem of connecting sovereign and people which fascinated him so much–that is why the General Will presents so many difficulties at anything but a very high level of abstraction. In spite of all the disagreements of many centuries, therefore, politics was considered essentially a means of forging a link between people and sovereign authority.[1] The norms that provided the old 'link' ('wise laws') were replaced from the seventeenth century onwards by structural concepts of various sorts, including inescapable and all-embracing ones like the power of the Leviathan, the General Will or Hegelian State or Marxist Class. These different structural links all helped to justify supreme authority, as well as linking it to people. They were the political equivalent of the Calvinist notion of a personal connection with God–the more direct the political link, the closer it bound the individual to institutionalized authority.

The analogy with religion holds a little farther as a means of understanding the subsequent development of what politics was about. The individual access to God promised by the Reformation did away with even the most neutral conveyances. God was changed to man's image, and man to God's–certainly in the view of man himself. By much the same token questions of metaphysical or legal legitimacy (divine right, original contract) gradually became problems–and, more important, *methods*–of continuous consent, just as the 'likeness' to God required man to labour totally and without ceasing on the Tantalus principle. In time political authority ceased to be viewed as a different and autonomous entity and became the potential

---

refracted into a composite blend is borrowed from Fred W. Riggs, initially in *The Ecology of Public Administration*, Bombay 1961; more fully worked out in *Administration in Developing Countries*, Boston 1964. We shall use the notion of prismatic further in this sense.

[1] For an excellent discussion of the intellectual history of sovereignty see recently F. H. Hinsley, *Sovereignty*, London 1965. This book emphasizes the purely Western (in our sense) application of this concept, and its irrelevance to large sections of the world. It also relates the intellectual and empirical history of the concept in a very original and lucid way.

self writ large–like the recreation of God in one's own image. A different order of priorities accordingly came to be established. Authority ceased to be a uniquely independent political factor but became a sum, a totality; what counted was the manner of reaching or creating it, or ratifying its institutional expression where it was seen patently to exist already. The interest of students accordingly became focused on the linking process to authority, and on its justification, rather than on the nature or function of authority itself. Inevitably there were both overemphasis and reductionism: authority now became something of an artifact, to be created or undone at will. While this view predominated, the perspectives of men like Burke, for whom political authority was not the product of specific and voluntary action but the accretion of evolving social structures, seemed petulantly deviant and old-fashioned; the discovery, or rediscovery, of social process in the creation and legitimation of authority by sociologists at the turn of the last century in turn appeared both modern and startling. The [re]discovery that a differentially structured society exists and plays an important part in the emergence of political authority is thus of relatively recent date. It is significant that it was not made by political theorists at all, taking up the threads provided by conservative thinkers like Burke and De Maistre, but by proponents of the new and strange science of sociology.[1] Its early proponents, like Comte, were considered cranks, even Durkheim enjoyed little contemporary echo and less real comprehension; it was not till the second decade of this century that Simmel, Weber and other Germans began to make an impact with their 'new' mode of analysis. Marx, who provided the only possible nineteenth-century integrative link between politics and society, only began to be dis-

[1] In grasping at this vision of society and articulating it methodologically and substantively in contrast to the emphasis of political philosophers, sociology has taken a hard look at its own forebears. These are now seen to go beyond the specifically sociological concerns of Comte and Durkheim, right back to Rousseau and Montesquieu–writers who hitherto had usually been considered as contributing to political theory rather than to sociology. Thus Montesquieu, though he articulated a very specific political theory, was also the first to base this on an equally specific notion of society, and to trace out the relationship between political and social phenomena as distinct entities. Rousseau is more difficult; like Marx he provides a starting point for both sociological and political theory, though he himself would not have considered such a distinction valid or necessary. These problems are discussed with great authority by Raymond Aron, *Main Currents in Sociological Thought*. Vol. I. *Montesquieu, Comte, Marx, de Tocqueville, the Sociologists and the Revolution of 1848*, Translation Richard Howard and Helen Weaver, London 1965. For present purposes it is instructive, however, to contrast the newness of this genealogy with the older and better-established descent-tree of political theorists.

covered as an academically valuable sociological thinker less than two decades ago.[1]

It is not surprising therefore that in political theory the notion of mobilization hardly existed as a specific function or process, just as there is no place for mobilization in 'respectable' theology: even Luther turned his thumbs firmly down on it.[2] In many dis-established sects, even as recent as the Salvation Army, mobilization is nonetheless assigned a very positive role and function. Sovereignty and individuals were two separate entities filling the known arena of politics: the problem was one of linking them by assertion rather than integrating them through an appropriate social process. As a recent study has emphasized, the notion of sovereignty requires both co-existence and co-extensiveness of a notion of community (sum of individuals) and sovereign authority (often but not always the state).[3] Because sovereign authority was first held to be autonomous,

---

[1] In a sense this division between classic political theory and sociology leads easily to question-begging and self-fulfilment; writers are simply *allocated* as belonging to one or other category in an over-facile manner. Yet there is more than a kernel of truth in these categories, particularly when we remember the long temporal dominance of the category labelled political theory. Moreover, what replaced political theory, though a process of gradual osmosis and shift in analytical method, was not sociology but partly economics–possessive individualism was given *analytical* as well as *empirical* free rein. See for instance C. B. MacPherson, *The Political Theory of Possessive Individualism*, Oxford 1962, a study, partly unintentional, of the *economic* implications of orthodox political theory, the historical accuracy of which, at least as far as Hobbes' intentions were concerned, has recently been strongly challenged. (See Keith Thomas' contribution in K. C. Brown (ed.), *Hobbes Studies*, Oxford 1966.) More recent examples of using economic methods and approaches on problems of political theory are J. M. Buchanan and E. Tullock, *The Calculus of Consent: The Logical Foundations of Constitutional Democracy*, Ann Arbor, Michigan, 1962, and Kenneth J. Arrow, *Social Choice and Individual Values*, Courts Commission for Research in Economics, Monograph No. 12, New York 1951.

[2] Luther did not, of course, frown on the psychological mobilization that brought individuals close to God by eliminating the structured access via other men–'how many men between God and myself'. No accident either that the nearest we get to political mobilization in classical political theory is Rousseau's romantic call for total political affectivity–with its very evangelical overtones; '. . . to feel themselves members of their country, to love it with that exquisite feeling which no isolated person has save for himself.' (*A Discourse on Political Economy*, London 1913, p. 268 [edition G. D. H. Cole].) Finally, no accident again that the transposition of this inchoate notion of psychological-political mobilization out of the realm of politics and into the area of scientific social integration provided by sociology should be accomplished by Durkheim, who read Rousseau closely and wrote *Montesquieu et Rousseau, précurseurs de la Sociologie*, new edition, Paris 1953.

[3] See Hinsley, *Sovereignty*, op. cit. Hinsley tends to see the state as the exclusive product of sovereign authority. This is, I think, neither historically true nor logically necessary. As the present discussion emphasizes, the state is one

then to emanate from, and finally became a sum of, the people, the structural link between them was declared innate on normative grounds–not requiring demonstration or proof, merely an adequate means of making it operational. Indeed, for many rationalist thinkers this link was bound to emerge naturally into full operational view once irrational obstacles to its emergence had been removed. In any case all that was needed was a visible, mechanically efficient means of embodying the link between people and sovereign authority–and one was found, in the shape of popular sovereignty expressed through elections.

Historically the spur to political mobilization has usually been a means of getting existing, autonomous authority to change its norms, values or structures–in other words, based on the articulation of interests. Through the long period of the Roman Empire, and again from the Middle Ages onwards, the 'lower' or lesser value-added–or even millenarian–type of collective behaviour periodically burst into an arena of orderly and settled normative relationships between sovereign and people.[1] Obsessed with a focus on authority and its justification, political theory was quite unable to accommodate these irruptions; correspondingly they were in practice suppressed as wholly 'dysfunctional' and unjustified. Only since the Puritan revolution in England and the French revolution a century later has the question of organized participation–the link problem–really arisen in practice. This important historical change broadly coincided with–and was almost certainly influenced by–the increasing concentration of political theory on the linkage problem. The function of interest articulation on the other hand, which gave rise to the mobilizations based on the noted historical cleavages discussed earlier, was hardly taken up in theoretical terms and was roundly condemned whenever it did arise–by Hobbes in theory, by the last States-General of 1789 in practice. Locke and Montesquieu, for instance, wrote at a time when group or class interest was a major cause of political, economic

---

possible version of institutionalized sovereign authority: an individual, a legislature (as the emanator of Austinian laws) or even a party, are other possible versions.

[1] It is worth noting that the 'normative' Middle Ages also had well-developed interest-oriented structure, which provided a very sophisticated form of interest articulation–representation by estates. These were however largely non-mobilizational; they embodied and maintained status in the social hierarchy and were quasi-selfregulating rather than attempting to mobilize latent interests into effective articulation for the purpose of influencing universal norms in their favour. Mobilization was indeed confined to 'lower', subnormative forms.

and religious mobilization; yet they do not discuss it except in terms of political institutions. Neither of course does Rousseau. From 1800 onwards the interest function of political mobilization, in so far as it was recognized at all, was in the conventional wisdom of political theory held to be subsumed in the 'linkage' function of authority legitimation. By voting for a contender for political power, interests were considered to have been adequately expressed and therefore bound by the result of the election. Democracy, in short, was dominated by collective representation; formally organized political parties for a long time continued to have a very bad Press.[1] Two essential but very different functions thus became in practice entangled and epistemologically confused in theoretical writing. It can be argued that this confusion has been the central bedevilment of the study, and also perhaps of the practice, of modern politics.[2]

[1] The literature of political theory on parties, with its high proportion of condemnation, is summarized and analysed very interestingly by Erwin Faul, 'Verfemung, Duldung and Anerkennung des Parteiwesens in der Geschichte des Politischen Denkens' ('Condemnation, Toleration and Approval of Parties in the History of Political Thought'), *Politische Vierteljahresschrift*, V, 1 (March 1964), pp. 60–80. The word party comes, of course, from part; as such it is often a polar concept to that of the whole. Cf. Giovanni Sartori, 'The Theory of Parties Revisited', in David Easton and Leonard Binder, *Theory and Method in Comparative Politics*, Englewood Cliffs (forthcoming); also 'Framework for a Typology of Parties and Party Systems', revised draft of paper for second CPS Conference, Cambridge, December 1965. The reflection of these attitudes in developing countries is discussed at some length below.

[2] Cf. Sigmund Neumann, *Parties*, op. cit., pp. 403–5. The extent to which this confusion continues to affect modern political theory or philosophy can be clearly seen in William Kornhauser's much cited *The Politics of Mass Society*, London 1960. Kornhauser sees mass society (the direct confrontation of sovereign and atomized individual) as something new, which it is not; Hobbes and Harrington held this view clearly–but not as a social fact. Kornhauser's great discovery (following Talmon, Arendt and the more pessimistic de Tocqueville tradition) is that 'mass society' (an extreme ideal-typical case of the exclusive application of my authority-legitimating function) can lead to 'the destruction of liberal democratic institutions; while in so far as a society is pluralistic, these institutions will be strong' (p. 7). The theory itself consists of the demonstration that mass society requires 'making available' elites for absorption by the mass, and 'making available non-elites' (a very odd, but under the circumstances necessary pseudo-sociological concept) 'for penetration by elites bent on total mobilization' (p. 22). This analysis is open to very serious methodological and ideological objections, not the least of which is the one most relevant to the present context; the transformation, by the merest assertive sleight-of-hand, of the purely political theory problem of linkage between society and people into a social category or type of society. Thus a type of analytical approach is confused with, and becomes, a type of society, and everything else follows from this–including other types of analysis (Durkheim's pluralism, Friedrich's totalitarianism) which in turn come alive for Kornhauser as contrasting types of society (pluralistic, totalitarian).

How has this confusion come about? We have noted the existence and mobilizational structuring of certain cleavages in recent European history. As long as sovereign authority was fixed, untouchable and autonomous beyond dispute, the articulation of interest based on these and other previous cleavages followed a progression of scale which ranged from small turbulence *ad homines* to a tussle for the normative attention and orientation of existing authority. Occasionally, in times of rapid social change or–in Marxist terms–revolutionary situations, the articulation of interests reached the level of value-orientation, and thus called in question the legitimacy of existing authority.[1] But until the late nineteenth century these articulations based on cleavage were random rather than structured; the interests articulated, however intense, were diffuse and not always related to specific collectivities. With the advent of the link ideology in theory as well as practical application, through extension of the franchise and the growing demand everywhere for this type of participation, the function and structure of interest articulation began to change significantly. In many European countries the interest articulating collectivities, who mobilized support based on cleavage identification, took over the new authority legitimation function in their stride, without altering their basic mobilizing potential. As orientation to cleavage became orientation to issues, the impact of mobilization became fixed at a normative level or below; the question of authority legitimation became functionally and processually separated from interest articulation either through plebiscites, etc., or through second-stage coalitions. Thus the formation of governments became an implicit consequence of elections, not an explicit and integral part of the electoral process; electoral mobilization was primarily based on the expression of interests–cleavages mediated by issues.

In England, however, the cleavages had not dominated mobilization based on collectivities. Indeed the cleavages, created by the process of the political subsystem, mostly focused on choices between competitors for political authority–a continuation of the process of selection by the crown in which the latter's role was merely transferred intact and unaltered to the sovereign people or voters (this is one country which turned its back firmly on the philosophy of the

[1] Some of the psychological implications of such collective behaviour on participants and leaders in times of rapid social change are elaborated in K. Baschwitz, *Du und die Masse–Studien zu einer exakten Massenpsychologie*, Leiden (Holland) 1951.

French revolution). The link between discrete individuals and authority was to remain as pure and unstructured as that between the crown
and its servants–choice was ideologically and sometimes even legis-
latively ordered to be *personal* and *rational*. Careful analysis of the
literature and the debates about the extension of the franchise seems
to indicate that groups, factions and associations were mostly condemned as reprehensible. Moreover, the individual-choice aspect of
voting is still inherent in the electoral laws and even in the form of
ballot papers in England and in some parts of the United States. The
link was not intended to be based on interest articulation.

But this exclusion was largely untenable in practice. First, political
authority now became accessible to competitition and was therefore
mise en cause. Instead of being tied to political collectivities that had
arisen from historical cleavages, the structure of interest articulation
became highly differentiated and largely untrammelled by the
formal electoral processes of politics; separate organizations were
able to develop outside the political parties and took the form of
groups related to, but not subsumed by, the electoral party structure
of authority legitimation. In particular the interest articulating groups
used the link structures as a means of communicating their demands
to authority.[1] In addition the legitimation of the link structures and
their emphasis on balloting helped to legitimize the interest articulation structures themselves. Hence the widely held ideological mystique
that voting at elections in England and the United States is primarily
a means of expressing individual and group interests. This legitimizes
the party system and the whole electoral process. It is very necessary
to be clear about the order of priorities here. Far from an electoral
process which serves its primary function of articulating interests
more or less badly, we have a process whose historical function is
that of authority legitimation but which has become accepted and
revered because it is regarded as a means of interest articulation.

This analysis points up the value of a functional approach to
problems in which the social scientists' view of function differs
radically from the perception of most participants, but where the
latter, properly evaluated by the observer, helps to crystallize the
correct view of function.[2] By suggesting the existence of two basic

[1] See the classic statement of this relationship in H. G. Wells, *The New
Machiavelli*, London (Penguin) 1946 edition, p. 238; quoted by Rokkan,
'Cleavage Structures . . .' op. cit. p. 8.
[2] I do not want deliberately to trail a methodological coat of structure-
functionalism too frequently. A good statement of the position and the
potential of functional analysis is in Theodore J. Lowi, 'American Business,

functions for political mobilization, and showing the extent to which they are served in different political systems, as well as the manner in which existing political processes handle them, we can more clearly assess the electoral process and its related party structures in the developed West. In particular we have noted the fusion or compression of the two functions into one electoral process to a greater or lesser extent, depending in large part on the historical evolution of cleavages and parties based on them. We are dealing with a more or less prismatic situation in which our empirical examples occupy only a limited central space on a large continuum of logical possibilities based on functional specificity or purity. But by investigating the different historical evolution of functional processes, the emphasis on one hand of the cleavage-issue dimension with its maintenance of the primacy of the interest articulating function, and on the other hand the emphasis on the link dimension with its priority for the authority legitimation function, we can analyse as well as classify two very different categories of tradition and functional priority. It is suggested that these functional imperatives tend to govern the historical evolution of structures.

This partly helps to explain the now well-documented historical fact that whereas in England there was much less of a ready-made cleavage public on which parties could build mass support, the crystallization of parties and party cleavages in many countries of Western Europe *preceded* the mass participation at elections through the extension of the suffrage. Indeed the latter confirmed rather than altered the existing party line-ups. In England and the United States yet again the form of party line-up was self-made, *ad hoc*; the Reform Bill of 1832 and the New Deal of 1933 themselves provided the basis for future party alignments and mobilization of support.[1]

Public Policy . . .' *World Politics*, op. cit.: 'Towards Functionalism in Political Science: The Case of Innovation in Party Systems', *Am. Pol. Sc. Rev.*, LVII, 3 (September 1963), pp. 570–83.
[1] For emphases on the crucial distinction between legitimation through voting and support for party (a somewhat similar distinction to my legitimacy-interest variable) see Stein Rokkan, 'Mass Suffrage, Secret Voting and Political Participation', *Archives Européennes de Sociologie*, II (1961), pp. 132–152; Talcott Parsons, 'Evolutionary Universals in Society', *American Sociological Review*, XXIX, 3 (June 1964), pp. 339–57. Case studies include H. Daalder, 'Parties and Politics in the Netherlands', *Political Studies*, III (1955), pp. 1–16; Ulf Torgerson, 'The Structure of Urban Parties in Norway during the First Period of Extended Suffrage, 1884–98', in Allardt and Littunen (eds), *Cleavages* . . . op. cit., pp. 377–99. The most recent and forceful general argument, covering Britain, Belgium, the Netherlands, Switzerland and Sweden is Hans Daalder, 'Parties, Elites and Political Development in Western Europe', in

Why has an understanding of these functional problems in their historical setting begun to be reached only so very recently? Perhaps the difficulty has been due partly to our own ideological false consciousness about the relationship between elections and political parties, grossly overvaluing the autonomy of the former and belittling the relative self-sufficiency of the latter.

> 'The trouble . . . is that we are not at the moment very certain of the function of elections in our own society. We have on the whole ceased to think that their function is to ensure government by the people . . . yet we continue to believe most heartily in their necessity; and this Western loyalty to elections has been strengthened by events of the last generation and of the last years.'[1]

Political parties in the electoral legitimation process are something of an ideological nuisance cluttering up the 'purity' of functional fulfilment. The fact that political leaders become ministers obscures the fact that ministers often remain political leaders.[2] It is only since

---

LaPalombara and Weiner (eds), *Political Parties and Political Development* op. cit. What these studies all bring out is that the electoral system may be a limiting factor on party structure and on the extent of interest articulation or authority legitimation, but does not govern basic party alignments in the legitimacy-interest pattern variable; nor can the ideal-typical interest-based mobilization *technique* of Western mass parties enable us to assess the *genuineness* of the interest component.

[1] W. J. M. Mackenzie, 'Export of Elections', op. cit., p. 255. I do not believe that the failure to analyse elections in their wider political context is a random matter of fashion or preference, but rather a compound of ideological unwillingness to use analysis as a means of investigating fundamentals, and of methodological self-satisfaction with areas amenable to facile quantification. The implications of both ideological and methodological easement are well expressed in the following quotation: 'The focus of the political behaviourist . . . does not seem to be the result of the state of political theory. Elections have been intensively studied because they lend themselves to the methodology of empirical research into politics.' Morris Janowitz, Deil Wright and William Delany, *Public Administration and the Public: Perspectives towards Government in a Metropolitan Community*, Ann Arbor, Michigan, 1958, p. 2. Cf. for the same implied criticism V. O. Key, Jnr., *Public Opinion and American Democracy*, New York 1961, and Richard Rose, *Influencing Voters*, London 1967.

[2] A very clear instance of this confusion has recently (October 1965) been provided by the complaints of George Brown, Minister for Economic Affairs, and of his cabinet colleagues, against the B.B.C. for failing instantaneously to recognize that the Five Year Plan, so long advertised as an electoral loss leader by the Labour Party, had transmogrified into a ministerial (legitimacy) document as soon as Labour had attained office and was thus no longer to be considered a 'mere' party plan. The problem arose because *government* statements may not be balanced by an opposition reply on Television or Sound Broadcasting, while *party* broadcasts must be if the opposition so desires.

constitutional or *de facto* leaders in newly independent countries have actually created *post hoc* political parties through institutionally inspired or elitist mobilization that students of politics–at least those with open eyes–have revalued political mobilization at the expense of elections as a means of *legitimization*. This in turn has led to the discovery that 'the elite/mass dichotomy postulated by most analysts is artificial and even misleading ... The ancient sense of community in Asia and Africa has not been dissolved into the individualism found in the modern West ... It is clear that ... power and influence go far beyond the conventional Western concept of leadership.'[1] Political mobilization from the top of the institutional pyramid downwards, instead of upwards towards authority from a cleavage base, has become the most significant contribution to politics by the 'new' countries. There is nothing remotely like it in the essentially constitutional form of power involved in the establishment of ancient and medieval tyrannies, and in the institutional mobilization in support of rulers like Napoleon and even Robespierre. Those who mark developing countries down on the conventional scale of pluralistic participation miss not only the significance of that contribution, but also miss the functional contribution of, say, the Soviet Communist Party and even the UNR in France.

Though the specific problem of mobilization in developing countries will be dealt with at greater length later, it is legitimate to ask at this stage to what extent the model of political mobilization in developed countries put forward here offers useful lessons and techniques to the Third World. At this stage such a confrontation will help to illuminate further the problems of analysis already outlined with regard to developed countries. To answer this question effectively, we need to know something of the bases of mobilization in developing countries; for the moment it is sufficient to assert the main differences in experience and expectations as compared with the West.[2]

[1] Hugh Tinker, *Ballot Box and Bayonet*, London 1964, pp. 96, 98–99. This suggestive little essay collides head-on with accepted American doctrine on the benefits of democratic or electoral participation. Cf. Daniel Lerner: 'Traditional society is non-participatory–it deploys people by kinship into communities isolated from each other and from a centre, while modern society is participant.' *The Passing of Traditional Society*, Glencoe 1958, pp. 48–50. In this sense cf. also Rupert Emerson, *From Empire to Nation*, Cambridge, Mass., 1960, ch. 15; Michael Brecher, *The New States of Asia*, London 1963, ch. 2.
[2] Cf. the present outline of political mobilization in developing countries with the more evolutionary definition and discussion of Dankwart A. Rustow, *Politics and Westernization in the Near East*, Princeton 1956, pp. 16–18.

THE FUNCTION OF POLITICAL MOBILIZATION

1. Most obviously the cleavage bases of the West simply do not exist in the Third World; indeed it is of the essence of political mobilization in most developing countries today that such cleavages as do exist–tribal, ethnic, etc.–should not be allowed to act as a base for mobilization and to develop into specific mobilizational structures. The cleavage-issue dimension is thus differently organized, its potential existence is recognized as a danger and every effort is made in terms of values, norms and collectivities to prevent its emergence as a historical factor in governing the political process. This means that any model of political process based on cleavages, in which interest articulation predominates, will not serve the elite values and goals of developing societies. A fairly typical example of such a model can be found in Fourth Republic France. Here the interest representation function of parties was strongly salient; elections hardly served as a form of authority legitimation at all. The plebiscitarian or legitimacy-orientated tradition had been broken after 1870, only to be revived for a time under the Vichy regime–but without any actual plebiscite! Meanwhile the choice of political authority had to be accommodated as best it could to this dysfunctional means, and did so uneasily for nearly ninety years.[1] The formation of government was only indirectly and in gross terms influenced by elections, taking place instead as a result of often prolonged bargaining by parties who used votes obtained rather like counters–or better, like firms in a merger who use capital assets as an 'objective' means of bargaining for seats on the new joint board.

2. Mobilization is largely from the top downwards in national-institutional terms through a government party. This places a strong accent, in value and normative terms, on authority legitimation; mobilization is overt, and every attempt is made to avoid conflict in commitment to party or state–either by having only one party, or by identifying the ruling party from among several with the special aura of such 'fused' legitimacy.[2] Hence models, which, though they may

[1] Cf. below pp. 318–9, 327–8. How dysfunctional it was can perhaps most readily be seen by the fact that the government 'crisis' became an institutionalized and carefully structured process of resolving the contradictory claims of the two roles–political representative and political authority–vested in one and the same cast of actors. See Philip Williams, 'Crisis as an Institution', *Crisis and Compromise*, London 1964, pp. 413–27. There is an analytical logic about this institutionalization of crisis which is noticeably absent from the more myth-proliferating British political process, though we shall find something like it in the institutionalization of coups in many developing countries.

[2] A recent discussion and analysis of this emphasis in the context of one particular society is C. A. Moore, *Tunisia Since Independence: The Dynamics of*

143

fulfil the functional requirements, do not possess the corresponding value emphasis, will not serve, especially where the ideological emphasis is on interest articulation. Britain is a pertinent instance. An electoral system for deciding between leaders of small groups competing for the institutionalized authority of the crown evolved in the course of the eighteenth century. The 'collective behaviours', the extra-institutional mobilization accompanying early industrialization up to the middle of the nineteenth century helped to bring about the extension of the benefit of these electoral techniques to much larger areas of the population. It was the peculiar genius of the Disraeli-Gladstone era to weld the mobilization potential of an industrial society on to the inchoate desire to exploit the possibilities of the ballot, thus trading once and for all the interest-articulating potential of political parties for structures of competition between the leadership of the parties for given periods of power. The myth of individual or local interest representation served to hide the fact that the real 'act' of voting was for a party and that this in turn was merely a method of legitimizing political authority from a very narrow range of choices.

3. In developing countries mobilization is focused on national perspectives. Intra-societal cleavages are to be subsumed by extra-societal or international ones. Mobilization is a functional process for the attainment of the goal of national integration; the required saliency and level of commitment are high. Accordingly no model which differentiates between cleavage mobilization and national perspectives, or whose national integration is the product of a historical transfer of symbolic sovereignty from ruler to people, and thus does not depend on specifically mobilized commitments, can serve as a useful example. This disbars all those Western models which do not make specific structural provision for national mobilization in terms of referenda, or referendum-type elections, in which intra-societal cleavage structures play only a marginal role. The Soviet Union is obviously an important source of ideas and orientation. The reconstitution of the French polity in 1958, with the constitutional amendments of 1962, also offers a possible model for

---

One-Party Government, Berkeley and Los Angeles 1965; a study specifically devoted to party-state conflict and its resolution. For the general problem in a theoretical perspective, cf. Sartori's discussion of various attempts by contributors to LaPalombara and Weiner, *Political Parties . . .* op. cit., to capture this problem conceptually, in 'The Theory of Parties Revisited', in Easton and Binder, *Theory and Method in Comparative Politics*, op. cit. Cf. also Nettl, 'Inheritance', and below, chapter 8.

developing countries; even though there is specific provision for interest-articulating elections in which parties are to play their role, this function (and the parties themselves) have been separated as far as possible from the authority-legitimation process with its operational emphasis on mobilization behind national perspectives. This differentiation is enshrined in having the two elections at different times, in the selection of different issues for the two elections (with the issues in the authority-legitimation election heavily weighted in terms of national and/or international content), finally by making it difficult for the existing cleavage-issue parties to intervene effectively as individual collectivities in presidential elections. Similarly the United States also offer a variant model of rather greater complexity in view of the fact that one and the same parties serve both functions at two different types of election. The limitations of the French and American models arise from the lack of sufficiently well-established universalistic perspectives in developing countries which can 'contain' both types of mobilization and their respective structures.

4. Finally developing countries are not dependent to anything like the same degree as the West on the historic legitimacy accorded to the result of an election held under formal rules designed, or at least believed, to enforce both a 'fair' and a 'rational' result. As we have already indicated, such legitimacy is particularly connected with the interest-articulation function; the ideological component is greater here than in the authority-legitimation function for which balloting seems in many ways more natural and logical (for this see note on elections at end of this chapter). Developing countries often retain non-electoral means of conferring legitimacy; especially in so far as the question of interest is held to be subsumed under that of authority legitimization. Just as mobilization is overt and manifest, and based on international rather than intra-national cleavages, so must any electoral process be as little manifestly divisive as possible. Since interest is held to be more divisive than roles for individual representatives of identical [national] interests, interest-articulating elections are not likely to commend themselves as models, and societies for whom such elections are considered to be the essential prism of legitimacy, through which any institutionalized authority must pass in order to obtain acceptance, will not commend themselves as models either.

This last point is worth elaborating. United Nations experts working on projects of 'improving' the Indian communities in Bolivia attempted (inevitably) to substitute democratic balloting techniques for the ancient but continuing processes of choosing village leaders by subterranean procedures out of which, slowly but inevitably, there emerged a unanimous consensus. The Indians were horrified, not only at the change itself, but its irrational inefficiency – above all at its built-in divisiveness. Their most interesting reaction was that henceforward they would just the same have to 'pretend' unanimity, even though none existed any more. Once more the Soviet Union, among developed countries, in this instance provides the most useful and appealing model of orientation and process. Though the legalistic appearance of authority-building ballots *outside* the party machinery through elections for Soviets had been carefully preserved, this is widely accepted as a fiction – little misapprehension remains except in the minds of a few legalistic apologists; even the party leaders have often bemoaned the inevitable lack of interest in the affairs of local and regional soviets. The real locus of authority legitimation is within the party, and the process takes place not in the election of party officials but in the prior search for, and creation of, a consensus – primarily with regard to who (legitimation), and only secondarily with regard to 'what' (interest articulation). Nowhere is the concept of interest representation more firmly depersonalized than in the Soviet Union (cf. below, p. 187, for the ideological basis of this). This is based on Lenin's insistence that public ratification of legitimacy need not be expressed by votes in order to be effective. Tacit approval (failure to rebel) is one extreme interpretation of this view of tacit consent, especially conducive to any materialist or historicist philosophy which claims that inevitable retribution comes down on the heads of those who force through any unripe or objectively unjustified expressions of norms or values. Nor are such notions of consent by any means confined to the Soviet Union and communists.[1]

Another, more positive, standard of legitimacy is the popular demonstration, so important in countries like Indonesia, Egypt, Ghana and Peron's Argentine. The 'permanent' crowd in the populous capitals of the Middle East is much more conducive to this form of legitimation than balloting – but notoriously just as fickle in

[1] A neat expression of this theory of consent was presented at a meeting of young Zionists. The speaker attempted to persuade his audience that it was Jews *not* interested in emigrating to Israel who were deviants from the norm. His justification for this was that since it should be presumed that all would go, not going required a specific assertion of dissent. The whole notion of tacit consent is also well established as a doctrine in divorce and contract law, and in many other areas of informal social behaviour. It is its specific denial in politics that may in this context perhaps be considered as abnormal and remarkable.

its own way as any electorate. If we look closely we can find this form of authority building and authority ratification employed as partial substitute for balloting (Greece, Turkey, Cyprus) and even as supplementary to balloting (France).[1] Popular turnout is held to legitimate or condemn dramatic performances perfectly adequately; no one calls for ballots on plays. In this respect the theatre presents a picture of politics both older and in some ways more accurate in defining a situation than modern political life itself. There is no *logical* reason why balloting should be peculiarly desirable as a means of signifying approval in political life.

As this discussion of the function of political mobilization shows, we are clearly still a long way away from an unbiased evaluation of our own political processes–and even farther from evaluating those of other societies in contrast to our own. Political mobilization has been particularly neglected–in spite of its by now evident importance. Its *functions* may be analysed as fairly clear cut; its role in the history of Western electoral and parliamentary democracy in developed politics is complex and contradictory. In the process of mass elections, interest articulation has become adapted to and differentiated from the formal party structure of the political system in various ways. The two functions of political mobilization have, to a greater or lesser extent, been subsumed within that of authority legitimation. What binds the interest articulation structures of developed, differentiated political subsystems to the authority-legitimizing structures is ideology; the more distinct the two sets of structures, as in Great Britain, the greater the need for ideological assertion of symbols and myths. In elitist societies especially, the fusion of functions can go a long way without undue strain by the massive use of myth and symbols–because constitutional forms tend anyhow to be only a second-order reflection of social reality. Secondly the almost universal reference to elections for purposes of deciding anything (or at least claiming that it has been decided) has helped to reduce the saliency and commitment involved in political mobilization. Though historically political mobilization has replaced both religious and military mobilization as the most efficient process for collective goal attainment, and political parties as the most efficient structures, both process and structure are ceasing to provide much evidence of goal attainment in terms of innovation and commitment. This may be because they are functionally less efficient (compared to other

[1] See for instance George Rudé, *The Crowd in History, 1730–1848*, New York 1965; also Baschwitz, *Du und die Masse*, op. cit.

THE FUNCTION OF POLITICAL MOBILIZATION

processes and structures), or because the goals of developed societies may be peculiarly evolving in the direction of simply maintaining the *status quo*, or because the diffuse overall commitment involved in intense and salient political mobilization may have become scattered into a form of specific issue-orientated commitments involving differentiated simultaneous mobilization across different subsystems. The question as to which of these is the main contributory factor, or whether all three are partly relevant, will be a major preoccupation in the later part of this analysis.

Meantime it is clear that the view which emphasizes the break up of diffuse mobilization into differentiated and more specific commitments, and equates this with stability and industrialized democracy, has noticeably failed to provide us with any useful analysis of political mobilization as a process of any significance. Political mobilization is presented as a crude and early version of modern, sophisticated pluralism, relevant only to certain peculiar societies today.

'"Mobilization of masses" is a phrase much used by Soviet political writers. What they understand by it is perhaps not too remote from what we mean by "public relations" . . . In the Soviet Union nearly all decisions are made in this way–that is, the members of the public are not led to an understanding of them by the processes of the market and need to have the decision "sold" to them *after it is taken*. Hence we have "mobilization", which aims at informing people as to what has been decided . . . and at building a positive attitude of acceptance of the decision. "Mobilization" is not left to the mass communications media; it is the main aim of thousands of *ad hoc* workplace and other meetings, and the pseudo-democratic processes of elections, meetings of Soviets, party conferences and congresses, have been largely shaped to serve its purposes.'[1]

Perhaps the most useful way of examining the problems raised by this characterization of, and negative judgement on, political mobilization is in terms of the saliency and process of politics in society as a whole; the role of the goal attainment subsystem in the social system.

Note to Chapter 5
Elections and Electors[2]

Elections have come to play a central role in the structuring of the

[1] T. H. Rigby, 'Traditional, Market and Organizational Societies and the USSR', *World Politics*, XVI, 4 (July 1964), pp. 553–4. My italics.
[2] This is a brief attempt to highlight some of the immediately relevant

political process in Western societies today; they are a crucial component in any analysis of function in the political subsystem. Though more has actually been written about elections in the last two decades than about any other aspect of politics, and though electors and voters are the most minutely analysed political individuals, there are still considerable lacunae–especially with regard to the function of elections in the wider social system, and the relationship between ideological attribution of function and the observed status of functions themselves. These are partly just empty, unresearched spaces. But they are also lacunae of underemphasis. Similarly, as regards voters, we have much knowledge about orientations, but hardly any about the relevant *roles* of voters. The present note cannot deal fully with these very substantial questions, but it attempts to discuss why some of these questions are relatively neglected, and why so much attention has been focused on elections even though the research effort is directed at very particular and limited questions. At the time of writing (March 1966) Britain is having another general election; this gives the problem a patina of contemporary as well as academic interest.

Very little examination of the philosophy underlying balloting or elections exists–except in a narrow, mathematical sense, concerned with the theoretical implication of method.[1] The substantial literature about electoral systems started from a particular set of assumptions (individual, free, rational choice expressed by means of a vote) and has since become increasingly concerned to demonstrate the restraints on that freedom. Perceptive analysts of voting and elections, realizing that their researches were undermining the rational assumptions of individual behaviour on which democratic theory was based, began some time ago to substitute for such individual

---

problems connected with elections and with electoral research. It is not a methodological or bibliographical survey, much less a critique, of the very substantial research in the field. For a useful bibliographical summary of the main behavioural work on elections and electors up to 1962, see Austin Ranney (ed.), *Essays on the Behavioral Study of Politics*, op. cit., notes 31–36, pp. 16–18. A bibliography of studies of British elections and electors is in Richard Rose (ed.), *Studies in British Politics*, London 1966, pp. 51–52, 332–4.

[1] For this see, most recently, Duncan Black, *The Theory of Committees and Elections*, Cambridge 1963; cf. W. H. Riker, 'Voting and the Summation of Preferences', *Am. Pol. Sc. Rev.*, LV, 4 (December 1961), pp. 900–11, and Riker, *The Theory of Political Coalitions*, New Haven 1962. A good though brief comment of recent date, which differentiates between the basic consensus and conflict aspects of elections, and discusses the latter according to mêlée, tournament and gladiator analogies, is by James Douglas, 'Consensus and Elections', *New Society*, 175, 3rd February 1966, pp. 11–14.

rationality the notion of *system* rationality–system in this case being simply the grossed-up mass of individuals. The classical statement of this was made as early as 1954: '*Individual voters* today seem unable to satisfy the requirements for a democratic system of government outlined by political theorists. But the *system of democracy* does meet certain requirements for a going political organization. The individual members may not meet all the standards, but the whole nevertheless survives and grows. This suggests that where the classical theory is defective is in its concentration on the *individual citizen*. What are undervalued are certain collective properties that reside in the electorate as a whole and in the political and social system in which it functions.'[1] But more recently still the theoretical 'rightness' of the system which makes good the 'wrongness' of the individual has been challenged in a formal sense as well; 'Insofar as [the theory of passive consent implicit in the adjustment of the democratic system to individual irrationality] suggests the existence of some harmonizing mechanism in the "system of democracy", a mechanism which systematically discounts errors or apathy in "individual voters" and synchronizes the parties' drive toward victory with the system's rightful aim of revealing a true consensus, the above hypothesis is wrong . . . What empirical study has done to [undermine] our confidence in the individual voter, pure theory seems similarly to be doing to our confidence in the ability of the party process to produce true consensus.'[2] It seems reasonable to suppose, therefore, that modern mathematical theories of elections coupled with empirical studies are raising grave doubts as to the functioning of the electoral process along the lines indicated by democratic political theory.

From another angle the assumptions of polling and surveys, when contrasted with observable reality, also give rise to doubts about their validity. Thus the origin of polling and surveys based on interviews was in a sense that of sibling to commercial market research. As a recent study shows, the underlying assumptions of such commercial effort were egalitarian and, what is more significant, plebiscitarian in that every respondent was assumed to be of equal weight and importance. Thus electoral surveys were to get behind the obtrusive *bric-à-brac* of party to the essential democratic, free and equal voter.[3] Some of this missionary zeal remains today, though it has become

[1] Bernard R. Berelson, Paul F. Lazarsfeld, William N. McPhee, *Voting*, Chicago 1954, p. 312. (Italics in the original.)

[2] Gerald Garvey, 'The Theory of Party Equilibrium', *Am. Pol. Sc. Rev.*, LX, 1 (March 1966), pp. 29–38, particularly p. 38.

[3] A very lucid analysis of the underlying assumptions of market research as

increasingly qualified by the recognition of structural factors limiting the freedom and rationality of the individual elector. Today the particular areas of interest, or problem areas, are: (1) the extent to which votes are choices made effective, (2) the effect of voting on the attitude of parties and vice versa, and (3) the social deductions that can be made from various voting and attitude patterns, as well as the reverse–the patterns that can be deduced from indices of social location and attitudes, such as class. In particular this third concern, namely the social/psychological bases of voting intentions and performance, is gaining ground. The following specific points seem to have been neglected and particularly to require investigation in terms of any system analysis.

1. What adjustments have been made, if any, to the changed circumstances of mass elections, in which voting takes place in conditions of very varying knowledge and evaluation but where each vote still has the same weight? Has the vacuum created by 'ignorant' voting induced the growth of party structures, who aggregate and simplify choices, on architectural or logistic grounds of stability? Does this mean that the peripheral level of political culture may actually be declining in developed societies as politics get more complex and electoral demands on rationality greater, with political parties increasing their simplification function and corresponding role, and thus actually obscuring the effect of declining involvement–in short the growth of indifference?

The shift in many modern societies from (party) structural emphasis on cleavage to emphasis on issues, which we have already noted as part of our model, may in fact provide evidence of declining involvement. This is in fact not so much an overall decline of political culture levels–a rare phenomenon–as a consumer-orientated shift in the form of involvement; the parties do more in the way of product advertising and sales, while the voter or consumer has to do less. *Choices* are simplified into *issues*. This is the para-economic model brilliantly sketched out by Downs.[1] Once more the perspectives of political science provide valuable evidence for rather fundamental changes in politics. The currently fashionable method of building spatial models of party competitition, in which electoral party politics are viewed in terms of different dimensions, each one of which

---

regards those polled is by Wilhelm Hennis, *Meinungsforschung und repräsentative Demokratie*, Tübingen 1957.

[1] *An Economic Theory of Democracy*, op. cit. Cf. also Joseph Schumpeter, *Capitalism, Socialism and Democracy*, New York 1950.

provides a notional space on which parties take up their respective positions on different issues, depends for its validity on the existence of issue rather than cleavage-orientated political systems.[1] But this in turn means making substantive adjustments in our view of involvement in, and commitment to, the political subsystem on the part of citizens, especially in the context of mobilization, to which research on participation, culture and other neighbouring subjects has not yet adapted itself.

2. How valid is the assumption, strongly implicit in the voting system as recommended by the Greeks, especially Artistotle, and taken over into the philosophy of the link between sovereign and people, that votes, being for *people* rather than issues, leave no trace, and have no social continuity other than putting the elected into office? More specifically, does voting create and institutionalize divisions as well as merely reflecting them in the political subsystem?

3. Has voting only one single function: do elections serve no other purpose than to elect someone? For instance, research on the symbolic function of elections exists, but as a separate rather than an integrated perspective.[2] Apart from this, elections also have other social functions, which have nothing directly to do with voting at all.[3] There is the party rally aspect, in which national elections provide the opportunity for symbolic or ideological articulation by parties for their members' benefit–the sort of thing analysed by Tingsten and Himmelstrand in Scandinavia, and by Günther Roth with regard to Germany.[4] Thus elections may be also latently functional in an

---

[1] The interrelationship of parties in this approach is viewed as systemic in that the position of each party is a combination of its own policies and those of its competitors. A good initial discussion of such models and their assumptions is Giovanni Sartori, 'Modelli spaziali di competizione tra partiti', *Rassegna italiana di sociologia*, VI, 1 (January–March 1965), pp. 7–29.

A constructive criticism of the Downs model in its application to the behavioural study of politics is Donald E. Stokes, 'Spatial Models of Party Competition', *Am. Pol. Sc. Rev.*, LVII, 2 (June 1963), pp. 368–77. Much recent work on elections has been influenced by this approach.

[2] See for instance Murray Edelman, *The Symbolic Uses of Politics*, op. cit.

[3] For this see e.g. Richard Rose, and Harvé H. Mossawir 'Voting and Elections: A Functional Analysis', in draft, due for publication in *Political Studies* 1967.

[4] Herbert Tingsten, 'Stability and Vitality in Swedish Democracy', *Political Quarterly*, XXVI, 2 (1955), pp. 140–51; cf. Himmelstrand, 'Depoliticization', op. cit.; also *Social Pressures, Attitudes and Democratic Processes*, Stockholm 1960. For Germany, Günther Roth, *The Social Democrats in Imperial Germany*, Totowa, New York 1963; cf. also J. P. Nettl, *Rosa Luxemburg*, London 1965, Chapter, IV, VIII and XII. For America see Murray Edelman, *The Symbolic Uses of Politics*, op. cit.

integrative sense, structuring and increasing cleavages or possibly lessening them. As autonomous social facts they can become political referents for the future, and help to generate particular social and political policies of their own which have hardly anything to do with the voters (e.g. the way that elections in Nigeria in 1964–5 seemed to define the entire political situation for a year, and eventually helped to generate a *coup d'état*). This becomes obvious when we look at developing countries where elections are also a means of collective inspection (how efficient is the party in organizing turnout and compliant voting?) as well as of information diffusion (putting across information to readily assembled audiences) and checking on information content (what has to be emphasized at the expense of what else?). We shall look at these electoral functions in developing societies more closely in chapters 8 and 9.

4. Whereas the original, small arenas of choice and participation made voting *against* fully equal in weight with voting *for*, modern electoral systems have (or think they have) eliminated the negative aspect, reserving it in a few societies to the referendum. But is this assumption justified? Another way of stating this problem is to assert that voting was originally intended to be confined to a sufficiently small group to permit every voting participant to be also a candidate if he wished. This assumption automatically doubles all the available choices (for as well as against).

5. Finally, to what extent does the function of voting presuppose the selection of one individual from among several, and therefore implicitly pervert any attempt to use the voting system for purposes of interest articulation through the graded choice of individuals in some order of preference? If the implicit function is so perverted, do techniques like proportional representation correct it, or do they imply quite a different function? This is the type of problem specifically raised by the variable interest articulation-authority legitimation put forward here. The research strategies suggested include an examination of electoral methods and techniques in the context of differently emphasized functional imperatives or requirements, and the choice of electoral methods in the light of the perception of electoral function or premise by the participants at the time.

Then there is the problem of the voter. Modern behavioural scholarship has increasingly focused on the elector as a member of a group or class, and deduced group attitudes from quantified coincidences. This focus varies widely according to the interests of the investigator, and relatively little precise correlation between the location of the voter and the casting of his vote still exists today. As one distinguished political scientist has suggested a few years ago, election surveys and the emphasis on classifying voter attitudes were threatening to take politics out of the study of elections altogether.[1] We have a growing plethora of facts, but it is not quite clear what we are looking *for*. Thus we have electors analysed by age, occupation, class, profession, income; on the basis of such hard, elicitable facts, modern techniques have developed sophisticated means of translating individual opinions and views into social group reference points – and even of predicting elections. But there is a big difference between attitudinal and sociological variables; the former ends with the analysis of attitudes quantified in terms of a total population (or sample), the latter begins with group action or process in a system. The type of summated whole embodied in the electorate, which Berelson and others have put forward in their 1954 study, does not make any adequate group, nor does their vote constitute any adequate action or process in a system for sociological purposes. Assignment of summated individuals to groups is a halfway house between them, and leads nowhere except the inflation of elections into the *terminus ad quem* of politics.[2]

[1] V. O. Key, Jr., and F. Munzer, 'Social Determinism and Electoral Decision: The Case of Indiana', in E. Burdick and A. J. Brodbeck (eds), *American Voting Behavior*, Glencoe 1959, pp. 281–99.

[2] Thus many of the big and sophisticated attitude studies like P. Lazarsfeld, B. Berelson and Helen Gaudet, *The People's Choice*, New York 1948; Berelson, Lazarsfeld, McPhee, *Voting*, Chicago 1954, and Angus Campbell *et al.*, *The American Voter*, New York 1960 (to name only three) neither set out to solve sociological questions in accordance with sociological variables, nor do they in fact do so. Other studies do both, like V. O. Key, Jr., *Public Opinion and American Democracy*, op. cit. It is obviously pointless to criticize research for failing to achieve what it never set out to do; it is however perfectly legitimate, and may well be important, to investigate why a certain research orientation may be strongly pursued in a field where different orientations suggest themselves as well but remain relatively neglected, and what, if any, consequence such research orientation may have on the priorities accorded to different processes in a social or political system. The impact of behavioural orientations on various aspects of political science is discussed and justified by H. Eulau, *Recent Development in the Behavioral Study of Politics*, Stanford 1961, and, more comprehensively, in Austin Ranney (ed.), *Essays on The Behavioral Study of Politics*, op. cit. But cf. Dahrendorf's critical comment in 'Three Symposia on Political Behavior', *American Sociological Review*, XXIX. 5 (October 1964), pp. 734–6. There remains the problem of whether attitudinal or structural (sociological) orientations are a matter of preference and emphasis, or whether they are methodologically incongruent. This is interestingly discussed by Paul F. Lazarsfeld in Lazarsfeld and Rosenberg, *Language of Social Research*, op. cit. and Lazarsfeld and Herbert Menzel in A. Etzioni (ed.), *Complex Organizations*, New York 1961, pp. 422–40, who attempt to relate the

THE FUNCTION OF POLITICAL MOBILIZATION

We are for instance frequently shown that the exercise of consistent rationality in elections is relatively low; while this may indicate very useful lines of enquiry in terms of level as well as quality of culture, the focus of such enquiries on elections as such does not tell us anything more than the limits of rationality in the case of one particular process. The consequential effects of the process on the system under the indicated circumstances are not pursued. To take an English example. When admitted Labour supporters in one constituency were confronted with specific Labour issues then relevant, only a third could be classified as supporting Labour on these issues and 39 per cent supported Conservatives. Among admitted supporters of the Conservative party only 38 per cent expressed official support of party policy on three major issues though only 4 per cent could be classified as actually pro-Labour. Almond's aggregation function of parties as offering a summation of choices thus turns out–at least in one study in depth–to be a myth; contradictions are summated along with choices.[1] If this lack of co-ordination between votes for parties on the one hand and evaluation of the parties' stand on various issues on the other correctly represents the situation of a significant proportion of the electorate in a highly developed or modern country, the spatial model of party competition operates in

method of investigating individual attributes with that of group attributes and process. On this subject see also the recent discussion by Raymond Boudon, 'Propriétés individuelles et propriétés collectives: un problème d'analyse écologique', *Revue Française de Sociologie*, IV (1963), pp. 275–99.

[1] R. S. Milne and H. C. Mackenzie, 'Straight Fight, a Study of Voting Behaviour in ... Bristol North-East at the General Election of 1951', *Parliamentary Affairs*, VIII, 1 (entire special issue). Further evidence of the lack of complete correspondence between party and class in Britain, which one would expect to be specially significant in two-party systems where such correspondence appears empirically most probable, is to be found in D. V. Glass (ed.), *Social Mobility in Britain*, London 1954; Jean Blondel, *Voters, Parties and Leaders*, London (Penguin) 1963, pp. 75–79. The evidence is summarized in Richard Rose, 'Social and Party Cleavages in Britain', article for special number of *Revue Française de Sociologie*, June 1966, p. 22 (in draft). Similar conclusions were reached with regard to America in a survey relating to political apathy–the avoidance of political discussion and commitment *except* in terms of voting; for a summary of the evidence of recent research see Lester W. Milbrath, *Political Participation*, Chicago 1965, chapter VI; Morris Rosenberg, 'Some Determinants of Political Apathy', *Public Opinion Quarterly*, XVIII (1954–5), pp. 349–66. See also Philip E. Converse, 'The Nature of Belief Systems in Mass Publics', in David E. Apter, *Ideology and Discontent*, New York 1964, pp. 206–61. The problem of self-conscious or deliberate apathy is discussed in Robert Agger, Marshall Goldstein and Stanley Pearl, 'Political Cynicism: Measurement and Meaning', *Journal of Politics*, XXIII (1961), pp. 477–506; Edgar Litt, 'Political Cynicism and Political Futility', *Journal of Politics*, XXV (1963), pp. 312–23.

a relative vacuum of ignorance–the model positing a degree of consumer rationality that is not borne out in practice. It follows that the occupation of 'space' by a party is only in part a maximization of electoral profit, and for the rest (to continue the economic analogy) is similar to a producer's adjustment to a highly imperfect, if not oligopolistic, market. To put it another way, electors either vote for someone *or* something; to quote one of the founders of British election research, Dr. Mark Abrams, in 1959: 'People do not vote for Mr. Macmillan or Mr. Gaitskell: they vote for themselves'. They are assumed to do one, they do the other–or at best the two alternatives (which correspond broadly to the two functions discussed earlier) are muddled and intertwined to an extent which makes it almost impossible to separate them. But until the two functions are separated at least as heuristic tools, we cannot even begin to separate them in any studies of concrete situations.

It can be argued that an elector must therefore always be considered from three different aspects at any one time. The first two are obvious by now; the elector as an autonomous individual, choosing a *representative* on allegedly objective merits (authority legitimation); the elector as a member of a social group or groups choosing a delegate for subjective reasons (this group membership is in fact a sociological requirement for any political interest articulation; that is why Abrams' statement is meaningless in this context). There is however a third, almost totally neglected aspect–the elector in a role, that of a [notional] games player. Everything said so far has treated the elector on the basis of his notional premise, as assuming or hoping that if sufficient numbers of other people think and feel as he (or his group) does, his and their wishes will prevail.[1] In other words, he casts his electoral bread upon the waters, without adjusting his own behaviour to any assessment of the likely behaviour of his fellow voters, or of the actual outcome of the election. Now this assumption is not likely to be universally valid. Games theory has shown us that among two or three players, a logical assessment of probabilities should make one player adjust his strategy according to an optimum compounded of his own wishes and his understanding of those of the other players. It has also shown that in all n-person non-zero sum game alliances are mandatory–not for reasons of common social location, nor because of any common social interest, but because the situation is

---

[1] A connection between role and premise as different approaches to the study of individual action is suggested by Herbert A. Simon, *Administrative Behavior*, second edition, New York 1957, pp. xxx ff.

defined and can only be defined in terms of collective winners and losers. A study of repeated small-scale voting situations shows that some–if not always the most rational–allowance is *always* made in these situations. (Papal elections are a good example, and have been historically analysed in detail, see e.g. Leopold von Ranke's *History of the Popes*; so are Board room and College Elections, e.g. C. P. Snow, *The Masters*.) Even in larger voting situations such compromises are frequent (Clemenceau's '*votez pour le plus bête*' in a ballot for the French Presidency, and the 13-count ballot for the presidency in 1953).[1] Some elements of this form of strategical adjustment are likely to be present in large-scale, national elections as well, though no means has been found of measuring and analysing them–and no great efforts have been made to find one. Thus in the 1966 British general election, the Liberal strategy as put forward by Grimond was clearly based on some such considerations; an assessment of the likely winner in each constituency where no Liberal was standing, with the recommendation that Liberal voters should support the weaker party, in order to ensure a national result as evenly balanced between the two major parties as possible, and consequent increase in the weight of the Liberal contingent in the new House of Commons. The moment people are asked who or what they are voting *against* as well as who or what they are voting *for*, those interviewed are being treated as potential if rudimentary games players.[2]

An interesting variant on the elector as games player is suggested by the conceptual possibility–which is fascinating a few social scientists as well as worrying rather more politicians–that electoral opinion polls may themselves influence attitudes and votes. Such effects, if they do exist in practice, would not operate as a single factor for which pollsters might conceivably allow in their mathematics, but are likely to be cumulative–i.e. each correction is again distorted by its own secondary effects on those polled.[3] The influence of polls, more or less neutral and on the whole purely empirical, thus

[1] Analysed in detail by C. Melnik and N. C. Leites, *House Without Windows*, New York 1958.

[2] Some investigation along these lines may be found in the Michigan Surveys, especially *The American Voter* (1960 edition). The problem of voting *against* has traditionally played an important and manifest part in elections in France.

[3] Nonetheless, it is *always* possible in principle to make accurate predictions that will be confirmed in theory, and *sometimes* also in practice, depending on the shape of the reaction function. See Herbert A. Simon, 'Bandwagon and Underdog Effects of Election Predictions', reprinted in Simon, *Models of Man, Social and Rational*, New York, 1957, pp. 79–87. A more general analysis of self-fulfilling and self-liquidating predictions in the context of group interests

conceptually creates a special sub-category of games-playing voters – not only playing against opponents but also against par. The strategy of choices in a bandwagon or underdog effect is similar to a golf match in which players are matched against each other and against par, and adjust to a varying preference or priority as between the live and the par opponent. (The prediction, of course, is par, the preference being between incorporating or ignoring the prediction when it comes to voting.)

Looking at elections and looking at electors are in any case two quite different things.[1] Hitherto the study of elections has been either technical – what happened: how could what happened have been made to happen more efficiently in a technological sense, or else social-functional – what were the voters trying to say, and why? In that sense an election is thus no more than a collective noun for a rather specific and unique action by individuals or groups of citizens. The actors for their part are viewed as having various orientations, which in turn (depending on the sociological perspectives of behavioural analysis) may be grossed up into group or class indices. Though obviously orientations need not depend on, or be related to, elections, and can be investigated quite independently of them, there is a remarkably high correlation between the timing and substance of behavioural analysis in politics, and the conceptual disjunction or caesura of an election. This does suggest that elections take on an importance in the methodology of studying politics which tends to translate itself into a corresponding – and possibly exaggerated – importance in the analysis of political process. In addition it makes the voter or elector an excessively important actor in politics; usually exaggerating his role where any assessment of its importance is undertaken.

Elections seem to have something of the quality of volcanoes; they bring to the surface knowledge about wishes and attitudes both

---

and values (unfortunately treated uniformly as ideologies) is in the as yet untranslated book by Stanislaw Ossowksi, *O osobliwościach nauk spolecznvch*, (On Personality in the Social Sciences), Warsaw 1962 especially pp. 214–15. The idea of *prophesies* affecting or weighting their own outcome, of course, dates back to ancient Greece at least. (Cf. Gibbon, *Decline and Fall*, Vol. I, Chapter 1, on the legend of Terminus.)

[1] Even a sophisticated and subtle analyst like Deutsch is still as firmly committed today (1963) to the use of 'voting data and perhaps sample surveys to obtain estimates of the political integration ratio' (*Nerves of Government*, p. 126) as in 1953, although he does not confuse this with, or treat it as, automatic evidence of according legitimacy.

primary (the result of electing someone) and secondary (the deeper analysis and the attempt, where made, to disentangle confusion between views held and votes cast). The fact that the surface product is overemphasized as an epiphenomenon and is not always evaluated correctly does not alter the very widespread view of elections as an occasional, though reliable and at least regular, means of geological enlightenment. It is noticeable that there is in most countries with 'democratic' elections a continuing and unresolved debate as to whether such elections ratify existing or proffered policies and the people that go with the policies, or whether they provide clues which future policies and people must take into account. Are elections an end or a beginning or both, and how much of each? (Note the difference between, say, England and the United States in this regard, as expressed by the two conceptions of 'standing' or 'running' for office.) If they are a means of sounding public opinion generally, are there not better ways of doing this, which do not impose their own situational patterns on the future–over and above the required expression of views? If they are not, but exist to choose a government from among one of a narrow range of choices, then why do behavioural analysts fasten on to them as an occasion on which soundings of orientations are somehow specially significant? In this context, is the unanimity-preserving or 'sounding' method of choosing a Conservative leader in Britain, recently modernized out of existence, or *any* form of achieving consensus, really so bad? Perhaps it would simplify the whole problem if we clearly separated the choice function of elections, with its overtones of optimal effectiveness in small group and multiple-choice situations, from the threat function which acts as a restraint on policy and adjusts the latter to the supposed load-bearing capacity of the potential electors. The latter is really a non-voting form of democratic involvement; it is this that provides the so-called sanction of restraint, the 'guarantee of our liberties', the complementary aspect of tacit approval.[1] As already mentioned, however, the idea that political apathy is either a continuing feature of permanent empirical validity in modern societies, or that it is theoretically conducive to any viable theory of equilibrium or democracy, is currently under strong challenge.[2]

[1] Cf. R. A. Dahl, *A Preface to Democratic Theory*, op. cit.; *Modern Political Analysis*, op. cit.

[2] For a summary of the evidence against political apathy and 'de-ideologization', see Jack L. Walker, 'A Critique of the Elitist Theory of Democracy', *Am. Pol. Sc. Rev.*, LX, 2 (June 1966), pp. 285–95; Joseph LaPalombara, 'Decline of Ideology', *Am. Pol. Sc. Rev.*, LX, 1 (March 1966), pp. 5–16. For

Finally there is the scale of dependence by parties on elections as a functional context. This is really a three-fold question.

1. In one respect it measures the adjustment of political mobilization to the electoral ideology through party structures (their 'democratic socialization'). American and British parties are primarily electoral collectivities in this sense. Though they fulfil a number of other functions in the political and integrative subsystems, the extent to which they are able to exercise these functions can only be assessed in accordance with their electoral 'efficiency'. The CPSU on the other hand is meaningless in such electoral terms. In many other countries the party systems probably fall somewhere in between these extremes of electoral relevance and electoral importance–and a variable scale on which parties could be placed in this context would be very useful.

2. In another sense the scale of dependence of parties on elections elucidates the integrative as against the external efficiency functions of political parties. The British Conservative party uses elections to gain votes (and organizes accordingly) while European far-right and left-wing parties and groups, as well as opposition parties in India and Pakistan, use elections as a means of increasing internal cohesion and external cleavage, and of strengthening their structures as a result (and organize electorally in accordance with this requirement). The fear that elections will be used to coalesce and integrate a value-orientated opposition is incidentally one of the reasons why military governments in South America delay, ban and pre-empt elections–as much as the direct threat of being voted out of office.

3. In yet a third respect the dependence of parties on elections measures the extent to which the latter are either stable articulations of cleavage or 'rotating' alignments and locations on continuum spaces according to different issues. Thus French parties in the Fourth Republic tended frequently to articulate ancient cleavages of the kind summarized earlier: the state revolution and the industrial revolution. The German parties since 1949 have tended on the other hand to adapt to issue orientations and have deliberately played down their cleavage origins. See also Norway for an example of cleavage parties adjusting gradually to issue orientations through time.

All these questions, somewhat schematically adumbrated here, do seem to indicate clearly that a broader conceptual approach is called

the theoretical implications of party position on equilibrium analysis see Gerald Garvey, 'The Theory of Party Equilibrium', ibid., pp. 29–38, op. cit.

for in the study of elections. The behavioural emphasis, with all its refinements, is not enough. First, elections and electors are *separate* foci for study, and the relationship between them must be clearly worked out. Secondly, the focus of analysis must aim at integrating not only electors but also elections into an ongoing social process after as well as before the great event. Finally–and perhaps most important–we must be clear as to the respective influence of ideology and of required function, elucidate the content and impact of the former and set it against the performance of the latter. There is no *a priori* reason why 'democratic' elections should be the centrepiece of modern politics, particularly once it is recognized that socio-political mobilization, which elections appear to call forth in practice, does not by any means always or wholly depend on elections and is not functionally subordinate to them, and finally that such mobilization is possible and can be studied without any elections at all.[1]

[1] Some of the most suggestive attacks on the behaviourists for not bringing into the open their latent ideological premises have come from philosophers– often from outside the discipline of politics, and competing with political science for the disputed catchment areas. If, the critics say, the false neutrality of these studies were abandoned, and the authors used their techniques frankly to examine normative democratic components in elections, both the discipline and the 'free world' would be better off. See Alfred Cobban, 'The Decline of Political Theory', *Political Science Quarterly*, LXVIII (1953), pp. 321–37, especially p. 335; more recently Christian Bay, 'Politics and Pseudopolitics: A Critical Evaluation of Some Behavioral Literature', *Am. Pol. Sc. Rev.*, LIX, (March 1965), pp 39–51, especially p. 39: 'much of the current work on political behavior generally fails to articulate its very real value biases, and the political impact of this supposedly neutral literature is generally conservative and in a special sense anti-political'. But, far from enjoining a broader investigation of political behaviour on a societal level based on process and function, which recognizes and evaluates the ideological component of culture and action, these critics often call for a return to a frankly democratic bias based on Aristotelean concerns with politics as leading to the good life. In the last resort the difference is alleged to be that political scientists believe 'the good life' to be here now (hence conservative), while the philosophers see it as a moving goal for which they must continue to strive. Hence they contrast the cited behavioural studies on elections unfavourably with works like Morris Janowitz and Dwaine Marvick, *Competitive Pressure and Democratic Consent*, Ann Arbor 1956, an analysis of the 1952 American Presidential election in accordance with the saliency of five explicitly stated criteria of *democratic* consent.

It is of the essence of this present essay that both these positions, as they have crystallized, leave much to be desired in their different ways, and that a new compromise position is essential if political analysis is to move forward. The problem of the connection between value or ideological bias in social analysis on the one hand, and the constraints of concepts and methodology on the other, will be raised again later when appropriate.

CHAPTER SIX

The Social Efficiency of Politics
in Developed Societies

SUMMARY

In the previous chapters two dimensions of variables relating to political mobilization were adumbrated and discussed. To facilitate the analysis the political subsystem was treated as a more or less autonomous system of its own; though mention was made of non-political factors such as cleavage, issue and interest bases, their translation into politics was not examined specifically as a theoretical problem. We now turn to this. First we shall investigate the relationship of the problem of authority with that of interest articulation in the analyses offered by different political theorists in the last two hundred years. Then we shall discuss authority in the context of greater or lesser autonomy of the political subsystem; how specifically *political* is the emphasis on authority legitimation as expressed through the process of political mobilization? Secondly, and closely connected with the first, is the social function of politics and particularly political mobilization; how does it relate to other social processes and orientations? In order to answer these questions, we shall return to the cultural variable of elitist and constitutional orientations, and discuss the interaction of this variable with that of interest articulation and authority legitimation as functions of political mobilization. A further assessment of empirical situations and societies in the light of the two variables will be attempted. More particularly we will investigate the extent to which the cultural variable governs the process of political mobilization, whether there is any pattern of correlation between a constitutionally oriented culture and a separation of functions on the one hand, and between an elitist culture and a fusion of functions on the other. Where we find a processual tendency towards functional fusion, which function can be said to predominate? In a brief methodological survey an assessment of the coverage of these specific problems in the literature is made, both with regard to empirical and to theoretical analyses.

Finally some conclusions from this analysis of political function, and its process-structural expression in the developed West, are drawn with regard to developing countries; how useful a model for political mobilization does the West provide? The analysis suggests that the Western model can offer only very limited help.

We might at this stage set down five hypotheses about political mobilization which partly summarize what has been said, and partly look forward to what is to come.

1. Political mobilization is related functionally to existing political authority, positively or negatively. Mobilization is either peripheral in origin, directed at or against existing authority in the course of its development, or it is structurally induced downwards, from an elite *towards* mass participation.

2. The functional dichotomy of interest articulation and authority legitimation distinguishes political mobilization historically and empirically from other forms of social mobilization.

3. In the West, the historical experience of different cleavages and their respective influence on the political process have resulted in widely varying tendencies towards fusion or differentiation in the way the two functions are carried out in terms of structures and process. Ideological myths are in some cases required to overcome strain and maintain the appearance that both functions are in fact served by one and the same structure.

4. A transfer or importation of party or electoral systems by one country from another means that these ideological accretions will not operate effectively, if at all; the dysfunctional aspects of fused mobilization structures appear more openly in new settings. Nonetheless, if the political culture orientation and the level of political culture of borrower and lender are similar, the ideological interpretation of process can be acquired somewhat more easily. This is seldom the case between a developed and a developing society since situations are defined quite differently, and for very different sections of the populations.

5. In most developed countries the development of politics has assigned functional primacy to authority legitimation over interest articulation. Since this conflicts with the latter as the main and proper perceived *purpose* or premise of political mobilization and of its

various structural components (like elections, political parties, etc.), we have a fairly clear example of ideological distortion.

The primacy of authority building over interest articulation as a function of party politics is not only the product of objective social forces, operating in some determined way. Much of it can be studied in the emphasis on, and preoccupation with, legitimacy on the part of political thinkers, who repeatedly stress the fundamental nature of this aspect. We have already noted the contribution of political philosophy in the creation of the notion of a link between individual and sovereign. But perhaps the weakest point of political philosophy has always been the historical *explanation* of what sovereign authority is. Once over this hump, political philosophers have produced sophisticated explanations of its proper *limits* (if any) and its proper *purposes*. These start in modern times from Hobbes with his prescription of narrow but complete sovereignty bent on self-maintenance, and can be seen in Locke with his divided sovereignty limited by and aligned to 'natural law'. Then the type of explanation of authority bifurcates; on the one hand into the various 'substitutionists' who, like Rousseau and Hegel, viewed the individual as attaining a meaningful existence only as participant in, or part of, a higher collective unity, and on the other hand into the Utilitarians with their notion of residual authority helping man – often in spite of himself – to achieve individual self-improvement by counteracting extraneous as well as psychological hindrances.[1] But the *origin* of sovereign authority, and more particularly the relationship of individuals to its original establishment, are not dealt with satisfactorily anywhere. The origin of sovereignty is assumed to have been inevitable and the relationship as coterminous (general will) or taken for granted as largely irrelevant (Bentham and the Utilitarians), or, most arbitrary of all, explained by a *single* and binding act of universal decision, (social contract). The fact that the form and extent of participation by future subjects in the original institutionalization of legitimate authority necessarily govern or at least affect the continuing relationship between sovereign and subject after the establishment of the state has tended to dis-

---

[1] Locke may be said to approach some notion of social limitation of, or constraint on, authority. But he also see these constraints as the result of the contractual origin of sovereign authority and not as arising from continuous interaction with institutionalized authority. 'Every man [by virtue of the social contract] puts himself under an obligation to everyone of that society to submit to the determination of the majority, and to be concluded by it . . .' The executive, for instance, is thus only 'acted' (activated) 'by the will of the society' etc. (*Two Treatises of Government*, II, pp. 96–97; 151.)

appear from view once the historical absurdities of the social contract theory, with its notion of enforceable legal obligation, brought it into disrepute.[1]

But there is an important conceptual difference between the form of sovereign authority (what it is like) and who has what share in it (participation). The legitimacy of authority, either episodically (for periods of time following an election) or qualitatively (according to prescriptions of good–or limited–government) tells us something about the innate nature of such authority. Indeed Locke and most subsequent political philosophers emphasized, by implication more often than by definition, that authority did not *lapse* through success-ful dissent or revolution, it merely passed into other hands–pre-sumably intact. The artificial nature of central authority and the residual threat, not of anarchic individualism but of a reversion to the 'base' of particularistic, even primary groups, came to be emphasized only in the last hundred years when societies were studied as wholes. Probably this is due to the long domination of legal think-ing even in political theory, with its search for sovereignty and some-where to locate it. In making no assumption about sovereignty but seeking to establish empirically observable units and structures in society–a common expressive function–sociology is only interested in central authority or sovereignty where it can genuinely be shown to exist and to function adequately. This may help to explain the relatively late arrival of modern systematic sociology in the political arena of the state–as opposed to the nation; the legal philosopher's conditions of sovereignty may historically not have been fulfilled in practice with regard to areas and people who did not share any common expressive function.

Perhaps the divorce of the preoccupation with sovereignty from any connected study of society in the modern sense can best be illustrated by a formula: Authority minus Community equals Sover-eignty. The notion of authority is taken to imply a sense of social community which, if removed or left out, merely leaves us with the legal notion of sovereignty which does not bear any such implication.

---

[1] Currently the notion that the social order is better explicable in terms of a revised version of social contract, in which certain concessions are held to have been made by the contractants in return for certain expectations regarding the future manner of dispensing justice and allocating rights and duties, is enjoying some revival. See particularly John Rawls, 'Justice as Fairness', in P. Laslett and W. G. Runciman, *Philosophy, Politics and Society*, Oxford 1962, pp. 132–57, and W. G. Runciman, *Relative Deprivation and Social Justice*, London 1966, Ch. 7.

We can consider the whole search for an answer to the classic political philosophers' question 'why should we obey?' as in fact already postulating a kind of answer; whether this be legal contract, or power, or natural law, or calculus of benefit, or even historical materialism, it is always an objective reason, rather than an expression of the sociological concept of participation summed up in its essential form by the Jewish (or Christian) formula–'I am he, he is I.'[1] In other words, none of the discussions of sovereignty indicated either identification with or–more important–continuous communication between, subject and sovereign–other than the artificial construct of representation in, for instance, J. S. Mill. Either there was sovereign power, somehow identifiable, or there was not, in which case the individual was in the last resort sovereign, autonomous and responsible for himself. No in-between position of simultaneous allegiance to self and community seemed viable. By the nineteenth century this vacuum was already producing a considerable and almost ubiquitous sense of unease among political writers; the artificial society as the sum total of individuals constructed by the *laissez-faire* economists, the frantic reconstitutions of a lost community through the search for scientific laws by Comte and Durkheim. But the point is that even then we are dealing with objective societies and objective laws incorporating scientific findings; solidarity is an observer's verdict, not that of the participants. In Marx, who recognizes the distinction quite clearly, sovereignty is in consequence most clearly counterpoised against community, and in the dictatorship of the proletariat we have the final, most logical extinction of communication between them.

In general the tools and philosophical constraints of sociology have tended to prevent the application of its methods and concepts to situations where no common expressive function or effective authority structure appears to exist. Though sociology is increasingly applying itself to the field of political sovereignty in studying problems of legitimate and effective power in whole societies, it has introspectively kept out of the field of so-called international relations until very recently.[2] Political philosophy, on the contrary–in so far as it postulates universal norms in the form of natural law, ethics

[1] I know no better illustration of this complete if painful substitutability among individuals in a genuine 'community', however divided, than Philip Roth's story, 'Eli the Fanatic' in *Goodbye Columbus*, New York, 1960, pp. 247–98.

[2] I owe this idea, which I have somewhat adapted, to Amitai Etzioni, who for some years has been investigating the potential of sociological explanation

or reason–has tended to bemoan the absence of an effectual international sovereign to *enforce* them. The substantial difference between approaches which respectively search for the existence *or* the enforcement of common norms and structures can readily be appreciated.

This is not to belittle political theory as such. Philosophical speculation about the causality and justification of things is one thing, but the obsessive preoccupation with sovereignty and its particular form of legitimacy in politics has in some ways helped to postpone our understanding of society by many decades. The problem of the continuing relationship between ultimate as well as intermediate authority and subject, the difference on the one hand between the political participation of subjects in the establishment of legitimate sovereignty, and on the other the inevitable presence and nature of social authority, finally the presence of intervening social structures between discrete individuals and central authority, have all largely been ignored. The influence of conservative thinkers like Burke and de Maistre, to whom the problems of community were real, has flowed unsuccessfully against the mainstream of convention; in any case their notion of political authority as merely the confirmation of 'natural' social processes has not prevented them from endowing the resultant sovereign authority with all the power of complete legitimacy. Instead of a linkage between two discrete entities, of which popular sovereignty is only a special case, these conservative thinkers have emphasized interdependence and mutual obligation. But they set this out in the form of natural (or normative) prescription; in the last resort they differ from their rationalist opponents in their *description* and *justification* of sovereignty rather than in their analysis of continued legitimacy and involvement. *In short the preoccupation with*

in the field of international relations. He divides the social sciences into those demanding systematic or at least orderly patterns (social anthropology, sociology, politics) and those which posit a plethora of random interacting collisions– or, in his terminology, 'bumper' sciences (economics, psychology). Another way of putting this is to call the two alternatives logical and probability system. The two disciplinary categories will tend to steer clear of incongruent research situations. It is then no accident that the most fruitful methodological lead into international relations was not provided directly by sociology at all, but by the mutant discipline of games theory on which general systems method, with its emphasis on a search for isomorphisms, has tried to build directly. Sociology has, as it were, been bypassed. The general systems approach makes possible the assumption and analysis of a systematic relationship between opponents (even casual ones whose interests and definitions clash temporarily or accidentally) *without* the implication of any common expressive function. Cf. James G. Miller, 'Living Systems', *Behavioral Science*, Vol. X, No. 3 (July 1965), pp. 201 ff.

sovereignty has until very recently pushed the problem of authority right out of sight.[1]

I would go so far as to suggest that the study of sovereignty, both as the focus of interest and as an intellectual method, actually prevents any understanding of authority in its intermediate and qualificatory sense. *This* is the real point of scission between political theory and sociology–a discrepancy which is latent in the basic difference of approach between Aristotle and Plato, and has come increasingly into the open ever since. Political theory essentially focuses on the relationship between individuals as self-sufficient units and the search for basic constraints on the randomness of their interaction. These constraints may take the form of natural law, reason, ethics, power or any other overriding regulation of behaviour –either as a direct influence on the individual through divine prescription, reason or moral sense, or by interpretation and personification in the form of sovereignty. In this context it matters little whether the sovereign is regarded as the agent or the source of overriding constraints. Sociology on the other hand is primarily concerned with the individual only in the context of his membership of differentiated groups, and with the interrelationship of these groups. Society is a summation of such groups–in that society can only be said to exist in so far as proof or evidence of common relationships in a universal framework exists. It is essentially comparative and relativistic; it abstracts common features of behaviour at different levels rather than postulating overall norms. What political theory on the whole assumes as fundamental, sociology attempts to establish as a final product.[2]

[1] This position is very penetratingly summarized by Sheldon S. Wolin, *Politics and Vision*, Boston 1960, pp. 289–91, especially p. 290. For emphasis on how one approach can inhibit the other see Rokkan's review of *Civic Culture*, *Am.Pol.Sc.Rev.* LVII, 3 (1964), op. cit.

[2] The issues between what are here described as sociological and political theory are incidentally and extremely brilliantly summed up in Lévi-Strauss's reply to Sartre's polemic in Claude Lévi-Strauss, *La pensée sauvage* (see 'History and Dialectic' in *The Savage Mind*, London 1966, p. 247): ' . . . I believe the ultimate goal of the human sciences to be not to constitute but to dissolve man. The pre-eminent value of anthropology [and sociology] is that they represent the first step in a procedure which involves others. [Such] analysis tries to arrive at invariants beyond the empirical diversity of human societies . . . However I am not blind to the fact that the verb 'dissolve' does not in any way imply (but even excludes) the destruction of the constituents of the body subjected to the action of another body. The solution of a solid into a liquid alters the disposition of its molecules. It also often provides an efficacious method of putting them by so that they can be recovered in case of need and their properties be better studied. The reductions I am envisaging are thus legitimate, or indeed

Political theory has thus for a long time been particularly preoccupied with questions of sovereign authority. Its methods and style of analysis as well as its implicit concerns have all contributed their share to the creation and continuing saliency of the electoral link between institutionalized authority and people at large which, as was suggested in the last chapter, became to a greater or lesser extent superimposed on the empirical processes of political mobilization in Europe and the United States–the developed West. The notion of cleavage mobilization transposed into interest articulation does not appear to have been a subject of legitimate concern to political thinkers until sociology became influential a few decades ago; where evidence of cleavage divisions was noted, it was more usually condemned as endangering sovereignty, especially where such divisions were institutionalized in terms of permanent factions or parties. Both intellectually and in terms of empirical process the mobilizing function of interest articulation was accommodated badly or not at all. It was not really until Schumpeter wrote *Capitalism, Socialism and Democracy* that an explanation of the political process in the West

possible, only if two conditions are satisfied. First, the phenomena subjected to reduction must not be impoverished; one must be certain that everything contributing to their distinctive richness and originality has been collected around them. For it is pointless to pick up a hammer unless to hit the nail on the head. Secondly, one must be ready to accept, as a consequence of each reduction, the total overturning of any preconceived idea concerning the level, whichever it may be, one is striving to attain.'

The difficulty for political theory to come to grips adequately with sociological problems, and vice versa, is also illustrated by two recent books. R. V. Sampson, *Equality and Power*, London 1965, relates the sociological problem of inequality in families to the political theory or nominalist problem of inequality in politics. He attempts to prove that since there is no *prima facie* reason for inequality in families, there is no such reason for it in politics either. The basic assumption that these are similarly structured relationships leads to the false application of similar criteria in order to resolve what is assumed to be the universally identical phenomenon of inequality.

The other example is W. G. Runciman, *Relative Deprivation and Social Justice*, London 1966. Like his previous *Social Science and Political Theory*, Cambridge 1963, this assumes that there need be no basic difference between one form of social analysis and another. Here an historical and contemporary analysis of the meaning and importance of class in Britain is attempted. But where a sociological approach would take the identification of classes as a starting point to examine group action, Runciman views them as a *terminus ad quem*, and uses the concept of class in order to investigate a primarily political philosophy problem about the fairness and acceptance of vertical differentiation or stratification in society. His research would lend itself equally well to a sociological theory about changes in group relations and structures; his preference, however, is for an ethical theory of fairness. The point is that he is unable to do both simultaneously.

based on economic interest articulation was provided, one moreover which suggested a stable relationship between interest articulation and authority legitimation–with the former as the structural base for competing elites offering themselves in the 'market' of the latter.

As time went by and the original cleavage structures became increasingly institutionalized as means or structures of authority legitimation, interest articulation had to find various other processes and channels of expression. Every second-year student of politics in developed countries is now familiar with the existence of a plethora of pressure and interest groups outside formal political parties, whether latent (as in the USSR) or manifest. Their apparent differentiation and specificity of function–as opposed to the aggregative diffuseness of the more extreme authority building political parties–have made them an increasingly attractive alternative to formal political mobilization as a means of articulating interest. In this context, therefore, what distinguishes pressure or interest groups from political parties is not so much any willingness to take *power* but rather their separateness as two distinct channels of participation in the political process, one of which can be concerned with the function of authority legitimation while the other is restricted to the articulation of specific interests. Interest articulation becomes structurally and processually differentiated from the formal political process; the function is carried out by pressure groups rather than parties in proportion as the latter act primarily as legitimacy builders. Liberated from the constraints of authority legitimation increasingly imposed by the electoral process, groups are able to 'revert' to efficient specificity–both in terms of their size and in the preciseness of direction in which they beam their demands. Thus motor car manufacturers initially form their own group. If they define their situation for one reason or another as requiring a normative level rather than that appropriate to action by a collectivity, they will attempt to mobilize fellow industrialists at the level of the widest entrepreneurial organization possible; a threat of higher taxation, free imports or nationalization mobilizes the Confederation of British Industries, the *Bundesverband der deutschen Industrie*, or *Confindustria* in Italy. At levels higher than normative mobilization, the differentiated functional channels of mobilization tend to converge once more. The threat of nationalization, probably located at the upper levels of normative impact or possibly already at a value level, is liable to produce a strategic merging of groups and parties into a temporarily diffuse process of defensive reaction. This scale of escalation is of course matched by the level of *impact* on government; motor manufacturers normally deal with departmental heads in ministries, at the normative level they talk to ministers, while in the case of some value addition they may talk (and listen) to the Prime Minister and/or appeal directly to the electorate over the government's head.

What is suggested here is that the simple equation of structural and processual differentiation with industrial development in the West is in many senses an oversimplification, if not indeed a major misunderstanding of function and process. The proliferation of interest-specific groups outside the formal political process is not only evidence of modernity, and to be welcomed as such, but also evidence that the formal political process as characterized by elections and election-orientated collectivities is not always effectively able to handle the articulation of interests. This has several important consequences. One is the relative inefficiency of the polity to act as the political subsystem for purposes of social goal attainment; the political subsystem may thus have a very different structural shape and range than the polity. This form of incongruence will be discussed further at a later point in this chapter. For the moment we will concentrate on the problem of interest-specific groups who do not formally participate in the electoral process at all; the more effective they are as vehicles for carrying out the function of interest articulation the greater may be the withdrawal of participants from the formal political process, left mainly with the 'interest-empty' function of providing a government. In elitist societies particularly, where the lack of subsystem differentiation provides less interest in the political subsystem as an alternative or competitive means of social mobility to the other subsystems, and where electoral choices provide little or no conflict between elites for the control of salient institutions, the lack of interest in formal politics may be considerable. Thus while it is empirically true enough that the difference between interest or pressure groups and parties is that the latter are concerned with taking power and the former not, it may be more fruitful to view groups as the residual form in which the function of interest articulation is carried out in the West, one which the formal political process, constrained by authority legitimating elections, is no longer able to handle efficiently.[1] What must be stressed is that there is nothing

[1] The classification of groups as differing from parties primarily in terms of willingness to take power is put forward most concisely by Harry Eckstein in 'The Determinants of Pressure Group Politics', in Eckstein and Apter (eds),

automatic, or necessarily synonymous with modernity, about this development. There is no reason why interest articulation should not have continued to form the more salient function of political mobilization and the political process generally. As has been pointed out, the structure of politics based on cleavages was, on the functional dimension, largely interest oriented; in many countries in Europe party mobilization is still primarily based on the articulation of interests. Even in England the non-cleavage politics of elite-participant groups in the eighteenth century had a strong interest element in it before the electoral link spread throughout the population as the suffrage came to be extended.[1] We must look to the link philosophy and the electoral institutionalization of it as the main explanation of the supremacy of the authority legitimation function.

The constraints imposed on political mobilization by electoral authority legitimation can be clearly seen if we consider the common case where mobilization takes place for the purpose of articulating interests which can neither be expressed through pressure groups (in the sense that these press for *ex parte* facilities or advantages) nor aggregated by the political parties into the process of authority legitimation. This is the situation that applies to what are often called attitude groups; they accordingly make for considerable conceptual awkwardness in conventional political analysis.[2] For our purposes, such movements (Know-Nothing Movement in America, CND in Britain, post-Peron *Peronismo* in the Argentine) illustrate precisely the functional constraints of political parties, especially in societies where parties are salient and largely exclusive authority legitimizers. The Civil Rights movement in the United States is a clear instance of this sort of group; like CND in Britain it focuses its manifest efforts on one issue even though the drive behind it is much wider in range. Indeed some of the value-oriented components of politics which have tended to disappear from the formal political process find their expression here. Attitude groups (other than those with limited or crank aims like the Lord's Day Observers, the Anti-

---

Comparative Politics, New York 1963, pp. 408–21, which summarizes the conclusions of his BMA case study, *Pressure Group Politics*, op. cit. See also the conclusions of S. H. Beer, 'Pressure Groups and Parties in Britain', *Am. Pol. Sc. Rev.*, L, 1 (March 1956), pp. 1–24.

[1] A recent discussion of some aspects of this problem is by Ian R. Christie, 'Was There a "New Toryism" in the Earlier Part of George III's Reign?', *The Journal of British Studies*, V, 1 (November 1965).

[2] See the discussion of the conceptual problem in F. G. Castles, 'Towards a Theoretical Analysis of Pressure Politics', *Political Studies*, XIV, 3, (October 1966), pp. 339–48.

Vivisectionists, and the Preservation of Rural England) are forced into legitimacy orientations, specifically denial of legitimacy. At the same time these movements, combining as they do a fusion of interest articulation with a distinct denial of legitimacy to the formal political collectivities, are unable to develop the structure of alternative authority-legitimizing collectivities. They may accordingly be defined partially as remedial legitimacy collectivities in a political system whose parties offer only narrow choices which are highly 'aggregable' and which in any case never exceed the level of normative conflict. Where such attitude groups exist they tend to escalate in their point of impact right up to a value level; they are structurally unstable and incongruent to the polity. Tending as they do to be formless and unstable, the interests they articulate find little chance of expression in society; they are accordingly often described (wrongly) as anomic.

By contrast in France, Italy, Belgium, India and Japan, accommodation of structured attitude groups into the polity is far easier. There is a more precise correlation between sectional interests and specifically interest-articulating political parties. Above all there is more political choice among parties; strategies of collaboration and bargains can more easily be worked out in an electoral context, and consequently the representation of group interests by politicians in the legislature *vis-à-vis* government is much more effective. As with the phenomenon of social cleavage representation in the political subsystem as evidence of subsystem differentiation, which will be discussed at greater length below, the specific reproduction of group interests in terms of parties, or quasi-groups within parties, also provides evidence of subsystem differentiation. This does not of course mean that organized interest or pressure groups will not exist, or exist to any lesser extent, in subsystems where party structures are mainly articulating interests, but that (1) they will be more readily integrated with the political process and the party system; (2) their existence and operations will be more manifest; (3) public awareness of their existence will accordingly be much more widespread and date back far longer than in countries where parties are mainly authority legitimating structures.[1]

---

[1] This becomes clear from the literature. In the United States, where social research is more attuned to the fads or preoccupations of the 'intelligent' public than anywhere else, group analysis was well under way in the first decade of the twentieth century with Bentley's *The Process of Government*. In the 1930's there was substantial French research on pressure groups; see the references in H. W. Ehrmann, *Organized Business in France*, Princeton 1957,

THE SOCIAL EFFICIENCY OF POLITICS

In developed countries part of the social function of political mobilization is in the end perhaps not 'fulfilled' at all. The pleasurable acclaim for interest specificities (as substituting for 'diffuse' general mobilization) by political scientists as well as sociologists seems implicitly to assume a concomitant growth of human rationality all round which empirical research on opinion formation and voting behaviour is continually showing to be non-existent. The missing element—social group cohesion—in these interest-specific mobilizations, which operate on one dimension only, is probably the factor for which so many social scientists are searching when they attempt to depict mass society. But in emphasizing its vulnerability to anomic or totalitarian tendencies, its allegedly unstable or transitory nature, they assign the cause to a lack of interest specificities instead of to their very existence and proliferation. It is all the more extraordinary to read Kornhauser, and find him cited so frequently as a major authority for the postulate of the relatively undifferentiated mass society, when we remember that Durkheim's model of organic solidarity, far from *equating* a plethora of interest-specific cross-pressures or commitments with social cohesion, actually postulates *both* as independent variables. His organic solidarity model has both the universal reference of solidarity *and* the specific commitments, and it is this model which he contrasts with mechanical and other solidarities.[1] If we take 'modern' society as interest-specific and look at the solidarity problem separately, we get a more accurate picture than by following Kornhauser in assuming that the conditions of mass society, because they lack organic solidarity, must also automatically lack commitment to interest-specific groups or quasi-groups. Organic solidarity may thus provide the clue to the missing component in our analysis of the formal political process as mainly

---

probably stimulated by the drive of Left-Wing suspicion of big business. Cf. also Jean Meynaud, 'I gruppi d'interesse in Francia', *Studi Politici*, IV (1957). A similar situation also existed in Italy. Where these European approaches differ from the American is in their unwillingness to posit general theories about such groups. But contrast this situation where parties mainly articulate interests with that of Britain, where public awareness of the existence of groups is very recent and largely originates from the attention of political scientists like Finer in the 1950's. Both general public and political scientists in England tend to share the same normative reservations about the activities of such groups.

[1] The implications of the much misunderstood Durkheim model are well set out in E. Allardt, 'Emile Durkheim—Deductions for Political Sociology', Paper presented to the Second Conference on Comparative Political Sociology, Cambridge, December 1965, cyclostyled.

providing authority legitimizing mobilization. The lack of interest-specific mobilization, and its 'scatter' in terms of issue-specific cross-pressures of low mobilization content, are compensated by the existence of conservative universalist perspectives with regard to nation and society.

This formulation also appears to provide an explanation of the frequently asserted phenomenon of ideological demobilization, to which reference has already been made. By putting forward the notion that the sum total of cultural commitment by citizens to society is constant instead of reducible, and that if we cannot find it in cleavage mobilizations we must look for the 'balance' elsewhere rather than write it off like losses in a balance sheet, the problem of depoliticization or reduction of ideology in politics assumes the quite different aspect of an enquiry into form and location rather than into quantity. As a substantive problem we shall discuss this aspect of mobilizational shortfall, the way the missing element is transferred to conservative universals, and how these are emphasized and structured in Western Societies, in greater detail in chapter 10. As a methodological problem, however, we have noted the inherent inhibitions of political theory and the conceptual gap, much greater than is often admitted, between it and sociological theory. Recently the variant of political theory known as – or calling itself – political science has been bridging this gap, at least in the United States; as such it has however raised the drawbridge between itself and its philosophical ancestor. And even today some of the intellectual disjunctions between sociology and politics remain; integration between them is still confined to a small social science elite. Few writers are concerned with any self-conscious effort to understand the difference and to bridge it.[1]

In the foregoing discussion of the functional imperatives of the political process we have abstracted from the problem of subsystem interrelationships. How should politics be viewed in its wider social setting? Any discussion of the articulation of interests must raise the problem of the relationship of politics with other social processes immediately. The articulation of interests in the political subsystem may or may not represent the political reflection of interests appertaining to all or any of the other subsystems. The more clearly

---

[1] An honourable exception is Francis X. Sutton; see particularly 'Social Theory and Comparative Politics', in Eckstein and Apter, *Comparative Politics*, op. cit., pp. 67–81. Cf. the discussion in Reinhard Bendix (ed.), *Nation-Building and Citizenship*, op. cit. pp. 15 ff.

differentiated the political subsystem, the more functionally specific will be the structures and processes through which interests are articulated with a view to influencing, and participating in, the formation of societal goals. Thus for instance the phrase 'what is good for General Motors is good for the United States, and what is good for the United States is good for General Motors', if taken literally, suggests a very diffuse identification of interests; the social goals of society find expression in the profitability of an industrial corporation (naturally in its widest sense, to include security and remunerativeness of a high level of employment etc.). A more differentiated expression of such identification of interests would be the support of members (employers and workers) of a corporation for a particular collectivity which is committed, within the political subsystem, to defend the interests of big business in general, of motor car manufacturers in greater particular, or even exclusively of the one firm, like some oil or fruit parties are in Latin America, and some local party organizations in the United States were some years ago. In terms of political mobilization this example suggests in the undifferentiated case little or no structured mobilization in the polity; the firm itself, an economic structure, would act directly in the political subsystem for goal attainment purposes.

This is a somewhat extreme example. But the same problem crops up–or should crop up–whenever we are studying political processes in the context of a whole society. Locating cleavages in Western societies in one or other of our subsystem boxes, and then investigating how and in what form an originally non-political cleavage like that between employers and unions, or manufacturers versus farmers, or Protestant versus Catholic, or even young versus elderly, becomes reflected in the political process, may not seem very interesting or important when there is still a mountain of other unsolved problems. But in any study of developing countries some answer to this problem is crucial, both for purposes of analysis and for policy making. For here we have a tense conflict between cleavage mobilizations of an intra- and inter-societal kind; between different cleavage mobilizations within society and national-social mobilization based on international cleavages. This is no dichotomy visible only to sophisticated analysts, but a deliberate struggle to prevent the crystallization and structuring of social cleavages by means of national counter mobilization. In consequence every effort is made to keep existing intra-societal cleavages out of the polity and the political subsystem; as we shall see later, this explains the emphasis on single-party states and the relative relegation of the electoral process from its sacrosanct position in the West.

As already suggested in chapter 3, the extent of differentiation and autonomy of the political subsystem is closely linked with an elitist or constitutional culture orientation. In elitist societies like Britain and the Soviet Union, the political subsystem is relatively undifferentiated; the style of action is similar in all subsystems, the evolution of elites is not specific and confined to the polity. Mobilization processes and structures therefore have a wider social basis than any specifically political structure. In the Soviet Union the mobilized commitment to the Communist Party is expressly and manifestly an overall, 'inter-system' one (the notion of subsystems can hardly be meaningful to those who assert an ideological hierarchy which assigns to politics a subordinate, mainly instrumental role). In Britain the emphasis on authority legitimation assigns a low priority to specifically political mobilization; the basis of electoral commitment to party is, on the whole, a reflection of social class in which deliberate and differentiated choices based on a view of social goals hardly arise. Those who speak of 'the Britain I want' are few and were usually considered slightly cranky extremists, like Bevan and Shinwell, or else their written declarations of faith are not directly programmatic, like those of Anthony Crosland. Most important of all, politics either provides little means of social mobility, or the only means; in both such cases the implication is that status crystallization will be high.[1]

---

[1] This, as noted above, is the term evolved by Gerhard Lenski, *American Sociological Review*, XIX (1954), pp. 405–13, op. cit. Its opposite in a directly political context, status polarization, is used by Angus Campbell *et al.*, *The American Voter*, op. cit., ch. XIII. The concepts signify an opposing judgement on congruence between the status of a person in different subsystems. Status crystallization is a measure of high simultaneous equivalence of status, while status polarization, or political crystallization (as it is sometimes called) implies a measure of low equivalence; high status in one subsystem coinciding with low status in another or others. *Prima facie*, therefore, status crystallization suggests a relatively undifferentiated political subsystem and an elitist culture, while status polarization suggests a differentiated or autonomous one, and a constitutional culture. This preliminary identification is in turn modified by the intervention of the functional variable; salient interest articulation in political structure and process suggests status polarization, while more salient authority legitimation in turn indicates a tendency to greater status crystallization. There will be societies like the United States where emphasis on authority legitimation in presidential elections combines with a constitutional culture; the two conflicting influences on status crystallization thus produce a middle position compared to, say, Norway which combines salient interest articulation on a cleavage base with an equally constitutional culture, and has therefore a higher incidence of status polarization. For evidence see the comparative

In France or the United States the political subsystem on the other hand is much more differentiated and autonomous in its crystallization of institutionalized authority. Thus in France, and indeed in many West European countries, the party structures and electoral cleavages are the institutionalized reflection of socio-economic cleavages in the political subsystem; the authority-legitimizing function is a post-electoral process in which only the elected may participate. Consequently both functions are carried out separately, at different times and through the assumption of different roles, by closely related and specifically political structures and processes. In the United States the functional differentiation is even carried to the extent of different elections of different individuals (as well as a differentiation of roles) for purposes of interest articulation and authority legitimation; though the collectivities involved in both types of elections are formally the same, it is by now a platitude that the two major parties act as one composite collectivity in presidential elections, but as fifty different collectivities for the purpose of electing state and federal legislatures. Interest articulation in the United States may not be based on as deeply ingrained historic socio-economic cleavages, and in any case not on the same cleavages as European party systems, but nonetheless the political subsystem is a strongly differentiated set of structures and processes which not only reflect social interests and attitudes transposed into goal-attainment terms, but also reflect the interests and authority attitudes relating to the specific subsystem itself. This is an important point. An undifferentiated, elitist political subsystem is not likely to produce specifically *political* issues nor specifically *political* interests and attitudes. Since in differentiated political subsystems like the United States and France differential mobility in different subsystems is high, the political process will provide a means of upward social movement within it for those whose opportunities in other subsystems may be blocked or entirely closed. Accordingly there will be a tendency to keep this channel of mobility open by retaining and perhaps extending the autonomy of the subsystem. Hence a *classe politique*. In elitist societies this self-generating tendency towards autonomy is largely absent; politics *reflects* the mobility opportunities in the rest

American-Norwegian study by Stein Rokkan and Angus Campbell, 'Citizen Participation in Political Life: Norway and the United States of America', *International Social Science Journal*, XII (1960) pp. 69–99; also Rokkan, 'Citizen Participation in Political Life: Introduction', ibid., especially pp. 13–14.

of society—or, as in the USSR, *creates* them—and therefore offers no possibilities of an alternative or differentiated channel of mobility.

This important problem of relating politics to society as a whole in some systematic way has had a certain amount of both theoretical and empirical attention in the last decade. But in the absence of any overarching attempt to apply Parsonian (or any other) social systems analysis the focus of research has varied considerably. Thus much of the empirical work, frequently based on the manageable area of community studies, has attempted to demonstrate the extent to which political cleavages reflect social cleavages, especially as expressed through parties and elections.[1] In particular, efforts have also been made to isolate the specific factor of economic power and contrast this with its reflection in, or differentiation from, political power.[2] These hard data analyses all concentrate on the reflection or non-reflection of elites as derivative of cleavages in different subsystems, taking the political subsystem as a 'base'. But this does not correspond precisely to our more structure-process oriented concerns. The latent but important difference between the behavioural and the structural-sociological approach can easily be lost when the area of interest is similar; nonetheless it is dangerous to confuse them.[3] Thus the cited studies see congruence between politics and society in terms of a lack of 'correspondence between the lines of socio-economic cleavage and the lines of political conflict', while

[1] See particularly the work of Peter H. Rossi, 'Theory and Method in the Study of Power in the Local Community', paper read to conference on Metropolitan Leadership, North Western University, April 1960; 'Power and Community Structure', *Midwest Journal of Political Science*, IV (1960), pp. 390–401; P. Cutright and P. H. Rossi, 'Grass Roots Politicians and the Vote', *American Sociological Review*, XXIII (1958), pp. 171–9; Rossi and Cutright, 'The Impact of Party Organization in an Industrial Setting', in Morris Janowitz (ed.), *Community Political Systems*, Glencoe Ill., 1961, pp. 81–116. See also D. Katz and S. J. Eldersveld, 'The Impact of Local Party Activity upon the Electorate' *Public Opinion Quarterly*, XXV (1961), pp. 1–27.

[2] R. O. Schulze, 'The Role of Economic Dominants in Community Power Structure', *American Sociological Review*, XIII (1958), pp. 3–9; Schulze, 'The Bifurcation of Power in a Satellite City' in Janowitz, *Community Political Systems*, op. cit., pp. 19–80; Andrew Hacker, 'The Elected and the Anointed', *American Political Science Review*, op. cit. Work has also been done on the correlation between membership of voluntary associations and political authority; see H. H. Hyman, 'Voluntary Association Memberships of American Adults', *American Sociological Review*, XIII (1958), pp. 284–94. Studies relating to Finland, Germany, Norway and Sweden are cited in S. Rokkan, 'Comparative Study of Political Participation' in Ranney, *Essays*, op. cit., p. 88, note 59.

[3] Some of the trenches between the two approaches are very fiercely drawn in Ralf Dahrendorf's review of Ranney, *Essays* in *American Sociological Review*, XXIX, 5 (October 1964), op. cit.

autonomy or substantial differentiation arises from 'a markedly class-distinct, "status-polarized" party system'. The former case applies to the United States, the latter to Norway.[1] In other words, it is the *ubiquitousness* of a set of cleavages throughout society that causes subsystem differentiation, while specificity of cleavage in each subsystem suggests relative fusion or lack of differentiation. Our present structure-process analysis in one sense suggests the opposite – at least on the cultural dimension; we have identified specific political elites and structures as evidence of differentiation, and multi-subsystem ones as evidence of fusion and lack of autonomy. The point is that in accordance with the variables suggested here, either of the behavioural cleavage cases can relate to a well-differentiated political subsystem. The Norwegian case is evidence of a strongly cleavage-oriented society, the American rather of an issue-oriented one; *both* have relatively well differentiated subsystems and *both* are societies with a constitutional culture. The Norwegian case presents an autonomous political subsystem in terms of social cleavages reflected by specific political structures; mobility is assured by the crystallization of *different* elites representing different cleavages to each one of which the political subsystem, and only the political subsystem, assures notional equality in access to power assured by elections. Political mobilization is thus a strongly interest-articulating process. The autonomy of the United States political subsystem is based, on the contrary, on authority-legitimating issues themselves differentiated from interest-oriented issues; all of these tend to be specific and confined to the political subsystem. Hence the lack of correspondence between social cleavage and political cleavage; the finding that worker participation in formal political activity is low does not mean – as it would in England – that the United States is an elitist society but that the political structures do not articulate interests based on socio-economic cleavages. The apparent correspondence of the behavioural data between Britain and the United States can be 'rectified' only by a functional variable which helps to differentiate the political mobilization process in accordance with its basic functions.[2]

---

[1] Rokkan, 'Comparative Study' in Ranney, *Essays*, op. cit., p. 84. The US-Norwegian study is Rokkan and Campbell, 'Citizen Participation ...', *International Social Science Journal*, op. cit.

[2] A more specifically process-oriented analysis of politics set against social processes as a whole is attempted in Nelson W. Polsby, Robert A. Deutler and Paul A. Smith (eds), *Politics and Social Life*, Boston 1963, especially P. Cutright, 'National Political Development: Its Measurement and Social Correlates', pp.

A theoretical model with which to study the relationship between polity and society has been offered by Harry Eckstein. This is a political scientist's model rather than that of a sociologist; polity and society are contrasted as equals rather than as a systemic political part in relation to a systemic social whole.[1] The argument is a modern version of Edmund Burke's; social stability and political stability (or instability) are interdependent, and the 'artificial' polity should if possible be so constructed as to reflect the 'natural' society, especially in its primary relations and groups (kinship subsystem and latency function). Politics is here seen as a special application of social action (without any assumptions about relative primacy or subordination). It is however assumed that democracy and stability are both desirable –to that extent it is a prescriptive view–and any adjustment in the prescribed direction will have to be made, or can more easily be made, by political rather than social change–a tribute to the goal-attainment function. The most interesting thing about this [incidental] evaluation of politics *vis-à-vis* sociology is the implied emphasis on the empirically quite verifiable tendency for political forms and structures to be traded freely between countries, to be as it were a matter of common property and knowledge [or misunderstanding], while social forms and structures are held to be endemic, subject to mercantilist restrictions on exports and imports. This means that formal social similarities probably reflect the 'real' similarities–a common expressive function. The view that the polity is more easily manipulable than society may also be related to the empirical proliferation of professional politicians who promise things, while professional sociologists on the whole keep out of promising, or trying, to alter society.

Such a view further implies that when polity and society are incongruent the social structure and the social process will generally prevail. There is thus the assumption either of a control hierarchy (social primacy) or of isolation between closed systems, which is the analytical equivalent of social fragmentation, and in fact undermines the basic assumptions of systems analysis. The depiction of society takes the form of an empirical polity and society as overlapping areas of decision-making. Eckstein uses Germany as the illustration of his thesis; the Weimar Republic is presented as a period of considerable incongruence between polity and society. In terms of our

569–82. A not very rigorous attempt to discuss the politics-society problem in developing countries is Fred R. von der Mehden, *Politics of the Developing Nations*, Englewood Cliffs, New Jersey, 1964, especially pp. 54–64.
[1] Harry Eckstein, *A Theory of Stable Democracy*, Princeton 1961.

systems analysis we would say that heavy and unexpected emphasis was placed after 1918 on a political system which suddenly acquired a density too great for the structures and roles which it embraced. An attempt was made to create, quite suddenly and arbitrarily, an autonomous, differentiated polity and assign to this somewhat artificial construct the goal-attainment function of German society. The democratic, election-based polity served mainly to articulate interests, in strong contrast to the essentially authority-legitimating tradition of German politics (the interest-articulation functions of the Reich elections before 1914 were usually played down by the participants, even though the parties had little say in the exercise of political authority). Finally the general notion of incongruence is reflected in the particular factor of conflict between an elitist political culture and an attempt to operate a political subsystem based on constitutionally oriented assumptions. It is accordingly suggested that a model based on congruence or incongruence between polity and society provides a somewhat gross form of analysis which can and should be broken down into more refined variables.

Another approach to the study of politics and society is that of Harold Lasswell. This is more directly concerned with the problem of the social efficiency of politics, hence it appears heuristically more interesting and fruitful in the present context. This view sees politics not as a special application of social action, but as a *corrective*, or *compensation*, for social relations and stratifications that are but dimly perceived, and are anyhow almost impossible to change. Politics now becomes precisely the opposite of the rational process *par excellence*. Lasswell summed this up in the now well-known phrase:

'Politics is the process by which the irrational bases of society are brought out into the open.'[1]

Like all aphorisms this is oversimple, but it does contain the seed of an important classification of the politics-society relationship. Irrational or not, politics clearly compensate and correct inchoate, latent social strains; political change is more 'open' than social change, and

---

[1] *The Political Writings of Harold Lasswell*, Glencoe 1951, p. 184. The emphasis here differs from the approach of many social scientists, to which Lasswell has also devoted a considerable amount of analysis: that political behaviour and the nature of politics are the consequence of certain common personality structure to be found in different societies; e.g. Adorno *et al.*, *The Authoritarian Personality*; Everitt E. Hagen, *On the Theory of Social Change*, Homewood, Ill., 1962. The two approaches complement each other considerably; the latter as it were providing the base, the former the superstructure.

the assignment of primacy to political action in society gives the desire for political participation a distinctly higher status than participation in other social processes (as for instance economic participation through industrial codetermination, equal rights for women in churches or families, etc.). Such a priority is quite distinct from any analytical priority we choose to allocate to the political subsystem and its goal-attainment function. This in turn is quite distinct from the problem of whether politics genuinely 'balance' social inequalities or merely pretend to do so–the idea that politics, by virtue of electoral mobilization, replaces religion as 'opium for the people'.[1] In societies with a constitutional culture, leadership is by definition clustered much more around institutions and therefore may not require so much 'compensatory' politics. This proposition is well brought out by the debate about strategy and tactics among the Negro leaders in the United States in 1965–6; the proponents of 'black power' (particularly the more radical leadership of the Committee of Racial Equality and the Students' Non-Violent Committee) appear to accept by implication a differentiated-elite model of the United States and to demand that a differentiated Negro elite should be specifically recognized. Viewed in this way, the radical leadership is accordingly more 'American', while Martin Luther King and the more 'moderate' groupings of the NAACP take a more 'elitist' view in attempting to obtain their demands from the existing white

---

[1] An interesting point emerges here. Politics is a more *manifest* process than most other social processes–hence in part the historical priority of political theory over sociology. At the same time its corrective function for social strains is clearly *latent*. This suggests that Merton's analysis of manifest and latent functions is only Round One in a long bout of analytical complexity. Latency and manifestness may first of all be interdependent concepts, in that a function may be capable of latency only if another and particular one is manifest, and vice versa; this suggests a diarchic relationship for each function. Secondly much interdependence may be connected with the relative position of outsider as opposed to participant observer, which has already been pointed up several times here. Thus politics may have the *manifest* function of goal attainment in the eye of the observer analysing the participant's evaluation of his own actions as part of a functional subsystem; the same function may become compensatory and *latent* in the direct judgement of the *observer* on the participant's actions within one subsystem in qualitative relation to other subsystems. In one case we are really observing a functional or 'vertical' relationship, in the other a qualitative or 'horizontal' relationship. This alternative may affect and possibly invert the status of a function's latency (observer's direct view of action or process) or manifestness (observer's indirect view of, and agreement with, participant's evaluation of action or process). Accordingly a function may move from latency to manifestness and back again depending on whether the function is vertical (as is usual) or horizontal as between qualitatively interrelated but same-level microsystems.

leadership.[1] Such a view assumes a qualitative difference between social and political action: social leaders 'happen' while political leaders are chosen or forcibly obtrude themselves, as with the economically anointed and the politically elected. Social legitimacy is proved by acceptance and social norms are defined by silence and hallowed by time, while political legitimation is a positive, carefully ordered act or process, and political norms are inscribed as laws and are *ipso facto* presumed to bind.

Because of its conceptual awkwardness, the compensatory definition of politics seems largely to have eluded political sociologists. Some very suggestive research in the United States correlated the growth of political activity among the underprivileged strata with a reduction of the crime rate.[2] More generally many of the studies of radical protest movements in developed societies indicate that there may well be a transfer of social deviance to political radicalism, and that one may be alternative to the other. In developing countries naturally this tends to work the other way round; lack of subsystem differentiation focuses on behaviour as the prime variable, irrespective of the area (political, economic, social, religion) within which it takes place.[3] In general, perceptive social scientists are well aware of the underlying function of politics as a compensation, though they usually hesitate to analyse it specifically. 'There are different adaptive mechanisms which have emerged to reconcile low-status individuals

[1] This analysis strongly conflicts with the more usual view of the NAACP as more typically American, while the radical elements are held to have introduced non-American perspectives into the struggle. Such an analysis ignores the traditions of radicalism – including violence – as well as that of polyarchies in American political history. Even a recent and sophisticated examination of the state of elitism vs. democracy, which attempts to accommodate peripheral social movements into the model of consensual elites, fails to make this point with regard to the traditional aspects of the radical Negro movement. See Jack L. Walker, 'A Critique of the Elitist Theory of Democracy', *Am. Pol. Sc. Rev.*, LX, 2 (June 1966), pp. 285-95.

[2] See Fredric Solomon, Walter L. Walker, Garrett O'Connor and Jacob Fishman, 'Civil Rights Activity and Reduction of Crime Among Negroes', *Archives of General Psychiatry*, XII (March 1965), pp. 227-36. The evidence for suicide is less clear, and may even show a correlation the other way; see Louis I. Dublin, *Suicide*, New York 1963, pp. 218-19; Herbert Jacob and Kenneth Vines (eds), *Politics in the American States*, Boston 1965, pp. 40 ff.

[3] Reference may be made to some of the literature on the British CND movement in this context; for America see also E. V. Essien-Udon, *Black Nationalism: A Search for an Identity in America*, Chicago 1962. The evidence of e.g. Colombia suggests for instance that while violence there may be analytically 'separated' according to subsystems, there is no suggestion of substitution; see most recently Richard S. Weinert, 'Violence in Pre-Modern Societies: Rural Colombia', *Am. Pol. Sc. Rev.*, LX, 2 (June 1966), pp. 340-7.

to their position and thus contribute to the stability and legitimacy of the larger system. The three most common ... 1. Religion, 2. [the belief in] social mobility, 3. political action-participation [but only as a means of compensation for inferior social status, even though the political movement may actually] "aim to raise the position of depressed groups".'[1]

Here the instrumental value of social mobility–real or imagined– in alternative three is different in kind to the other two. It is not external and compensatory but (as an explanation of social contentment and harmony) almost self-justificatory: if you believe that you can get to the top in a system you accept that system; you are likely to be loyal to any system that enables you to get to the top. To that extent 'proof' that a society is achievement-oriented from top to bottom is also by definition proof of social stability. (Incidentally, the way Lipset's point about America (*The First New Nation*) could be made in accordance with the present analysis is not merely to take Parsons' pattern of achievement orientation and then discuss its effect on political roles and culture, but once more to subsume this by referring to America as a highly constitutional society. Leadership there is not so much a matter of 'flexible', 'variable', 'inter-penetrative' elites–which explains nothing and can anyhow be challenged– but is provided by elites which themselves emerge (as legitimate) by occupying known positions in the political and social structure; in fact elites based on institutions.)[2] This compensatory emphasis incidentally has peculiar relevance to the 'difficult' case of Japan, with its intractably pre-developmental or law-mobilizational social system, combined nonetheless with an achievement orientation so strongly marked as to balance other factors. One could also stress post-war Japan as a case of strong political 'compensation', with politics offering channels of mobility and access to influence (e.g. to students) unavailable in a somewhat rigid, stratified society. Political roles are sharply defined and the political subsystem is fairly dense. Another way of making the same point is to explain the density of the political subsystem and its sharp incongruity with the rest of the social system in terms of the Japanese capacity and need to define every situation sharply and uniquely. Japanese social life in all its aspects accordingly becomes a strongly differentiated series of carefully defined tableaux,

---

[1] S. M. Lipset, *The First New Nation*, p. 272.

[2] These points have most recently been made yet again by E. Digby Baltzell, *The Protestant Establishment*, London 1965, with its accent on institution-based invasion and erosion of the White Anglo-Saxon Protestant elite through time.

each one of which to some extent defines the subsystem location for the participant, and with it the proper roles, the correct processes and above all the boundaries of action.

Politics and *religion* are, on the other hand, alternatives on the same dimension concerned with the same compensatory end. Except in theocracies (and even in potential theocracies like Pakistan before Ayub Khan) religion is now almost universally out-dated as a means of social compensation, or as a higher-level form of social mobilization–though it is still common to find religious riots at personal or collectivity level, especially when aggravated by questions of race. Historically, politics has replaced it. But there is still one important difference between the two forms of mobilization. Religion with its aspect of trans-valuation has in its social effect been largely compensatory in the West since the Middle Ages; it has hardly ever itself ordered a society's social status and values, but merely provided alternatives. Politics, on the other hand, whether in [social] fact compensatory or not, claims to be equal if not superior to 'mere' social action; in the conventional wisdom political legitimacy is by general definition the highest, if not indeed the only, societal legitimacy there is (the 'supremacy' of sovereignty once again). This is implicit in the different analytical status of integration and goal attainment as social functions. Hence the general swing to the authority-building function of politics, its distillation as a unique process different from 'mere' social relations. In the last resort politics has in many cases become a partial means of emasculating social action. Parsons, with particular reference to the United States, summarizes it like this: Politics and political leaders are the advance guard of social action and social leaders in setting and achieving collective goals. This function is acknowledged by various social groups who now give legitimacy and support to these goals. Within the polity special social groups crystallize to push particular policies which eventually become binding on everyone. Since these groups compete, those outside the formal structure of authority gain access to political power. The implication clearly is that the relatively confined structure of politics drains off energies that might otherwise be used to create strains in the broader social system.[1] This analysis has much obvious relevance to the European cases of an established, autonomous state. Here interest articulation dominates the party

[1] Talcott Parsons, 'Voting and the Equilibrium of the American Political System', in Eugene Burdick and Arthur Brodbeck (eds), *American Voting Behavior*, Glencoe, Illinois, 1959, pp. 80–120.

system. It is the articulation of interests that 'compensates' for the failure to give adequate expression to the legitimation of state authority; the characterization of institutionalized authority in Third and Fourth Republic France and postwar Italy as *'plus ça change, plus c'est la même chose'* expresses this compensatory element very well.

But does politics really provide alternative compensation, or is its claim to objective, here-and-now compensation as slender as religion's claim to a transvaluational one? Marx certainly described politics as the religion of the capitalist era; both religion and politics deluded their devotees in their different epochs instead of satisfying them substantially. Marx postulated that any given political system reflected the interests, not of all participants, but only of the ruling class–class being in this case the defined common denominator of economic relationships. In the Marxist analysis legitimacy (voting) and interest articulation here and only here coincide; legitimacy now *is* the expression of the dominant interest. In short, the entire 'modern' preoccupation with ballot-box authority building is a fraud. The election dominated party system legitimates political authority *a priori*, based as it is on outside control of the means of production, by persuading the electorate that in legitimating authority it is in fact articulating its interests. This once more presupposes a 'fit' between society and polity–or rather between socio-politics and economics, just as Eckstein's theory bases stable democracy on a fit between authority relations in primary or secondary groups (which he calls society) and those in the polity. The difference however is that Marx's 'politics' have a surface appearance of 'correcting' social relations and it is only the core below the surface which 'fits' into the dominating class relationship (base and super-structure) while in Eckstein's theory politics are 'real' in purpose as well as effect, but may yet be tailored to 'fit' social realities.

The reality or illusoriness of politics seems in the event to vary most significantly accordingly to whether we are dealing with constitutional or elitist cultures. In England and Russia politics do have a good deal of compensatory quality about them, and detailed examination of functions, ritual and symbols show that things get done *behind* the overt acts of doing. In this connection reference should be made once more to the transition of Imperial to Weimar Germany after the First World War, a transition compressed into a relatively short space of time, and therefore easy to analyse. A moderately elitist society here became 'dislocated' into a strongly elitist one–in spite of, and behind, a strongly constitution-oriented political 'front'. Thus socio-political congruence in a constitutional form becomes elitist in the observer's view *not* because of any change in culture overnight (an empirical impossibility) but because the reality of legitimacy orientations and structures continued to be latently maintained in spite of a 'new' polity which demanded but did not receive a widespread reorientation towards institutionalized authority. Legitimacy now came to be vested in outside structures like the civil and military bureaucracies. This example has significant relevance to many 'new' countries and to the *jolie laide* politics of South America where politics are so often a front and no more. On the other hand the American and post-1958 French polities clearly are examples of processes of functional allocation of legitimacy–though in many ways very different processes. Not only does politics have its well-defined and–by the actors–well-understood place in the wider drama of society, and politicians assume their social place as *politicians* (the political system is clearly differentiated), but the functions of interest and legitimacy are actually *separated* as *processes*.[1] In particular, political mobilization is based on various communities and specifici-

[1] An acute comment by Philip Williams in a private communication points up once more some of the methodological confusion between students of politics and those of sociological orientation. Williams points out that professional entry, exit and re-entry into politics at all levels are much more frequent in France than in England, and that consequently it would be truer to speak of politicians having a distinct social place in England than in France or the United States. 'In the United States politicians become judges, and businessmen go into the cabinet, and generals win the presidency. In France civil servants stay in the Assembly and return to the civil service on losing their seats; civil servants become ministers or govern Algeria; Pompidou goes from *Conseil d'Etat* to politics, to banking and back to politics again; the Courts of Law are among the main arenas of political conflict; writers are expected to exercise political influence and so are military men–especially when retired; prefects go into Parliament, and in the Fifth Republic the presidential nomination is even suggested for technocrats (Louis Armand) or Professors (Georges Vedel).' Cf. the discussion in Andrew Shonfield, *Modern Capitalism*, op. cit., pp. 151–75.

All this is beyond dispute. But we are here concerned with the differentiation or diffuseness of systems and roles, not with the exclusiveness of occupations or professions; with the de-personalization of behaviour-patterns in a process rather than with their identification with particular individuals, or kinds of individuals. Thus it can and should still be argued that the political role of a civil servant (or of any other deputy for that matter) in the French Assembly is more sharply defined than that of the fairly rare ex-civil servant in the British Parliament.

This is incidentally also a good illustration of the difference between the levels of the concepts of polity and political system. The judicial example given above crystallizes the boundary between the polity and the political system; courts of law, for instance, would not normally be part of the polity (except conceivably in the USSR), but may well be part of the political system at

ties of interest (class, religion, colour, occupation, language) whereas for purposes of authority building the emphasis is on choice pure and simple without any large-scale mobilization at all. De Gaulle for instance disdains the UNR for his referenda, while in the United States the political parties represent a convenience for the emergence of presidential candidates, ebbing out of the picture the instant the candidate has been chosen; their strongest and most continuous impact is in city and state elections and in elections to Congress, where the interest-articulation pattern is most salient.

One way of tackling the problem of the polity/society relationship in this context of compensation–and the tendency for societies to be constitutional or elitist–for the purpose of empirical analysis is to study the chronology according to which any particular polity was 'built' into any particular society. One fairly extreme case is the United States. Though American society predated independence (Lipset partially exaggerates the 'newness' of American society after independence), the process of creating a specifically American polity did have considerable social consequences. The political system was well differentiated, if not from the start, at least from the 1830's onwards. Though not congruent with society in the formal, Eckstein sense, it did express the achievement orientation of the wider social culture. Above all it provided a substantial and efficient compensation factor at city and state level which catered for the social needs of the otherwise underprivileged immigrant communities and groups, and in due course enabled American society to tackle and survive the later problems of the extending frontier, of industrialization, of secession and slavery. Social change in the last resort kept step with political change; though social and political norms at times conflicted strongly, the acceptance of institutionalized leadership in the political system not only survived but won through in its turn to influence and guide economic *laissez-faire* (or elitist) norms in the economy and the latency subsystem into a direction of congruence with the polity–in spite of, or because of, a well-maintained system differentiation. The United States thus provide us with one of the ideal-typical examples of a constitutional society–even though it is currently meeting a major challenge to the genuineness of its constitutionality in the interest-articulation-versus-legitimacy campaign of the Negro community.

---

particular moments and for particular purposes. Thus structure, role consensus and action premise are judicial (however differently this may be defined); but the function may be integrative *or* goal-attaining.

At the other end of the scale is the Soviet Union, where a social revolution was activated by–and then largely contained by–political means. At least until recently, social stratification was rigidly encapsulated in a political framework. This enforced encapsulation and identification of society and politics have given rise to an extremely elitist society. Nonetheless, as in America, there is substantial polity/society congruence–though for very different reasons (and one of the less obvious consequences of the post-Stalin era is the partial escape and independence of society from, and into occasional opposition to, the polity). The case of Germany and its 'cartellized' elites has already been mentioned. England is a third extreme in this analysis of dual-pattern variables; to *save* society, the existing structure and processes of the polity were repeatedly sacrificed by the ruling elite from the seventeenth century onwards.

> 'After 1848 the position of the old leaders was stronger than it had been before, for they had abandoned what was indefensible in their position and retained what was material for their power.'[1]

Congruence between society and polity is limited, and England is strongly elitist. The same is now largely true of Japan, though that country was once an example of extreme socio-political congruence. Here the new and separate (from society) *political* norms imposed since 1945 have not yet been internalized by the participants, who partly 'misuse' the political process in a direction of congruence with the social structure which is justified neither by the formal mechanics of 'democratic' politics nor by the definition of the situation that goes with it. This unstable situation will need to be resolved.

The problems of socio-political congruence, and the compensatory status and function of politics in society, both raise important substantive issues in the comparative study of whole societies and of political subsystems. Analysis along these lines helps to explain certain tendencies and emphases, both in the cultural elitist-constitutional pattern and in the functional emphasis on interest articulation and authority legitimation. But at the same time they highlight the considerable difference between politics in developed and developing countries; as approaches to the analysis of politics they are mainly

[1] G. Kitson Clark, *The Making of Victorian England*, London 1962, p. 43. What better description than this could be given of an elitist society? For a concrete instance of this in bureaucratic terms, with reference to the Northcote-Trevelyan report, cf. also below, p. 353.

relevant to the former and do not by themselves provide the same cross-national as well as developmental cross-level tools as the variables we have elaborated earlier.

Before we examine some of these problems in the context of developing countries more specifically in the next chapter, it may be useful to highlight the discussion of the last two chapters by way of summary contrast with what we might expect to find in developing countries. This may show the gap between the Western experience and the needs of the Third World most forcibly; by showing the irrelevance of the Western experience, the ground is cleared for looking at the cleavage and functional imperatives of developing countries, and the political processes and structures they are creating to cope with them. This can best be done in the form of six propositions.

1. The historical cleavage bases of the West, and the structures that have arisen from them, do not exist in developing countries today.

2. The institutionalization of interest articulation based on cleavages, in so far as the latter exist in their particular form in developing countries, is held to be divisive and hence to be discouraged by all possible means. Since no stable political authority relationships exist, within which interest articulation can take place, such interest articulation collectivities would endanger the precarious existence of political authority.

3. Political mobilization accordingly takes place almost exclusively on the basis of authority legitimation. Even though this holds true of some Western models, like that of England, the strong ideological component which presents authority legitimation in terms of interest articulation makes the model almost impossible to transplant. The functions, status and validity of elections accordingly differ strongly from that generally accepted in the West.

4. The problem of social-political congruence, and the compensation function of politics, do not arise in the same way in developing countries; society and polity are viewed as conflicting, the former as backward, the latter as modern. Consequently the polity serves to restructure society. Hence a distinctly elitist model of mobilization, based on Soviet experience, is often seen as necessary, and culture production takes place in such a context, often in conflict with the existing social culture.

5. The differentiation and autonomy of the political subsystem are

viewed as undesirable, and objectively appear as impossible in relation to perceived goals. Instead we have deliberate dedifferentiation under elite surveillance. The political system must not reflect social cleavages, nor must it articulate specific, differentiated cleavages of its own. Instead the political system attempts to reconcile existing cleavages by counter-mobilization, and directs all counter-mobilization from above towards the obliteration of such cleavage mobilization as already exists (tribal or ethnic structures, etc.).

6. Finally, the emphasis on dedifferentiated mobilization extends to the prevention of interest-specific group mobilizations as well as more directly political cleavage structures. Nonetheless such groups exist, especially within authoritative mobilization structures such as the single party, as well as within the military or civil bureaucracy.

CHAPTER SEVEN

The Problem of Developing Countries

SUMMARY

In this chapter we move from the discussion of developed societies, with occasional reference to developing countries by way of obvious contrast, to a central focus on the latter. Initially the proposition is put forward that in discussing the difficulties of adapting the political processes and institutions of the West to the needs of developing countries, especially competitive democratic elections and parties, we must look as much at the innate assumptions and problems of Western processes as at any alleged failures or shortcomings in developing countries. These assumptions and problems have been highlighted in the previous discussion; a brief survey is now sketched out of the methodological approaches of Western social and political scientists to the study of developing countries which suggests that these approaches often assume that developing countries are infant or deviant examples of the Western experience and can be studied in terms of shortfall from a norm. The possible benefit of the system-function approach, developed earlier for studying problems of development, is pointed up, with one or two examples of societies where the conventional method creates particular heuristic difficulties.

Two basic problems concerning authority relationships and the institutionalization of political authority in developing countries are then adumbrated: first the newness of national existence and hence of national authority; secondly the conflict between association with the demands of legitimacy imposed by an often colonial past, and the renunciation of this past in connection with the establishment and maintenance of a new legitimacy of dissociation. The implications of these problems on the political process are examined, with particular reference to the functional or dysfunctional nature of imported Western processes, institutions and ideas. The Western desire to impart its political experience is discussed as an ideological phenomenon; by imposing or offering its own means of interest articulation

193

and especially authority legitimation, the West attempted expressly or inadvertently to predetermine the norms and values of developing societies. It also hindered the actual advent of independence by making itself the arbiter of conflicts which proved much more divisive than the structural experience of cleavage and authority choices in the West had led those who propagated Western political structures and processes to believe. Where developing countries needed legitimacy structures to support the beneficiary leaders of new or newly independent nations, who had reached precarious power without any profound commitment by members of the society to their rule, the West was able to offer only party structures and electoral processes based on 'containable' cleavages or compensatory politics of authority legitimation in symbolic and confused form. These would either have proved impossibly divisive or would have failed to provide the basis of legitimacy appropriate to the social situation of developing countries.

Finally, in a separate note or excursus, an important variant of political or structural advice by the West is examined – that of administrative science. It is suggested that this, though concerned with a somewhat different emphasis than straightforward political advice or examples, does nevertheless deal with the same order of problems and tends in part to reflect the same ideological perspectives on the part of the exporter. Possibly because developing countries take more readily to such 'scientific' advice than to the more overtly biased political kind, there has been a great expansion of interest and effort in the output of writing on development administration.

We have frequently lamented the difficulties, shortcomings and perversions of imported democracy in 'new' countries. More recently Western observers, while still regretting the difficulties faced by democracy, do see them as more than just pig-headedness, evil intentions or human incompetence due simply to lack of education; they admit the structural shortcomings, the lack of democratic tradition and of a suitable social or economic base.[1] But hardly anyone except Marxist looks for any shortcomings in electoral democracy itself. This remains ideologically almost sacrosanct; it is merely the gap

[1] Two well-known proponents of the 'erosion of democracy' and 'erosion of administration' schools of analysis are Rupert Emerson, *From Empire to Nation*, Chapter XV; and Michael Brecher, *The New States of Asia*, London 1963, Chapter II respectively.

between desire and attainment that widens. Democracy is seen as the end of a continuum of economic development; accordingly the sophisticated advice today is: develop your economy, only then can stable or 'real' democracy become possible. In terms of the present analysis the core assumption of such advice must necessarily be an assignment of primacy to the economic or adaptive subsystem, to which the political subsystem will in turn [democratically] adapt. Economic priorities govern political decisions. Democracy is viewed as the natural or congruent form for a sophisticated economy.

The analytical apparatus of this particular comparative approach, in which developing countries are seen as unformed (or malformed) infants when measured against developed or adult societies in the West, stems from a particular type of economic model of development first worked out fully by Rostow. It is based on the experience of industrialization in the West, and extrapolates the historic Western model into a modern context and for universal application.[1] From this and other seminal works of the period there grew a substantial literature of economic development in which the developed West was increasingly established as a norm, and its socio-economic system as a means, which developing countries were advised to copy and make their own. There are four main aspects to this.

1. The notion of economic development as desirable *per se*.

2. The firm installation of the West as a comparative reference, and a source of ideas and institutions.

3. The focus on liberal democracy as typical of the West, and therefore either an essential *prerequisite* for, or an essential *consequence* of, economic development.

4. The subordination of political and social goals, and the desire for social change, to economic priorities and modes of thought; the former being viewed as an automatic consequence of the latter.

---

[1] W. W. Rostow, *The Stages of Economic Growth*, Cambridge 1960. The notion of irreversible industrialization following a single universal process which is characterized by broad and comparative stages is much older than Rostow (though he formalized it in modern economic terms); similar notions may be found in the work of List and Schmoller in the last century, as well as Bruno Hildebrand. For Rostow's translation of economic analysis into specific policy recommendations (for the United States), see Max F. Millikan and W. W. Rostow, *A Proposal: Key to Effective Foreign Policy*, New York 1957. A similar approach, but with all the authority of the UN behind it, is taken by *U.N. Analyses and Projections of Economic Development*, New York 1955. A recent proponent of this type of convergence theory is Cyril A. Zebot, *The Economics of Competitive Coexistence: Convergence Through Growth*, New York 1964.

THE PROBLEM OF DEVELOPING COUNTRIES

A good deal of writing has been devoted, not only to pushing this thesis in whole or in part, but also to examining its implications in detail, both critically and approvingly. Recently many sociologists and political scientists concerned with problems of development have been trying to liberate their disciplines from the priorities of econ-omics; one characterization of this version of economism has recently pronounced it as pathological.[1] Instead an attempt has been made to articulate a political 'equivalent' to economic development in terms of specifically political criteria by which such development might be judged. These range from the attempt to define greater attainment of democracy in terms of 'a greater distribution and reciprocity of power' to the elaboration of specific political 'goods' which the polity must increasingly deliver as its develops.[2] Simultaneously however the attack on democratic determinism has also shifted to a more aggressive posture. There have recently appeared a number of studies on the [American] horizon questioning the *desirability* as well as the *possibility* of applying democracy to developing countries.[3]

[1] Ann Ruth Willner, 'The Underdeveloped Study of Political Development', *World Politics*, XVI (April 1964), pp. 48 ff. Cf. Manfred Halpern, 'Toward Further Modernization of the Study of New Nations', *World Politics*, XVII (October 1964), pp. 157–81; R. A. Packenham, 'Approaches to the Study of Political Development', ibid., pp. 108–20, which is an attempt *inter alia* to integrate the study of development with modern organization theory.

[2] For the notion of greater distribution and reciprocity of power see Frederick W. Frey, 'Political Development, Power and Communications in Turkey' in Lucian W. Pye, *Communications and Political Development*, Princeton 1963, p. 301. For the notion of specific political goods described as mere security, justice, liberty and welfare, see J. Roland Pennock, 'Political Development, Political Systems and Political Goods', *World Politics*, XVIII, 3 (April 1966), pp. 415–34, particularly p. 433. Various definitions of specifically political development are reviewed in this article.

[3] See for instance Karl de Schweinitz, *Industrialization and Democracy; Economic Necessities and Political Consequences*, New York 1964, who argues that the political possibilities of developing countries do not permit democracy, but that this need not be an obstacle to economic growth as such. To a con-siderable extent research interest in convergence through development, and in the relative status of economic and political priorities in developing countries, arose–at least in the United States–as a byproduct of the ideologically much more significant problem of convergence or divergence between the developed giants, the United States and the Soviet Union. The case for economic conver-gence coupled with continuing political divergence is argued most forcefully by Zbigniew Brzezinski and Samuel P. Huntington, *Political Power: USA/USSR*, New York 1964. This book incidentally provides an interesting analysis of subsystem differentiation. A useful discussion of the relationship of political and economic development, and of convergence or divergence between the developed and the developing world, is Mancur Olsen, Jr., 'Some Social and Political Implications of Economic Development', *World Politics*, XVII, 3 (April 1965), pp. 525–54.

Frequently this normative or ideological concession has not been made openly, but via a 'neutrally' methodological or conceptual channel.

It is worth while briefly glancing at the main sources of current analysis of development in its broadest sense, and attempting to classify these under distinctive heads. In fact there are four distinct approaches currently in vogue; they naturally overlap considerably but do have recognizably different starting points and concepts.

1. The great impact of empirical and theoretical analysis of social *change*; in short the strongly emphasized move in the last decade from static to dynamic perspectives in sociology, with a corresponding growth of concepts and methodology. This has tended to subsume both purely economic perspectives (the departure from which is discussed under heading 2) and has particularly helped the study of development to get away from the over-simplistic and ideological identification of development with the orthodox concerns of democratic theory–justice, liberty, responsibility, representation, etc.[1]

2. The attempt to analyse *development* more autonomously and specifically as a political and sociological problem, and not only as a series of second-order determinacies following on economic development or industrialization. This approach concentrates on the specifically political and sociological determinants and causations of change; though these are not necessarily abstracted from economic development, an attempt is made to treat the economic and socio-political components as distinct though interrelated variables. The relationship has been well summarized in the phrase of the MIT study on developing countries: 'The very innovational spirit which is itself an essential source of economic change is at the same time in part a product and consequence of such change'.[2]

[1] There is of course an enormous amount of literature on this, and it would be futile to attempt to summarize it briefly. Reference may, however, be made to one very recent outstanding contribution; Amitai Etzioni, *Studies in Social Change*, New York 1966. This work is of course built on the contributions of major sociologists like Parsons and others over the last two decades.

[2] Max F. Millikan and Donald L. M. Blackmer (eds), *The Emerging Nations*, Cambridge (Mass.) 1961, p. 44. In a more political context see Samuel P. Huntington, 'Political Development or Political Decay', op. cit., and especially David E. Apter, *The Politics of Modernization*, Chicago 1965, perhaps the most comprehensive discussion of problems and approaches to date. Ten definitions of political development in this context are briefly surveyed by Lucian W. Pye in 'The Concept of Political Development', *Annals of the American Academy of Political and Social Science*, CCCLVIII (March 1965), pp. 1–13; see also contributions by Karl von Vorys and discussion *passim* in this volume. On the whole this is a disappointing discussion which does not do justice to the subject. Some valuable methodological suggestions about the comparative

3. The study of individual developing societies in their particular culture and ideological setting. There is now a substantial collection of area studies, obviously of varying quality, but increasingly focusing on the analysis of similar variables and the solution of similar problems.[1]

4. Finally, and very important, is the recent work of economic historians to develop the results of their empirical cross-national studies into a conceptual framework for the analysis of industrialization.[2]

For our purposes here the important issue is still the extent to which *methods*–however neutrally conceived–for analysing Western 'democratic' development are relevant and suitable for analysing development in today's Third World. We have already attempted to isolate the core assumption of modern democratic theory–voting, or formal participation in the ratification of legitimacy. If we now transpose this assumption on to developing countries, together with the mechanisms of political and social change offered by the West, the discrepancies and differences in the functional requirements of the two types of polities soon become clear. The problem of ranking developing countries in accordance with some scale of Western attainment loses its significance. Before legitimacy can be ratified, it must exist; before authority can become legitimate, it must be or at one time have been effective and must be recognized as such. Western political theory tells us about the nature and ownership, or occupancy, or authority, its extent and form, but not how to create it–

study of changes are made in Richard L. Merritt and Stein Rokkan (eds), *Comparing Nations*, New Haven 1966.

[1] Particularly relevant in this context are the already quoted works of Lucian W. Pye, *Politics, Personality and Nation Building, Burma's Search for Identity*, New Haven and London 1962; David E. Apter, *Ghana in Transition*, second edition, New York 1963; *The Political Kingdom of Uganda: A Study in Bureaucratic Nationalism*, Princeton 1961. For some of the problems posed by the appearance of different approaches see the discussion of three major authors by Leonard Binder, 'National Integration and Political Development', *Am. Pol. Sc. Rev.*, LVIII, 3 (September 1964), pp. 622–31.

[2] One most outstanding contribution perhaps is Alexander Gershenkron, 'Typology of Industrial Development as a Tool of Analysis', in the collected papers of *Second International Conference of Economic History: Aix-en-Provence 1962*, The Hague 1965, II, pp. 487–505. This approach puts forward as a possible tool of analysis eight pairs of variables, which accommodate political and social as well as economic factors. In addition Gershenkron recognizes the need for an 'organizing principle' for the study of development–an important concession of sociological method; for this he suggests the degree of a country's backwardness on the eve of its industrialization. See also the outline provided by Cyril S. Belshaw, *Traditional Exchange and Modern Markets*, Englewood Cliffs (N.J.) 1965, particularly chapter V, and the brief conspectus of theories in Wilfred Malenbaum, 'Government, Entrepreneurship and Economic Growth in Poor Lands,' *World Politics*, XIX, 1 (October 1966), pp. 54 ff.

because authority is confused with sovereignty. The structural technology of Western politics is not much help either. Elections and parliamentary parties are not designed to *build* legitimate sovereignty (as opposed to political *authority*), but merely to ratify or occupy it [as an institution]. Ratification takes place within the narrow confines of modern 'democratic' party politics, especially in 'alternative' two-party polities; these are machines for ratifying *existing* or *alternative* occupancy of sovereign institutions. In so doing, they create and legitimate the notion of sovereignty itself. By confusing these two functions the confusion between authority and sovereignty also increases; success at elections substitutes sovereignty for authority but still avoids any need to distinguish between them and indeed for recognizing the existence of authority at all (for which Aristotle with his organic or natural progression from social authority to political sovereignty is perhaps partly to blame). No electoral system has ever created authority out of a void, at best it has brought it to the fore by labelling it sovereign. By way of example we need only look at the creation of the state of Israel and its first government; essentially an electoral acknowledgement of a victory previously won–partly by force of arms, and partly in the United Nations. This situation is quite common in developing countries, and has special implications which we shall examine in more detail later.[1]

What is true of the need to create authority is equally true of a common stock of information. The whole concept of democracy implies such a stock; it is a parameter of the adequate functioning of Western electoral mobilization as viewed by its apologists and advocates. Mobilization supplies some of the critical minima of information, just as it builds a support structure for new authority. The information in question will, indeed must, be crude and the manner of communicating it blaring and repetitive if it is to succeed in fulfilling its purpose. And, just as with authority, elections and electoral politics by themselves do not fill this basic need for information except over a very long period. On the macro-level it is supplied by the accretion of historic cleavages and their mobilization structures;

---

[1] The problems of elections in new nations have not been adequately discussed on a comparative cross-national basis, and with due weight to their wider socio-political consequences. See for instance W. J. M. Mackenzie and K. E. Robinson (eds), *Five Elections in Africa*, London 1960, and Mackenzie, 'The Export of Electoral Systems', op. cit. One important case study which does justice to the wider social problems is J. J. Maquet and M. d'Hertefelt, *Elections en société féodale: une étude sur l'introduction du vote populaire au Ruanda-Urundi*, Brussels 1959.

on the micro-level by individual socialization into politics through parents, schools, peergroups, etc.[1] These sources provide an induction into loyalties for the individual without any personal experience of cleavage; while they cannot predetermine opinion formation over issues (these, as has been noted, often contradict mobilized electoral or cleavage alignments), they do constrain the self-identification with structures of aggregated choices represented by political parties at elections. Thus for purposes of comparison with developing countries electoral politics in developed countries, West or East, may be said to rest on a long-standing accretion of information which can, whenever required, be referred to by the articulation of symbols, and to which the process of electoral politics makes only surface adjustments at any one time. The common stock of information is accordingly as much a prior assumption as it is a product of elections in the West.

The same sort of assumption is true of influence, the political exercise of which also requires a sophisticated level of shared information. This indeed is one of the ways of distinguishing influence from power, the latter requiring a much lower common stock of information shared by the participants. Karl Deutsch and Parsons have highlighted this important distinction with a cash-credit analogy; power corresponds to the glistening specie of cash, influence to the equivalent in credit; a transposition from the exercise of influence in politics to the use of power is thus similar to the conversion of credit into cash, a form of response, say, to having one's bluff called.[2] This again suggests that in developing countries the absence of a stock of suitable political influence, based on political information of long standing, must tend to favour the exercise of power to a much greater and more frequent extent. The lack of information stock in developing countries, and the need for relatively crude methods and symbols of mobilization, indicate a crucial relationship between educational differentials and the likelihood of success for one of the elites competing for power before or after inheritance. A recent

[1] There is a substantial literature on this. For the basic argument see H. H. Hyman, *Political Socialization*, Glencoe 1959. For a more specifically political approach, see R. E. Lane, 'Political Character and Political Analysis', *Psychiatry*, XVI (1953), pp. 387–98; 'Depth Interviews on the Personal Meaning of Politics', *PROD*, I (1957), pp. 10–13; 'The Fear of Equality', *Am. Pol. Sc. Rev.*, LIII (1959), pp. 36–51; *Political Life*, Glencoe 1959; also Herbert McClosky, 'Conservatism and Personality', *Am. Pol. Sc. Rev.*, LII (1959), pp. 27–45.

[2] Karl W. Deutsch, *Nerves of Government*, pp. 120 ff.; Talcott Parsons, 'On the Concept of Political Power', op. cit.

study of Ghana has identified an educational factor in the emergence of the CPP from the Gold Coast Convention as a distinct group. The CPP was mainly composed of elementary school leavers from a limited number of schools, where the parent GCC had been more mixed in educational composition; this produced a nationalism in the former party with a distinct–and, as it turned out, more popular– flavour.[1]

These factors of socialization and education, all of which indicate a very different relationship of the political to the social systems as between developed and developing countries, seem to offer a much surer guide to the so-called 'democratic' difficulties–if such they be– in new states than constant emphasis on human or economic under-development. No doubt the very mechanisms of democratic participation, whether compensatory or real, cannot be applied meaningfully without a certain minimum of what sociologists call universalism (as opposed to particularism), without some tendency to achievement orientation. *Some* correlation between Western democracy and economic development has now been established beyond doubt–in terms of historical coincidence if nothing else (i.e. some societies industrialized simultaneously with the spread of parliamentary democracy). Similarly the psychological attributes of democratic politics–and more particularly those of 'undemocratic' or authoritarian politics– have also been established in convincing hypotheses. But there is no reason why either economic development or democratic psychological attributes on their own should necessarily lead or even tend to democracy. In the field of psychological studies particularly we analyse the known authoritarian or democrat *a posteriori*; there is little than can lead us to predict authoritarian probabilities in the future. Nobody foresaw Hitler, and especially no psychologist.[2]

[1] Dennis Austin, *Politics in Ghana, 1946–60*, London 1964; David E. Apter, *Ghana in Transition*, New York 1963, pp. 165–6, 207–8. More recently see the study by Philip J. Foster, *Education and Social Change in Ghana*, London 1966. More comparatively James S. Coleman (ed.), *Education and Political Development*, Princeton 1966.

[2] One cannot therefore help being somewhat suspicious of T. W. Adorno *et al.*, *The Authoritarian Personality*, New York 1950, not so much as a piece of research, but of its subsequent rather facile use by sociologists as a simple radar device for monitoring quickly a very complex catchment area. What is essentially an abstraction based on empirical observation and study tends to be turned upside down, into a functional explanation of certain types of polities. Cf. e.g. the large literature on Soviet 'diaperology': Margaret Mead, *Soviet Attitudes toward Authority*, New York 1951; G. Gorer and J. Rickman, *The People of Great Russia*, London 1949; Henry V. Dicks, 'Observations on Contemporary Russian Behaviour', *Human Relations*, V, 2 (1952), pp. 111–75;

The difficulty of incorporating the past history of the West and the current history of the Third World into an adequate and objective analysis or study of development thus appears at least in large part methodological, a problem of our own making as a result of our intellectual ordering of priorities. If we insist on moving electoral democracy into the forefront of our value system by identifying it with the 'proper' manner of evolving and ratifying authority structures in the social system as a whole, a way must then clearly be found to make electoral democracy an automatic accompaniment of any well-ordered and developed society. In this way social scientists have become almost as historically determinist as Marxists–in the sense that any verdict of historical or developmental unreadiness (making the essential differentiation one of *time*) is determinist.[1] But

---

Dinko Tomašić, *The Impact of Russian Culture on Soviet Communism*, Glencoe 1953, and many others. The symbolic invocation of psychology (catchment area!) seems to increase in direct proportion to the dilemma of academic confrontation with the socially or politically inexplicable in traditional terms.

It is worth noting that Soviet critics of Western, particularly American, sociology have concentrated their fire on these psychological explanations of deviant and above all revolutionary behaviour. See for instance A. K. Uledov, *Obshchestvennoe mnenie sovetskovo obshchestva*, Moscow 1963, especially p. 194; cf. Lewis S. Feuer, 'Problems and Unproblems in Soviet Social Theory', *Slavic Review*, March 1964, p. 122. See in general the discussion in *Problems of Communism*, XIV, 6 (November-December 1965), pp. 34–47.

The parallel development to this psychological 'anti'-literature in the West is the substantial 'pro'-literature on achievement inculcation in childhood, based on the work of David McClelland, *The Achieving Society*, New York 1961, and many others since (most recently Orvis F. Collins, David G. Moore and Darab B. Unwalla, *The Enterprising Man*, East Lansing 1964). This approach is perhaps more directly the reflection of an existing ideology than its sibling on authoritarianism, since it starts with the initial, almost Jules Verne-like, assumption that achievement is *normally* or *best* expressed in the form of entrepreneurial action, and then proceeds on an international scale to relate an achievement-oriented youth with entrepreneurial success in life. The latent or secondary assumption must be, of course, that entrepreneurship finds its best or easiest expression in liberal democracies. For a critique of this approach stressing value prerequisites and psychological predispositions of achievement motivation, see John H. Kunkel, 'Values and Behavior in Economic Development', *Economic Development and Cultural Change*, XII, 3 (April 1965), pp. 257–77. Cf. also below p. 235, note 2.

[1] A good–and highly respected example–of 'democratic determinism' is the analogy of democracy with wealth (e.g. S. M. Lipset, *Political Man*, New York 1960, Chapter II, pp. 45–72). This tells us about a *relationship* valid in itself but to be variously explained, but not about a *causality*–democracy does not produce wealth, wealth does not produce democracy. It also produces a commitment to the *status quo*. If this happens to be democratic, then . . . Equally determinist is the classification of stable democracies on one side versus unstable democracies plus dictatorships on the other–which, as may become clearer, is *in part* a more normative variant for the more neutral elitist-constitu-

whereas Marxists superordinate class conflict to all other social action, many Western political sociologists similarly superordinate political democracy as a solvent of social relations. And just as Stalinism was a positivist vulgarization of Marxism, so does any excessive preoccupation with the shortfall (as yet) of democracy in any society vulgarize the real nature and social function of politics.

The sort of problems that arise when apparently electoral-democratic forms in a society under consideration lead to a Western 'type' of analysis, as opposed to the more fatalistic acceptance of deformations in the study of 'proper' developing countries, can be seen when we look at Greece today. It is not a developed country, yet it appears since the war to have a fairly stable democracy of at least medium-term duration. Democracy and its apparatus (political parties, elections, etc.) are asserted by participants in the form of constant ideological reference to the Hellenic past and the deeply ingrained democratic component in the political psychology of modern Greeks. If anything democracy in Greece is held by analysts to be *excessively* anchored in culture and tradition, to such an extent as to make the emergence of stable political authority difficult, and lead to indiscipline. Thus social-psychological rather than economic determinism among many Western as well as Greek commentators causes the contribution of Greek tradition and the heritage of the Hellenic spirit to be emphasized, rather than the existence of any economic base for democracy. The real content of Greek *political* democracy, its role, its place in the social scale of saliency and relevance, remain largely unexamined like the Stalinist claim to Leninism; just as Leninism is universal and indivisible, so is democracy. In fact Greece is a highly authoritarian society. The political system is narrow and not nearly as salient as the Greek psychological preoccupation with political discussion might lead one to believe. The kinship system on the other hand is broad and very salient. Greek politics are compensatory *par*

---

tional pattern suggested here. This is the basic Almond focus ('Comparative Political Systems', *Journal of Politics*, XVIII (1956), pp. 392 ff.); cf. also Philip Cutright, 'National Political Development', *American Sociological Review*, XXVIII (1963), pp. 253–64. For the general parallel of Western and Marxist scientific determinism, cf. Bernard Crick, *The American Science of Politics*, London 1959, pp. 220–7, particularly p. 226: 'The freest people on earth have a strangely morbid taste for determinism'; also Christian Bay, 'Behavioral Literature', op. cit. It is worth noting that behaviourists, whose language is normally the epitome of neutrality and politeness, become extraordinarily sensitive when accused of determinism by those with a more philosophical bent. See the brief and very *engagé* comments on Crick by Evron M. Kirkpatrick in Austin Ranney, *Essays*, pp. 28–29.

excellence—at the bottom of the social scale; at the top the political system is more closely congruent in style and process to the other subsystems.[1] Any attempt to relate democracy with economic development in the case of Greece is clearly ill-founded; the attempt to co-ordinate Greek political democracy with any congruent features of the social structure no less so. Greece thus does not fit either the conventional Western or the conventional Third World case. What is suggested is that only an analysis in terms of subsystem function and subsystem differentiation can incorporate this particular case into any comparative study of nations or societies; more particularly the study of how the two functions of political mobilization are fulfilled in the subsystem, the way in which the cultural emphasis of social elitism corrodes or dominates the apparently constitutional framework of the polity, and finally the extent to which politics serves as a manner of compensating for a social system with low mobility. Hence the problem of economic development ought to be viewed, not as an autonomous problem, but as one of relatively low priority in social goal attainment; compared to other developing countries there is little willingness to adopt the process and structures of mobilization which intensive economic development requires.

We can now elaborate in greater detail on these general remarks about developing countries, and the manner in which analysis of them must depart from conventional comparison with the developed West. The first problem of developing countries is that of *creating* political authority—then only does the question of legitimizing and

---

[1] A useful 'participant' discussion of the psychological determinants of Greek society, which stresses the personality aspect in relation to modern group formation in Greek society, may be found in A. Pollis, 'Political Implications of the Modern Greek Concept of Self', *British Journal of Sociology*, XVI, 1 (March 1965), pp. 29–47. This discussion centres round the concept of *philotima* or self-regard. This, though specifically applied to Greece, is a useful rationality-destroying concept which might be relevant to the analysis of many other societies. Its obverse, *atimia*, has been well used by Gustavo Lagos, *International Stratification and Underdeveloped Countries*, Chapel Hill (North Carolina) 1963, pp. 22–25, in the context of national status in the international system. The concept of *philotima* may be understood as a strong imposition of a normative reference group on personal attitudes, thus stifling the adequate use of comparative reference groups in self-evaluations of status.

There are no adequate studies of modern Greek politics or society in English to my knowledge; a brief introduction to the problem is Y. Daphnis, *Ta Ellenika Politika Komata* (*Greek Political Parties*), Athens 1961. Most of the 'views' of Greece put forward here as conventional are based on various reports by academics submitted to the Greek government concerned with specific administrative and economic problems.

ratifying it arise. From the start the nature of political authority is constrained by two unique factors: (1) the need for continuity with the past on the one hand coupled with the desire for maximum dissociation from it on the other, and (2) the imposition of a valid and universalistic authority on often highly particularistic societies – a new form of authority rather than a summated or extended one. Before going on to discuss the means of achieving this two-fold legitimacy the problem can be restated in functional terms: (1) is a normative problem of establishing a set of values and of pursuing the goals that follow from it; (2) is a problem of efficiency, in mobilization as well as counter-mobilization against particularistic collectivities and structures, and also in terms of a compression of time. Let us take these in turn.

(1) The achievement of independence is normally a transfer of sovereignty. *Existing* authorities – more or less efficacious, more or less legitimate – suddenly become sovereign. But this transfer is not neutral or colourless; rather the achievement of an urgent right hitherto deemed to have been denied – it carries strong connotations of affect. Consequently even the most peaceful handover involves a period and process of formal dissociation from the former rulers by the beneficiary or 'inheritance' elite as an essential means of establishing its legitimacy. In the case where independence is won as a result of an anti-colonial war of independence the achievement of dissociation is automatic or revolutionary, otherwise it has to be carefully created. In British ex-colonies the party or parties created more or less expressly to exploit the processes of legitimization made available by the colonial ruler's value system ('democratic elections') often had to go through the formal motion of dissociation: the nearer the actual date of independence, the firmer this dissociative posture – for instance the embracing of ex-Mau Mau Kikuyu by KANU in Kenya, the respective flourishes of dissociative symbols by Presidents Banda and Nyerere, and the competitively dissociative drive of the CPP in the old Gold Coast. Very often the process of dissociation is in fact *post hoc* rather than – or as well as – *propter hoc*. Ghana is the most striking example of this – the 'incomprehensible' deterioration of relations between the governments of Ghana and Britain some years *after* independence. More recently TANU and President Nyerere have undertaken the same retroactive process. The increasingly dissociative or revolutionary posture of the Cuban regime *vis-à-vis* the Americans, with its positing of Cuba's previous colonial situation in relation to the United States, can also be cited.

In this fairly common *ex-post* variant an inheritance situation takes on an increasingly revolutionary orientation.[1]

There are obvious, built-in elements of schizophrenia in this situation–on two levels, which we might call norm-oriented or cognitive, and value-oriented or ideological. Most colonial powers–except the Dutch, Spanish and Portuguese, who rarely leave voluntarily–appear to feel that the test of readiness for independence is a willingness and ability to work the political system in accordance with the value assumptions of the home country. Many colonies–except perhaps those who achieved their independence through victory in a revolutionary war–accept the implicit identification of their colonial masters' domestic 'democratic' processes and ideas with their perceived status of power and modernity, and thus begin by adopting the core of their imperial masters' constitutional principles as well as furniture; at least they appear to try.[2] Even the conception of

---

[1] The inheritance situation and its subsequent socio-political probabilities are explained in detail in Nettl, 'Inheritance', op. cit. The terminology used comes from the analogy with legal inheritance–hence the notion of beneficiary.

[2] The voluntaristic aspect of this adoption of process and norms, important though it is, can be overstated. 'An ingenious person might construe this attempt to establish Western constitutions in developing countries as the march of a new type of imperialism–a device for captivation. On the contrary the 'imperialists'–British, French, Dutch, Belgian, Australian, and to a slightly lesser extent American–are no longer Wilsonian. They insist nowadays that it is absurd to suppose that Western institutions can possibly be made to work in Oriental or African countries without long apprenticeship. *We have not imposed Western institutions, they have demanded, one might say extorted, them from us,* and we are thus committed against our will to an extraordinary adventure. We share the commitment because we furnish the model and will be involved in the consequences of success or failure. [And] now that the experiment is launched we are not invited to participate . . .' (W. J. M. Mackenzie, 'The Export of Electoral Systems', op. cit., p. 241; my italics.) This combination of scepticism and regret–instead of personal offence and annoyance–may be described as typically English. A more general discussion, along the same lines, of the difficulties of inherited Western democracy in developing countries can be found in I. R. Sinai, *The Challenge of Modernization*, London 1964.

At first sight the implication seems to be that Western colonial powers have had their democratic techniques gouged out of them reluctantly by their ex-colonies. However the key to the meaning of the passage quoted is in the phrase 'without long apprenticeship'; in the last resort this is merely a sophisticated version of the notion that much 'improvement' in developing countries is necessary before they can 'safely' operate democratic systems. Cf. Sékou Touré; 'This "theory of maturity" becomes the ideological basis for the continuing slogan by which they (the imperialists) try to justify keeping their colonies enslaved.' *Independent Guinea; Articles and Speeches*, Moscow 1960, p. 53. The genuineness and consistency of the attempt to 'prepare' ex-colonies for such suitable independence in accordance with the political and administrative prescriptions of the imperial power are examined in the perceptive

négritude, and the development of a distinct socio-cultural African-ism in many Francophone African republics, were largely created in, and diffused from, Paris–an adaptation of a distinctly French tradi-tion. The only significant exceptions are the countries of Latin America, who turned their back almost completely on the constitu-tion and polity of Spain and Portugal in favour of the rationalist prescriptions emanating from revolutionary France. Though the United States of America also did not adopt the British constitution in detail, their efforts at constitution-making were in part intended to improve on the spirit of the British system rather than provide a completely dissociative approach. In general, therefore, inheritors usually undertake to accept and try to work a foreign system from whose *local* application and representatives they strongly dissociate themselves. Since at the same time dissociation is an increasingly essential component of inheritance legitimacy–*ex ante* or *ex post*–it tends to clash with the conflicting commitment to the colonial power's political structure or process. Sometimes this results in considerable strain, resolved either dramatically by political coups or revolution (Pakistan, Sudan, Burma), or by a slower adaptation of the borrowed constitution in spirit and even in form to local or anyhow different conditions and values (Ghana, Nigeria, some French ex-colonies like Congo-Brazzaville and Mali). The strain, it might be added, is greatly increased in cases where countries intending to be constitutional unwittingly adopt the methods and structure of an elitist society like the United Kingdom.

However there are also some strong norm-oriented counter-forces to the over-rapid dissolution of the alien political heritage. One of these is the preoccupation with legality, for instance in the ready acceptance of territorial *status quo*, together with the willing takeover of such territorial claims as the colonial power might have had against the country's neighbours. Surprisingly this has proved one of the most obstinate and stable continuities in all 'new' polities. The governments of Kenya, China, Algeria and even India, both the most and the least 'indebted' of ex-colonies, have emphas-ized the sacrosanct nature of their territorial boundaries and claims at almost any cost, even though both boundaries and claims on neighbours were often the expansionist, whimsical or merely

---

analysis of Bernard Schaffer, 'The Concept of Preparation: Some Questions about the Transfer of Systems of Government', *World Politics,* XVIII, 1 (October 1965), pp. 42–67. For particular emphasis on the administrative aspect of this problem see in greater detail below, pp. 212–6.

'convenient' creation of a colonial power repudiated in almost every other sense. Since it is difficult to argue logically for precise geographical continuity at the same time as claiming political, social and intellectual repudiation, the dissociation has necessarily become ideological and highly assertive, value rather than norm-oriented.

The second value-oriented cause of instability results directly from the adoption of economic growth as an overriding priority. The strain of combining this with the assertion that beneath the overlay of imposed foreign values there exists an indigenous and long-suppressed, therefore traditional, personality peculiar to the 'liberated' country is considerable. Here too strain produces myth—for instance the implied 'solution' that vast state economic enterprises somehow synthesize the traditional (anti-capitalist) values with the acceptance of developmental goals set, at least in part, by the West.[1] Economic development thus serves a highly political function; we have here an extension of political roles, and of the actions and premises of the political system, at the expense of those normally thought of as economic. This is analogous to the apparently similar experience of the Soviet Union, from whom much of the politico-economic process model is borrowed; there too the political system was wide in range, extending to its maximum during the rapid industrialization of the Stalin era (see above, p. 73). The point is important as this similarity is crucial in deciding the extent to which the Soviet Union provided and provides the model for today's developing countries. Systems analysis here offers a useful way of distinguishing the communist and Third World forms of economic development from that of the West. In the latter case the adaptive subsystem and function grew in range and saliency at the expense of goal attainment, integration and latency, while in the former case it was and is the goal-attainment subsystem which had primacy in range and saliency.

In the main the situation in ex-colonial countries around the moment of independence and for some considerable time afterwards provides an interesting parallel with both the dissociative expectations and the 'compromises' of historical Marxism.[2] The basic strain

[1] One of the major elements of instability in many post-inheritance situations is the fact that values, norms, collectivities and roles are as a rule strongly dissociational from the benefactor (actual former colonial power, or *any* ex-colonial or neo-imperialist power), while goals tend to be far less dissociational in view of the common world-wide 'culture' of, or commitment to, economic development and national independence. See Nettl, 'Inheritance'.

[2] For the essentially 'inheritance' aspect of the mass Social Democratic parties of the Second International, particularly the German Social Democrats.

between the value-orientation of committed party members on the one hand, and the demands of integrative control or constraint of members on the other, each one of which developed contradictory goals of its own, is precisely the same as the schizophrenic element of the inheritance aspect of colonial parties and elites; dissociation versus acceptance and continuity. The parallel can be carried still farther. The Bolshevik revolution was the extreme example of dissociation in modern times—perhaps since the Mongol and Turkish invasions of Europe in the fourteenth and fifteenth centuries. Both territorial integrity and constitutional structure were deliberately thrown into the melting pot, and every effort concomitant with physical survival was made to renew the social structure as well. The period from the beginning of the New Economic Policy in 1921 to Socialism in One Country and the First Five-Year Plan in 1928 represents a reversal of this dissociative momentum, until today (in relation to China) the full reassertion of Russian territorial 'rights' has perhaps helped to set the seal on the reversal of the original negation of 'old' norms and values by the Bolshevik revolutionaries. Neither post-Bolshevik communist revolutions nor ex-colonial inheritors have ever tried to emulate the extreme dissociative aspects of the 1917 revolution, but all have found some kind of compromise. In the communist world under Stalin the basis of such compromise was usually the convenience of the Soviet Union, tempered since the mid-1950's by some concessions to domestic legitimacy (the notion of national or historic rights is figuring strongly in disputes between communist nations, e.g. Rumania versus Hungary and the USSR, China versus USSR). In ex-colonial countries, on the other hand, both norm- and value-oriented assertions of territorial integrity and, for instance, rights of suzerainty (Nagas, Karens), as well as assertion of a moral right to economic privileges to be wrung out of the former colonial power, are all essential functions of legitimacy. Legitimacy— or, if one prefers in this instance, national integration—is optionally compounded out of dissociation and continuity; the 'best' balance is the most efficient—in achieving and maintaining legitimacy. The inherent contradiction in political inheritance between dissociation and continuity is a general and structural problem wherever high-level dissociative factors are present, and not a peculiar and merely 'chronological' feature of dying colonialism.

---

see J. P. Nettl, 'The German Social Democratic Party as a Political Model, 1890–1914', *Past and Present*, op. cit., particularly p. 67.

(2) This same dilemma in a way largely governs the creation of an indigenous universalistic authority in the first place. The plenitude of powers of the colonial rulers is taken over in full as a matter of course–no one even considers a *more* limited government than that existing in the colonial era. In retrospect, and by way of continuative legitimacy, these powers of the colonial rulers are often exaggerated considerably. This dichotomous attitude, in which the colonial power is retrospectively accused of wielding arbitrary power[1] and at the same time of flagrant failure to exercise this power constructively–or more precisely for some form of national development–is very noticeable in Indian and African writing on British imperialism, and in the more rational portions of Indonesian writing on the Dutch. The *potential* of plenitude which colonial powers in fact hardly ever used now becomes meticulously stated in law or claimed as political fact. Even in India and Malaysia, both of whom assiduously attempted to build on the higgledy-piggledy British *status quo*, the stronger moral claim of the new indigenous central power has, until recently, been legalistically tempered by careful reference to suitable British precedent. Algeria is another rather more remarkable example of continuity in this and other ways; in spite of the dissociative effect of a long revolutionary war, the Algerians adopted a constitution largely copied from that of the Fifth Republic, and retained a substantial part of the French administrative system of Prefectures. To use a latter-day Marxist analogy once more, the administrative structure of the preceding bourgeois state has been largely preserved wherever it was found to be efficient, a feature peculiar to the Peoples' Democracies of Eastern Europe in contrast to the Soviet Union.

But how was it that no social structure sufficiently broad or solid to take over these inherited functions emerged with similar facility? The dissociative requirement of legitimacy was felt to be strong enough to ensure that a simple handing over of office to some group of individuals arbitrarily selected by the colonial power, using the powers inherent in the existing colonial structure to make their rule effective, would prove to be entirely insufficient. It is very significant that such a situation, in which a small group of individuals literally

---

[1] 'The civil service, the police, justice, defence, foreign relations–all were in the hands of the governor', wrote Kwame Nkrumah bitterly; *Ghana: The Autobiography of Kwame Nkrumah*, Edinburgh 1959, p. 122. For the Soviet emphasis on this colonial discretion or arbitrariness, see generally T. P. Thornton (ed.), *The Third World in Soviet Perspective*, Princeton 1964, pp. 252–75.

'found' themselves in power, was much more typical of coups (Egypt, Sudan, Latin America) than of either the formal handover of power at independence or of revolutionary wars; inevitably even in the case of successful coups or *cuertelazos* there was a need for some downward projection of a 'legitimacy structure' if the new government was to survive for any length of time. This is where French and British commitment to the structure of democratic politics—elections and parties—provided an apparently handy solution. Usually two or more political parties emerged with more or less official colonial blessing, pressing for ever speedier independence (dissociation) but accepting either of the colonial power's preparation for elections as a test of legitimacy, or at least the constitutional principles which contained provisions for such elections (continuity). In accordance with Western value-orientations and traditional political theory, this should have been sufficient to ensure effectiveness and legitimacy.[1]

However, these legitimacy-oriented creations—moreover a manner of legitimation and a form of legitimacy that were themselves foreign importations—could not provide a stable basis for commitments and mobilization. The diffuse reflection of society provided by legitimacy-oriented politics, which obscured rather than crystallized interest orientations based on issues, could not be reproduced in societies where the polity was not the product of gradual adaptation over time but a newly created set of institutions and structures concerned manifestly with the major tasks of social problem-solving, where society was not viewed as something requiring political compensation but rather political supremacy and reconstruction through the political process. Secondly, cleavages based on political mobilization in developing countries could not even remotely be contained within the control of formally institutionalized authority—the *état* or *Staat*, the role of which was itself one of the bases of cleavage in many Western societies; instead such cleavages as existed in newly independent countries were readily understood to be capable of disrupting the newly created state altogether once they were permitted to serve as bases for mobilization structures. Thus the cleavages themselves, far from serving as the basis of political mobilization, were viewed as capable of making the operation of a more or less differentiated political system impossible. We shall examine some empirical examples of such mobilization in developing countries in the following chapter. Meantime, however, the social situation of developing

[1] The implications of this are elaborated in 'Inheritance', op. cit.

211

countries appears to have precluded the efficient application of the available basic Western models—'elitist' authority legitimation and 'constitutional' interest articulation. Yet such Western models were initially adopted in many ex-colonial and also non-colonial developing countries—partly because of imperial rather than indigenous prescriptions of legitimacy, partly because the Western models were viewed as functionally efficient both for authority legitimation as well as interest articulation, primarily by Western advisers or benefactors themselves, derivatively by many beneficiaries who initially also viewed their main task as one of 'catching up' the developed West.

Excursus: The Administrative Variant

So far the argument has been largely concerned with political structures and collectivities. It is worth noting that exactly the same points can be made with regard to administrative problems. The development of administrative studies in Western Europe and America is an interesting and logical outcrop of the general tendency towards regulation of the economy by the government.[1] The fruits of these studies have been, and are, also on offer to developing countries as part of post-inheritance aid. Though efficient administration and functional democracy are offered as separate wisdoms by different sets of advisers, this is a symptom of the academic and structural differentiation already referred to; as far as the recipients are concerned, they are complementary and come basically from the same value source. There is thus no reason why they should continue to be treated as separate aspects; in the colonial period certainly no such distinction between political and administrative training was ever attempted. Nor indeed need they be separated analytically by those who study the relationship between developed and developing societies—for efficient administration is, in the age of modern capitalism, held to be an integral part of functioning democracy and is propagated as such.

The problem of transferring one's experience and ideas of administration from a developed to a developing situation runs into exactly the same difficulties as those we have noted with regard to the attempt to impose or prescribe the electoral choices of political

[1] For this see outstandingly Andrew Shonfield, *Modern Capitalism: The Changing Balance of Public and Private Power*, London 1965. For the theoretical implications of the imposition of organizational theory on democracy see Wolin, *Politics and Vision*, Chapter X.

democracy.[1] The science or technique of efficient administration as evolved in developed societies, unlike the propagation of democratic and particularly electoral procedures, need not itself have dysfunctional elements in its normative context. Clearly it is still mainly an abstract problem rather than a concrete one, and is in the West still located in the area of techniques rather than basic philosophies. Certainly there are those who suggest that the study of administration and organization, with its predictive and manipulative possibilities, should be raised from the level of techniques to the level of philosophy, but they are as yet the exception.[2] Until this happens, the relevance of the present discussion is not in the basic ideological problems posed by administrative studies and the science of administration as such, but in what happens when they are transplanted *tel quel* to developing societies.

It is not perhaps so surprising that the status of administrative science has on the whole not been compounded with the ideology of democracy by its developing recipients; even those who have questioned the validity of Western democracy are still showing themselves to be willing recipients of administrative advice and techniques, and continue to send their civil servants to Western schools of administration and universities even though their politicians have long since ceased to pay lipservice to Westminster, and keep their cere-

[1] A very similar argument to mine, based largely on these administrative problems, and setting out from the same starting point in terms of a situational definition as my concept of 'Inheritance', may be found in B. B. Schaffer, 'The Concept of Preparation', *World Politics*, XVIII, 1 (October 1965), pp. 42–67, op. cit. Among other things, the author of this article refers to compartmentalism–the unjustified separation of administration from political questions–as the main difficulty involved in the handing down of Western administrative wisdom to developing societies, though he does not clearly identify the ideological purpose in making this division. He also argues convincingly that the whole concept of preparation, in its wider political as well as administrative aspects, was both a means of retarding independence *and* of guiding it into strongly reform-oriented or non-revolutionary channels (for the implications of this see once more Nettl, 'Inheritance'). For further discussion of the administrative aspect of this problem, see Victor Thompson, 'Objectives for Development Administration', *Administrative Science Quarterly*, IX, 1 (June 1964), pp. 91–108; Y. Dror, 'Muddling Through–Science or Inertia', *Public Administration Review*, XXIV, 3 (September 1964), pp. 154–7; see also C. E. Lindblom, 'Policy Analysis', *American Economic Review*, XLVIII (June 1958), pp. 298–312.

[2] Herbert A. Simon, *Administrative Behavior*, New York 1947. Philip Selznick, 'Foundations of the Theory of Organization', *American Sociological Review*, XII (1948), pp. 23–35. Philip Selznick, *Leadership in Administration: A Sociological Interpretation*, Evanston, Ill., 1957. Cf. E. W. Bakke, *Bonds of Organization*, New York 1950; L. Gullick and L. Urwick (eds), *Papers on the Science of Administration*, New York 1937.

monial expressions of solidarity and political admiration for Belgrade, Moscow and Peking as well as London. What we have here are the results of a remarkable rescue operation. For in the colonial period problems of administration were not only identified with the colonial power's values and norms, but the notion of preparing colonies for independence was an indissoluble compound of administrative and political decisions and attitudes – and viewed as such by the dissociative inheritance elements. One recent author indeed goes so far as to suggest that the concentration on party-political aspects of readiness of independence – the kind of political legitimation procedures through elections we have been discussing here – was an original admission of failure for the administrative variant in the imposition of Western norms.[1] It is in this context, therefore, that the separation of the apparently value-laden political prescriptions from the allegedly neutral problems of administration, followed by the acceptance on the part of developing countries of advice on the latter while maintaining and even sharpening opposition to the former, must be viewed and analysed. This post-independence separation and reassessment of the relationship between two components which were previously viewed as part and parcel of the same process of colonialism are one of the significant features of what might be called inheritance. All this makes the urgency of discussing the ideological impact of current administrative techniques even greater. Studies relating purely administrative problems to the wider context of their ideological implications are therefore to be very much welcomed, for the colonial period as well as for the post-colonial era.[2]

[1] 'The theory [of administrative preparation for independence] was a combination of Marx and Whigs . . . The *non-political conditions* for the transfer of power were surrendered.' Schaffer, 'Preparation', p. 62 (my italics).

[2] One such study, in the context of Papua and New Guinea, is Schaffer, 'The World Bank Report on the Economic Development of the Territory of Papua and New Guinea', cyclostyled in preparation for publication. In general the approach of Fred W. Riggs is very significant in this context; particularly *The Ecology of Public Administration*, Bombay 1961; *Administration in Developing Countries*, Boston 1964, and 'Trends in the Comparative Study of Public Administration', *International Review of Administrative Sciences*, XXVII, (1962), pp. 9–15. Cf. also Riggs in Joseph LaPalombara (ed.), *Bureaucracy and Political Development*, Princeton 1963, and LaPalombara, 'An Overview . . .' in ibid., pp. 3–33. For some illuminating comments on the connection between ideology and the direction of (as well as finance for) research into development administration, see Riggs, 'Relearning Old Lessons: The Political Context of Development Administration', *Public Administration Review*, XXV (1965), pp. 70–79.

It is not, of course, suggested that all those who have discussed administrative problems in developing societies have been slavish propagators of Western models, though some certainly have. Nonetheless the shrewder observers have tended to take a purely *ad hoc* line and have attempted, with the minimum of possible prejudice, to apply their general experience of administrative questions to the particular context of their enquiry, without much attempt to investigate the possibility of formulating general propositions or theories of administration with specific reference not so much to the *needs* as to the *common situation* of developing countries.[1] Their underlying assumption seems to be that administration *as a science* (if indeed it is one) can be indifferently useful to all types of societies providing that the necessary allowance for individual social contexts is made. Certainly the numbers of case studies and of textbooks of allegedly universal validity offering advice on how administration can become efficient in all circumstances have increased phenomenally in the last few years – in proportion to the decline in the number of books offering advice on how to be democratic. But the assumption that there are universally valid criteria of administrative efficiency may itself not be valid. In chapter 12 it will be argued that the very notion of administration, its function and structure, indeed the whole 'modern' concept of bureaucracy, differs so fundamentally between developed and developing countries that the very notion of an overall administrative science, with its implications of rational (as opposed to political) problem solving, seems hardly to apply in developing countries.[2] Consequently the problem of efficient administration should, in my view, take a much lower priority in policy recommendation to developing countries than it currently has – particularly in so far as it is a 'neutral' substitute of efficiency for the more

[1] In this regard mention must specially be made of the work of A. H. Hanson, *Public Enterprise and Economic Development*, second edition, London, 1965; good area studies of particular geographical application are A. D. Gorwala, *Report on the Efficient Conduct of State Enterprise*, New Delhi 1951; A. H. Hanson, *The Process of Planning*, London 1966 (both on India); Mahbub Ul Haq, *The Strategy of Economic Planning: A Case Study of Pakistan*, Oxford 1965; Albert Waterston, *Planning in Pakistan: Organization and Implementation*, Oxford 1965. In general see Waterston, *Development Planning: Lessons of Experience*, Baltimore 1965.
[2] One of the very few approaches which accords partial recognition to the specific and unique problem of administration in a context of under-development, both as a general problem in itself and as one generically different from administration in developed societies, is that of Fred W. Riggs. Cf. also Victor Thompson, 'Objectives for Development Administration', op. cit.

directly ideological focus on democratic procedure in government. The kind of efficiency criteria discussed in the next chapter are related, not to governmental administration at all, but to political mobilization – on the grounds that this criterion of need may have a greater priority for developing countries.

Part III

PROCESS

CHAPTER EIGHT

The Structure and Process of Mobilization in Developing Countries

SUMMARY

In this chapter the processes of mobilization in developing countries are examined in greater detail and a classification is worked out according to which such processes of mobilization may be structurally distinguished. First we have party-based mobilization, in which the structure of commitment and authority legitimation is based primarily on a single or predominant party. Secondly and alternatively, there is the somewhat more diffuse process of mobilizing on the basis of national-constitutional integration. This is a broader framework based frequently on the charismatic arbitrage between institutions by a leader, whose charisma is routinized and dispersed in favour of the newly created offices of state, the military, the bureaucracy, etc., all within the context of national integration and identity. The bases of commitment to the nation–necessarily *nations trouvées* in the absence of a long historical period of national integration–are examined in some detail in terms of commitment resulting from mobilized support against designated opponents. Imperialism is taken as an example of such a mobilizing referent.

A special variant of this type of mobilization, and the process *par excellence* by which commitment and support are mobilized, is the development plan. The process and structures of planning are analysed in some detail in accordance with their political and social rather than their economic functions, the plan being viewed under various headings such as means of ideological control, means of socio-political communication, symbol of legitimacy and means of role recruitment. Though the analysis is primarily concerned here with developing countries, glimpses of differences from the situation in developed countries are pointed up.

The chapter ends with a brief assessment of the relative roles which the Western and communist models can play in the structuring of mobilization as outlined in the chapter; the advantages of the Soviet model are tempered by certain differences which are highlighted. In this context, reference is made to the contribution of Soviet analysis of developing countries, particularly with regard to mobilization and the concept of the National-Democratic state. This takes up the threads of the discussion of Soviet analysis initiated in chapter 7.

In discussing the manner in which developing countries try to attain their goals, and particularly the extent to which they are able and willing to adopt Western values, norms and collectivities, we have to be clear about the particular relationship between capacity and goal attainment which exists in developing countries today. This can perhaps best be summed up by adapting to the present context a proposition relating to international conflict. 'If a state's perception of injury (or frustration, dissatisfaction, hostility, threat or fear) to itself is "sufficiently" great [it] will offset perception of insufficient capability, making the perception of capability much less important a factor in a decision to go to war [or modernize].'[1] As much of the foregoing discussion has shown, the same limitations on 'realistic' assumptions of capability and accurate self-consciousness apply to development problems in the Third World, given a sufficient feeling of *atimia* or need.

Following the basic cultural classification of societies into elitist and constitutional, we shall divide the present discussion of means of mobilization in developing countries into two main classifications; mobilization through party on the one hand, and mobilization through national-economic or national-constitutional norms and structures on the other. The phrase national-constitutional is used in preference to that of state to point up the essentially non-European tradition and to emphasize the empirically observable primacy of the concept of nation.

1. *Party Mobilization*

Western political parties, at least those whose goals lie within the area of accepting the basic value system of society (i.e. other than right-wing 'negation' parties and communists during ultra-left spells)

[1] Robert C. North, Ole R. Holsti *et al.*, *Content Analysis, A Handbook with Application for the Study of International Crises*, Evanston, Illinois, 1963, appendix B, pp. 171–2.

tend necessarily to be *both* authority building *and* interest articulation instruments. The extreme cases of pure interest articulation and authority legitimation are ideal-typical abstractions. But one or other of these divergent functions dominates at any one period. To operate successfully as authority legitimizers, political parties must use the techniques of interest articulation forced on them by systems of election which, however they may otherwise vary, all demand some mobilization. Even in those presidential systems where authority building and interest articulation are structurally and processually separated, the individual to be elected as Chief Executive still needs the logistic support of a party–even though, like de Gaulle in France, he may deny them thrice. In a situation of inheritance such routinized, specific possibilities of mobilization do not usually exist, and neither therefore does any readily available logistic support; this has usually to be created. A long-standing, value-oriented and highly structured movement like Congress in India may seem to approximate it but cannot, under the umbrella of overall, often rather simplistic, dissociational values, provide the norm-oriented and differentiated infra-structure which makes European parties viable. Whatever the possibility of cleavage mobilization in developing countries–and this certainly exists, though it is strongly de-emphasized by the goal-formulating elites–the issue end of the dimension is largely lacking; as suggested, a spatial model of party competition makes no empirical sense. The dominant single issue continues to be inheritance–national independence and existence. To this extent political conflict has strongly consummatory overtones; normative orientations tend to be resisted or supported in value-oriented terms and symbols. Thus even where some shared commitment to common values exists, as in India, the structuring of conflict in norm-oriented terms is difficult; the search will be for consensus rather than accommodation of conflict which, in the view of the participants, cannot always be 'contained'. Moreover the basis of political legitimacy is anchored in inheritance; any challenge to the legitimacy of the ruling party is viewed as a challenge to inheritance itself. This identification of legitimacy with inheritance is highly personal in many developing countries. Commitment to party is either based on communal, religious or racial interest, or a limited transfer to a party structure of the personal legitimacy of a small inheritance elite or a single charismatic leader. Where the Indian Congress has developed some of the competitive, issue-oriented features of Western political parties, which it combines with many typical inheritance elements, it is one of the rare cases of such adaptation; in many developing countries the predominance of value-oriented mobilization in favour of nation or party and against all manifestations of cleavage, in combination with highly personal, charismatic leadership, prevents the emergence of anything resembling a Western political party.

Inheritance situations have therefore given rise to political parties of a special type, fulfilling (objectively) rather special functions in the political system. (1) The most important of these is to provide logistic support strong enough (*a*) to impress the departing colonial power, often oriented to the visible manifestations of mass support as proof of legitimacy, with the strength of the party's claim to become its political successor–or alternatively to make the party strong enough to throw the colonial power out of force; (*b*) to overcome its various social and economic as well as political opponents (no one but Western political scientists and constitutional advisers ever expect the new constitutional game to be played wholeheartedly for long); (*c*) to move the country forward up the steep slope demanded by the current, almost universally accepted, developmental goals. This obviously requires a high degree of mobilization– both in terms of the numerical proportion of the politically acculturated and in terms of devotion and compliance within the party. Speed is also essential; the 'natural' (Western, particularly British) transformation of political interest articulation gradually into aggregated authority legitimation is too slow. The time factor is an important element in the rejection of Western political norms and electoral processes.

On the face of it Western political democracy–which is a compromise fusion of these two functions with a legitimacy base, and a symbolic interest superstructure, or vice versa–has thus little to offer except an outward shell of techniques and structural forms. Developing societies adapt and transform these as quickly as possible. First, the dissociative element discussed earlier must be sharply emphasized. Under cover of this, an alternative legitimacy structure has often evolved (Congress in India, CPP in the Gold Coast, Mapai in Israel) very like the 'state within the state' of pre-1914 Social Democracy in Germany, and, of course, the Bolsheviks prior to 1917. This serves to rally the strong but diffuse anti-colonial feeling of the acculturated as well as pre-empting legitimacy away from those indigenous collaborators with the colonial power who are often technically best qualified to take over. The breakout of the CPP from the United Gold Coast Convention is a good example of this dissociative competition; others can be found in Algeria–the CRUA-FLN alliance ousting VDMA and Centralists as competitors for popular support– and also in French West Africa. It has often proved possible to combine both dissociation and technical collaboration with the colonial power, as in India and for example pre-independence Palestine, but the mobilizational aspect of dissociation is always present to a large extent.

(2) Secondly the emphasis on rapid mass mobilization deliberately dispenses with the self-conscious appeal to rationality which, in the West, is a major symbolic reference point to the function of political parties as means of interest articulation, however vestigial this function may really be in the case of many political parties nowadays. At local levels every divisive issue is exploited against the colonial *status quo;* caste, tribe, ethnic groups, language, recent immigrants against old inhabitants, rich versus poor, young versus old. The ability to weld this confusion of appeals in different areas into one nationally cohesive party depends:

(*a*) on poor interregional and intervillage communication; the lines of communication run to and from the centre, and therefore the new 'national' symbols tend to obliterate local competitors.

(*b*) on the overriding assertion of broad values: developmental, nationalist, neutralist, anti-selected-enemy.

The dichotomy between grass roots and centre, which is present to a greater or lesser extent in all but strongly legitimizing political parties everywhere (whose existence effectively depends upon elections), is one of the significant features of politics in developing countries. In developed countries the patronage or pork barrel interests of party functionaries (Mapai, Italian Christian Democrats, MRP, Austrian parties) or luminaries (French Radical Party, Italian Liberals, German FDP) are generally able to overcome most of the centre-periphery difficulties–with some exceptions like Norway, where the centre-periphery cleavage still exists, though it is now declining there as well. But in developing countries the divergence is different, both in orientation and in kind. For one thing, local politics in tribal or caste societies are almost exactly zero-sum games, in which strategy is to a large extent predetermined–if the Reddi [caste] candidate is a Communist, then the Kamma candidate will often automatically be Congress.[1] In much the same way as in the

[1] The example is taken at random from the analysis (not of course in terms of games theory) of Selig S. Harrison, *India, The Most Dangerous Decades*, London 1960. Cf. in this context the elections in Nigeria 1964–5. For a very

United States (an analogy curiously neglected until recently by American theorists) the combination of one set of attitudes to local issues with an often quite contradictory attitude to the same or similar issues at national level on the part of senators and representatives, and the attempt to present these divergences as a consistent whole, helps to explain the apparently illogical but smilingly easy tergiversations of African and Asian politicians, of which the early history of the independent Congo is such a striking example.[1] The logic of top-to-bottom consistency, which accepts as permissible only differences in range but not in *apparent* direction of opinion or policy, is common to both democratic and Communist ideologies but has little empirical application to the 'issue publics' of developed countries and even less to developing countries as a whole. Nor does its negative corollary: that built-in inconsistency is mechanically self-cancelling, and therefore equivalent to being immobile, i.e. conservative.[2]

---

acute and relevant analysis of the relationship between the 'natural' local factors and the 'artificial' aspects of national identification in developing countries, both in terms of contrasts and contradictions, see C. Geertz' contribution 'The Integrative Revolution', in Clifford Geertz (ed.), *Old Societies and New States*, New York 1963, pp. 105–57.

[1] Significantly many studies of this contradiction in the United States relate to the manner in which particular business interests are aligned against the institutionalized representatives of the Public. For sophisticated empirical treatment see Bauer, Pool, Dexter, *American Business and Public Policy*, op. cit.; Francis X. Sutton, *et al.*, *The American Business Creed*, Cambridge, Mass., 1956. A masterly theoretical statement of the problem is by Robert A. Dahl, 'A Critique of the Ruling Elite Model', *Am. Pol. Sc. Rev.* LII (1958), pp. 463–9. All these studies come up with the conclusion that there are no hard and fast lines between public authority and private interests. Instead the lines are constantly shifting over each issue; each side has varying fifth columnists or open supporters in the other 'camp', as formally delineated by institutional factors!

[2] For developed countries see above, ch. 5. For developing ones several examples are given by Ruth Schachter, 'Single-Party Systems in West Africa', *Am. Pol. Sc. Rev.*, LV (June 1961), pp. 294–307. Other African references, where this problem is ventilated, may be found in G. M. Carter and W. O. Brown, *Transition in Africa*, Boston, Mass., 1958; D. P. Ray (ed.), *The Political Economy of Contemporary Conflict*, Washington 1959; most recently and systematically in the excellent compendium by James S. Coleman and Carl G. Rosberg, *Political Parties and National Integration in Tropical Africa*, Berkeley and Los Angeles 1964.

The prevalence of this type of directional contradiction in all societies where local autonomy is substantial has not been studied enough. In the United States the congressional habit of speaking for a measure and then voting against it (or vice versa) is not a functional lacuna but a logical fulfilment of role expectation (representative versus delegate). The same problem exists in Norway, France and Italy, which seems to suggest that the problem is really one of interest articulation versus authority legitimizing rather than providing evidence either for over-vigorous grassroot influence on the centre, or for the notion that such examples are confined specifically to federal as opposed to unitary politics.

(3) Further, the construction and rapid build-up of inheritance parties initially make the distribution of charismatic and other authority or legitimacy *independent* of the constitutional structure of the state system eventually to be 'inherited'. This is a problem peculiar to inheritance situations and absent from Western 'input' parties, whose claim to convey legitimacy depends formally on their voting 'weight' within the polity, and more essentially on the extent to which they reflect the cleavages of the more differentiated political system or the less differentiated total social system. The inheritance situation presents substitution problems after the attainment of inheritance, during which constitutional rather than party norms are emphasized, and constitutional rather than party structures tend to carry legitimacy. Optimally, the two forms of mobilization, party and national-constitutional, are merged both evaluatively and structurally –from the top downwards (values-norms-collectivities; leadership-legislation-executive administration). But often the merger is confined to the top leadership and its own consensus over the composite or distinct roles involved, while the two structures develop rival interests and clusters of goals–with the party claiming not only a veteran's primacy but the guardianship of the ideological conscience, and the government structure claiming the legitimacy and efficiency of continuity. And at times the fused top leadership in fact helps to perpetuate this dualism for the all-important reason that party still provides a more efficient means of mobilization (logistic support and impetus) than the constitutional structure. The top leadership aims to get the best of both worlds by combining both aspects in some such capacity as 'supreme leader' or 'saviour' or Party Praesidium. In any case personal charisma, in Max Weber's terms, tends to become institutionalized or routinized in favour of one or other structure.[1] To symbolize the relations between party as dynamo and state bureaucracy as vehicle in the form of a permanent conflict is a useful means both of crystallizing and routinizing the function of supreme arbiter, as well as enhancing it.[2]

This situation is familiar from the classical post-revolutionary situation of Bolshevik Russia and Nazi Germany, as well as Italy and Spain. The party/state conflict was at the same time both inhibiting

[1] For a discussion of Ghana in this context, see W. G. Runciman, 'Charismatic Legitimacy and One-Party Rule in Ghana', *European Journal of Sociology*, IV, 1 (1963), pp. 148–65.
[2] This example provides one good illustration of the notion of social conflict as a stabilizing or routinizing factor, in accordance with the ideas of Simmel. See Lewis A. Coser, *The Functions of Social Conflict*, op. cit.

and productive. In each case the distinctive mobilizing potential of party was assigned the greatest weight and priority at moments of crisis: 1944–5 in Germany and Italy, when the previous, mainly national appeal was breaking down; 1932–3 in Germany, as well as 1917 in Russia, when a combined party-national appeal to mobilized commitment could not yet be made. But it might well be argued that maximum efficiency in a dichotomous, post-inheritance situation can be obtained only if there is a comprehensible difference – at least in emphasis – between the articulated value system of party and state. If these are fused entirely, then one cannot survive the defeat or popular dilapidation of the other. If, on the other hand, they operate in harmony rather than unison, and one can be played up more forcibly than the other for a time, then the leadership's options can be kept open and its possibilities of action are more flexible (for instance the modulation Socialism-Russia-Socialism-Russia from 1936–66 in the Soviet Union). In developing countries the natural tendency has been initially to try and merge the two forms of mobilization as fully as possible, though both Ghana, Guinea, the Ivory Coast and Tunisia as one-party states, India (Congress), Israel (Mapai) as well as the Ba'ath Socialists in Syria and Iraq as multi-party states are examples of partly contrived, partly – in the circumstances inevitable – separation. This identification of the two channels of mobilization as one and the same is, of course, part of the need to underpin a new, as yet precarious, form of institutionalized legitimacy; the attempt to provide a visible demonstration of a universal authority structure which developed societies have generally internalized in the form of 'the state', and hence take for granted. It is this that in the latter cases provides the basis of the universal perspectives within which cleavage or interest-specific mobilization may safely take place. Developing societies, on the other hand, lack the perspectives or internalization; hence the need for structural synonymity and ideological postulate.[1]

(4) Finally, political party mobilization has to provide an effective means of countering the particularistic, non-competitive, essentially self-sufficient or unadaptive social structure of many developing countries. It mixes achievement with ascription. It is this aspect

[1] This tendency towards initial 'collapse' of party mobilization into national mobilization, and increasing identification between them, is also one of the significant differences between inheritance and revolution from below. Sometimes they separate out again after independence. This may be taken as evidence of an inheritance situation moving in a more revolution-oriented direction. For an analysis of this see 'Inheritance', op. cit.

particularly that gives mass parties an advantage over *coteries* parties (i.e. patron parties or their more progressive siblings, modernizing oligarchies). For these latter cannot, with odd exceptions, offer structural alternatives to the old primary social structure, but merely a new central authority at the top and a source for new but barely internalized norms and values—political fishbones that stick in social throats. Such coteries can and do try to adapt the traditional social structure—and often get transformed and emasculated by it in turn (some of the reforming coteries in Arab countries, in Burma and in Thailand are examples). This 'logistic vacuum' leads even initially successful modernizing oligarchies, whose advent to power may already have been a reaction to the immobility and inefficiency of an inherited democratic political system which proved unable to articulate, and much less put into practice, development goals, to return sooner or later to political mobilization based on party or near-party structures (Egypt). We shall discuss this stalactite effect in greater detail later. As the example of India has shown, mere denunciation of caste, religious prejudice, etc., as unmodern and appeals against them are not enough, however authoritatively they may be made. Such barriers to development can be mobilized or transformed out of existence, not by unstructured charismatic movements like Gandhi-ism, but only by political mobilization.[1]

These considerations govern the structure and process of party mobilization in almost all developing countries. In nearly every case there will be a dominant party acting as a major vehicle of mobilization. It may be exclusive, in that no other political parties exist. It may merely be dominant; although other political parties exist both the legitimacy function and much of the interest-articulation function of the system are subsumed in the dominant party, and its competitors are identified as no more than marginal

---

[1] There have been four specific attempts at creating such mobilizing collectivities in Egypt since 1952: the Liberation Rally of 1953, the National Union which emerged from the 1956 constitution, the Arab Socialist Union of 1962, and most recently (1964) the Government Party—the latter being the most aptly or 'functionally' named. (See the discussion in the *Washington Post*, 9 February 1964.)

A rather vague definition of the specific instrumentality of party in nation-building—as one of several alternatives— is given by Foltz, 'Building the Newest Nations: Short-run Strategies and Long-run Problems', in Karl W. Deutsch and William J. Foltz (eds), *Nation Building*, New York 1963, especially p. 121. An intelligent discussion which emphasizes the therapeutic (under the guise of the word 'functional') benefits of *institutionalization* offered by parties rather than their mobilizing instrumentality is contained in Huntington, 'Political Development and Political Decay', op. cit.

mobilizers of sectional minority interests without any claim to legitimacy.

We cannot therefore expect to find a reproduction of European party systems in the multi-party situation of developing countries. The Western system, functionally analysed, postulates identical functions for different parties–though the full implications of this model are open to challenge.[1] The spatial model of party competition, as has been noted, carries implications of issue orientations which again are usually not relevant to developing countries. Finally the integrated cleavage model, in which political parties are based on interlocking and summated historical cleavages within the context of firmly established universals, can also not be applied adequately to the *nation trouvée*. Even those who dislike and attack the mobilizing and dictatorial tendencies of African single-party states recognize that the full implications of Western electoral systems and ideology cannot be met in Africa; political parties based on communal divisions would never succeed in persuading anybody to change their minds and would therefore make elections pointless.[2] All that would be required to settle the composition of the government on such a basis would be a communal census count. Instead the difference between single-party systems and multi-party systems in developing situations ceases to have the significance usually attributed to it by Western analysts, and represents essentially a variation of degree rather than of kind. The implications of this are discussed at greater length below in chapter XI.

As regards the structural aspect of exclusive or dominant inheritance parties, this can conceptually be divided into two categories; the centralizing model and the pluralistic model.[3]

1. *The centralizing model*–sometimes referred to as the revolutionary type of party–is the extreme attempt to provide a political structure of a new type. The basis of commitment departs radically from the existing cleavages in traditional systems. Structurally it resembles the mobilizing parties of the communist model; it is hierarchical, closely organized and extends into every geographical and functional area. It also adapts from the communist model a good deal of the notion of

[1] The most complete functional model is put forward by Almond. For a critique, see Nettl, 'Are Two-Party Systems Symmetrical?', *Parliamentary Affairs*, XIX, 2 (Spring 1966), pp. 218–23.

[2] See W. Arthur Lewis, *Politics in West Africa*, London 1966.

[3] The typology is adapted from that used in James S. Coleman and Carl G. Rosberg, *Political Parties and National Integration in Tropical Africa*. op. cit.

party autonomy; every attempt is made to crystallize separate and exclusive party channels of commitment and decision, which are then imposed as legitimate for society in general. Loyalty to the party has primacy over loyalty to other institutions and structures.

At the same time these structures, whose early development usually arises in connection with inheritance or independence, provide a link to more traditional components. They attempt to routinize the legitimacy of an individual leader, and are viewed as personal extensions of the charismatic leader's legitimacy. Instead of the tendency towards anonymity, which provides one of the bases of the communist experience, identification of party with individuals in developing countries is very high. Like communist parties there is also an attempt to articulate a philosophy as ideology–but again this is not mainly based on a corpus of objective historical truth as interpreted by the leadership, but is viewed rather as the product of the superior intelligence of the leader himself. The implications of these tendencies are examined in greater detail and with empirical examples in the next three chapters.

At the same time the fact that such parties attempt to counter-mobilize against existing cleavage structures and orientations does not prevent a reverse flow in the group composition of these parties; the tendency towards domination or colonization of the party structure, or at least important parts of it, by representatives of individual communities or groups of tribes, is well documented.[1] We have therefore to distinguish between the functional premise of counter-mobilization against divisive elements and orientations, and its empirical translation into single community domination within the single party. The domination of a single group or community under the umbrella of an anti-communal mobilization structure is frequently an important cause of direct communal counter-mobilization on the part of minorities who see all access to power denied.

[1] See particularly the three country studies in Coleman and Rosberg, *Political Parties*, op. cit.; Victor D. du Bois, 'Guinea', pp. 186–215; Thomas Hodgkin and Ruth Schachter Morgenthau, 'Mali', pp. 216–58; David E. Apter, 'Ghana', pp. 259–317. A similar tendency is indicated in the relative domination of the Uganda Peoples' Congress by the Nilotic peoples of Northern Uganda at the expense of the Bantu, and the domination of the Kenya African National Union by Bantu peoples at the expense of the Nilotic element. For a discussion relating to Uganda in the context of the attempt to develop national perspectives and mobilization, see David E. Apter, *The Political Kingdom in Uganda*, op. cit.; L. A. Fallers, 'Ideology and Culture in Uganda Nationalism', *American Anthropologist*, LXIII, pp. 677–86. Similar types of stratification can be observed in Algeria and Malaysia.

Nonetheless, whatever the facts of the situation, the legitimacy orientations of a centralizing mobilization structure can be symbolically wielded against directly community-oriented opponents, even though the single party may in fact, objectively speaking, represent the comination of one such community.

2. *The pluralistic model.* Single parties in many countries attempt to provide a more pragmatic or gradual approach to the creation of universals and the de-emphasis of communal and other cleavages. This is done by making the single party into a more or less competitive 'universe' within which various interests and cleavages can be represented – but within a common structure and without the institutionalization of divisive tendencies through elections. Where this type of single party exists it is held that the conflict of interests should, at an early stage of socio-political development, be confined to well-acculturated participants only, and should not involve the larger, peripheral sections of society. Examples of this type of party may be found in Tunisia, Kenya, Tanzania, Senegal, Ivory Coast and Cameroun.[1] This pattern also corresponds to dominant party structures as in India, Mexico and Malaysia.

These parties can therefore be viewed both as mobilizing and as reconciling.[2] Precisely because they attempt to keep conflict internal and to prevent it from 'leaking' out into an electoral context, these parties use elections as means of mobilization. They differ from the centralized parties mainly in that they do not easily articulate any philosophy. The role of the leader is more one of arbitration within the party than supreme philosopher or inspirer. Above all, such relatively pluralistically single parties provide a more balanced form of mobilization as between party and national-constitutional channels.

While this distinction between the two types of parties is useful, too much should not be made of it. Both types of parties are mobilization structures, both use the traditional form of legitimacy institutionalized in the leader, both identify the party as the main legitimacy structure of the *nation trouvée*. The difference between both of them on one hand, and Western systems on the other, is considerably

[1] See Coleman and Rosberg, pp. 16–185.

[2] To this extent the present classification differs from that of David E. Apter, who posits mobilization and reconciliation as opposite functions and concepts for the classification of political systems. See 'System, Process and Politics of Economic Development', in B. F. Hoselitz and William Moore, *Industrialization and Society*, The Hague 1963, pp. 135–58, and at greater length, *The Politics of Modernization.* Chicago 1966.

greater than the difference between the two types themselves. This may be seen from the very different function of elections in developing and developed countries, to which we have already referred briefly (note to chapter V). Thus both types of parties use elections not as a means of offering choices (except, in a few cases like Tanzania, between individuals representing the party) but as means of inspecting party structure, of mobilizing support, of creating symbolically integrative occasions for asserting the legitimacy of inheritance and the reality of the nation, etc. The possibilities of articulation by the electorate consists not of expressing interests, nor of legitimizing alternative elites, but in providing a sounding board for opinions, wishes and interests which will enable the party to adjust (or not to adjust) its future policies. Elections are thus a form of two-way communication rather than an economic market situation of offer and purchase. Finally elections provide a means of making available audiences for a dramatic performance. Because of the perceived solemnity of electoral occasions, imported from the West but without the corresponding emphasis on electoral legitimacy, the electoral audiences may be expected to be in a particularly receptive frame of mind. Naturally this works both ways; if the performance is disappointing a great deal of legitimacy of a consummatory kind may be lost–as the Nigerian elections of 1964–5 showed clearly. In this context, therefore, single parties in developing countries can be viewed as major agents of political culture production.

Moreover the tendency towards centralizing or pluralistic single parties is not necessarily stable. In Uganda Obote's constitutional coup of 1966 represents a move towards a greater tendency of centralization, as does the official KANU reaction to the Oginga revolt in Kenya. At the same time the recent tendency in Tanzania has been for a stronger accent on reconciliation and less on centralization. Indeed, the evolution of party attitudes and structures as between these two types cannot really be discussed in terms of internal factors only; it depends also on the balance between party and national-constitutional channels of mobilization, and the relationship or conflict of the relevant structures.

The value system of dissociation following upon inheritance provides important possibilities of mobilization which can often be developed through the constitutional structure. These, it should be noted, are not vested exclusively in institutions alone, but are often activated or at least enhanced by an inheritance party structure. The most effective type of inheritance mobilization is therefore based on a combination of constitutional and inheritance–party structures.[1] In those countries, however, where relatively divisive multi-party systems exist, or where no mobilizing party structure has developed, the alternative constitutional means will to that extent be emphasized more strongly (India, Pakistan, Egypt, Indonesia). These constitutional means of mobilization can be classified for purposes of analysis into two main categories.

2. *National Constitutional Mobilization*

a. *Economic Planning*

We are not here primarily concerned with the economic aspects of development planning but with the socio-political ones, especially in the context of mobilization. The relationship between *purposive* economic development and national integration has been strongly stressed both in the academic literature as well as in the writings of political justification (or explanation) by leaders and participants. As such this focus already represents a considerable shift and advance from the conceptual commitment to a causal, almost automatic, relationship between national autonomy and industrialization; national independence made possible industrial growth, hence if a country was independent, it was bound to develop industrially towards take-off and maturity, and therefore the most certain path to industrialization was national independence.[2] The new emphasis is on

[1] This analysis may be contrasted with the rather crude dichotomy (or does he mean polarity, as his chart indicates?) between Socialism and Nationalism as alternatives to mobilization, given by David E. Apter, in *Ideology and Discontent*, op. cit., pp. 23–30, especially p. 23. Cf. John H. Kautsky, 'An Essay in the Politics of Development', in Kautsky (ed.), *Political Change in Underdeveloped Countries*, New York 1962, pp. 30–90, who develops a more detailed version of the same argument. As the present analysis attempts to show, the distinction between Socialism and Nationalism is meaningless in the context of developing countries, and represents another confusing conceptual importation from the situation of the developed West to the entirely different one of developing countries.

[2] One of the classic statements of the relationship between nationalism and industrialization in the developed West is Alfred Cobban, *National Self-Determination*, Chicago 1944; cf. also E. H. Carr (ed.), *Nationalism: An RIIA Report*, London 1939, reprinted 1963. A recent study which specifically attempts to relate political change in the national states of the developed West to the imperatives of economic development is the series of case studies by Robert T. Holt and John E. Turner, *The Political Basis of Economic Development: An Exploration in Comparative Political Analysis*, London/New York 1966. The trendsetting discussion of the problem as it applies to the contemporary Third World may be found in B. F. Hoselitz (ed.), *The progress of Underdeveloped Areas*, Chicago 1952 (particularly essays by Gershenkron and Linton). One of the best definitions of the relationship is by K. Davis 'Social and Democratic Aspects of Economic Development in India', in S.

the planning and manipulation of growth. As with the relationship between national independence and 'natural' economic growth, there are two alternative ways of arranging the priorities; those who assign primacy to the right socio-political conditions and derive the possibility and analysis of planned economic development from them, and those who give conceptual priority to economic planning and chronological priority to industrialization, and then derive socio-political change from economic change in both a conceptual and a chronological sense.[1]

Kuznets, W. E. Moore and J. J. Spengler (eds), *Economic Growth: Brazil, India, Japan*, Durham (North Carolina) 1955, p. 294; cf. also the other essays in this volume. Reference should also be made to K. H. Silvert, *Expectant Peoples: Nationalism and Development*, New York 1964; the most recent and sophisticated analysis of the interplay between national aspirations and economic development, largely based on Latin American experience. This work is particularly valuable in that it gives no hostages to any *ab ovo* economic priorities, and does not attempt to impose economistic norms on recalcitrant socio-political data or problems.

A discussion of the *retarding* effects of nationalism on economic growth, suggesting a somewhat catholic interpretation of nationalism and representative of a more economistic approach to development problems, is in B. F. Hoselitz, 'Non-Economic Barriers to Economic Development', *Economic Development and Cultural Change*, I, 1, pp. 8–21; J. Van der Kroef, ibid., IV, 2, pp. 116–33. Conversely it has been argued, with perhaps more justification, that industrialization can hinder or retard integration, and hence be objectively dysfunctional to nationalism. For this argument in a succinct form, see Mancur Olson, Jnr., 'Rapid Growth as a Destabilizing Force', *Journal of Economic History*, XXVII (December 1963), pp. 529–52. The only attempt to destroy completely the connection between nationalism and economic development is Elie Kedourie, *Nationalism*, second revised edition, London 1961, an argument based on the extraordinary assertion that nationalism is merely the brainchild of a few overheated intellectuals.

There is also a recent attempt to evolve, if not yet a political theory of economic development, at least an economists' theory of the political factors in such development. This analyses the consequences of autarchic do-it-yourself policies in terms of comparative cost theory. See Harry G. Johnson, 'A Theoretical Model of Economic Nationalism in New and Developing States', *Political Science Quarterly*, LXXX, 2 (June 1965), pp. 169–85. The important core definition of such economic nationalism is that it is more concerned with redistribution towards the middle class or elite than with net growth. This very vital point, which challenges the whole framework of economic rationality postulated by development economics, was first elaborated by Albert Breton, 'The Economics of Nationalism', *Journal of Political Economy*, LXXII (1964), pp. 376–86.

For an extensive reference to the literature see Neil J. Smelser, 'Mechanisms of Change and Adjustment to Change', in B. F. Hoselitz and W. E. Moore, *Industrialization and Society*, Paris/The Hague (Unesco) 1963, pp. 49–54.

[1] The 'state of the discipline' with regard to the second alternative, where the socio-political consequences of development in emerging countries are at issue, can most readily be found in Hoselitz and Moore, *Industrialization and Society*, op. cit. Cf. also W. E. Moore and A. S. Feldman, *Labor Commitment and Social*

Though this is already a great step forward from the past of mutual ignorance and ignoring referred to in chapter I, the present analysis attempts to go farther still. Instead of presenting alternative disciplinary and conceptual approaches, it is suggested that both orders of priority represent correct possible analyses of empirical situations; the case of economic development preceding and causing socio-political change represents the typical historical situation of the West, the case of socio-political change and priorities preceding and in turn bringing about economic development represents the more recent historical situation of Communist countries and the current needs of the Third World. Hence it is in this context of socio-political priority that developmental planning will be discussed – not in the terms of economists measuring its failures and successes by economic standards, but as instruments of socio-political change towards a situation that may then make industrialization and economic development possible.

As regards economic planning, therefore, we are dealing with the emergence of goals which, if not always different from those of the West, are at least differently emphasized from those which the West intended to leave as its bequest. The democratic politics which are seen in the West as a value-oriented *end* now tend to become merely the first and possibly handiest means to the achievement of certain *purposes* – to be discarded in case of strain between ends and means,

---

Change in Developing Areas, New York 1960. The argument for the first case is made by a number of economists who have looked to an adjustment in the polity, and in politics, as a necessary *precondition* for economic development. This may be described as a notion of political development which, though still related to economic development, precedes it in terms of time. For this see Paul A. Baran, *The Political Economy of Growth*, 1957, Norman S. Buchanan and Howard S. Ellis, *Approaches to Economic Development*, New York 1955; Benjamin Higgins, *Economic Development: Principles, Problems and Policies*, New York 1959. Cf. discussion and literature cited in Malenbaum, *World Politics*, op. cit.

The methodological implications of these two approaches are interesting, since they relate directly to the problem of catchment areas discussed in chapter I. Contrary to what might be supposed, economists are more likely to assign temporal and even conceptual priority to socio-political factors; these are the independent variables, or catchment area, through delimitation and ordering of which an analysis of the dependent variable, the heartland of the discipline, can then be undertaken with the appropriate and sharpened tools. Similarly political scientists will give temporal and possibly conceptual priority to the factors of economic change; these then enable socio-political effects to be discussed. Both approaches demand the 'right' preconditions from the 'other' disciplines – and, of course, the 'other' social subsystems – without which their analysis cannot begin. Accordingly neither need question the status or validity of the other.

or if they do not quickly prove instrumental. The general misunderstanding of democracy as a means to development rather than an end unto itself is one of the oddest and most significant myths in the recent dialogue between the developed and developing world–the West was democratic and *is* developed, therefore the one is viewed as leading to the other. This nonsense is encouraged by the work of empirical social scientists in the general context of 'Industrialization and Democracy': an apparent synthesis on one hand of Marxist determinism, with its breakdown of historical development into distinct stages, and the transformation of the correlation of Protestant ethic with capitalist development which locates economic goals in the value system–a transformation oversimply ascribed *in toto* to Weber.[1]

This type of approach is strongly in evidence in the current interpretation of development capabilities in terms of personality structures–methodologically more directly Weberian than the older democracy-development equation.[2] What seems to have escaped notice is that this type of analysis resembles, in the context of psychology, the *laissez-faire* economics of, say, Ricardo. The word 'society' becomes merely the sum total of individual achievements– without any sense of community; an interpretation already familiar. The role of politics becomes essentially negative, to remove obstacles, etc. Incidentally it is also worth noting that this analysis of economic

[1] The problem of determinism versus hard facts in the interpretation of economic change is well illustrated by the debate about living standards in the middle period of the English Industrial Revolution. See W. Woodruff, 'Capitalism and the Historians: A Contribution to the Discussion on the Industrial Revolution in England', *Journal of Economic History*, XVI, 1 (1956), pp. 1–17; R. M. Hartwell, 'Interpretations of the Industrial Revolution in England: A Methodological Enquiry', ibid., XIX (1959), pp. 229–49; E. J. Hobsbawm, 'The British Standard of Living, 1790–1850', *Economic History Review*, X, 1 (1957), pp. 46–69; S. Pollard, 'Investment, Consumption and the Industrial Revolution', ibid., XI, 2 (1958), pp. 215–27; R. M. Hartwell, 'The Rising Standard of Living in England, 1800–1850', ibid., XIII, 3 (1961), pp. 397–417; E. J. Hobsbawm and R. M. Hartwell, 'The Standard of Living During the Industrial Revolution: A Discussion, XVI, 1 (1963); A. J. Taylor, 'Progress and Poverty in Britain, 1780–1850: A Reappraisal', *History*, XLV (1960), pp. 16–31.

The most recent treatment of the problem is in E. P. Thompson, *The Making of the English Working Class*, London 1964.

[2] See for instance David C. McClelland, *The Achieving Society*, New York 1963; also McClelland, 'The Achievement Motive in Economic Growth', Hoselitz and Moore, op. cit., particularly p. 83. An older appraisal of entrepreneurial behaviour as much more bureaucratic is George Katona, *The Psychological Analysis of Economic Behavior*, New York 1951. It is noticeable that this work is now quite unjustifiably out of fashion and is hardly ever cited in any of the social and psychological literature on entrepreneurial behaviour.

change based on *n* Achievement, anchored as it is in the psychological behaviour patterns of individuals, has therefore to reintroduce the necessary notion of social collectivity by using Riesman's 'other-directedness' as a substitute for the missing function of community.

But the problem is not solved by the introduction of a piece of handy jargon about different value systems and different goals. Just as some of the strange mutations of Western politics tell us interesting things not only about the adapters but about the tools, so does an examination of an inherited and adapted value system shed much light on the original. It has for instance been shown convincingly that the modern welfare state is functionally and closely correlated to the contemporary form of nationalism of which neutralism is merely the acutest expression.[1] Thus for all their internal differences, developing and developed countries act in certain significant ways as blocs in the international field, which indicates that they share certain important 'bloc' values. For instance, the modern tendency for associations is between likes (European Common Market, Latin America and Central American Common Markets) instead of between unlikes (Empires, Commonwealth); this is the defensive aspect of welfare nationalism (the French community is the brilliantly 'old-fashioned' exception). This tendency also explains the weakness of military pacts like SEATO and CENTO as opposed to NATO, the strains in Comecon, as well as the ineffectualness of GATT.[2] In pseudo-Leninist but effective jargon: *nationalism is neutralism in the age of*

[1] See, for instance, Gunnar Myrdal, *An International Economy, Problems and Prospects*, London 1956 and *Beyond the Welfare State*, London 1960; also *Economic Theory and Underdeveloped Regions*, London 1957.

[2] An academic reflection of this empirical congruence-seeking may be found in recent developments in the sociology of international relations. The transition from empire to bloc may be seen as a transition from one kind of constraint (power and the symbols of gold-backed credit) to another (influence based on the credit of common knowledge and common expressive function). This appears to correspond, at least chronologically, to the transition from an approach to international relations based on diplomacy, political factors and deterrence analysis to one positing the possibility of an international social system. An analysis which brilliantly pioneers the exploitation of these new factors is Karl W. Deutsch, S. A. Burrell *et al.* (eds), *Political Community and the North Atlantic Area*, Princeton 1957. Cf. the somewhat sour reaction of a traditional political specialist defending, moreover, the sacrosanct British field of federalism as a subject of study: A. H. Birch, 'Approaches to the Study of Federalism', *Political Studies*, XIV, 1 (February 1966), pp. 15–33. For a discussion of both methodological and existential aspects of this problem see Amitai Etzioni, 'The Epigenesis of Political Communities at the International Level', *American Journal of Sociology*, LXVIII (1963), pp. 407–21. The general trend and much of the literature is surveyed in Nettl and Robertson, 'Modernization and International Systems', op. cit.

imperialism. Beneath the surface of a continuing commitment to orthodox political democracy, great changes have been wrought in the real processes of participation and decision-making in the West by an increasing orientation to welfare-state nationalism; pressure groups of producers as against consumers, bureaucracies growing in size and importance, emasculation of representative assemblies – above all the realignment of East versus West into North (rich) against South (poor). Of course the process of change in the value system of advanced societies has been gradual rather than abrupt, masked by the conservative ideology which inhibits the recognition of change and by the retention of symbols which are no more than shorthand based on a common stock of knowledge usually acquired in the past. In emerging countries this formidable apparatus of conservatism built into the political and economic processes does not exist; both are new. The adaptation of Western-type development goals has therefore been more direct, more brutal and much easier to study. Nonetheless the basic notion of development is a Western concept; it would be an error to assume that the developmental values system of each new nation has arisen spontaneously or autonomously.

Electoral democracy in the West is based on a commitment to values which include the maintenance of democratic means as well as the attainment of welfare ends. Yet it has been criticised for not offering any adequate solution for the efficient achievement of both effective representation and the provision of adequate welfare services. In England we hear a good deal today about the difficulty of combining the commitment to worthwhile electoral choices with the growth of the demands, or at least alleged demands, on the state, and the consequent increase in bureaucratic decision-making together with the growth of the power of the executive at the expense of the representative legislature.[1] But these are the criticisms of academic observers; the system continues to enjoy the legitimacy accorded by participants who are satisfied both with the growing provision of welfare and with the unchanging maintenance of competitive as well as representative democracy. Visible change in terms of increasing welfare is thus combined with the symbols of changeless electoral

[1] Apart from the arguments of Bernard Crick, *The Reform of Parliament*, op. cit., the British situation has recently been summarized concisely by H. V. Wiseman, *Parliament and the Executive*, London 1966. Cf. also David Coombes, *The Member of Parliament and the Administration*, London 1966, for a case study of parliamentary control of the executive as exercised or not exercised by one particular committee – that on Nationalized Industries.

democracy–the maintenance of the *status quo*. The emerging value systems of developing countries have to find more dynamic means of attaining their goals: international status and prestige, domestic development for national integration and for the possession of visible items of modernity. The developmental value system becomes itself a means of political mobilization, so that the different levels of values, goals and norms become dedifferentiated or compressed. For this purpose a value system needs sharply focused reference points, hence much symbolic crystallization, in order to become an 'actionable' pattern of goals and norms. The 'democratic' West provides few recent and successful examples of such mobilizational value systems. The French Revolution is perhaps the last great one, the failure of German nineteenth-century Liberalism the last unsuccessful one. The model of a value system being used expressly as a means of political mobilization in terms of an official ideology comes to developing countries mainly from the Soviet Union. Perhaps the most important import from Russia is not after all the single monolithic party as the keeper of society's conscience–which is neither peculiar to the Soviet Union nor applicable in all developing countries–but the use of the economic plan as a means both of building a developmental value system and as a framework for mobilizing commitment. Planning as part of the value system serves the function of ideological control, while planning as means of mobilization provides a structure of commitment, information and communication. We can examine these functions in turn.

i. *The Plan as Means of Ideological Control*

Economic planning of the Soviet or near-Soviet type is an excellent way of articulating values and aligning goals and even norms tightly to values. Soviet planners have always been most concerned with ensuring that their sector expectations are clearly made to relate to the total plan, so that individual failures can be made to symbolize the full brunt of endangering the collective whole–a highly political whole. Countries like Egypt, Ghana and Algeria have adopted this technique, with all its draconian sanctions for economic sabotage– indeed they have gone one better by using economic sabotage as a means of political pressure on groups and individuals with which the Soviet Union usually deals politically (though not always, e.g. Jews, 'parasitic' artists, etc.). We need only compare the political destruction of the capital- and property-owning middle classes in Eastern Europe after the war, often on the grounds of collaboration with, or support for, Fascist and Nazi regimes, with the piecemeal economic expropriation of capitalists in Egypt, Iraq and Indonesia, community by community. Only when all the foreigners had been eliminated did the Egyptian government come to deal with Lebanese, Syrians and Copts, and finally Arab Egyptians. What we have here is nothing less than the 'economicization' of general norms; as in the Soviet Union the language and relevance of a wide area of norms becomes economic, so that the whole socio-political cosmos tends at one stage to become primarily economic. The *function*, however, remains political. This emphasis is accompanied by a corresponding upgrading in status for those closely involved in making plans (planners, economists), those fulfilling them (engineers, managers, especially Stakhanovites) and above all those *enforcing* them (control commissions generally).[1] Economists usually divide planning into *indicative* (Western type, particularly French) and *allocational* (Soviet Union). Once the vital political functions of planning are taken into account, however, this categorization loses its aptness. Instead the categories *distributive* (including both indicative and allocational in a primarily economic sense) and *value-oriented* (the objectification of socio-political norms and values in economic terms) may appear more appropriate for present purposes. Thus instead of classifying planning in accordance with its *form or manner or application*, we would classify it according to its *social relevance or saliency*.

It is worth noting that Soviet analysts sometimes see the political mobilization possibilities of planning—even of the non-Soviet variety —more clearly than Western writers, fragmented as the latter are into the separate, often non-communicating disciplines of economics, sociology and politics.[2] Soviet writing has been much helped by the

[1] None of the research on Egyptian or Indian bureaucracies since independence with which I am familiar seems to stress this important point. It is for instance noticeable that both in India and Egypt the Revenue authorities have benefited relatively more than most from upward mobility in status and income. In New Delhi the Revenue authorities are almost as sacrosanct as the British Inland Revenue Department. With regard to planners the point has been made somewhat more adequately. It is perhaps significant that in many developing countries planners enjoy relatively greater security than in the Soviet Union; Indian and Egyptian planners for instance show an extraordinary tenacity for personal survival in office.

[2] We may accordingly need a self-conscious discipline of political economy which would after all be no more than a return to a previous, less differentiated, past. There are still several Chairs of Political Economy in England but only one genuinely and self-consciously qualified incumbent, Alec Nove in Glasgow. Cf. his 'Hirschman, "Reform-Mongering" and Development Economics', in *Scottish Journal of Political Economy*, XI, 1 (February 1964), pp. 25–31.

official (if still hesitant) blessing bestowed on so-called anti-imperial-ist National Democracies, with their non-capitalist but also non-Soviet methods of planning and state enterprise.[1] It should perhaps be stressed that for purposes of the present analysis the difference between Soviet and, say, Cuban, Algerian and Egyptian planning relates to their socio-political premises and consequences, not to any criteria of economic effectiveness. These different criteria will lead to very different judgements of merit. Nor is it proposed to evaluate the individual plans of different developing countries according to either set of criteria. The main purpose here is to sketch out socio-political mobilization criteria of a structural kind according to which empirical evaluations might be attempted. What the examples cited here have in common is that they are all value-oriented instruments of social and political mobilization. The fact that the state or nation for which they mobilize may be Socialist, National-Democratic or plain incapable of any such classification is irrelevant.

ii. *The Plan as a Means of Socio-political Communication*

Planning may in addition provide a means of communication of a uniquely universal kind in many emerging societies. Most imme-diately there is the provision of a neutral jargon or cluster of symbols which helps to overcome language barriers – both in kind and in level of sophistication.[2] The influence of the Indian plans in socializing sectors of the population into universal-national perspectives, though little studied, have probably been considerable. And apart from welding potentially rival social structures into the polity (business, unions, etc.), planning has helped to carry the concept of government into areas hitherto at the margin of acculturation.[3] Planning thus affects both the quality and the extent of acculturation.[4] As suggested

[1] For this see particularly N. P. Shmelev, 'Bourgeois Economists on the Role of the Public Sector in Underdeveloped Countries', *Mirovaya Ekonomika i Mezhdunarodniye Otnosheniya* (Moscow) No. 4 (1962), pp. 87–91, and Shmelev, *Idiologiya imperializma i problemy slaborazvitikh stran*, Moscow 1962; also M. S. Dzhumusov, *O nekapitalisticheskom puti razvitiya*, Moscow 1963.

[2] Cf. in this connection the rather interesting plea for technical jargon as a means of overcoming the language disabilities of a strong minority of foreign refugee scholars in the United States put forward by Deutsch, 'On Models', op. cit., pp. 29–30 (in draft).

[3] Some of the aspects of this form of acculturation are discussed, at an anthropological level of very primitive contact, by E. M. Chilver and P. M. Kaberry, 'From Tribute to Tax in a Tikar Chiefdom', in Immanuel Wallerstein (ed.), *Social Change: The Colonial Situation*, London 1966. Cf. also L. A. Fallers, 'The Predicament of the Modern African Chief: An Instance from Uganda', in the same volume.

[4] One interesting and little highlighted socializing aspect of planning is that

earlier in chapter II, the extent of political culture in developing countries should be measured, not by any amount of voting at elections, nor yet by the efficacy with which a limited metropolitan elite may operate any system, but by the view of government at the social periphery along the progression from total ignorance–pre-ordained tyrant–active authority–respondent to normative involvement. Planning as an instrument of political mobilization tends to drive the peripheral members of the polity farther along this continuum.

This function of increasing communication offered by economic planning will naturally be greatly enhanced in so far as there is participation in making as well as carrying out the plans. The effectiveness of such participation may to a considerable extent prove to be a secondary consideration; the sense of participation provides the means of communication. It is in this light that the elaborate mechanism of formal discussion of plans in the Soviet Union, their despatch downwards for discussion and then back up the party and Soviet administrative hierarchy, should be considered. This too is one of the important latent functions of the much despised *panchayati raj* in India. Critics of the economic inadequacy of Chinese plans for rural industrialization–'walking on two legs'–often tend to ignore their enormous potential for socio-political communication with the most 'backward' areas of the country. There is less excuse for this ignorance as regards China in view of the fact that the Chinese leadership is quite specific about the multi-functionality of its policies and their related social structures.[1] This is in part what the

---

it provides important new criteria of legitimacy–not in a Soviet sense of plan-fulfilment, but by making businessmen adopt new and sometimes apparently disadvantageous norms. It can for instance be argued that the prevailing, and officially encouraged, tendency for Indian firms to seek foreign associates is not only a means of importing foreign capital and technical knowhow (and proving that one has done so) but of gaining respectability–and with it security from nationalization, penal regulation and/or taxation–in the eyes of government. Foreign associates, instead of being kept discreetly in the background as an inescapable technical necessity, are as a rule paraded in Delhi with discreet pride. On the implications of this see also Michael Kidron, *Foreign Investments in India*, London 1965.

[1] For a perceptive economist's view nonetheless divorced from these wider perspectives, see Yuan-Li Wu, *The Economy of Communist China*, New York 1965. An analysis of the policy of deliberate non-specificity in Communist China, especially with regard to the army, is by Ellis Joffe, *Party and Army: Professionalism and Political Control in the Chinese Officer Corps 1949–1964*, Cambridge (Mass.) 1965. The general ideological implications are acutely analysed in H. F. Shurmann, *Ideology and Organization in Communist China*, Berkeley/Los Angeles 1965.

whole 'cultural' revolution of 1966 was about. Finally, even in cases of one-way communication only, like Egypt and Algeria, part of the communication function is achieved through wide publicity and visits to villages for purposes of personal and verbal explanation.

iii. *The Plan as Symbol of Legitimacy*

Planning, particularly as adapted by developing countries, greatly enhances audience participation in the political show. We shall later examine in greater detail the important component of this aspect of participation in the creation of legitimacy in developing countries, in contrast to the Western notions of electoral participation as supplying evidence of legitimacy. This aspect obviously affects the pattern of planning in certain definable directions; the emphasis will be on the spectacular and concentrated rather than on the derivatively instru-mental and dispersed. Such emphasis on the spectacular has many political advantages of participation which remain lost on foreign economic advisers. Certain dramatic devices seem to have gained the universal approval of fashion–steelworks, jet airlines, large public buildings in the capital. What is not generally known is that much of this audience potential of planning was also developed in the Soviet Union (the Dnepr dam, the Moscow Underground and, recently and most spectacularly, the Soviet space programme). It is interesting in this context to note the extent to which attacks on liberal writers before and during the Twenty-third Party Congress in March 1966 were buttressed by pointing to Soviet space achievements as evidence of an enlightened educational system. Where planning comes in is that these manifestation do not just happen, they are programmed and consequently become part of the legitimacy of a planned society.

The fact that planning in developing countries takes place in conditions of greater or lesser audience participation affects the impact very considerably. Most obviously plans tend to be heavily urban; rural and agricultural rehabilitation, necessarily dispersed and inefficient in terms of socio-political participatory response, remains relatively neglected. Here may be found another important distinc-tion between Western and Third World plans. The former tend to be evaluated in terms of *figures*, and remain an experts' preserve– twenty years of trying to interest the British public in even the crudest economic statistics like Trade Gap figures provide a substan-tial monument to public disinterest. Third World Plans on the contrary are poor on figures, even poorer on matching target figures with achievement–'a statistical nightmare', in the words of one development economist – but achieve their impact, both in terms of target and achievement, through more obvious, prestige-oriented symbols. Only the Soviet Union has perhaps succeeded in marrying the two types of symbols into a combined epistemology of planning, but it has taken a brutal fifty years to do it.

iv. *The Plan as Means of Role Recruitment*

Finally, planning provides a means of socialization into a variety of modern political and bureaucratic roles and techniques. For one thing it facilitates the mobilization of economic interest groups with a speed not to be achieved in orthodox capitalist societies, where they are more likely to 'mobilize' defensively on a class or sector basis, institutionalized initially through the political process and separating out from it only to the extent that it fails to accommodate them adequately. One of the first criteria of effective mobilization is a precise focus of impact – clearly provided by government agencies in planning economies. In India, for instance, the incipient and still embryonic transformation of age-old, essentially *hierarchical* and *non-competitive* castes into *interchangeable* and *competitive* caste associations is not merely some vague adjunct of economic development, but a direct consequence of (*a*) the specifically political acculturation of growing sectors of society since independence (which provides the vehicle), and (*b*) the planning process (which provides much of the incentive). This hierarchy-competition variable, which is an operationalized reflection of the familiar ascription-achievement pattern of values, is essential tool to the study of India; without it any discussion of caste, however extensive and otherwise perceptive, will explain nothing.[1] For another thing planning can carry the experience of a choice/allocation/implementation technology down to peripheral levels which remain untouched by the more orthodox

[1] One of the best analyses of these caste functions and changes is F. G. Bailey, 'Closed Social Stratification in India', *European Journal of Sociology*, IV, 1 (1963), pp. 107–41; see also at greater length his earlier *Caste and the Economic Frontier*, Manchester 1957. There is considerable literature on the transformation of the caste structure into political-economic interest groups – an area of research particularly conducive to the pressures of pluralistic determinism which move many American researchers into problems of development. See for instance Lloyd I. and Susanne Holber Rudolph, 'The Political Role of India's Caste Associations', *Pacific Affairs*, XXXIII (March 1960), pp. 5–22; Lloyd I. Rudolph, 'The Modernity of Tradition: The Democratic Incarnation of Caste in India', *Am. Pol. Sc. Rev.*, LIX (December 1965), pp. 975–89. Cf. also Myron Weiner, *The Politics of Scarcity: Public Pressure and Political Response in India*, Chicago 1962. A. H. Hanson, *The Process of Planning*, op. cit., chapter VII, also gives an account of the effect of planning on caste structure and vice versa.

forms of political mobilization. Thus *panchayati raj*, in the immortal words of an advertisement for a lavatory disinfectant, reaches down to rural nooks and crannies where neither the Congress nor the Communist brush have always reached effectively. Caste and sub-caste provide partly vehicles and partly resistant insulations, without by any means stifling the countervailing and wider functions of mobilization entailed by the system of 'planning from below'.[1]

It will be obvious that, as with the Soviet model, economic planning techniques in developing countries should at least be con-sidered in the context of political purposes, or at least functions, as well as economic ones.[2] This may not have been intended in the Soviet Union—though with the emphasis on economic action and priorities which is so significant for Marxism, and which was institutionalized in turn by the necessarily practical simplifiers who implemented Marxism in the Soviet Union, it was probably inevit-able. But with the emergence of a value system in which a rather special kind of economic development figures large, the predominance of economic *techniques* even for political and social *purposes* in developing countries appears a more logical relationship. Dare we perhaps adapt Eckstein's theory of social/political 'fit' in a functional direction by postulating that the priority ordering of goals as between income (economics), status (sociology) and power (politics) must also govern the orientation towards primary means? In other words, if the goals are economic (or social) the means of achievement should most efficaciously be oriented towards the relevant techniques, so that the necessary goal attainment functions will be carried out by economic

[1] For one study of how local distribution of resources was undertaken and the caste responses to them, see Adrian C. Mayer, 'Some Political Implications of Community Development in India', *European Journal of Sociology*, IV, 1 (1963), pp. 86–106. See also Baldev Raj Nayar, 'Community Development Programme; Its Political Impact', [Bombay] *Economic Weekly*, 17th September 1960. Hanson, op. cit., preoccupied with the contradiction between orthodox democracy on the one hand and economic efficiency on the other, condemns *panchayati raj* far too severely in my opinion.

[2] For a good general discussion of state intervention in a developing economy with a somewhat different approach, see Alexander Eckstein, 'Individualism and the Role of the State in Economic Growth', *Economic Development and Cultural Change*, VI, 2 (January 1958), pp. 81–99. The author stresses the 'last resort' function of the state in making up for deficiencies in skills, factor endowment, time, social facilities. For him not mobilization but state inter-vention is the extraneous balancing factor. However, in typical situations of development today the notion of state intervention by itself explains little; the notion of the state as such is an unjustified Hegelianism since the state itself has neither tradition nor authority.

(or social) means. This, if correct, would seem to suggest that the contraction or expansion of any system range in society is governed by the ordering of goals, though the density of the system may in turn be more a matter of cultural style, not necessarily moving in the same direction.[1]

Another conclusion is that our whole conceptual framework of the politics of development may need revising. David Apter has addressed himself specifically to this problem, and his attempt at classification has probably been the most successful to date.[2] His three main categories are: *mobilization, modernizing autocracy, reconciliation.* The latter is clearly 'best'–India approximates to it most closely. But there is some difficulty in applying these concepts in practice– is the Indian Civil Service not a modernizing autocracy? is [mobilized] reconciliation and balance not as effective in Indonesia, in spite of its violence, as [consensual] reconciliation in India? (Cf. above, pp. 228–31, with regard to parties.) The deeply ingrained preoccupation of Western social scientists with non-violent change, and the deprecation and downgrading of violence, are common to otherwise even the most divergent approaches; few are even prepared to accommodate it as a normal style of political behaviour but only as extreme or deviant.[3] We shall have to deal with this problem at greater length in the discussion of legitimacy in the next chapter. Moreover Apter offers the *option* of mobilization as one of several alternatives, whereas everything argued so far here is intended to show the *inevitability* of mobilization; the variables are concerned with extent, structure and process. Electoral democracy as generally understood in the West is *not* always highly efficient in this regard– for reasons of structural and processual fusion and de-emphasis; but in no sense does it appear to be an *alternative* to mobilization. Even in India mobilization is essential, and planning (among other means) helps to bring it about. 'Extensive self-discipline, civic devotion' etc.

[1] Cf. the analysis of two-tier social stratification in South America with the lower tier using status and power to obtain income, and the upper tier using income to attain power and status, in Richard N. Adams, 'Dual Sectors . . .' op. cit.

[2] 'System, Process and the Politics of Economic Development', in B. F. Hoselitz and W. E. Moore, *Industrialization and Society*, The Hague, 1963, pp. 135–58. Cf. also Apter's fuller and more systematic elaboration of his basic classifications, with detailed discussion of many empirical examples of developing countries, in *The Politics of Modernization*, Chicago 1966. In spite of the reservations about Apter's categories expressed here, this book undoubtedly represents the most specific and comprehensive discussion of the problems of political modernization at present available.

[3] But cf. Spiro, 'Comparative Politics', op. cit., as an honourable exception.

−the qualities required for an efficient reconciliation system−do not grow on trees. Apter's analysis, however neutral and scientific in intention, may nonetheless lead in the last resort to the explanation of shortfall from desirable democratic norms by lamenting inadequate social personality once more.[1]

b. *National Integration*

This is the other essential form of Third World mobilization. Its reference points, symbols and selection of goals, in fact the whole content of modern nationalism, are relevant here (however interesting the evidence of the substantial literature on the subject) only in so far as it is a means of mobilization, and/or concerns factors of efficiency.

In the first place national-constitutional mobilization emphasizes all the old-fashioned tenets of national identity which the West now takes largely for granted; internalization there is such that symbols only are needed for occasional reference. In developing countries this 'taking for granted' notion also exists but as a specific assertion which often does not correspond to the facts; we have here an interesting use of myth by backward projection. In colonial situations the assertion of national identity, even of national existence, is not so much a matter of a desirable *future*, but a case of asserting historical and abstract rights of which the country concerned has in the [recent] past been deprived by the foreign colonial power. African leaders, for instance, see evidence of this in the colonial powers' (in this case British) preoccupation with local administration as opposed to central government−and of course in the whole divisive technique of indirect rule.[2] But the basic justification or 'proof' of national existence is not so much history (though it *is* history wherever possible, which is not often), but morality−and morality by liberal as well as Marxist standards.[3] Thus we have the assertion of a logical/legal right in the form of an historical one. This can be compared with the Zionist arguments for the recreation of Israel

[1] Cf. Ann Ruth Willner, 'The Underdeveloped Study of Political Development', op. cit.

[2] See Kenneth Kaunda, *Zambia Shall Be Free*, London 1962, pp. 20–21 (local government); Obafemi Awolowo, *The Path to Nigerian Freedom*, London 1947 (indirect rule); cf. the discussion in L. P. Mair, *Native Politics in Africa*, London 1936, especially pp. 12–13, and Wallerstein, *Social Change*, op. cit., part I.

[3] See for instance the use of pseudo-philosophical/logical techniques to 'prove' the right as well as the need of African independence in Kwame Nkrumah, *Consciencism*, London 1964, and his subsequent statements on this issue in *Neo-Colonialism: The Last Stage of Imperialism*, London 1965. I suspect the exercise to be largely meaningless, but the interest is in the technical effort rather than in its 'objective' success.

which are in their origin mainly historical and therefore fall on the deaf, or rather *legalistically* oriented, ears of many other developing countries. The emphasis of Israeli argument has accordingly shifted in the last decade. Towards the West, *Zionist* arguments continue to be historical, towards Africa and Asia they have become logistic and legal, but above all achievement-oriented *Israeli* arguments.[1]

One of the reasons for this emphasis on legalism is a curious and only recently re-discovered fact (by observers; participants are very conscious of this aspect)– that one of the most successful elementary forms of mobilization of otherwise unacculturated sections of the periphery of society is the claim for the return of rights believed to have been illegally removed or denied. It has, for instance, been found that preaching the inequity of land distribution, and the resultant glaring discrepancies in social status and economic return to peasants in North East Brazil, are far less remunerative (in terms of resentment, generalized belief and therefore mobilized commitment) than the much 'narrower' presentation of ancient legal rights with regard to land and water unjustly or illegally taken away.[2] This desire for a return to some previous *status quo* rather than any genuine advance (which is equivalent to demanding a just and equitable present to which one is entitled rather than a demand for change in the direction of a new and better future which one may hope for), coupled with the

[1] Reference may be made in this connection to the distinction between state preserving, state building and nation building set out in Karl W. Deutsch and William J. Foltz (eds), *Nation Building*, New York 1963; cf. also H. K. Jacobson, 'ONUC's Civilian Operations: State Preserving and State Building', *World Politics*, Vol. XVII, No. 1, October 1964. This distinction does not seem to me to be very useful with regard to developing countries. It is the Hegelian problem once more; no concept of state separate from nation can generally be found to exist there–or to flourish where it exists. The essence of the inheritance situation is that the state as such has little meaning, and that the existence of colonial government in fact prevented its emergence. Thus state and nation are, in development situations, wholly fused, and attempts to separate them cannot but lead into a cul-de-sac of legalistic quibble. Cf. once more in this context the problem of state intervention as something of an abstract Public Administration construct by the relevant academic specialists.

[2] The point emerges from discussions with Brazilian sociologists, but has not been emphasized in print as far as I know. The phenomenon of primitive legal mobilization has been confirmed by E. J. Hobsbawm, *Primitive Rebels: Studies in Archaic Forms of Social Movement in the 19th and 20th Centuries*, Manchester 1959. Compare this with the cry of 'Norman Yoke' by English revolutionaries in the seventeenth century, emphasized by Christopher Hill. Cf. also the discussion of symbolic projection away from current issues to both distant past and approaching future in S. N. Eisenstadt, 'Sociological Aspects of Political Development in Underdeveloped Countries, *Economic Development and Cultural Change*, V, 4, pp. 294–8; M. Matossian, 'Ideologies of Delayed Industrialization', ibid., VI, 3, pp. 217–28.

vital ability to verify rights by learning to read, is the dynamo behind much rural discontent in developing countries, and served the same purpose a century or more ago in Western Europe and America–summed up in the famous phrase 'Raise more hell and less corn'. This is of course a sectional or class mobilization of a 'low', often 'anomic' or riotous, order.[1] The intrumentality of denied rights as a mobilizing factor applies just as strongly to the higher norm and value-oriented mobilizations of assertive nationalism in whole societies. Following inheritance, the rulers find the reassertion of denied or obliterated national rights an efficient means of mobilization.[2]

[1] A point about the word anomie, literally rulelessness or mindlessness (Durkheim), nowadays 'professionalized' by sociologists into what political philosophers call irrationalism, indicating a pattern of behaviour for which no valid reason or interest can be deduced [by the observer!!] or where the means seem in no way instrumental to the ends. Historically, the notion of irrational or anomic behaviour is under scrutiny and attack by an analytical offensive on the part of Marxist historians who show (at any rate to my satisfaction) that many of the classic instances of such behaviour can in fact be very instrumental and rational. See e.g. E. J. Hobsbawm, 'The Machine Breakers' in *Labouring Men*, London 1964, pp. 5–22, also Hobsbawm, *Primitive Rebels*, op. cit. This reassessment has not, in general terms, yet affected the sociologists' comfortably continuing preference for anomie, crazes, etc. To stick to the example of Brazil for the moment: it seems to me that whether one classifies the often messianic peasant movements there as a rationally violent response to poverty and exploitation, or as an example of anomie in accordance with Merton's definition of a too rapid restructuring of previously stable reference groups (*Social Theory and Social Structure*, chapter IV) depends more on the preferences of the observer than on any difference in the observable facts. A variant of Merton's anomie classification (which incidentally is far too often used as a lazy explicatory symbol instead of an explanation) is the analysis of 'misled' peasant violence as the product of corrupt, selfseeking and treacherous leaders. Cf. Anthony Leeds, 'Brazil and the Myth of Francisco Julião', in Joseph Maier and R. W. Weatherhead (eds), *Politics of Change in Latin America*, New York 1964; and Benno Galjart, 'Class and "Following" in Rural Brazil', *America Latina*, op. cit. A general indictment of corruption of peasants recently arrived in cities by demagogues and a reprehensible urban environment is Carlo Alberto de Medina, *A Favela e o Demagogo*, São Paulo 1964.

[2] This assertion of denied rights can fruitfully be analysed in terms of pumping information into a relative vacuum–a process of forcibly creating consciousness not very different from the notion used by Marxists. In this sense consciousness is not, of course, merely an awareness of things or events, but an awareness of oneself (person or collectivity) being aware; cf. C. Kluckhohn and H. A. Murray (eds), *Personality in Nature, Society and Culture*, New York 1947, Chapter I. This problem has been known to philosophy for a long time; cf. Sartre on Descartes: 'Human Consciousness must always be directed upon some object; but further, in being aware of this object, it will also be aware of itself perceiving, or being aware.' The point about denied individual rights, and the denied right of national existence in colonial or ex-colonial situations, is that they take on validity and concreteness only in so far as their denial is stridently and universally asserted.

It is worth stressing in this particular connection that students in developing countries have been among the most sensitive groups in becoming aware of, and asserting, allegedly deprived rights. Accordingly they have played a significant and increasing role both in providing successful support for mobilizing regimes, as well as in opposing and often overthrowing unsuccessful ones.[1] The symbolically articulated value system of national development is perceived by them as a right, and their privileged access to information probably enables them to scan and evaluate performance more accurately than any other single group–other than the ruling elite. In Burma, the Sudan, Colombia, and most dramatically and successfully in Indonesia at the beginning of 1966–to take four widely separated examples –students have protested against regimes which share a noticeable lag in achieving the visible criteria of development. In each case the symbols become *too* crude, and were too obviously at variance with perceived reality. Moreover, in only one of these countries, Indonesia, was there any overriding mobilization based on a clear and present foreign or imperialist danger. Thus we may conclude that students are less willing to accept information dissonance or incongruence and that they require a greater level of information constraint than that at which the ruling elite are accustomed to operate for the benefit of the peripherally mobilized population. Yet the students cannot manipulate symbols and assert goals in a manner capable of producing such congruence. This may hold particularly in those cases where the ruling elite is self-consciously operating at low educational levels. Similarly the foreign students who protested in Moscow, as well as the Spanish students who went on strike for university autonomy, may be said to have been galvanized by a dissonance of information and a crudity of symbols which failed to take into account the wide gap which had developed between their stock of information and acculturation level and that which their own or their host society considered appropriate for them. This may in fact be a reaction to excessively 'distended' subsystems; the excessive economization of symbols and norms may raise economic rather than political expectations which

[1] The evidence is surveyed by S. M. Lipset, 'University Students and Politics in Underdeveloped Countries', *Minerva*, III, 1 (Autumn 1964). One of Lipset's conclusions, that students *either* study well and contentedly (as in America– *pace* the Berkeley Campus of the University of California in 1965) *or* play at politics, and should preferably concentrate on the former, seems to me an unexpected simplification for such a highly sophisticated analyst. Cf. S. N. Eisenstadt, *From Generation to Generation*, op. cit.

remain unfulfilled and produce dissatisfaction and a challenge to legitimacy.

There is of course more to the role of students in developing countries than this; only those aspects relevant to the discussion of asserted rights as means of mobilization have been touched upon. Any analysis of the important role students play in the politics of developing countries, particularly with regard to inducing change, must also deal with the aspect of institutional facilities for collective behaviour provided by universities and their central–hence convenient–location. In addition, it must deal with the ideology of direct action which is related both to the particular life chances of students in societies with limited absorptive capacity for graduates, giving these students the sense of being at the end or height of their influence rather than at the beginning as in the West. This is where the analogy with the Populist and Marxist émigré students from Russia and China at the turn of the last century is relevant.[1] Finally there is the purely generational aspect; the sharp cleavage between young and old which is not confined to developing countries, though it takes distinctly violent form there.

Naturally the assertion of rights is greatly strengthened (in terms of mobilizational efficiency, not in accretion of evidence) if the negator of rights, the *passé* colonial ruler kept alive as an ongoing menace, can be positively identified. This is the mobilizational function of the conceptual symbol of imperialism. Though the technique of using diffuse, collective labels as a means of carting different opponents off to one and the same auto-da-fé is clearly borrowed from a Marxist tradition (it goes back well beyond the Soviet Union and even Lenin), its application in developing countries serves a somewhat different purpose. In the Marxist tradition it was for one thing always applied against individuals or groups on the basis of expressed views, from which possible actions were then deduced–except at the height of the Stalin purges, when expressed views were no longer needed for such deduction. Precisely because the certainties attaching to known

[1] See J. M. Meijer, *Knowledge and Revolution*: *The Russian Colony in Zurich 1870–1873*, Assen (Holland) 1955. An analysis of this problem more directly concerned with the formation of modern anti-imperialist ideologies among Afro-Asian students studying in the West is Prodosh Aich, *Farbige unter Weissen*, Cologne 1962; A. K. Singh, *Indian Students in Britain*, Bombay 1963. In general Lipset, 'University Students . . .' op. cit., also Robert Waalder, 'Protest and Revolution against Western Societies', in Morton A. Kaplan (ed.), *The Revolution in World Politics*, New York 1962; some important comments in Harold D. Lasswell and Daniel Lerner (eds), *World Revolutionary Elites, Studies in Coercive Ideological Movements*, Cambridge (Mass.) 1965.

individuals were being frequently and violently restructured, heroes becoming criminals and unpersons overnight, the impersonal 'isms' may have assumed importance as information anchors in their stead. In developing countries by contrast the epithet 'colonialist' or 'imperialist' is, with a few exceptions, more often reserved for use in national rather than individual confrontations, and in the latter instance does not carry any permanent stigma. Moise Tshombe, imperialist agent *par excellence*–one of the few instances of specific *ad personam* application–was Prime Minister of the Congo for over a year until the autumn of 1965. The concept of imperialism has here mainly a mobilizing function and is not merely a means of eliminating an opponent–though this purpose has some mobilizational possibilities too.

It is highly instructive to trace the effect of increasing specificity of symbolic imperialism on different proportions of mobilized population. To present this graphically we might first make a scale of specificity thresholds.

Specificity 1 = imperialism as a notion without any particular attribution;

Specificity 2 = general attribution to colonial and ex-colonial powers;

Specificity 3 = a specific colonial power at a distance (Ghana → Britain, Guinea → France, Indonesia → Holland since 'liberation' of West Irian);

Specificity 4 = a specific neighbouring colonial power (Egypt → Britain in the Yemen, Cyprus → Britain [bases], Indonesia → Holland, before 'liberation' of West Irian, Egypt → Israel, Cuba → U.S.A).

Specificity 5 = full personalization of imperialism (identification with individuals or dissident groups within society, or focus on individual imperialists outside it).

These thresholds may be taken, purely for purposes of representation, to correspond to equivalent thresholds of intensity of commitment. Thus specificity 1 corresponds to low commitment on the part of those mobilized, while each threshold of increasing specificity corresponds to an 'equivalent' increase in commitment. Plotting this scale on one axis against the percentage of total population mobilized (diagram 4), we would then get a curve which shows an optimum point at x of specificity/intensity and maximum proportion of population mobilized. Specificity beyond this point particularizes the referent to an extent which reduces the range of its impact on the population.[1] It must of course be emphasized that this diagram is not based on, nor represents, any quantitative data on mobilization, but is a purely theoretical representation of probabilities based on analogy with research on Soviet newspapers, and on empirical observation of the effects of symbol diffusion in various developing countries.

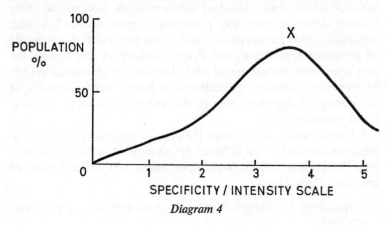

Diagram 4

With such a scale it is possible to relate the search for specificity to the mobilization factor on a national, rather than party, basis. The propaganda assault on a neighbour under the flag of fighting a local agent of imperialism can be shown to be one of the most effective forms of national mobilization available. It introduces the tension of *guerre à outrance*, not in terms of a danger of ethnic or economic extermination, but on the grounds that the newly won national independence is threatened with a return to colonial or neo-colonial status. This is a significant example of a value system and one of its symbols (anti-imperialism) imposing its own norms and processes on societies; the compression or dedifferentiation effect mentioned earlier. The mobilizing technique has been found so efficient that it seems to pay the rulers of countries which have been independent for a considerable time to claim that until recently they were no better than colonies in disguise–neo-imperialism–so as to be able to denigrate as imperialists the supporters of a recently overthrown domestic government, and to benefit from the plethora of mobiliza-

[1] A somewhat similar falling-off effect with regard to the increasing specificity of targets is suggested by Smelser, *Collective Behaviour*, op. cit. Thus diffuse symbols mobilize up to value levels, while more specific ones relate to collectivities and individuals. Here the scale of impact falls off and not, as in my example, the proportion of the population mobilized. These may, but need not, come to the same thing.

tional possibilities that anti-imperialism provides. Egypt is one example of such definitional anti-colonialism, the Yemen is an even more marked one, because whatever the Imam's regime might have been it was not a colonial sub-administration. This technique has also become increasingly common practice in Latin America, following Cuba's example.[1] On the other hand the optimal specificity of focus in terms of mobilized commitment is reached with this threshold; from then on mobilizational potential declines with wholly personal specification. Intensity of commitment will increase with maximal specificity, but such mobilization will be limited in range, affecting only a small part of the population (crowd, caste, ethnic group). Also it will become increasingly limited in duration of time. Riots against very specific phenomena often exhaust themselves quickly by their very violence. This can be seen from the collective behaviour of mobilized groups in Indonesia which recently (October 1965–April 1966) have rioted against the Chinese and the Communists where only a short time before they were rioting against quite different 'agents of imperialism'. Similarly there is a lack of stability and permanence in the mobilizing potential of violent anti-Moslem behaviour in India and anti-Tamil behaviour in Ceylon. The focus may be said to be too narrow for the limits of intense mobilization to be reached other than intermittently and temporarily even for limited sectors of the population.

National-constitutional mobilization presents the great structural

---

[1] See for instance R. Avakov and L. Stepanov, 'Sotsialniye problemy natsional'no–osvoboditel'noi revoliutsii', *Mirovaya Ekonomika i Mezhdunarodniye Otnosheniya* V (May 1963), pp. 46–54. For more extensive analysis of this phenomenon, see Nettl, 'Inheritance'. It should be obvious that the manœuvring and adaptation of linguistic symbols for mobilizational purposes–of which this is but an instance–deserve much further study, both in the particular context of deliberate mobilization, and in the wider one of the relationship between social structure and action on the one hand and linguistic symbols on the other. The possibilities of a vigorous taxonomy of 'style' and its socio-personal implications–together with a lament for so much empty research space which no one seems interested in filling–are set out in W. Percy, 'The Symbolic Structure of Interpersonal Process', *Psychiatry*, XXIV (1961), pp. 39–52. There is also the work of Edward Sapir in Linguistics, partly reprinted in D. Mandelbaum (ed.), E. Sapir, *Selected Writings in Language, Culture and Personality*, Los Angeles 1949. The philosophers have, of course, done much work on this (Peirce, Weldon, Cassirer, Wittgenstein), though their work has been little used by social scientists–a catchment area problem once more. Such linguistic analysis is of critical importance for the sociological use of cybernetics, to which Deutsch does less than justice, but cf. his recent paper 'On Theories, Taxonomies and Models as Communication Codes for Organizing Information', *Behavioral Science* op. cit., Section III; also his argument about matching structures relates to this problem–*Nerves*, pp. 87–88.

advantage of making possible the use of conventional military processes and techniques. The more military values, norms and methods can be used and are accepted as legitimate the greater becomes the compression factor in the process of mobilizing commitment; acculturation, though necessarily narrow, can be deliberately and intensely applied, resistance more legitimately broken. This military aspect of national mobilization is most clearly in evidence in the case of Indonesia, where one armed confrontation has followed another (first over West Irian, then against Malaysia), and where the overriding imperatives of a prolonged national crisis enabled Sukarno and his immediate colleagues to maintain the delicate balance of *charismatic arbiters* between latently divisive factions and territories whose centrifugal cleavages might otherwise have torn the unwieldy state apart. From this point of view confrontation is an ideal solution; it provides all the domestic social advantages of warlike mobilization without the economically ruinous and socially dangerous commitment to actual war. It also helped to keep going an army to balance the powerful communist party and thus made the arbiters more secure. Other countries have tried this solution too; Egypt was caught in actual and ruinously expensive fighting in the Yemen, while Algeria and Morocco found the stakes too high and preferred to call off their confrontation in 1963 without any corresponding social demobilization; indeed the Algerians may well have been attempting to mobilize Moroccan students in the 1965 crisis there with the suggestion that the royal Moroccan government was in fact no more than an imperialist relic. This method had the advantage of hindering any Moroccan anti-imperialist counter-mobilization. In its extreme version national mobilization is in fact an incompatible alternative to economic planning; though Sukarno on the whole managed to avoid full-scale war he openly stated many times that he preferred to opt for national-military mobilization at the expense of planning mobilization.

It would be naïve to suggest that confrontation can always be maintained without the risk of conflict—especially where a particular confrontation with another country, rather than the concept of confrontation with a generalized other (imperialist, communist, racist), has become part of the ideology or value system. It might be argued for instance that imperialist-revolutionary or colonial-liberation confrontations between nations lead to war less frequently than particular, arch-enemy conflicts like those of Syria versus Israel and especially India versus Pakistan. However, the latter type of conflict may also be more stoppable, precisely because confrontation is in that case not so much a structural form of mobilization, but represents instead a cultural component of hostility to a particular enemy which short-circuits or bypasses all structural considerations of capability. This however is within the area of conjecture–recently elevated to a respectable exercise on the part of political scientists.[1]

Two basic forms of constitutional/national–as opposed to party–mobilization available after inheritance–and, to a lesser extent, after revolution–have been set out at some length. There are of course others: the legalistic and uncompromising obstinacy over often arbitrary boundaries frequently drawn for no other reason than the convenience of an alien colonial administration (Kenya ⇆ Somalia, Algeria ⇆ Morocco, India ⇆ China).[2] Secondly, and perhaps more important, there has been a shift away from the ethnic considerations which were so much in vogue between 1918–45 and are still professed as conventional wisdom in the West; the emphasis in developing countries is on the *nation trouvée* while ethnic, tribal and linguistic differences are played down. We have therefore a form of nationalism that is very different from traditional Western concepts.[3] The

---

[1] See Bertrand de Jouvenel, *L'art de la conjecture*, Paris 1964, and the *Futuribles* volumes published in Paris since 1961.

[2] A recent, forcefully argued article suggests that, with the one exception of Somalia, the preconditions of conflict over 'national' boundaries do not exist in Africa. Ravi L. Kapil, 'On the Conflict Potential of Inherited Boundaries in Africa', *World Politics*, XVIII, 4 (July 1966), pp. 656–673. These preconditions are defined as (a) cultural homogeneity of the affected nations, (b) boundaries approaching but not coinciding with population discontinuities (thus creating small minorities). Kapil argues that in most African cases frontiers do not create barriers between 'valued continuities of interaction', but are 'irrelevant' to them. He also emphasises that boundaries 'have become essential reference points in the definition of a *non-traditional* concept of political legitimacy.' (p. 671, my italics). These points are important and valid, but apply only to peripherally induced conflict; they ignore the fact that frontier conflicts can be artificially manufactured if the very preoccupation with internal problems of legitimacy on which Kapil relies for his thesis demands foreign diversions. See for instance the previous dispute between the Congo and Uganda as a factor in Obote's coup d'état in 1966.

[3] For a discussion of this, see Ernest Gellner, *Thought and Change*, pp. 147 ff., especially p. 168: 'Nationalism invents nations where they do not exist.' (Kedourie, *Nationalism*, op. cit., of course maintains that this inventiveness also holds true in the West.) There is accordingly considerable justification in a recent suggestion that the notion of nation building (as used by Deutsch and Foltz, *Nation Building*, op. cit., and Bendix, *Nation-building and Citizenship*, op. cit.) are really misnomers; empire-building would be more appropriate, were it not for the ideologically unfortunate connotations of this term. See Günther Roth, 'Personal Rulership, Patrimonialism and Empire-Building in the New States', Paper presented to the Political Sociology Section of the Sixth World Congress of Sociology, Evian, September 1966 (mimeographed), pp. 15–18.

examples of Cyprus and Israel are significant in this context. The Cyprus government emphatically insisted on Cypriot integrity and nationality, at times *against* both Enosis and partition. The division between Cypriot Turks and Greeks was primarily ethnic and religious –though there are small but significant groups of Greek-speaking Muslims. But the emphasis of Cypriot Greek and Turkish distinctiveness is not exclusively a Cypriot problem; it appears to be chronologically correlated to the relative vicissitudes of Greece and Turkey respectively as countries, in their general situation as well as in their relation with each other. This feature of dependence on outside considerations and support is significant in almost all cases of nationalistic irredentism–Sudetenland, South Tyrol, Vorarlberg, etc. In the case of Israel the attempt, however limited in success, to build an Israeli nationality *inclusive* of resident Arabs is interesting, when one considers the enormous outside pressure on that country's 250,000 Arabs. In Syria and Egypt, Palestinian nationality is being deliberately kept alive by refusing many of the attributes of citizenship to refugees, even though reference to a national Palestinian citizenship effectively means no citizenship status at all for the beneficiaries of this solicitude.

Those who lament–or merely stress–the continuing strength of nationalism in the West and the Third World fail to recognize the recent shift in its emphasis, symbols and content–particularly in developing countries.[1] The reason for the revival of nationalism in *developed* countries is of course the failure of the great alternative–class–between 1860 and 1930; a failure which made a relapse into nationalism inevitable. This, in the case of the emerging countries, was in turn enhanced by the special and urgent demands which they made on their particular version of nationalism in terms of functional

---

[1] But cf. Karl W. Deutsch, 'The Future of World Politics, *Political Quarterly*, XXXVII, 1 (January/March 1966), pp. 9–32. This excursion into informed *futurismo*, based on the Yale Data Programme and extrapolations of its findings into the next two decades, suggests a common tendency towards national-constitutional mobilization, for both developed and developing countries. No attempt is made there to distinguish between party and national forms; Deutsch would presumably include both means as conducive to the same end without assigning as much weight to their alternative and conflicting character as I have done here. His main evidence is what might be called the growing tendency towards introspection; the increasing concern of each nation with its own affairs. Thus participatory or mobilized nationalism is likely to increase overall. Deutsch concludes that this increasing internal participation factor makes all countries increasingly hard to govern (communication overload), and makes the rule of foreign countries (colonialism) substantially harder still.

and communicative *need*, which could not be satisfied by reference to a, in their case, largely meaningless concept of class. Developing countries have been the pace-setters in moving from ethnic, linguistic and cultural considerations (*nations introuvables*) to the *nation trouvée*.[1] What they do have in common with Western nationalism however is the broadly inclusive purpose of the so-called Welfare State, which identifies national progress with economic development and therefore tends in the last resort to be autarchic towards countries, even neighbours, who have different economic structures, different standards of living and different economic problems—however much else there might be in common between 'blocs'. The real cleavages on which mobilization in developing countries is based are thus not intra-societal but international, inter-societal; the more successful the induction into the latter, the less salient and divisive the former. Yet the extent of mobilized commitment bears little relation to the distribution of economic rewards; in developing countries one might legitimately ask: whose welfare?[2] The impact of nationalism is therefore manifest and primary for developing countries—for the attainment of integration, modernization and mobilization.

We have already emphasized strongly the failure of Western electoral mobilization and its processes in providing adequate 'tools' for the mobilizational requirements of developing countries. The communist model, arising as it does from a revolutionary-inheritance situation, is more conducive to adaptation in the Third World. But in stressing this greater conduciveness, it should not be thought that inheritance and revolutionary situations are identical, or that the requirements of developing countries today can be met by the simple transfer of communist structural and processual experiences and techniques. There are substantial ideological as well as structural

[1] This idea was expressed by Sukarno as long ago as 1933 (*For a Free Indonesia*) 'We shall . . . attain independence . . . by waging a struggle in which all the people participate . . .' in order to construct a nation 'that has no aristocracy, no bourgeoisie, no classes, no capitalism.' Reprinted in Sukarno, *Indonesia Accuses*, Moscow 1956, p. 246; quoted with approval by A. A. Guber, 'Introduction to Indonesia', in T. P. Thornton, *Soviet Perspective*, p. 74. A similar assessment of the progression in the national idea under very different circumstances and from a different angle is Hélio Jaguaribe, *O Nacionalismo na Atualidade Brasileira*, Rio de Janeiro 1958.

[2] It can in fact be argued that internally the meaning of 'welfare' in many developing countries means a redistribution of wealth from the poor [working class] to that sector of the middle classes that provides the new elites and the intelligentsia. See Albert Breton, 'The Economics of Nationalism', and Harry G. Johnson, 'A Theoretical Model of Economic Nationalism', both op. cit.

differences. Communist parties always lead valid and highly autonomous internal lives. The important socio-political decisions are usually intra-party decisions. They act as an enclave in, if not indeed a replacement for, their host societies as far as the commitment and orientation of their members are concerned, even where they are in power. That is why many francophone Republicans in Africa have tended to look to the socialist parties of metropolitan France as an example – with their history of successful adaptation to the Republic. The autonomy and structural substitution for society implied in the communist model do not apply to developing countries; indeed mobilizing parties there are of necessity more strongly 'adaptive'. This role is not likely to change as long as developmental-national goals exist; only when and if these goals change, together with the value system from which they spring, is the life of parties likely to become more autonomous and less adaptive – unless of course such presently developing societies move in the direction of electoral legitimacy according to the European or American model.[1]

Bearing in mind both the natural affinities and differences between mobilization in communist and developing countries, it is instructive to glance briefly at the contribution of Soviet analysis of developing countries and their problems. Such analysis is always strongly related to, and conscious of, policy requirements. We may therefore expect to find there a good deal of reference to Soviet experience and comparison of it with that of the countries analysed. The study of developing societies in the Soviet Union falls under the category of relatively non-specialized philosophy, and divisions of competence or interest are geographical rather than functional or academic, with the possible exception of economics, recently advancing apace towards academic specialization. Nonetheless Soviet analysis has managed to approach an understanding of the *specific* nature of socio-political development in the Third World – though not without difficulty and hesitation. The concept of National Democracy is the result. Though party and national mobilizations are not separated as dichotomous patterns – this would be too great a concession to Western sociological method – development mobilization is nonetheless presented as a special pattern of fusion, in which the old emphasis on party is played down

[1] I have argued (*Rosa Luxemburg*, II, London 1966, pp. 539–40, 704) that the period of intense industrialization in Russia from 1928 onwards, culminating in the great purges, was in fact an attempt to destroy the autonomy of the party as represented by the traditionally integrative cadres of old Bolsheviks, in order to make the party more adaptive to the social system as a whole and instrumental in the attainment of developmental values and goals.

to allow recognition and partial approval of a national framework. The concession is made acceptable by emphasizing the situational opposition of National Democracies to the current version of imperialism. Naturally National Democracy is not a *terminus ad quem* but a stage on the road to Socialism. There is however no absolute demand for revolution; National Democracy may, it is emphasized, emerge peacefully.[1]

Where all this differs from, and improves upon, some Western analysis is mainly in recognizing that contemporary underdevelopment, and the escape from it through industrialization, are situationally and structurally unique–different from past industrialization in the West and Russia, but at the same time providing enough common elements to make what has here been termed development a comparable pattern all over the contemporary world. Western writing, with its attachment to democratic-industrial norms and values, has only in part and very recently begun to escape from the ideological cul-de-sac of analysing modern development by reference to its own industrial genesis; it still, for instance, cannot fully internalize the notion and concept of aid (much less that of imperialism) in the elaboration of its development models, political or for that matter economic.[2] Where Soviet writing often produces an overfacile connection between political and social change, Western academic autonomy at best produces 'equivalent' analyses in one discipline for changes demonstrated by the other (see chapter 1); at worst it ignores

[1] See the summary of Soviet writing in William Shinn, 'The National-Democratic State: A Communist Program for the Less Developed Areas', *World Politics*, XV, 4 (April 1963), pp. 377–89. Also A. Sobolev in *World Marxist Review*, 2 (1963), pp. 39–48; V. I. Pavlov and I. B. Rediko, 'The National Democratic State and the Transition to Non-Capitalist Development', *Narody Azii i Afriki*, 1 (1963), pp. 29–40. There are also a number of specialist studies on Algeria, Burma, Guinea, etc., which stress this model. For emphasis on peaceful transition see G. Starushenko in *Kommunist*, No. 13 (1962), p. 107; also 'The 20th CPSU Congress and Problems of Study in the East Today', *Sovetskoe Vostokovedeniye*, 1, (1956), p. 7.

[2] For aid, and the difficulty of giving any systematic explanations of its effects on the socio-political structure of different countries, see Charles Wolf, Jnr., *Foreign Aid: Theory and Practice in Southern Asia*, Princeton 1960, particularly chapter VIII. But cf. Celso Furtado, *Desenvolvimento e Subdesenvolvimento*, Rio de Janeiro 1961, particularly chapters IV and V. It is worth pondering that the theoretical analysis of aid in economics has not really progressed beyond the notion of miraculous (non-autonomous) investment, appearing in the growth model like a husband popping up in a three-cornered bedroom farce. Thus aid is either seen as an import substitute for the recipient, or more rarely as an export substitute for the giver, or a Christian duty, but hardly ever as a systemic relationship of a special kind. This *ad hoc* approach is especially typical of Britain, both in terms of policy and economic analysis.

interconnections by insisting on the complete autonomy of problems in sociology, politics and economics.[1]

[1] There has, in the course of 1965 and 1966, been something of a campaign in the Soviet Union for more scientific comparative study of politics as an officially recognized academic social science. Far from being unique, this may best be viewed as a special–and perhaps specially significant–part of a revival of interest in and demand for a more adequate study of social science generally. Except within a purely legal framework, there is as yet no Soviet conception of a specialized role for political science, though there is for instance in Poland. For social scientists in the West this has a threefold interest.

1. It has led to a more intense Soviet examination of theory and methodology of the social sciences in the West, especially American and French, and confronted these with Soviet approaches. A recent overview and discussion may be found in *Markzistskaya i burzhuaznaya sotsiologiya sevodnya*, Moscow 1964; also G. V. Osipov, *Sovremennaya burzhuaznaya sotsiologiya* (*Kriticheskii ocherk*), Moscow 1964; cf. also *Sotsiologiya V SSSR*, 2 vols., Moscow 1965; and *Sotsial'niye issledovaniya*, Moscow (Academy of Sciences) 1965.

2. The areas of interest on which Soviet sociology has concentrated: sociology of work (inevitably), sociology of leisure (less inevitably), some educational and rather more medical sociology. For this see the translated abstracts printed in *Soviet Sociology*, issued by the International Arts and Sciences Press, New York.

3. The areas which Soviet sociology ignores; class analysis, national differentiation, political sociology, the application of systems analysis (which has been *methodologically* well received in the Soviet Union) to social and political life, though there has been some interest in its application to psychology. A discussion of the state of the social sciences in the Soviet Union, which includes economics, is in *Problems of Communism*, XIV, 6 (November-December 1965), a special number devoted to the social sciences in the USSR. Special reference to emphasis and omissions in Soviet sociology is made by Paul Hollander, 'The Dilemmas of Soviet Sociology', pp. 34–46.

It should be emphasized that what we would call socio-political analysis of foreign countries, especially capitalist and developing societies, is structurally and intellectually differentiated from self-confessed sociological analysis of the USSR, and still belongs in the Soviet Union to the generic category of philosophy. Thus the Soviet writers on developing countries cited in the present book come from quite a different intellectual background and have a different premise and purpose from those writing on sociological topics in the Soviet Union; they are by definition less specialized and also more 'political' or ideological. The recent shift to empirical factfinding in Soviet sociology is primarily located in Soviet self-examination and as yet applies much less to the analysis of foreign countries.

CHAPTER NINE

Legitimacy, Mobilization and Political Change in Developing Countries

SUMMARY

The bases of legitimation in developing countries, anchored in traditional forms of according legitimacy, are discussed and contrasted with the legitimacy of Western electoral systems. Traditional forms of legitimacy are characterized in terms of an analogy with the theatre; the relationship between rulers and ruled being presented as an actor-audience relationship. It is argued that although developmental nationalism is the specific product of an inheritance situation, the orientation towards legitimacy often continues in a more traditional style. Consequently there is a conflict between the value system and its goals on the one hand, and the methods of according legitimacy on the other.

In terms of mobilization the forms discussed in chapter 8 can be incorporated in a variable. This organizes the direction of mobilization from the top downwards, which is typical of the cases discussed in chapter 8, and from the bottom upwards–against or towards established authority which–England apart–represents the Western experience of political mobilization. This directional variable is called stalactite-stalagmite. It is applied to a discussion of the problem of change in developing societies, more particularly of the means available for making change possible in systems of traditional legitimacy.

Since electoral mobilization is a divisive influence whose structural crystallization is strongly de-emphasized in most developing countries, the two means of change available are reorientation by the rulers on the one hand, and coups on the other. These processes are examined at some length, both in terms of their form and their effectiveness. Change is analysed on two dimensions: the relative emphasis on one or other forms of internal mobilization discussed in chapter 8, and a movement along the international spectrum of orientations ranging from strong association with the former colonial power and the West generally, to dissociation from them and greater alignment with the communist powers at the other end.

The discussion of legitimacy is then related to the two forms of mobilization in the context of the postulated value system of developmental nationalism. According to various empirical examples, an attempt is made to assess the extent to which the two methods, party and national-constitutional, are compatible and can be combined. The extent to which stalactite mobilization can be carried out in accordance with emphasis on party or national-constitutional structures is examined. In this connection the role of the charismatic arbiter is emphasized, as a necessary component in enabling options for mobilization to be kept open and conflict between them to be resolved. The role of the charismatic arbiter is presented as an adaptation of a traditional function into the context of developmental nationalism.

Beneath the new and adapted means of mobilization in developing countries, both ideological and structural, there lurks a concept of legitimacy substantially different from that of the West. The latter postulates a notion of the state or nation and its legitimacy embodied in a historical tradition and based on a long period of national development and autonomy which has been internalized by the participants (what we have briefly referred to as Hegelianism). In developing countries, however, we must look to a very different source of legitimacy. First there are the aspects of association and dissociation already discussed earlier in an inheritance context. However, they can only be understood as part of a synthesis with more traditional styles of authority legitimation. These are based on a strong articulation of social distance – not entirely unlike the clothing of legitimate authority with divine sanction which formed the basis of rule in classical Egypt, Mesopotamia, Greece and also Rome.[1] We need not investigate too closely the relationship between religious and political components in developing countries; for our purpose it is sufficient to note that the style of legitimacy sought and accorded tends

---

[1] The most comprehensive discussion of the relationship between religion and legitimate rule in its social context is Henri Frankfort, *Kingship and the Gods: A Study of Ancient Near Eastern Religion as the Instigator of Society and Nature*, Chicago 1948. A very lucid recent discussion of the changing aspects of this concept in the ancient world is by Mario Attilio Levi, *Political Power in the Ancient World*, London 1965.

to accentuate individual supremacy, at least in symbolic terms—what has summarily been referred to so far as charisma, but also contains substantial elements of patrimonialism as defined by Weber as part of his concept of *Herrschaft*. It should be understood, however, that such charisma is not only related to a particular person and his standing and achievement, but to a social style and social setting which make the emergence of such leaders probable or even necessary.

But it is not merely a matter of personal leadership, whether institutionalized in terms of an office or not. Legitimacy in developing countries is a particular combination of authoritative legitimacy personified by an outstanding leader, and a structure or structures through which such charisma is routinized. Such structures may be parties, bureaucracies, or both—in collaboration or in conflict. While, therefore, the various structures appear to suggest some similarity with the authority-legitimation parties and state bureaucracies of Western countries, the former in cases like Britain, the latter in countries like France and Germany with a long tradition of *étatisme*, it is the additional presence of the charismatic leader which limits the analogy with the Western case (the structural and functional differences have already been noted). The mobilization structures do not ultimately derive their legitimacy from elections, nor from the accretion of Hegelian legitimacy accorded to a state bureaucracy, but from the values and norms of dissociation emphasized by the structure, and personified by the continuative legitimacy taken over by the charismatic leader. Hence we have referred here to this type of leadership as that of charismatic arbiter.[1]

There is, of course, a wide range in the relative components of the traditional and the inheritance aspects of such legitimacy on the part of charismatic arbiters. Empirical cases range from a leader of almost

---

[1] The first sociological definition and analysis of charisma is, of course, Max Weber's, and is most readily accessible in English under the relevant sections in Max Weber, *The Theory of Social and Economic Organization*, New York 1964 (translation A. M. Henderson and Talcott Parsons). A recent discussion of the concept and its interpretation is W. H. Friedland, 'For a Sociological Concept of Charisma', *Social Forces*, XLIV (October 1964), which includes a survey of recent literature (pp. 18–19). See also some remarks in Mattei Dogan, 'Le personnel politique et la personnalité charismatique', *Revue Française de Sociologie*, VI (1965), pp. 305–24, dealing mainly with de Gaulle in the recent French elections. The problem of dispersal and routinization is specifically analysed and discussed by W. G. Runciman, 'Charismatic Legitimacy and One-Party Rule', op. cit.; also by Edward Shils, 'The Concentration and Dispersion of Charisma: Its Bearing upon Economic Policy in Underdeveloped Countries', *World Politics*, XI, 1 (October 1958), pp. 1–19.

purely traditional authority like Prince Sihanouk of Cambodia or the Shah of Persia, both acting in a personally modern role, to the greater emphasis on the arbitration aspect of leadership as in the case of President Sukarno of Indonesia. Even in those cases where the leader is associated primarily with one structure, whether party like the CPP in Ghana or military bureaucracy like Ayub Khan in Pakistan, the arbitration element is nonetheless present, even if latently; this is a necessary remnant of the traditional role of leadership in many societies with its emphasis on providing a final means of resolving disputes. The main difference here is that the merely personal aspect of disputes to be arbitrated has become collectivized; instead of persons the supplicant disputants are parties, bureaucracies – collectivities generally.

In a recent essay, based on a long experience of India in particular and South-East Asia in general, Tinker has highlighted the dramaturgical basis of legitimacy in these countries – in order to contrast it most firmly with the electoral legitimacy of the West, and to emphasize the West's tendency to regard the needs of developing polities exclusively in its own terms.[1] It is worth summarizing this argument and even extending it somewhat, in order to contrast the very different basis of legitimacy in the developed and developing world. On this difference ultimately depend not only the various forms of political structure, but also their functions, style and processes.

Essentially the structure of legitimacy orientations in many traditional as well as developing societies is based on the ability of the ruler to provide a show, whose symbols and processes are held to be in keeping with the ascribed status of legitimate rule. The extent to which such a show maintains the interest and involvement of participating spectators also governs the legitimacy which the ruler will be accorded; if the show is boring or irrelevant, or the symbols are unsuitable to expectations which themselves may be conservative or changing, legitimacy may begin to be withdrawn. This is not, however, a manifest process. The audience will still attend, but with reduced commitment or greater indifference. Since an actor-audience relationship does not possess a structured means of giving approval to legitimate authority through positive acts like voting, the orientations towards authority are, from an analyst's point of view, latent or

---

[1] Hugh Tinker, *Ballot Box and Bayonet*, London 1964. For more extended treatment, see Tinker, *Reorientations: Studies on Asia in Transition*, London 1965.

residual. They do not find expression in positive acts of authority legitimation of the sort discussed in the early chapters, but in a latent complex of attitudes towards authority which may become activated only when and if its legitimacy is challenged from outside. Thus the legitimacy of institutionalized authority may erode gradually in the course of time, though there may not be any ready means by which outside observers can assess the erosion. When, however, a challenge arises the latent orientations of the audience will be translated either into willingness to support the regime, passive indifference or possibly hostility responsive to the outside threat. The cash-credit analogy mentioned earlier in the context of power and influence has substantial relevance to this situation. We may summarize this kind of legitimacy orientation under three headings.[1]

1. *Saliency or Relevance.* Much of the discussion about the saliency of politics, which we have already raised in earlier chapters in the context of political subsystem density, is here concerned not only with functional predominance but also with dramaturgical impact. The debate about the end of ideology appears on the whole to tackle problems of commitment in terms of dramaturgical indices. In fact the saliency of politics and its dramaturgical functions are different things; they tell us about different styles of politics rather than different levels of impact or commitment. Thus the fact that much of the impact of interest articulation has shifted from the formal and expressive symbolism of party politics to confidential negotiations between organized interest-specific groups and government does not indicate any decline of the function and importance of politics as such. The example of the Soviet Union has shown us that there elections are ratifications of decisions already taken, but that the saliency of conflict in making these decisions, indeed the violence often connected with this process, is nonetheless an important factor of Soviet politics – at any rate historically. It might therefore be preferable to concentrate on the relevance of symbolic as opposed to functional political processes without treating them as evidence of political saliency.

The dramaturgical analogy of the theatre provides considerable insights into the legitimacy bases of authority in developing

[1] The following analysis of legitimacy in developing countries is a summary of a longer version; see J. P. Nettl, 'The "Show" of Politics' (forthcoming). This is an attempt to extend Tinker's *obiter dicta* by using some of the concepts and ideas put forward by Erving Goffman in his work on the symbolism of interpersonal relations (see particularly *The Presentation of Self in Everyday Life*, *Stigma*, and *Personal Behavior in Public Places*).

countries.[1] For one thing greater familiarity with the relevant show, in terms of more frequent performances, may mean less involvement and hence less relevance; in this sense more is definitely worse since scarcity may be a function of preciousness in traditional forms of leadership, as Weber pointed out. This suggests an explanation for the long spells of mystical withdrawal by, for instance, Ghana's Osagyefo and Indonesia's Bung Karno, to commune with the *Amanat Penderitaan Rakjat*–the Mandate of the People's Suffering– while the newspapers were deliberately encouraged to speculate. The traditional basis of legitimacy and the more frequent, sectorally specific commitments involved, for instance in planning, tend to conflict. The two forms do not accord easily. The more traditional charismatic leaders in many developing countries have tended to abstain from too much personal reference to, and involvement in, the development plans for which their own governments have made themselves responsible. Nkrumah, Nasser and others have not followed the Soviet example according to which the overall leadership spends a good deal of time and words on the pedestrian business of economic facts and figures; they hold themselves and their authority to be 'above' such a mundane basis. Indeed, Sukarno has gone one further and himself deliberately and repeatedly played down the importance of such instrumental, uninspired concerns.

Overall the development component of developmental nationalism as a *process* does not lend itself readily to dramaturgical presentation. Just as the content of theatrical plays has tended, over the years, to reduce the possibility of structured audience participation in terms of clapping, shouting and singing, so the preoccupations with administration and economic development for the purpose of providing welfare offer little means for audience participation but demand a different form of involvement. There is consequently a latent form of conflict over legitimacy orientations implicated in the concept of developmental nationalism. Even development plans themselves represent a compromise in this respect, with adjustment to economic rationality often sacrificed to traditional elements of ascription involved in the maintenance of legitimacy. This is another argument for the conspicuous piece of public expenditure which makes so little sense in an economic context.

[1] The relevance of this analogy is in fact quite old. Adam Smith talked of politics in terms of the need for actors to adjust to the evaluated capacity for emotion on the part of their audience; see *Theory on Moral Sentiments*, London 1812, in *Works*, I, pp. 188–90.

Any attempt to institute electoral legitimacy orientations must appear as a means of reducing the dramatic impact of politics. The history of elections in Britain in the eighteenth and nineteenth centuries, and more recently still in the United States, shows that the traditional function of elections has frequently been one of *articulating* the symbolic drama of politics. But the adoption of electoral legitimacy orientations from the West by developing countries is not based on a symbolism relevant to the period when such dramatic articulation partially substituted for the institutionalization of choices; the electoral ideas and methods initially available for adoption by *nations trouvées* in the last twenty years are those existing in the West today. Once again this provides evidence of the inherent difficulty of relating the chronology of 'modern' economic development processes on the one hand with the use of 'modern' political methods and processes on the other. In many ways the socio-economic situation of developing countries today might have justified the adoption of electoral systems more akin to those of the English eighteenth century. But it is impossible for a country seeking to import ideas or processes from another to do so by looking back into the exporter's past; instead only current processes viewed as fully up to date are ever imported. By adopting the electoral attitudes and processes of polities with mass parties concerned either with authority legitimation or interest articulation within a formal, established universe of national existence, and placed more towards the issue end of the cleavage-issue dimension, hardly any provision can be made for articulating the dramatic symbols of politics of traditional societies. Moreover, as we have seen, the structural means of articulating cleavages, without which electoral legitimacy can hardly function, are frequently suppressed or de-emphasized as well.

The value orientations of developmental nationalism, together with the adoption of the electoral processes of the West, thus help to erode and constrain the traditional expressions of participation on which much of the legitimacy of inheritance rulers and elites in developing countries ultimately rest. In this respect the present situation of developing countries is a stage of transition. The former bases of legitimacy remain valid to a considerable extent, but the imported means of authority legitimation and interest articulation make the expression of traditional legitimacy difficult, without as yet providing a viable alternative on which a new structured form of authority legitimation can emerge.

2. *Roles.* The symbols of a professional *classe politique* do not

appear to accord well with the symbols of traditional legitimacy. Developing countries resist the concept of a professional class of politicians and the notion of a professionalization of politics. That is why a number of writers have chosen to discuss ruling elites in developing countries in terms of broad, undifferentiated, multi-role classifications like intellectuals.[1] Increasing differentiation of a political subsystem is almost certainly related to the emergence of professional politicians. Consequently we would expect to find constitution-oriented cultures to accommodate more easily the notion of professional politicians than elitist cultures.

Political professionalization always presents difficulties. How, for instance, can the frequently diffuse role of British politicians be evaluated, when by any standards they spend more actual time on politics than many of their continental colleagues who yet have a much more sharply defined and professional role? The answer may lie in distinguishing between action and role in this context, and the theatre may be once again a useful analogy. For here too the notion of a star suggests quite a different role to that of a professional actor, and the basis of 'stardom' is differently distributed between the emergence of an actor at the top of his profession on the one hand, and the stereotyped image of an all-round superman on the other. It can be argued for instance that constitutional cultures will tend to produce the former type of star role, while elitist cultures will produce the latter. There may consequently be a connection between the well-known aspect of professionalization in politics on the one hand and the culture variable on the other, expressed in terms of a tendency for subsystem differentiation.

Traditional forms of legitimacy correspond ill with subsystem differentiation and professionalization. Accordingly we find that the growth of structural differentiation is resisted in many developing countries. The charismatic arbiter is not a well-defined role nor can it be crystallized in terms of professional evaluations. Instead it is a function capable of being carried out in a variety of ways and with varying role emphasis. Similarly the dedifferentiated or compressed

---

[1] Particularly Edward Shils, *Political Development in the New States; The Intellectual between Tradition and Modernity*, op. cit.; 'The Intellectuals in the Political Development of the New States', *World Politics*, XII, 3 (April 1960), pp. 329–68; John H. Kautsky, *Political Change in Underdeveloped Countries: Nationalism and Communism*, New York 1962, pp. 44 ff., 90. The unstable nature of the compound and aggregate concept of intellectual in a modern setting are discussed briefly by J. P. Nettl, 'Rosa Luxemburg Today', *New Society*, 184 (7th April 1966) pp. 11–13.

form of elite surveillance of mobilization in many developing countries under the aegis of a party inhibits the crystallization of distinct roles and of subsystem differentiation. There is perhaps some correlation between emphasis on elitist mobilization through party and the maintenance of traditional symbols of legitimacy, while a more constitutional orientation would appear to support a tendency for more rapid erosion of the traditional legitimacy base. Routinization of charisma would thus be more readily accomplished in favour of a hierarchical party structure than in favour of the more competitive, less tightly structured national-constitutional framework.[1]

3. *Participation and Involvement.* Finally the form in which participation and involvement in processes of according legitimacy find expression in traditional societies can also be understood more readily by analogy with the theatre. Communication between leaders and followers is akin to that between actors and audience, while the verdict of political legitimacy is also somewhat similar to that provided by the response of a theatrical audience. If we look at the manner in which many major decisions are made in the Soviet Union in terms of sensitizing, familiarization and dramatic explication rather than through processes of formally competitive offers anticipating or following on electoral verdicts, we have a situation much more like the theatre than Western democratic politics. The Soviet party leader at a congress, as much as the humble party worker in a cell or factory meeting, is expected to transform a cold audience to enthusiastic response by a performance, instead of providing an explanation in competition with other and contrary explanations on which those present have recently voted, or are subsequently expected to vote. Moreover, the Soviet party official is expected to have the same 'sense' of the meeting–and has to report on this–as the actor has of his audience. Naturally in the Soviet Union this process of dramatic explication has been eroded through time, but it probably explains the early relationship of government and people more adequately than the more common explanation of deception or skulduggery. Such processes resemble the decision-making in non-voting, informal committees in Britain, in which it is the chairman's job both to place views before the meeting and to translate its 'sense' into resolutions–avoiding, if possible, any formal voting procedure. The British small-group tradition maintains a distinction between consensual decision-making on the one hand, and electoral legitimacy

[1] This is indeed implied by both Shils, 'Concentration and Dispersal of Charisma', and Runciman, 'Charismatic Legitimacy', op. cit.

with regard to choosing officers. This distinction captures the flavour of elitist orientations far more accurately than the formal political processes based on mass elections. It is in small-group processes that the culture base can be observed, to which the formal electoral processes of mass parties are merely a symbolic superstructure.

A similar but much more openly articulated basis of participation and involvement exists in many developing countries. Once again the audience potential of a performance is considered vital. Indeed, one of the reasons for a preoccupation with international affairs on the part of leaders in developing countries, quite in excess of any genuine international status, wealth or power potential, is a search for more dramatic material with which to compensate for the relative dullness of much domestic 'development' politics. This is borne out by the remarkably ample space devoted to the international postures of leaders by the local press. It is helpful, therefore, to view the international system from the point of view of developing countries as a stage on which a performance may be provided for the benefit of a local audience no longer able to find adequate satisfaction in the 'traditional' performance composed only of domestic affairs.

Much of the critique of Western democracy by writers in developing countries stresses this failure to provide adequate participation in the traditional processes of according legitimacy. They challenge frontally the assertion of Western analysts that the difference between Western electoral legitimacy and traditional forms of politics is that of participation as against non-participation.[1] Western analysis, based on its own experience of electoral legitimacy, has tended to break down the relatively gross concept of *participation* into an *orientational* notion of involvement and a *processual* notion of participation. Involvement is generally assessed in two different ways (*a*) attitudinal (the cultural variables outlined in chapters 2 and 3), and (*b*) mobilizational (the indices of familiarization or socialization put forward by Deutsch). While it is perfectly legitimate to use these tools on developing countries, and deduce comparative characterizations of developing countries from any data obtained, it would be

[1] For a strong case against Western democracy see for instance Jayaprakash Narayan, *A Plea for the Reconstruction of Indian Polity*, Benares 1961. The analysis of Western democracy by Narayan and others is in fact remarkably like that of Robert Michels, *Political Parties*, first English edition, London 1915. For another analysis stressing the audience aspect of participation in developing countries see Masikh-uz-Zaman, *Community Development and its Audience*, Lahore 1960.

The classic statement of the Western position is cited above, p. 142, note 1.

dangerous to use this form of analysis and its results for the purpose of making judgements on legitimacy, and hence to explain from them basic patterns of political processes. This applies particularly to the context of political mobilization, with which we are here primarily concerned. Just as the bases of legitimacy vary considerably between the West and the Third World, so the bases and means of mobilizing are substantially different.

Our discussion of mobilization in the previous chapter has indicated the dangers of cleavage mobilization in developing countries in the absence of established universals. Cleavages are based on highly divisive structures like ethnic communities, race, religions, etc. As we have noted, every effort is made to prevent this form of cleavage mobilization gaining strength through the use of structural or situational facilities. In so far as Western electoral processes have been adopted, they tend to articulate such cleavage mobilizations. The basic direction of mobilization in developing countries has been from the top downwards; a means of structuring existing legitimacy based on traditional audience participation in support of inheritance leaders and elites. In order to accommodate this particular form of mobilization into a comparative analysis we require a directional variable which will differentiate between upward cleavage mobilization and induced downwards mobilization from an inheritance leader or elite. This variable will be called *stalagmite-stalactite*.

Stalactite mobilization reflects the type of constitutional-national or inheritance party mobilization discussed in the previous chapter. It is essentially induced, and is intended to provide a basis of structural support in terms of commitment and orientation on the part of those mobilized. It also seeks to counter-mobilize, where applicable, against established or nascent cleavage mobilizations based on regions, tribes, ethnic communities, religions, etc. One form of such mobilization is the inheritance party. Though its mobilizing processes almost invariably began before independence as a peripheral assault on the legitimacy of colonial government, the inheritance component is precisely the fact that, with independence and the take-over by the new legitimate inheritance party, the direction of mobilization changes to a downward aim. Indeed in many cases this anticipated change of direction was an essential part of the legitimacy basis of commitment at a time when the party was still mobilizing against established colonial authority. In stalactite mobilization the charisma of the leader, with its traditional component, will be dispersed in favour of the party structure. Another, though more diffuse means, is the national-constitutional framework, where the charisma of the leader may be partially dispersed in favour of a party, the constitutional structure, and the military and/or the civil bureaucracy. This represents a crucial distinction between traditional-developing countries on the one hand and Western countries on the other. In the developed countries of the West the legitimacy of leaders, elites or parties on the one hand, or of individuals occupying important offices on the other, is based on and reflects the overall legitimacy of the nation and its constitutional framework. In traditional-developing countries legitimacy of the nation itself, and of the political or constitutional structures appertaining to it, is partly the product of the legitimacy of a ruler. Even though chronologically the nation may be created by inheritance or revolution before a charismatic leader emerges, the priorities of legitimacy nonetheless suggest that the very creation of a charismatic arbiter is needed in order to provide legitimacy for the national or political structures. This is the basis of stalactite mobilization in developing countries.

Stalagmite mobilization, as we have noted, represents cleavage-based mobilization against or towards an existing authority and is more typical of the Western situation. In developing countries such mobilization applies to the structures based on communal groupings of the kind outlined above, acting as foci of mobilization against the stalactite mobilization structure. In some cases such mobilization in an electoral form has been partially accommodated into the system, as for instance in India, in Ceylon, and in Nigeria before 1965. In other countries such mobilization has not been accommodated, and represents a norm or even value-oriented response, often underground, to stalactite mobilization. Thus the activities of the East Pakistan Awami League are an instance of such stalagmite counter-mobilization against the national-constitutional orientation of Ayub Khan (hence his statement in Dacca in April 1966 that such mobilization represented an attempt to break up the state of Pakistan). Similarly the mobilization of collectivities like the army and its supporters in Nigeria, Ghana and Algeria against the inheritance leadership may be viewed as a form of stalagmite counter mobilization.

This directional variable has very great relevance to the problem of social and particularly political change in developing countries. Electoral mobilization among other things does provide for formal, institutionalized means of political change, or lack of it as the case may be. We know that this is not socially as effective as is often supposed; this problem has already been discussed at some length in terms of congruence between the social system and the political subsystem (chapter 6) and also in terms of the autonomy and differentiation of the political subsystem from other subsystems (chapter 3). In the absence of electoral mobilization, or at least its considerable de-emphasis in terms of values and objectively viewed function in much of the Third World, we must look elsewhere for the mechanisms of political and social change. It is noticeable that even in those developing countries where elections exist and their results are accepted by the participants, they cause little change either in policy or personnel; either the ruling legitimacy party continues more or less stably in power as in India, Mexico and Israel, or elections provide a mere façade for decisions which may bring about changes but are taken irrespective of electoral results and considerations. There are, of course, exceptions to this. In Ceylon for instance electoral results brought about a substantial change of the ruling elite; the newcomers introduced different policies from those of their predecessors following upon the general election of 1956 when the Shri Lanka Freedom Party took over from the United Party. But at the same time this was not an electoral change in the Western sense; the basis of Bandaranaike's electoral victory was a form of stalagmite counter mobilization whose basis was not primarily electoral but diffusely violent; the electoral victory was almost a confirmation of an effective coup rather than an alternative to it. In general electoral changes are not a common or effective means of inducing change.

Instead change comes from two sources, (1) the reorientation of the leader and elite in power, (2) the removal of individual or elite leadership through coups.

1. *Reorientation of Leadership*

In terms of the actor-audience relationship indicated earlier in this chapter, leaders in developing countries are perhaps more sensitive to the changing requirements of their audience than might be supposed. The inheritance situation in general suggests a balance between associational and dissociational factors with regard to the former ex-colonial power often generalized conceptually into a relationship with the ex-colonial or neo-imperialist West as a whole. Too strong an associational emphasis by the leadership towards alignment with the West produces a counter movement in a more dissociational direction; similarly too strong an emphasis on dissociation and apparent alignment and identification with the revolutionary-communist opponents of the West may produce a negative response in a more associational direction. It is not suggested that such realignments on the part of ruling elites or leaders in developing countries are the result of a search for some optimal mean in each individual case. Taking an overall view of the Third World, however, it is possible to discern certain basic pressures in both directions which indicate a tendency towards equilibrium.[1] Thus for instance Nkrumah and Sukarno may well have passed the acceptable limits of a dissociational-revolutionary direction, even though the original pressure for a more dissociative attitude was probably based on a reasonable assessment of legitimacy expectations. Similarly murmurings in, and resignations from, KANU in Kenya in March/April 1966 indicate at least the possibility of a negative response to the increasingly associational attitudes of Kenyatta, as well as being a reflection of interest–oriented communal conflict. One of the most carefully articulated attempts to find an equilibrium position in this context is that of Nyerere in Tanzania; indeed this leader appears more conscious than most of the precise demands of an equilibrium position, and is prepared to respond very readily in either direction to perceived needs in order to maintain maximum legitimacy for his rule. The international policies of King Hassan of Morocco appear to be guided by similar perspectives.[2] It is not possible here to do full justice to this important problem of adjustment to equilibrium between bloc association and dissociation, or to the means of assessing where the equilibrium position lies–precisely because we are dealing with a form of participation more akin to an actor-audience relationship than with more formal processes of electoral legitimacy, which makes the expression of approval or disapproval very hard to measure. The whole problem of association and dissociation spelt out here is of course merely one aspect of the general drive towards modernity–defined for present purposes as a changing goal largely connected with the reduction of atimia in the international system according to the dimensions of power, status and wealth.[3] The

[1] The bases for this equilibrium, and the pressures in both directions are analysed at some length in 'Inheritance', op. cit.

[2] See for example Douglas E. Ashford, *Political Change in Morocco*, New York 1961.

[3] This analytical approach to international modernity is spelt out at length in the admirable discussion by Gustavo Lagos, *International Stratification and Underdeveloped Countries*, Chapel Hill (North Carolina) 1963. For atimia see particularly pp. 22–25. A wider overview of these problems and their affect on the perception of actor-nations in an international context is attempted in Robertson and Nettl, 'Modernization and International Systems'.

establishment of such categories, which arrange as well as sharpen everyone's view of self in order that remedial action may be applied, requires diffusion of elite orientations through society and corresponding participation and involvement by these sectors. It is in this context, therefore, that participation in the creation of a climate of opinion becomes important. This climate of opinion, once established, may generate further constraints on elite and leadership action with a view to producing or accelerating social change.

It is perhaps significant that the most manifest processes of adjustment and change should relate to the international field, and that governments should on the whole be less responsive to purely internal demands for reorientation or change. But many effective demands for change are also generated internally. Again we do not find them in any anticipatory offerings by parties in the electoral market place. Instead they are residual responses to felt needs, generally in the context of deprivation. A sense of deprivation of promised or inherent rights provides the main basis for the relatively unstructured phenomena of persuasion–riots, demonstrations, strikes. Even though India and Malaysia have structural means of opposition in the polity, their unimportance *vis-à-vis* the dominant legitimacy party is such that effective demands for changes in policy will be articulated in the streets rather than the Lok Sabha; the opposition follow such expressions of dissent rather than leading them. This was the manner in which successful pressure for the creation of linguistic states was articulated, and has in fact become the established means of persuading or dissuading the government. The case of Ceylon has already been mentioned in this context. But the element of compression, to which we have repeatedly referred, tends to escalate such unstructured or diffuse opposition rapidly beyond facility (or role) and collectivity level; these movements often generate norm and value-oriented pressure, and thus call in question the legitimacy of ruling parties, elites and individual leaders. Precisely because of the latent or residual manner of according legitimacy, the status of rulers in this regard can often only be tested when such confrontations take place. This leads to consideration of the other effective means of creating change in developing countries.

2. *Coups as a Means of Change*

In the absence of more formal electoral mechanisms, it is particularly the function of coups to provide fairly regular tests of legitimacy orientations in developing countries. There is no need to investigate here the situational and structural facilities available to particular groups for the seizure of power; the articulate value system of national consciousness and honour, the access to rapid mobilization, the possibility of delivering individuals quickly at strategic points, and the possession of weapons by the army have all been documented sufficiently as factors which enable the armed forces in developing countries to play a major role in supporting or overthrowing governments.[1] However the structural conduciveness to coups in developing countries has perhaps been over-stressed; coups have become one of the major features in the characterization of developing polities, both empirically and as a form (and as an excuse for the absence) of analysis.[2] What is important for our purpose here is not so much the existence and frequency of coups, but their function in the legitimation process.

The moral condemnation of coups is a feature of political style peculiar to the West; such convictions are not shared either in communist or developing countries. Instead there may well be an acceptance of coups as an integral functional component both in the process of according and denying legitimacy, and as a means of achieving change. There is considerable difference in the classic type of coup immortalized under the name *Cuertalazo* in Latin America, and the type of coup more common in inheritance situations in the *nations trouvées*; the former producing almost no change of a political or social kind, the latter often adjusting both the manner of mobilization as between national-constitutional and party emphasis, and changing the attitude of the country concerned as between association and dissociation with regard to the West. A coup producing little or no change in any of these factors is rare in developing countries. In almost all the cases of coups over the last decade, the result has either been a radically different emphasis on mobilizational structures (Sudan, Nigeria, Ghana, Algeria) and/or in the competitive situation as between the West and the communist world (Algeria, Ghana, Indonesia). It is for instance significant that though the rate

[1] See particularly S. E. Finer, *Tne Man on Horseback*, London 1962; John J. Johnson (ed.), *The Role of the Military in Underdeveloped Countries*. See also S. P. Huntington, *Changing Patterns of Military Politics*, New York 1962, and Morris Janowitz, *The Military in the Political Development of New Nations*, Chicago 1964. A recent integrated discussion of structural and broader social factors making for military influence in Latin America is by S. Andreski, *Parasitism and Subversion: The Case of Latin America*, London 1966.

[2] See for instance R. van der Mehden, *Politics of the Developing Nations*, Englewood Cliffs, New Jersey, 1964, especially pp. 54–64.

of frequency of coups has changed little in Syria before and after the Second World War, the changes in government as a result of coups since 1956 have tended to produce changes more like those which we have suggested as typical for developing countries instead of the basic changelessness of *cuertalazos*. In present-day Latin America itself we also find both types of coups, but still with relatively high emphasis on the traditional type of coup. The reasons for this are not hard to seek, since the army has retained much of the tradition and orientations of a long period of *cuertalazos*. This identification of coups as one situationally functional means of change does throw doubt on the more traditional explanation which identifies military coups with some peculiarly cultural or psychological tradition in Latin America and certain countries of the Middle East. Instead it is suggested that the difference between *types* of coups may be significant, and that those common in developing countries today ought to be viewed as having a necessary function for inducing change in a certain stage of socio-political development.

It is of course difficult to assess, by the common means of measurement of political orientation in the West, the response of the typical participatory audience in developing countries to such coups. Given the compact organization of a military group successfully challenging a government, and the latent residual form of participatory response to legitimacy claims, no structured opposition to a successful coup on the part of the previous government's supporters can usually be expected. Yet there are some indices for measuring popular responses with regard to legitimacy challenges through coups. For one thing the unanimity of the army in organizing a coup is an important factor; there is a great deal of difference between the army acting as a collectivity, and certain regiments or units acting as an armed but otherwise informal group. Similarly we may find some evidence of audience attitude to the legitimacy of the previous government in the reaction of students—the most vocal group with its own basis of rapid mobilization and its own facilities for collective action. Finally in this context the subsequent behaviour of successful military challengers may provide important clues to the legitimacy situation; their ability and willingness to mobilize support by either of the basic structural alternatives, their readmission of previous members of the government to office, their continuation or disruption of previous policies. It is of course perfectly possible for coups to take place in an atmosphere of complete passivity, which give little indication of relative legitimacy orientations. In many ways legitimacy is a product of gradual familiarization; where coups are frequent the attitude of those not directly involved will be a mixture of non-committal caution and reinsurance, by keeping open links with all possible parties, elites or institutions.

Some of the difficulties which Western analysts have in evaluating change in developing countries also apply to the formulation of adequate judgements on 'good' or 'bad' government. Corruption is often considered to be a significant factor. A recent study has attempted to show that there may be a connection between colonial government and corruption–the Rousseau-like purity of Africans (in this case Nigerians) responding to evil Western colonial influence in much the same defenceless manner as Polynesians responded to the importation of European syphilis.[1] This may however be a doubtful importation of Western values into irrelevant circumstances. Certainly the attitude towards personal gain from public office is not as censorious in traditional and traditional-developing societies as in the West, where the two roles and actions have become sharply differentiated. Corruption in the West is typically associated with, and made reprehensible by, the temporary nature of public office; since personal gain cannot conceptually be made 'relinquishable', it cannot be electorally accommodated and therefore obstructs both the interest articulation and the legitimacy functions of elections.[2] In any situation where leadership and legitimacy are not subject to formally processual means of change, and are based on the *assumption* of permanence, this is likely to be reflected in an acceptance of the need to purchase services or favours from authority. Since those who have legitimate authority are not viewed as temporary occupants of posts, but as permanent incumbents, the division between private wealth and public authority is somewhat meaningless. It may well be, therefore, that the tendency in developing countries for those who have been overthrown in a coup to be accused *inter alia* of corruption is more an instance of imported Western polemical window-dressing which usually goes with electoral mobilization, than any genuine reflection on the legitimacy of previous rulers. Just as it is dangerous to take too literally the polemics of Bolsheviks as signifying hostility,

[1] See Ronald Wraith and Edgar Simpkins, *Corruption in Developing Countries*, London 1963. A recent graphic description of Western influence on Tahiti is Alan Moorehead, *The Fatal Impact*, London 1966.

[2] The most valuable discussion of the problem of corruption in developed countries, specifically in the United States, is still provided by *The Autobiography of Lincoln Steffens*–in spite of, or because of, its diffuse and rambling introspections.

so the phraseology of political change in developing countries should not be taken as having attained reified reality.

This broader discussion of the nature of legitimacy, its effects on mobilizational direction and on the processes of change, makes it possible to connect more meaningfully the two types of mobilization structures contrasted and analysed in the previous chapter with the broader aspect of legitimacy in developing countries as incorporated in the value system of developmental nationalism.[1] The basic forms of according legitimacy must obviously be related to the value system. As we have noted, there is a latent conflict between the traditional forms of according legitimacy and the influence of inheritance with its crystallization of developmental and national perspectives, based increasingly on the *nation trouvée*. The means of according legitimacy have to adjust themselves to the changing values. More particularly we must investigate the possibility of relating if possible the two forms of mobilization to each other and should try to examine their function as a means of giving expression to, as well as maintaining, legitimacy under circumstances of development. Is the choice between them historically and functionally haphazard? It would seem at first glance that in one important sense historical accident has been decisive: in all those cases where independence has been hastened either through dissociation or revolution, political parties or movements have been the most important factor of mobilization. In those countries, on the other hand, where social action and developmental consciousness have had little or nothing to do with independence (South America), or where party political mobilization has either been ineffective or nationally divisive (Egypt, Pakistan) national mobilization has been superordinated to party or movement. But national mobilization presents structural difficulties as well as instrumental benefits. The value system and its goals may be capable of being articulated and made operational in terms of norms, but the vertical hierarchy of control, communication and participation is far more complex and difficult to structure in constitutional form than through a dominant political party. The latter is after all the modern instrument *par excellence* of mobilization from top to bottom. Generally, attempts to build suitably simple constitutional structures take the form of 'basic' or 'guided'

[1] The phrase development nationalism was, as far as I know, first used in Brazil in the early 1950's (*O nacionalismo desenvolvimentista*) by an intellectual group called Itatiaia, which formed first the Economic Institute known as IBSEP in 1953 and then the ISEB (Instituto Superior de Estudos Brasileiros) in 1956.

democracy.[1] These latter types of political systems are really an attempt to knock the interest-articulation function out of politics altogether and make elections into 'pure' authority legitimating; we need only compare Ayub Khan and De Gaulle in this context. The mere fact of having electors share in the choices and decisions – at several removes – of the central consultative or legislative assembly is held to be a form of evaluative commitment to, and participation in, the construction of authority. This is a 'pure' instance of the General Will, in the sense that no party considerations of majority or minority are supposed to arise (but still do, both in France and during the last presidential elections in Pakistan). The original Soviets in early post-revolutionary Russia worked on the same principle. This pure legitimization, however, has its great drawbacks, since the very depersonalization or colourlessness of elections (merely choosing or ratifying individual, unrelated, largely unprogrammatic candidates) fails to mobilize people effectively and thus does not provide the required structural connection between authority and subject.[2] Emphasis on legitimizing elections has proved to weaken mobilized political commitment even in countries where parties play an electoral role, like Britain, Sweden, U.S.A.; too much emphasis on this function corrodes the cleavage bases of mobilization which electorally find more adequate expression in interest articulation and corresponding party structure. In developing countries with a constitutional orientation, where stalactite or downward mobilization

[1] Thousands of words have been wasted on semantic and classificatory arguments about this type of polity – 'tutelatory democracy (oligarchy)', 'modernizing bureaucracy (elite)' etc. This is the descriptive ideology at its worse, 'absolutizing the relative or peculiar, that is, being parochial' (Leo Strauss, 'An Epilogue' in H. J. Storing (ed.), *Essays on the Scientific Study of Politics*, New York 1962, p. 320). One cannot help feeling that the essentially transitory nature of these types, in terms of legitimacy as much as physical survival, makes them much more comprehensible as a phase in the post-inheritance national/party mobilization analysis – using functional rather than descriptive categories.

[2] 'However, these political leaders [in utopian, xenophobic developing countries] should not take their claim to legitimacy too literally. They should not rely on their nationalistic commitment as being strong enough to enable them to ignore or smother grievances completely. They should "play politics" in the usual sense with aggrieved groups, thus giving these groups access to responsible political agencies, and thereby reducing the conditions that pave counter claims to legitimacy.' (Neil J. Smelser, 'Mechanisms of Change . . .' op. cit., p. 47.)

Though one may not necessarily agree with this prescription, it will be noted that this extract implicitly recognizes the *difference* as well as the *relationship* between interest – articulation and legitimacy functions, and urges empirical as well as analytical reconciliation between them.

is the salient direction, a mainly electoral form of legitimacy tends to create a vacuum, especially where such legitimizing elections are indirect or in tiers, as in Pakistan.

This vacuum can best be illustrated in a purely formal way. A standard text on voting systems illustrates the so-called alternative vote by referring to various ways in which graded preferences between three candidates for office in a small-group situation can be most satisfactorily set off against each other (weighting the differences between first, second and third choices).[1] The assumption implicit in this particular manner of expressing unstructured, purely personal, preferences in the course of choosing *ex pluribus unus* is fairly obvious; such a method is clearly ideal for authority legitimation rather than interest articulation in the present context. What may be less obvious but just as important is the assumption that an election is a single act of will, meaningless in any continuum; it leaves no trace other than the election of X. Conversely the assumption is that there need be no continuing legitimacy for X other than his historic election. He is structurally unsupported–except in so far as a new *ex post* support structure arises which now may have nothing to do with the original election. *This* is the dangerous vacuum in elections that are unstructured choices of individuals and little else. A good example of how deeply ingrained into the culture a system of election may become–and how much it may influence the process of popular democratic elections in politics–is the British system of what I will call royalty-type selection–in fact a throwback to a practice prevalent in certain parts of ancient Greece, and incorporating some aspects of feudal practice. This is the process of choosing leaders with all the trappings and roles of elections, including application to signify willingness to stand, interview, semi-public evaluation, canvassing, etc. Once elected, however, these leaders or officials exercise not so much power (which is variable) but enjoy the status and influence of an emerged superior, expecting and getting the deference and title of a quasi-monarch. This is the case with heads of Oxbridge Colleges, Vice Chancellors and other [working] life offices. Compare this with, say, Bishops, who exercise the same type of authority on the basis of appointment rather than election. The manner of selection loses much of its relevance in so far as the basis of continuing legitimacy is concerned. Legitimacy in these 'royalty' cases is based neither on the office as such, nor on the fact that the candidate

[1] E. Lakeman and J. D. Lambert, *Voting in Democracies*, London 1955, pp. 288 ff.

was democratically elected; it is apparently an attribute of the person or, better, of the *type* of person. This might accordingly be described as an example of elitist [cultural] 'shaping' of formal electoral legitimacy.

Continued insistence on more or less *purely* national mobilization with, say, formal prohibition of any kind of party may lead to a rather diffuse, partial and above all *passive* acceptance of the national value system without evidence of any active or perceived mobilized commitment. At the same time this type of emphasis tends also to bring about a countervailing retreat into *oppositional* party mobilization. Perhaps the whole notion of national-constitutional mobilization—i.e. with nation, state and constitution as its main referent instead of more specific collectivities or structures, but under the umbrella of an assumed general value system—is peculiarly typical of British-trained soldiers and administrators; if a government of soldiers and civil servants ever took over in New Delhi they would perhaps approach the legitimacy problem similarly to Ayub Khan. It is thus somewhat ironical that the colonial servants of an elitist society like the British should have attempted to operate and inculcate such 'pure' constitutional forms. In any case examples of such mobilization based on ideal-typically constitutional forms are rare and usually of short duration. Pakistan and Burma were relatively durable examples, while the Sudan of General Abboud proved no more than a short interlude, liquidated by a party-mobilized opposition which, once in power, soon disintegrated in its turn.

More common is the case where an early preference for national mobilization by inheritance leaders has tended to revert to more specific emphasis on party structure in order to improve the process of mobilization more effectively and to channel it into a more specifically ideological direction. Malaysia provides an interesting example of such a shift through time. The creation of the Alliance Government was apparently meant to achieve, and appeared to succeed in achieving, a nation-oriented mobilization in favour of Malaysia (a *nation trouvée* if ever there was one), among the top and some of the middle sectors of the different communities in the federation. Originally this mobilized commitment was to overcome the strong communalism of Malaya itself, and was adapted to Malaysian problems on a larger scale only after 1963. The policy of the Alliance leadership may therefore be seen as creating a specific legitimacy orientation and a constitutional structure which both contained, and was superordinate to, the interest articulation of purely communal parties. But more recent evidence suggests that the legitimacy orientation of the ruling party has been eroded by continued emphasis on communal interest articulation within it; there is now a real fear that the government of Tunku Abdul Rahman may be turned into an increasingly Malayan communal interest structure at the expense of Chinese, Indians and others. We can see in the dominance of the Alliance a desire for such a legitimacy structure over and above the communal interest articulation, and in Singapore's secession from the federation a verdict of failure on this attempt (a similar secession was brewing during 1965 in Sabah).[1] A specific attempt at national mobilization has therefore been eroded by communal interest articulation—in spite of the confrontation with Indonesia. This analysis reflects in particularly acute form the same problems which we have already noted with regard to tribes in Uganda and Kenya, and caste in India. Such situations also provide an illustration of the important difference in cleavage bases and mobilizations between developed and developing societies. In the latter the bases are not based on intranational experience and structured by at least partially abstract commitments like class, religion, attitudes to issues, but by more concrete and deeply divisive factors like race, colour, ethnic community or caste. These abstractions can, of course, always become realities in developed countries given the right circumstances, as has become evident in the sharpening of community conflict in Belgium in the last few years. The colour problem, moreover, is anything but an abstraction even in highly developed countries. But at least neither problem has as yet been reflected by precisely related cleavages in the political system, as would have been the case in many new nations.

In most developing countries there is, moreover, no historical experience of national integration, and no authoritative state. A legitimacy orientation subsumed by interest articulation will, in terms of mobilized commitment, erode the structural basis of legitimacy on which the authority of an inheritance party, and possibly that of a charismatic leader or arbiter, must rest. As we shall see, an inheritance party must, if it is to maintain its effective claim to legitimacy, also maintain its emphasis on the saliency of the authority legitimizing

---

[1] The struggle for, and early success in, establishing a political legitimacy structure over and above the divisive communal conflict of interests in Malaysia is well analysed in K. J. Ratnam, *Communism and the Political Process in Malaya*, London 1965.

function. This appears crucial if inheritance parties are to remain dominant or exclusive in developing countries.

Indonesia provides an interesting variant of these models, combining interest-cleavage structures and overarching national-constitutional mobilization. The three major political groups–Army, Religious Nationalists and Communists–have over the last decade been welded into partial political agencies of the government–at least as long as this remained under the legitimate leadership of Sukarno. With all their differences, they did not [set out to] offer any alternative government; instead they mobilized their various supporters ostensibly on the leadership's behalf. This was the basis of *Nasakom*.[1] The position has been altered and the balance upset by the insurrection of the Communist Party (October 1965) which may be seen as an attempt to break up the *Nasakom* troika. Sukarno and his immediate followers attempted to maintain the symbols of the *Nasakom* arrangement as the essential vehicle of the revolution, in spite of the brief but bloody civil war. Sukarno continued to play down the apparent withdrawal of the communists from the troika as merely part of a policy of 'adjustment of balance'. It may be possible that if and when the communists are reduced to a less preponderant share in the legitimacy structure, a Sukarno-type compromise may well be re-established, with or without him; certainly he and his immediate supporters were loath to accept the imbalance which must result from any excessive weakening of the communist component. But probably this solution has been (and can only be) achieved at the cost of continual foreign confrontations; without them the constituent components of the polity are likely to become too particularistic, dissensual, and finally disruptive. The end of confrontation with Malaysia has therefore been matched during 1966 with strenuous efforts by Suharto's government to create an internal consensus by maintaining some of the *Nasakom* structure intact. The extent to which the insurrection was genuinely an attempt by the KPI to seize power, or merely a tactical move within *Nasakom* which got out of hand, is not yet clear; we cannot take the victors' evidence fully at face value. One eventual solution may still be some form of re-admission of the communist component, possibly under a thin disguise, to a reconstituted tripartite mobilization structure in the polity.

[1] For Indonesia in this context see Herbert Feith, 'Indonesia's Political Symbols and their Wielders', *World Politics*, XIII, 1 (October 1960), pp. 79–97; *The Decline of Constitutional Democracy in Indonesia*, New York 1962; most recently Herbert Luethy, 'Indonesia Confronted', *Encounter*, XXV, 6 (December 1965), pp. 80–89, XXVI, 1 (January 1966), pp. 75–83.

A somewhat similar situation existed in Iraq, where Kassem began with no structured political support at all but tried to mobilize commitment on an Indonesian-type national balance between two hitherto antagonistic groups, both committed to the basic tenets of the 'revolution'. His successors have tried various alternatives, ranging from dominant party mobilization (Ba'ath) to Aref's version of an Egyptian-type national mobilization in 1964. But none of these variants or combinations has yet produced any evidence of stable commitment, and therefore of long-term durability.

But perhaps the most significant example of a deliberate and controlled attempt to shift the basis of mobilized commitment from a national-constitutional to a party base was Egypt. For years Nasser was trying to establish a political movement of logistic support on a broad national basis, but at the same time without the colourlessness and lack of cohesion of Pakistan's basic democracy–an attempt to have the best of both forms of mobilization.[1] Broad as it is, Nasser's version of party mobilization requires from participants a certain minimum commitment to the current *status quo* and specifically to the revolution. That 'optimal' solution, though by no means entirely successful, may nonetheless help in part to explain the relatively high stability of the regime.

There are many other examples of this type of shift from an early, but often narrow, constitutional legitimacy base–the consequence of a coup–to a broader party basis of mobilization and support for legitimacy. Peron provided the most typical example in Latin America of such stalactite mobilization, proliferating from the top downwards after inheritance and combining in varying degrees national orientations with party structures and techniques.

We have already classified the two directions of mobilization as stalagmites and stalactites respectively, in accordance with the direction, timing and source of mobilization. Stalactites are the most common case of post-inheritance structures mobilizing from the top downwards. They may be the consequence of coups in favour of officers or other elites with development orientations, looking for the necessary mobilizing tools after they have gained power. The

[1] A need perceived at least as clearly by Soviet analysts as by those of the West. 'These measures [expropriation, planning, etc.] do not themselves go beyond the limitations of state capitalism. The social base of the regime is still narrow, and the popular masses are no more allowed to participate in making decisions about their country than they were before . . .' R. Avakov and G. Mirsky, 'The Structure of Classes in Underdeveloped Countries', in *Mirovaya Ekonomika i Mezhdunarodniya Otnosheniya*, No. 4 (1962), p. 79.

relationship between party and state will be uneasy and shifting.[1] A relatively late, post-inheritance appearance of parties would thus set them at a disadvantage compared to national, constitutional and administrative norms. As we have noted stalagmites in developing countries are, on the other hand, opposition parties, whether based on on a breakaway from the ruling elite like that of the KANU deputies in Kenya who attempted to form an opposition under Oginga Odinga in April 1966, or on cleavage-based counter mobilization–ethnic, tribal or religious–against the stalactite mobilization of the ruling party, or the national-constitutional or military structure. Such counter mobilization may also be based on a region or sub-culture, not unlike the Norwegian cleavage basis mentioned earlier. It should, of course, be emphasized again that in colonial, pre-independence situations even eventual stalactite inheritance parties will often begin as stalagmites at the periphery, like the FLN and the Indian Congress before 1947, though in other cases, where such parties are at least partially inspired by the colonial power, as in Ceylon or in the case of the Muslim League in India, they will already have begun life as stalactites.

The often difficult and conflicting relationship between party and national-constitutional structures enhances the vital role of the charismatic arbiter. We have already introduced the concept of charismatic arbitrage earlier as peculiarly relevant to developing countries in connection with mobilization and legitimacy. The particular function of this type of leadership in reconciling conflict between alternative and competing mobilization structures in many developing countries will be clear from the immediately foregoing discussion of actual and potential conflict between them. In quite a number of countries the conflict has been institutionalized, and with it the role of the charismatic arbiter; Bourguiba in Tunisia, at one time Sukarno in Indonesia, Modibo Keita in Mali and Houphouet-Boigny in the Ivory Coast–above all Nyerere in Tanzania and Kenyatta in Kenya. Even in situations where realistic arbitrage is less institutionalized, some aspects of such a role must inevitably devolve on the leader who is both head of his party and chief of state. Elsewhere the effective national leader may be genuinely 'above' party and play a more traditional role of king or prince as in Iran or in Cambodia. The existence of this arbitrage aspect of leadership in a situation of developmental nationalism has to be recognized. Precisely where

---

[1] See C. A. Moore, *Tunisia*, op. cit., for evidence of this in one of the most 'orderly' developing countries.

arbitrage is relatively lacking and a preponderant alignment with party has taken place, as in Ghana, an important function in the attainment of equilibrium between mobilization structures and commitments may be lacking. Any adequate analysis of legitimacy and mobilization must therefore stress the component of arbitrage in all such situations where both forms of mobilization are structurally represented and ideologically emphasized.

CHAPTER TEN

Mobilization and the Quality of Political Culture

SUMMARY

We now come back to the classification of political cultures into constitutional and elitist, which was established for developed countries in chapter 3. Does such a classification apply also to the developmental situations we have just been examining, and if so how? Can we relate stalactite mobilization in any general and systematic way to these two types of social culture?[1] An attempt is made in this chapter to isolate the factors which indicate the nature of emerging political cultures in situations of development. Then possible future developments are discussed under four headings: 1. The relationship between forms of mobilization, patterns of culture and social change. 2. The relationship of form, direction and structure of mobilization with legitimacy. 3. The instrumentality of different forms of mobilization for economic growth. 4. The chances of autonomous (as opposed to induced) democratization in the form of choice-accommodation.

[1] There has recently been an increasing effort to analyse the problem of developing countries more specifically in terms of political culture. A cultural emphasis is implied in many area studies of developing countries. Culture has also played an important part in many historical studies of social change in different societies, especially where particular dramatic events like the Bolshevik Revolution or the Meiji restoration in Japan were at issue. For the latter see particularly R. P. Dore, *Education in Tokugawa, Japan*, London 1965, who concludes that 'where the notion of individual self-improvement is widely diffused, the notion of *national* improvement can readily be understood and accepted' (though he does not, of course, suggest self-improvement to have entrepreneurial connotations like e.g. McClelland). See also R. N. Bellah, *Tokugawa Religion*, Glencoe 1957; R. A. Scalapino and J. Masuri, *Parties and Politics in Contemporary Japan*, Berkeley and Los Angeles 1962; Robert E. Ward and Dankwart A. Rustow (eds.), *Political Modernization in Japan and Turkey*, Princeton 1964. Particularly important in this field is the work of Clifford Geertz, who has tied in religion as a vital component of culture formation. See his recent general outline in 'Religion as a Cultural System', in Michael Banton (ed.), *Anthropological Approaches to the Study of Religion*, London 1966. Geertz also provides perhaps the best 'bridge' between anthropological and sociological approaches to the empirical study of culture.

For a start it appears likely that there is a *prima facie* relationship between constitutional or national *mobilization* on the one hand, and what we have called a constitutional pattern of culture on the other. Both have the same symbols and structural referents. Successful mobilization of a developing country on a national-constitutional basis would enhance the legitimacy of the existing constitutional structure. In so far as inheritance leadership is, in the early stages, charismatic, it is the top constitutional office or structure that will benefit from both the routinization of charisma and the successful initial implementation of developmental nationalism. It is this type of expectation that seems to have guided leaders like the Shah of Persia, Ayub Khan, Sukarno and Prince Sihanouk of Cambodia in their emphasis on being arbiters-'above' party. Some of this emphasis also seems to apply to Nehru's successors; the assertion that it is the *office* of Prime Minister that has benefited from Nehru's charisma, rather than expecting that the *person* of Shastri or Mrs. Gandhi-or for that matter the top leaders of the Congress party-should attempt to develop a new charisma of their own. Certainly both of Nehru's successors hitherto have gone out of their way to stress the difference in style between themselves and their predecessor-Shastri almost comically so. Yet this point has not always been adequately understood in the West. Thus, for instance, the British press coverage of post-Nehru India provides an interesting slant on the premises and ideology of what are really quite sophisticated and knowledgeable journalists-India being, in Britain, traditionally the best-reported developing country. For one thing, the comparison Nehru-Shastri is made almost entirely in personal terms. Secondly, too much was made of the confrontation Prime Minister-Party Boss (Shastri-Kamaraj Nadar) with the former at first depicted as the creature of the latter. No one seems to have suggested that the routinization of

Directly comparative work on socio-political culture is rarer and more recent. One such attempt at a diarchic confrontation is David E. Apter, 'The Role of Traditionalism in the Political Modernization of Ghana and Uganda', *World Politics*, XIII, 1 (October 1960), pp. 45-68. General theoretical approaches by political scientists are also rare. The first perhaps was Gabriel A. Almond in 'Comparative Political Systems', *Journal of Politics*, XVIII, 3 (August 1956), pp. 391-409. More recently there has been a compendium of analyses of political culture specifically tied to problems of development; Lucian W. Pye and Sydney Verba (eds), *Political Culture and Political Development*, Princeton 1965, op. cit., including studies of Russia, Japan, England, Germany, Turkey, India, Ethiopia, Italy, Mexico and Egypt. This project followed on the five-country study of *The Civic Culture*. Cf. R. A. Packenham, 'Approaches to the Study of Political Development', *World Politics*, XVII, 1 (October 1964), pp. 108-20, who also stresses the possibility of a comparative cultural approach.

charisma, and the subsequent reluctance to re-personalize it, were essentially situational – not some unfortunate shortcoming in the new incumbent's personality (cf. Eshkol and Ben Gurion in Israel, Erhard and Adenauer in Germany). Charismatic leaders thus attempt to ensure the succession for themselves in deliberately structural or institutional rather than personal terms; even if they do not, the situation frequently does it for them. This is part of the wider problem of inheritance parties tending to break up as a result of fission generated from within, which we shall examine at the beginning of chapter 11.

The American revolution in the eighteenth century is one very marked example of national mobilization leading directly to a strongly constitutional orientation in political culture. The case for arguing that American political culture is constitution- rather than elitist-oriented has already been argued at some length in chapter 3. Naturally we must make allowances for the very different ideological orientations of the time; the legalistic perspectives of the inheritance leadership, the almost universal antipathy to faction, the absence of any sense of an inclusive international system within which the search for status affected the legitimacy of the government at home, and finally the lack of structural means of stalactite mobilization. Even so, this was the first modern inheritance situation *par excellence*. Yet the situation of today's *nations trouvées* is very different. The developmental value system on an international scale both constrains and gears internal mobilization in certain directions of instrumentality. Secondly the technological means of communication have changed enormously, so that forms of mobilization are sought which compress into a short space of time the long-run effects of national integration in the West, for instance in the United States. Where American social and intellectual historians tend to stress the components of integration in their own past, developing countries are acutely aware 'that despite its advantages [for establishing an integrated national society], the United States came very close to failing in its effort to establish a unified legitimate authority ... it is fairly obvious that conditions in the early United States were quite different from those faced by most of the new nations of today'.[1] Today's developing

---

[1] Lipset, *First New Nations*, op. cit., p. 91. For American stress on basic cultural and structural integrative factors, see ibid; also Daniel Boorstin, *The Genius of American Politics*, Chicago 1953; Louis M. Hartz, *The Liberal Tradition in America: An Interpretation of American Political Thought since the Revolution*, New York 1955; Ralph H. Gabriel, *The Course of American Democratic Thought*, New York 1956; cf. Henry Steele Commager, *Living Ideas in America*, New York 1951 for a selection of foreign statements on this point.

ex-colonies need some kind of mobilizing party to facilitate legitimacy articulation and to combine inheritance with development. The building and structuring of such stalactite parties suggest the need for a clearly defined elite; if they do not exist the political system will tend to create them, very much in accordance with Lasswell's prescription.[1] Developing societies with stalactite mobilizing parties are culturally much less likely to be constitution-oriented than the historical United States, even when they do opt for a national-constitutional emphasis in mobilization. We can see the problems created by a cultural orientation towards constitutionalism in a developmental situation very clearly in Egypt. The constitutional structure is deficient insofar as, for instance, the civil administration at higher levels continues to be too much identified with the army. There is a felt lack of mobilized commitment and of a suitable structure for remedying this need. A party political form of mobilization in stalactite form was being gingerly attempted for the fourth time in 1964–5. The difficulty in this context with personal charisma is that, instead of *assisting* political mobilization, it sometimes *substitutes* for it to a considerable degree. Frequent public expressions of popular approval, the articulation of accorded legitimacy by enthusiastic urban crowds, are not themselves evidence of mobilized commitment, at best a crude unstructured form of it; only the lower indices of acculturation mentioned in chapter 2 are reached in such a way. There is in the case of Egypt a strong argument for seeing in the persistence of a national-constitutional form of mobilization, and in the corresponding difficulty in the emergence of a more directly elitist stalactite party, a reflection of a particular historical tradition that has produced a strongly hierarchical culture based on the identification of institutional legitimacy with personal leadership. This appears to hinder the kind of orientational change towards more acculturated involvement outlined in chapter 2.[2] In other words there may be distinct historical and structural reasons why neither a distinctly political culture nor a distinct political subsystem can develop in Egypt. Empirically, in accordance with our cultural classification, both the United States and Egypt might initially be classified as constitutionalist cultures; but whereas the United States meets the important definitional criteria of a differentiated political subsystem

---

[1] Lasswell and Kaplan, *Power and Society*, op. cit.; 'The Elite Concept' in Lasswell *et al.*, *The Comparative Study of Elites*, op. cit.

[2] For an acute analysis of this tradition see A. Abdel-Malek, *Egypte: société militaire?*, Paris 1963. A more extended discussion of this view in the context of bureaucracy is given below, p. 379f.

with its own specific institutions to which considerable weight and reverence are attached, Egypt is a 'peculiar' instance where these criteria do not yet apply, but where the historical socio-political tradition happens to be strongly institutional for other reasons.

There are also significant instances of strong bias towards constitutional-national forms of mobilization in situations where the socio-political culture might have led us to expect an elitist, party-based mobilization structure. Thus Pakistan appears to be strongly anchored in the Indian tradition of crystallized status ascription which leads to the emergence of elites little differentiated as between subsystems. This is not primarily a matter of religion so much as of social stratification; Islam, though basically egalitarian, has not proved a barrier to the formation of cohesive elites and of marked social disjunction in terms of class stratification. It is one of the strongly compensatory religions.[1] Where the constitutional orientation of the polity in India appears to aim at the creation of a differentiated political elite distinct from the established social elites, using the inheritance legitimacy of the Congress party and especially the dispersed and institutionalized charisma of the inheritance elite around Nehru, the constitutional orientation of the polity in Pakistan since the advent to power of Ayub Khan has attempted to make a clean sweep; not to create a differentiated political elite but to prevent political elite formation altogether by emphasizing the role of the administration, and by legitimizing the administrative-constitutional structure through direct democracy. This does not necessarily mean that political elites do not emerge; there is also evidence of party-based counter mobilization, especially in East Pakistan.[2] As yet it is by no means certain that a constitutional socio-political culture in a wider sense is emerging in Pakistan.

In the Arab Middle East and in Latin America the same lack of congruence can be observed; constitutional emphasis on mobilization –in some cases even differentiated and strongly conflicting political elites as in Syria–struggling with a cultural orientation towards elitism.[3] To a considerable degree this incongruence is simply the

[1] For the relationship between social structure, economic development and religion in the Middle East, see A. J. Meyer, *Middle Eastern Capitalism: Nine Essays*, Cambridge (Mass.) 1959; Reuben Levy, *The Social Structure of Islam*, Cambridge 1962, and most recently a very different analysis by Maxime Rodinson, *Islam et capitalisme*, Paris 1965.

[2] See for instance Karl von Vorys, *Political Development in Pakistan*, Princeton 1965.

[3] For Syria see Patrick Seale, *The Struggle for Syria*, Oxford 1965.

consequence of the narrow range of political culture. Elite formation is a widespread social phenomenon, while conflict and differentiation are confined to the 'narrow' political system in which only a limited number of elite participants are meaningfully involved. It may well be that the conflictual nature of politics is directly the result of this two-tier system: the stable basis of social elite formation makes possible a more risky policy of conflict at the centre which does not however endanger the wider social legitimacy base of these elites. The corollary of this is that the consequences and outcomes of such political conflicts shall not seriously disturb the social base. Such a situation represents a 'game' of politics in the truest sense, and certainly helps to explain a long period of Latin American politics prior to the advent of effective Populism and its subsequent transformation into developmental nationalism; strong remnants of this situation may still be found in many countries like Colombia, Ecuador and Bolivia. We have already noted the existence of such a problem in the context of socio-political congruence or incongruence in developed countries in chapter 6. In developing countries the problem is much more acute. A new polity, attempting to articulate structures and processes conducive to the attainment of developmental goals, will have to struggle in order not to be stifled by a social culture with which it may be strongly incongruent. The history of Burma in the last two decades is a good example of what is in many ways a relapse into non-developmental, withdrawn isolation, under the surveillance of a military regime dedicated mainly, it would seem, to the prevention of the emergence of any mobilization structures.

We have in fact to be very careful, in the study of *nations trouvées* and development, to avoid deducing cultural orientations too readily from evidence of structure and process in politics. There is first the problem of an international, global-minus culture of developmental nationalism created by the existence of the Third World which certainly inhibits and constrains the development of national political cultures in the individual manner in which this took place in the West.[1] The 'gap' of several hundred years of national independence and autonomy in the West between the end of the Middle Ages and today, during which the notion of an international culture largely lost its validity, may globally prove to be the historical exception rather than the rule. Secondly there is the obvious problem of newness; a distinctly political culture can hardly be said to have emerged

[1] See 'Inheritance', op. cit., for a discussion of this international culture and value system.

293

without some evidence of corresponding subsystem differentiation. Culture is no doubt confirmed by political processes; initially, however, it is the orientational setting within which structures and processes are shaped that to a large extent defines a culture. It is perfectly feasible to analyse politics in developing countries in terms of different cultural influences and constraints, and to contrast the instrumentality of political structure and process towards goal attainment with the concessions imposed by history and tradition, but it would be naïve to confine this to a purely or even mainly political context. Elitism and constitutionalism as cultural orientations are useful patterns primarily for the analysis of developed societies; there is some evidence of similar crystallization in developing countries, particularly where emphasis on one or other of the two major forms of mobilization may be due to cultural influences rather than mere circumstantial causes. Thus there may be a *prima facie* relationship between emphasis on constitutional mobilization and a constitutional culture, and between a party emphasis and an elitist culture, and such emphasis maintained through time may well help to produce a corresponding cultural orientation. But we have already seen in chapters 8 and 9 that the emphasis in developing countries is rarely sustained or stable, that it frequently swings and rebounds from one to the other–that in fact excessive emphasis on one form tends to produce a reaction in favour of the other. This is one of the main causes of instability in the new nations. Consequently any over-facile identification of structure and process with culture must be avoided.

The need for caution will be all the more evident if we jump out of our frame of reference for a moment and look at pre-development or traditional societies. The notion of such a category of societies is used with all due reservation since it is by no means certain that today an analytically separate category of this sort still makes any sense.[1] In these would-be societies politics hardly emerges in any differentiated concreteness (although anthropologists, with their own definition of politics–nothing to do with roles–have no difficulty in separating and analysing politics and a version of the political

[1] Nonetheless the need for 'a speculative paradigm of groups', which separates pre-development, developing and developed societies into 'traditional, transitional and modern' for purposes of analysis, is convincingly stressed in the scheme offered by F. W. Riggs, 'The Theory of Developing Polities', *World Politics*, XVI, 1 (October 1963), pp. 151 ff. But much more thought needs to be given to the meaning and organizing power of these categories in present circumstances.

system).[1] There is thus hardly any political culture to speak of except around the centre, amongst the major participants. Accordingly we cannot apply our political culture categories meaningfully to countries like Basutoland and the pre-revolutionary Yemen. Even in such cases where the use of the patterns constitutional-elitist is meaningful at all, it would appear pointless to try and work out any hierarchical order of causality in order to apply one or other category; conceptually we do not seem to have in pre-development societies any real means of ordering our two dichotomies. On one hand many of these societies have distinct elites (in the form of dominant families or age groups), on the other their ascriptive selection is expressed in terms of institutions, ranks, offices. Where elites can be said to exist, as among the Buganda, there is a snug, long-established fit between them and the social institutions – indeed elites and institutions are almost indistinguishable from each other. Both help to emphasize and demarcate each other. But the whole notion of opinion as a means of overcrowding or reinforcing cleavage, of specific mobilizing structures and of a constitutional framework to embody them, are all alien to these societies. Yet on a small scale (tribe, clan) mobilization is relatively easy within such societies because of this fit – though of course it is not political but military or religious mobilization – in defence or emphasis of the existing. The point that is often missed by modern analysts of mobilization is that traditional societies do have highly efficient and rapid means of mobilization relating to their particular reference groups. The common if limited stock of information permits the instant identification of the alien and the hostile.[2]

While it is therefore perfectly possible to discover more or less

[1] There is a large literature on this. For the most comprehensive comparative statement, see M. Fortes and E. E. Evans-Pritchard (eds), *African Political Systems*, London 1940; more recently Michael Banton (ed.), *Political Systems and the Distribution of Power*, ASA Monograph 2, London 1965.

[2] A relevant problem which has never ceased to intrigue me is the instant certainty with which enemies are identified in periods of communal rioting in e.g. India, Africa, etc. In developed, pluralistic societies this takes us much longer; dress and smell for instance are deceptive. Moreover, we make frequent mistakes in our hostile identifications. The records of Section IV of the German RSHA in the Nazi era, charged with the solution of the Jewish problem, clearly show this difficulty of accurate identification; hence the reliance on documentary evidence. So does the evidence of marginal cases in *apartheid* enforcement, where there is no criterion of visible colour. The problem is illuminated in a fascinating way by Sinclair Lewis, *Kingsblood Royal*, 1947, where this novelist describes the progress of a man at first recognized universally as white to a situation in which he becomes equally universally considered as coloured – without, of course, any change in pigmentation. Such a story would be quite impossible in India.

elitist tendencies in traditional societies, these can be compared only in terms of some notional scale of egalitarianism – or, better, of closed or open access. The present confrontation of cultural orientations in developed societies, between elitism and constitutionalism according to the relative weighting of institutional structures, and the differentiated or undifferentiated nature of the political subsystems, is in the main pointless. Developing countries are necessarily a transitional category with regard to political culture; new polities created by an inheritance situation emerging from a diffuse socio-cultural environment. Nonetheless the relationship between party and state in the political system of developing countries, where both forms of mobilization are temporarily 'in balance' (it would be absurd to speak of equilibrium in situations of such instability), may help to provide some evidence of nascent or established cultural orientations provided we do not strain its weight.

The history of Nigeria since independence, for instance, suggests the emergence of a constitutional culture; the overthrow of the Northern-dominated federal government of Sir Abubakar Tafewa Balawa, and the subsequent introduction of military government in all provinces with apparently strong centralizing tendencies, do appear to represent an anti-elitist affirmation against the attempt to use the constitutional structure of the Federation, and the electoral mobilization system, in an elitist direction by the North-West regional alliance. The Northern Party, the NPC, and its allies were beginning to behave in many ways like the stalactite parties of party-oriented mobilization systems. Notwithstanding the peculiar tribal divisions of this very large and loose *nation trouvée*, it is conceivable that a more widespread elitist orientation among some of the main tribes might have produced a more openly stalactite party orientation, resulting in the formation of a single alliance party throughout Nigeria – or a disruption of the Federation altogether – rather than a strongly renewed emphasis on centralized national-constitutional forms of mobilization and the virtual prescription of parties. In this sense the events of 1965–6 in Nigeria may legitimately be viewed as conservative or restorative.

The majority of cases show some kind of balance between the two forms of simultaneous mobilization; such simultaneous and dynamically competitive situations are in a sense the ideal-typical case of the developmental *nation trouvée*. It is usually very difficult to decide where power and ultimate decision-making between party and state are really located, especially where a charismatic arbiter presides over both. The jostling for position among Kenyatta's lieutenants in Kenya between 1964 and 1966 is an illustration of these uncertainties, the position of Odinga and Mboya sometimes appearing more firmly anchored in their party role than in their ministerial position. The decision in May 1965 in Zanzibar to make responsibility to party formal and exclusive, and thus strongly downgrade the autonomous authority of ministerial office and its dependence on the President, can also be viewed in the light of this basic party-constitution dichotomy; yet the subsequent policy of President Nyerere on the mainland once more suggests a contrary emphasis. Sometimes it would almost seem as though Nyerere were trying objectively to make up his mind as between party and national forms of mobilization.

This uncertainty and conflict are, of course, a reflection of the dual nature of mobilization itself; there is overlap and competition between, say, KANU and Kenyatta's government as means of mobilizing Kenya, overlap that has become still greater and more confusing since KADU, then the only opposition party, went into liquidation in 1964–a liquidation of an unwanted and out-dated *structure* as much as of an unviable opposition role. It is important to distinguish between this conflict–usually hidden but occasionally overt–and the much more common phenomenon of inter-party struggle for power. In Turkey, one of the most manifest cases, Republicans and Democrats (Justice Party) compete within an elitist setting–a struggle between two different political elites that have been crystallizing ever since one sprang out from the body of the other more than twenty-five years ago, after several false starts under the aegis of Ataturk. But beneath this struggle there was an attempt on the part of the army leadership under Gursel and the Revolutionary Council to impose a constitutional orientation on both parties after 1961, to implement the Ataturk direction of turning an elitist system into a constitutional one.[1]

If we take countries like Ghana, Algeria or Tunisia, the relative neglect of national mobilization in the early inheritance stage was

---

[1] An attempt to discuss Imperial Turkish society in accordance with our elitist/constitutional classification presents some intriguing problems. As in most traditional empires which had been in existence for a long time, and whose constitutional structure was weakening towards the end, the basis of support toward the end became an increasingly elitist one. The growing tendency in such a situation for elites to form *outside* the formal institutional structure (or as a result of one institution growing at the expense of others), and then supporting and controlling the structure as a whole, was especially noticeable in Turkey (compared to, say, China). The rise of the Nationalist movement should thus be seen, not as the beginning of a new tendency, but as the final

accentuated by an increasingly pronounced elitist orientation. As in the case of countries with a more constitutional mobilization, the dust-storm of personal charisma at first obscured much of the eventual orientation. But the evidence does suggest that it was the party rather than the state which was the main beneficiary of the routinization and dispersion of charisma.[1] As already suggested, the mobilizational demands of inheritance–particularly where resisted by the colonial power–followed directly by the demands of development nationalism, make an elitist orientation a quicker and more flexible means of achieving the goals postulated by the value system. The counter pressures are also greater, and may lead to counter-mobilizations–often on the part of the military, like the 1965 coup against Ben Bella in Algeria and the overthrow of Nkrumah early in 1966. In many cases we should therefore view military intervention as the spearhead of a constitutional counter mobilization against an excessive emphasis on the structure–and, where applicable, ideology –of a stalactite party. The latent conflict between party and national-constitutional forms and structures of mobilization then comes out into the open through a manifest clash between party and military. Students of the Soviet Union know well how conscious the party leadership has always been of this possibility, and how carefully every opportunity for creating ideological, structural or situational facilities for such a conflict has been blocked.

We might perhaps conclude the enquiry into mobilization in developing countries so far by stating four hypotheses about future

---

and successful breakthrough of an elitist counter mobilization that had begun with the Janissaries and almost succeeded in breaking through at the time of Enver Pasha and the Young Turks. It is the particular contribution of Ataturk that he attempted to force this explosion back into constitutional channels–by eroding, somewhat like Stalin, the elite which had brought him to power–though he never succeeded in taming it to the same extent. This problem remained, and remains, largely unsolved in Turkey today. The best discussion of these problems is Bernard Lewis, *The Emergence of Modern Turkey*, London 1961, especially chapter X.

[1] For Ghana, see Runciman, 'Charisma', Apter, *Ghana in Transition*, Austin, *Politics in Ghana*, all op. cit.; for Tunisia, the valuable recent analysis by Moore, *Tunisia*, op. cit. There is no book particularly on the structure of politics in Algeria; some information may be gathered from the recent historical study by David C. Gordon, *The Passing of French Algeria*, Oxford 1965, Claude Estier, *Pour L'Algérie*, Paris 1964. Cf. the overview in Arslan Humbaraci, *Algeria: A Revolution that Failed*, London 1966. Another useful case history of the problem is provided by Aristide R. Zolberg, *One-Party Government in the Ivory Coast*, Princeton 1965. Coleman and Rosberg, *Political Parties in Africa*, op. cit., provides useful comparative evidence.

developments in the context of the main topics discussed here. 1. The first concerns the wider implications for the future of the relationship between the two forms of mobilization and the two patterns of culture, especially with regard to the production of a specific pattern of culture for political development and political change. This hypothesis is mainly concerned with sociological criteria of analysis rather than practical criteria of instrumentality for given goals. The notion that the immediate impetus for any rapid social change comes through the emergence of new elites and through their onslaught on the existing incumbents, to penetrate or to replace them, is by now almost a sociological truism. In saying this we have said everything–and nothing. In the inheritance-developmental, or more revolutionary-developmental situations which we have been discussing, the emergence of new elites may sometimes be pre-empted or aborted by the premature imposition of a constitutional orientation on an unready society–as in some ex-colonial territories emerging by peaceful negotiation. The constitutional-national frame-work and resultant mobilizational techniques have, as we have seen, sometimes a very arbitrary or manufactured appearance. New inheri-tance elites have hardly had time to become established before they have to adapt themselves to–and worse, identify themselves with–imported political institutions and processes. Early post-independence Ceylon is a good illustration of this, as are a number of Francophone African states; the Congo is the archetypal example of the problem.[1]

It can therefore be argued that a more traditional basis of support for inheritance elites–new in the sense of their function and role in an inheritance and developmental context–may be desirable to give them the early logistic support which will enable them in time to develop a wider legitimacy and an effective stalactite mobilizing structure. This may mean precisely the type of communal stratifica-tion described earlier in chapter 8, where a new legitimacy collec-tivity with a cross- or even anti-communal orientation rests in effect on a particular communal base; the objective effect being that one communal group has privileged access to power and authority positions at the expense of others. This kind of communal reservoir of latent legitimacy support has been very aptly called a vote bank–though, of course, it applies also to non-electoral situations.[2] Mobilizational

[1] For the relationship between the 'set' tribes, structures and elites, and the new political processes and institutions relating to independence in the Congo, see most recently Paule Bouvier, *L'accession du Congo belge a l'indépendance: Essai d'analyse sociologique*, Brussels 1966.

[2] See F. G. Bailey, *Caste and the Economic Frontier*, op. cit.

possibilities exist in pre-development societies, and the rapid adaptation of these possibilities in the political sphere is liable to be useful as a means of initial legitimacy support. In other words the legitimizing principles of pre-development societies, with their search for community-based consensus, probably suit inheritance political mobilization better than Western systems. This community base for initial elite formation must of course be at least partially open, so that access will not be altogether denied to candidates from other communities, even though these may be in a minority. This partially open elite structure for mobilizing purposes is best attained through an inheritance party. In time this elite party may disintegrate and produce intra- or inter-party competition or conflict. But initially the function of mobilization is best served through an elite-controlled mobilizing party. In this one respect, therefore, the modern consensus in developed nations or states resembles the traditional consensus in families and tribes and even castes. *Elites and consensus are positively and functionally correlated.* This relationship also has some important consequences for developed countries, which will be further discussed in chapter 11.

The primary mobilizing units of pre-development societies are thus communal. This suggests an initial predisposition to the creation of extra-institutional elites in the new polity and its structure. The scale of mobilization may increase in the process of nation-building; it is one of the objects and consequences of national integration, also one of its major difficulties. The first measuring variable that can usefully be brought to bear on the problem of range of the mobilizing referents is particularism-universalism; the location of people (and things) according to a narrower or larger frame of reference. In a political sense it is a measure of the increase in the extent of a differentiated political culture, a factor of cohesion—at least of social communication. At the same time (or rather independently though often simultaneously) development may, but need not, produce a shift along another pattern variable; diffuseness-specificity. For this is *not necessarily* a cohesive factor. The most developed and successful modern system of sustained long-term political mobilization—Communism—has resisted the proliferation of structural and orientational specificity and differentiation, apart from technical functions and roles in the narrower economic sense. In the Soviet Union the break in the progress towards specificity seems to come, in sociological terms, between professionalization of administrative, technical or political *knowledge and activity* on the one hand, and the definition of the corresponding *role* on the other; an interesting problem of role location which deserves further investigation. In some elitist Western democracies this counter-function to specificity and differentiation is, it might be argued, carried out by what will be here called an elite-based consensus (Durkheim's organic solidarity?). It would thus be reasonable to assume that since cohesiveness is greater in elitist than in constitutional polities and societies, the latent possibilities of *any form of* mobilization (stalactite or stalagmite) are also greater in the former. And empirically this appears to be well borne out; for instance the pattern of social behaviour of the various Western European nations in the most recent common experience of mobilization, the Second World War, seems to show a greater tendency to rapid, long-term mobilization and commitment in elitist societies like Britain, the Soviet Union and Nazi Germany than relatively constitutional ones like France and the United States.

This greater mobilizational efficiency of elitist societies might be expected to apply to *any* form of social mobilization—not merely political. The First, and even more the Second, World War provided *the* mobilizational experience of the century for Western Europe. Yet total war—as it was called—was translated into very different norms in different societies, though the value orientation of a fight for survival or extinction was broadly and remarkably similar in all of them. To compare accurately a special scale of indices would have to be set up, but such socio-economic studies as exist indicate a remarkable relationship between intensity of mobilization and the criteria of 'elitism' put forward here. Russia was clearly the most intensely mobilized country, followed by Britain rather than Germany (the elitist orientation of Germany being of recent vintage), followed by America and finally France—though the situation of the latter as a combatant clearly differed strongly from that of the others. This pattern may thus not just be a statistical accident but a structured hierarchy. This hypothesis would run directly counter to the definition and examples of totalitarianism as the most highly developed form of mobilization, put forward by a number of eminent American scholars.[1]

---

[1] See for instance Carl J. Friedrich and Z. K. Brzezinski, *Totalitarian Dictatorship and Autocracy*, Cambridge (Mass.) 1956. There has been a substantial amount of recent research which has put the claim of a highly mobilized Nazi Germany in a proper perspective, and has shown the shortfall in totalitarian mobilizing efficiency even in wartime. See for instance B. H. Klein, *Germany's Economic Preparations for War*, Cambridge (Mass.) 1959, David Schoenbaum, *Class and Status in the Third Reich* (unpublished doctoral dissertation, Oxford

Mobilization and social change are not the same thing, nor even of the same order of social magnitude. While one may reasonably assert that elitist societies are more easily capable of mobilization, the functional relationship of mobilization with the larger concept of social change is more complex. Highly constitutional societies like the United States have industrialized, and undergone both the prior and consequent social changes, at least as effectively as elitist societies like Britain. For our purpose, however, it may be said that the kind of *directed* and–in terms of time as well as control–*compressed* development we have been discussing in the context of *nations trouvées* requires political mobilization on a scale which primarily constitution-oriented societies would find difficult–and still remain constitutional.

For in the last resort the difference in functional efficiency between constitutional and elitist societies is not merely technical–a matter of mobilizational facility. We have already discussed at some length the etiolation of politics in Western democracies, not so much in terms of values and norms but in relation to structural and functional dispersal or fusion. A similar tendency can be observed, though to a lesser extent, in the Soviet Union, where a somewhat more constitutional orientation has been emerging in recent times.[1] But the problem can–indeed should–be examined also in terms of values. Western democracy is essentially a value system in its own right, to which both 'its' political philosophy and the sophisticated proliferation of apparently neutral and especially scientific techniques and concepts have greatly contributed. Though not conservative in a crude, obvious sense, this value system admits changes only in so far as they do not endanger the structure of the social system as reflected

---

1964, with its excellent 'elitist' characterization of the leadership situation as 'institutional Darwinism'). See most recently T. W. Mason, 'Labour in the Third Reich, 1933–1939', *Past and Present*, 33, April 1966, pp. 112–41, and Mason's further work on the war period yet unpublished.

Some of the problems of comparative mobilization as between Nazi Germany and the Soviet Union are raised in J. P. Nettl, 'The Economy of the Soviet Zone of Germany', in Carl J. Friedrich (ed.), *Totalitarianism*, Cambridge (Mass.) 1954, pp. 296–307 and discussion passim.

[1] Khrushchev's difficulty in getting party and administrative officials to go out to the virgin lands in the late 1950's is illustrative of this. The elite has preserved many of the old mobilizing goals and techniques largely intact, the lower echelons have 'lost' some of them. The increasing and stable (so far) separation of top party and government posts is also a pointer in a more constitutional direction, though too much should not be made of this–the preservation of collective leadership is also a means of preserving and strengthening the elite at the expense of political institutions.

OF POLITICAL CULTURE

in its technical or constitutional–above all electoral–layout. This means that the primary task of the socio-political structure is to accord legitimacy *within the system* and to translate its expression into policies and laws. Secondly, changes must not substitute any order of priority for that of maintaining the system itself. This, as has been so forcibly and perhaps excessively pointed out by his critics, is the underlying assumption and technological purpose of Lasswell's prescriptions for the social, or policy, sciences.[1]

To avoid oversimplification once more, two qualifications to this hypothesis need to be made at once. One is that the order of magnitude of changes permitted within the social system by Western democracy and its sociological conceptualization is of course substantial. There is necessarily no great advantage in strict system homeostasis for those in power–or those analysing systems.[2] But the point is that changes must be capable of being accompanied within the system–not necessarily by one *particular* constitution, but by any constitution that maintains the basic process of according legitimacy. Given a situation in which the processes of according legitimacy have become too dilapidated for this purpose, as in the French Fourth Republic, a constitutional society seems often to prefer to create a single powerful office capable of charismatic exploitation–with the latent expectation or premise that the charisma will become *constitutionally routinized*–rather than make any move towards a more elitist orientation. In 1958 such an elitist solution was mooted, as we know, in France. But de Gaulle himself continues to opt for the expected, constitutional solution and plays down the instrument which is proffered with a view to channelling and dispersing his charisma towards a party elite, preferring to concentrate and embody it in the constitutional office of the Presidency–even though he treats the legal-constitutional inhibitions of the office somewhat flexibly as long as it is occupied by himself.

The second qualification is to repeat once more what has already

[1] See most recently Harold D. Lasswell, *The Future of Political Science*, London 1964. Cf. also the section on Lasswell in H. J. Storing (ed.), *Essays on the Scientific Study of Politics*, op. cit., and Bernard Crick, *The American Science of Politics*, pp. 176–97. Not only Lasswell; the whole proliferation of a certain type of systems analysis is anchored in the same ideological assumption.
[2] Reference may be made in this connection to the debate on the extent to which sociological structure-functionalism is, or is not, able to accommodate social change. See e.g. E. Nagel, 'A Formalization of Functionalism' in Nagel (ed.), *Logic Without Metaphysics*, Chicago 1956, pp. 247–83; F. Cancian, 'Functional Analysis of Change', *American Sociological Review*, XXV (1960), pp. 818–27.

been said earlier. Constitutional societies and polities are not 'elite-free'. The difference is that in constitution-oriented cultures elites are functionally associated with, and identifiable from, social, administrative and political institutions—the formal structure. By way of illustration we may compare one important, apparently similarly placed elite in two different societies, elitist England and constitutional France: the higher civil service. The great French administrative reorganization of the early nineteenth century was accompanied by the creation of a specific educational and recruitment structure to feed the new civil service. The creation of these educational institutions in turn required means of recruiting a specific elite to staff them. These measures were so successful that the education and selection process spilt over from the polity to the rest of society; those qualified through the new process became a social elite as well. In the long run we thus have in France a form of substitution; the elite reference group is now no longer so much the higher civil service, the *haute fonction d'état*, as the *grandes écoles*. With this core qualification, the hierarchical specificity of the civil service has become diffuse. Entry at the top, variety of career, temporary departure into politics or elsewhere and possible later return, are all frequent enough in France—*with the necessary educational qualification*. In England, by contrast, the civil service has attained political, and later still social, status only very gradually. Until recently there was little specific recruitment, and even today no special educational process. But as the political importance and social status of the higher Administrative Class increased (Foreign Service first, Home Civil Service later), it also became a focus for social elite colonization until, here again, a different direction and form of substitution took place; the civil service became one of the major institutional reference groups and even sources of recruitment for an extraneous social elite sustained, among other things, by a long-established, exogenous educational system.

The same point can probably be made about the armies of these respective countries, and perhaps about their churches. There could have been no Dreyfus case in England because Dreyfus would not have reached such rank or position—or indeed would have been less likely to join the army in the first place. If he had, he would also have been more fully 'accepted', and would not have been singled out for suspicion. One might thus contrast Dreyfus with Burgess and Maclean—different attitudes to a remarkably similar situation or alleged betrayal of a social 'caste'.

The use of the cultural variable of elites and constitutions thus seems to provide some useful indices not only for the classification of cultures as an abstract phenomenon for analytical purposes, but also in analysing mobilization processes and structures in different societies. With regard to the latter, however, we are much more in the realm of hypothesis due to lack of empirical, not to mention quantifiable, data. This is especially true, and therefore imposes extra caution, when we come to be dealing with developing countries; a transitional category in this context which is still closely linked to a traditional base where the variable really has no firm grip. In the long run some kind of a correlation between certain cultural orientations and corresponding structures and processes of mobilization will no doubt emerge. Conversely, sustained emphasis in any one direction is likely to lead to culture production of the corresponding kind. Thus a successful stalactite mobilization party, remaining in power for a considerable time and able to impose its structural and value orientations on the society in question, is likely to lead to something of an elitist political culture. Similarly, a successful form of dispersed charisma in a national-constitutional direction, able to mobilize commitment and attain adequate levels of development, may well bring in its trail a constitutional orientation in its political culture production—even though such an orientation may be imposed on an otherwise elitist society, drawing its orientation from socio-religious and other long-established bases. In general in the case of *nations trouvées*, we have to contrast the creation and life-chance of new mobilization structures, whether emphasizing party or constitutional forms, with a well-established social structure with which they may be in conflict. Culture production in the political system is by definition *at the expense of* the catchment area diffusely occupied by an undifferentiated socio-political culture.[1]

All we can therefore do at this stage is to point up, in terms of empirical analysis as well as hypothesis, the possible ways in which the relationship between culture orientations and structural-processual factors might be related—with all due reservation to the difficulties of generalizing in this matter.

2. The second concerns intensity and direction of mobilization, types of mobilization structure, and the relationship of mobilization

[1] Some of these points are raised, both retrospectively and predictively, in a recent comparative area discussion of political and social development in the Muslim world; M. Halpern, *The Politics of Social Change in the Middle East and North Africa*, Princeton 1966. In general see also the discussion in Apter, *Politics of Modernization*, op. cit.

and legitimacy. At present levels of development in the Third World– which means for a long time–the demands of developmental nation- alism will surely impose a priority on efficient mobilization; if one structure or process fails to provide it, another will be tried. The barriers to maximizing mobilizational efficiency arise not so much from any *a priori* attachment to orthodox democracy, but from the existence of strong particularistic social structures like ethnic and tribal loyalties and caste autonomies, and the consequent lack of a common information stock of any size. The experience of Com- munist one-party mobilization has been simply to ignore the rele- vance of such factors, to subordinate them in the main to a class definition, and to encourage head-on confrontation with them. The only particularistic concession that Communism has traditionally made has been to ethnic groups with distinct language and cultures– providing the latter keep to the folk (or folsky) variety (which a good deal of old Jewishness did, but new Zionism does not). Mobilization in the Soviet Union has in large part been based on a party structure precisely because this appeared the only effective counterforce to a national mobilization which, by emphasizing Russian chauvinism, inevitably led to non-Russian counter mobilization–so useful to the Bolsheviks before 1917. Hence national-constitutionalism forms of mobilizing commitment were attempted only at moments of great crisis like the Second World War, and quickly de-emphasized after- wards; it might be argued that national irredentism was and is the prevailing nightmare of the Soviet leadership since the mid 1920's.[1]

Developing countries cannot pose the antithesis as strongly and neatly as the USSR; the party structures either do not exist or are too brittle to stand a strongly conflictual load (Ghana and Algeria). Even though single parties, where they exist, do emphasize structural support for the *nation trouvée* and opposition to the emphasis of ethnic particularism, the situation compels them to insist on a struc- tural rather than an ideological emphasis; rather than deny the historical or prescriptive validity of ethnic or tribal self-assertion, it is the structural means of cleavage mobilization that are denied. There is much substance in the undertone of Soviet criticism that the structural emphasis on mobilization in developing countries is not matched by any corresponding emphasis on, and articulation of, ideology; Nkrumah's consciencism and the utterances of Sukarno, however deficient in worthwhile *content*, at least attempted to fill this

[1] See e.g. *The Guardian*, 22nd April 1966.

vacuum. In the context of party mobilization, therefore, pragmatism is viewed as a deficiency–a practical concession to the ubiquitously threatening realities of strong ethnic and tribal sensitivities perhaps, but at the same time also a concession to their survival and strengthening.

In spite of these differences from, and reservations about, the Soviet model, the socio-political mobilization experience of the West, based as it is mainly on cleavage structures or on a form of authority legitimation which integrates and thus compensates for interest articulation, is of far less use to developing countries than the Soviet experience. This has already been argued in a variety of structural and goal-related contexts. Electoral mobilization would, if adopted, provide just the structural base for cleavages which no-party or single-party systems are so anxious to avoid. Though Indian parties, like American, are more properly electoral confederations than directly regional or ethnic structures,[1] the political subsystem does cater for *orientational* accommodation to ethnic and linguistic separatism; while collective behaviour, riots, religious agitation, authoritative self-immolation through fasting, etc., provide the focus for action which the party system fails to articulate (a further instance of the problem of structural accommodation for issue conflicts in narrow-choice political systems abased on electoral mobilization outlined earlier, above, pp. 170 ff).[2]

One of the most dramatic examples of the articulation and structuring of ethnic divisions through the adoption of electoral mobilization is the recent history of [British] Guyana. Here three ethnic communities are represented precisely by electoral parties, elections

[1] See most recently Paul F. Brass, *Factional Politics in an Indian State*, Cambridge 1965.

[2] In the Indian case, it is sometimes argued that the establishment of particularities in the shape of linguistic states has actually helped to strengthen identification with an All-Indian 'universe'; see for instance Lucian W. Pye, *Aspects of Political Development*, Boston 1966, p. 27. But this argument contains difficulties. For one thing, the proliferation of linguistic states has not by any means been public policy; the first round after independence was the result of violence and bloodshed in bilingual Bombay State (Gujerati and Mahrathi) which the government did not expect. Since then further application of the principle, demanded for instance by Nagas and Sikhs, has been fiercely resisted, though in the latter case eventually conceded too. Secondly any real benefit for the Indian Union arises not from the fact that linguistic states have been founded, but that so many have been founded that they balance each other out. The federal government has thus increasingly become umpire and arbiter. Third, and perhaps most important, India is the exception, not the rule; it is an error to cite India as illustration of any general theory of political development or developmental nationalism, as does Pye.

are almost entirely predictable and the function of authority legitimation is obliterated by that of interest articulation. It should be noted that this was in addition a colonial situation where the problem of legitimacy was hedged with special difficulties; associative legitimacy, in the sense in which legitimacy is established in accordance with beneficiary-imposed norms and roles, was constrained by the limited functions assigned to the elected government as opposed to the colonial administration. It seems clear that even in British Guiana an early attempt was made in 1952–3 to develop the People's Progressive Party as a stalagmite legitimacy structure with the intention to act as a stalactite party after inheritance. This suggests that the inheritance situation also imposed itself here to a considerable extent. However fear of Jagan personally, and the pressures of the colonial administration, between them forced this attempt back into a purely interest articulating channel.[1] Since 1953 there has thus been a twofold difficulty; associative legitimacy limited by the long delay in impending inheritance or independence, dissociative legitimacy counteracted by a cleavage-oriented electoral system which emphasized interest articulation as against authority legitimation. In this context the institution of proportional representation in 1962 only helped to structure the cleavage bases still further; on the other hand the basic structure-functional components of this situation would not have been altered by a return to the majority constituency method. Jagan's demand for this on behalf of the largest and most strongly dissociative potential inheritance party, the People's Progressive Party (PPP), might have created greater numbers in the assembly for the winning party, but could not by itself have reproduced the bases of an authority legitimation process subsuming interest articulation functions within an accepted and internalized national universe, on which the import of the British electoral system would have to rest in order to function adequately.

Other examples of this situation in less ideal-typical form have been cited. In Africa it is a frequent phenomenon, based more specifically on tribal divisions which 'capture' electoral mobilization parties even if they did not provide their original basis. The case of Malaysia has also been discussed. In general we may consider that *nations trouvées*, unless they happen to be strongly ethnocentric from the start – and it must be stressed that in an ex-colonial situation this *is* an accident –

[1] See Peter Simms, *Trouble in Guyana*, London 1966. Though this book is notably anti-Jagan, who becomes the villain of the Guyana show, the author shows clearly how the early attempt to make the PPP into a 'typical' inheritance party was frustrated by fears of Jagan's Marxist associations.

are bound to find electoral mobilization structures dangerously divisive. The reasons for adopting it in a whole number of cases, initially at any rate, have already been mentioned: direct imposition by the colonial power as a means of proving 'readiness for independence', the ideological diffusion of the notion that [electoral] democracy is causally geared to economic development, the diffusion of the more subtle but also more widespread identification of electoral democracy with political modernity, finally the sheer difficulty of finding any alternative, other than through gradual evolution, which accommodates balloting without assigning a primary value-function to elections. In a sense we should view the development of many *nations trouvées* with emphasis on one-party or multi-structure mobilization as attempts to find such an alternative through time. All this does imply, however, that the pressures in favour of electoral mobilization are concentrated on the historic moment of scission from colonial status to independence, and will for the rest decline increasingly as the Third World becomes a separate, itself culture-producing, partly even institutionalized structure in the international system, with increasing autonomy and a growing supra-national value system.[1] In so far as electoral mobilization is viewed as an *adaptation* from developed countries, it is likely to decline rather than increase. In this sense the tendency for electoral democracy will wither rather than grow, while the Soviet Union and the People's Democracies will continue to supply a more suitable model. But more probably there will be an increasingly indigenous Third World solution or solutions, anchored in its particular forms of legitimacy and processes for legitimizing authority, as well as its own means of providing structures for mobilizing support.

Remains the possibility of an autonomous development of electoral democracy and electoral forms of mobilization as the Third World develops economically. To deal with this possibility more adequately we must have a further look at the recent evolution of developed societies. This we shall do in chapters 11 and 12.

3. The third hypothesis is concerned with the instrumentality of existing processes of political mobilization for the attainment of economic development. We have in this analysis frequently referred to the notion of developmental nationalism as a concept for characterizing the particular value system of the Third World – a value

[1] See Peter Worsley, *The Third World*, London 1964, for a somewhat over-argued case for homogeneity and autonomy. The problem is surveyed in Nettl and Robertson, 'Modernization and International Systems', op. cit.

system that must not be confused with economic development in its formal sense, of which it is only one component. Developmental nationalism is a complex configuration of strongly felt desires in which international status and power play an important part, together with the securing of national integration, the development of the economy as well as the modernization of society. International and internal perspectives are closely interconnected; there is a good deal of substitution in short-run goals between the various components.[1] For the moment, however, we must look at the instrumentality of the various processes of political mobilization for economic development in its formal or narrow technical sense.

There are many approaches to the study of economic development. One important approach views economic development as a general process which, to be successful, must achieve an adequate balance between all sectors of the economy; any extreme disproportion between advanced and retarded sectors within one and the same economy is likely to frustrate overall growth. This is the implication of the Harrod-Domar growth model. An alternative theory views sectoral disproportion, both functional and geographical, as instrumental in overall economic growth, and suggests that the potential results of conflict between such sectors in different stages of development are likely to provide a better means of overall growth than any attempt artificially to level out such sectoral disequilibria. The latter approach is more closely tied to sociological perspectives and also appears to correspond better with empirical reality.[2] What relationship if any may be deduced between the different types and structures of developmental mobilization and these two basic approaches to economic development?

A developing society that relies largely on private initiative, whether domestic or foreign, to invest in and develop industry is liable to find a very differential distribution of growth in different geographical and industrial sectors. As the analysis of Brazil by Celso

[1] The crystallization of the developmental value system in its national and international context is discussed in 'Inheritance', op. cit., also 'Modernization and International Systems', op. cit.

[2] For an economist's analysis along these lines see A. O. Hirschmann, *The Strategy of Economic Development*, New Haven 1958; Bert F. Hoselitz, *Sociological Aspects of Economic Growth*, Glencoe 1960; and Jacques Perroux, *La Coexistence Pacifique*, Paris 1958; cf. also Celso Furtado, *Desenvolvimento*, op. cit., *Dialética do Desenvolvimento*, Rio de Janeiro 1964, and Hélio Jaguaribe, *Desenvolvimento Econômico e Desenvolvimento Político*, Rio de Janeiro 1962. For a country study of the specific impact of a highly developed, foreign-owned oil industry on an otherwise backward society, see R. Betancourt, *Venezuela: Política y Petroleo*, Mexico City 1956.

Furtado has shown, this type of development, if left to proliferate on its own, produces secondary socio-economic consequences in which it would be more accurate to speak of two societies within one nation or country rather than one: a highly developed 'imperialist' sector and a poorly developed traditional and local sector. Moreover the mutual interaction and its effect are just as liable to produce still greater differences rather than eventual synthesis; such a development is therefore self-reinforcing even though *overall* national indices of growth may rise.

Economic planning in conditions of socio-political mobilization of a stalactite kind is also likely to produce sectoral and geographical unevenness. Here it is the structures of mobilization for authority legitimation, and the mobilized commitment to the goals and norms of the ruling elite, which should act as a cohesive, integrative influence in preventing excessive distortion between more and less economically developed sectors and geographical areas. National-constitutional mobilization is less directly structured than the party-based variant, and hence tends to articulate demands and pressures for a more balanced distribution of economic effort; the framework is overall-national rather than party-elitist. In developing countries where a national-constitutional orientation prevails, therefore, we might expect to find a greater welfare slant to planning, as in India, or less intensive planning altogether, as in Pakistan. India is particularly instructive in this regard; a federal system where, in a strictly economic rather than mobilizing sense, the government reconciles and balances the conflicting claims of various sectors and regions. Moreover since the mobilization structures attempt to encompass and transform existing caste and ethnic cleavages as much as mobilize against them, economic planning and development must take into account, and align itself to, these social realities. The party system will in fact emphasize not only sectoral interests and cleavages structured by the electoral system of mobilization, but will also articulate various economic choices with regard to planning emphasis and comprehensiveness. Intensity of planning or freedom of action for private enterprise is still to some extent an issue in Indian electoral politics. As critics of India's planning have pointed out, there is a distinct conflict both in conception and application between the demands of planning, with its imperatives of stalactite mobilization on the one hand, and the reconciliation and electoral demands of Indian politics on the other.[1]

[1] See most recently Hanson, *Process of Planning*, op. cit.

There are, of course, strong anti-economic components in the development plans of many party mobilizing systems, some of which have already been discussed in terms of socio-political mobilization and communication. Frequently the ends or goals of economic development, objectively viewed, are lost in the transformation of means of mobilization into ends *tout court*. While the effectiveness of mobilization for the implementation of economic planning and development is greater in party-mobilized systems, the pursuit of more directly economic goals–in terms of national product, *per capita* production and *per capita* income–in the formulation of development plans is probably greater in national-constitutional systems of mobilization. We have thus a paradoxical situation, in which the likelihood of adopting economic criteria in one system is to some extent balanced by a greater capacity for effectiveness in the other. From the point of view of objective growth in accordance with established economic indices, the possibility of successful economic development is greatest in a situation of party-based mobilization with strong economic perspectives instead of the more common values of developmental nationalism with its socio-political as well as economic components. Such cases are rare–and it is worth noting how rare they are. Even among developed countries the emphasis on primarily economic perspectives is unusual; Denmark, Switzerland and Sweden come to mind–all of them countries with an established tradition of neutrality or neutralism of a kind very different to that common to the Third World. Nor is there any visible trend among developing countries towards more directly economic perspectives coupled with emphasis on party mobilization systems. The most likely prospect of adequate economic development, therefore, may not be found in party mobilization systems after all, but in the rather less 'efficient' systems based on national-constitutional orientations and mobilizing emphases. This suggests another important divergence from the communist model.

4. The fourth hypothesis concerns the ability of the political sub-system in today's developing countries eventually to accommodate openly structured choices–the 'democratic' preoccupation. Obviously the further any hypothesis projects into the future, away from the known (or not too well known) facts of today, the more Boolean choices have to be accommodated into the analysis–a difficulty that corresponds to the sort of problem involved in translating a game of chess into a computer programme: fine for three moves, but unmanageably complex beyond that.

Nonetheless, let us look one stage farther into the future. Assuming effective mobilization does take place, and development is being achieved, will the demand for political *choices* then become a new superordinate orientation, a new priority or goal? The example of the Soviet Union would suggest that this is likely only in part. The Soviet Union today ranks as a fully developed society. There are certainly strong demands for consumer choices in the economy, which are being gradually accommodated. But the political debate is much more in terms of areas of free comment than in favour of structural provision for political alternatives which might provide a basis for *political* consumer choices. Stalactite mobilization remains the dominant socio-political mode, not a demand for its transformation into electoral mobilization based on cleavages or issues–let alone interests. As has already been pointed out, there are in any case important differences between the Soviet model and the developing countries. One of them is the balance in the latter between party and national mobilization; the long-term validity of the Soviet model implies a continuous and weighted option for party mobilization. Another is the nature of the party in question; the *raison d'être* of Communist parties is not merely a functional one of mobilizing for development under the umbrella of inheritance legitimacy, but is anchored in an overall, ubiquitous and above all permanent (or at least very-long-term) legitimacy based on historical necessity–the philosophical-ideological component mentioned ealier. This distinguishes it from the much more pragmatic national and inheritance parties in developing countries–whatever the other, structural similarities. The pan-African claims of Nkrumah as well as those of francophone *négritude*, the pan-Arabism of Nasser, the Socialism of Ba'ath can perhaps all best be understood as attempts to develop ubiquitous and permanent claims for historical necessity and validity–and therefore to legitimacy. These claims accept the finite nature of the inheritance/development situation and of 'its' parties, and accordingly try to aim higher towards a supra-national, even quasi-continental legitimacy. This similarity between them holds even though Nasser disclaims the possession of philosophic truth, while Nkrumah, Sukarno and Sékou Touré revel in it.[1] This is one example of a post-inheritance situation sharpened into a more revolutionary configuration, with the *techniques* approximating more closely once more to the Communist model, however different the *values* and *claims* for

[1] Compare Nkrumah's *Consciencism* with Nasser's *The Philosophy of the Revolution*, Buffalo (N.Y.), 1959, especially pp. 20 ff.

legitimacy may be (contrast for instance Nasser's 'invasion' of the Yemen on defensive anti-imperialist grounds, and the Soviet invasion of Poland in 1920 on revolutionary grounds).

The future of mobilizing parties in developing societies hinges to a considerable extent on the ability to provide a minimum of choice–not in accordance with any objective criteria of need, but to satisfy the requirements of mobilized participants. This is especially important as the role of charismatic arbiter declines; no country can expect a succession of Nkrumahs, Ben Bellas, Nassers or Sukarnos–in fact the overthrow of three out of four of these articulators of mobilizing philosophies rather than aggregators of interests shows the poverty of their philosophy and also their transgression beyond the frontiers of the irreducible minimum of choice. Nonetheless our analysis suggests that the need to provide choice will in developing countries be accommodated more satisfactorily in terms of choice between people and only secondarily in terms of choices between policies. The tradition of legitimacy in most developing countries as we have outlined it on the one hand, and the fact that issue orientations as well as empirical issue publics are peculiar to the Western experience, indicate that choices will be viewed primarily in terms of different personalities. The two forms of producing change in the leadership of developing countries (characterized here as shifting leadership orientations and coups respectively) will give way–if at all–to a growing acceptance of personal rotation in leadership rather than to any institutionalized crystallization of issue line-ups. There is clearly an important correlation between these two forms of choice, which has neither been investigated theoretically nor empirically to date. In practical terms inheritance parties are likely to disintegrate precisely through pressures for greater choice among people. The Indian Congress Party has already pollinated the leadership of much of India's political life. As we shall see, similar processes of disintegration have taken place in inheritance-type parties in Italy and Israel. Of course the accommodation of choices between people can be more easily contained within the framework of one party than choices which are based on more divisive *combinations* of issues and people. The attempt to accommodate purely personal choices for electors within the continued legitimacy of single-party rule was most clearly expressed in the Tanzanian elections of September 1965. Thus 'democratic' choices between candidates are the most likely form of accommodating any future demand for greater choice in developing countries.

Social specificities of traditional societies undergoing development.

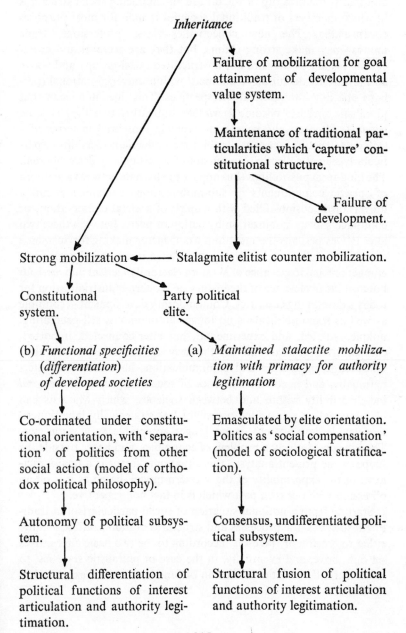

Inheritance

Failure of mobilization for goal attainment of developmental value system.

Maintenance of traditional particularities which 'capture' constitutional structure.

Failure of development.

Strong mobilization ◄——— Stalagmite elitist counter mobilization.

Constitutional system.

Party political elite.

(b) *Functional specificities (differentiation) of developed societies*

(a) *Maintained stalactite mobilization with primacy for authority legitimation*

Co-ordinated under constitutional orientation, with 'separation' of politics from other social action (model of orthodox political philosophy).

Emasculated by elite orientation. Politics as 'social compensation' (model of sociological stratification).

Autonomy of political subsystem.

Consensus, undifferentiated political subsystem.

Structural differentiation of political functions of interest articulation and authority legitimation.

Structural fusion of political functions of interest articulation and authority legitimation.

315

But one thing does follow inevitably from economic development, and that is the breakup of the diffuse all-embracing social structures in which members of traditional societies remain for most purposes encapsulated. The new collectivities–class, professions, trade unions–may make strong claims, but they are sectoral and cross-cutting insofar as they are not unstructured quasi-groups, and above all they are by definition 'contained' within universal-national (perhaps one day international) perspectives. This does not mean that pluralistic societies become *inevitable*, but rather that they become *possible*. Alternatively, people may remain mobilized in terms of a stalactite structure for a considerable time, under the leadership of a particularly salient collectivity in pursuit of a particularly desirable goal. The long-term possibilities thus appear to alternate between a plethora of specific commitments or sub-mobilizations contained within a universalistic cosmos filled with a spirit of societal conservation, or continued salient mobilization by nation or party. Between these two alternatives perhaps the most important factor making for sustained stalactite mobilization in developing societies is not only the relatively epiphenomenal irrelevance of Western electoral *functions* and *methods* but also the irrelevance of the history of Western industrialization for today's developing countries. Contemporary development–economic as well as socio-political–is no longer autonomous, self-generating, unique, isolated, and experimental, but inter-connected, imported, comparative, general and on the way to becoming measurable. Knowledge, impatience and communications have increased internationally, and hence the existence of social and economic *sectoral* incompatibility within and between societies, which Marxists call neo-imperialism and which we might less strategically label inheritance underdevelopment, is no longer acceptable as a *status quo*. Though substantively a problem of economics, and hence outside the scope of the present analysis, this situational factor is a final indictment of the exportability of the Western model, based as it is on an obsession with our own past which is in fact non-repetitive.

Starting from a notional situation of social particularism in traditional societies, the processes and structures of mobilization, leading either to erosion or 'take-off' according to the two basic alternatives set out above, and eventually, in the case of pluralistic societies, to structural differentiation or fusion of functions, can be expressed in the flowchart on p. 315.

CHAPTER ELEVEN

Mobilization Structures in Different Stages of Development: Parties and Organized Groups

SUMMARY

We have contrasted mobilization processes in developed and developing societies, and evolved an apparatus of variables that aided the comparative study of structures and processes. An attempt can now be made to integrate the analysis in terms of politcal subsystems viewed as symmetrical or asymmetrical wholes. Using the variable evolved, a functional theory of polities is sketched out, with application to both developed and developing societies. According to this theory political subsystems are classified into either interest-articulation and authority-legitimation systems on one hand, and those asymmetrical ones in which dominant authority legitimizing parties are confronted by a constellation of smaller interest articulating ones. Symmetry and asymmetry are related to various stages of development. Developed societies, especially Britain, the United States and France, are discussed at some length in the context if the functional emphasis of their polities.

Next, the same subsystem classification is applied to developing societies, and a dynamic theory of change is put forward according to which socio-political development may be analysed. This theory consists of the notion of a required level of commitment to maintain societies which are either in the process of development or more or less fully developed. As formal mobilizing processes and structures decline in importance or efficiency their function is increasingly taken over by differentiated, interest- or issue-specific mobilizations. But the sum of mobilized commitment provided by these specificities leaves a shortfall in the required amount of commitment, especially in terms of structured support for the universal referent of nation or society. This, it is suggested, is provided by the concept of bureaucracy.

MOBILIZATION STRUCTURE:

We take up again the functions of political mobilization–interest articulation and authority legitimation on one dimension, cleavage and issue bases of commitment on the other. These dimensions were tested out in chapters 4 to 6 as a functional approach to the study of political structure and process; some of the reasons for evolving these variables rather than following up the conceptual possibilities of previous analyses were spelled out in some detail. We now apply this functional variable to the analysis of party and group systems–the polity. Taking the classic configuration of single-, dual- and multi-party systems, it would appear that the more aggregative parties are, the more strongly they are likely to emphasize authority legitimation in a functional sense. Thus systems with strongly aggregative parties are likely to be primarily authority legitimizing systems. One- or two-party systems tend at first sight to be aggregative and thus will appear to be oriented towards legitimation rather than articulation. Exclusive single parties in power are invariably stalactites, almost by definition, while two-party systems can be either but will tend more often to be stalagmites; nonetheless both are aggregative–or perhaps better, arrogative–and legitimizing rather than interest articulating. On the other hand the type of party that intends to act as an exclusive single stalactite party in power (Communist and Fascist) tries to achieve legitimacy before attaining power in a multi-party situation through the articulation of interest– by identifying the two functions, and above all the two orientations, as one and the same thing. In this they partially fit the surrounding pattern; multi-party systems tend to articulate sectional cleavage and issue-oriented interests, whether economic, ethnic, religious or even just the particular interest of the party cadres and professionals. These systems are all symmetrical to a considerable extent.

This type of symmetry between either legitimacy and interest articulation parties within one polity is in fact quite a reliable index of a certain fairly advanced stage of development. A developed political system will tend in its entirety either towards authority legitimation *or* interest articulation in the long run; if the system changes, *all* major parties will change as well. Compare Britain and Fourth Republic France; in Britain even the third-party Liberals must try to be authority legitimizers even though a self-conscious appeal to sectional interests might appear to provide greater stability and a better guarantee of survival for a minority party (e.g. Celtic Fringe). Since the institution of the Fifth Republic in France, even very traditional interest-articulating parties like the Socialist Radicals

318

and MRP, are beginning painfully to try and compete with the UNR in providing an alternative legitimacy by combining for the purpose of presidential elections (e.g. the June 1965 negotiations for a coalition to support Deferre followed in September by a tentative socialist-communist alignment in favour of Mitterand). Note also the virtual disappearance of interest-articulating parties in West Germany like the BHE, the Refugee party. The function of Communist parties is significant in this respect. They are interest articulators in multi-party systems; partly at least this congruence explains their success in countries such as Italy and France, in addition, of course, to a number of other and unique historical factors there. In Britain and the United States, as well as Scandinavia and post-war Western Germany, where the tendency is towards more or less salient authority legitimization, communist parties fail to attract more than a minute membership; they are unable to fulfil their 'natural' minority function of articulating interests and transforming this into a claim to legitimacy.

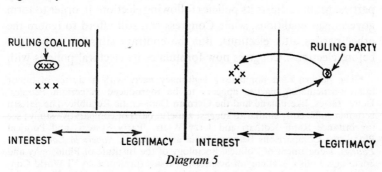

RULING COALITION   RULING PARTY

INTEREST   LEGITIMACY   INTEREST   LEGITIMACY

Diagram 5

In traditional polities political parties, where they exist at all, are also largely interest articulators—interest being defined here as the shared wishes of collectivities like tribes, castes, etc. Here too party systems tend to be symmetrical; the bases and processes of authority legitimation have nothing to do with party mobilization or structure and consequently the problem of authority legitimation in a party sense does not arise.

In contrast there are a whole number of polities in which one party dominates through its aggregative legitimacy orientation, while the others are more or less confined to a fringe position of sectional interest articulation—a defensive posture which keeps them in being but also prevents them from competing for effective power. Such asymmetry of party functions in the polity is one of the interesting features of a certain stage in the process of development–closely related to the inheritance situation. The co-existence of one large (and generally ruling) legitimacy party with a cluster of small, strongly interest-oriented parties is quite a common pattern in the Third World. Such asymmetrical situations exist or existed in India (Congress), Israel (Mapai), Mexico (PRI); in Pakistan (Muslim League) and Burma (AFPL). Thus the 'developed' situation looks like the left-hand side of diagram, while the 'developing' situation would look like the right-hand side.[1]

It is sometimes suggested that the stability of the ruling legitimacy party is mainly due to the advantages it enjoys under simple majority electoral rules; the opposition parties cancel each other out in most constituencies, leaving the ruling party effectively (or ineffectively) in command.[2] But the same situation applies *across* electoral systems; in Israel, which has almost pure proportional representation, Mapai too goes on and on. Where elections become significant in this context is in explaining the attitudes and policies of the legitimacy parties. Mapai adjusts its policies following elections in order to form government coalitions, while Congress can still afford to ignore the other parties after elections. But the contrary situation appertains before elections. Congress now formulates its electoral policies with

[1] The pattern of a dominating legitimacy party with a cluster of minor interest-articulating parties appears to be reproduced in certain Peoples' Democracies, like Poland and the German Democratic Republic. The pattern is in fact sufficiently similar to suggest a useful basis of comparative study; see for instance Rajni Kothari and Jerzy Wjatr, 'Party Systems and Political Pluralism: Comparisons Between India and Poland', *Papers in Comparative Politics*, Department of Political Sociology of the Institute of Philosophy and Sociology, Polish Academy of Sciences, Warsaw (presented to VI World Congress of Sociology, Evian, September 1966); also Wjatr and Adam Przeworski, 'Control Without Opposition', *Government and Opposition*. I, 2 (January 1966); Kothari, 'Form and Substance in Indian Politics–Party System', *The Economic Weekly* (Bombay), June 1961. A larger comparative project of research into social values and local politics is announced, based on India, Poland, USA and Yugoslavia.

However, the analogy between this type of party pluralism and the one described above for developing countries cannot be carried too far. In Third World countries, the complementary system of parties is competitive, in the Peoples' Democracies consensual–no real opposition is possible. Thus the interest-articulating function of the 'bloc' partners is extremely limited–personal but no interest representation. The Indian and Polish authors of the study cited here are well aware of these differences. In the interesting classification of party systems put forward on p. 3 of the joint paper the Polish system is described as 'Regemonical'.

[2] An illustration is given by Brass *Factional Politics*, op. cit.; Congress in UP State took 48 per cent of the vote and 90 per cent of seats in 1952, 35 per cent and 58 per cent respectively in 1962.

due regard for the policies of its opponents (in accordance with a spatial model as do British and American parties), thus using opponents as a partial reference; while Mapai and other legitimacy parties in multi-party or interest articulating polities can afford to ignore opponents to a much greater extent, knowing that a further post-coalition round of bargaining is coming anyhow.

The eventual break-up of the ruling legitimacy party faced by a series of smaller interest-articulation parties also seems to mark a particular stage in political development, and is therefore important. A good example is in fact that of a developed country, post-war Italy, where the gradual erosion of the Christian Democrats' legitimacy is very noticeable. Apart from the few monarchists and the neo-fascists, this was the only real legitimacy-oriented party since the end of the war. Though some of the other parties have authority-legitimating pretensions, they are in fact quite narrow interest articulators. Recently various DC factions have shown signs of restiveness in articulating a more salient section interest. The constraints of discipline imposed by authority legitimation, which had moreover to be defended at regular elections against interest-articulating competitors, proved a strain; a study of the conflicts and debates within the DC as reported in the newspapers indicates the pressures for a reversion to an interest orientation within the party more typical of the system. This pressure may appear particularly relevant to a developed society and therefore to a naturally more symmetrical political system. The pressures in fact came to a head during the choice of a presidential successor to Segni. In that instance the Christian Democrats as a party significantly refused to act as authority legitimizers. Other examples like the German CDU/CSU, Mapai and possibly the Indian Congress further suggest that asymmetry within a single system of simultaneous legitimizing and interest-articulation parties may be unstable in the long run following upon the exhaustion of direct inheritance legitimacy; either the interest-oriented opponents to the legitimizing party in power will join together to become alternative legitimizers (or wither away altogether as in Germany), or else the ruling legitimacy-oriented party will split—first into undisciplined coteries at the top (in the legislature, with *legislative* and *party* leadership often in opposition), and later possibly into different and distinct interest-articulating parties. This in turn means greater reliance on post-election coalitions. It thus appears that in the long run, and barring revolutionary changes, the political party system will tend towards symmetry rather than complementarity of functions. But, apart from some People's Democracies, one example of enduring asymmetry is the PRI in Mexico. There the peripheral interest-articulation parties are quite unimportant in size and influence. At the same time they are not mere shadows like the 'coalition' or 'front' parties in e.g. East Germany or Poland, which simply coexist symbolically with the ruling party; they have a definite function to perform.[1]

Historically political parties usually began as a means of rallying common interests against existing authority – the Crown in Britain, the State in Western Europe: to nudge that authority in required directions, to limit it but not primarily to legitimize it or reconstruct it. But the legitimating function crept in very early; after the civil war in England in the seventeenth century the 'corruption' of the interest representatives began, with the Crown increasingly 'selecting' those most prominently exposed in the forum of interests, the two Houses of Parliament and more particularly the House of Commons. This 'corruption' reached its height in the second half of the eighteenth century, when faction – anti-government mobilization within the still narrow extent of the polity – was considered a deplorable abuse. Note that this disapproval was confined to structured *mobilization* not to individual dissent by representatives; the ballot was still seen in its old function of choosing known individuals from among a few candidates by a few electors – the essence of the notion of representative government. It was at this time that the United States gained its independence, and the same individualistic attitude to elections as well as the cultural disapproval of faction also took hold strongly on the other side of the Atlantic. The extension of the suffrage in Britain as a democratic 'right' in the nineteenth century produced an extension downwards (stalactite) of the factional mobilization already

[1] It is not very clear to what extent a structure-functional systems analysis (or any systems analysis in the social sciences) assumes symmetry with regard so structures serving similar functions. Parsons, Almond, Easton and othetr appear to suggest that structures serving identical functions are symmetrical – i.e. functionally 'the same', and hence substitutable for purposes of fulfilling functions without causing change in the system. The present analysis suggests that complementarity may be a better overall approach; compensation between subfunctions serving broadly similar main functions – in this case interest articulation and authority legitimation processes and structures of mobilization within the system. Within such overall complementarity a situation of symmetry becomes a special case, as outlined above.

The postulate of symmetry is open to challenge on other grounds. See Alvin W. Gouldner, 'Reciprocity and Autonomy in Functional Theory' in Llewellyn L. Gross (ed.), *Symposium on Sociological Theory*, Evanston (Ill.) 1959, pp. 241–70. Cf. J. P. Nettl, 'Are Two-Party Systems Symmetrical?', *Parliamentary Affairs*, XIX, 2 (Spring 1966), pp. 218–23 for a brief empirical investigation of this problem in the Anglo-American context.

common at the top; the modern party system grew up to legitimate the sovereign's selection, first of a whole cabinet and later of the Prime Minister alone, since Crown appointment was now no longer a sufficient legitimization by itself. Today in Britain the process is almost complete; the formation of a government is now exclusively related to an election. Conversely everyone who votes in an English general election knows that he is trying to help elect a government. Only a relatively small, five to ten per cent minority (Liberals) vote in the certain knowledge that they will not do so.

Historians sometimes marvel at the fact that the highly conservative, authoritarian Bismarck should have introduced adult manhood suffrage in the Second Reich in 1871, a considerable time before liberal democratic Britain or Belgium. But German political parties in the Wilhelmian Reich were in no sense legitimizers, but merely articulated sectional interests. Election results every four or five years did not in the least influence the choice of Chancellor or ministers. Consequently an Imperial government in the shrewd hands of Bismarck would not anticipate any likelihood of having to hand over any power to the population at large, to the mob as so many Prussian Conservatives fearfully lamented. In some otherwise more liberal German states and provinces, where elections *did* exercise more influence on the choice of ministers, the extension of the suffrage to Reich universality was thus quite logically resisted until the end of the Empire. Indeed the whole British tradition of functional fusion in elections is much less in evidence on the Continent. In France, during the revolution and afterwards (except between 1830 and 1848), authority see-sawed between King or Emperor on one hand, who appointed his own ministers at random (1800–15, 1815–30, 1851–70), and an assembly on the other which did not so much control or guide authority as in effect elect an executive committee in the form of the cabinet to administer the country (1793–9, 1848–51, 1870 onwards). In the latter case parties still went into elections as interest articulators, but their *representatives* became authority legitimizers within the aegis of the state once they entered the National Assembly. The apparent confusion between the two processes and orientations is due more to a visual compression, a *trompe l'œil* of cause and effect, than to any functional compression or fusion into one electoral process as in England.

As defined in chapter 3, a society with a constitutional culture will tend to separate functions, and articulate them through differentiated structures, more than an elitist one. Interest-articulating parties suit, and are more likely to be found in, constitutional societies, while aggregative, legitimizing parties with their tendency towards 'compensatory' politics are more at home in elitist societies. In other words multi-party systems would tend to be constitutional, and two- or one-party systems elitist. But this could clearly lead to a considerable over-simplification. What about the United States with its constitutional culture in politics and its traditional two-party system? But in fact the two functions are quite distinct and separate in the United States; though there are two parties only, there are at least two *types* of elections at different times – and where they are simultaneous, as in the year of a Presidential election, the functional difference is made clear to the elector; senators and governors do often ride into office on Presidential coat-tails, but not always and not necessarily. A vote for a President is an authority legitimizing vote in which the party serves as a vehicle for aggregation. Theoretically it should be the same with a vote for governor of a state, but the extent of legitimacy orientation is probably lower at this level – itself an interesting indicator of the ideological assessment of the federal balance. Votes for representatives, senators and most state offices are interest-oriented votes with strong local or particularistic influences. There are in effect fifty different Democratic and Republican parties in the United States.

The clearest evidence for these propositions comes from the differences in behaviour of the *elected* during and after elections. The President necessarily concentrates his campaign on mainly national issues, though often on local personalities – especially during whistle-stop tours. American senators and representatives concentrate heavily on local issues while British constituency candidates rely on their party manifesto and play down local issues; indeed *Lokalpatriotismus* is a form of deviant political behaviour among parliamentary candidates in Britain. Once elected, these differences are extended still further; British MPs form disciplined party cohorts, while American Senators and representatives do not. This suggests that the basis of compliance will vary as between legitimizing and interest-articulating parties, and that compliance is related to electoral functions; compliance in legitimacy parties must relate to *government*, while compliance in interest-articulating parties relates to *representation*. But in itself this tells us nothing about the form or strength of compliance, the enforcement of discipline, the emergence of leadership – all the aspects of political parties other than those directly concerned with elections.

The conceptual priority of functional requirements over formal electoral or constitutional processes can vividly be illustrated from the Canadian case. Here we have a parliament and cabinet polity somewhat similar to that of Britain. Yet the fact that the foci of interest-articulation and authority-legitimation are fused into one and the same collectivity, in the shape of political parties, does not obscure the tendency to functional separation, and consequent stress. The very instability of Canadian constituency voting in recent times crystallizes the search for functional separation (in the decade 1954–64, 75 per cent of the 265 constituencies changed hands at some time, twice as many as in Britain, almost twice as many as in the United States). As a recent study has indicated this is due to a conflict on one side between a desire to accord legitimacy at different times to specific alternative leaders (this is especially true of the Conservative leader John Diefenbaker), and on the other side the enforced channelling of this desire into elections and structures strongly concerned with interest articulation. The evidence suggests that had such a thing been possible, voters might well have preferred to elect Diefenbaker simultaneously with a liberal (interest-articulated) legislature.[1]

In the American Presidential system we thus have a limiting case to the notion of party functions as an analytical *polarity* of interest articulation and authority legitimation. The differentiated fulfilment of both functions within a single party structure in the major American parties – a factor making for *functional* efficiency – makes them less tightly structured than would be the case with a more emphatic bias towards one of our two functions. A similar tendency can be observed in a federation like Brazil, where parties have to serve both central legitimacy and regional as well as national interest articulation. Here too Presidential elections tend to crystallize functionally in

---

[1] See Peter Regenstreif, *The Diefenbaker Interlude,* Toronto 1965. This analysis indicates the breakthrough of latent functional imperatives from a constitutional society into a polity whose main features were borrowed from elitist Britain. In this connection the particular role of a federal constitution or, say, a federal polity should be noted. This almost always implies a constitutional orientation. Elections at provincial levels, and for provincial governments, have a far higher interest-articulation content than their national counterparts. To this extent therefore the federal polity in Canada mediates a difficulty of the 'elitist' type party and electoral structure; at provincial levels the interest established is relatively unaffected by legitimacy considerations (this also explains the survival of the Social Credit Party). A similar point may be made about Australia which is more elitist in culture, and where interest and legitimacy functions have more effectively been fused by symbols of representation in national elections. There is much greater stability in constituency results in Australia than in Canada.

the direction of legitimacy, while regional elections and those for Congress are interest-articulating. The party system is not as cohesive as in the United States with the result that Presidential elections are on the whole much more obviously personal. But at the same time the failure to provide for really effective functional differentiation can be seen in the suspension of the constitution by President Castelo Branco in 1965, who felt his potential legitimacy threatened by the interest-articulation elections for provincial governors. Whereas in the United States Congress majority and President may legitimately be opposed to each other, in Brazil the different verdicts of the two elections are not readily accepted, and expressions of interest articulation at provincial levels were taken by both voters and government as a hidden form of legitimacy denial in a situation where free 'legitimacy' elections were unlikely to take place. Thus the process of functionally differentiated elections can serve to transpose the perceived functions from legitimacy to interest and vice versa (Cf. the U.S. mid-term elections in 1966).

We can reasonably draw the general conclusion that effective dual-function parties like those in the United States and elsewhere, which in fact carry out both major modern functions of politics within one and the same collectivity even though at different times or places, will lose in ideological cohesion and tight structuring. This loss will ultimately be reflected in their *mobilizational* efficiency, even within the limited definition of that process in the context of a modern constitutional society. The same loss of mobilizational efficiency occurs in developing countries with dual-function parties (Congress in India, Mapai in Israel). But the loss is relative; value systems in such societies require a much greater general mobilized commitment to parties or other mobilizing structures than in the West.

Within one and the same party, therefore, the alternative or even simultaneous carrying out of the two separate functions does lessen the cohesiveness and mobilizational efficiency of the party. Hence the particular and peculiar American emphasis (and that of many similarly situated constitutional societies) on elections as a symbolic *show*, which always strikes European observers so forcibly. This is another way of commanding sympathetic participation, by engaging *attention* to overcome weak mobilizing potential. The difference in the theatrical quality of politics between this type of show and that in developing countries is that in the latter case we have a show by institutionalized actors asserting accepted symbols of legitimacy, while in developed countries it is the *process* of

326

elections which provides the dramatic content, and governs the actors' roles.

It is worth investigating further at least one aspect of this inherent duality of function in one single party. If, as in America, the cohesiveness of party suffers, what happens in the legislatures? Though recent research has shown that the commonly held British view of American party fissiparousness in Congress may be much exaggerated,[1] party discipline is weak compared to Britain, especially with regard to the executive–considered in this context as an extrapolation of party; congressmen and senators vote the public interest as evaluated by their private consciences, balancing this against the accountable and demonstrable wishes of their constituents. To this extent the relationship between electors and representatives is in part a carry-over from a pre-party situation; the elected 'represent' discrete individuals from a given geographical area *irrespective* of whether they voted for him, irrespective also of any programmatic combinations or formal mobilization on his behalf. The elected representative's immediate loyalties are to his 'friends'–that highly political word of 150 years ago–as well as to the public interest, the commonwealth. This is part of the 'knowledge' implicit in the theory and ideology of balloting; a constitutional society accords more readily with the logic of its techniques than an elitist one. All of which does not prevent many of these same representatives and friends turning themselves into actors and enthusiastic spectators in as ideological and mobilizing a ritual as an American convention to nominate a presidential candidate.

The French Fifth Republic has attempted to embody an even 'purer' functional specificity and structural differentiation than the American model. Instead of dual-function parties we have here parties confined as far as possible to interest-articulation only–and the National Assembly reduced from an authority-building forum to one of interest articulation. According to de Gaulle, political parties should not participate in presidential elections or referenda–not even the UNR pledged to ensure his own continuance and authority as its main *raison d'être*; though formally parties are permitted to participate in such elections *qua* parties, perhaps in the hope that their difficulties in functioning successfully under such authority-legitimating circumstances may help to discredit them further. Clearly de Gaulle has to be less sweeping with the use of normative prescription

[1] See Truman, *The Congressional Party*, op. cit.; also Truman (ed.), *The Congress and America's Future*, Englewood Cliffs 1965.

or law in his attack on parties than someone like Ayub Khan in Pakistan, where the party tradition is much less well established and also relatively more divisive. Instead of the parties carrying out a dual function, as in America, which de Gaulle believes to be impossible in the well-entrenched French multi-party system, the duality reverts to its basic, theoretically 'proper' level—to the individual voter mobilized by party for his interests, but 'unattached' for the purpose of authority legitimation. Not quite unattached, however; de Gaulle's identification of himself as the unique personification of the national interest enables him to justify constitutional-national symbols of mobilization of the kind we have described earlier, on behalf of himself in the roles both of candidate and president. It also explains the morality of his unabashed usurpation of the technical means of communication like the mass media and other instruments of constitutional or national mobilization for the purposes of his legitimation. There is no attempt to view these organizations as neutral or uncommitted as in Britain. But we must wait some years yet before we can judge the extent to which this attempt to institutionalize relatively pure processual and functional differentiation in France has succeeded.

As we have seen, many developing countries, particularly in the context of inheritance situations, tend initially to adopt the polity model of their benefactor or former colonial power—especially, but not only, where independence has been attained reasonably amicably. The most difficult model for a developing country to import is the presidential polity of the American or Fifth Republic type. Of course 'president' may be taken as the euphemistic title for a military leader or charismatic arbiter; in that case the position naturally changes and much of the difficulty is eliminated by a display of constitutional symbols. The Philippines (ex-US colony) have adopted the genuine model, so far with apparent stability and success. One would like to know how developmental mobilization functions there—if at all—and more about the role of the parties.[1] In general, however, this type of constitution, if properly run, 'delivers' little mobilization, and balances the two political functions closely against each other. The

---

[1] One recent analysis puts forward the political process in the Philippines as a working illustration of Almond's thesis that parties function primarily as input aggregators of demand and supports. Among developing countries the Philippines thus approximate most closely to functioning Western democracy. See Jean Grossholtz, *Politics in the Philippines*, Boston 1964. This analysis however does not indicate much progress in terms of development or change; the picture emerges as one of relating stagnant 'stability'.

primary 'goal' of the polity is to keep itself in balance and in being as *a priori* a good thing.

Much of the mobilization that does take place in the United States is concerned to redress alleged imbalances between interest and legitimacy. Thus for instance we may legitimately view the Republican rally under Eisenhower's candidature in 1952 partly as an attempt to mobilize on behalf of a conservative interest function (Congress) against an allegedly excessive assertion of central authority legitimation under the Democrats. Because of this inbuilt institutional equilibrium change cannot easily come from the formal constitutional structure itself, but *either* from outside *or* informally from inside. We must now look at some of these lubricating informalities.

The Smelser scale of mobilized groups discussed in chapter 6 told us something about the extent of mobilization, by reference to the extent or level in society of the thing mobilized *against*; the social order as a whole (values), the rule and policies of society (norms), groups within society (collectivities) and finally individuals. For purposes of the polity, we must now construct a somewhat different scale, as we are here dealing with a slightly different problem. First, a scale of *intensity of commitment to informal mobilization*. This is not concerned with different levels of societal impact, like Smelser's scale, but with degrees of saliency at any given level. It will have been obvious already that, though mobilization changes its intensity, as well as its scale, in developed countries, the level and intensity of mobilization needed in emerging countries rarely exist in developed ones, except in times of crisis or war. On the whole, the spur to sudden increases in mobilization and levels of commitment in developed countries is a defensive one, in protection of *existing* interests. Even where this is not the case, and people do in fact mobilize for improvement or advantage, the mobilizational *reference* is still presented as defensive. Thus some of the most violent mobilizations for change have in the past been initiated *in defence of* the Republic, the revolution, a group's status or standard of living, etc. The assumption is that 'they' are aiming at a restoration; we can see this emphasis during 1792–4 in France, and in the mobilizing tactics of the Russian Communist Party under Stalin. Similarly the mobilization that takes place in many industrial strikes – and some of the greatest resultant changes – are often based on the symbolic *restoration* of some position, balance or differential said to have been objectively altered or eroded. The same considerations apply to such associations as CND, which again does not quite fit into Smelser's categories; it seems to cover all levels from values down to anomic behaviour, but at the same time it is both *informal* as well as *defensive* – to 'protect' society as much as to change it. All this may be an echo of the hypothesis about denied rights as one of the major mobilizing stimulants mentioned earlier (above, p. 247): evidence of the essentially conservative nature of social action. But in the context of developed societies an increase in mobilization and commitment is a late recourse, not a normal function of achievement. Any analysis of the intensity of mobilization and commitment must thus cater for stalagmite or stalactite mobilization in defence of the *status quo*, whether latent or manifest, as well as for offensive mobilizations.

Secondly, a measure of *increasing specificity or differentiation*. This measure of increasing specificity organizes the sociologists' common depiction of modern society: a multiplicity of cross-cutting interests and commitments of lower intensity than the encapsulated 'ideological' conflicts and commitments of a less differentiated past. The whole pattern of interest or issue groups in developed societies is but one of a number of specific, limited mobilizations which cover merely a small segment of the participating individuals' total 'interests' and attitudes, and similarly impinge only on a few of government's receptive surfaces. Intensity of commitment decreases as functional specificity and structural differentiation increase. At the same time specificity narrows the target area of impact of any mobilization. We are thus dealing here with a scale of impact quite different from Smelser's adaptation of the Parsonian societal hierarchy of values, norms, etc. Perhaps the difference between levels of commitment or intensity, and measures of specificity or differentiation can best be explained by reference to the two well-known Parsonian pattern variables specificity-diffuseness and particularism-universality. Smelser's scale of intensity levels is mainly concerned with the latter, while measures of differentiation are more directly relevant to the former. But there is a latent contradiction here. By itself specificity seems initially to imply particularism, while diffuseness implies universality. This will have become clear from the discussion of traditional and developing countries; the 'particularity' of communal, tribal, etc. commitments corresponds, in such a context, to a specificity of reference. It is not that there are no universals in traditional societies, but that *these* are the universals. Either the pattern variables have no meaning except in application to pluralistic, large-scale societies of integrated nations, or we must recognize that their

330

universal application to all societies requires the meaning of the patterns to change in different situations. What is the element of change in the implication or meaning of the patterns as between traditional-developing and developed societies?

This, it is suggested, may be supplied by the concept of notion of porousness. Only if we qualify the meaning of specificity with some notion of porousness–to permit location of things or people in a universal context through the frontiers of the specific commitment or collectivity–can universality be combined with specificity in a real social situation, instead of contradicting it. That is to say, specificities of interest must be porous enough to admit knowledge of, and orientation towards, universal referents, and not bottle them up within a particularity or adapt them to relatively 'particular' symbols. In terms of mobilization, this porousness means that the pursuit of specific interests, even if frustrated, can be prevented from escalating sufficiently in range to threaten broader targets than those 'particular' ones originally aimed at. In developed societies, specificity therefore implies an interacting and stable pattern of interests, operating within relatively limited parameters of scale and impact.[1] We have already encountered this situation in dealing with cleavage mobilization in developed nations, which 'admit' the universal referent of nation or state and which are stabilized and contained by it.

Even more is this precisely the situation with regard to interest groups in developed societies. Generally they will try to avoid any conflict with government escalating beyond the 'level' of the institution which is the appropriate target for their interest. Let us take trade unions. Their militancy (in say, the, US where it is particularly marked) has always aimed at a given, limited target–the employers, occasionally the government. In Britain, where the unions are less militant but traditionally more political, the same broadly holds true; since the end of the New Unionism after the 1926 General Strike the politics of trade unions have become increasingly differentiated from the visible processes and actions relating to their self-interest. For

[1] Talcott Parsons himself distinguishes the use of the specificity-diffuseness variable from that of particularism-universality by placing the first in the category of orientation, and the second in the category of modality. Orientation relates to the actor's view of the situation, modality to a bird's-eye (or theorist's) view of the actor in his situation. These definitions and his model are in 'Pattern Variables Revisited: A Response to Robert Dubin', in *American Sociological Review*, XXV (1960), pp. 467–83, especially pp. 467–9. A partial restatement is in 'On the Concept of Political Power', op. cit., and a further extensive restatement is expected shortly.

example the law with regard to the political levy embodies this differentiation, and is universally accepted. Since the wave of French syndicalism receded fifty years ago, a somewhat similar differentiation has become established there through the separation of 'economic' negotiations at the shop-floor level from the national level of politics. Free participation in the latter is tacitly accepted by the employers only in return for acceptance by the unions that shop-floor bargaining must steer clear of politics.[1] A similar situation exists in Italy.[2]

The unions are in any case a relatively militant example of interest groups. The same argument applies to professional and business associations. The extraordinary weakness of the top aggregative bodies, which various kinds of interest groups have established for themselves on a class or professional basis, is also worth noting. The general Council of the TUC, the Confederation of British Industry, the Council of Churches in this country and America rarely succeed in articulating effectively any aggregated interest on behalf of their constituent bodies–precisely because they are not political parties but clusters of interest groups. Even in those cases where the top confederate body is more powerful, because the group appears more homogeneous (doctors, accountants), strong economic and status disjunctions within the profession are rapidly reflected in the loss of aggregative potential by the top body. The growing differences between medical specialists and general practitioners, which at first resulted in protracted and bitter negotiations with the government in 1965, was soon followed by murmurs of dissent within the British

[1] This point has been stressed particularly by Michael Crozier in various studies on French trade unions.

[2] See Murray Edelman and R. W. Fleming, *The Politics of Wage Price Decisions, A Four-Country Analysis*, Urbana, Illinois, 1965, for evidence that in many countries where unions are politically active such activity takes place at the expense of the overall interest representation for their members–at least unless there is clear differentiation between the level of the two activities. If the unions want to engage in national politics their interest articulation, to be effective, must aim at workshop not national level. Alternatively, if plants are to be politically organized, economic negotiations must be confined to the national level in the framework of general negotiations of wage levels. A recent and suggestive book (Frank Tannenbaum, *The True Society*, London 1964) attempts to subsume the British trade unions' manifest role as interest groups under their function as status hierarchies. The author presents trade unions as the modern equivalent of the defensive–or better protective–status hierarchies of the Middle Ages, broken up by subsequent economic and technological change. For present purposes the accuracy of this analogy hardly matters; the evidence of their limited capacity for sectional mobilization is fairly conclusive irrespective of whether Tannenbaum's thesis is correct or not.

Medical Association. The lawyers have long had two professional bodies representing solicitors and barristers respectively. On the continent this tendency is less well developed, and gross aggregative associations are still relatively much more effective in playing a more directly political role within more strongly differentiated political subsystems.

The tendency to specific and porous mobilization develops certain definite patterns. For one thing, interest groups tend to separate out from political parties as much as possible–a tendency that can perhaps carry a greater weight of explanation than the mere assertion of structural differentiation normally associated with modernity. In countries where political parties are aggregative (like Britain, Sweden and now Western Germany), political interest articulation tends to have given way to the search for authority legitimization. It is the interest groups who take over many of the articulation functions. In presidential systems like the American the interest-articulation function, though relatively efficiently expressed by political representatives, is often based on perceptions of geographical and individual attributes like religion, race and language, as much as on any rational evaluation of group interest. The same has long been partially true of French or Italian parties too. Another variant of a snug fit between interest-articulation and political party structures is Holland–where some of the cleavage basis is religious as well as geographical, economic, and purely 'political'. The Dutch party system has a religious base, which has not been seriously eroded by crosscutting cleavages created by the advent of a socialist party.[1]

Most important of all, however, is the question of efficiency. The porous interest of social groups (as opposed to the interests of geographical units in federal polities) is not always served most effectively by political representation. This raises once more the question of social-political congruence. A snug fit will avoid the need for the political system to reproduce structurally the expression of particular social and economic interests; socio-economic groups will simply adapt to the functional requirements of the political subsystem. An interesting point here is that the only type of interest that appears absolutely to require specific structural expression in political terms is the territorial or geographical unit; hence a federation may be viewed as the specific political form of giving expression to one particular kind of interests–that of geographical units. A crucial

[1] For Holland see Hans Daalder, 'Parties and Politics . . .' *Political Studies*, op. cit.; also his chapter in R. A. Dahl (ed.), *Oppositions* . . . op. cit.

determinant in the relative efficiency of parties and groups in articulating interests is the question of roles. Political representatives can represent political interest, and do so in a political manner. The role demands a certain type of action with a certain type of response, from which party considerations can never be far absent. But many of the group interests are fulfilled by latent actions; watching briefs, consultation, informal representation as contrasted with formal legislative and political processes. These then are often social, legal and even kinship or peer-group roles; only occasionally do they become political roles over particular issues. In a welfare state, with its growing responsibilities and bureaucracies, interest groups have sought and found 'their' relevant or corresponding decision-making institutions or 'targets' at various levels of the state bureaucracy. They find that the best way to conduct their particular business is to duplicate the bureaucratic organization of their targets, by employing permanent officials working under elected 'political' heads with occasional general meetings–vestigial concessions to a legitimization function which, in interest groups, has no role to play at all other than a theatrical or symbolic one, at annual meetings and dinners.[1] The bureaucratic role is more efficient for expressing such porous interests than the political one.

At first sight this tendency looks–in the classical sense–fairly 'unpolitical'; the activities of interest groups take place outside party politics, and hence outside political mobilization. But there are no stable vacuums in politics. In the relative absence of stalagmites we shall find stalactites; *where interest groups flourish we shall find constitutional mobilization from above–in favour of the status quo*. This is often referred to as the consensus. In direction and purpose this type of stalactite mobilization resembles somewhat the stalactite constitutional-national mobilization of developing societies. In terms of goals, symbols, process and structure it is very different. Let us look more closely at what this notion of consensus implies.

Essentially it means an agreement on values; the sum of common components in the universal referents that makes sense of, and orders, the range of porous specificities in modern societies. But often it also

---

[1] For a full spelling out of this apparatus, see PEP, *Industrial Trade Associations*, London 1957, also J. W. Grove, *Government and Industry in Britain*, London 1962, pp. 125–61; more theoretically, Harry Eckstein, *Pressure Group Politics*, London 1960, introduction; S. H. Beer, 'Pressure Groups and Parties in Britain', *Am. Pol. Sc. Rev.*, L, 1 (March 1956), pp. 1–23; *Modern British Politics*, op. cit.

carries a sense of residual or spontaneous agreement, and is therefore contrasted by 'democratic' commentators with the enforced or blatant consensus that comes from single-party or national mobilization in communist or corporative fascist societies–voluntary [social] cohesion as opposed to enforced [political] control. Consensus is thus generally a strongly ideological word (although it need not be), and carries a positive value-judgement. It is a collective state of mind abstracted from, and made effective by, a state of social balance–but it is *not* a function. In fact the notion of consensus with its de-emphasis of stratification and conflict,[1] implies almost a negation of functional analysis. Most commonly we find it used by those political scientists and sociologists concerned with problems of horizontal rather than vertical differentiation.[2]

The argument for the existence of a consensus is based on the recession of ideological politics (usually defined in this context as the process of conflict for the creation and legitimation of sovereignty and its value system), and on a corresponding growth of normative conflict for the satisfaction of, or compromise between, different interests. According to this approach groups represent interest-specific political collectivities whose actions are not based on ideology, while political parties aggregate to a greater or lesser extent the normative desires and interests of unorganized individuals and possibly of interest-specific groups and quasi-groups. Such aggregation is equivalent to the competitive search for electoral legitimacy.

[1] We have to distinguish between Parsons' first-order concept of shared values in any social system, which underlie his entire conceptual scheme or model of society, and the notion of consensus which is an objective abstraction relating to the action product of empirically harmonious polities or societies. Here again we have on the one hand the common pool of beliefs and desires of the participants, analytically collectivized by the observer as a value system (never mind whether the Parsonian assumption of common values as sufficiently cohesive to integrate the social system is empirically applicable to all or even most societies). On the other hand we have the observer's direct judgement of participants' actions–consensus–which shortcircuits one of the three steps of social analysis outlined earlier (above, p. 20). The critique of consensus that follows here is not intended to be synonymous with any criticism of the notion of value systems.

[2] These two approaches consist of (a) either asserting the reality and validity of class conflict in Marxist, neo-Marxist or quasi-group terms (Dahrendorf), *or* denying it in terms of consensus, (b) jettisoning the vertical model altogether in favour of a horizontal model of differentiation which emphasizes wealth, power and status in terms of social rewards in return for function, according to a common normative ordering (Bernard Barber, Parsons). In the latter case the problem of consensus hardly arises because the starting point of derived order, according to which rewards are distributed, emanates in the last resort from the notion of an effective consensus.

Legitimacy is accorded through spontaneous, 'rational' agreement by individuals or social groups; no special authority-legitimating function is perceived or needed.[1] The opposing argument concentrates its efforts on denying that depoliticization exists or is possible in this context, and stresses instead the presence of the particular ideology of pluralism. This view stresses the pervasiveness of institutional brokerage within a vertically differentiated elite-controlled society, in which ideological control overcomes and etiolates the competitive choices of elections. Such ideological control is exercised for instance through the obstinate inequalities of the British school system and the selectiveness of American school curricula. Moreover the fact that the same problem has been discovered in the Soviet Union is held to provide yet further evidence for the universality of such latent forms of ideological control.[2] Both views, however, miss the vital structural aspect of consensus: bureaucracy. This is the means by which the stalactite-mobilizing potential of the consensus is made operational in developed societies. Or, to be more precise, bureaucracy is the stalactite structure substituting for mobilization.

[1] The debate over the status of consensus in England, as expressed by the attitudes and policies of the two major parties, begins to make good sense if viewed in this context. Both Beer (*Modern British Politics*) and McKenzie (*British Political Parties*) are therefore 'right', and it makes little sense to pick out a winner, as many recent commentators have done. Beer draws his conclusions from the manner in which parties carry out the legitimacy function, and finds a good deal of 'fundamental difference'. McKenzie focuses on the interest-articulation function, and finds consensus and overlap in the area of normative dispute. *Wenn Zwei sich streiten, lacht der Dritte*–what better proof could there be for my thesis of functional confusion, when two acute and accurate observers appear to meet head on?

[2] See V. Shubkin, 'Molodezh vstupaet v zhizn' (Youth on the Threshold of Life), *Voprosy filosofii*, 1965, 5, pp. 57–70; cf. 'Class Struggle Looming in Russia', the *Guardian*, 2nd July 1965, p. 12.

CHAPTER TWELVE

Mobilization Structures in Different Stages of Development: Bureaucracy

SUMMARY

We take up the conclusion of the previous chapter: that bureaucracy is the structural expression of consensus and serves the function of substituting for the missing quantitative factor in the sum total of mobilized commitments in developed societies. Bureaucracy is first defined in a Weberian sense–as a phenomenon or modernity but not necessarily as the product of, or synonymous with, organizational and even social rationality. Its function as a substitute for mobilization is then investigated more specifically in different Western societies, and it is noted that bureaucracy too has a mobilizing potential–albeit a fairly weak and above all conservative one. Such a conception conflicts with the frequent depiction of Soviet bureaucracy as mobilizing *par excellence*; the problems, both conceptual and empirical, posed by this contradiction are examined at some length. This in turn leads to the historical analysis of bureaucracy and its relationship with broader theories of society held by different schools of thought. In order to avoid breaking the thread of the main argument, this discussion is confined to an appendix at the end of the chapter.

Since bureaucracy has been defined as a phenomenon of development or modernity the central administrative structures, both civil and military, in developing countries today pose special problems of analysis, which are looked into–both as internal problems of collectivities and as an external factor in the operation of social systems. A hypothesis of future developments is put forward, and finally an attempt is made to explain civil-military relations in certain countries, especially Latin America, within the framework of the theory of bureaucracy put forward here.

If the phenomenon of bureaucracy is to be allocated a major social function, it will first be necessary to define it adequately for present purposes, and to justify this definition. We take as a starting point the work of Max Weber, who first isolated a particular form of bureaucracy as an essential feature of modernity, using it specifically as a means of contrasting modern societies with traditional ones. Weber viewed bureaucracy as the structural product of a certain type of leadership, again anchored in modernity, which he contrasted with traditional and charismatic types of leadership. Since much of the analysis presented here has implicitly followed the conceptual distinction between traditional and developed, and has tended to crystallize the contemporary notion of development as a transition stage with different structural components (though at a higher level of abstraction the uniqueness of today's Third World justifies the creation of a specific developmental concept or category of society) the notion of bureaucracy as relating to modernity is not difficult to accommodate.[1]

However, the present analysis differs from Weber's characterization of bureaucracy in one important respect—which moreover has always given rise to a number of difficulties, and is still the subject of academic debate. This concerns the identification of bureaucracy with rationality or rational behaviour. According to this view the proliferation of bureaucracy as a phenomenon corresponds to an increasingly rational approach to the problems of society; presumably a completely rational approach would be completely bureaucratic. Such an approach has to a considerable extent been the spur to much modern American organization theory which seeks to raise bureaucratization (though not under that name) to the level of rational organization and behaviour, and suggests that most social problems of conflict will be resolved by such 'bureaucratization'. Thus organization has been described as 'the most rationally contrived unit of human association'; organization or administrative theory is one without which 'effective rational choice can hardly exist'.[2] But we shall here concentrate instead on the phenomenon of bureaucracy without these teleological perspectives; and merely confine ourselves to the notion of an hierarchical, tightly structured collectivity acting with a view to solving problems. Instead of objectively rational criteria, the influence of bureaucracy on society will be treated as a *cultural* phenomenon, connected with acceptance by, and commit-

[1] Further reference to Weber's concept of bureaucracy can be found in the appendix to this chapter, specifically pp. 365-9 ff.

[2] H. A. Simon, *Models of Man*, op. cit., p. 196, Cf. Simon, *Administrative Behavior*, second edition, Glencoe 1957; Philip Selznick, *Leadership in Administration: A Sociological Interpretation*, Evanston, Ill., 1957.

ment to, large-scale organized activity. In this way there will be no need to make any objective assessment of the phenomena, other than noting its influence. This approach is akin to that of Michel Crozier.[1]

There is naturally some overlap between these different approaches. Bureaucratic behaviour is anchored in the internal situation of a bureaucracy as a collectivity as well as in its external situation as a social structure, while administrative behaviour is a problem-solving approach constrained in particular by its own situation. Thus bureaucratic behaviour might be said to arise from the bureaucratic function or role in society, and the term will be used here whenever the derived behavioural aspects of bureaucracy in modern society are in question. Administrative behaviour, on the other hand, would result from membership of large-scale organizations, whether bureaucratic or not, in which an element of rationality or at least success in solving the problems 'put into' it is implied. Bureaucratic behaviour is concerned with function in a cultural setting, administrative behaviour with the attainment of manifest goals.

It has been suggested earlier that bureaucratic behaviour tends towards conservatism; that the function of bureaucracy in society is to provide a structural means of mobilizing commitment to the maintenance of the *status quo*. This has been characterized by Crozier as follows: 'People on top theoretically have a great deal of power and often much more power than they would have in other, more authoritarian societies. But these powers are not very useful, since people on top can act only in an impersonal way and can in no way interfere with the subordinate strata. They cannot, therefore, provide real leadership on a daily basis. If they want to introduce change, they must go through the long and difficult ordeal of a crisis. Thus, although they are all-powerful because they are at the apex of the whole centralized system, they are made so weak by the pattern of resistance of the different isolated strata that they can use their power only in truly exceptional circumstances.'[2] Though the application of this hypothesis is intended to apply mainly to the internal context, it may be taken as relevant also to the external or societal one within which modern bureaucracy operates. Here too formal power is not very 'useful', and a crisis is often required to produce changes.

The effective operation of bureaucracy in modern society depends largely on the existence of a consensus. This provides for agreement

---

[1] *The Bureaucratic Phenomenon*, London 1964.
[2] ibid., p. 225.

on social values and goals in society in the form of a positive narrowing or limiting of conflictual issues; as noted, it transposes an abstract concept created by social scientists and based on their observation of limited conflict into concrete, structural effectiveness. In this way the notion of consensus discussed here approaches the characteristics of a quasi-group,[1] whose main determinant here is the functional relationship between a particular arrangement of the patterns of specificity and universalism on the one hand and certain particular features of large-scale activity on the other—largely but not exclusively related to the activity of central government. Consensus thus provides the link between effective political power and influence as means of defining situations on the one hand, and bureaucracy on the other.

In this context the notion of consensus is both a constraint on, as well as the product of, bureaucratic behaviour. A crisis induced by sudden demands for change will transform the credit-based relationship between consensus and bureaucracy into a cash demand and may undermine and threaten the consensus itself.[2]

It should be evident that this suggested functional relationship between bureaucracy and liberal democracy, or (as we have preferred to call it) electoral mobilization, is in some ways the opposite to the conventional wisdom of democratic theory. This is based largely on

[1] For this concept see Ralf Dahrendorf, *Class and Class Conflict in an Industrial Society*, pp. 179 ff., 237 ff.

[2] This characterization of bureaucracy, its function of substituting for mobilization and its relationship to political leadership differs somewhat from that put forward by Ralf Dahrendorf, 'Bureaucracy Without Liberty: An Essay on the Politics of Other-Directed Man' in S. M. Lipset and Leo Lowenthal (eds), *Culture and Social Character*, New York 1961, pp. 175–206. Dahrendorf depicts modern bureaucracy particularly as the 'neutral' repository of power, which it maintains by relying on the provision of outside political policies which it can then administer. This suggests that bureaucracy requires political leadership to 'activate' it. The question of any congruence or incongruence between bureacratic values and mobilizing potential on the one hand, and the existence and orientation of a socio-political consensus on the other, does not arise.

Dahrendorf for instance explains the acquisition of power by the National Socialists in Germany as due in part to the failure of the Weimar parties to provide policies which the bureaucracy could administer; the latter accordingly turned to more effective totalitarianism alternatives. The present argument would suggest that German bureaucracy had a well-developed and articulated standard of consensus requirement against which it measured the policies offered by the parties or coalitions in the Weimar Republic. Finding the parties dissensual and the coalitions ineffective, the bureaucracy tended to desert its political masters. Moreover, Hitler's strict adherence at the beginning to formal legality and to electoral channels of legitimation made the adherence of the conservative bureaucracy to the new pseudo-consensus that much easier.

the pioneering work of Michels. The two sides of this same coin are represented by those who find bureaucratic substitution for democracy inevitable–whether regretfully or appreciatively–and those who believe that it can and should be counteracted.[1] We have here taken the view that the growth of bureaucracy is in direct proportion to the decline of cleavage mobilization and conflict through the establishment of a consensus; however, we see this as the inevitable hallmark of one type of political development, that of the West, based on a particular form of political mobilization. The transformation of cleavage mobilization into expressions of electoral legitimacy within the framework of a universal perspective of nationality or statehood is due to historical reasons which have been analysed at some length in chapters 5 and 6. Bureaucracy is a product of this development, not its cause. According to the present analysis a contrast between bureaucracy on the one hand, and 'democracy' as expressed through electoral legitimacy on the other, would be a meaningless, indeed false, dichotomy–assuming as it does a notional capacity for modern electoral legitimacy to provide choices which previously never existed, and upon which the growth of bureaucracy has therefore had little effect. To say as Gouldner does that 'if oligarchical waves repeatedly wash away the bridges of democracy, its eternal recurrence can happen only because men doggedly rebuild them after each inundation' is mere semantics. Such a statement fails to take into account the vital delegatory component of bureaucracy, which we shall examine in greater detail below. It is in short an intellectual concession to certain trends in organization theory which cannot be justified by a meaningful definition of modern bureaucracy. The contrast we have preferred to emphasize is between *bureaucracy* on the one hand and *mobilization* on the other.[2]

[1] Robert Michels, *Political Parties*, op. cit. Outstanding among those who regret the inevitability of democratic decline through the growth of bureaucracy is Philip Selznick, e.g. *TVA and the Grass Roots*, Berkeley and Los Angeles 1949. Some other American organization theorists, like Simon, evaluate the growth of bureaucracy at the expense of electoral competition somewhat more positively as evidence of modernity. A good example of those who believe that bureaucraticization is inimical to democracy but can and should be resisted is Alvin W. Gouldner, 'Metaphysical Pathos and the Theory of Bureaucracy', *Am. Pol. Sc. Rev.*, XLVIII (1955), pp. 496–507, and *Patterns of Industrial Bureaucracy*, Glencoe, Ill., 1954.

[2] One of the difficulties in using Michels as the source for the idea that bureaucracy and democracy are to be treated as dichotomies or incompatibilities is that Michels was not at all concerned with problems of bureaucracy *per se*. The notion of oligarchy as a negation of democratic control in terms of

The suggested characterization of bureaucracy as a structure particularly suited to supporting the *status quo*, and mobilizing commitment on its behalf, also conflicts strongly with the characterization of the Soviet Union as an example of a mobilizing bureaucracy.[1] It has become common practice to refer to the party official in the Soviet Union as a bureaucrat; we need only glance at the title of many Western studies of the Soviet Union to note the frequent emphasis of the term bureaucrat or bureaucracy. Presumably this emphasis is due to the communist preoccupation with organization, and the strictly hierarchical manner in which communist parties are organized. But such a characterization leaves many problems unsolved. For one thing the emphasis on bureaucracy fails entirely to do justice to the political component of decision-making, or to the whole problem of authority legitimation and interest articulation. It is tied far too much to the assumption that all decisions are simply made 'at the top'. Moreover, it is based on a misconception of roles. Though it is the members of the party organization who are responsible for the substantial technical business of mobilization, they do *not* carry out this function in terms of bureaucratic roles by any conceivable definition. The study of Russian newspapers makes it clear that there is a very real role conflict between bureaucrat and party worker; Marxist social analysis has in fact never admitted the concept of bureaucracy in the Weberian sense, but uses it only in the sense of an immobilistic behavioural deviation.

---

policy formulation and execution—which was the real concern of Michels—initially has nothing to do with bureaucracy at all, but only with the institutionalization of 'democratic' leadership. In any case Michels also postulated a dichotomy between democracy and oligarchy which may have been meaningful at a time when the party he analysed *claimed* to be the only democratic structure in an autocratic system, but which has long ceased to represent empirical reality anywhere. Finally it is meaningless to speak of the pre-1914 SPD, which was Michels' object of analysis, as bureaucratic in the formal sense, since its full-time paid staff in 1912 was less than a hundred against a membership of many tens of thousands, and against the four and a quarter million votes obtained in 1912.

[1] For this see for instance Helen Constas, 'Max Weber's Two Conceptions of Bureaucracy', *American Journal of Sociology*, LXIII, 4 (January 1958), pp. 400–9; also Constas, *The Soviet Union as a Charismatic Bureaucracy—Viewed Comparatively*, Paper read to the American Sociological Society, August 1958, Seattle, Washington. Cf. also recently Merle Fainsod, 'Bureaucracy and Modernization: The Russian and Soviet Case', in Joseph LaPalombara, *Bureaucracy and Political Development*, op. cit., pp. 233–67. This analysis exploits the Weberian concept of dispersed and routinized charisma, with bureaucracy as its recipient. A similar combination of two normally incongruent concepts like bureaucracy and mobilization is made in the sociological analysis of certain religious movements by talking about the 'deification' of the structure—(e.g. Salvation Army).

In terms of mobilization many of the formal assumptions about the Soviet Union are also rather dubious. Instead of some notion of participation and involvement–an orientational perspective perfectly well expressed by the Soviet word *partiinost*–many analysts of the Soviet Union implicitly assume that mobilization in the Soviet context differs little from the actions of a cowboy dealing with a herd of cattle. And even when some orientational perspectives are added to the analysis, the notion of 'bureaucratic mobilization' immediately comes up against the fact that wherever members of bureaucracies acting in bureaucratic roles have attempted to mobilize people, they have done so very inefficiently. This can be seen for instance by a study of the circumstances and instructions (or lack of them) under which the party sent its members into the country for the collectivization drive of 1928–9.[1]

The notion of bureaucraticization begins to make more sense in the Soviet Union since the death of Stalin. For one thing an element of pluralism has begun to creep in, even though this is institutional rather than cleavage-based and group-organized. Secondly, and more important, the role of the Soviet administration has taken on a distinctively conservative tinge. Many of those who could have been characterized as political mobilizers in the days of the first two five-year plans have now, for generational and other reasons, become supporters of the *status quo* against further changes, and are thus taking on a more distinctly bureaucratic role. The conflict between the leadership under Khrushchev and the *apparat* over regionalization and the required move into the provinces demonstrates very clearly the widespread normative shift in the party from emphasis on mobilization to a bureaucratic emphasis on administration.

The identification of the notion of bureaucracy with mobilization, anchored in the very widespread Western view of Soviet society as essentially bureaucratic, has given rise to a related approach to the study of developing countries. This is the one put forward by Shils, Kautsky and others to which we have already referred above, pp. 95, 268; a view of developing societies 'stratified' into an intellectual layer at the top and a bureaucratic layer covering the lower rungs of the administrative ladder. In this context there is no specific attempt to crystallize a differentiated concept of bureaucracy at all;

[1] For this see M. Lewin, 'The Immediate Background of Soviet Collectivization', *Soviet Studies*, XVII (October 1965), pp. 162–97; Alec Nove, 'The Decision to Collectivize', Paper read to the Soviet Affairs Seminar at the London School of Economics, November 1964.

indeed the main emphasis is placed on parties and the top institutional structure of the state without any clear distinction between them. Though this analytical disjunction between intellectuals and others is useful as a means of investigating the value orientations of elite groups, no very clear indication of the structural differentiation between intellectuals and bureaucrats is attempted. Bureaucracy in this context becomes a residual category to which all the inefficient, conservative and 'mindless' elements are consigned, while the analysis can proceed to concentrate on the influential elite components of society without any awkward lumber. In the present context this approach does not offer much help, however, since it assumes as valid what we have attempted to deny–namely the passive and manipulatable 'mass' made up of middle and lower sectors of society, as well as the relative unimportance of structural and functional differentiation as between different structures of control, communication and mobilization.

Another conceptualization of bureaucracy from which the present analysis partially dissents is that offered by Eisenstadt.[1] Here the issue is not a difference in substantive interpretation, but in terminology. Eisenstadt's characterization and analysis of traditional empires are impeccable, and provide a basis for viewing the administrative structures in these situations as a form of system substitutes, handling the processes of input-conversion-output without any participation by the significant sections of the population at large. This situation undoubtedly existed and partially exists today, though it does not accord with the definition of bureaucracy that has been given here. In the present context Eisenstadt's bureaucracies are not concerned with mobilization but with self-sufficient substitution. This raises the problem of totally bureaucratic societies, in which a larger or smaller section of the population is hierarchically organized in a traditional form of administration (or bureaucracy) but where the problem of mobilization, either stalactite or stalagmite, supportive or oppositional, does not arise. The Marxist notion of oriental despotism as a depiction of such societies, both as an empirical fact and as a form of analysis, becomes relevant here; these problems will be discussed at greater length in the appendix on different characterizations of bureaucracy at the end of this chapter.

Eisenstadt has also made a specific attempt to relate the concept of

---

[1] S. N. Eisenstadt, *The Political Systems of Empires*, Glencoe 1963. See also Almond, 'A Developmental Approach to Political Systems', *World Politics*, XVII, 2 (January 1965), pp. 199 ff.

traditional bureaucracy to situations of development, and has identified bureaucracy in this context as one of the most important
phenomena in the development situation; 'diverse bureaucratic
organizations and mechanisms existing in most institutional spheres,
increased extension of the central administration's legal and political
activities and their permeation into all society'.[1] We shall be dealing
with the substantive problem of bureaucracy in developing countries
in greater detail later in the chapter; for definitional purposes at this
stage it is sufficient to note that the prismatic situation of development imposes a multiplicity of roles on administrative structures.
However, the main function of bureaucracy in developed societies, as
a means of mobilizing commitment to established values in a
conservative direction, exists only occasionally and vestigially in
situations of development – more so where the national/constitutional
channel is emphasized than in the case of party-based mobilization.
Bureaucracies do not contribute materially to the mobilizing imperatives outlined in chapters 8 and 9; on the whole they hinder them.
Where they are drawn into the mobilization process, they are
not efficient. 'No bureaucracy in the world will ever transform itself
into self-government ... Its very virtues are inimical to a party
system' as Austen Chamberlain wrote more than half a century ago
in connection with the political expectations of the Indian Civil
Service.[2] No very clear or general function and role emerges for
bureaucracy in the typical contemporary context of development; in
fact in so far as the concept of bureaucracy can be assigned any
consistent and universal definition of a functional kind it cannot be
meaningfully applied to situations of developmental nationalism.
Remains the large problem area of central administrations with which
Eisenstadt and others have dealt analytically and descriptively –
problems of structure, of collective norms, of integration, of instrumental efficiency, of cultural influence. These are not solved or
removed by distinguishing them from problems of bureaucracy,
nor by suggesting that they do not easily lend themselves to cross-

[1] 'Sociological Aspects of Political Development in Underdeveloped Countries', *Economic Development and Cultural Change*, V, 4 (1957), pp. 289–307,
more particularly 'Bureaucracy and Political Development: A Paradoxical
View' in LaPalombara (ed.), *Bureaucracy and Political Development*, op. cit.,
and 'Initial Institutional Patterns of Political Modernization: A Comparative
Study', *Civilizations*, XII, 4 (1962), pp. 461–73. Eisenstadt's latest restatement
is in 'Modernization and Conditions of Sustained Growth', *World Politics*,
XVI, 4 (July 1964), pp. 576–94.
[2] B. R. Nanda, *The Nehrus: Motilal and Jawaharlal*, Bombay 1952, p.
144.

national conceptualization and generalization. Because the *nation trouvée* provides a feeble and uncertain universality, and because change in developing societies is often the consequence of varying emphasis on different or competing structures as a result of coups or intra-elite reorientations, the administrative structures in developing societies do play a very important part in politics. But this is very different from the function which we have assigned to bureaucracy in developed or modern societies.

Yet there appears to be one crucial exception to the general proposition that central administrative structures can play little part in the mobilizing processes of development – namely Japan. In this instance we do appear to have a case of stalactite bureaucratic mobilization consequent upon the Meiji Restoration, in favour of something very like developmental nationalism. This took place at a period when the value system of developmental nationalism can hardly be said to have existed anywhere, and it is therefore not surprising that the Japanese case, as a remarkable example of economic development, went almost entirely unnoticed at the time. In fact the usual standard of comparison with Japan has not been the case of other developing countries, but the remarkably dissimilar and contrasting history of late nineteenth and early twentieth-century China – possibly an example of the limitations of regional perspectives in the search for historical comparisons.[1] The discovery of Japan as a possible model for others is of very recent origin – and even then the discoverers were comparative social scientists rather than ruling elites in developing countries. In any case the Japanese model poses substantial difficulties. For present purposes its main features are (1) the fact that Japanese industrialization was 'induced'; far from being a spontaneous and largely unrecognized effort, the effects of which flowed in course of time from the periphery towards the centre, the notion and implementation of development were deliberately pushed from the centre outwards. (2) the combination of economic growth *per se* with nationalistic perspectives. Economic growth, with a particular accent on heavy industry, was firmly linked to national self-assertion and status in the international system. Recent analyses of Japanese economic development by economists stress the 'distortion' of 'pure' or rational economic perspectives by nationalistic

---

[1] A very interesting and useful analysis of these differences is provided by John K. Fairbank, Edwin O. Reischauer and Albert M. Craig, *East Asia: The Modern Transformation*, London 1966, which is extremely illuminating both on Japan and China in an Asian context.

demands like military growth etc.[1] The uniqueness of Japan as an example of successful development, both in terms of dates and achievement, is well brought out in a recent comparative analysis between Japan and Turkey, where similarities are pointed up which in fact relate to a temporal difference of some fifty or more years.[2] As far as the problem of bureaucracy is concerned Japan is thus probably an exceptional example of effective bureaucratic mobilization within the values of developmental nationalism–though the exception is explained at least in part by the very concrete and widely perceived reality of national universals at the time, and their important, almost total, personalization in the form of the Emperor.[3] These factors are replicated in few of today's developing countries.[4]

Instead developing countries constitute a transitional category in this context, in which the 'substitutionist' central administration of traditional empires is gradually being transformed into either the non-bureaucratic or political mobilizing form of society characterized

[1] See most recently William W. Lockwood (ed.), *The State and Economic Enterprise in Japan*, Princeton 1965, particularly contributions by Landes, Crawcour and Oshima. Cf. also Lockwood, *Economic Development of Japan*, Princeton 1954.

[2] See Ward and Rustow, *Political Modernization in Japan and Turkey*, op. cit.

[3] There is no specific discussion of Japanese bureaucracy in a developmental context. The nearest specific analysis is Thomas C. Smith, *Political Change and Industrial Development in Japan; Government Enterprise 1868–80*, Stanford 1955. Though this deals with the specific problem, the discussion is limited to a short if crucial period in time. Different aspects of Japanese bureaucracy may be gleaned from Kurt Steiner, 'The Japanese Village and its Government', *Far Eastern Quarterly*, XV, 2 (1956), pp. 185–291; R. P. Dore, *City Life in Japan*, Berkeley and Los Angeles 1958; Ruth Benedict, *The Chrysanthemum and the Sword*, Boston 1946; Jean Stoetzel, *Jeunesse sans chrysanthème ni sabre*, Paris 1954.

[4] A possible example of one developing country in which somewhat similar preconditions of identification of nationhood with ruler might be found is Iran. The Shah appears to try and play a role somewhat like that of the Japanese Emperor. This suggests that a more obvious comparative study of development with Japan might have been Iran rather than Turkey. However there are also limits to this analogy, since the Shah of Persia's family does not have the ancient legitimacy of the Japanese ruling house (though the period of effective Meiji rule in the 1870's in Japan was about of the same duration as that of the Pahlevis today). Also the sense of nationhood is not as strong in Persia as in Japan, nor is it supported by an intensive programme of education and an equally intense use of religion. See L. Binder, *Iran*, op. cit.; Norman Jacobs, *The Sociology of Development: Iran as an Asian Case Study*, New York 1966.

A potentially somewhat similar situation exists in Ethiopia–though again with great shortfalls in educational and agricultural effort, the latter being one precondition of successful industrialization. However both the factors of a high degree of national integration, and of personalization in the form of religious–politically legitimate emperor, are present there. See most recently Richard Greenfield, *Ethiopia: A New Political History*, London 1965.

by the Soviet Union, or the consensual type of society of the West with their differentiated, specific group mobilizations and bureaucratic structures which take up the 'slack' of the shortfall in total mobilized commitment. The central administrations of developing countries, whether labelled bureaucracies or not, contain prismatic elements—i.e. combinations of traditional and development components—which are better separated analytically and contrasted than subsumed under some concept of developmental bureaucracy.[1] In the present analysis, with its implicit definition of modernity or development as being attainable through two very different forms of social values and processes, the prismatic approach must accommodate a three-way perspective: traditional central administration (where it exists) being adapted to, and contrasted with, stalactite political mobilization structures on the one hand, and stalagmite cleavage or electoral mobilization structures on the other. The central administrations of developing countries have therefore to be analysed in relation to political mobilization as set out in chapters 8 and 9, as well as in terms of indices of modernity of the Western type in situations of electoral mobilization.

Having defined the concept of bureaucracy, and tested this definition out on a number of empirical cases, we can now examine in greater detail how it relates to developed societies, particularly how and in what manner it provides the 'missing' quantity of mobilization in situations of multiple, specific, differentiated group mobilizations.

There are two main arguments for the function of bureaucracy as a substitution factor for formal mobilization processes and structures as well as a partial means of providing a focus for mobilized commitments. First, we have seen that the growth of non-party interest groups is positively related to the growth of bureaucracy—certainly in terms of chronological coincidence, probably in functional terms also.[2] Such interest groups are porous, interest-specific or issue-oriented

[1] It is not without significance that the origin of the notion of prisms as a means of separating the traditional from the modern components in situations of development should have originated in the study of bureaucracy or public administration *before* it was inflated to provide a conceptual framework for the study of whole societies and even international systems in the course of development. See Fred W. Riggs, 'The Theory of Developing Polities', *World Politics*, XVI, 1 (October 1963), pp. 147–71; 'International Relations as a Prismatic System', ibid., XIV, 1 (October 1961), pp. 144–81; Roger D. Masters, 'World Politics as a Primitive Political System', ibid., XVI, 4 (July 1964), pp. 595–619.

[2] The purely functional analysis of bureaucracy in a similar context is stressed by Talcott Parsons, who considers bureaucracy as a 'complex organization of supervision' resulting from 'the need for minute co-ordination of the different

-hence occasional-mobilizing structures; their function for mobilization declines as their own bureaucratic organization becomes more efficient. Bureaucratic norms and processes here substitute for mobilization-just as a series of porous, specific mobilizations, pluralistically involving the same participants, substitute for a wider ranging and more diffusely *aimed* but also more intense or salient political mobilization. It was suggested earlier that the *sum* of any one person's -or of many persons'-specific mobilizations does not qualitatively or quantitatively equal that of mobilized political commitment, and that in developing countries there is accordingly a distinct tendency to fix the content of symbols at that level of specificity where the proportion of the population mobilized is at its maximum. To restore the balance, and return Parsons' two-pattern variables to their proper direction of social change, we need an x in the equation which balances the weight of all the pieces (specificities) with the weight of the social whole (universe).[1] In other words something that holds the universe of a developed society together. This is the role of the consensus; *it becomes logically necessary to contain the pressure through the open pores of the 'specific'*. But consensus implies the existence of bureaucratic structures which take over the function of maintaining the *status quo*. In doing so, they also take over the missing part of the political function of mobilization, and permit the 'safe' pursuit of specificities.[2]

The porousness of specific mobilizations in developed societies can

---

functions' which follow upon 'the elaborate differentiation of functions' implicit in 'the elaborate division of labour'. (Talcott Parsons, *The Social System*, op. cit., pp. 507-8.) Though his analysis has obviously substantial similarities with that adumbrated here, we have allocated to bureaucracy a more specific socio-cultural and socio-political function than Parsons, who seems to take a more deterministically *economic* view in equating bureaucratic organization with the division of labour in its widest and all-embracing sense. He thus lays himself open to logical and empirical criticism of the kind offered by Peter Drucker, *Concept of the Corporation*, New York 1946, pp. 189 ff., and Reinhard Bendix, 'Bureaucracy: The Problem and its Setting', *American Sociological Review*, XII (October 1947), pp. 507-9, also Bendix, 'Bureaucraticization in Industry', in Kornhauser *et al.* (eds.), *Industrial Conflict*, New York 1954. These criticisms are elaborated by Gouldner, 'Metaphysical Pathos and the Theory of Bureaucracy', op. cit., pp. 82-86.

[1] 'Proper direction of social change' in the modernizing or developmental sense in which others (for instance G. A. Almond in the introduction to *The Politics of the Developing Areas*) use the pattern variables-a use which Parsons, who uses them as dichotomies as much as directions of historical evolution, has in fact disclaimed.

[2] The identification of consensus with bureaucracy in the context of pluralism has received support from an unexpected quarter: political theory-but of a kind unusually suffused by sociological awareness. 'Modern pluralism . . .

be interestingly illustrated from an extreme case, Holland. Supporters of movements based on religious cleavage were and are 'encapsulated' to the extent of *apparent* particularism combined with specificity; not only religion-based parties but ancillary schools, youth movements, confessional trade unions, sports clubs, newspapers and even radio stations. On the face of it this situation resembles that of pre-1914 German Social Democracy, which has become known as *verzuiling*–literally columnization, or encapsulation into rigid hierarchies. But where German Social Democracy was the epitome of a specific particularism which explicitly rejected any social universals, preferring to concentrate on millenarian perspectives, the Dutch social system combines specificity with universalism by the existence of a consensus–and an extremely effective one at that.[1] If we compare this to a developing country with a somewhat similar phenomenon of *verzuiling* like the Lebanon, the difference between specific and porous mobilization in a developed society, and the more thoroughly particularistic and unporous mobilization in a developing one, emerges clearly. The Lebanon appears to be a good example of a society in delicate balance between a universalistic perspective threatened periodically by the closing of the pores of particularistic mobilization. Thus when the rules of the rather narrow game are broken (as they were by Camille Chamoun in 1956–7) the pores quickly close and commitments revert to the 'columns' of par-

---

represents still another offshoot [of the tradition of trying to replace the political order with social bookkeeping or the administration of things] ... society was the repository of groups and issues which, to the pluralists, constituted the primary social loyalties. The pre-eminence of the political order was viewed as the consequence of the mistaken belief that society required a supreme sovereign authority ... the shadow of the political order was preserved because, in a society of autonomous groups, some kind of co-ordinating power was needed–which is to say the political order is justified more out of weariness than design ... modern political thought converts political problems into administrative ones.' Wolin, *Politics and Vision*, p. 314. For the notion of 'political order' and 'some kind of co-ordinating power' read bureaucracy. Note also the mandatory reference to sovereignty, equated in this context once more with the political order–identifying the source unmistakably as political theory.

[1] For this concept and its reverse, *ontzuiling*, see J. P. Kruijt, *Verzuiling*, Zaandijk 1959; J. P. Kruijt and W. Goddijn, 'Verzuiling an ontzuiling als soziologisch process', in A. den Hollander *et al.* (eds.), *Drift en Koers*, Assen 1962, pp. 227–63. For Germany see Günther Roth, *The Social Democrats in Imperial Germany*, Totowa (New York) 1963; also J. P. Nettl, 'The German Social Democratic Party ...' *Past and Present*, op. cit. A recent discussion which highlights the effectiveness of the Dutch consensus in the important context of wage-price negotiations may be found in Edelman and Fleming, *Wage-Price Decisions*, op. cit., pp. 220–78.

ticularistic mobilization. There is hardly any consensus in existence, but rather a narrow constitutional type of 'game' which has already been identified as typical of a number of developing countries.[1]

Secondly, and developing the implications of this, the point can be argued in terms of value orientation. The conservative perspectives of bureaucracy have already been mentioned. In the first place it is the product of a particular orientation–that of *delegation*–and it will attempt to maintain this delegative orientation (common information stock and 'credit agreement' of informal consensus between delegates and those they represent). This incidentally illuminates once more the incompatibility of participation and delegation inherent in electoral legitimacy–in contrast to the more conventional view of compatibility between delegation and participation through 'free' elections. Bureaucracies are themselves institutional interest groups with their own interests and goals to defend; the success of bureaucracies, unlike that of the cleavage structures of political mobilization, is self-perpetuating and does not tend to be self-liquidating even in the long run. Secondly the internal process of action in a bureaucracy– and by derivation in any society in which bureaucratic behaviour has obtained major cultural significance–is so structured as to tend much more easily towards conservation than change. Etzioni has summed up this position very well. 'The ultimate justification of the administrative [or bureaucratic] act . . . is that it is in line with the organization's rules and regulations, and that it has been approved–directly or by implication–by a superior rank.'[2] The structural relationship within bureaucracies spelled out here is, of course, reinforced by symbolic articulation of individual subordination often called 'bureaucratic ritual', which enhances the functional significance of the structured composition of action itself.[3] This is a different tendency to conservatism from that involved in the notion of delegation; in

[1] For a recent discussion of the Lebanon in this context, which appeared after this text was completed, see L. Binder (ed.), *Politics in Lebanon*, New York and London 1966. A comparative study of Holland and the Lebanon would make an interesting contribution to the study of in some respects similar social structure in very different stages of development.

[2] Amitai Etzioni, *Modern Organizations*, New York 1964. This definition is raised in contrast to professional action which Etzioni defines as follows: 'The ultimate justification for a professional act is that it is, to the best of the professional's knowledge, the right act. He might consult his colleagues before he acts, but the decision is his. If he errs, he will still be defended by his peers'–on the basis of his professional standing.

[3] This ritualistic concept has been stressed by Robert K. Merton, 'Bureaucratic Structure and Personality', in Merton, *Social Theory and Social Structure*, Glencoe, Ill., 1957.

many 'modern' societies the disobedient civil servant will be disciplined by his bureaucratic superiors, but covered and defended by his political superiors. Together, however, the delegatory aspects of the relationship between lower and upper bureaucrats both differentially result in the articulation of the *status quo* at different levels of action. Both structures of action diffuse conservative tendencies into their social environment at their different levels.

Finally, and perhaps most important, is the allegedly 'neutral' and instrumental behaviour of bureaucracy. This leaves the overt *articulation* of official values and norms, and the manipulations of the relevant symbols, to other, more suitably political institutions, and makes bureaucracy essentially the guardian of the fundamental values, of the 'real public interest', of that General Will that can be 'discovered' or 'found' but cannot be synthetically created. This *underlies* so many of the choices of politics. The more closely the political articulation of values, norms and symbols resembles the bureaucratic conception of the public interest, the tighter and more intimate the effectiveness of the sense of delegation. The direction of collective bureaucratic behaviour is therefore towards preservation, and as such is conservative. It is also a subtle, secondary instrument in much stalactite mobilization.[1]

The order of priorities has, of course, to be correctly understood. The development of bureaucracy was not followed by the growth of interest specificities but the proliferation of interest specificities in turn induced modern bureaucracy. This is important because it distinguishes developed from developing societies; in many of the latter centralized administrative structures, where these existed at all, were operating long before there was any economic development, differentiation of structures or of roles. In the developed West on the other hand the historic English and American pattern was one in which bureaucracy followed upon, and was the consequence of, industrial development and the concomitant structural differentiation

---

[1] This sense of guardianship is clearly implied in the comparative, conceptual classification of national bureaucracies in F. M. Marx, *The Administrative State*, Chicago 1957. But it may be taken to apply just as much to the bureaucracies of large firms, trade unions and churches. Even trade union traditions of militancy become routinized, hallowed and bureaucratic, as do traditions of informality in certain large firms. The *techniques* of governmental bureaucratic mobilization under the umbrella of a value system are discussed in Nettl, 'Consensus or Elite Domination: The Case of Business', op. cit. This study applies largely to Britain; the reverse case can be made for America, where *business* bureaucracies seem to be more influential in establishing or perpetuating the social value system.

as outlined in the classical Smelser model.[1] The French and German experience followed the pattern of today's Third World more closely; 'Empire' or traditional bureaucracy preceding, and helping to induce, industrialization, which in turn modernized and transformed the bureaucracy and brought it 'into line'. There is of course an enormous difference between the French State, which by the end of the eighteenth century had lost its personification and had become impersonal (in Germany it retained strong elements of personification with the King of Prussia and Emperor until almost the end of the century), and the relative abstraction and repersonalization of the *nation trouvée*. But even in the more *étatiste* European countries it was the proliferation of specificities and differentiations that eventually produced the modern type of bureaucracy; the *coincidence* of these two factors is the overriding consideration and cannot be ignored.

This bureaucratic equalization function appears to be indifferently applicable to both elitist and constitutional society; it is apparently necessary in all developed societies that proliferate specificities. If one were to venture beyond this safe generalization, the function of the *central* bureaucracy is probably somewhat greater and more salient in elitist cultures where consensus is also more strongly in evidence. The debate in Britain over the provisions of the Northcote-Trevelyan report in 1854 illustrate very well the problem of bureaucratic mobilization in an elitist setting. 'The reform will strengthen and multiply the ties between the higher classes and the possession of administrative power. As member of parliament for Oxford I look forward eagerly to its operation', said Gladstone. An opponent's description of the same reform was 'rational class nepotism'.[2] It is also significant that the Northcote-Trevelyan report was the beginning of the end (at least until very recently and except for the period of wartime crisis) of the habit of bringing outsiders into Civil Service posts. This can, of course, be taken as evidence for the fact that

[1] Neil J. Smelser, *Social Change in the Industrial Revolution*, op. cit.

[2] See Edward Hughes, 'Civil Service Reform 1853–1855', *Public Administration*, XXXVII (Spring 1954), p. 28; also H. G. R. Greaves, *The British Constitution*, London 1948, second edition, p. 164.

A recent commentator who quotes these sources and discussed them sums up the effect of the Civil Service reform in a precisely contrary sense: 'The reforms were intended to strengthen the influence of political institutions upon the socio-economic system.' (Richard Rose, 'England: A Traditionally Modern Political Culture', in Sidney Verba and Lucian W. Pye (eds), *Political Culture and Political Development*, Princeton 1965, p. 83 f.) The present analysis suggests that the correct conclusion was the opposite–that it was the influence of the socio-economic system upon the political institutions which was strengthened.

broader initial elite recruitment makes later *ad hoc* recruitment unnecessary and 'tidies up', as it were, the institutionalization of the elite. It is a fairly typical feature of an elitist society that the institutions are tailor-made for the elite rather than the other way about (cf. France above, p. 304). Further evidence in the same direction is provided by the extraordinary myth which has plagued discussion of the role and function of the Civil Service in Britain over the problems of policy versus administration. The British system rests on the assumption that policy will be provided by political authority at the top while administration will be carried out by 'non-political' (which is usually confused with non-party) officials from very near the top to the bottom.[1] In fact this separation is both empirically meaningless and theoretically absurd. In practice civil servants do establish policy to a very great extent. Such a view also ignores the vital problem of bureaucratic goals; almost every empirical study of bureaucratic organization has now shown beyond doubt that this factor can be discounted only at great peril. The existence of this myth, and its maintenance in the face of all evidence, are one of the many sources of elitist self-definition in Britain and largely explain the 'inexplicable' influence of bureaucratic goals and values. In France, by contrast, there is general recognition that no such separation between policy and administration is possible, and they interact to an extent that makes their separation meaningless except at an advanced level of sociological analysis like that of Crozier. This avoidance of an unreal distinction of functions in France is reinforced sociologically by a widely perceived view of bureaucracy as a self-contained collectivity which is not arbitrarily carved up into political and administrative components. The French system of administrative law shows that the adjudication of problems arising out of the existence of the state bureaucracy is and should be made in full cognizance of the autonomy of the act or acts in question, rather than follow a purely arbitrary separation of administrative problems–with quasi-legal remedies or no remedies at all–from policy problems with political remedies only.

The growth of modern bureaucracy is almost certainly a reflection of a growing achievement orientation in developed societies–so much so that the connection between, say, central bureaucracy and achievement becomes in itself ascriptive. This is a significant conceptual

[1] In fact very much like the excessively 'anglophile' definition of bureaucracy offered by Dahrendorf in the German context in 'Bureaucracy without Liberty', in Lipset and Lowenthal, op. cit.; see above, p. 340.

difficulty posed by the variable achievement-ascription.[1] In England for instance the upper Civil Service demonstrably carries differentiated ascriptive status (Foreign Office Clerk, High Treasury Official, Scotland Yard, Secret Service – the latter recently combining a good deal of fictional boosting with simultaneous real-life ridicule). Yet this status location is in part clearly based on a present evaluation of historic achievement. In England as elsewhere the word bureaucracy carries a certain amount of *a priori* stigma in the popular imagination; bureaucracy is not an immediately obvious habitat for ascriptive status. Something of the same tendency is visible in France too, where *fonctionnaire* is still a pejorative word in middle and lower social circles (including many *petit-bourgeois* who long for their sons to become one). On the other hand *haut-fonctionnaire* is not a stigma but an ascriptive acknowledgement of deference based on historical achievement. Clearly an accumulated, routinized capital of evaluated achievement in time becomes ascriptive; we may suggest that perhaps it is the application of this accumulated capital to a person rather than an institution that makes it ascriptive.

But what about America? A tradition of egalitarian individualism clearly militates against the acceptance of bureaucratic status – irrespective of the empirical proliferation of bureaucracy itself which is, as one might expect, substantial. Bureaucracy there carries rather less evaluated achievement status, though its low status has now begun to rise substantially; as the decision-making structure of rationally sanctified large-scale organizations it is beginning to be recognized as a locus of achievement. Nonetheless central government services as a particular form of bureaucracy perhaps still have lower ascriptive status compared to business organizations. In the Soviet Union the party 'bureaucracy' still has considerably more status, power and influence than the Soviet bureaucracy at all corresponding levels except the very top, and seems to provide a better channel of social mobility.[2] The special difficulties of discussing

---

[1] Cf. Dubin, 'Parsons' Actor', op. cit., who emphasizes universality and specificity for the adaptive modality, and distributes achievement-affectivity and ascription-neutrality between the modalities of goal attainment and pattern maintenance. It could in that case logically follow that goal attainment and pattern maintenance become almost incongruent.

[2] See Z. Brzezinski and S. P. Huntington, 'Cincinnatus and the Apparatchik', *World Politics*, XVI, 1 (October 1963), pp. 52–78, for some comparative analyses of US and USSR careers. The authors however insist on contrasting US *politicians* with Soviet *bureaucrats* – a somewhat misleading *a priori* categorization which somewhat limits the value of the comparison. Cf. also the approach of Alex H. Inkeles and Peter Rossi, 'National Comparisons of

bureaucracy in the Soviet Union have already been noted. The elitist/constitutional variable does not therefore seem greatly to affect the role of bureaucracy in this context; compared to Britain and France the central government bureaucracy *proprio dictu* in both the United States and the Soviet Union seems constrained in its actions and initiatives, as well as somewhat limited in its social status.

On the other hand, a country like Germany seems to have both mobilizing potential and a stock of capitalized achievement for its bureaucracy, as well as a strong ascriptive element. Oddly enough, the change from latent to overt mobilization in Germany corresponds to an increase in the positive evaluation of bureaucracy (1918–45) while a decrease in the positive evaluation of bureaucracy (1945–64) corresponds to an apparent slackening of national mobilization.[1] It will be interesting to see whether a country like Italy, with a tradition of low esteem for bureaucracy, will also come to evaluate bureaucracy more positively than in the past now that a dramatically successful rate of economic development has been attained and the capacity for political mobilization appears to have slackened. There are a few individual examples of it–Enrico Mattei, and the management of IRI and ENI, though it may well be said that these bureaucracies are viewed as commercial rather than governmental, and therefore belong to the same big *azienda* reference group as FIAT, Montecatini, Edison, etc. (This possibility arises from the peculiar structure and anatomy of many Italian State enterprises, which are run very like any commercial firm, and may even be quoted on the Stock Exchange.[2] The fact that the present discussion has focused on government bureaucracy may perhaps have narrowed the argument overmuch. As a recent study of modern capitalism shows, a growing bureaucratic element is visible in all societies–both manifestly in terms of size and influence as well as latently in terms of setting goals which serve as foci for mobilized commitment and culture production. But while it is central government bureaucracy that is in question in France and, though somewhat less obviously, in Britain, the corres-

---

Occupational Prestige', *American Journal of Sociology*, LXI (1956), pp. 329–39.

[1] Cf. Ralf Dahrendorf, *Gesellschaft und Demokratie in Deutschland*, op. cit., pp. 249 ff., 280 ff., 347 ff.

[2] Useful insight into the Italian situation may be obtained from Joseph LaPalombara, *Interest Groups in Italian Politics*, Princeton 1964, particularly pp. 252–394, and LaPalombara and Gianfranco Poggi, 'I gruppi di pressione e la burocrazia italiana', *Rassegna italiana di sociologia*, 1 (October-December 1960), pp. 31–35.

ponding element in the United States is partly central government, partly the large commercial corporations, while in Germany it is to some extent the bureaucracy of banking institutions that fulfils many of the same value-mobilizing functions.[1] The relative downgrading of government bureaucracy in Germany, corresponding to a slackening of national mobilization in the period 1945–64, may thus be explained not in terms of decline of bureaucratic mobilization generally but by a shift of emphasis from one *type* of bureaucracy to another. This formulation provides a lead into the situation in countries like Japan where there is evidence of inter-bureaucratic competition for social goal-setting. In Holland too it can be argued that we should not look only at the central government bureaucracy as the main locus of goal setting, but also at the increasingly important structures of co-operative organizations like the Foundation of Labour and the Socio-Economic Council. Finally it can be argued that the displacing of one bureaucracy by another may help partially to explain the situation of the military in Latin America (see below, pp. 361–4).

Further illumination of the modern bureaucratic phenomenon may finally be provided by direct contrast with the situation in developing countries. It is hardly surprising, if developed countries with vast bureaucracies have not fully succeeded in internalizing and evaluating this structural and cultural phenomenon as a recognized and acceptable part of social life (as they have internalized armies, executives, legislatures, judiciaries), that developing countries should find it even more difficult. The notion of modern society as bureaucratic, it must be remembered, is a social scientist's view, not a participant's. Actually the difficulty is existential and real, not merely a matter of evaluation or of finding the right analytical framework. The inheritance situation hardly fosters bureaucracy: only if inheritance becomes long drawn-out and almost stagnant, as in India, does it engender bureaucratic forms of substitution. (In this context the ruinous variant of inheritance stagnation which overtook the pre-1914 German Social Democrats must be remembered.) After inheritance the administrative service originally recruited by the colonial power usually occupies an ambivalent position: technically indispensable, yet viewed with suspicion and disdain–somewhat like Trotsky's former Tsarist officers and the scientist-technicians having to be protected by Lenin against the majority of revolutionary Bolsheviks. Such a bureaucracy may conceivably lend itself to national-constitutional mobilization, particularly where economic planning is promi-

[1] See Andrew Shonfield, *Modern Capitalism*, op. cit.

nent (India), but if the orientation is towards party mobilization any existing bureaucracy 'taken over' by the inheritors will merely be another particularistic structure to be broken up, eroded or neutralized. Once more the prevailing anti-bureaucratic orientation is complementary to mobilization, and bureaucracy is synonymous in this context with static conservatism and failure to contribute to the goals of developmental nationalism; a tendency for dichotomous oversimplification unconsciously adopted from Soviet ideology together with some of the processes of party mobilization itself.

But the clearest evidence of unsuccessful 'grafting' of bureaucracy on to developing societies is the fact that the central government bureaucracy, where it exists, is not a general social phenomenon, reproduced in the form of complementary bureaucracies in other social collectivities like business, trade unions, churches or associations–a diffused component of society and of social behaviour as in developed countries. Instead we have a number of more or less rigid status hierarchies. This is perhaps the essential difference between traditional administration and modern bureaucracy. In a developing society, as Eisenstadt shows, the two forms of structure tend to conflict; the central government administration, to some extent under pressure to act as though under the umbrella of pluralistic or multispecific consensus, is faced by a social environment demanding the functions and processes of a status hierarchy. Instead of a functional imperative in a social environment of differentiated structures and functional specificities, 'bureaucracy' in developing countries is a particularistic, self-sufficient element–still partially substituting for mobilized commitment altogether as in traditional empires, partially displaced by the typical mobilizing structures of developmental nationalism. As in the case of the relationship between traditional legitimacy orientations and developmental values, bureaucracy in a developmental situation represents a conflictual stage of transition between the traditional and the 'modern'.

What about bureaucratic behaviour? In this transitional situation administrators in developing countries often take on roles that have little or no relation to the administration's goals–goals, moreover, that often cannot be attained or even assessed in administrative forms.[1]

[1] From among the substantial literature on bureaucracy in developing countries reference may be made to Victor A. Thompson, 'Administrative Objectives of Development Administration', *Administrative Science Quarterly*, IX (1964), pp. 91–108, where the relevance of the modern, Weberian model of bureaucracy to developing countries is examined and criticized. Cf. also Schaffer, 'The Concept of Preparation', op. cit., and literature cited there.

For one thing, the central government administration tends to resemble not only a status hierarchy but a caste of scribes–the nearest social equivalent to a bureaucratic class in countries like India, Burma and the Middle East. This is more like 'pure' ascription, without any even moderately recent capitalization of achievement; the type of bureaucratic class crystallization of which Imperial China was the archetype. Another important aspect of administrations in many developing countries is that they are means of rewarding political supporters by providing a permanent source of employment for the constituents of the 'vote bank', and at the same time induce further support and compliance through the promise of further employment. In this regard also government administration (in e.g. South America) traditionally and frequently supplements and re-places the pork barrel of political parties, trade unions and other associations.[1] Local and personal allegiance becomes redeemable through the guarantee of jobs in the civil bureaucracy for an influen-tial man's 'retinue'. As a means of integration and commitment the central administration thus partially substitutes for other collectivi-ties in developing countries, and the administrative role often subsumes that of a party worker, *militant* or trade union official. It is in this context that Eisenstadt's emphasis on the role of bureaucracy in developing countries is significant–as an extension of socially integrative functions and as a diffuse cluster of associated roles, rather than in terms of specific functions in the *political* subsystem as in modern societies.

This diffuse administrative complex of roles is faithfully reproduced both in the prismatic or mixed nature of the consensus of role expectations with regard to individuals and in the way in which individual 'bureaucrats' actually play their roles. The new district officers in ex-British Africa–according to a hostile press–sit on the same verandah with the same drinks at sundown as their colonial predecessors. In India one of the observable realities about economic administration is the ritualistic emphasis on status differentials between administrators and others; however a government decision

[1] As might be expected, the national-constitutional emphasis in mobilization in Egypt is correlated with an extraordinary high percentage of government or bureaucratic employment. Indeed, it can be argued that the inability to succeed with a more party-political manner of mobilization is not the cause but the consequence of such bureaucraticization; cf. below, p. 379. In the decade 1947–57, nearly 35 per cent of all Egyptians with primary or better education were government employees, nearly 50 per cent of all expenditure went on their salaries and wages, figures that have increased still further since then. (Morroe Berger; *Bureaucracy and Society in Modern Egypt*, Princeton 1957, p. 83.)

on any one of the innumerable licence applications by business firms may go in the end, the ritual of applicant humility and bureaucratic arrogance is followed faithfully—often down to the final paradox of almost gratuitous official rudeness *in spite of* the certainty on both sides that the application will go through. A number of countries even find it necessary to buttress the roles of their administrators with legislation that makes public incivility to government servants into a mild form of *lèse majesté*. The consequence of such a role consensus is that bureaucracy finds it difficult to convert to a different, more instrumental role when and if the latter becomes appropriate as development proceeds; in countries like Greece and Turkey collective bureaucratic self-sufficiency in an integrative social structure has removed the bureaucracy from that contact with society which underlies its adaptive or *administrative* purpose in society. The same problem of self-sufficiency and distance would seem to apply to pre-revolutionary China or indeed any society with a 'bureaucratic' caste system.[1]

Certain types of traditional society, perhaps best described summarily as empires, in fact have a well-developed system of central administration which benefits from the legitimacy of the ruler not so much by charismatic dispersion but by being viewed as integral parts of the ruler himself (see below, p. 373). These are non-mobilized societies. The administration is an autonomous system of its own consisting of, and substituting in large part for, the political sub-system. Between such societies and modern ones, in which bureaucracy has the function of equalizing the amount of mobilized commitment provided by differentiated specific group mobilizations, developing societies are a transitional category, though distinctive and widespread enough to justify distinct conceptual characterization of their own. Even though one of the major forms or channels of mobilization is what has here been called national-constitutional,

---

[1] I have participated in a number of training courses for Greek and Turkish civil servants, and some of these observations are based on this experience. One of the interesting phenomena in such government administrations is the obsession of the younger members with the *science* of administration—the search for a panacea which is both achievement-oriented product, as well as intellectual justification, of their special status hierarchy. But it is often divorced from any knowledge of the realities of the thing to be administered. For instance, they tend to view agricultural administration exclusively as a problem of how to administer agriculture, but in no way connected with providing more food more efficiently. Cf. the CPSU which has usually been guilty of the opposite scientism; that of excessive preoccupation with the technical problems of agriculture, and the attempt to raise production by command.

central administrations have only a limited role to play in mobilizing commitment within the value system of developmental nationalism. In situations where mobilization is a functional imperative, 'bureaucracy' will have a correspondingly reduced function in the political or goal-attainment subsystem. Moreover, the administrative or bureaucratic role is not instrumental for developmental nationalism. Instead it tends to be a prismatic, undifferentiated complex of roles. Nonetheless, administrations are an important phenomenon in developing countries, emphasizing integrative functions and providing a substitute for many welfare functions in developed societies—instead of the goal-attainment function which bureaucracy has both in traditional empires and in modern societies. The problem of administration or bureaucracy in developing countries, though conceptually awkward, is crucial, and fully justifies the empirical and theoretical attention of social scientists.

Excursus: Bureaucracy in Latin America and the Periodization of Developmental Nationalism

This analysis of bureaucracy in development situations may incidentally be of some help in explaining the peculiar but widespread incursion into government of the military in Latin America. One sees all kinds of explanations; some are compounds of common factors arising out of particular area studies, some are descriptive, some are psychological, some socio-economic. An almost universal phenomenon in a rather isolated continent is likely to have a cause capable of general conceptualization—and not merely to represent an abstract sum of various local accidents of history. An analysis based on the foregoing discussion accordingly might follow these lines:

The attainment of South American independence early in the nineteenth century—i.e. prior to any sign of local economic development and developmental nationalism—was largely reflected in, and structured by, a military form of mobilization which, in the continued absence of socio-economic development, remained dominant for a long time. Though undoubtedly an inheritance situation, South American national independence antedated the historical emergence of more precise developmental goals; industrialization, in so far as it was understood at all, was something that 'happened'—in a certain and particular part of the world far away (and even then was widely viewed as despicable and undesirable). A situation can be *defined* as an inheritance situation by participants irrespective of the developmental goals that nowadays go with it. The typical pattern of an inheritance party was historically not mature in an era of military mobilization which certainly survived longer in the Spanish than probably in any other European tradition. This does not mean that the period was one of intense military mobilization, but merely that such mobilization as did take place took a military rather than political form.

This raises the problem of historical dating for the beginning of what has here been called developmental nationalism—a particular blend of nationalism with perspectives and orientations towards purposive economic development. The history of Japan in the nineteenth century, so difficult to accommodate in any comparative analysis of economic growth and of conditions conducive to it, is significant as regards dating, for Japan almost certainly provides the first historical example of developmental nationalism—even though the emphases were not identical with the value system of the present Third World. Recent analysis justifies the dating of the beginning of developmental nationalism in Japan at about 1870–80; emphasis on economic growth but always with nationalistic priorities —even when the latter contradicted the former, as in the case of military expenditure. It is thus clear that the growth and triumph of Latin American nationalism predated the emergence of developmental nationalism anywhere by fifty years. What is more remarkable perhaps is the isolation of the Japanese example; only twenty years later do we find a partially similar phenomenon in Wilhelmian Germany, which most contemporaries regarded as unique and which they themselves sought to emulate (e.g. Vitte in Russia).[1] Even today Japan provides an outstanding *example* of economic and technological growth rates in the developed World, but there is hardly any evidence of it providing a socio-economic *model*—least of all with regard to processes of mobilization. There is certainly no structural or processual analogy to be drawn between Latin America and Japan; the problems of the former being firmly rooted in its own past of predevelopmental nationalism.

The post-inheritance pattern in newly independent Latin America thus lay not between party and national-constitutional mobilization, but between military and national-constitutional forms, with the military carrying out the function of the party elite—though without

[1] For this see the admirable discussion by David Landes, 'Technological Change and Development in Western Europe 1750–1914', in Vol. VI of the *Cambridge Economic History of Europe: The Industrial Revolutions and After*, Cambridge 1965.

the latter's mobilizing efficiency. The value system which we have characterized as developmental nationalism there remained incarcerated in pre-developmental, military terms and the *nation trouvée* attained legitimacy and structural reality in terms of mainly military symbols. Strong traces of this can still be found in the way that quite improbable rumours of impending attack from abroad echo through many Latin American societies at frequent and regular intervals, and in the willingness of civilian militias to take up arms on these and all other occasions; also in the ideological hangover of very sharp situational definitions which today are still based on minor wars between one country and another a relatively long time ago. The notion of a traditional national enemy is very strong in Latin America. Mobilization thus still tends to take military forms relatively often; society has remained oriented in the direction of military mobilization.

The goals and attitudes of central government administrations similarly have remained immured in a military rather than a civilian context. The reaction against this was never strong enough to upset the self-interested pressure of the military as a dominant group, and just as we have described bureaucracy in a pre-developmental situation in terms of a caste of scribes, so the military in South America were for long a dominant caste of soldiers. The role is here also superordinated to the function; the *civil* bureaucracies of Greece and Turkey have the same difficulty in adapting to a developmental function as do many of the *military* in South America – except perhaps in Brazil and to a lesser extent in the Argentine. Compare this with the role of the military in Turkey as frequently *supplanting* the civil bureaucracy in a developmental function, and generally articulating the values of national integration and development.[1] The comparison between the two types of military and civil bureaucracy goes farther. Bureaucracies in developing countries are employment agencies for the educated unemployable. On the whole the military have fulfilled a similar role in South America – though the education is often, if not always, of a specialized kind. Add to this the difficulty of economic advancement in countries where the substantial profits from entrepreneurship have tended for many decades to go into short-term lending or refuge abroad rather than into sustained long-term indus-

---

[1] See Dankwart A. Rustow, 'The Army and the Founding of the Turkish Republic', *World Politics*, XI (1959), pp. 513–52; Daniel Lerner and Richard D. Robinson, 'Swords and Ploughshares: The Turkish Army as a Modernizing Force', ibid., XIII (1960), pp. 19–45; generally S. P. Huntington (ed.), *Changing Patterns of Military Politics*, op. cit.

trial expansion. High profits have, as it were, bought off the entrepreneurial class from socio-political involvement and from status competition in power terms. Moreover land, perhaps the prime source of status, is very narrowly distributed.[1] Many of the usual avenues capable of draining away some of the status-seeking groups and individuals from a military career were therefore blocked. The politics of the Populist era provided the first modern alternative for low-status groups.

Partially at least we can see political instability in Latin America in terms of a struggle between military and civilian bureaucracies. In those countries where the military have been confined to a more 'typical' role, the civilian bureaucracy has gained in status and importance (Mexico, Cuba, Uruguay, to a lesser extent Brazil). In other countries the military, to preserve their special status and power, have somewhat creakingly adapted to a developmental role–once more in opposition to a civilian bureaucracy (Argentine, Brazil). This hypothesis, which attempts to explain the predominance of military bureaucracies as related to weakness and low status on the part of civilian bureaucracy, at any rate meets the foregoing analysis as a whole and seems to provide the possibility of explaining rather than merely describing a more or less universal phenomenon in Latin America.[2]

Note to Chapter 12
The Historical Analysis and Conceptualization of Bureaucracy

Two important implications are involved in the present definition of bureaucracy. One is the concept of mobilizational shortfall, arising from the notional confrontation of the sum of differentiated specific mobilizations with that of relatively undifferentiated and salient political mobilizations. This has already been discussed at some

[1] The importance of this economic aspect of military strength is analysed by Merle Kling, 'Towards a Theory of Power and Political Instability in Latin America', *Western Political Quarterly*, IX, 1 (March 1956), pp. 21–35. Cf. Andreski, *Parasitism and Subversion*, op. cit.

[2] There is no need to cite here the substantial literature on the Latin American military, or the even larger literature on the military and militarism as a comparative phenomenon. Theories abound–treating Latin America all the way from being a special case of a general problem to being unique. Similarly explanations vary from broadly social to specifically military. See S. E. Finer, *The Man on Horseback*, London 1962; John J. Johnson (ed.), *The Role of the Military in Underdeveloped Countries*, Princeton 1962; S. P. Huntington, *Changing Patterns of Military Politics*, New York 1962. The most recent general analysis is Morris Janowitz, *The Military in the Political Development of New Nations*, Chicago 1964.

length.[1] The other is that bureaucracy under such circumstances becomes in part a form of equalization and substitution–if not conceptual substitutionism–for political mobilization. Though a function of ideological conservation in the form of 'bureaucratic mobilization' on behalf of the *status quo* has here been assigned to modern bureaucracy, this has been found as a rule to be weak and in any case unstructured–i.e. an ideological and value reinforcement. The main aspect of bureaucracy is thus one of substituting for, as well as making good, a missing quantity of political commitment.[2] It is this second aspect of substitution that requires some further discussion.

Apart from defining bureaucracy as a modern phenomenon, any analysis of bureaucracy in the context of–and especially in contrast to–political mobilization means giving bureaucracy a modern setting. Political mobilization is historically a recent phenomenon, dating back two hundred years at most. Bureaucracy is much older; not so much as a specific concept (even in its older, purely organizational sense rather than the present, socio-cultural one) but as what we would now describe as a salient form of goal attainment or politics. The notion that bureaucracy is the concrete or structural expression of rational problem-solving, illuminated by legality and rationality (the twin headlamps of modernity, as it were) begins with Max Weber. And it was Weber, too, who first differentiated between this type of bureaucracy and the immense bureaucratic *apparat* of more

---

[1] It is not a new idea, though I think the case has perhaps been argued here in a new way. The idea of equating pluralism with the growth of bureaucracy can be traced right back to some of the implications of Durkheim's organic solidarity (see especially *De la Division du Travail*, second edition, Paris 1902). Similarly, and the other way about, the unspoken implications of what we now call pluralism can probably be read into the work of Michels and Ostrogorskil in which the bureaucratic component and its influence in democratic political parties were first identified. See S. M. Lipset, 'Ostrogorski and the Analytical Approach to the Comparative Study of Political Parties', *Institute of International Studies*, General Series, Berkeley, California, 1964; (Introduction to re-edition of Ostrogorski, *Democracy and the Organization of Political Parties*, New York 1964); Erik Allardt, 'Emile Durkheim–Deductions for Political Sociology', paper read at second Comparative Political Sociology Conference, Cambridge, December 1965, p. 10.

[2] Cf. Trotsky's analysis of ideological substitutionism in a specifically Russian context of 'social unripeness'; according to this Marxist canon the Decembrists projected the ideology of an as yet non-existent bourgeoisie, the Populists projected the ideology of a silent and unconscious peasantry. Both collectivities to some extent substitute themselves for a class or quasi-group. L. Trotsky, *Itogi i Perspektivy*, Moscow 1919; *Sochinenya*, Vol. II, *Nasha Pervaya Revolutisiya*.

ancient empires in the sense that here, as elsewhere, he was the first to treat structural phenomena as a central referent for geographically wide-ranging comparisons.[1] As in so many other cases, Weber drew attention to a problem with which we have been grappling ever since.

In fact the problem is not merely one of historical continuity, in the form of some timeless social phenomenon that remains while so many other things change. Rather it is an antithesis: bureaucracy has been, in one conceptual sense and according to one very seductive mode of analysis, the epitome of the most 'unmodern' type of society, its main criterion of identification and its concrete historical form–oriental despotism. This is the type of society which adapts to the stringency of its environment (the hydraulic society organized around the need to exploit its scarcest resource, water) by a closely structured, hierarchical ordering of status and function depending on, and subject to, the complete though institutionalized dictatorship of a supreme being. Slow to evolve but very durable and homeostatic once established, it is, to that extent, a variant from the normal Marxist scheme of changing social forms whose peculiarity is that it is admittedly *hors dialectique*.[2] The question of where Marxist historical

[1] The comparative analysis of bureaucracy is relatively incidental and marginal to Weber's main social analyses. It is mostly to be found in *Wirtschaft und Gesellschaft*, especially in those parts of this major work translated in *The Theory of Social and Economic Organization*, New York 1947. A specific discussion of Weber's alternative types of bureaucracy is by Helen Constas, 'Max Weber's Two Conceptions of Bureaucracy', *American Journal of Sociology*, LXIII, 4 (January 1958), pp. 400–9; for a critique of the manner of extrapolating and allocating these categories to various contemporary societies see Renate Mayntz, 'Max Weber's Idealtypus der Burokratie and die Organizationssoziologie', *Kölner Zeitschrift für Soziologie und Sozialpsychologie*, XVII, 3 (1965), pp. 493–502. Almost every writer on modern bureaucracy, administrative or organization theory pays tribute, often of a rather ritual kind, to Weber's ideas. In any case there is no intention of turning this brief discussion of bureaucracy into yet another of the 'what Weber really meant' essays which clutter up the editorial desks of British sociological journals–and which incidentally provide further evidence of the shackles of an unreconstructed training in the form of textual exegesis so depressingly typical of British political theory–based on what are hopefully and arrogantly called the classics –Hobbes, Locke, etc.

[2] Marx himself devoted a certain amount of time and effort to the problem: 'Formen die der kapitalistischen Produktion vorhergehen', in *Grundrisse der Kritik der Politischen Oekonomie (Rohentwurf)*, first edition, Moscow 1939; English version Eric Hobsbawm (ed.), *Karl Marx–Precapitalist Economic Formations*, London 1965. See also *Capital*, (Trans. Eden and Cedar Paul, London 1933), I, chapter XII, pp. 377 ff. As so often the plummiest comments are *obiter dicta*–including the joyful claim that the 'absence of private land ownership . . . is the real key to the heaven of the Orient' (Letter to Engels, 2nd June 1853, Engels' reply on 6th June and Marx once more on 14th June).

analysis stops, and concretization of current political problems into dogma in communist situations begins, is fascinating but regretfully irrelevant here.[1] What is important here, however, is not the status of the debate in the history of Marxist polemics but the analysis itself— in so far as it contributes to the contemporary problem of bureaucracy. Here Wittfogel's book makes an important contribution through the attempt to relate his concept of a bureaucratic society to the present day. He certainly intended to characterize Stalin's Russia as an oriental despotism–and the more so since Stalin had exorcised and outlawed this concept in Soviet historiography as inapplicable both to the Soviet Union as well as to China–Wittfogel's central example.[2] Hence the heat of the Marxist debate. Was Wittfogel right–empirically as regards the Soviet Union, theoretically as regards the applicability and conceptualization of oriental despotism to modern circumstances?

The answer hinges on just what you want the concept of bureaucracy to do. In the Marxist canon it has, *inter alia* and in its extreme form, to substitute for a class analysis altogether. For it brings forward the state as a factor, not merely of epiphenomenal significance, but of absolute social and above all economic primacy. So much so that some Marxists have made the concept respectable–and at the same time have tried to force it back on to the highway of

---

These references may be found in 'Orientdiskussion', *Marx/Engels, Werke*, XXVIII, Berlin 1963, pp. 254, 259–61, 266–9. The basic Marx-Engels references on this whole theme are most readily accessible in B. Maffi (ed.), *K. Marx, F. Engels: India, Cina, Russia*, Milan 1960. Cf. also G. Lichtheim, 'Marx and the Asiatic Mode of Production', *St. Antony's Papers*, XIV, London 1963, pp. 86–112.

[1] A summary of the literature and a discussion of its political relevance can be found in the reviews and prefaces to the various editions of Karl Wittfogel's classic, *Oriental Despotism* (English edition 1957, second edition 1962). Particularly valuable in this regard are Franco Venturi's review in the *Journal of the History of Ideas*, XXIV (January-March), pp. 133–42, and the preface to the 1963 French edition by Pierre Vidal-Naquet (will be cited as 'Avant-propos').

[2] This was done by making China and Russia 'feudal' instead, and thus susceptible to dialectic change. It also excused Stalin's support for the KuoMinTang up to 1930. For China, see K. Wittfogel in *China Quarterly*, 12, October/December 1962, pp. 159–67. For Russia, Walter S. Laqueur, *The Soviet Union and the Middle East*, London 1959, pp. 91–92. The argument culminated in the so-called Leningrad Discussion of 1931, (reported in *Diskussiya ob aziatskom sposobe proizvodstra*, Moscow/Leningrad 1931), about the existence of a specific Asian mode of production. Support for such a view was in fact condemned as heresy. Much the same argument was applied to Soviet Egyptology; see Maxime Rodinson in *Les Temps Modernes*, April 1963, pp. 1872–4; *Islam et capitalisme*, Paris 1965.

dialectic manageability by designating such a state and its minions as themselves an oppressing and exploiting class.[1] It will be readily understood that such identification with, or substitution for, class is the greatest concession to epistemological primacy in the Marxist armoury. Not possessing as salient a means of arranging the priorities of social stage scenery, bourgeois analysis has to deal with the phenomenon in a much more relativistic manner. There is no distinct Asiatic mode of production, no residual or specific category of oriental despotism (the distinction between these two is also a peculiarly Marxist problem); instead there is more or less bureaucracy. And at once the whole problem changes focus. We are now topic- (or problem-) oriented, the distinctions become quantifications of a structural phenomenon or a social abstraction, and instead of distinguishing between types of societies we differentiate between the kinds and amounts of bureaucracy or bureaucratic structure. The problem is no longer whether there is such a thing as a wholly bureaucratic society but what sort of and how much bureaucracy fits different societies. And these last two sets of problems also crystallize, not only into different modes of analysis but into distinct and in some ways incompatible views about the essential nature of society.

At one extreme is the type of analysis that characterizes bureaucracy essentially as the institutionalized form of state activity or intervention, as distinct from what might loosely be called private enterprise. This is not, of course, confined to the economic sector, but covers all forms of activity which are centrally controlled and depend on central or governmental initiatives. The aspect of initiative is probably the crucial one; bureaucracy is not only a structure implementing a particular regulatory function, but also a phen-

---

[1] This was the starting point of the historical analysis of Russia of both Plekhanov and Trotsky–though they drew very different political conclusions. A variant was the idea of Pokrovsky, that in Russia (and only in Russia) the state autocracy and its apparatus were the peculiar instrument of the capitalist class which evolved in the Sixteenth Century (M. N. Pokrovsky in *Krasnaya Nov*, May and August 1922, pp. 144–51, 275 ff.). Lenin veered backwards and forwards on this point at various times, and never committed himself unequivocally either to the identification of the autocracy (bureaucracy) as a distinct class of its own, or as the peculiarly Russian instrument of a more 'normal' class. The view of Russia as an orthodox feudal state, which was Stalin's contribution, naturally prohibits the elevation of the bureaucracy to the status of a separate class, or even of a class factor; it becomes merely a low-grade epiphenomenon. But it is not hard to see how sensitive Stalin was bound to be in the 1930's towards the accusation that he was building a monstrously bureaucratized society, which echoed all the way from the Trotskyite Left to the American Social Science Right.

omenon resulting from the primacy of state initiative–in whatever direction and for whatever purpose or function. Such a definition closely relates what appear, in other forms of analysis, to be very different societies–traditional, largely bureaucratized societies qualifying (or almost qualifying) as oriental despotisms (like China and Egypt), much less fully organized societies (like the Turkish or Russian Empires), European pre-participatory or absolute monarchies like France and Spain, and finally most of today's developing countries which substitute state or state-party for private or boureois class initiative.[1] The only major omissions are communist countries and the developed West.

The other type of analysis is that of Weber, and the large corpus of work based on it. This is the rational view of bureaucracy, which anchors the concept in a particular social environment–one of large-scale organization governed by criteria of efficiency, and by legitimately articulated as well as widely diffused norms.[2] Far from looking for continuity through state initiative across time, oriental despotism and all its watered-down or partial variants are lumped together in the category of the traditional, and contrasted with the modern legal-regional societies with their distinct phenomenon of bureaucracy.[3] Indeed the main emphasis is on contrast. In East

[1] The main and most persuasive proponent of this type of analysis is S. N. Eisenstadt. The comparative study of empires is in *The Political Systems of Empires*, op. cit., that of development bureaucracies in the literature cited above, p. 345, note 1. Some relevant discussion of traditional societies in this context is in Eisenstadt, 'Primitive Political Systems: A Preliminary Comparative Analysis', *American Anthropologist*, LXI, pp. 200–20. As the title suggests, there is no contrast between politics and bureaucracy; the former is by implication defined as concerned with power and its use as a determinant for action. For Marxists this is a complete obfuscation of any distinction between the important and the unimportant; bureaucracy as an autonomous feature of societies which otherwise appear very disparate becomes an inadmissible, valueless and obscurantist abstraction. Thus Eisenstadt's *Political Systems* is described as an attempt 'to define as bureaucratic the monarchy of Louis XIV just as much as that of the Pharaohs. The only value of the work is its bibliography.' (Vidal-Naquet, 'Avant-propos', op. cit., p. 17, note 2.)

[2] Weber's analysis of 'ideal' rationality–and consequential bureaucratic form and behaviour–is also in *Wirtschaft und Gesellschaft*. See Reinhard Bendix, *Max Weber: An Intellectual Portrait*, London 1960, pp. 418–25. But he also expressed fears and reservations about the implications of such trends; see J. P. Mayer, *Max Weber and German Politics*, London 1944, pp. 127–8.

[3] For the discussion of the exclusiveness or inclusiveness of the category of oriental despotism see e.g. E. R. Leach, 'Hydraulic Society in Ceylon', *Past and Present*, 15, April 1959, pp. 2–26; P. Barton, 'Du despotisme oriental', *Contrat Social*, 1959, pp. 135–40; D. D. Kosambi in *The Economic Weekly* (Bombay), 2nd November 1957 (on India); A. Abdel-Malek, *Egypte: société militaire?*

Africa, lineage bureaucracy and its norms are seen by those anthropologists influenced by Weber as incompatible and in conflict with central or state bureaucracy and its norms; the transformation from the former to the latter is evidence of the initiation of Weberian modernity in this context.[1] It may be worth noting in passing that the Marxist approach has here been stood on its head; instead of state bureaucracy substituting for, and/or preventing the emergence of, class-based conflict, its emergence now becomes a sign of modernity which makes politics of stratification and conflict *possible*.

On this approach and its somewhat evolutionary perspectives has been constructed the substantial edifice of modern administrative science, ranging from the relatively modest concerns of the empirical study of public administration to the development of administrative science in America by writers like Selznick, Gulick, Urwick, March, Chester, Barnard, Simon and Blau. This orientation has, moreover, shifted the focus of study from the whole social setting, which Weber, Simon and Eisenstadt shared, to the internal, integrative aspect of bureaucracy as representing a microcosm of society called organizations. Simon's work is one of the links in this transition; the implication is that if you understand modern organizations, you understand modern society.[2] In this context there is, too, a form of convergence between modern American organization theory and Lenin's development of Marxism—both stress the primacy of organizational perspectives in the successful adaptation of society to the environmental demands of modernity. This congruence between ideological polari-

---

Paris 1963. For oriental despotism in Africa see especially G. P. Murdock, *Africa: Its Peoples and their Culture History*, New York 1959.

Wittfogel's own contribution to the further debate is in 'The Legend of "Maoism" ', *China Quarterly*, 1 (April/June 1960), pp. 72–86; 'The Legend of "Maoism" Concluded', ibid., 2, pp. 16–34; 'The Marxist View of China (Part 1)', ibid., 11 (July/September 1962), pp. 1–20; 'The Marxist View of China (Part 2)', ibid., 12 (October/December 1962), pp. 154–69. See also *Slavic Review*, XXI, 4 (December 1962), pp. 678–99.

[1] L. A. Fallers, *Bantu Bureaucracy, A Study of Integration and Conflict in the Politics of an East African People*, Cambridge 1956, pp. 12 ff., 277 ff. Cf. also Fallers, 'Despotism, Status Culture and Social Mobility in an African Kingdom', *Comparative Studies in Society and History*, II (1959), pp. 11–32.

[2] Cf. also Etzioni, *Complex Organizations*, op. cit., and *Modern Organizations*, New York 1964; generally Wolin, *Politics and Vision*, op. cit., chapter X. A recent critique of the adaptation of Weber's concept of bureaucracy for the purposes of modern American organization theory is Renate Mayntz, 'Max Weber's Idealtypus der Bürokratie und die Organizationssoziologie', *Kölner Zeitschrift für Soziologie und Sozialpsychologie*, XVII, 3 (1965), pp. 493–502. This focuses on the excessive formalization and systematization of Weber's purely classificatory criteria of modern bureaucracy (see especially pp. 497–8).

ties has not gone unnoticed among critical American theorists; it is a special bureaucratic component of the general convergence theory to which we have already referred.[1] It is perhaps worth pointing out as being more than an historical curiosity that the notion of bureaucratic convergence between America and the Soviet Union was not in fact discovered on the Western side at all but formed part of the attack by left-wing communist critics on the 'petrification' of Leninism practised by Lenin's successors in the 1920's. Thus perhaps the most interesting and distinguished left-wing communist theorist of the time, Karl Korsch, was talking about the 'Americanization of state and factory' in the Soviet Union as early as 1926.[2] Though there has been much talk, both among bourgeois writers and by Trotsky and his followers, of the bureaucratization of Soviet society, this quite common characterization of the *peculiar* bureaucratic nature of the Soviet Union (to which Wittfogel's particular contribution also belongs) must be distinguished from the type of convergence approach of a few left-wing communists and modern American analysts. It is only the latter who admit of a *common* bureaucratic problem connected with modernity and industrialization.[3]

Here we have, then, three distinct approaches: (1) bureaucracy as a form of society (the Marxist view); (2) bureaucracy as the component of state activity in any society, and (3) bureaucracy as the organizational form of modern systems. How much of the difference between

[1] See for instance Allen Kassof, 'The Administered Society: Totalitarianism Without Terror', *World Politics*, XVI (July 1964), pp. 558 ff. The only concession to ideological difference between the USA and the USSR in this context is that American writers on organization theory tend to describe the Soviet individual as 'helpless' and the American individual by implication as 'pointless'. See in general H. Gordon Skilling, 'Interest Groups and Common Politics', *World Politics*, XVIII, 3 (April 1966), pp. 452–73, particularly pp. 456 ff.

[2] See *Kommunistische Politik*, (Berlin) 1926, I, 13–14, p. 3.

[3] In its extreme version, based on anarchist perspectives and stimulated by disappointment with the Soviet Union in failing to provide the promised liberation of man, some left-wing communist or anarchist criticism has of course identified all forms of organized political activity with bureaucracy. This attitude represents a final shift from Trotskyite and left-wing communist criticism of the Soviet Union as a bureaucratic deformation to the indictment of Marxism itself as essentially a bureaucratic philosophy. For this see *inter alia* Bruno Rizzi, *La bureaucratisation du monde*, Paris 1939. In this respect the wheel has turned full circle; such a view corresponds like an inverted mirror image to the American analysis of convergence as an inevitable bureaucratization of society, necessarily implicated in any attainment of modernity. But these are both extreme views at the margin of sociological analysis; neither attempts to make valid distinctions between fundamentally different functions in different political systems today.

them is real and how much ideological? In more precise terms, are there societies in which all basic decision-making flows from a single centre, where the only 'political' component is that central supreme authority, and where (in hydraulic terms) the whole structure is ultimately designed to extract and allocate a single but fundamental scarce resource? Or is this only a way of looking at a problem? For our purpose, which is confined to examining bureaucracy in the contemporary world, the argument about the Soviet Union under Stalin thus is not merely so much sectarian juggling with esoteric concepts but a real and vital problem.[1] For contained in the broader stage-of-society framework of the debate is the more immediate question: can a ruling political party, one of whose priorities is political mobilization, be described as a bureaucracy? If mobilizing bureaucracy is a valid concept, then the present definition of bureaucracy, as well as the suggested polarity between political mobilization parties on the one hand and bureaucracy on the other, are both clearly invalid.[2] Reasons have already been given for dissenting from both the general attempt to identify Stalin's Russia as a version of oriental despotism, or the (implicitly connected) *particular* compound concept of a mobilizing bureaucracy. Briefly, there is a serious role conflict involved—even though a particular collectivity may be both mobilizing and bureaucratic at different times, particularly in a situation of compressed differentiation. It has also been suggested that bureaucratic mobilization, in so far as this exists as a distinct form, is of a diffusely ideological kind, and is conservative. This also seems to hold true for many of the classical situations to which oriental despotism appears applicable; there the essence of mobilization is religious-ideological rather than political-participant or collec-

[1] However sectarian the manner of its presentation. Apart from Wittfogel, Trotsky's own contribution can be found in *The Revolution Betrayed*, London 1937, and in the collection of articles and letters from 1939–40, *In Defence of Marxism*, New York 1965 (Trotsky's reply to Burnham). Cf. Max Schachtman, *The Bureaucratic Revolution: The Rise of the Stalinist State*, New York 1962, also recently Tony Cliff, *Russia: A Marxist Analysis*, London 1964.

[2] The African cases cited above (in general see Peter C. Lloyd,-'The Political Structure of African Kingdoms', in *Political Systems and the Distribution of Power*, ASA Monograph 2, London 1965, pp. 63–112) create a difficulty; in a situation of normative conflict like that described between lineage and state norms, an element of mobilization must be involved in any change towards one or other type. But though a change towards state or central norms may be the threshold of Weberian modernity it does not by any means satisfy its full implications. From the point of view of the present analysis, the situation is still 'more' traditional rather than modern. The problem is therefore one of deciding whether the single concept bureaucracy can legitimately be used across this span, and this will be discussed below.

tive. The legitimacy accorded to the head of the bureaucracy–the sole 'political' office–is that of God (as priest-king in Mesopotamia, as God-king in Egypt), with some routinized dispersal of legitimacy to the bureaucratic structure.[1] But though Weber's notion of routinization of individual charisma may apply to bureaucracies of a traditional kind, it also applies to parties and to religious organizations–the deification of a structure.[2] The problem is one of routinization from an individual to a structure, which may be bureaucratic but need not be. Moreover it can be argued that far from any routinization of personal charisma towards the party in the USSR, Stalin's personality cult was the opposite–the personalization of a collective charisma. In spite of all the personal accretion of power in the hands of Stalin, legitimacy continued to be vested in the party as an autonomous collectivity, and no one will suggest that the great mobilization phenomena of the period, industrialization and collectivization, were either conservative or non-political. If anything, a bureaucratic evolution–in the present sense–has become evident in the USSR since the late 1940's, more especially since the deposition of Khrushchev. The notion of a personality cult suggests a still greater departure from oriental despotism than any movement towards it from 'orthodox' political mobilization. In short, whatever the extent and nature of Stalin's personalization of power, the existence and nature of the CPSU prevents it, and the society that contains it, from being identified as primarily bureaucratic.[3]

[1] See Henri Frankfort, *Kingship and the Gods*, op. cit., G. Posener, *De la divinité du Pharaon*, Paris 1960; most recently Mario Attilio Levi, *Political Power in the Ancient World*, op. cit.

[2] W. G. Runciman, 'Routinization of Charisma', *European Journal of Sociology*, op. cit., is not specifically concerned with bureaucracy but with investigating the empirical evidence for structural routinization of Nkrumah's charisma for the benefit of the CPP in Ghana. For an example concerned with a religious structure see R. Robertson's chapter on the Salvation Army in Bryan Wilson (ed.), *Patterns of English Sectarianism*, forthcoming.

[3] In her discussion of Weber on bureaucracy Helen Constas ('Max Weber's Two Conceptions of Bureaucracy', op. cit.), suggests that the idea of evolution from the traditional type of bureaucracy to the modern type may be misplaced. Instead the traditional form may persist in societies which otherwise might be classified as modern. Like Wittfogel, though from an anti-Marxist perspective, she cites Egypt, Incan Peru and the USSR as examples of charismatic or traditional bureaucracies (her own orientation comes to the fore with the description of this bureaucratic form as 'irresponsible'). Leaving aside the question of whether she reads Weber right, her analysis does pose the problem of characterizing bureaucracy in its most acute form; if she is right, then the concept of bureaucracy does cover a much wider field across traditional, developing and modern societies, and the dichotomy mobilization-bureaucracy becomes meaningless. Even Weber's alleged middle position, in which one

A similar difficulty arises with the analysis of bureaucracy as the component of state activity in any society. Are we really able to discard qualitative discussion in favour of asking questions about more or less of such activity? Is the bureaucracy of ancient empires, absolute monarchies and contemporary developing countries really to be encapsulated within one concept, however broadly defined? And if so ought we not better to call it central government administration? For if administration as such, analytically separate from mobilized politics, is the primary referent, if in fact the notion of a distinct bureaucratic category is anchored in the absence of manifest ideology vested in or propagated by specific collectivities, then and only then does this method of analysis come into its own. In one sense it then even corresponds to the Marxist approach, as it were its reflection in a dialectical mirror; both approaches focus on the same problem as presented by the social conditions of their respective environments. In one case the state and 'its' peculiar structure is autonomous and can *ipso facto* be studied as a greater or lesser phenomenon, abstracted from other things; in the other case there is no autonomy but different kinds of society based in the last resort on different productive relations. Unless some specific and relevant form of productive relations can be identified it is possible to argue that there can be no 'equivalent' kind of society (the Leningrad discussion). In the terms we have been using in the present essay, the structural focus emphasizes functional autonomy (as the critique of Gouldner has suggested) while the Marxist focus emphasizes the predominance of the adaptive function over the [three] others.[1] But both substitute bureaucracy for politics, or see it as a particular form of politics (hence *The Political System of Empires*).

The problem of the relationship between bureaucracy and mobilization, and of the validity of the boundary between the societal and structural analyses of bureaucracy in a traditional or development situation, is posed most urgently by the example of Japan. Here we have an *historical* example (its relevance to contemporary Japan has somewhat diminished) of something very like the phenomenon of a mobilizing bureaucracy, structurally replicating the intervention of a central government in an industrial context. Japan is the first

type evolves historically into the other, is no longer tenable. To my mind, this approach links the comparative analysis of a component (Eisenstadt) to the comparative analysis of societies (Marxist), so that bureaucracy ceases to be a variable and becomes merely a substitute for classifying societies; democratic equals rational-legal bureaucracy, dictatorship equals charismatic bureaucracy.
[1] 'Reciprocity and Autonomy in Functional Analysis', op. cit.

historical example of developmental nationalism, a value system for which the bureaucracy helped to mobilize commitment. This was not, then, conservative and processually 'weak', but intense and tied to perspectives of change. Secondly, while the structure of Japanese bureaucracy was distinct and readily identifiable, the notion of a bureaucratized society in its broadest, cultural aspect also finds strong empirical justification here. Accordingly, whether the reason is time–the premature glimpse, in the second half of the nineteenth century, of the phenomenon of developmental nationalism that was to reach international maturity only almost a hundred years later–or a unique social structure–a traditional bureaucratic system, deliberately restored, yet capable of adapting to the mobilizing demands of developmental-national perspectives–or both, the Japanese case is a severe test for the analytical disjunctions of the categories we have enumerated. It is perhaps significant and certainly depressing that none of the analysts whose work has been cited in the context of bureaucracy–beginning with Marx down to the modern organization theorists–makes more than marginal reference to Japan.[1]

Finally there are the implications of neo-Weberian analysis. As in the Marxist canon, bureaucracy, instead of being an autonomous phenomenon, once more has a firm social referent. But where this analysis in turn differs from the Marxist one is in the type of society for which bureaucracy is typical. From being an unregeneratedly ancient social form it has now been moved to become the hallmark of modernity; from a residual category to an evolutionary one. It no longer contrasts with, substitutes for, or *is* a form of, politics, but becomes instead the specific by-product of a certain type of politics. It has been integrated into a broader form of social analysis. The fact that this type of analysis has to some extent regressed from the societal reference of Weber back to a more structural one in the course of time may perhaps be due to its 'bourgeois' framework; the shift from Weber to Simon and Blau may therefore not be random or idiosyncratic. But in one very important sense at least the Weberian societal perspective has been retained; only this form of analysis recognizes implicitly that the concept of bureaucracy is not exclusively tied to government or state but finds application indifferently in churches, businesses, government departments and voluntary or professional associations. In this

---

[1] LaPalombara, *Bureaucracy and Political Development*, op. cit., for instance has all of two pages on Japan, part of a brief Asian travelogue by Riggs (pp. 160–1).

respect at least it still follows on the societal perspectives of Marxist analysis. Where it also differs once more is that it too creates a residual category, albeit of a special type–the designated problem-solving component of a norm-oriented society. The buck stops there. The cultural problems created *by* bureaucracy are not a very salient feature of modern organization theory.

From all this the intellectual sources of our own definition of bureaucracy here can now more clearly be identified. The identification of bureaucracy with modernity–more specifically, industrialization and pluralism–comes from Weber. So does the integration of bureaucracy into the analysis of politics, of which it is a partial and special component. But it has not been used here as a residual concept–either as a structural prototype identified with a particular form of productive relations or type of society, or as an 'ideal' structure for fulfilling the special functions demanded by a particular type of society. Instead, like the second of the variants discussed, it has merely been given a specific structural reference. To this extent, the present definition cuts across both the second and third methods of analysing bureaucracy. But in emphasizing at the same time the cultural aspect of bureaucracy, the social problems it creates and the effect these have on society, a somewhat more Marxist perspective has been adopted–or, more accurately, a perspective based on a number of recent analyses of the bureaucratic phenomenon.[1]

The important element taken over from this tradition is the essentially conservative nature of bureaucracy. In the first instance,

---

[1] Reference has already been made to the work of Michel Crozier. It should be noted that Crozier does not see bureaucracy as a static form or even as a sort of hardening or self-reinforcing social tendency, but as a phenomenon capable of adjustment to changing social conditions (of course on a relatively minor scale compared to, say, the Marxist approach). Moreover it is a flexible analysis that makes allowance for a wide variety of cultural peculiarities in different societies. The relationship between this analysis and that of Weber is well set out in Crozier, *Bureaucratic Phenomenon*, op. cit., p. 297.

Crozier is not, of course, the sole proponent of such a theory or analysis of bureaucracy, combining structural focus with a two-way relationship with culture–influencing it and being modified by it. Merton has touched on this ('The Unanticipated Consequences of Purposive Social Action', *American Sociological Review*, I (1936), pp. 894–904; 'Bureaucratic Structure and Personality', *Social Forces*, XVIII (1940), pp. 560–8). So has Dahrendorf ('Democracy without Liberty', op. cit.), who examines bureaucracy as a phenomenon of other-directedness–five bureaucrats in search of an authoritative policy on which to exercise their power. Cultural perspectives have been firmly incorporated into the important work of Peter Blau, *The Dynamics of Bureaucracy*, Chicago 1963; *Exchange and Power in Social Life*, London 1964; and, with W. Richard Scott, *Formal Organizations*, San Francisco 1962.

political pressure for change will be resisted by more articulation of conservative bureaucratic values and norms – the dysfunctional element emphasized by Crozier. In the longer run, bureaucracy may prove more adaptable and the phenomena of resistance to change will decline in impact and extent, but there will always be a time lag. But where Crozier, with admittedly special reference to France, sees the demand for change as normal or 'functional', and bureaucratic resistance to it as 'dysfunctional', the emphasis here has been to view developed Western society as 'normally' stable and change as abnormal (dysfunctional has normative, or rather prescriptive, overtones and has accordingly been little used here). This is not primarily due to any difference in interpretation but to the horizon of comparative perspectives; Crozier's analysis is confined to the developed West, the *Abendländer*, while we have been here mainly concerned with the contrast between the categories of developed and developing nations. Hence bureaucracy has been viewed not only as the major structural component of conservation, but also the vehicle of ideological mobilization in favour of the *status quo*. Crozier emphasizes the conservatism arising from bureaucracy's internal structure while we have concentrated on the societal decline of the overall quantity of political mobilization, and the transfer to bureaucracy of the notional shortfall in 'required' total mobilization in any society, without in any way denying the importance of the internal aspect. It is readily accepted that in one sense our approach to bureaucratic conservatism implicitly invalidates the futuristic perspectives summed up by Crozier in the words that 'bureaucratization in the Weberian sense [of rationality] is truly increasing, perhaps at an accelerated rate, but without entailing the dysfunctional consequences that Weber feared and all his successors prophesied . . . In other words, the elimination of the "bureaucratic systems of organization" in the dysfunctional sense is the condition for the growth of "bureaucratization" in the Weberian sense'.[1]

Dysfunctional, it should be emphasized, in this context means resistant to change *in a change-oriented modern society* – hence ultimately unable to 'satisfice', in the words of Simon. Remove the social change-orientation (as in empires) and bureaucracy of course at once ceases to be 'dysfunctional'. The connection with the second form of analysis mentioned above, and with Eisenstadt in particular, becomes very clear at this point. Change, too, is a very relative term. In Crozier's sense of tending towards the Weberian form of rational

---

[1] *Bureaucratic Phenomenon*, p. 299.

bureaucratization, change seems to imply the growth of immediate and internal criteria of efficiency and rationality, related to the environment mainly in terms of being a microcosmic reflection of it. In the context of wider social goals and their implementation, change is, as we have tried to show, directly and proportionately related to mobilization; bureaucracy in this context implies not only consensus and pluralism, but also a social value commitment to conservation rather than change. A non-conservative, or even mobilizing, bureaucracy is not so much impossible, but ceases to be a bureaucracy within the scope of the present definition.

In the last resort we are left with two differences over the meaning of words: a smaller difference with Crozier over the scope of change, another and larger difference with the Marxists as well as Eisenstadt over the meaning of bureaucracy. As regards the first of these, we have noted that this is partly a matter of perspective. In confronting developed and developing societies as two categories possessing very different and often conflicting sets of conditions, and reflecting different situations, it is hardly surprising that developing countries emerge as primarily committed to great and rapid changes, both in their own terms and in the analysts' view of them as belonging to a transitional category, while developed countries appear stable, if not static–especially as the value emphasis is in the main so clearly conservative. This certainly does not mean complete statism or homeostasis, a frozen state. But it does on the whole suggest change confined to the form of remedy, of catching up in lagging sectors, of change in *balance*. The notion of stability and conservative value-emphasis is highly relativistic; it will be recalled that one of the starting points and references for the present analysis was the usefulness of the Western model as an import by developing countries. To this extent, therefore, the two analyses overlap; Crozier himself states that he is mainly concerned to compare one society through time, not different societies at any one moment. Changes that appear substantial in one analysis will appear relatively insignificant in the other.[1]

[1] Nonetheless it is not quite clear how far Crozier intends to take the optimistic neo-Weberian perspectives adumbrated at the end of his book. This is a recurrent problem with any book, however brilliant, which draws theoretical conclusions from empirical material and then, at the end, ventilates the implications of the analysis with a little prescriptive fresh air from farther afield. This *futurismo* is a perfectly reasonable proceeding–one wishes British and recent American 'objectivity' would permit it a bit oftener; the only trouble is the difficulty of 'weighting' these conclusions against the main body of the study itself. As already stated, if it is Crozier's intention to open out his definition of bureaucracy to its full Weber-Simon logic, to describe it as a

The other, more fundamental difference follows directly. Though modern central government administration has been used here as the most relevant example of bureaucracy, there is no question of any exclusive identification with it. Repeated reference has been made to other forms. Bureaucracy, then, is conceptually distinct from central administration–from any administration for that matter. Bureaucratic behaviour is not administrative behaviour. This distinguishes the scope of the present analysis from that implied by the second category of bureaucracy discussed earlier, which is mainly interested in central government administration. At the same time, as regards the Marxist approach, the present analysis has not contributed anything useful to the discussion of the historical validity of either oriental despotism or the Asiatic mode of production. The problem is not dealt with by excising the USSR and consigning the rest to ancient history. For one thing, it has recently been suggested that the difficulties of political mobilization in Egypt, to which reference has already been made several times, should in fact be seen as evidence for the survival of the objective conditions, as well as the appropriate form of polity, for oriental despotism.[1] Where the notion of oriental despotism is not merely an analytical category but represents structural constraints on mobilizing possibilities; where we have a society apparently unable to develop the sort of *political* stalactite mobilizing structures common in the rest of the Third World; there bureaucracy seems a good concept for capturing the realities of such a situation of purely state institutional mobilization–were it not for the fact that we already have a different and contradictory definition of the concept. This would suggest the benefit of a minor indulgence in the academic game of creating neologisms. But instead I have preferred merely to point up the different meanings possible for the concept of bureaucracy–both those available in the widest inclusive sense as well as the limited choice which remains once the more rigorous demands and conditions set out here have been applied. All

temporarily lagging but eventually full-blooded organizational rationalization of social goal attainments, irrespective of whether static or change-oriented, then we certainly part company.

[1] Maxime Rodinson, 'L'Egypte nassérienne au miroir marxiste', *Les Temps Modernes*, April 1962, pp. 1859–87; A. Abdel-Malek, *Egypte: société militaire?*, op. cit., Morroe Berger, *Bureaucracy and Society in Modern Egypt*, Princeton 1957. Cf. also the writings of Hassan Riad cited by Rodinson, and in Vidal-Naquet, 'Avant-propos', pp. 42–43. Not a peep out of Moscow about Egypt along these lines, incidentally; cf. L. A. Gordon and L. A. Fridman, 'Composition and Structure of the Working Class in Asia and Africa', *Narody Azii i Afriki*, op. cit., more generally Thornton, *Soviet Perspective*, op. cit.

are possible uses of bureaucracy, but they are neither interchangeable nor are they necessarily alternative. There is considerable overlap, especially as far as the ideological implications of their respective frameworks are concerned; focus on a type of society versus focus on a structural component; substitute for–or microcosm of–politics versus evolutionary byproduct of politics. As with the concept of system we need a deliberate choice based on clear definition. A possible one has been suggested.

Conclusion

Conclusion

I. *The Conceptual Framework*

a. *The Variables*

Four variables have emerged from the foregoing discussion for classifying political subsystems, structures and processes. Though the differences between developed and developing societies are categorical and go beyond problems of scale, amount or sophistication, the variables evolved here are intended to apply to both types of society, though not necessarily with equal sharpness of definition in each case.

1. The first is the political culture pattern-variable *constitutional/elitist*. This emphasizes the relevance of the institutional structure in the polity as against the primacy of socio-political elites. The main criteria are the location, saliency and role of constitutional or elite leadership, the differentiation or diffuseness of roles – indeed the differentiation or diffuseness of the political subsystem as a whole. Finally, the relationship between political and social life as a whole, seen in terms of density and range of the political subsystem as well as congruence and incongruence, is relevant to the characterization of a political subsystem in accordance with this variable.

2. The second variable relates more narrowly to the function of political or goal-attainment structures and processes and has been termed *interest articulation/authority legitimation*. These two functions are viewed as imperatives for the political subsystem. The main object of this variable is to break down the problem of representation into its two basic components: representation of interests and means of according legitimacy. The criteria here are the premises as well as the functions of political action, particularly with regard to electoral behaviour and the role of the elected. The discussion has concentrated mainly on mobilization structures in the context of this functional variable, and the classification of structures and processes

suggested by it has been organized further by the application of an additional dimension concerned with cleavage or issue orientations. This covers the flexibility of mobilizing structures; retention and saliency of an original cleavage base or capacity to adjust to different issues. The determinants of this dimension are the relationships between information and action.

3. The third variable is a locational and directional one, which we have called *stalagmite/stalactite*. The main determinant is the original direction of mobilization as between centre and periphery, which is necessarily affected by the purpose or premise of mobilization – against or on behalf of the existing values, norms, collectivities, etc.; upwards from a cleavage base or downwards from the locus of formally institutionalized authority.

4. Finally, there is an important residual pattern variable which has specifically been little touched upon in the foregoing discussion. It is again related to the function of political collectivities in their environment and might be termed extrovert/introvert or, in more Parsonian terms, *adaptive/integrative*.

This terminology is, of course, a misappropriation from Parsons. His adaptive and integrative functions are two out of four functional imperatives for the survival of social systems. In Parsons' analysis the terms adaptive and integrative relate to specific subsystem functions and are associated with the economic and rule-making subsystems respectively. But perhaps we may legitimately use the notion of adaptive and integrative functions also in a case where we are dealing, not with social subsystems, but with specific collectivities. Adaptation and integration are functions which must be fulfilled for all social and political collectivities *to some degree*. But at a certain level of analysis we are no longer dealing with a simple classification of functions, but with a dichotomy – for beyond a certain minimum of essential adaptation to environment and minimal preservation of autonomy, more adaptation or more integration become alternatives; more of one may mean less of the other. This is specially relevant to bureaucracy.

Analytically this can be highlighted by an examination of the extent to which the social consciousness and the compliance of individuals are related to symbols of status, mobility and identity emanating from either the structure in question or from society as a whole, particularism as opposed to universalism. This too is a stretch of Parsons' pattern variables in that, as has been pointed out earlier, a connotation of modernity has, under certain circumstances, been

CONCLUSION

assigned to particularism as well as to universalism, and the progression from particularism to universalism cannot thus be taken *purely* and by itself as evidence of progress towards 'modernity'.[1]

The reason why this variable, or one dealing with these problems, has hardly been used in the present analysis is simply that the ground has been fairly extensively covered in the existing literature already. As reference to research on political parties and bureaucracy showed, much stress has been placed on problems of integration. The internal structure of parties and groups, the form and extent of compliance to their norms, the hierarchical division into leaders, activists or militants, members and voters and the interrelationships between all these, are presently a major focus of research on both sides of the Atlantic. Perhaps more important, however, is the conceptual location of integrative problems in systems analysis. In structure-functionalism, integration is a major subsystem function, separate from the goal-attainment problems with which we have here been primarily concerned. Obviously mobilization has important integrative aspects and functions, both in terms of some notion of an overall integrative function for the social system as a whole, as well as in the sense of assessing the relative importance and contribution of the alternative functional component of integration or goal attainment implicated in the analysis of any political structure or collectivity. It is in the latter, alternative sense that the proposed variable is required, rather than from the point of view of more specifically integrative perspectives at a social system level. Also, we have here abstracted from this problem or dimension because its 'integration' into the present analysis on a comparative basis would have greatly increased the length. Nonetheless any apparatus of variables for the study of politics in general, and political mobilization in particular, must clearly include such a variable. The 'level-of-commitment' approach of Deutsch obviously has great relevance to this dimension. The

[1] Reference in this connection should be made once more to the recent development of the ideas of Gabriel Almond, 'Political Systems and Political Change', *American Behavioral Scientist*, VI, 10 (June 1963), pp. 3–10; 'A Developmental Approach to Political Systems', *World Politics*, XVII, 2 (January 1965), pp. 183–214; and Gabriel A. Almond and G. Bingham Powell, *Comparative Politics: A Developmental Approach*, Boston 1966. This last work is a full-blown operationalization of the approach sketched out in *World Politics* 1965. It only came to hand just as the present manuscript was nearing completion, and therefore can only be cited rather than properly evaluated in the present discussion. It is Almond's most Parsonian approach to date, and relates to the present model– though Almond's concern is with political *systems*, a concept he uses in a manner hovering halfway between the present definition of system and polity.

CONCLUSION

theoretical approach of Stein Rokkan to cleavage bases and electoral mobilization in the developed West, on which the present discussion has heavily relied, is also essentially an operationalization of the integrative sector of the social system notionally mapped out by Parsons as the I quadrant of his basic paradigm.[1] Finally we have not pursued the systemic status of integration more fully here because recent theoretical formulations suggest that I (Integration) and G (goal attainment) functions can fruitfully be collapsed into one and the same subsystem.[2]

With this four-variable apparatus it should be possible to attempt a genuinely comparative approach to political subsystems in their wider social setting which will include, or integrate into one form of analysis, developed as well as developing societies. Apart from the multitude of questions raised in the present context, such an apparatus may help to tackle a host of problems which have not specifically been raised here. An important one is that of coalitions. There are pre-electoral coalitions as represented by British and American parties, emphasizing authority legitimation as well as social 'adaptation' to goal attainment, and by communist parties who also emphasize authority legitimation but with a much greater stress on integration. As against this there are post-electoral coalitions as in Italy and Fourth Republic France, electorally stressing interest articulation with a varied emphasis on adaptation or integration across the spectrum from right (adaptation–except for fascists) to left (integration). These differentiations can in turn be organized by the broader cultural elitist-constitutional variable, which distinguishes Britain strongly from the United States. The four-variable apparatus is accordingly offered as a tool for the comparative study of political subsystems albeit at a fairly high level of abstraction.

[1] See Talcott Parsons and Neil J. Smelser, *Economy and Society*, London 1956; Parsons, 'General Theory in Sociology', in Robert K. Merton *et al.* (eds), *Sociology Today*, New York 1959, pp. 39–78; 'Pattern Variables Revisited', *American Sociological Review*, op. cit.; 'On the Concept of Political Power', *Proceedings of the American Philosophical Society*, op. cit.; Rokkan's formulation is 'Cleavage Structures, Party Systems and Voter Alignments: An Introduction', in Lipset and Rokkan (eds), *Party Systems and Voter Alignments*, op. cit., especially pp. 10 ff. (in draft). One of the theoretical problems raised by Rokkan's approach is due to his need for rigorous selection of problems for detailed discussion; he illustrates these integrative problems almost exclusively in terms of political collectivities and structures, and ignores the vital role of non-political structures in this functional area.

[2] This is implicit in the theoretical introduction to Amitai Etzioni, *Political Unification: A Comparative Study of Leaders and Forces*, op. cit.

CONCLUSION

b. *A Formalization of Political Functions*

It has been assumed throughout the preceding argument that both the two political functions of interest articulation and authority legitimation are functional imperatives, and as such essential to any political system. The way political systems deal with these two functions can perhaps be formally summarized from the foregoing discussion in the following terms and illustrated in a diagram:

1. The two functions can be *compressed*. This means that both functions are fulfilled by one structure and/or one [electoral] process. This is the case in developing societies with stalactite mobilization.

		STALACTITE MOBILIZATION	STALAGMITE/ELECTORAL MOBILIZATION
DEVELOPING SOCIETIES		COMPRESSION	DISPERSAL
DEVELOPED SOCIETIES	CONSTITUTIONAL CULTURE		SEPARATION
	ELITIST CULTURE	SUPERIMPOSITION	CONFUSION

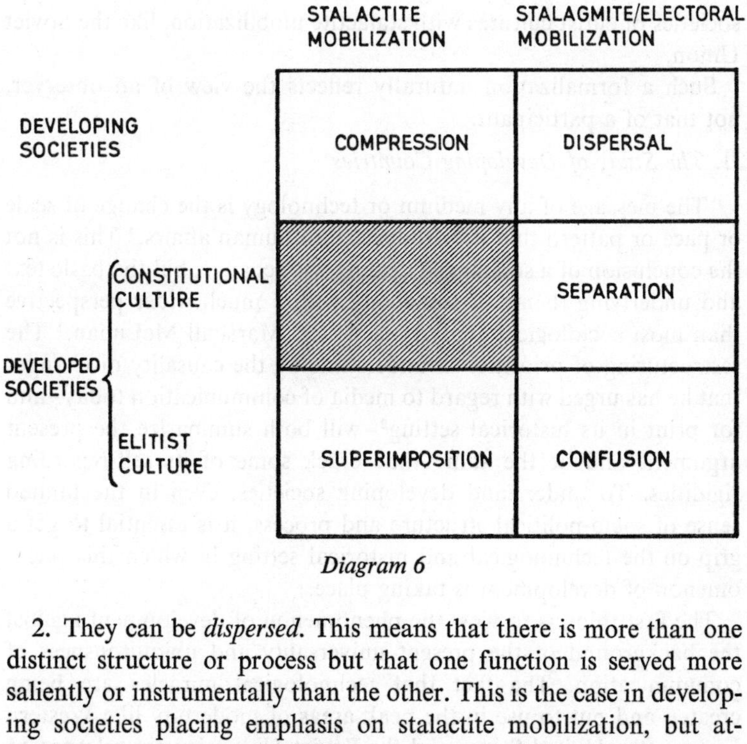

Diagram 6

2. They can be *dispersed*. This means that there is more than one distinct structure or process but that one function is served more saliently or instrumentally than the other. This is the case in developing societies placing emphasis on stalactite mobilization, but attempting to operate the Western electoral process without the 'corresponding' basis of cleavage mobilization integrated within a national-universal framework.

3. They can be *separated*. This again means that there is more than one process and one or several types of electoral structures, but that both functions are 'balanced' and manifestly articulated. This is the case

387

in developed societies with constitutional cultures in which elections serve as cleavage mobilizing processes within a universal framework.

4. They can be *confused*. This means that there is only one type of structure and one process in which one function manifestly predominates over the other. This is the case in developed societies of elitist cultures and with electoral mobilization. Here the function of symbols in obliterating the effects of confusion, and in restoring a sense of balance, becomes important.

5. They can be *superimposed*. This means that there is only one type of structure but more than one process, and both functions are manifestly carried out. This is done by viewing them as *identical*; one function automatically serving the other. This is the case in developed societies of elitist cultures with stalactite mobilization, like the Soviet Union.

Such a formalization naturally reflects the view of an observer, not that of a participant.

II. *The Study of Developing Countries*

'The message of any medium or technology is the change of scale or pace or pattern that it introduces into human affairs.' This is not the conclusion of a sociologist dealing with change, but the basic text and underlying theme of somebody with a much wider perspective than most sociological analysts—a writer, Marshall McLuhan.[1] The restructuring of priorities in understanding the causality of changes that he has urged with regard to media of communication today—and for print in its historical setting[2]—will both summarize the present argument and at the same time crack some of its self-regarding rigidities. To understand developing societies, even in the limited sense of socio-political structure and process, it is essential to get a grip on the technological and historical setting in which this phenomenon of development is taking place.

The first thing is to view the phenomenon of development against the background of the present universality and ubiquitousness of communication. The fact that technological miracles are being created and put to use in the peak areas of modernity like Western Europe, the United States and the Soviet Union is very relevant to developing countries. They may not have all the technological apparatus of modernity—though they have some. But they do have

---

[1] *Understanding Media*, London 1964. For a more empirical discussion cf. [Eric Hobsbawm], 'Pop Goes the Artist', *Times Literary Supplement*, 17th December 1964.

[2] *The Gutenberg Galaxy*, London 1962.

knowledge of its existence, a demand for its benefits and very often the means of appreciating its effect–all acquired through indirect communication. This means that the relationship between society on the one hand and technology in communication, industry, weapons and for that matter in means of repression in developing countries, cannot be viewed in the same terms as we apply to the societies which first produced them. The business of producing them has its own consequences on the socio-political situation, quite different from those which obtain in countries whose knowledge and benefits are obtained at second hand. Use of such instruments in circumstances of development changes both the physical objects of modernity themselves as well as their influence on society. The sociological confrontation of 'modern' elements, whether they be social, economic or technical, with traditional or ancient phenomena gives a 'cold' composition which can only come alive when we understand the particular synthesis that such confrontations produce. With this in mind the severe limitations of the prismatic or classification-of-variables model become clear. We may get analytical clarity and the possibility of comparisons from them–but not necessarily understanding. Hence the need to see developing countries *simultaneously* as both a transitional and a unique category.

One of the important and direct consequences is that the time element, which has usually provided a remarkably reliable tool in the comparative study of our own history, becomes almost useless when we study developing countries. For many of them modernity is the blunt impact of other people's history compressed and objectified in the form of hard and indigestible lumps of physical objects and social processes. Studying the adaptation of societies to modernity is therefore not merely a matter of confronting items that we label modern or traditional, but of understanding the confrontation between one's own history and the concentrated though always partial essence of experience extruded and communicated by other countries. The breakdown of isolation in the international community is probably the most important single factor with which we must grapple in any attempt to evaluate developing countries today. It explains the remarkably similar if not common developmental value system in a large part of the world, coupled with the physical imbalances in development right across differentiated subsystems and functions in single societies–indeed it explains the very notions of imbalance and underdevelopment. It further explains the discrepancy between our view of the Third World and its own view of itself and us. The cybernetic model of political processes is peculiarly apt in this context, since the ruling elites of developing countries, whatever else they are, have certainly become crucial elements in the diffusion and prismatic refraction of information from the modern areas of the world into their own environment, and vice versa. More than that, their selection of what theses, techniques and objects of foreign modernity shall be imported has enormous consequences for the development of their societies. The manner in which they acquire 'modern' notions and objects, the way in which they install and use them, all set the basic pattern for the phenomenon we have described as development. The message is therefore not the 'state of the nation'–modern, intermediate or traditional, in whole or in part–but the process of change itself, particularly the process of adaptation from and interrelationships with the processes and objectified or verbalized experiences of others. The medium of change is the message.

The most obvious and familiar tools of analysis–simple, well-defined words–threaten to lose all sharpness of definition and with it their usefulness at this point. We talk of the army, the police, the civil service; parties and groups; governments. As the foregoing discussion has perhaps begun to show, such words are not very adequate in any comparative analysis which seeks to confront developed with developing countries. The word 'police' means quite different things to the traffic-bound Londoner, to the refractory writer from Leningrad serving out a period of rehabilitation in a labour camp, to the applicant for a passport in Lagos. The notion of a political party again has completely different referents and connotations to a Democrat in Chicago, to the chairman of a peasant commune in China and to a voter in Nairobi. This provides a partial explanation and excuse for the heavy use of jargon in the present book –and also the absence of good old standbys like state, parliament and law. Words, like mechanical objects, work differently in different environments. Any discussion of party in a developing country must take account not only of the root of the word in its language of origin but also of its particular application in the country of destination, and must accommodate the difference in meaning in each of the two cases as well as the particular synthesis produced by the emigration. Nor ought this synthesis to be viewed only as a transition stage between the notionally traditional and the notionally modern aspects of any situation, but also as a unique blend of the two which, whatever directions of change may result from it in the future, justifies treating the present as a distinct and unique category. The study of developing countries, therefore, is the study of a blend of known components which is both some sort of an equilibrium position between them as well as the basis of something totally new.

In postulating such high requirements for any real understanding of developing societies the role of the sociologist, or of any other specialized social scientist, must necessarily be pedestrian. He cannot understand, and therefore cannot depict or explain, 'all'; he can merely seize upon certain aspects and analyse them. But though his task is relatively mundane in relation to the requirements of total understanding, the context within which he works is crucial. Unless he is aware of certain overall if abstract features of the whole world today, such as the universality of communication, the fact that perhaps societies have put their central nervous systems outside of themselves and are therefore 'possessed' by international communication structures rather than fully autonomous beings with wills and choices of their own, his work is likely to be parochial. That is why the study of mass media and its relationship to the status of the individual in society is one of the most important requirements in the modern world, in that it indicates the parameters of understanding which any social scientist dealing in whole societies must observe in his work. Within or between societies, he must compare. The study of development becomes in the last resort a study of the way in which universal factors and objects are internalized and used by different societies. What characterizes developing countries today is the range of social and physical technology with which they have to cope and which they have to incorporate.

The present study has taken one sector of this broad problem – that of socio-political technology – and has attempted to analyse the impact of modernity on traditional societies. The conclusion that has been reached is that in a social context the usefulness of such imports as a means of reproducing the conditions of the exporting society is limited, and that the experience of modernity offered by one type of developmental process may be more readily internalized and therefore more 'useful' than that offered by others. Though analytically the social processes and structures of modernity have been treated as autonomous, we have tried to relate them at the same time to the historical experience of the exporters as well as to the functional requirements of the importers. Even so the sector treated is very small and the whole exercise closes with the assertion of a big question-mark; can any attempt to do justice to the phenomenon of development in the world today be made without at the same time

CONCLUSION

incorporating the possibly much more important area of physical and technological phenomena without which social change cannot really be understood at all? By limiting the focus to social processes and structures, are we not perhaps attempting to assess modernity in terms of the problems and with the analytical techniques of an historical period which has already passed for ever?

Bibliography

Abdel-Malek, A., *Egypte: société militaire?*, Paris 1963. Cited pp. 291, 369, 379

Adams, Richard N., 'Dual Sectors and Power in Latin American Social Structure', Conference Paper, London RIIA, February 1965. Cited pp. 98, 245

Adorno, T. W. *et al.*, *The Authoritarian Personality: Studies in Prejudice*, New York 1950. Cited pp. 52, 182, 201

Agger, Robert; Goldstein, Marshall, and Pearl, Stanley, 'Political Cynicism: Measurement and Meaning', *Journal of Politics*, XXIII (1961), pp. 477–506. Cited p. 155

Aich, Prodosh, *Farbige unter Weissen*, Cologne 1962. Cited p. 250

Akzin, B., 'The Role of Parties in Israeli Democracy', *Journal of Politics*, XVII (1955), pp. 507–45. Cited p. 108

Allardt, E. and Himmelstrand, U. in S. Rokkan (ed.), *Approaches to the Study of Political Participation*, Bergen 1962. Cited p. 79

Allardt, E. and Littunan, Y. (eds.), *Cleavages, Ideologies and Party Systems: Contributions to Comparative Political Sociology*, Helsinki 1964. Cited p. 66

Allardt, E., 'Emile Durkheim–Deductions for Political Sociology', Paper presented to the Second Conference on Comparative Political Sociology, Cambridge, December 1965, cyclostyled. Cited pp. 174, 365

Almond, Gabriel A., 'Comparative Political Systems', *Journal of Politics*, XVIII, 3 (August 1956), pp. 391–409. Cited pp. 14, 203, 289

Almond, Gabriel A. and Coleman, James S. (eds.), *The Politics of the Developing Areas*, Princeton 1960. Cited pp. 14, 51, 349

Almond, Gabriel A. and Sydney Verba, *The Civic Culture: Political Attitudes and Democracy in Five Nations*, Princeton 1963. Cited pp. 14, 27, 42, 50, 51, 55, 56, 62, 63

Almond, Gabriel A., 'Political Systems and Political Change', *American Behavioral Scientist*, VI, 10 (June 1963), pp. 3–10. Cited pp. 14, 385

Almond, Gabriel A., 'A Developmental Approach to Political Systems', *World Politics*, XVII, 2 (January 1965), pp. 183–214. Cited pp. 14. 53, 103, 110, 344, 385

Almond, Gabriel A. and Powell, C. Bingham, *Comparative Politics:*

BIBLIOGRAPHY

A Developmental Approach, Boston 1966. Cited pp. 14, 27, 110, 385

Andreski, S., *Parasitism and Subversion: The Case of Latin America*, London 1966. Cited pp. 276, 364

Angell, Robert C. and Singer, J. David, 'Social Values and Foreign Policy Attitudes of Soviet and American Elites', *Journal of Conflict Resolution* VII (December 1964), pp. 329–91. Cited p. 76

Apter, David E., 'The Role of Traditionalism in the Political Modernization of Ghana and Uganda', *World Politics*, XIII, 1 (October 1960), pp. 45–68. Cited pp. 75, 84, 117, 289

Apter, David E., *The Political Kingdom of Uganda: A Study in Bureaucratic Nationalism*, Princeton 1961. Cited pp. 198, 229

Apter, David E., *Ghana in Transition*, New York 1963. Cited pp. 94, 198, 201, 298

Apter, David E., 'System, Process and Politics of Economic Development', in B. F. Hoselitz and William Moore, *Industrialization and Society*, The Hague 1963, pp. 135–58. Cited pp. 230, 245

Apter, David E. (ed.), *Ideology and Discontent*, New York 1964. Cited pp. 102, 155, 232

Apter, David E., 'Ghana', in James S. Coleman and Carl G. Rosberg, *Political Parties and National Integration in Tropical Africa*, Berkeley and Los Angeles 1964. Cited p. 229

Apter, David E., *The Politics of Modernization*, Chicago 1965. Cited pp. 16, 84, 197, 245, 305

Aron, Raymond, 'Social Structure and the Ruling Class', *British Journal of Sociology*, I, 1 (1950), pp. 1–16, and I, 2 (1950), pp. 126–43. Cited p. 93

Aron, Raymond, 'Classe sociale, classe politique, classe dirigeante', *European Journal of Sociology*, 1, 2 (1960), pp. 260–81. Cited p. 93

Aron, Raymond, *The Opium of the Intellectuals*, New York 1962. Cited p. 74

Aron, Raymond, *Main Currents in Sociological Thought*, Vol. 1, *Montesquieu, Comte, Marx, de Tocqueville, the Sociologists and the Revolution of 1848*, Translation Richard Howard and Helen Weaver, London 1965. Cited pp. 14, 134

Arrow, Kenneth J., *Social Choice and Individual Values*, Courts Commission for Research in Economics, Monograph No. 12, New York 1951. Cited p. 169

Ashford, Douglas E., *Political Change in Morocco*, New York 1961. Cited p. 274

Aspaturian, V. V. in Roy C. Macridis and Robert E. Ward (eds.), *Modern Political Systems: Europe*, Englewood Cliffs 1963. Cited p. 76

Austin, Dennis, *Politics in Ghana, 1946–1960*, London 1964. Cited pp. 201, 298

Avakov, R. and Mirsky, G., 'O klassovoi strukture v slaborazvitikh stranakh', *Mirovaya Ekonomika i Mezhdunarodinye Otnosheniya*, No. 4 (1962). Cited p. 285

Avakov, R. and Stepanov, L., 'Sotsialniye problemy natsional'no–

osvoboditel'noi revoliutsii', *Mirovaya Ekonomika i Mezhdunaro-dinye Otnosheniya*, V (May 1963), pp. 46–54. Cited p. 253

Awolowo, Obafemi, *The Path to Nigerian Freedom*, London 1947. Cited p. 246

Bailey, F. G., *Caste and the Economic Frontier: A Village in Highland Orissa*, Manchester 1957. Cited pp. 243, 299

Bailey, F. G., 'Closed Social Stratification in India', *European Journal of Sociology*, IV, 1 (1963), pp. 107–41. Cited p. 243

Bakke, E. W., *Bonds of Organization*, New York 1950. Cited p. 213

Balogh, Thomas in Hugh Thomas (ed.), *The Establishment: A Symposium*, London 1959. Cited p. 77

Baltzell, E. Digby, *The Protestant Establishment*, London 1965. Cited p. 185

Banton, Michael (ed.), *Political Systems and the Distribution of Power*, ASA Monograph 2, London 1965. Cited p. 295

Baran, Paul A., *The Political Economy of Growth*, London 1957. Cited p. 234

Barber, Bernard, *Social Stratification: A Comparative Analysis of Structure and Process*, New York 1957. Cited p. 86

Barton, P., 'Du Despotisme oriental', *Contrat Social*, III, 3 (May 1959). Cited p. 369

Baschwitz, K., *Du und die Masse–Studien zu einer exakten Massen-psychologie*, Leiden (Holland) 1951. Cited pp. 138, 147

Bauer, A.; de Sola Pool, Ithiel, and Dexter, Lewis A., *American Business and Public Policy: The Politics of Foreign Trade*, New York 1963. Cited pp. 102, 224

Bay, Christian, 'Politics and Pseudopolitics: A Critical Evaluation of some Behavioral Literature', *Am. Pol. Sc. Rev.*, LIX, 1 (March 1965), pp. 39–51. Cited pp. 102, 161, 203

Beer, S. H., 'Pressure Groups and Parties in Britain', *Am. Pol. Sc. Rev.*, L, 1 (March 1956), pp. 1–24. Cited pp. 172, 334

Beer, S. H., *Modern British Politics: A Study of Parties and Pressure Groups*, London 1965. Cited pp. 105, 335

Bell, Daniel, *The End of Ideology: On the Exhaustion of Political Ideas in the Fifties*, Glencoe 1960. Cited p. 74

Bellah, R. N., *Tokugawa Religion: The Values of Pre-Industrial Japan*, Glencoe 1957. Cited p. 288

Belshaw, Cyril S., *Traditional Exchange and Modern Markets*, Englewood Cliffs 1965. Cited p. 198

Bendix, Reinhard, 'Bureaucracy: The Problem and its Setting', *American Sociological Review*, XII (October 1947), pp. 493–507. Cited p. 349

Bendix, Reinhard, 'Bureaucraticization in Industry', in Kornhauser *et al.* (eds.), *Industrial Conflict*, New York 1954. Cited p. 349

Bendix, Reinhard and Lipset, Seymour Martin, 'Political Sociology: An Essay and Bibliography', *Current Sociology*, VI (1957), pp. 79–169. Cited p. 37

Bendix, Reinhard, *Max Weber: An Intellectual Portrait*, London 1960. Cited p. 369

BIBLIOGRAPHY

Bendix, Reinhard (ed.), *Nation-Building and Citizenship: Studies of our Changing Social Order*, New York 1964. Cited pp. 74, 175, 255

Benedict, Ruth, *The Chrysanthemum and the Sword*, Boston 1946. Cited p. 347

Bentley, *The Process of Government*, Bloomington (Indiana) 1949 (first edition 1908). Cited p. 173

Berelson, B.; Lazarsfeld, P. and McPhee, William, *Voting: A Study of Opinion Formation in a Presidential Campaign*, Chicago 1954. Cited pp. 150, 154

Berger, Morrow, *Bureaucracy and Society in Modern Egypt*, Princeton 1957. Cited pp. 359, 379

Bergson, H., 'Die Wahrnehmung der Veränderung', in Bergson, *Denken und Schöpferisches Werden*, Meisenheim 1948. Cited p. 19

Berlin, Isaiah, 'Does Political Theory Still Exist?', in P. Laslett and W. G. Runciman (eds.), *Philosophy, Politics and Society*, second series, Oxford 1962. Cited p. 49

Betancourt, R., *Venezuela: Política v Petroleo*, Mexico City 1956. Cited p. 310

Binder, Leonard, *Iran: Political Development in a Changing Society*, Berkeley and Los Angeles 1962. Cited pp. 51, 94, 347

Binder, Leonard, 'National Integration and Political Development', *Am. Pol. Sc. Rev.*, LVIII, 3 (September 1964), pp. 622–31. Cited p. 198

Binder, Leonard (ed.), *Politics in Lebanon*, New York and London 1966. Cited p. 351

Birch, A. H., 'Approaches to the Study of Federalism', *Political Studies*, XIV, 1 (February 1966), pp. 15–33. Cited p. 236

Black, Duncan, *The Theory of Committees and Elections*, Cambridge 1963. Cited p. 149

Blau, Peter and Scott, W. Richard, *Formal Organizations: A Comparative Approach*, San Francisco 1962. Cited p. 376

Blau, Peter, *The Dynamics of Bureaucracy: A Study of Interpersonal Relations in Two Government Agencies*, Chicago 1963. Cited p. 376

Blau, Peter, *Exchange and Power in Social Life*, London 1964. Cited p. 376

Blondel, Jean, *Voters, Parties and Leaders*, London (Penguin) 1963. Cited p. 155

Boorstin, Daniel, *The Genius of American Politics*, Chicago 1953. Cited p. 290

Bott, Elizabeth, *Family and Social Network: Roles, Norms and External Relationships in Ordinary Urban Families*, London 1957. Cited p. 97

Bottomore, T. B., *Elites and Society*, London 1964. Cited pp. 92, 93

Boudon, Raymond, 'Propriétés individuelles et propriétés collectives: un problème d'analyse écologique', *Revue Française de Sociologie*, IV (1963), pp. 275–99. Cited p. 155

Boulding, Kenneth E., 'Political Implications of General Systems Research', *General Systems*, VI (1961). Cited p. 102

BIBLIOGRAPHY

Bouvier, Paule, *L'accession du Congo belge a l'indépendance: essai d'analyse sociologique*, Brussels 1966. Cited p. 299

Brass, Paul F., *Factional Politics in an Indian State*, Cambridge 1965. Cited pp. 307, 320

Braybrooke, D. and Lindblom, C. E., *A Strategy of Decision: Policy Evaluation as a Social Process*, New York 1963. Cited p. 130

Brecher, Michael, *The New States of Asia: A Political Analysis*, London 1963. Cited pp. 142, 194

Breton, Albert, 'The Economics of Nationalism', *Journal of Political Economy*, LXII (1964), pp. 376–86. Cited pp. 49, 233, 257

Brzezinski, Z. and Huntington, S. P., 'Cincinnatus and the Apparatchik', *World Politics*, XVI, 1 (October 1963), pp. 52–78. Cited p. 355

Brzezinski, Z. and Huntington, S. P., *Political Power: USA/USSR*, New York 1964. Cited pp. 17, 196

Buchanan, J. M. and Tullock, E., *The Calculus of Consent: The Logical Foundations of Constitutional Democracy*, Ann Arbor, Michigan, 1962. Cited p. 169

Buchanan, Norman S. and Ellis, Howard S., *Approaches to Economic Development*, New York 1955. Cited p. 234

de Caillavet, de Flers and Arène, *Le roi s'amuse*, Paris 1908. Cited p. 80

Campbell, A. *et al.*, *The American Voter*, New York 1960. Cited pp. 112, 154, 177

Cancian, F., 'Functional Analysis of Change', *American Sociological Review*, XXV (1960), pp. 818–27. Cited p. 303

Carr, E. H., *What is History?*, London 1962. Cited p. 46

Carr, E. H. (ed.), *Nationalism: An RIIA Report*, London 1939, reprinted 1963. Cited p. 232

Carter, G. M. and Brown, W. O., *Transition in Africa: Studies in Political Adaptation*, Boston 1958. Cited p. 224

Castles, F. G., 'Towards a Theoretical Analysis of Pressure Politics', *Political Studies* XIV, 3 (October 1966), pp. 339–48. Cited p. 172

Cherry, Colin, *On Human Communications*, New York 1957. Cited p. 56

Chilver, E. M. and Kaberry, P. M., 'From Tribute to Tax in a Tikar Chiefdom', in Immanual Wallerstein (ed.), *Social Change: The Colonial Situation*, London 1966. Cited p. 240

Christie, Ian R., 'Was There a "New Toryism" in the Earlier Part of George III's Reign?', *The Journal of British Studies*, V, 1 (November 1965), pp. 60–76. Cited p. 172

Clark, G. Kitson, *The Making of Victorian England*, London 1962. Cited p. 190

Cliff, Tony, *Russia: A Marxist Analysis*, London 1964. Cited p. 372

Cobban, Alfred, *National Self-Determination*, Chicago, 1944. Cited p. 232

Cobban, Alfred, 'The Decline of Political Theory', *Political Science Quarterly*, LXVIII (1953), pp. 321–37. Cited p. 161

Coleman, James S. and Rosberg, Carl G., *Political Parties and*

397

National Integration in Tropical Africa, Berkeley and Los Angeles 1964. Cited pp. 224, 228, 229, 230, 298

Coleman, James S. (ed.), *Education and Political Development*, Princeton 1966. Cited p. 201

Collins, Orvis F.; Moore, David G. and Unwalla, Darab B., *The Enterprising Man*, East Lansing (Michigan) 1964. Cited p. 202

Commager, Henry Steele, *Living Ideas in America*, New York 1951. Cited p. 290

Constas, Helen, 'Max Weber's Two Conceptions of Bureaucracy', *American Journal of Sociology*, LXIII, 4 (January 1958), pp. 400–9. Cited pp. 342, 366, 373

Constas, Helen, 'The Soviet Union as a Charismatic Bureaucracy–Viewed Comparatively', Paper read to the American Sociological Society, August 1958, Seattle, Washington. Cited p. 342

Converse, Philip E., 'The Nature of Belief Systems in Mass Publics', in Apter (ed.), *Ideology and Discontent*, New York 1964, pp, 206–61. Cited p. 155

Coombes, David, *The Member of Parliament and the Administration*, London 1966. Cited p. 237

Cornford, J., 'The Transformation of Conservatism in the late Nineteenth Century', *Victorian Studies*, VII (1963), pp. 35–66. Cited pp. 60, 127

Coser, Lewis A., *The Functions of Social Conflict*, London 1956. Cited p. 225

Crick, Bernard, *The American Science of Politics*, London 1959. Cited pp. 203, 303

Crick, Bernard, *In Defence of Politics*, London 1962. Cited p. 115

Crick, Bernard, *The Reform of Parliament*, London 1964. Cited pp. 115, 237

Cropsey, Joseph, 'On the Relation of Political Science and Economics', *Am. Pol. Sc. Rev.*, LIV, 1 (March 1960), pp. 3–14. Cited p. 50

Crozier, Michel, 'De l'étude des relations humaines à l'étude des relations de pouvoir', *Sociologie du Travail*, I, 1961. Cited p. 16

Crozier, Michel, *The Bureaucratic Phenomenon*, London 1964. Cited pp. 16, 339, 376, 377

Cutright, P. and Rossi, P. H., 'Grass Roots Politicians and the Vote', *American Sociological Review*, XXIII (1958), pp. 171–9. Cited p. 179

Cutright, P., 'National Political Development: Its Measurement and Social Correlates', in Nelson W. Polsby, Robert A. Deutler and Paul A. Smith (eds.), *Politics and Social Life: An Introduction to Political Behavior*, Boston 1963, pp. 569–82. Cited pp. 180, 203

Cutright, P., 'National Political Development', *American Sociological Review*, XXVIII (1963), pp. 253–64. Cited p. 203

Daalder, H., 'Parties and Politics in the Netherlands', *Political Studies*, III (1955), pp. 1–16. Cited pp. 140, 333

Daalder, H., 'Parties, Elites and Political Development in Western Europe', in LaPalombara and Weiner (eds.), *Political Parties and Political Development*, Princeton 1966. Cited pp. 140–1

Dahl, Robert A., and Lindblom, Charles E., *Politics, Economics and Welfare*, New York 1953. Cited p. 130

Dahl, Robert A., *A Preface to Democratic Theory*, Chicago 1956. Cited pp. 93, 159

Dahl, Robert A., 'The Concept of Power', *Behavioral Science*, II, 3 (July 1957), pp. 201–15. Cited pp. 30, 93

Dahl, Robert A., 'A Critique of the Ruling Elite Model', *Am. Pol. Sc. Rev.*, LII, 2 (June 1958), pp. 463–9. Cited pp. 93, 224

Dahl, Robert A., *Who Governs? Democracy and Power in an American City*, New Haven 1961. Cited pp. 30. 93

Dahl, Robert A., *Modern Political Analysis*, New York 1963. Cited p. 30

Dahl, Robert A. (ed.), *Political Opposition in Western Democracies*, New Haven 1965. Cited pp. 66, 74, 333

Dahrendorf, Ralf, *Class and Class Conflict in Industrial Society*, London 1959. Cited pp. 15, 22, 97, 98, 340

Dahrendorf, Ralf, 'Bureaucracy Without Liberty: An Essay on the Politics of Other-Directed Man', in S. M. Lipset and Leo Lowenthal (eds.), *Culture and Social Character*, New York 1961, pp. 175–206. Cited pp. 340, 354, 376

Dahrendorf, Ralf, *Gesellschaft und Freiheit*, Munich 1961. Cited pp. 15, 78

Dahrendorf, Ralf, 'Three Symposia on Political Behavior', *American Sociological Review*, XXIX, 5 (October 1964), pp. 734–6. Cited pp. 154, 179

Dahrendorf, Ralf, *Gesellschaft und Demokratie in Deutschland*, Munich 1965. Cited pp. 15, 22, 356

Daphnis, Y., *Ta Ellenika Politika Komata (Greek Political Parties)*, Athens 1961. Cited p. 204

Davidson, James F., 'Political Science and Political Fiction', *Am. Pol. Sc. Rev.*, LV, 4 (December 1961), pp. 851–60. Cited p. 49

Davis, Kingsley and Moore, Wilbert E., 'Some Principles of Stratification', *American Sociological Review*, X (1945), pp. 242–9. Cited p. 86

Davis, Kingsley, 'Social and Democratic Aspects of Economic Development in India', in S. Kuznets, W. E. Moore and J. J. Spengler (eds.), *Economic Growth: Brazil, India, Japan*, Durham (North Carolina) 1955. Cited pp. 222–3

Davis, Lane, 'The Cost of Realism: Contemporary Restatements of Democracy', *Western Political Quarterly*, XVII (1964). pp. 37–46. Cited p. 102

Deutsch, Karl W., *Nationalism and Social Communication*, Cambridge (Mass.), 1953. Cited pp. 13, 66

Deutsch, Karl W., Burrell, S. A. *et al.* (eds.), *Political Community and the North Atlantic Area*, Princeton 1957. Cited p. 236

Deutsch, Karl W., 'Social Mobilization and Political Development', *Am. Pol. Sc. Rev.*, LV, 3 (September 1961), pp. 493–514. Cited pp. 13, 64

Deutsch, Karl W., *Nerves of Government: Models of Political*

Communication and Control, Glencoe 1963. Cited pp. 13, 31, 56, 66, 114, 158, 200, 240

Deutsch, Karl W. and Foltz, William J. (eds.), *Nation Building*, New York 1963. Cited pp. 227, 255

Deutsch, Karl W.; Singer, J. David and Smith, Keith, 'The Organizing Efficiency of Theories: The N/V Ratio as a Crude Rank Order Measure', *American Behavioral Scientist*, IX, 2 (October 1965), pp. 30–33. Cited p. 106

Deutsch, Karl W., 'The Future of World Politics', *Political Quarterly*, XXVII (January/March 1966). Cited pp. 61, 256

Deutsch, Karl W., 'On Theories, Taxonomies and Models as Communication Codes for Organizing Information', *Behavioral Science*, XI, 1 (January 1966), pp. 1–17. Cited p. 105

Dicks, Henry V., 'Observations on Contemporary Russian Behaviour', *Human Relations*, V, 2 (1952), pp. 111–75. Cited p. 201

Dore, R. P., *City Life in Japan*, Berkeley and Los Angeles 1958. Cited p. 347

Dore, R. P., *Education in Tokugawa, Japan*, London 1965. Cited p. 288

Douglas, James, 'Consensus and Elections', *New Society*, 175, February 1966, pp. 11–14. Cited p. 149

Downs, Anthony, *An Economic Theory of Democracy*, New York 1957. Cited pp. 112, 151

Downs, Anthony, 'An Economic Theory of Political Action in a Democracy', *Journal of Political Economy*, LXV (April 1957), pp. 135–50. Cited p. 130

Dror, Y., 'Muddling Through–Science or Inertia?', *Public Administration Review*, XXIV, 3 (September 1964), pp. 154–7. Cited p. 213

Drucker, Peter, *Concept of the Corporation*, New York 1946. Cited p. 349

Dublin, Louis I., *Suicide*, New York 1963. Cited p. 184

du Bois, Victor D., 'Guinea' in Coleman and Rosberg (eds.), *Political Parties and National Integration in Tropical Africa*, Berkeley and Los Angeles 1964, pp. 186–215. Cited p. 229

Duncan, Graeme, and Lukes, Steven, 'The New Democracy', *Political Studies*, XI, 2 (June 1963), pp. 156–77. Cited p. 102

Durkheim, E., *De la Division du Travail*, second edition, Paris 1902. Cited p. 365

Durkheim, E., *Montesquieu et Rousseau, précurseurs de la sociologie*, new edition, Paris 1953. Cited p. 135

Duverger, M., *Political Parties*, London 1954. Cited p. 108

Dzhunusov, M. S., *O nekapitalisticheskom puti razvitiya*, Moscow 1963. Cited p. 240

Easton, David, *The Political System: An Enquiry into the State of Political Science*, New York 1953. Cited pp. 14, 103

Easton, David, 'An Approach to the Analysis of Political Systems', *World Politics*, IX, 1957. Cited p. 14

Easton, David, *A Framework for Political Analysis*, Englewood Cliffs, 1965. Cited p. 14

Easton, David, *A Systems Analysis of Political Life*, New York 1965. Cited pp. 14, 66

Eckstein, Alexander, 'Individualism and the Role of the State in Economic Growth', *Economic Development and Cultural Change*, VI, 2 (January 1958), pp. 81–99. Cited p. 244

Eckstein, Harry, *Pressure Group Politics: The Case of the British Medical Association*, London 1960. Cited pp. 15, 172, 334

Eckstein, Harry, *A Theory of Stable Democracy*, Princeton 1961. Cited pp. 15, 181

Eckstein, Harry, 'The Determinants of Pressure Group Politics', in Eckstein and Apter (eds.), *Comparative Politics*, New York 1963, pp. 408–21. Cited p. 171

Eckstein, Harry (ed.), *Internal War: Problems and Approaches*, London 1964. Cited p. 15

Edelman, Murray, *The Symbolic Uses of Politics*, Urbana (Illinois) 1964. Cited pp. 64, 152

Edelman, Murray and Fleming, R. W., *The Politics of Wage Price Decisions: A Four-Country Analysis*, Urbana (Illinois) 1965. Cited pp. 64, 332, 350

Edinger, Lewis J., 'Post Totalitarian Leadership: Elites in the German Federal Republic', *Am. Pol. Sc. Rev.*, LIV, 1 (March 1964), pp. 58–82. Cited p. 80

Ehrmann, H. W., *Organized Business in France*, Princeton 1957. Cited p. 173

Eisenstadt, S. N., 'Sociological Aspects of Political Development in Underdeveloped Countries', *Economic Development and Cultural Change*, V, 4, pp. 294–8. Cited pp. 247, 345.

Eisenstadt, S. N., *From Generation to Generation: Age Groups and Social Structure*, Glencoe 1956. Cited pp. 95, 249

Eisenstadt, S. N., 'Primitive Political Systems: A Preliminary Comparative Analysis', *American Anthropologist*, LXI, 1959, pp. 200–20. Cited p. 369

Eisenstadt, S. N., 'Initial Institutional Patterns of Political Modernization: A Comparative Study', *Civilizations*, XII, 4 (1962), pp. 461–73. Cited p. 345

Eisenstadt, S. N., *The Political Systems of Empires*, Glencoe 1963. Cited pp. 344, 369

Eisenstadt, S. N., 'Bureaucracy and Political Development', in Joseph LaPalombara (ed.), *Bureaucracy and Political Development*, Princeton 1963. Cited p. 345

Eisenstadt, S. N., 'Modernization and Conditions of Sustained Growth', *World Politics*, XVI, 4 (July 1964), pp. 576–94. Cited p. 345

Eldersveld, Samuel J., *Political Parties: A Behavioral Analysis*, Chicago 1964, Cited p. 108

Emerson, Rupert, *From Empire to Nation: The Rise to Self-Assertion of Asian and African Peoples*, New York 1962. Cited pp. 95, 142, 194

Engelmann, Frederick C., 'A Critique of Recent Writings on

Political Parties', *The Journal of Politics*, XIX (1959), pp. 423–40. Cited p. 108

Essien-Udon, E. V., *Black Nationalism: A Search for an Identity in America*, Chicago 1962. Cited p. 184

Estier, Claude, *Pour L'Algérie*, Paris 1964. Cited p. 298

Etzioni, Amitai, 'Kulturkampf ou coalition: Le cas d'Israël', *Revue Française de Science Politique*, II (1958), pp. 311–35. Cited p. 108

Etzioni, Amitai, *A Comparative Analysis of Complex Organizations: On Power, Involvement and their Correlates*, Glencoe 1961. Cited pp. 15, 370

Etzioni, Amitai, *The Hard Way to Peace*, New York 1962. Cited p. 15

Etzioni, Amitai, 'The Epigenesis of Political Communities at the International Level', *American Journal of Sociology*, LXVIII (1963), pp. 407–21. Cited pp. 15, 236

Etzioni, Amitai, *Modern Organizations*, New York 1964. Cited p. 351

Etzioni, Amitai, *Political Unification: A Comparative Study of Leaders and Forces*, New York, Chicago, London 1965. Cited pp. 15, 386

Etzioni, Amitai, *Studies in Social Change*, New York 1966. Cited pp. 166, 197

Eulau, H., *Recent Development in the Behavioral Study of Politics*, Stanford 1961. Cited p. 154

Eulau, H., in Austin Ranney (ed.), *Essays on the Behavioral Study of Politics*, Urbana 1962. Cited p. 154

Fainsod, Merle, 'Bureaucracy and Modernization: The Russian and Soviet Case', in Joseph LaPalombara (ed.), *Bureaucracy and Political Development*, Princeton 1963, pp. 233–67. Cited p. 342

Fairbank, John K.; Reischauer, Edwin O. and Craig, Albert M., *East Asia: The Modern Transformation*, London 1966. Cited p. 346

Fallers, L. A., 'Ideology and Culture in Uganda Nationalism', *American Anthropologist*, LXIII, pp. 677–86. Cited p. 229

Fallers, L. A., *Bantu Bureaucracy, A Study of Integration and Conflict in the Politics of an East African People*, Cambridge 1956. Cited p. 370

Fallers, L. A., 'Despotism, Status Culture and Social Mobility in an African Kingdom', *Comparative Studies in Society and History*, II (1959), pp. 11–32. Cited p. 370.

Fallers, L. A., 'The Predicament of the Modern African Chief: An Instance from Uganda', in Immanual Wallerstein (ed.), *Social Change: The Colonial Situation*, London 1966. Cited p. 240

Faul, Erwin, 'Verfemung, Duldung und Anerkennung des Parteiwesens in der Geschichte des politischen Denkens' ('Condemnation, Toleration and Approval of Parties in the History of Political Thought'), *Politische Vierteljahresschrift*, V, 1 (March 1964), pp. 60–80. Cited p. 137

Feith, Herbert, 'Indonesia's Political Symbols and their Wielders', *World Politics*, XIII, 1 (October 1960), pp. 79–97. Cited p. 284

Feith, Herbert, *The Decline of Constitutional Democracy in Indonesia*, New York 1962. Cited p. 284

BIBLIOGRAPHY

Feuer, Lewis S., 'Problems and Unproblems in Soviet Social Theory', *Slavic Review*, XXIII, 1 (March 1964), pp. 117–25. Cited p. 202

Finer, S. E., *Anonymous Empire: A Study of the Lobby in Great Britain*, London 1958, second edition 1965. Cited p. 105

Finer, S. E., *The Man on Horseback: The Role of the Military in Politics*, London 1962. Cited pp. 276, 364

Floud, Jean, in *History and Theory*, IV, 2 (1965), pp. 271–5. Cited p. 46

Foltz, William J., 'Building the Newest Nations: Short-run Strategies and Long-run Problems', in Karl W. Deutsch and William J. Foltz (eds.), *Nation Building*, New York 1963. Cited pp. 227, 247

Fortes, M. and Evans-Pritchard, E. E. (eds.), *African Political Systems*, London 1940. Cited p. 295

Foster, Philip J., *Education and Social Change in Ghana*, London 1966. Cited p. 201

Frankfort, Henri, *Kingship and the Gods: A Study of Ancient Near Eastern Religion as the Instigator of Society and Nature*, Chicago 1948. Cited pp. 262, 373

Franks, Lord, *Report of Commission of Enquiry*, Vol. I, Oxford 1966. Cited p. 87

Frey, Frederick W., 'Political Development, Power and Communications in Turkey', in Lucian W. Pye (ed.), *Communications and Political Development*, Princeton 1963. Cited p. 196

Friedland, W. H., 'For a Sociological Concept of Charisma', *Social Forces*, XLIV (October 1964), pp. 18–26. Cited p. 263

Friedrich, Carl J., 'Philosophy and the Social Sciences', in H. Feigl and M. Brodbeck (eds.), *Readings in the Philosophy of Science*, Minneapolis 1953. Cited p. 36

Friedrich, Carl J. and Brzezinski, Z. K., *Totalitarian Dictatorship and Autocracy*, Cambridge (Mass.) 1956. Cited pp. 301, 302

Friedrich, Carl J., 'Political Philosophy and the Science of Politics', in R. Young (ed.), *Approaches to the Study of Politics*, Evanston (Illinois) 1958, pp. 172–89. Cited p. 36

Friedrich, Carl J., *Man and His Government: An Empirical Theory of Politics*, New York 1963. Cited pp. 14, 78, 117

Friedrich, Carl J., 'Political Pathology', *Political Quarterly*, XXXVII, 1 (1966). Cited p. 117

Furtado, Celso, *Desenvolvimento e Subdesenvolvimento*, Rio de Janeiro 1961. Cited pp. 259, 310

Furtado, Celso, *Dialética do Desenvolvimento*, Rio de Janeiro 1964. Cited p. 310

Gabriel, Ralph H., *The Course of American Democratic Thought*, New York 1956. Cited p. 290

Galjart, Benno, 'Class and "Following" in Rural Brazil', *America Latina*, VII (1964), pp. 2–24. Cited pp. 98, 248

Garvey, Gerald, 'The Theory of Party Equilibrium', *Am. Pol. Sc. Rev.*, IX, 1 (March 1966)., pp. 29–38. Cited pp. 150, 159

Gash, N., *Politics in the Age of Peel*, London 1953. Cited p. 60

Geertz, Clifford, 'The Integrative Revolution', in Clifford Geertz

BIBLIOGRAPHY

(ed.), *Old Societies and New States: The Quest for Modernity in Asia and Africa*, New York 1963, pp. 105–57. Cited pp. 62, 224

Geertz, Clifford, *Peddlers and Princes: Social Change and Economic Modernization in Two Indonesian Towns*, Chicago 1963. Cited p. 62

Geertz, Clifford, 'Ideology as a Cultural System', in David E. Apter (ed.), *Ideology and Discontent*, New York 1964, pp. 47–76. Cited p. 62

Geertz, Clifford, 'Religion as a Cultural System', in Michael Banton (ed.), *Anthropological Approaches to the Study of Religion*, London 1966. Cited p. 288

Geiger, Theodor, *Aufgaben und Stellung der Intelligenz in der Gesellschaft*, Stuttgart 1949. Cited p. 95

Gellner, Ernest, *Words and Things*, London 1959. Cited p. 17

Gellner, Ernest, *Thought and Change*, London 1964. Cited pp. 17, 110, 255

Gershenkron, Alexander, 'Typology of Industrial Development as a Tool of Analysis', in collected papers of *Second International Conference of Economic History: Aix-en-Provence 1962*, The Hague 1965, II, pp. 487–505. Cited p. 198

Glaser, Barney G., and Strauss, Anselm L., *Awareness of Dying: A Sociological Study of Attitudes towards the Patient Dying in Hospital*, London 1966. Cited p. 19

Glass, D. V., *Social Mobility in Britain*, London 1954. Cited p. 155

Gluckman, Max (ed.), *Closed Systems and Open Minds: The Limits of Naïvety in Social Anthropology*, Edinburgh 1964. Cited p. 44

Goffman, Erving, *The Presentation of Self in Everyday Life*, New York 1959. Cited pp. 15. 265

Goffman, Erving, *Stigma: Notes on the Management of Spoiled Identity*, Englewood Cliffs 1963. Cited p. 265

Goffman, Erving, *Personal Behavior in Public Places: Notes on the Social Organization of Gatherings*, London 1963. Cited p. 265

Gordon, David C., *The Passing of French Algeria*, Oxford 1965. Cited p. 298

Gordon, L. A. and Fridman, L. A., 'Ossobennosti sostava i struktury rabochego klassa v ekonomicheski slaborazvitikh stranakh Azii i Afriki (na primere Indii i OAR)', *Narody Azii i Afriki*, 2 (1963), pp. 3–22. Cited p. 379

Gorer, G. and Rickman, J., *The People of Great Russia*, London 1949. Cited p. 201

Gorwala, A. D., *Report on the Efficient Conduct of State Enterprise*, New Delhi 1951. Cited p. 215

Gouldner, Alvin W., *Patterns of Industrial Bureaucracy*, Glencoe 1954. Cited p. 341

Gouldner, Alvin W., 'Metaphysical Pathos and the Theory of Bureaucracy', *Am. Pol. Sc. Rev.*, XLVIII (1955), pp. 496–507. Cited pp. 341, 349

Gouldner, Alvin W., 'Reciprocity and Autonomy in Functional Theory', in Llewellyn L. Gross (ed.), *Symposium on Sociological Theory*, Evanston (Illinois) 1959, pp. 241–70. Cited pp. 322, 374

BIBLIOGRAPHY

Greaves, H. G. R., *The British Constitution*, second edition, London 1948. Cited p. 353

Greenfield, Richard, *Ethiopia: A New Political History*, London 1965. Cited p. 347

Grossholtz, Jean, *Politics in the Philippines*, Boston 1964. Cited p. 328

Grove, J. W., *Government and Industry in Britain*, London 1962. Cited p. 334

Guber, A. A., 'Introduction to Indonesia', in T. P. Thornton (ed.), *The Third World in Soviet Perspective: Studies by Soviet Writers on the Developing Areas*, Princeton 1964. Cited p. 256

Gullick, L. and Urwick, L. (eds.), *Papers on the Science of Administration*, New York 1937. Cited p. 213

Guttsmann, W. L., *The British Political Elite*, London 1963. Cited p. 77

Hacker, Andrew, 'The Elected and the Anointed: Two American Elites', *Am. Pol. Sc. Rev.*, LV, 3 (September 1961), pp. 539–49. Cited pp. 81, 93, 179

Hagen, Everitt E., *On the Theory of Social Change: How Economic Growth Begins*, Homewood (Illinois) 1962. Cited p. 182

Halpern, Manfred, 'Toward Further Modernization of the Study of New Nations', *World Politics*, XVII (October 1964), pp. 157–81. Cited p. 196

Halpern, Manfred, *The Politics of Social Change in the Middle East and North Africa*, Princeton 1966. Cited p. 305

Hanham, H. J., *Elections and Electoral Management: Politics in the Time of Disraeli and Gladstone*, London 1959. Cited p. 60

Hanson, A. H., *Public Enterprise and Economic Development*, second edition, London 1965. Cited p. 215

Hanson, A. H., *The Process of Planning: A Study of India's Five Year Plans 1950–63*, London 1966. Cited pp. 215, 243, 244, 312

Haq, Mahbub ul, *The Strategy of Economic Planning: A Case Study of Pakistan*, Oxford 1965. Cited p. 215

Harrison, Selig H., *India: The Most Dangerous Decades*, Princeton 1960. Cited pp. 118, 223

Hartwell, R. M., 'Interpretations of the Industrial Revolution in England: A Methodological Enquiry', *Journal of Economic History*, XIX (1959), pp. 229–49. Cited p. 235

Hartwell, R. M., 'The Rising Standard of Living in England, 1800–1850', *Economic History Review*, XIII, 3 (1961), pp. 397–417. Cited p. 235

Hartz, Lewis M., *The Liberal Tradition in America: An Interpretation of American Political Thought since the Revolution*, New York 1955. Cited p. 290

Hennis, Wilhelm, *Meinungsforschung und repräsentative Demokratie*, Tübingen 1957. Cited p. 151

Higgins, Benjamin, *Economic Development: Principles, Problems and Policies*, New York 1959. Cited p. 234

Himmelstrand, Ulf, *Social Pressures, Attitudes and Democratic Processes*, Stockholm 1960. Cited p. 152

Himmelstrand, Ulf, 'A Theoretical and Empirical Approach to Depoliticization and Political Involvement', *Acta Sociologica*, VI (1962), pp. 83–110. Cited pp. 74, 152

Hinsley, F. H., *Sovereignty*, London 1965. Cited pp. 133, 135

Hirschmann, A. O., *The Strategy of Economic Development*, New Haven 1958. Cited p. 310

Hobsbawm, Eric J., 'The British Standard of Living, 1790–1850', *Economic History Review*, X, 1 (1957), pp. 46–69. Cited p. 235

Hobsbawm, Eric J., *Primitive Rebels: Studies in Archaic Forms of Social Movement in the 19th and 20th Centuries*, Manchester 1959. Cited pp. 247, 248

Hobsbawm, Eric J., and Hartwell, R. M., 'The Standard of Living During the Industrial Revolution: A Discussion', *Economic History Review*, XVI, 1 (1963). Cited p. 235

Hobsbawm, Eric J., *Labouring Men: Studies in the History of Labour*, London 1964. Cited pp. 16, 248

[Hobsbawm, Eric J.], 'Pop Goes the Artist', *Times Literary Supplement*, 17 December 1964. Cited p. 388

Hodgkin, Thomas, and Schachter Morgenthau, Ruth, 'Mali' in Coleman and Rosberg (eds.), *Political Parties and National Integration in Tropical Africa*, Berkeley and Los Angeles 1964, pp. 216–58. Cited p. 229

Holt, Robert T. and Turner, John E., *The Political Basis of Economic Development: An Exploration in Comparative Political Analysis*, London/New York 1966. Cited p. 232

Hopkins, Keith, 'Elite Mobility in the Roman Empire', *Past and Present*, No. 32 (December 1965), pp. 12–26. Cited p. 96

Hoselitz, B. F. (ed.), *The Progress of Underdeveloped Areas*, Chicago 1952. Cited p. 232

Hoselitz, B. F., *Sociological Aspects of Economic Growth*, Glencoe 1960. Cited p. 310

Hoselitz, B. F., 'Non-economic Barriers to Economic Development', *Economic Development and Cultural Change*, I, 1, pp. 8–21. Cited p. 233

Hughes, Edward, 'Civil Service Reform 1853–1855', *Public Administration*, XXXII (Spring 1954), pp. 17–51. Cited p. 353

Humbaraci, Arslan, *Algeria: A Revolution that Failed*, London 1966. Cited p. 298

Huntington, Samuel P. (ed.), *Changing Patterns of Military Politics*, New York 1962. Cited pp. 276, 363, 364

Huntington, Samuel P., 'Political Development and Political Decay', *World Politics*, XVII, 3 (April 1965), pp. 386–430. Cited pp. 17, 124, 197, 227

Huntington, Samuel P., 'Political Modernization: America vs. Europe', *World Politics*, XVIII, 3 (April 1966), pp. 378–414. Cited pp. 17, 75

Hyman, H. H., 'Voluntary Association Memberships of American Adults', *American Sociological Review*, XIII (1958), pp. 284–94. Cited p. 179

Hyman, H. H., *Political Socialization: A Study in the Psychology of Political Behavior*, Glencoe 1959. Cited p. 200

Inkeles, Alex H., and Rossi, Peter, 'National Comparisons of Occupational Prestige', *American Journal of Sociology*, LXI (1956), pp. 329–39. Cited pp. 355–6

Jacob, Herbert, and Vines, Kenneth (eds.), *Politics in the American States*, Boston 1965. Cited p. 184

Jacobs, Norman, *The Sociology of Development: Iran as an Asian Case Study*, New York 1966. Cited p. 347

Jacobson, H. K., 'ONUC's Civilian Operations: State Preserving and State Building', *World Politics*, XVII, 1 (October 1964), pp. 75–107. Cited p. 247

Jaguaribe, Hélio, *O Nacionalismo na Atualidade Brasileira*, Rio de Janeiro 1958. Cited p. 256

Jaguaribe, Hélio, *Desenvolvimento Económico e Desenvolvimento Politico*, Rio de Janeiro 1962. Cited p. 310

Janowitz, Morris and Marvick, Dwaine, *Competitive Pressure and Democratic Consent: An Interpretation of the 1952 Presidential Election*, Ann Arbor 1956. Cited p. 161

Janowitz, Morris; Wright, Deil, and Delany, William, *Public Administration and the Public: Perspectives toward Government in a Metropolitan Community*, Ann Arbor (Michigan), 1958. Cited p. 141

Janowitz, Morris, *The Military in the Political Development of New Nations*, Chicago 1964. Cited pp. 276, 364

Joffe, Ellis, *Party and Army: Professionalism and Political Control in the Chinese Officer Corps 1949–64*, Cambridge (Mass.) 1965. Cited p. 241

Johnson, Harry G., 'A Theoretical Model of Economic Nationalism in New and Developing States', *Political Science Quarterly*, LXXX, 2 (June 1965), pp. 169–85. Cited pp. 233, 257

Johnson, John J. (ed.), *The Role of the Military in Underdeveloped Countries*, Princeton 1926. Cited pp. 276, 364

de Jouvenel, Bertrand, *L'art de la conjecture*, Paris 1964. Cited p. 255

Kapil, Ravi L., 'On the Conflict Potential of Inherited Boundaries in Africa', *World Politics*, XVIII, 4 (July 1966), pp. 656–73. Cited p. 255

Kassof, Allen, 'The Administered Society: Totalitarianism Without Terror', *World Politics*, XVI, 4 (July 1964), pp. 558–75. Cited p. 371

Katona, George, *The Psychological Analysis of Economic Behavior*, New York 1951. Cited p. 235

Katz, D. and Eldersveld, S. J., 'The Impact of Local Party Activity upon the Electorate', *Public Opinion Quarterly*, XXV (1961), pp. 1–27. Cited p. 179

Kaunda, Kenneth, *Zambia Shall be Free*, London 1962. Cited p. 246

Kautsky, John H., 'An Essay in the Politics of Development', in Kautsky (ed.), *Political Change in Underdeveloped Countries*, New York 1962. Cited pp. 95, 232, 268

BIBLIOGRAPHY

Kedourie, Elie, *Nationalism*, second revised edition, London 1961. Cited pp. 233, 255

Key, Jnr., V. O., and Munzer, F., 'Social Determinism and Electoral Decision: The Case of Indiana', in E. Burdick and A. J. Brodbeck (eds.), *American Voting Behavior*, Glencoe 1959, pp. 281–99. Cited p. 154

Key, Jnr., V. O., *Public Opinion and American Democracy*, New York 1961. Cited pp. 141, 154

Kidron, Michael, *Foreign Investments in India*, London 1965. Cited p. 241

Klein, B. H., *Germany's Economic Preparations for War*, Cambridge (Mass.), 1959. Cited p. 301

Kling, Merle, 'Towards a Theory of Power and Political Instability in Latin America', *Western Political Quarterly*, IX (1956), pp. 21–35. Cited pp. 94, 364

Kluckhohn, C. and Murray, H. A. (eds.), *Personality in Nature, Society and Culture*, New York 1947. Cited p. 248

Koestler, Arthur, *The Act of Creation*, London 1964. Cited p. 49

Kommunistische Politik (Berlin) 1926, I, 13/14. Cited p. 371

Kornhauser, William, *The Politics of Mass Society*, London 1960. Cited pp. 75, 137

Kosambi, D. D. in *The Economic Weekly* (Bombay), 2 November 1957. Cited p. 369

Kothari, Rajni, 'Form and Substance in Indian Politics–Party System', *The Economic Weekly* (Bombay), June 1961. Cited p. 320

Kothari, Rajni, and Wjatr, Jerzy, 'Party Systems and Political Pluralism: Comparisons Between India and Poland', *Papers in Comparative Politics*, Department of Political Sociology of the Institute of Philosophy and Sociology, Polish Academy of Sciences, Warsaw (presented to VI World Congress of Sociology, Evian, September 1966). Cited p. 320

Kroeber, A. L., *The Nature of Culture*, Chicago 1952. Cited p. 27

Kroeber, A. L. and Kluckhohn, Clyde, *Culture: A Critical Review of Concepts and Definitions*, Papers of the Peabody Museum of American Archaeology and Ethnology, XLVII (1952). Cited p. 27

Kruijt, J. P., *Verzuiling*, Zaandijk 1959. Cited p. 350

Kruijt, J. P., and Goddijn, W., 'Verzuiling an ontzuiling als soziologisch process', in A. den Hollander *et al.* (eds.), *Drift en Koers*, Assen 1962, pp. 227–63. Cited p. 350

Kunkel, John H., 'Values and Behavior in Economic Development', *Economic Development and Cultural Change*, XII, 3 (April 1965), pp. 257–77. Cited p. 202

Lagos, Gustavo, *International Stratification and Underdeveloped Countries*, Chapel Hill (North Carolina) 1963. Cited pp. 204, 274

Lakeman, E. and Lambert, J. D., *Voting in Democracies*, London 1955. Cited p. 281

Landau, M., 'On the Use of Metaphor in Political Analysis', *Social Research*, XXVIII (1961), pp. 331–53. Cited p. 49

Landes, David, 'Technological Change and Development in Western

Europe 1750–1914', in Vol. VI of the *Cambridge Economic History of Europe: The Industrial Revolution and After*, Cambridge 1965. Cited p. 362

Lane, Robert E., 'Political Character and Political Analysis', *Psychiatry*, XVI (1953), pp. 387–98. Cited p. 200

Lane, Robert E., 'Depth Interviews on the Personal Meaning of Politics', *PROD*, I (1957), pp. 10–13. Cited p. 200

Lane, Robert E., *Political Life: How People Get Involved in Politics*, Glencoe 1959. Cited p. 92

Lane, Robert E., 'The Fear of Equality', *Am. Pol. Sc. Rev.*, LIII, (1959), pp. 36–51. Cited p. 200

Lane, Robert E. and Sears, David, *Public Opinion*, Englewood Cliffs 1964. Cited p. 83

LaPalombara, Joseph and Poggi, Gianfranco, 'I gruppi di pressione e la burocrazia italiana', *Rassegna italiana di sociologia*, 1 (October–December 1960), pp. 31–35. Cited p. 356

LaPalombara, Joseph, 'An Overview . . .' in LaPalombara (ed.), *Bureaucracy and Political Development*, Princeton 1963, pp. 3–33. Cited pp. 214, 375

LaPalombara, Joseph, *Interest Groups in Italian Politics*, Princeton 1964. Cited p. 356

LaPalombara, Joseph, 'Decline of Ideology: A Dissent and an Interpretation', *Am. Pol. Sc. Rev.*, LX, 1 (March 1966), pp. 5–16. Cited pp. 62, 100, 101, 159

LaPalombara, Joseph, and Weiner, Myron (eds.), *Political Parties and Political Development*, Princeton 1966. Cited pp. 66, 108, 141, 144

Laqueur, Walter S., *The Soviet Union and the Middle East*, London 1959. Cited p. 367

Lasswell, Harold D.; Leites, Nathan *et al.*, *Language of Politics*, New York 1949. Cited p. 51

Lasswell, Harold D. and Kaplan, Morton A., *Power and Society: A Framework for Political Inquiry*, New Haven 1950. Cited pp. 30, 92, 93, 291

Lasswell, Harold D., *The Political Writings of Harold Lasswell*, Glencoe 1951. Cited pp. 115, 182

Lasswell, Harold D., *Psychopathology and Politics* (1930), reprinted in *The Political Writings of Harold Lasswell*, Glencoe 1951. Cited p. 114

Lasswell, Harold D.; Lerner, Daniel, and de Sola Pool I., *The Comparative Study of Symbols: An Introduction*, Stanford 1952. Cited p. 51

Lasswell, Harold D.; Lerner, Daniel and Rothwell, C. Easton, *The Comparative Study of Elites*, Stanford 1952. Cited pp. 93, 291

Lasswell, Harold D., 'Political Constitution and Character', *Psychoanalysis and Psychoanalytical Review*, XLVI (1959), pp. 3–18. Cited p. 114

Lasswell, Harold D., 'The Garrison-state Hypothesis Today', in S. P. Huntington (ed.), *Changing Patterns of Military Politics*, Glencoe 1962. Cited p. 114

BIBLIOGRAPHY

Lasswell, Harold D., *The Future of Political Science*, London 1964. Cited p. 303

Lasswell, Harold D. and Lerner, Daniel (eds.), *World Revolutionary Elites: Studies in Coercive Ideological Movements*, Cambridge (Mass.) 1965. Cited pp. 92, 250

Lazarsfeld, Paul F.; Berelson, B. and Gaudet, Helen, *The People's Choice: How the Voter Makes up his Mind in a Presidential Campaign*, New York 1948. Cited p. 154

Lazarsfeld, Paul F. and Rosenberg, Morris (eds.), *The Language of Social Research*, Glencoe 1955. Cited pp. 92, 154

Lazarsfeld, Paul F. and Menzel, Herbert A. in A. Etzioni (ed.), *Complex Organizations: A Sociological Reader*, New York 1961, pp. 422–40. Cited p. 154

Leach, E. R., 'Hydraulic Society in Ceylon', *Past and Present*, No. 15 (April 1959), pp. 2–26. Cited p. 369

Leeds, Anthony, 'Brazil and the Myth of Francisco Julião', in Joseph Maier and R. W. Weatherhead (eds.), *Politics of Change in Latin America*, New York 1964. Cited pp. 98, 248

Leiserson, Avery, *Parties and Politics: An Institutional and Behavioral Approach*, New York 1958. Cited p. 108

Lenski, Gerhard E., 'Status Crystallization: A Non-Vertical Dimension of Social Status', *American Sociological Review*, XIX (1954), pp. 405–13. Cited p. 177

Lenski, Gerhard E., 'Social Participation and Status Crystallization', *American Sociological Review*, XXI (1956), pp. 458–64. Cited p. 78

Lerner, Daniel, *The Passing of Traditional Society: Modernizing the Middle East*, Chicago 1958. Cited pp. 95, 142

Lerner, Daniel, and Robinson, Richard D., 'Swords and Ploughshares: The Turkish Army as a Modernizing Force', *World Politics*, XIII (1960), pp. 19–45. Cited p. 363

Lerner, Daniel, 'Some Comments on Center-Periphery Relations', in Richard L. Merritt and Stein Rokkan (eds.), *Comparing Nations: The Use of Quantitative Data in Cross-National Research*, New Haven 1966, pp. 259–65. Cited p. 66

Levi, Mario Attilio, *Political Power in the Ancient World*, London 1965. Cited pp. 262, 373

Lévi-Strauss, Claude, *La pensée sauvage*, English translation *The Savage Mind*, London 1966. Cited p. 168

Levy, Reuben, *The Social Structure of Islam*, Cambridge 1962. Cited p. 292

Lewin, M., 'The Immediate Background of Soviet Collectivization', *Soviet Studies*, XVII (October 1965), pp. 162–97. Cited p. 343

Lewis, Bernard, *The Emergence of Modern Turkey*, London 1961. Cited p. 298

Lewis, Sinclair, *Kingsblood Royal*, New York 1947. Cited p. 295

Lewis, W. Arthur, *Politics in West Africa*, London 1966. Cited p. 228

Leys, Colin, 'Models, Theories and the Theory of Political Parties', in Harry Eckstein and David E. Apter, *Comparative Politics: A Reader*, New York 1963, pp. 305–15. Cited p. 108

Lichtheim, G., 'Marx and the Asiatic Mode of Production', *St. Antony's Papers*, XIV (London 1963), pp. 86–112. Cited p. 367

Lindblom, C. E., 'Policy Analysis', *American Economic Review*, XLVIII (June 1958), pp. 298–312. Cited p. 213

Lipset, Seymour Martin, and Linz, J., *The Social Bases of Political Diversity*, Stanford 1956. Cited p. 74

Lipset, Seymour Martin, *Political Man: The Social Bases of Politics*, New York 1960. Cited pp. 74, 75, 94, 202

Lipset, Seymour Martin, *The First New Nation: The United States in Historical and Comparative Perspective*, London 1964. Cited pp. 51, 95, 184, 290

Lipset, Seymour Martin, introduction to M. Ostrogorski, *Democracy and the Organization of Political Parties*, New York 1964 (first published in France in 1903). Cited pp. 129, 365

Lipset, Seymour Martin, 'The Changing Class Structure and Contemporary European Politics', *Daedalus*, XCIII, 1 (1964), pp. 271–303. Cited p. 74

Lipset, Seymour Martin, 'University Students and Politics in Underdeveloped Countries', *Minerva*, III, 1, Autumn 1964. Cited pp. 249, 250

Lipset, Seymour Martin, 'Some Further Comments on "The End of Ideology"', *Am. Pol. Sc. Rev.*, LX, 1 (March 1966), pp. 17–18. Cited pp. 62, 75

Lipset, Seymour Martin, and Rokkan, Stein (eds.), *Party Systems and Voter Alignments*, forthcoming 1967. Cited pp. 66, 115, 386

Litt, Edgar, 'Political Cynicism and Political Futility', *Journal of Politics* XXV (1963), pp. 312–23. Cited p. 155

Lloyd, Peter C., 'The Political Structure of African Kingdoms', in *Political Systems and the Distribution of Power*, ASA Monograph 2, London 1965, pp. 63–112. Cited p. 372

Locke, *Two Treatises of Government*, Vol. II of the *Works* of John Locke, twelfth edition, London 1824. Cited p. 164

Lockwood, William W., *Economic Development of Japan*, Princeton 1954. Cited p. 347

Lockwood, William W. (ed.), *The State and Economic Enterprises in Japan*, Princeton 1965. Cited p. 347

Lowi, Theodore, J., 'Towards Functionalism in Political Science: The Case of Innovation in Party Systems', *Am. Pol. Sc. Rev.*, LVIII, 3 (September 1963), pp. 570–83. Cited p. 140

Lowi, Theodore J., 'American Business, Public Policy, Case Studies and Political Theory', *World Politics*, XVI (July 1964), pp. 677–715. Cited pp. 102, 139

Luethy, Herbert, 'Indonesia Confronted', *Encounter*, XXV, 6 (December 1965), pp. 80–90; XXVI, 1 (January 1966), pp. 75–83. Cited p. 284

Lupton, T. and Wilson, C. Shirley, 'The Social Background and Connections of "Top Decision-Makers"', *The Manchester School*, XXVII, 1 (January 1959), pp. 30–51. Cited p. 77

BIBLIOGRAPHY

Mackenzie, W. J. M., 'The Export of Electoral Systems', *Political Studies*, V, 3 (1957), pp. 240–57. Cited pp. 17, 110, 141, 206

Mackenzie, W. J. M. and Robinson, K. E. (eds.), *Five Elections in Africa*, London 1960. Cited p. 199

MacPherson, C. B., *The Political Theory of Possessive Individualism*, Oxford 1962. Cited p. 135

Maffi, B. (ed.), *K. Marx, F. Engels: India, Cina, Russia*, Milan 1960. Cited pp. 366–7

Mair, L. P., *Native Politics in Africa*, London 1936. Cited p. 246

Malenbaum, Wilfred, 'Government, Entrepreneurship and Economic Growth in Poor Lands', *World Politics*, XIX (October 1966). Cited pp. 198, 234

Mannheim, Karl, *Ideology and Utopia: An Introduction to the Sociology of Knowledge*, London 1936. Cited pp. 14, 62

Maquet, J. J. and d'Hertefelt, M., *Elections en société féodale: une étude sur l'introduction du vote populaire au Ruanda-Urundi*, Brussels 1959. Cited p. 199

Markzistskaya i burzhuaznaya sotsiologiya sevodnya, Moscow 1964. Cited p. 259

Martin, F. M., 'Social Status and Electoral Choice in two Constituencies', *British Journal of Sociology*, III, 3 (1952), pp. 231–41. Cited p. 97

Marx, F. M., *The Administrative State: An Introduction to Bureaucracy*, Chicago 1957. Cited p. 352

Marx, Karl, *Capital*, translation Eden and Cedar Paul, London 1933. Cited p. 366

Marx, Karl, 'Formen die der kapitalistischen Produktion vorhergehen', *Grundrisse der Kritik der Politischen Oekonomie (Rohentwurf)*, first edition Moscow 1939, English edition E. J. Hobsbawm, *Karl Marx: Precapitalist Economic Formations*, London 1965. Cited p. 366

Marx, Karl, *Marx/Engels, Werke*, XXVIII, Berlin, 1963. Cited p. 366

Masikh-uz-Zaman, *Community Development and its Audience*, Lahore 1960. Cited p. 270

Mason, T. W., 'Labour in the Third Reich, 1933–1939', *Past and Present*, No. 33 (April 1966), pp. 112–41. Cited p. 302

Masters, Roger D., 'World Politics as a Primitive Political System', *World Politics*, XVI, 4 (July 1964), pp. 595–619. Cited p. 348

Matossian, M., 'Ideologies of Delayed Industrialization', *Economic Development and Cultural Change*, VI, 3, pp. 217–28. Cited p. 247

Mayer, Adrian C., 'Some Political Implications of Community Development in India', *European Journal of Sociology*, IV, 1 (1963), pp. 86–106. Cited p. 244

Mayer, J. P., *Max Weber and German Politics: A Study in Political Sociology*, London 1944. Cited p. 369

Mayntz, Renate, 'Max Weber's Idealtypus der Bürokratie und die Organizationssoziologie', *Kölner Zeitschrift für Soziologie und Sozialpsychologie*, XVII, 3 (1965), pp. 493–502. Cited pp. 366, 370

McClelland, David, *The Achieving Society*, New York 1961. Cited pp. 202, 235

BIBLIOGRAPHY

McClelland, David, 'The Achievement Motive in Economic Growth', in Hoselitz and Moore (eds.), *Industrialization and Society*, The Hague 1963. Cited p. 235

McClosky, Herbert, 'Conservatism and Personality', *Am. Pol. Sc. Rev.*, LII, 1 (March 1959), pp. 27–45. Cited p. 200

McKenzie, R. T., *British Political Parties*, second edition, London 1963. Cited pp. 77, 335

McKenzie, Robert, 'Perils of the Party Game', *Observer*, 6 December 1964. Cited p. 113

McLuhan, Marshall, *The Gutenberg Galaxy: The Making of Typographic Man*, London 1962. Cited p. 388

McLuhan, Marshall, *Understanding Media: The Extensions of Man*, London 1964. Cited p. 388

Mead, Margaret, *Soviet Attitudes Toward Authority: An Interdisciplinary Approach to Problems of Soviet Character*, New York 1951. Cited p. 201

de Medina, Carlo Alberto, *A Favela e o Demagogo*, São Paulo 1964. Cited p. 248

Mehden, von der, Fred R., *Politics of the Developing Nations*, Englewood Cliffs 1964. Cited pp. 180, 276

Meijer, J. M., *Knowledge and Revolution: The Russian Colony in Zurich 1870–1873*, Assen (Holland) 1955. Cited p. 250

Melnik, C. and Leites, N. C., *House Without Windows*, New York 1958. Cited p. 157

Merritt, Richard L. and Rokkan, Stein (eds.), *Comparing Nations: The Use of Quantitative Data in Cross-National Research*, New Haven 1966. Cited pp. 65–6, 92, 197

Merton, R. K., 'The Unanticipated Consequences of Purposive Social Action', *American Sociological Review*, I (1936), pp. 894–904. Cited p. 376

Merton, R. K., 'Bureaucratic Structure and Personality', *Social Forces*, XVIII (1940), pp. 560–8. Cited pp. 351, 376

Merton, R. K., *Social Theory and Social Structure*, second revised edition, Glencoe 1957. Cited p. 248

Meyer, A. J., *Middle Eastern Capitalism: Nine Essays*, Cambridge (Mass.) 1959. Cited p. 292

Meynaud, Jean, 'I gruppi d'interesse in Francia', *Studi Politici*, IV (1957). Cited p. 174

Michels, Robert, *Political Parties*, first English edition, London 1915. Cited pp. 270, 341–2

Milbrath, Lester W., *Political Participation*, Chicago 1965. Cited p. 155

Miller, James G., 'Living Systems: Basic Concepts', *Behavioral Science*, X, 3 (July 1965), pp. 193–237. Cited pp. 27–8, 167

Miller, James G., *Living Systems*, forthcoming. Cited p. 28

Millikan, Max F. and Rostow, W. W., *A Proposal: Key to Effective Foreign Policy*, New York 1957. Cited p. 195

Millikan, Max F. and Blackmer, Donald L. M. (eds.), *The Emerging Nations: Their Growth and U.S. Policy*, Cambridge (Mass.) 1961. Cited p. 197

413

BIBLIOGRAPHY

Mills, C. Wright, *The Power Elite*, New York 1959. Cited p. 93

Milne, R. S. and Mackenzie, H. C., 'Straight Fight, a Study of Voting Behaviour in the Constituency of Bristol North East at the General Election of 1951', *Parliamentary Affairs*, VIII, 1 (entire special issue). Cited p. 155

Mitchell, William C., *The American Polity: A Social and Cultural Interpretation*, New York/London 1962. Cited p. 28

Moore, C. H., *Tunisia Since Independence: The Dynamics of One-Party Government*, Berkeley and Los Angeles 1965. Cited pp. 143, 286, 298

Moore, F. W. (ed.), *Readings in Cross-Cultural Methodology*, New Haven 1961 (Human Relations Area Files). Cited p. 51

Moore, W. E. and Feldman, A. S., *Labor Commitment and Social Change in Developing Areas*, New York 1960. Cited p. 234

Moorehead, Alan, *The Fatal Impact*, London 1966. Cited p. 278

Murdock, G. P., *Africa: Its Peoples and their Culture History*, New York 1959. Cited p. 370

Myrdal, Gunnar, *An International Economy, Problems and Prospects*, London 1956. Cited p. 236

Myrdal, Gunnar, *Economic Theory and Underdeveloped Regions*, London 1957. Cited p. 236

Myrdal, Gunnar, *Beyond the Welfare State*, London 1960. Cited p. 236

Nadel, S. F., 'The Concept of Social Elites', *International Social Science Bulletin*, VIII, 3 (1956), pp. 413–24. Cited p. 92

Nagel, E., 'A Formalization of Functionalism', in Nagel (ed.), *Logic Without Metaphysics*, Chicago 1956, pp. 247–83. Cited p. 303

Nanda, B. R., *The Nehrus: Motilal and Jawaharlal*, Bombay 1952. Cited p. 345

Narayan, Jayaprakash, *A Plan for the Reconstruction of Indian Polity*, Benares 1961. Cited p. 270

Nash, M., *Machine Age Maya: The Industrialization of a Guatemalan Community*, New York 1948. Cited p. 112

Nasser, Gamal A., *The Philosophy of the Revolution*, Buffalo (New York) 1959. Cited p. 313

Nayar, Baldev Raj, 'Community Development Programme: Its Political Impact', [Bombay] *Economic Weekly*, 17 September 1960. Cited p. 244

Nettl, J. P., 'The Economy of the Soviet Zone of Germany' in Carl J. Friedrich (ed.), *Totalitarianism*, Cambridge (Mass.) 1954, pp. 296–307. Cited p. 302

Nettl, J. P., 'The German Social Democratic Party as a Political Model 1890–1914', *Past and Present*, No. 30 (April 1965), pp. 65–95. Cited pp. 18, 208, 350

Nettl, J. P., 'Consensus or Elite Domination: The Case of Business', *Political Studies*, XIII, 1 (February 1965), pp. 22–44. Cited pp. 77, 352

Nettl, J. P., *Rosa Luxemburg*, London, 1966. Cited pp. 21, 152, 257

Nettl, J. P., 'Rosa Luxemburg Today', *New Society*, 184 (7 April 1966), pp. 11–13. Cited pp. 115, 268

BIBLIOGRAPHY

Nettl, J. P., 'Are Two-Party Systems Symmetrical?', *Parliamentary Affairs*, XIX, 2 (Spring 1966), pp. 218–23. Cited pp. 228, 322

Nettl, J. P. 'Centre and Periphery in Social Science: The Problem of Political Culture', *American Behavioral Scientist*, IX, 10 (June 1966), pp. 39–46

Nettl, J. P., 'The Concept of System in Political Science', *Political Studies*, XIV, 3 (October 1966), pp. 305–38. Cited pp. 18, 29, 109, 303

Nettl, J. P. and Robertson, Roland, 'Industrialization, Development or Modernization?', *British Journal of Sociology*, XVII, 3 (September 1966), pp. 274–91. Cited pp. 18, 31, 35, 50, 91

Nettl, J. P. and Robertson, Roland, *The International Context of Modernization*, forthcoming 1967; contains 'Industrialization, Development or Modernization?'; 'Inheritance'; and 'Modernization and International Systems'. Cited pp. 18, 91

Nettl, J. P. and Shapiro, David, 'Appearances or Realities–A British Approach', *Journal of Common Market Studies*, II, 1 (1963), pp. 24–36. Cited p. 99

Neumann, Sigmund, 'Toward a Comparative Study of Political Parties', in Neumann (ed.), *Modern Political Parties: Approaches to Comparative Politics*, Chicago 1956. Cited pp. 108, 137

Nkrumah, Kwame, *Ghana: The Autobiography of Kwame Nkrumah*, Edinburgh 1959. Cited p. 210

Nkrumah, Kwame, *Consciencism: Philosophy and Ideology for Decolonization and Development with Particular Reference to the African Revolution*, London 1964. Cited pp. 246, 313

Nkrumah, Kwame, *Neo-Colonialism: The Last Stage of Imperialism*, London 1965. Cited p. 246

North, Robert C.; Holsti, Ole R., *et al.* (eds.). *Content Analysis, A Handbook with Application for the Study of International Crises*, Evanston (Illinois) 1963. Cited p. 220

Nove, Alec, 'Hirschman, "Reform-Mongering" and Development Economics', *Scottish Journal of Political Economy*, XI, 1 (February 1964), pp. 25–31. Cited p. 239

Nove, Alec, 'The Decision to Collectivize', Paper read to the Soviet Affairs Seminar at the London School of Economics, November 1964 (cyclostyled). Cited p. 343

Oakeshott, Michael, *Rationalism in Politics and Other Essays*, London 1962. Cited p. 110

Olsen, Mancur, Jnr., 'Rapid Growth as a Destabilizing Force', *Journal of Economic History*, XXVII (December 1963), pp. 529–52. Cited p. 233

Olsen, Mancur, Jnr., 'Some Social and Political Implications of Economic Development', *World Politics*, XVII, 3 (April 1965), pp. 525–54. Cited p. 196

Osipov, G. V., *Sovremennaya burzhuaznaya sotsiologiya* (*Kriticheskii ocherk*), Moscow 1964. Cited p. 259

Ossowski, Stanislaw, *O osobliwościach nauk spolecznych* (On Personality in the Social Sciences), Warsaw 1962. Cited p. 158

BIBLIOGRAPHY

Ossowski, Stanislaw, *Class Structure in the Social Consciousness*, London 1963. Cited p. 97

Ostrogorski, *Democracy and the Organization of Political Parties*, New York 1964 (Edition S. M. Lipset). Cited p. 129

Packenham, R. A., 'Approaches to the Study of Political Development', *World Politics*, XVII (October 1964), pp. 108–20. Cited pp. 196, 289

Parry, Geraint, 'Elites and Polyarchies', Paper read at the Political Studies Conference, London, March 1966 (cyclostyled). Cited p. 93

Parsons, Talcott, *The Structure of Social Action: A Study in Social Theory, with Special Reference to a Group of Recent European Writers*, New York 1937. Cited p. 12

Parsons, Talcott, 'An Analytical Approach to the Theory of Stratification' (1940), and 'A Revised Analytical Approach to the Theory of Stratification' (1953), both in Parsons, *Essays in Sociological Theory* (revised edition), Glencoe 1954. Cited p. 86

Parsons, Talcott, *Essays in Sociological Theory*, Glencoe 1947, revised edition 1954. Cited p. 12

Parsons, Talcott and Shils, Edward (eds.), *Toward a General Theory of Action*, Cambridge (Mass.) 1951. Cited p. 12

Parsons, Talcott, *The Social System*, London 1952. Cited pp. 12, 348–9

Parsons, Talcott, Bales, Robert and Shils, Edward (eds.), *Working Papers in the Theory of Action*, Glencoe 1953. Cited p. 12

Parsons, Talcott, (Robert Bales *et al.*), *Family Socialization and Interaction Process*, Chicago 1955. Cited pp. 12, 47

Parsons, Talcott and Smelser, Neil J., *Economy and Society: A Study in the Integration of Economic and Social Theory*, London 1956. Cited pp. 12, 47, 386

Parsons, Talcott, 'Voting and the Equilibrium of the American Political System', in E. Burdick and A. J. Brodbeck (eds.), *American Voting Behavior*, Glencoe 1959, pp. 80–120. Cited pp. 13, 186

Parsons, Talcott, 'Some Problems Confronting Sociology as a Profession', *American Sociological Review*, XXIV (1959), pp. 547–59. Cited p. 50

Parsons, Talcott, 'General Theory in Sociology', in Robert K. Merton *et al.* (eds.), *Sociology Today*, New York 1959, pp. 39–78. Cited p. 386

Parsons, Talcott, *Structure and Process in Modern Societies*, New York 1960. Cited pp. 12, 103

Parsons, Talcott, 'Social Structure and Political Orientation', *World Politics*, XIII, 1 (October 1960), pp. 112–29. Cited p. 75

Parsons, Talcott, 'Pattern Variables Revisited: A Response to Robert Dubin, *American Sociological Review*, XXV (1960), pp. 467–83. Cited pp. 12, 331, 386

Parsons, Talcott, 'An Approach to the Sociology of Knowledge', *Transactions of the Fourth World Congress of Sociology*, Milan 1959, pp. 25–49. Cited p. 74

Parsons, Talcott (Edward Shils *et al.*), *Theories of Society: Formations of Modern Sociological Theory*, Glencoe (Illinois) 1931. Cited p. 12

Parsons, Talcott, 'The Point of View of the Author', in Max Black (ed.), *The Social Theories of Talcott Parsons: A Critical Examination*, Glencoe 1961. Cited p. 13

Parsons, Talcott, 'On the Concept of Influence', *Public Opinion Quarterly*, XXVII, 1 (Spring 1963), pp. 37–63. Cited p. 13

Parsons, Talcott, 'On the Concept of Political Power', *Proceedings of the American Philosophical Society*, CVII (1963), pp. 232–62. Cited pp. 13, 31, 200, 331, 386

Parsons, Talcott, *Social Structure and Personality*, Glencoe 1964. Cited p. 13

Parsons, Talcott, 'Evolutionary Universals in Society', *American Sociological Review*, XXIX, 3 (June 1964), pp. 339–57. Cited p. 140

Pavlov, V. I., and Rediko, I. B., 'Gosudarstvo natsional'noi demokratii i perekhod K nekapitalicheskom razvitiyn', *Narody Azii i Afriki*, 1 (1963), pp. 29–40. Cited p. 258

Pennock, J. Roland, 'Political Development, Political Systems and Political Goods', *World Politics*, XVIII, 3 (April 1966), pp. 415–34. Cited p. 196

PEP, *Industrial Trade Associations*, London 1957. Cited p. 334

Percy, W., 'The Symbolic Structure of Interpersonal Process', *Psychiatry*, XXIV (1961), pp. 30–52. Cited p. 253

Perrot, Michelle and Kriegel, Annie, *Le Socialisme français et le pouvoir*, Paris 1966. Cited p. 101

Perroux, Jacques, *La Coexistence Pacifique*, Paris 1958. Cited p. 310

Ploss, Sidney I., 'Soviet Politics Since the Fall of Khrushchev', Foreign Policy Research Institute, Philadelphia 1965 (cyclostyled). Cited p. 76

Pollard, S., 'Investment, Consumption and the Industrial Revolution', *Economic History Review*, XI, 2 (1958), pp. 215–27. Cited p. 235

Pollis, A., 'Political Implications of the Modern Greek Concept of Self', *British Journal of Sociology*, XVI, 1 (March 1965), pp. 29–47. Cited p. 204

Polsby, Nelson W., *Community Power and Political Theory*, New Haven 1963. Cited p. 93

Polsby, Nelson W., Deutler, Robert A. and Smith, Paul A. (eds.), *Politics and Social Life: An Introduction to Political Behavior*, Boston 1963. Cited p. 180

Posener, G., *De la divinité du Pharaon*, Paris 1960. Cited p. 373

Potter, A. M., *Organized Groups in British National Politics*, London 1961. Cited p. 105

Problems of Communism, XIV, 6 (November/December 1965), pp. 34–47 (Symposium on the Social Sciences in the USSR). Cited p. 259

Pye, Lucian W., *Politics, Personality and Nationbuilding: Burma's Search for Identity*, New Haven and London 1962. Cited pp. 51, 94–5, 198, 288

Pye, Lucian W. and Verba, Sidney (eds.), *Political Culture and Political Development*, Princeton 1965. Cited pp. 51, 97, 289

BIBLIOGRAPHY

Pye, Lucian W., 'The Concept of Political Development', *Annals of the American Academy of Political and Social Science*, CCCLVIII (March 1965), pp. 1–13. Cited p. 197

Pye, Lucian W., *Aspects of Political Development: An Analytic Study*, Boston 1966. Cited p. 307

Ranke, Leopold von, *The History of the Popes, Their Church and State, and Especially of their Conflicts with Protestantism in the Sixteenth and Seventeenth Centuries* (translation E. Foster), London 1896. Cited p. 157

Ranney, Austin (ed.), *Essays on the Behavioral Study of Politics*, Urbana 1962. Cited pp. 65, 149, 154, 203

Rapoport, David S., 'A Comparative Theory of Military and Political Types', in S. P. Huntington (ed.), *Changing Patterns of Military Politics*, New York 1962, pp. 77–96. Cited p. 125

Ratnam, K. J., *Communalism and the Political Process in Malaya*, London 1965. Cited p. 283

Rawls, John, 'Justice as Fairness', in P. Laslett and W. G. Runciman (eds.), *Philosophy, Politics and Society*, Oxford 1962, pp. 132–57. Cited p. 165

Ray, D. P. (ed.), *The Political Economy of Contemporary Africa*, Washington 1959. Cited p. 224

Regenstreif, Peter, *The Diefenbaker Interlude*, Toronto 1965. Cited p. 325

Rigby, T. H., 'Traditional, Market and Organizational Societies and the USSR', *World Politics*, XVI, 4 (July 1964), pp. 539–57. Cited p. 148

Riggs, Fred W., *The Ecology of Public Administration*, Bombay 1961. Cited pp. 133, 214

Riggs, Fred W., 'International Relations as a Prismatic System', *World Politics*, XIV, 1 (October 1961), pp. 144–81. Cited p. 348

Riggs, Fred W., 'Trends in the Comparative Study of Public Administration', *Revue internationale des sciences administratives*, XXVIII, 1 (1962), pp. 9–15. Cited p. 214

Riggs, Fred W., 'Bureaucracy and Political Development: A Paradoxical View', in Joseph LaPalombara (ed.), *Bureaucracy and Political Development*, Princeton 1963, pp. 120–67. Cited p. 214

Riggs, Fred W., 'The Theory of Developing Polities', *World Politics*, XVI, 1 (October 1963), pp. 147–71. Cited pp. 294, 348

Riggs, Fred W., *Administration in Developing Countries*, Boston 1964. Cited pp. 133, 214

Riggs, Fred W., 'Relearning Old Lessons: The Political Context of Development Administration', *Public Administration Review*, XXV (1965), pp. 70–79. Cited p. 214

Riker, W. H., 'Voting and the Summation of Preferences', *Am. Pol. Sc. Rev.*, LV, 4 (December 1961), pp. 900–11. Cited p. 149

Riker, W. H., *The Theory of Political Coalitions*, New Haven 1962. Cited p. 149

Rizzi, Bruno, *La bureaucratisation du monde*, Paris 1939. Cited p. 371

Robertson, R. in Bryan Wilson (ed.), *Patterns of English Sectarianism*, forthcoming. Cited p. 373

Rodinson, Maxime, 'L'Egypte nassérienne au miroir marxiste', *Les Temps Modernes* (April 1962), pp. 1859–87. Cited pp. 367, 379

Rodinson, Maxime, *Islam et capitalisme*, Paris 1965. Cited pp. 292, 367

Rogers, Everett M., *Diffusion of Innovations*, New York 1962. Cited pp. 47, 49

Rokkan, Stein, 'Citizen Participation in Political Life: Introduction', *International Social Science Journal*, XII, 1 (1960), pp. 7–14. Cited p. 177

Rokkan, Stein, and Campbell, Angus, 'Citizen Participation in Political Life: Norway and the United States of America', *International Social Science Journal*, XII, 1 (1960), pp. 69–99. Cited pp. 177, 179

Rokkan, Stein, 'Mass Suffrage, Secret Voting and Political Participation', *Archives Européennes de sociologie*, II (1961), pp. 132–52. Cited p. 140

Rokkan, Stein and Valen, H., 'The Mobilization of the Periphery', in S. Rokkan (ed.), *Approaches to the Study of Political Participation*, Bergen 1962, pp. 111–58. Cited p. 60

Rokkan, Stein, 'The Comparative Study of Political Participation: Notes Toward a Perspective on Current Research', in Austin Ranney (ed.), *Essays on the Behavioral Study of Politics*, Urbana 1962, pp. 47–90. Cited pp. 42, 179

Rokkan, Stein, Review of G. A. Almond and S. Verba, *The Civic Culture* in *Am. Pol. Sc. Rev.*, LVII, 3 (1964), pp. 676–9. Cited pp. 63, 168

Rokkan, Stein, 'Comparative Cross-National Research', in Merritt, Richard, L. and Rokkan, S. (eds.), *Comparing Nations: The use of Quantitative Data in Cross-National Research*, New Haven 1966, pp. 3–26. Cited p. 65

Rokkan, Stein, 'Electoral Mobilization, Party Competition and National Integration', in Joseph LaPalombara and Myron Weiner (eds.), *Political Parties and Political Development*, Princeton 1966. Cited p. 115

Rokkan, Stein, 'Cleavage Structures: Party Systems and Voter Alignments: An Introduction', in Lipset and Rokkan (eds.), *Party Systems and Voter Alignments*, Glencoe 1967 (forthcoming). Cited pp. 108, 115; *see* Lipset 128, 130, 139, 386

Rose, Richard, *Politics in England*, Boston 1964. Cited p. 97

Rose, Richard, 'England: A Traditionally Modern Political Culture', in Pye and Verba (eds.), *Political Culture and Political Development*, Princeton 1965, pp. 83–129. Cited pp. 75, 97, 353

Rose, Richard (ed.), *Studies in British Politics*, London 1966. Cited pp. 149, 152

Rose, Richard, 'Social and Party Cleavages in Britain', article for special number of *Revue Française de sociologie*, June 1966 (in draft). Cited p. 155

BIBLIOGRAPHY

Rose, Richard, *Influencing Voters: A Study of Campaign Rationality*, London 1967. Cited p. 141

Rose, Richard, and Mossawir, Harvé H., 'Voting and Elections: A Functional Analysis', *Political Studies* 1967 (forthcoming). Cited p. 152

Rosenberg, Maurice, 'Some Determinants of Political Apathy', *Public Opinion Quarterly*, XVIII (1954–5), pp. 349–66. Cited p. 155

Rossi, Peter H., 'Power and Community Structure', *Midwest Journal of Political Science*, IV (1960), pp. 390–401. Cited p. 179

Rossi, Peter H., 'Theory and Method in the Study of Power in the Local Community', Paper read to conference on Metropolitan Leadership, North Western University, April 1960. Cited p. 179

Rossi, Peter H. and Cutright, P., 'The Impact of Party Organization in an Industrial Setting', in Morris Janowitz (ed.), *Community Political Systems*, Glencoe 1961, pp. 81–116. Cited p. 179

Rossiter, Clinton, *Parties and Politics in America*, Ithaca (New York) 1960. Cited p. 108

Rostow, W. W., *The Stages of Economic Growth*, Cambridge 1960. Cited p. 195

Roth, Günther, 'Personal Rulership, Patrimonialism and Empire-Building in the New States', Paper presented to the Political Sociology Section of the Sixth World Congress of Sociology, Evian, September 1966 (mimeographed). Cited p. 255

Roth, Günther, *The Social Democrats in Imperial Germany*, Totowa (New York) 1963. Cited pp. 152, 350

Roth, Philip, 'Eli the Fanatic', in *Goodbye Columbus*, New York 1960, pp. 247–98. Cited p. 166

Rousseau, *A Discourse on Political Economy* (edition G. D. H. Cole), London 1913. Cited p. 135

Rudé, George, *The Crowd in History, 1730–1848*, New York 1965. Cited p. 147

Rudolph, Lloyd I. and Susanne Holber, 'The Political Role of India's Caste Associations', *Pacific Affairs*, XXXIII (March 1960), pp. 5–22. Cited p. 243

Rudolph, Lloyd I., 'The Modernity of Tradition: The Democratic Incarnation of Caste In India', *Am. Pol. Sc. Rev.*, LIX, 4 (December 1965), pp. 975–89. Cited p. 243

Runciman, W. G., *Social Science and Political Theory*, Cambridge 1963. Cited p. 37

Runciman, W. G., 'Charismatic Legitimacy and One-Party Rule in Ghana', *European Journal of Sociology*, IV, 1 (1963), pp. 148–65. Cited pp. 225, 263, 269, 298, 373

Runciman, W. G., 'Sociologese', *Encounter*, XXV, 6 (December 1965), pp. 45–47. Cited p. 50

Runciman, W. G., *Relative Deprivation and Social Justice*, London 1966. Cited pp. 22, 165, 168

Rustow, Dankwart A., *Politics and Westernization in the Near East*, Princeton 1956. Cited p. 142

420

BIBLIOGRAPHY

Rustow, Dankwart A., 'The Army and the Founding of the Turkish Republic', *World Politics*, XI (1959), pp. 513–52. Cited p. 363

Sampson, Anthony, *The Anatomy of Britain*, London 1962. Cited p. 77

Sampson, Anthony, *The Anatomy of Britain Today*, London, 1965. Cited p. 77

Sampson, R. V., *Equality and Power*, London 1965. Cited p. 168

[Sapir, Edward]; D. Mandelbaum (ed.), Edward Sapir: *Selected Writings in Language, Culture and Personality*, Los Angeles 1949. Cited p. 253

Sartori, Giovanni, *Democratic Theory*, Detroit 1962. Cited p. 93

Sartori, Giovanni, 'Constitutionalism: A Preliminary Discussion', *Am. Pol. Sc. Rev.*, LVI, 4 (December 1962), pp. 853–64. Cited p. 82

Sartori, Giovanni, *Partiti e Sistemi di partito*, Florence 1965. Cited p. 108

Sartori, Giovanni, 'Modelli spaziali di competizione tra partiti', *Rassegna italiana di sociologia*, VI, 1 (January/March 1965), pp. 7–29. Cited p. 152

Sartori, Giovanni, 'Framework for a Typology of Parties and Party Systems', Revised draft of paper for Second CPS Conference, Cambridge, December 1965. Cited p. 137

Sartori, Giovanni, 'The Theory of Parties Revisited', in David Easton and Leonard Binder, *Theory and Method in Comparative Politics*, Englewood Cliffs, forthcoming. Cited pp. 108, 137

Scalapino, R. A. and Masuri, J., *Parties and Politics in Contemporary Japan*, Berkeley and Los Angeles 1962. Cited p. 288

Schachter, Ruth, 'Single-Party Systems in West Africa', *Am. Pol. Sc. Rev.*, LV, 2 (June 1961), pp. 294–307. Cited p. 224

Schachtman, Max, *The Bureaucratic Revolution: The Rise of the Stalinist State*, New York 1962. Cited p. 372

Schaffer, Bernard, 'The Concept of Preparation: Some Questions about the Transfer of Systems of Government', *World Politics*, XVIII, 1 (October 1965), pp. 42–67. Cited pp. 206, 213, 214

Schaffer, Bernard, 'The World Bank Report on the Economic Development of the Territory of Papua and New Guinea', cyclostyled in preparation for publication. Cited p. 214

Schoenbaum, David, 'Class and Status in the Third Reich'. Unpublished Oxford Doctoral Thesis 1964. Cited pp. 87, 301

Schulze, R. O., 'The Role of Economic Dominants in Community Power Structure', *American Sociological Review*, XIII (1958), pp. 3–9. Cited p. 179

Schulze, R. O., 'The Bifurcation of Power in a Satellite City', in Morris Janowitz (ed.), *Community Political Systems*, Glencoe 1961, pp. 19–80. Cited p. 179

Schumpeter, Josef, *Capitalism, Socialism and Democracy*, third edition, New York 1950. Cited pp. 102, 151

Schweinitz, Karl de, *Industrialization and Democracy: Economic Necessities and Political Consequences*, New York 1964. Cited p. 196

BIBLIOGRAPHY

Seale, Patrick, *The Struggle for Syria*, Oxford 1965. Cited p. 292

Seligman, Lester G., *Leadership in a New Nation: Political Development in Israel*, New York 1964. Cited p. 108

Selvin, Hanan C. and Hagstrom, W. O., 'The Empirical Classification of Formal Groups', *American Sociological Review*, XXVIII (1963), pp. 399–411. Cited p. 92

Selznick, Philip, 'Foundations of the Theory of Organization', *American Sociological Review*, XII (1948), pp. 23–35. Cited p. 213

Selznick, Philip, *TVA and the Grass Roots*, Berkeley and Los Angeles 1949. Cited p. 341

Selznick, Philip, *Leadership in Administration: A Sociological Interpretation*, Evanston (Illinois) 1957. Cited pp. 213, 338

Shils, Edward, 'The End of Ideology?', *Encounter*, V (November 1955), pp. 52–58. Cited p. 74

Shils, Edward, *The Torment of Secrecy: The Background and Consequences of American Security Policies*, Glencoe 1956. Cited p. 86

Shils, Edward, 'Intellectuals, Public Opinion and Economic Development', *World Politics*, X (1958), pp. 232–255. Cited p. 95

Shils, Edward, 'The Concentration and Dispersion of Charisma: Its Bearing upon Economic Policy in Underdeveloped Countries', *World Politics*, XI, 1 (October 1958), pp. 1–19. Cited pp. 263, 269

Shils, Edward, 'The Intellectuals and the Powers: Some Perspectives for Comparative Analysis', *Comparative Studies in Society and History*, I (1958–9), pp. 5–22. Cited p. 95

Shils, Edward, 'Political Development in the New States' (in two parts), *Comparative Studies in Society and History*, II (1959–60), part I, pp. 265–92; part II, pp. 379–411. Cited p. 16

Shils, Edward, 'The Intellectuals in the Political Development of the New States', *World Politics*, XII, 3 (April 1960), pp. 329–68. Cited p. 16

Shils, Edward, *The Intellectual Between Tradition and Modernity*, The Hague 1961. Cited pp. 16, 95

Shils, Edward, 'Centre and Periphery' in *The Logic of Personal Knowledge: Essays Presented to Michael Polanyi on his Seventieth Birthday*, London 1961, pp. 117–30. Cited p. 58

Shils, Edward, *Political Development in the New States*, The Hague 1962. Cited pp. 16, 94, 95, 268

Shils, Edward, 'Opposition in the New States of Asia and Africa', *Government and Opposition*, I, 2 (January 1966), pp. 175–205. Cited p. 16

Shinn, William, 'The National-Democratic State: A Communist Program for the Less Developed Areas', *World Politics*, XV, 4 (April 1963), pp. 377–89. Cited p. 258

Shmelev, N. P., *Idiologiya imperializma i problemy slaborazyitikh stran*, Moscow 1962. Cited p. 240

Shmelev, N. P., 'Burzhuazuiye ekonomisti o roli gosudarstvennogo sektora v slaborazvitikh stranakh', *Mirovaya Ekonomika i Mezhdunarodniye Otnosheniya*, No. 4 (1962), pp. 87–91. Cited p. 240

BIBLIOGRAPHY

Shonfield, Andrew, *Modern Capitalism: The Changing Balance of Public and Private Power*, London 1965. Cited pp. 100, 188, 212, 357

Shubkin, V., 'Molodezh vstupaet v zhizn' (Youth on the Threshold of Life), *Voprosy filosofii*, 5 (1965), pp. 57–70. Cited p. 336

Shurmann, H. F., *Ideology and Organization in Communist China*, Berkeley/Los Angeles 1965. Cited p. 241

Silvert, K. H., *Expectant Peoples: Nationalism and Development*, New York 1964. Cited p. 233

Silvert, K. H., 'The Politics of Economic Change', Paper presented to a Conference on Latin America at the Royal Institute of International Affairs, London, February 1965. Cited pp. 34, 94

Simmel, Georg, *Grundfragen der Soziologie*, Leipzig 1917. Cited p. 50

Simms, Peter, *Trouble in Guyana*, London 1966. Cited p. 308

Simon, Herbert, *Administrative Behavior: A Study of Decision-Making Processes in Administrative Organizations*, 1945, second edition, New York 1957. Cited pp. 16, 156, 213, 338

Simon, Herbert, *Models of Man: Social and Rational: Mathematical Essays on Rational Human Behavior in a Social Setting*, New York 1957. Cited pp. 16, 338

Simon, Herbert, 'Bandwagon and Underdog Effects of Election Predictions', in Simon, *Models of Man, Social and Rational*, New York 1957, pp. 79–87. Cited p. 157

Simon, Herbert and March, James, *Organizations*, 1958. Cited p. 16

Sinai, I. R., *The Challenge of Modernization*, London 1964. Cited p. 206

Singh, A. K., *Indian Students in Britain*, Bombay 1963. Cited p. 250

Skilling, H. Gordon, 'Interest Groups and Communist Politics', *World Politics*, XVIII, 3 (April 1966), pp. 452–73. Cited p. 371

Smelser, Neil J., *Social Change in the Industrial Revolution: An Application of Theory to the Lancashire Cotton Industry*, London 1959. Cited pp. 13, 113, 353

Smelser, Neil J., *Theory of Collective Behavior*, London 1962. Cited pp. 13, 113, 251

Smelser, Neil J., 'Mechanisms of Change and Adjustment to Change', in B. F. Hoselitz and W. E. Moore (eds.), *Industrialization and Society*, Paris/The Hague (Unesco) 1963, pp. 49–54. Cited pp. 233, 280

Smelser, Neil J., 'Toward a Theory of Modernization' in Amitai and Eva Etzioni (eds.), *Social Change*, New York 1964, pp. 258–74. Cited p. 47

Smith, Adam, *Theory on Moral Sentiments*, London 1812, in Smith, *Works*, I. Cited p. 266

Smith, Thomas C., *Political Change and Industrial Development in Japan: Government Enterprise 1868–1880*, Stanford (California) 1955. Cited p. 347

Snow, C. P., *The Masters*, London 1954. Cited p. 157

Sobolev, A., in *World Marxist Review*, 2 (1963), pp. 39–48. Cited p. 258

BIBLIOGRAPHY

Solomon, Frederic, Walker, Walter L., O'Connor, Garrett, and Fishman, Jacob, 'Civil Rights Activity and Reduction of Crime Among Negroes', *Archives of General Psychiatry*, XII (March 1965), pp. 227–36. Cited p. 184

Sorokin, Pitirim A., *Society, Culture and Personality: Their Structure and Dynamics*, New York 1947. Cited p. 27

Sotsial'niye issledovaniya, Moscow (Academy of Sciences) 1965. Cited p. 259

Sotsiologiya V USSR, 2 vols. Moscow 1965. Cited p. 259

Spengler, Joseph J., 'Theory, Ideology, Non-Economic Values, and Politico-Economic Development', in Ralph Braibanti and J. J. Spengler (eds.), *Tradition, Values and Socio-Economic Development*, Durham (North Carolina) 1961, pp. 3–56. Cited p. 100

Spiro, Herbert J., *Government by Constitution: The Political Systems of Democracy*, New York 1959. Cited pp. 30, 84

Spiro, Herbert J., 'Comparative Politics: A Comprehensive Approach', *Am. Pol. Sc. Rev.*, LVI, 3 (September 1962), pp. 577–95. Cited pp. 30, 51, 57, 84, 130, 245

Stammer, Otto (ed.), *Politische Forschung*, Cologne 1960. Cited p. 65

Steffens, Joseph Lincoln, *The Autobiography of Lincoln Steffens*, New York 1931 edition. Cited p. 278

Steiner, Kurt, 'The Japanese Village and its Government', *Far Eastern Quarterly*, XV, 2 (1956), pp. 185–291. Cited p. 347

Stoetzel, Jean, *Jeunesse sans chrysanthème ni sabre*, Paris 1954. Cited p. 347

Stokes, Donald E., 'Spatial Models of Party Competition', *Am. Pol. Sc. Rev.*, LVII, 2 (June 1963), pp. 368–77. Cited p. 152

Stone, Lawrence, *The Crisis of the Aristocracy 1558–1641*, Oxford 1965. Cited p. 96

Storing, H. J. (ed.), *Essays on the Scientific Study of Politics*, New York 1962. Cited pp. 280, 303

Strauss, Leo, 'An Epilogue' in H. J. Storing (ed.), *Essays on the Scientific Study of Politics*, New York 1962, pp. 305–28. Cited p. 280

Sukarno, *Indoneziya obuinyaet* (*Indonesia Accuses,*) Moscow 1956. Cited p. 256

Sukarno, *For a Free Indonesia*, 1933. Cited p. 256

Sutton, Francis X. *et al.*, *The American Business Creed*, Cambridge (Mass.) 1956. Cited p. 224

Sutton, Francis X., 'Social Theory and Comparative Politics', in Eckstein, H. and Apter, David E. (eds.), *Comparative Politics: A Reader*, New York 1963, pp. 67–81. Cited pp. 103, 175

Tannenbaum, Frank, *The True Society: A Philosophy of Labour*, London 1964. Cited p. 332

Taylor, A. J., 'Progress and Poverty in Britain, 1780–1850: A Reappraisal', *History*, XLV (1960), pp. 16–31. Cited p. 235

Thomas, Keith, in K. C. Brown (ed.), *Hobbes Studies*, Oxford 1966, pp. 185–237. Cited p. 135

Thompson, E. P., *The Making of the English Working Classes*, London 1964. Cited pp. 21, 235

BIBLIOGRAPHY

Thompson, Victor, 'Objectives for Development Administration, *Administrative Science Quarterly*, IX, 1 (June 1964), pp. 91–108. Cited pp. 213, 215, 358

Thornton, T. P. (ed.), *The Third World in Soviet Perspective: Studies by Soviet Writers on the Developing Areas*, Princeton 1964. Cited pp. 95, 210, 256, 379

Thrall, R. M., Coombs, C. H. and Davis, R. L. (eds.), *Decision Processes*, New York 1954. Cited p. 130

Thurdock, George P., 'The Cross-Cultural Survey', *American Sociological Review*, V (1940), pp. 361–70. Cited p. 51

Thurdock, George P., *An Outline of World Cultures*, third edition, New Haven 1963. Cited p. 51

Tingsten, Herbert, 'Stability and Vitality in Swedish Democracy', *Political Quarterly*, XXVI, 2 (1955), pp. 140–51. Cited p. 152

Tinker, Hugh, *Ballot Box and Bayonet*, London 1964. Cited pp. 142, 264

Tinker, Hugh, *Reorientations: Studies on Asia in Transition*, London 1965. Cited p. 264

Tiryakian, Edward A. (ed.), *Sociological Theory, Values and Sociocultural Change*, Glencoe 1963. Cited p. 62

Tomasić, Dinko, *The Impact of Russian Culture on Soviet Communism*, Glencoe 1953. Cited pp. 201–2

Torgerson, Ulf, 'The Structure of Urban Parties in Norway during the First Period of Extended Suffrage, 1884–1898', in Allardt, E. and Littunen, Y. (eds.), *Cleavages, Ideologies and Party Systems: Contributions to Comparative Political Sociology*, Helsinki 1964, pp. 377–99. Cited p. 140

Touraine, Alain, *Sociologie de l'action*, Paris 1966. Cited p. 124

Touré, Sékou, *Independent Guinea: Articles and Speeches*, Moscow 1960. Cited p. 206

Trotsky, L., *Sochineniya*, Vol. II Moscow/Leningrad 1926, *Nasha Pervaya Revoliutsiya*. Cited p. 365

Trotsky, L., *Itogi i Perspektivy*, Moscow 1919. Cited p. 365

Trotsky, L., *The Revolution Betrayed*, London 1937. Cited p. 372

Trotsky, L., *In Defense of Marxism (Against the Petty-Bourgeois Opposition)*, New York 1965 (Reprinted Collection). Cited p. 372

Truman, David B., *The Congressional Party: A Case Study*, Englewood Cliffs 1959. Cited pp. 108, 327

Truman, David B. (ed.), *The Congress and America's Future*, Englewood Cliffs 1965. Cited p. 327

Turner, Ralph H., 'Modes of Social Ascent Through Education: Sponsored and Contest Mobility', Reprinted in A. H. Halsey, Jean Floud and C. A. Anderson (eds.), *Education, Economy and Society*, New York 1961, pp. 121–39. Cited p. 86

Uledov, A. K., *Obshchestvennoe mnenie sovetskogo obshchestva*, Moscow 1963. Cited p. 202

U.N. *Analyses and Projections of Economic Development*, New York 1955. Cited p. 195

BIBLIOGRAPHY

Urquidi, Victor L., *The Challenge of Development in Latin America*, New York 1964. Cited p. 43

Valen, H. and Katz, K., *Political Parties in Norway*, Oslo 1964. Cited p. 108

Van der Kroef, J., 'Economic Development in Indonesia: Some Social and Cultural Impediments', *Economic Development and Cultural Change*, IV, 2 (January 1956), pp. 116–33. Cited p. 233

Venturi, Franco, 'Oriental Despotism', review in *Journal of the History of Ideas*, XXIV (January-March), pp. 133–42. Cited p. 367

Vidal-Naquet, Pierre, 'Avant-propos', (introduction) to French edition of Wittfogel, *Oriental Despotism*, Paris 1965. Cited pp. 367, 369, 379

Vincent, John, *The Formation of the Liberal Party, 1857–1868*, London 1966. Cited p. 127

von Vorys, Karl, *Political Development in Pakistan*, Princeton 1965. Cited p. 292

Waalder, Robert, 'Protest and Revolution against Western Societies', in Morton A. Kaplan (ed.), *The Revolution in World Politics*, New York 1962. Cited p. 250

Walker, Jack L., 'A Critique of the Elitist Theory of Democracy', *Am. Pol. Sc. Rev.*, LX, 2 (June 1966), pp. 285–95. Cited pp. 159, 183

Ward, Robert E., and Rustow, Dankwart, A. (eds.), *Political Modernization in Japan and Turkey*, Princeton 1964. Cited pp. 288, 347

Waterston, Albert, *Planning in Pakistan: Organization and Implementation*, Oxford 1965. Cited p. 215

Waterston, Albert, *Development Planning: Lessons of Experience*, Baltimore 1965. Cited p. 215

Watson, Andrew M., and Dirlam, Joel B., 'The Impact of Underdevelopment on Economic Planning', *Quarterly Journal of Economics*, LXXIX, 2 (May 1965), pp. 167–94. Cited p. 49

Weber, Max, *Wirtschaft und Gesellschaft*, second edition, Tübingen 1925. Cited pp. 366, 369

Weber, Max, *The Theory of Social and Economic Organization* (translation A. M. Henderson and Talcott Parsons), New York 1964. Cited p. 263

Weil, Eric, 'Philosophie politique, théorie politique', *Revue française de science politique*, IX (1961), pp. 267–94. Cited p. 36

Weiner, Myron, *The Politics of Scarcity: Public Pressure and Political Response in India*, Chicago 1962. Cited p. 243

Weinert, Richard S., 'Violence in Pre-Modern Societies: Rural Colombia', *Am. Pol. Sc. Rev.*, LX, 2 (June 1966), pp. 340–7. Cited p. 184

Wells, H. G., *The New Machiavelli*, London (Penguin edition) 1946. Cited p. 139

Williams, Philip, 'Crisis as an Institution', in Williams, *Crisis and Compromise*, London 1964, pp. 413–27. Cited p. 143

Williamson, G. Scott, and Pearce, Innes H., *Science, Synthesis and Sanity*, London 1965. Cited p. 57

426

BIBLIOGRAPHY

Willner, Ann Ruth, 'The Underdeveloped Study of Political Development', *World Politics*, XVI, 3 (April 1964), pp. 468–82. Cited pp. 196, 246

Wiseman, H. V., *Parliament and the Executive*, London 1966. Cited p. 237

Wittfogel, Karl, *Oriental Despotism*, first English edition 1957, second edition 1962. Cited p. 367

Wittfogel, Karl, 'The Legend of "Maoism"', *China Quarterly*, 1 (April/June 1960), pp. 72–86. Cited p. 370

Wittfogel, Karl, 'The Legend of "Maoism" Concluded', *China Quarterly*, 2 (July/September 1960), pp. 16–34. Cited p. 370

Wittfogel, Karl, 'The Marxist View of China (Part 1)', *China Quarterly*, 11 (July/September 1962), pp. 1–20. Cited p. 370

Wittfogel, Karl, 'The Marxist View of China (Part 2)', *China Quarterly*, 12 (October/December 1962), pp. 154–69. Cited pp. 367, 370

Wittfogel, Karl, 'Agrarian Problems and the Moscow-Peking Axis', *Slavic Review*, XXI, 4 (December 1962), pp. 678–99. Cited p. 370

Wjatr, Jerzy, and Przeworski, Adam, 'Control Without Opposition', *Government and Opposition*, I, 2 (January 1966). Cited p. 320

Wolf, Jnr., Charles, *Foreign Aid: Theory and Practice in Southern Asia*, Princeton 1960. Cited p. 259

Wolin, Sheldon S., *Politics and Vision, Continuity and Innovation in Western Political Thought*, Boston 1960. Cited pp. 14, 92, 168, 212, 350, 370

Woodruff, W., 'Capitalism and the Historians: A Contribution to the Discussion on the Industrial Revolution in England', *Journal of Economic History*, XVI, 1 (1956), pp. 1–17. Cited p. 235

Worsley, Peter, *The Third World*, London 1964. Cited p. 309

Wraith, Ronald, and Simpkins, Edgar, *Corruption in Developing Countries*, London 1963. Cited p. 278

Wu, Yuan-Li, *The Economy of Communist China*, New York 1965. Cited p. 241

Zapf, Wolfgang, *Wandlungen der deutschen Elite: Ein Zirkulationsmodell deutscher Führungsgruppen 1919–1961*, Munich 1965. Cited pp. 80, 95

Zebot, Cyril A., *The Economics of Competitive Coexistence: Convergence Through Growth*, New York 1964. Cited p. 195

Zetterburg, Hans L., *Social Theory and Social Practice*, New York 1962. Cited p. 55

Zolberg, Aristide R., *One-Party Government in the Ivory Coast*, Princeton 1965. Cited p. 298

Index

Reference to sources and citations of authors will be found in the Bibliography which gives page references to the present text.

INDEX

Legitimacy, legitimation of authority: concept of, 198–9, 205 *seqq.*, 211, 221 *seqq.*; economic plan as symbol of, 241–3; bases of, in developing countries, 261 *seqq.*; dramaturgical impact of, 264–6; drawbacks of over-emphasis on 'pure', 280–1; elitist shaping of formal electoral, 281–2; legitimizing-mobilization relationship, 305–9; and participation, 269–71; and professionalization notion in politics, 268–9

Lenin, Leninism, 120, 146, 203

Leningrad discussion of 'Asian Mode of Production', 374

Liberal vote in Britain, 318, 323

Liberation Rally of 1953 (Egypt), 227 n.

Lipset, on nature of American society, 185, 189

Lloyd, Selwyn, 119

Locke, J.: concept of divided sovereignty, 164, 165; view of general constraint on authority, 164 n.; notion of mobilization, 136

Lord's Day Observance Society, 172

Luther, Martin, and aversion to mobilization notion, 135

de Maistre, on community problems, 134, 167

Malaysia: Alliance Government created in, 282; building on British *status quo*, 210; dominant party structure in, 230; communalism and electoral mobilization problem in, 308–9; rioting in, 275

Mali, 207, 229 n

Mapai, *see* Israel

Marx, Marxism, 30, 35 n., 53, 101, 114, 117, 133, 134–5, 166, 202, 203, 244; a comparison with Rousseau, 134 n.; concept of bureaucracy, 342, 366–8, 371 n.; convergence with modern American organization theory, 370–1; historical, in newly-emergent countries, 208–9; ideal-typical society of, 68–9; nature of 'politics as religion' (capitalist era) as seen by, 186–7; on political systems as reflection of ruling-class interests, 187

Mass society, analysis of theories of, 137 n.

Mattei, Enrico, and Italian form of bureaucracy, 356

Maturity, theory of (democracy in developing countries), 206 n.

Mboya, Tom (Kenya), 297

Merton's *anomie* classification, 248 n.

Mexico: dominant party structure of, 230; strength of ruling legitimacy party in, 273; enhanced status of civilian, over military, bureaucracy, 364; PRI as part of asymmetrical party pattern, 320, 321–2

Military structures, role of, in national-constitutional mobilization, 253–4

Mill, J. S., attitude of to sovereignty, 166

Millenarianism, of Latin America, 59

Mitterand, François, as French Presidential candidate, 319

Mobilization: three methods of analysing political, 115–20; constitutional, 232 *seqq.*: *national economic planning*, 232–46, *national constitutional integration*, 246–60; in context of roles, norms, collectivities, values, 119–20; as core concept, 32–33; as possibly disappearing concept, 107, 109 *seqq.*; electoral, 138, *and see* Elections; and economic development, 309–12; four hypotheses on future development of, in emerging countries, 299–316; intensity and direction of, and relation with legitimacy, 305–9; manipulated and participatory, 111 *seqq.*; 'of masses' (Soviet writers), 148; military, serving political functions, 125; military, as a cleavage mobilization, 125–6; national military, 253–5; party-based, 219–32; purely political replacing both military and religious, 147; political as distinct from social, 115 *seqq.*; religious, as cleavage mobilization, 125, 128, 133 *seqq.*; some posited alternatives to, 231 n., 232 n.; *see also* Stalactite, Stalagmite

Modernization, concept of, 35

Modibo Keita, as charismatic arbiter, 286

Montesquieu, links of with modern sociology, 134 n., 136

437